# The Sound of Vultures' Wings

SUNY series in Religious Studies

Harold Coward, editor

# The Sound of Vultures' Wings

## The Tibetan Buddhist Chöd Ritual Practice of the Female Buddha Machik Labdrön

Jeffrey W. Cupchik

Foreword by
Pencho Rabgey, M.S.C.

SUNY
PRESS

Cover photo: Machik Labdrön, Tibetan female ascetic, founder of the Chöd tradition.

Published by State University of New York Press, Albany



Printed in the United States of America



For information, contact State University of New York Press, Albany, NY
www.sunypress.edu

**Library of Congress Cataloging-in-Publication Data**

Names: Cupchik, Jeffrey W., 1967– author.
Title: The sound of vultures' wings : the Tibetan Buddhist chöd ritual practice of the female Buddha Machik Labdrön / Jeffrey W. Cupchik ; foreword by Pencho Rabgey.
Description: Albany : State University of New York Press, [2024]. | Series: SUNY series in religious studies | Includes bibliographical references and index.
Identifiers: LCCN 2016031437 (print) | LCCN 2016057871 (ebook) | ISBN 9781438464435 (ebook) | ISBN 9781438464411 (hardcover : alk. paper)
Subjects: LCSH: Gcod (Buddhist rite) | Buddhist music—China—Tibet Religion—History and criticism. | Ma-gcig Lab-sgron, 1055–1149.
Classification: LCC BQ7699.G36 (ebook) | LCC BQ7699.G36 C87 2017 (print) | DDC 294.3/4446—dc23
LC record available at https://lccn.loc.gov/2016031437

10 9 8 7 6 5 4 3 2 1

*To Pala (Ven. Pencho Rabgey)*

*and*

*to Chöd ritual masters and students*

*engaging in the practice . . .*

# Note to the Reader

*Chöd is a Vajrayāna Buddhist practice, from the class of highest yoga tantra, passed down in unbroken lineages from teacher to disciple over many generations—through its founder Machik Labdrön in 12th century Tibet—and reaches us today through transmissions of sacred instructions on its meditational and musical practices.*

*A person who wishes to practice Chöd must first receive the appropriate initiation from a qualified teacher who retains all the initiations and permissions.*

*Importantly, as a foundation, one must first study and practice the three principle aspects of the Buddhist path under the guidance of a qualified teacher before engaging in Chöd practice.*

*The Chöd melodies are held sacred, transmitted to disciples by lineage masters, and should not be the basis of creative compositions outside of the context of Chöd practice.*

# Contents


List of Illustrations ix

Note on Terminology xiii

Note on the Meaning of the Title xv

Foreword xix

Preface xxiii

Acknowledgments xxvii

Introduction: Approaching Chöd Ritual Studies 1

**Part I: Chöd Ritual Practice in Context**

Chapter 1 Ritual Efficacy: Musical Performance in Chöd Practice 29

Chapter 2 Musical Character of the Chöd Genre 75

**Part II: Elements of Chöd Practice**

Chapter 3 The Sound of Vultures' Wings: Ritual Mapping the Chöd Practice 113

Chapter 4 The Chöd *Ḍamaru* Drum: Symbolism, Function, and Variation in an Interpretive Community 139

Chapter 5 Mantric Utterance in Chöd 165

Chapter 6 The Four Ritual Activities 185

## Part III. Meaning and Application of Chöd Practice

Chapter 7 Mind and Sound in Chöd 195

Chapter 8 Transmission and Transformation 211

Chapter 9 Gift of the Body in Chöd: Healing the Suffering from "Self-Interest" 255

Conclusion: Continuity of the Chöd Ritual Tradition 279

Note on Chöd Research 291

Notes 293

Glossary 357

Bibliography 363

Index 379

# Illustrations

## Tables


| | | |
|---|---|---|
| 2.1 | Contrasting Tibetan Ritual Music: Monastic Ensemble vs. Chöd Ritual | 79 |
| 2.2 | Stages of the Actual Practice | 86 |
| 2.3 | Ritual Structure of the Chöd Sādhana, *Dedicating the Illusory Body* | 89 |
| 2.4 | During Meditation Sessions: Actual and Mentally Performed Ritual | 105 |
| 2.5 | Post-meditation Periods: Disposition of Mind In-between Sessions | 105 |
| 5.1 | Perfection of Wisdom Mantra with *Ḍamaru*: Variation 1 | 175 |
| 5.2 | Mantra of the Perfection of Wisdom with *Ḍamaru*: Variation 2 | 175 |
| 5.3 | Calling Forth Beings with the Thighbone Trumpet (*Kangling*) | 178 |
| 5.4 | Layers of Depth in Mantric Visualization: Interpreting Symbolism | 179 |
| 5.5 | Utterance of the Mantric Syllable "*Āḥ*" (21x): Variation 1 | 182 |
| 5.6 | Utterance of the Mantric Syllable "*Āḥ*" (21x): Variation 2 | 182 |
| 9.1 | Mauss's Gift Economy vs. Market Economy | 270 |
| 9.2 | Gift Economy with the Mahāyāna Buddhist *Bodhicitta* Motivation | 270 |

## Figures


Vulture Peak—rock formation resembling a vulture on the sacred mountain at Rājgṛha xii

Vulture Peak with Tibetan prayer flag offerings xii

1.1 Machik Labdrön (Ma gcig lab sgron), founder of the Chöd Tradition 34

1.2 Machik Labdrön, central figure, Merit Field of the Chöd Tradition 35

1.3 Padampa Sangyé (Pha dam pa sang rgyas) 37

1.4 Varjayoginī (Tib. Rdo rje rnal 'byor ma) 39

1.5 Tibetan liturgy: Transliteration, Romanization, and translation (line 1) 59

1.6 Tibetan liturgy: Transliteration, Romanization, and translation (line 2) 59

1.7 "Going for Refuge": Musical transcription 60

2.1 General structure of a moment within Chöd performance 99

2.2 Ritual elements experienced during a moment of Chöd performance 100

3.1 "The White Distribution" melody (*dkar 'gyed*) 115

3.2 "Seven Branch Offering Practice" (*yan lag bdun pa*) 130

3.3 The "Seven Branch Offering Practice" 132

3.4 "Devotion to the Spiritual Guide" (*bshes gnyen tshul bzhin*) 137

4.1 Machik Labdrön, holding the drum (*ḍamaru*) and Tibetan bell (*dril bu*) 145

4.2 Relative stability of tradition: Core beliefs and the extent of variation 150

4.3 His Eminence the Ninth Khalkha Jetsun Dampa Rinpoché, Jampel Namdröl Chökyi Gyaltsen (1932–2012), head of the Ganden Chöd lineage 153

4.4 Position of the Chöd *ḍamaru's* suspended pellets and length of the strings, as modified by Ven. Pencho Rabgey 158

4.5 Ven. Pencho Rabgey "Pala" demonstrating how to practice with the *ḍamaru* 162

4.6 Ven. Pencho Rabgey adjusting the drum's rotation subtly with arm, hand, and wrist 162

8.1 Ven. Pencho Rabgey, "Pala," giving an invited lecture in the Interfaith Chapel, University of Rochester, at the event "Music, Healing & Ritual in Tibetan Cultural Contexts" 227

## Companion Website*

*See Companion Website / www.soundofvultureswings.com*

*Traditionally, the Chöd melodies are held sacred, passed from master to disciple through many generations of Chöd practitioners, and should not be taken as the basis for compositions outside the Chöd tradition.

According to tradition, a person who wishes to practice the meditational and musical aspects of the Chöd tradition, must receive the oral transmission of sacred liturgical Chöd melodies from a qualified teacher who possesses all the appropriate initiations and permissions.

The music notations and transcriptions that appear in this book also should not be taken as the basis for creative compositions outside the context of the Chöd traditional practices.

With thanks for your compassionate understanding.

Top photo: Vulture Peak—rock formation resembling a vulture on the mountain at Rājgīr (Rājgṛha), India. Bottom photo: Vulture Peak with Tibetan prayer flag offerings. (Photos by Iria Crespo)

# Note on Terminology

## Gcod or Chöd?

The title of this book does not retain the widely accepted Tibetological system of Wylie transliteration.[1] The Tibetan spelling of the ritual is rendered gCod, with the letter "ga" as a prefix, the root letter being "ca" (pronounced "cha") which takes the vowel *naro* (pronounced "o," but modified here by the suffix "da" to sound "ö," with an umlaut).

To facilitate ease of reading for the non-Tibetanist, throughout the book we have rendered gCod phonetically as Chöd. In terms of pronunciation, Chöd is uttered with an unaspirated high tone "Chö" without the "d" being sounded at all. However, due to the frequency with which the spelling "Chöd" has been employed in liturgical texts used at Tibetan Buddhist Dharma centers, and in recent article and book publications, the "d" suffix is retained.

## Writing Conventions: Tibetan and Sanskrit Terminology

In addition to Wylie, we use common English phonetic renderings of Tibetan and Sanskrit terms so that the reader's experience will flow more easily.

Proper names are capitalized in the first letter, and rendered according to the Wylie transliteration system in parentheses, and preceded by the name in Romanized English Phonetics: e.g., Machik (Ma gcig Lab sgron). Similarly, the renowned eleventh-century Tibetan poet-saint Milarepa is spelled in Wylie as Mi la ras pa and pronounced according to the phoneticized "Milarepa," e.g., Milarepa (Mi la ras pa).

Tibetan and Sanskrit terms are italicized in parentheses following the term given in English translation: e.g., "meditation deity" (*yidam*).

If both Sanskrit and Tibetan terms are in common usage, Sanskrit is given first, followed by Tibetan, e.g., "cyclic existence" (Skt. *saṃsāra*, Tib. *'khor ba*).

Some of the most common terms used throughout the book have not been placed in italics to facilitate one's ease in reading. These include terms which, although Sanskrit or Tibetan, have become so frequently encountered in the literature that the reader will quickly grow to become familiar with them. For example, the term "sādhana," which literally means "method of accomplishment" and refers to a liturgical text; and "ḍākinī" which refers to a "female sky goer" or enlightened female buddha.

## Note on Gender in Language

Initially, at the time of writing most of this book's content, it was considered respectful to use the pronouns "she" and "her" when discussing individual practitioners.

Amidst a collective new and growing awareness and respect for diversity and inclusion initiatives to accommodate the wish for increased gender neutrality in language—and with sensitivity to gender attributions when writing of contemplatives and their ritual traditions, as practiced in Buddhist societies—this book joins efforts in the creating of a space for consciously articulated modifications in language. Respectfully, in numerous instances, passages in this book are rendered gender-neutral.

Yet, some passages do not allow for a smooth conveyance of meanings and comprehensibility when the use of "they" is invoked to replace "she/her." Where the practitioner invites all beings to the *Gaṇacakra* feast, frequent use of the term "they" would be too confusing.

In this context, where language can bring Machik's Chod practice closer to the reader's immediate experience, the passage sometimes utilizes the gender pronouns "she" or "her." This is intended to be read as neutralizing or at least balancing gendered norms, signaling Machik's achievements within the historically predominantly patriarchal religious society—as there are many women contemplatives in the Chod tradition.

Since, to all conventional appearances, the Tibetan woman founder of this tantric practice tradition achieved the highest spiritual attainment through her Chod practice; and, among her five children, she entrusted two of her sons to become the lineage holders of her transmitted teachings, it is hoped the effort to convey gender parity in language will be read in context.

# Note on the Meaning of the Title

Some brief explanation of the title of this book may be useful at the outset, since the mention of "vultures" in different Buddhist contexts has varied significance related with both philosophy and practice. Even when the term "vultures" is invoked metaphorically, as it is in some instances, it nevertheless carries with it an apprehensive feeling. Yet, the term has distinctive and important meanings in relation to different aspects of the path to enlightenment, as the following relates.

## Vulture Peak

The image of vultures has been emblematic at least since the historical origin of what has come to be known as Buddhism.

Buddha Śākyamuni turned the Dharma wheel for the second time atop Vulture Peak near the town of Rājgīr (Rājgṛha), in ancient Magadha, now Bihar State, in North India. This hill is so named because of its rocky summit (some 600 steps to walk up), where boulders resembling the shape of a vulture's head and hooked beak can be seen from certain vantage points. The peak is a pilgrimage place for Buddhists today, as it is widely recognized as the site of the dialogue recounted in *The Heart Sutra.*

Dwelling in this sacred place, the Buddha taught the meaning of "emptiness" (Skt. *śūnyatā*, Tib. *stong pa nyid*)—the lack of inherent existence of persons and phenomena—and how realizing this "ultimate truth" is prerequisite to one's attainment of enlightenment. To eliminate suffering both for oneself and all other beings, it would be impossible, he taught, without this realization.

In this context, "vultures" serves as a representative image, evoking the Buddha's instructions on the cultivation of the realization of "emptiness," the interdependent nature of reality.

## Śāntideva: Vultures as a Sign of Impermanence

Later, in the eighth century, Śāntideva, a renowned Indian master adept at Nālandā University, mentions "vultures" no less than six times in his well-known text, *Guide to the Bodhisattva's Way of Life* (Skt. *Bodhicaryāvatāra*): twice in chapter 5 on Guarding Alertness (verses 58 and 66), three times in chapter 8 on Meditation (verses 44, 46, and 181), and once during the Dedicatory chapter 10 (v.11).

At each instance, he refers to vultures not to highlight Vulture Peak, but rather to conjure up the fearful imagery regarding the pending demise of one's body. Vultures are a sign of impermanence, and a reminder of the fear-induced urgency to practice.

Customarily, in Buddhist communities of Central Asia, vultures are invited to a "sky burial," the funerary rite which takes place in a designated open site atop a mountain—the final offering of one's body of this life.

## Machik Labdrön

Approximately 1,600 years following Prince Siddhārtha's birth (by some accounts, around 563 BCE), Machik Labdrön, the eleventh-century Tibetan female adept, is said to have realized emptiness while reciting the *Perfection of Wisdom Sūtra* (Skt. *Prajñāpāramitā Sūtra*) in a benefactor's home. She later received teachings and guidance directly from the Indian Buddhist master Padampa Sangyé, who founded the Pacification (Tib. *zhi byed*) Tradition.

Thereafter, she developed the Chöd ("cutting") Tradition: a method of *bodhicitta* practice that combines sūtra and tantra, through which one is said to be able to achieve enlightenment by cutting-off the root of "self-grasping ignorance" (Tib. *bdag 'dzin ma rig pa*).

## The Sound of a Vulture's Wings

Three years before encountering Machik's Chöd Tradition, I had personally experienced the intimate fear roused by the sound of the wind passing through the feathered wings of a vulture gliding overhead while hiking beside a narrow mountain ledge behind Rizong Monastery in Ladakh, India. This visceral experience of the sound-image of vultures descending to explore whether I was their next meal later suffused with my Chöd studies, and became absorbed thereafter into my memory.

After three years, I was introduced to Machik Labdrön's Chöd ritual practices while receiving the initiation and practice instructions from His Eminence Khalkha Jetsun Dampa Rinpoché. I then received transmissions into Chöd practice from various lamas, and entered into an apprenticeship for many years with renowned Chöd master practitioner, Ven. Phuntsok "Pencho" Rabgey,* or "Pala."

## Musical Imagery

My study of the Chöd Tradition, initially through traditional pedagogical methods, and subsequently through the interdisciplinary lens of ethnomusicology, provided opportunities to receive the musical transmission as well as the scriptural and oral transmission (Tib. *lung*).

One day, while writing my doctoral dissertation on this subject, I encountered a Chöd lama's pith instructions (Tib. *man ngag*) that revealed Machik Labdrön had composed several melodies herself, including a melody designed to represent a sound-image: "the sound of vultures' flapping their wings as they arrive at a sky burial." Machik had set this melody to the subritual section in a Chöd liturgy when one's body is at its most vulnerable.

Her melody exhibits use of the music compositional device of "tone painting," enlivening the practitioner's meditative visualization at this key

*When Venerable Pencho Rabgey arrived in Canada in 1971 with his family, together with the first wave of 221 Tibetan refugees ever to emigrate to the country, the immigration officer on that occasion apparently misheard the pronunciation of Phuntsok as "Pencho," and inscribed that name. Since then, Pencho has been his official first name, as registered in his Canadian passport, preceding his surname Rabgey. When he and his family were awarded the Meritorious Service Cross and Medal, Canada's highest civilian honor, by the Office of the Governor General in 2019, his official name Pencho Rabgey was decorated accordingly with M.S.C. Although the Library of Tibetan Works and Archives published his autobiography in 2017 under his Tibetan name, Phuntsok, written in Tibetan language, which is appropriate for Tibetan audiences, he has requested that we use his name as it appears in his passport, Pencho, which we will do forthwith. In some sections where an expressed instruction or teaching of Chöd is conveyed to me directly, the reader will find that I switch over to the familiar "Pala," as otherwise it feels too distanced from the actual context.

moment. This shows an effective composition technique utilized by one of the most important Tibetan adepts and artists of Buddhist ritual music.

## Sonic Iconography

Depicting meditative symbolism through a melody—in ways utterly harmonious with the liturgical poetry—corrects a mistaken earlier impression that music-text relationships in Chöd rituals are of relatively minimal importance.

These symbolic concordances conveyed performatively through the Buddhist sound arts ought to now be considered far from anomalous. Additional such instances of music-text relationships can be found in various liturgies.

These instances may be thought of as "sonic iconography," akin to the purposeful use of thangka paintings as an aid in meditation—cueing the aural, or visual, sensorium respectively, to deepen one's practice. Such findings led me to engage in "ritual mapping," an analytical technique for exploring the many and varied ways in which the outer musical performance and inner meditation practice elements cohere in the context of Chöd ritual liturgies and practices.

One of the goals in writing this book is to relay to its readers, some of whom could be future scholar-practitioners of Buddhist ritual, observations and techniques for mapping the performative architecture of Chöd rituals themselves—as they encounter them.

By mapping the symbolic meaning of "the sound of vultures' wings," and other examples to be shown, we come to understand that symbolism is expressed as an evocative instrument of Chöd practice that can be accomplished through the creative conjoining of the interdependent ritual elements of melody, poetry, and mental visualization with emotion, culture, and consciousness.

Exploring how Buddhist ritual arts are designed to augment the practitioner's internal and external transformation can perhaps become, at once, both a goal and a path.

# སྔོན་འགྲོའི་གཏམ།

༄༅། །བར་ལམ་ནས་ཟབ་མོ་གཅོད་ཀྱི་ཆོས་འཁོར་མང་པོ་མང་དག་ཅིག་དབྱིན་སྐད་དུ་འགྱུར་བ་དག་རྗེ་ཕེས་རིས་འཛམ་དཔལ་རིགས་བཟང་རང་ཉིད་ཀྱིས་ལྷ་ཀློག་བྱས་རྗེས་ཤིན་ཏུ་དད་ནས། ཁོ་བོར་གཅོད་ཀྱི་སྐོར་དྲི་བ་མང་པོ་བྱུང་བ་མ་ཚད་གཅོད་ཀྱི་མན་ངག་ལ་སྦྱོང་འདོད་ཡོད་པའི་སྐོར་ཁ་བརྡ་བྱུང་། དེ་ལ་ངས་བསམ་ཚོད་ཐོག་མར་གཅོད་ཀྱི་དབང་ལུང་མན་ངག་ཚད་ཀྱི་བླ་མའི་དྲུང་ནས་ཞུ་དགོས་པ་ལས། གང་བྱུང་དཔེ་དེབ་ཀློག་པ་ཙམ་གྱིས་མི་དྲུང་བས་དོན་རྟགས་ཚང་མ་གསལ་བཤད་བྱས་ནས་ཁོང་རང་རྒྱ་གར་གང་སར་དུ་གཅོད་པ་མང་པོ་དང་བླ་མ་རྗེ་བཙུན་དམ་པའི་ཞལ་ནས། གཅོད་དབང་ནམ་མཁའ་སྒོ་འབྱེད་དབང་དང་ཁྲིད་བཅས་ཐོབ་འདུག རྒྱ་གར་ལྷོ་ཕྱོགས་སུ་གཅོད་ཁྲིད་མང་ཙམ་ཐོབ་འདུག དེ་ནས་རིམ་གྱིས་རང་ངོས་ནས་གཅོད་ཀྱི་རྒྱུད་པ་རྒྱུད་ཐབས་ཀྱི་བརྒྱུད་མ་རྒྱུད་ཤེས་རབ་བརྒྱུད་སྨས་རྒྱུད་ཟུང་འཇུག་བརྒྱུད་ཉེ་རྒྱུད་བྱིན་རླབས་བརྒྱུད་ཀྱི་རིམ་པ་དང་། ཚིག་གའི་ཚིག་འབྲེལ་དང་རྟ་དབྱངས་རྟུང་ལེན་སོགས་གཙོ་བོ་ཡོངས་འཛིན་བྱམས་པ་རིན་པོ་ཆེས་བདེ་ཆེན་སྙིང་པོ་དགྱེས་པའི་དགའ་སྟོན་གཞིར་བཟུང་ནས་སློབ་ཁྲིད་བྱས། དེ་ཡང་གཅོད་ཀྱི་དགོངས་དོན་བྱམས་སྙིང་རྗེ་བྱང་ཆུབ་ཀྱི་སེམས་དང་འབྲེལ་བའི་སྒོ་ནས། ཡང་དག་པའི་ལྟ་བས་བདག་འཛིན་གཅོད་པ་དེ་གཅོད་ཀྱི་དོན། དེ་ལ་ཕྱི་ནང་གསང་གསུམ་དེ་ཁོ་ན་ཉིད་ཀྱི་གཅོད་སོགས་སློབ་གསོ་གང་ཐུབ་བརྟོད་ཡོད། དེ་ཡང་གལ་ཆེ་བ་ཁོང་རང་བོད་སྐད་དང་བོད་ཡིག་ལ་ཉམས་སྦྱོང་གང་ལེགས་ཡོད་པ་དེའི་ཆོས་ཕྱོགས་ཀྱི་སློབ་གཉེར་ལ་ཕན་ཐོག་གང་ལེགས་བྱུང་ཡོད་པ་བཅས།

ཀ་ཤར་ལིན་མཛེས་ནས་ ༢༠༡༨ ཟླ་ ༣ ཚེས་ ༩ ལ།

ཕུན་ཚོགས་རབ་དགས།

# Foreword

Pencho Rabgey, M.S.C.

In recent times there have been many English translations of texts regarding the profound teaching cycles of Chöd. Jeffrey (Jampel Rigsang) had himself read many of these translations, and developed immense faith in them. He came to me with numerous questions about the teachings of Chöd; but not only that: he wished to train in the secret instructions of Chöd, and we discussed this. In my estimation, I thought that Jeffrey should begin by requesting the empowerments, oral transmissions, and secret instructions from a teacher who was qualified to grant all of these. In any case, since it is not sufficient merely to read from a book, I explained all the meanings and symbolism to him clearly.

Then he himself went to various places in India, and received the empowerment of Chöd known as "Opening the Door of the Sky," along with the instructions for practice, face to face with the Lama [Khalkha] Jetsun Dampa and many practitioners of Chöd. In South India he received quite a number of teachings on Chöd. Then gradually, step-by-step, from my side I taught him the tantra of Chöd: the father tantras (the lineage of method), the mother tantras (the lineage of wisdom), the son tantras (the lineage of the union of the two), and the close family tantras (the lineage of blessing). I taught him the melodies, the connections between the words of the rituals, how to strike the drum, and so on, taking as my principle source the *Banquet Set to Please Dechen Nyingpo* written by the Tutor [to the Twelfth and Thirteenth Dalai Lamas], Yongdzin Jampa Rinpoché.

On top of that I imparted to him, to the best of my ability, education in the real meaning of Chöd: in constant relationship to love, compassion, and the wish for enlightenment, one gains the perfect view. With this, one cuts off grasping to a self—this is the meaning of "cutting." Then, I also imparted to him the outer, inner, and secret Chöd, as well as the Chöd of reality such as it is. Furthermore, which is very important, he himself has excellent experience in both spoken and literary Tibetan language, and this will bring splendid benefit to the study of the Dharma.

Phuntsok Rabgey [Ven. Pencho Rabgey]
March 8, 2016
Lindsay, Ontario

Foreword translated by Eva Natanya, PhD

# Preface

The Tibetan female ascetic Machik Labdrön (Ma gcig lab sgron, 1055–1153), developed a Vajrayāna (tantric) Buddhist meditation method called Chöd (Tib. *gCod*, Eng. "to cut"), and associated ritual meditation practices as a method through which a practitioner can rapidly increase their level of *bodhicitta* (altruistic awakening mind) and "cut" (Chöd) attachment to the habitually mistaken notion of a truly-existent "self" with the antidote to "self-grasping" ignorance: the realization of the emptiness of all phenomena. The Chöd practitioner learns to develop *bodhicitta* by operationalizing the experience of fear and reversing the habitual tendency to cherish oneself above others to thereby attain enlightenment. Inviting all beings throughout the universe with the human thighbone trumpet (*rkang gling*), drum (*ḍamaru*), bell (*dril bu*), and sung melodies (*rta*) for a feast and to pay down one's karmic debt to them, the Chöd practitioner plays the symbolic ritual instruments and sings liturgies set in the "songs of meditation experience" *gur* (Tib. *mgur*) style, the same genre in which the Tibetan poet-saint Milarepa (Mi la ras pa) composed.

Chöd practice involves the detailed visualizing of giving the body away in a succession of "distributions" or "banquets" (*'gyed*) to various guests, including: the buddhas, bodhisattvas, Dharma protectors, and the invited spirits. Giving away the mentally transformed body to the spirit guests to pay down the practitioner's karmic debt to them, even in visualization, may conjure up the experience of fear and attachment, which the practitioner aims to recognize as habitual self-preservation. At a critical moment in the ritual dramaturgy, when the practitioner is most protective of the "self," they aim to "cut" the habitual grasping to this apparently existent "self." When unable to find a "self" to protect, the practitioner is faced with the erroneous basis for "self-grasping" (*bdag 'dzin*), and thereby has an opportunity to realize the truth of "emptiness" which is understood as the absence of inherent existence of all phenomena.

Although the Chöd ritual has increasingly received Western scholarly attention during the past few decades from Buddhist studies scholars working in the areas of historiography, translation, and hagiography, a gap remains with respect to the study of the musical and performance aspects of the practice. Researching Chöd utilizing the tools of ethnomusicology, this multisite ethnographic study combines a musical apprenticeship under recognized masters of the Chöd Tradition with musical analysis to explore, for the first time, the various functions served by the music in the Chöd ritual. This approach has yielded a fascinating discovery about the relationship between the melodies and the textual liturgy. Based on a case study of Chöd sādhana practices, including *Dedicating the Illusory Body as a Heaped Offering* and *Offering Gaṇacakra in Connection with the Yoga of the Profound Path of Chöd*, there is substantial evidence that music-text (performance-visualization) correspondences exist in the main liturgical texts of the Chöd Tradition's lineages. This corrects an earlier impression that the *gur* genre of spiritual song-poetry is the result solely of spontaneous compositions with the insight that Chöd lamas appear to have deliberately crafted Chöd music and poetry in ways to enhance the meditative experience for practitioners of the ritual and augment the efficacy of Chöd as a transformative event.

## Audiences, Intentions, Readership

As discussed in greater detail throughout the Introduction, the intended readership for this book is diverse and interdisciplinary, and primarily includes: (1) Buddhist Studies scholars and Indo-Tibetan and Himalayan Studies specialists; (2) music scholars—ethnomusicologists, musicologists, and music theorists—who are exploring the roles of music and sound in the context of liturgical rituals as they are performed in Buddhist practice traditions; (3) Chöd practitioners, as well as contemplatives engaged in ritual music practices informed by other Buddhist tantric traditions; and, (4) scholars of anthropology of religion, ritual studies, and performance studies who might find here approaches to exploring Buddhist ritual music traditions that emerge from glimpses of insights into traditional teachings. Whichever their disciplinary starting point, all of these readerships will be introduced to methods and tools for mapping performative meanings undergirding a Chöd liturgy—a tantric ritual that *embodies* the Mahāyāna Buddhist Perfection of Wisdom sūtras, while leading to "severance" and *disembodiment*—which is the central focus of chapter 1 and most subsequent chapters.

Since each of these readerships will approach Chöd in their own ways, seeing through their respective lenses, I recognize that each will also have a somewhat different locus of interest at first. That said, nearly every section intends to speak to at least two of these readerships at the same time. Both Buddhist Studies scholars and Chöd practitioners, for example, will be familiar with the philosophical terminology, while being perhaps less acquainted with an approach to liturgical music that explores sound and music experiences as performed/practiced during a ritual occasion. By the same reasoning, ethnomusicologists and anthropologists conducting ethnographic research in Buddhist communities, and while there exploring ritual events, could discover something analytically useful in this book for how to investigate the roles of musical elements in Chöd practices, and other Buddhist tantric practices more generally. Finally, practitioners who are deeply engaged in Chöd rituals, as well as those just emerging into the depth of its study and practice, may find here some glue that adheres to their early experiences—perhaps making sense of connections they have already intuited.

In essence, I hope researchers involved in mapping a multi-faceted Buddhist tantric tradition such as Chöd can benefit from a guide that helps them to ground a cross-disciplinary approach when attending to the use of music, sound, and visualization in its ritual performances. Similarly, I wish that practitioners may also find useful the broader exercise here: taking an analytical approach toward expressing, in language and illustration, nothing other than the ineffable (*śūnyatā*), which can be more fully appreciated in the context of practice through performance. To go even one step further, perhaps it is not Chöd that needs to be considered in both its epistemological and performative dimensions, but rather traditional disciplinary boundaries that need to be relaxed in order to allow the vibrancy and numinosity of the Chöd Tradition to be better appreciated.

My goal in addressing these diverse readerships, at once or in turn, emerges from my wish that the explorations and discoveries conveyed in this book will help contribute to creating a new space—a space in which analyses of a Buddhist tantric ritual music tradition through an "integrated" approach can be of practical use to interdisciplinary researchers and practitioners alike. Notwithstanding the false distinction between researchers and practitioners suggested above, some renowned scholar-practitioners are known to be creative contributors to the performative aspects of Chöd sādhanas, and other traditions where Tibetan tantric rituals are practiced (see the discussion about the "Interpretive Community" of Chöd adepts in chapter 4).

An immediate aim is to ask the reader to consider the Chöd Tradition with respect to aurality, and how its philosophical foundation and performative architecture combine to make visceral the experience of mental transformation through sound. If that is achieved satisfactorily, it will be an important boon, offering potentially increased efficacy once the reader knows the interdependent layers of such practices—such as how the internal meditation practices cohere with the external musical performance elements.

Additionally, my hope is that the approaches suggested on these pages will assist in expanding the scope of subsequent research into Buddhist ritual music, and thus enhance future inquiries by treating such musical practices as living traditions with varied performances. It would be especially gratifying to those involved in this project, I think, if readers engage in exploring the mapping techniques themselves, and examine whether their analyses gel with their own understanding and practice of Chöd, and perhaps other Buddhist tantric rituals.

At this juncture, I would like to address the third readership noted above, who have already received some direct instruction into this musical-meditation tradition from their Chöd lamas, and have begun to encounter some of the commentarial literature on Chöd, referred to in the coming pages. And here I write from the perspective of someone who has had the fortunate circumstances arise *first* to become immersed in the traditional transmission process, and *then* to engage in interdisciplinary detailed musical and textual analysis. In the context of traversing a gradual path, I would like to suggest the following: if those who wish to practice Chöd could *first* engender the possibility for transformation by experiencing the practice under the tutelage of a qualified lama, and *then* combine this traditional perspective with this book's new analytical understandings of how the performative architecture of a Chöd sādhana echoes with the renunciation that supports cultivating the inner wisdom of *bodhicitta* imbued with the correct view of emptiness, then this book's project of conveying insights across disciplinary boundaries would have obtained some functional value.

Jeffrey W. Cupchik
Toronto, Canada

# Acknowledgments

This research project has benefited from the generosity and assistance of many people. In this study, both textual work and ethnographic study have been combined. The work of translation and musical transcription together with cultural immersion involved many individuals and communities. First and foremost, my deepest appreciation to the Rabgey family of Ontario, Canada: "Pala" (Ven. Pencho Rabgey, M.S.C.), a renowned exponent of the Chöd Tradition and former monk of Sera Mey Monastic College, who instructed me by tirelessly transmitting the Chöd Tradition with its varied musical aspects and textual meanings. "Amala" (Tsering Dolker Rabgey, M.S.C.), Pala's life partner, who supported this work in many original and heartfelt ways, setting an example of support that always echoed of Sarasvatī's plucked strings to Mañjuśri's sung songs of wisdom. Gratitude to their esteemed daughters, my college friends at the University of Toronto: Dr. Losang C. Rabgey, M.S.C. (DPhil, SOAS), who initially taught me the Tibetan lute "dranyen" (Tib. *sgra snyan*), and Dr. Tashi Y. Rabgey, M.S.C. (Rhodes Scholar, PhD, Harvard), who advised me to "receive as complete a transmission of Chöd as possible." The Rabgey family founded Machik (machik.org), whose mission is to foster compassionate, innovative approaches to strengthening Tibetan communities in Tibet and globally. Their work is emblematic of Machik Labdrön's practice of going to challenging places and engaging generously and compassionately, amidst complex situations.

Oftentimes, things become clearer to a critical eye from a distance. I thank Geshé Thupten Jinpa Langri (PhD, Cambridge, UK; Principal English Translator to His Holiness the Fourteenth Dalai Lama), who advised me to transcribe the Chöd melodies in musical notation. It must be said again here that I did not expect to find such close correspondences between poetic text, musical gesture, and formal design in the Chöd liturgical corpus. While subsequent research may find additional correspondences, the findings here are merely my insights into the phenomena of a little-studied but most profound of yogas, the thousand-year-old song-poetry tradition of Machik Labdrön, her tantric Chöd ritual meditation practice and performance tradition.

I would like to thank the Tibetan lamas of the Chöd Tradition who assisted with this project. His Eminence Khalkha Jetsun Dampa Rinpoché for giving initiations and teachings into Chöd meditation and ritual performance practices, always focusing on the Mahāyāna motivation of *bodhicitta*, and for welcoming me into Takten House in Dharamsala. Gratitude to Kyabje Zong Chogtul Rinpoché, Changdzö Tenzin Wangchuk, Geshé Lobsang Tsultrim and all the monks at Ganden Shartse Monastic College. In particular, I am grateful to Changchub Rabgey for generously lending precious time for Chöd instruction, and everyone at Tayön Khangtsen. Many thanks to Venerable Kusho Kundeling and his Chöd student group in Bylakuppe, Karnataka, India. I also thank Tramtro Rinpoché and Ari-Khensur Rinpoché Lobsang Tharchin for inspiring, albeit brief, teachings on Chöd. Much gratitude to Zasep Rinpoché for wisdom and insights into Chöd practices, and to Gaden Choling Mahayana Buddhist Center in Toronto and Zuru Ling in Vancouver, Canada.

In addition, I thank the Former Abbot of Sera Mey Monastic University (1996–2007), Khensur Rinpoché Lobsang Jamyang, who led the Sera Mey North American Monk Tour. I am grateful for his daily mentorship and instruction during our one year together on the road performing rituals and fundraising for Sera Monastic University in India while living in and serving North American Diasporic Vietnamese and Chinese Buddhist communities. By working with Khensur Rinpoché and his delegation of ten monk ritual experts, I learned more about Buddhist ritual and its roles in community contexts than I ever could have otherwise. I am grateful to Ngawang Nyendrak, *dbu mdzad* (chanting master) of the Sera Mey North American Monk Tour for musical instruction and many years of friendship. My heartfelt thanks to Acharya Thupten Kelsang Champa in Toronto for his clear and profound instruction in Tibetan language, and his translation expertise.

For invitations to deliver conference and colloquium papers on earlier versions of chapters of this work, I thank the following scholars and unique settings: Frances Garrett, Henry Shui, and Bill Bowen (University of Toronto, *Tung Lin Kok Yuen International Conference Visualizing and Performing Buddhist Worlds*); Phyllis Granoff (Yale, *South Asian Studies Council Colloquium Series*); José Cabezón (University of California–Santa Barbara, *International Conference on Tibetan Ritual*); Mark Blum (University of California–Berkeley, *Symposium on Buddhist Ritual Music*); and, Sarah Morelli and Richard Wolf (Harvard University, *Conference on the Music of Central, West and South Asia*).

I would like to thank esteemed colleagues in Tibetan Studies and Buddhist Studies whose guidance helped inform this research: Jake Dalton (Yale/UC Berkeley), David Germano (University of Virginia), Janet Gyatso (Harvard Divinity School), Elliot Sperling (Indiana University), Robert Thurman (Columbia), and Eugene Wang (Harvard). As well, I have benefited from counsel given by Ethnomusicologists working in South Asia: James Kippen (University of Toronto), Sarah Morelli (University of Denver), Regula Quereshi (University of Alberta), Rob Simms (York University), and Sarah Weiss (Yale). Special thanks to Ter Ellingson (University of Washington–Seattle), the preeminent Ethnomusicologist-Tibetologist who served as external examiner at my dissertation oral defense, and then championed the work with strong encouragement during its final stages.

At York University, my deepest appreciation is to my supervisor, Rob Bowman, who continuously set an example of bi-musicality and integrity in negotiating multiple identities as the rigorous historical musicologist while wearing popular music historian scholar's clothes and brandishing the ethnomusicologist's weapons of methodological strengths, disciplinary enthusiasm for musical arts, and an analytic mission to research the guiding aesthetic logic of any musical tradition. As well, much deep gratitude to my co-supervisor David Mott, who gave a range of supportive feedback from perspectives on Tibetan Buddhist practice, Chöd meditation rituals, music lineage transmission, to insights into "music as energy"—as a jazz improviser, composer, and working practitioner and teacher of qi gong. I am grateful to David Lidov, for sharing his expertise in musical semiotics, showing me that "a sign is something that points to something else," and for introducing Naomi Cumming's project of exploring the ineffable in sonic/musical experience, and what it might mean to musically "emote." I am also grateful to Austin Clarkson for special insight into pedagogical issues in art and music, and to Saroj Charwa for a meaningful introduction to the sociological study of religion.

In Philosophy at York, I thank Evan Thompson who encouraged me to audit two of his courses on the Mind and Buddhism, and to present a paper in that forum. I thank Shannon Bell for her course in Social and Political Thought, which fostered a rethinking of identity politics, and exposed me to the post-humanist vision of feminist thought. Bell also introduced me to the work on Emmanuel Levinas's notion of "substitution," as understood by political philosophers Asher Horowitz and Gad Horowitz—both of whom gave time to discuss this project, which informed chapter 9 of this book. Many thanks also to Rosemary Coombe for introducing the current literature on cultural intangibles as intellectual property, and the consideration of cultural rights as human rights.

I thank my colleagues who first welcomed me to the Eastman School of Music, at the University of Rochester: musicologist Ralph P. Locke, whose incisive explorations of musical symbolism are an ongoing inspiration, and whose editorial support and encouragement have been invaluable. Gratitude to ethnomusicologist Ellen Koskoff, who invited me to design courses on music, health and culture (medical ethnomusicology), Tibetan musical cultures, and ethnographic research methodologies.

Support for this research was generously provided through the Social Sciences and Humanities Research Council with a Doctoral Research Fellowship. I am also grateful to the Shastri Indo-Canadian Institute for awarding an India Studies Fellowship to undertake this research. A Trudeau Fellowship was awarded to this research project, allowing research travel to study with Chöd lamas, monks, and lay practitioners in South and North India. I thank the School of Oriental and African Studies (University of London) for awarding a Commonwealth Scholarship at an early stage of the PhD research. The Canada Council for the Arts kindly gave a Travel Grant in support of my studies of Tibetan music. Research funding was also provided through York University's internal sources: the Fieldwork Costs Fund, Graduate Development Fund, and Research Costs Fund. In addition, the incredible Chamba Tibetan Summer Language and Culture Immersion Program designed and taught by the Rabgey family, offered seven weeks of essential training in modern colloquial Tibetan language, which was invaluable.

Many thanks to the editorial and production staff at the international journal *Asian Music,* University of Texas Press (special thanks to Editor, Ricardo D. Trimillos). Much gratitude to the *Yale Journal of Music & Religion* (General Editor, Robin A. Leaver; Managing Editor, Joanna Murdoch; and, Associate Editor, Phil Bohlman) for kind assistance in preparing the work, and to Robin for inviting me to contribute an article to the inaugural issue for the purposes of conveying an analytical understanding of a Himalayan tradition of liturgical song poetry to a wider interdisciplinary audience. Thus, an earlier version of chapter 4 appeared as "The Tibetan *gCod Ḍamaru*—A Reprise: Symbolism, Function, and Difference in a Tibetan Adept's Interpretive Community," *Asian Music*, Vol. 44, No. 1 (Winter/Spring 2013): 113–139. It is included here, with minor revisions, by permission of the *Journal of the Society for Asian Music* at University of Texas Press. Portions of chapters 1, 2, and 3 appeared in "Buddhism as Performing Art: Visualizing Music in the Tibetan Sacred Ritual Music Liturgies," *Yale Journal of Music & Religion*: Vol. 1, Iss. 1, Article 4 (2015), 31–62, http://dx.doi.org/10.17132/2377-231X.1010. A further article of musical analysis will be forthcoming in the *Journal of Musicological Research*, "Melodies for Dissolving the Self: Tibetan Songs of Meditative Experience."

I wish to express my sincere gratitude to the many people at SUNY Press (Albany, NY) who worked on bringing this book project to fruition. A mountain of gratitude to Harold Coward, Editor of the SUNY Series in Religious Studies, whose strong support of my research in music and religion led to his interest in reading the book manuscript and his welcoming the volume within this esteemed series. I convey my deep appreciation to Nancy Ellegate, Acquisitions Editor, who initially championed the project with Harold, and saw it through the key early stages of publication at SUNY. Many warm and sincere thanks to Jessica Kirschner, Nancy's Editorial Assistant, and Amanda Lanne-Camilli who subsequently worked with Jessica to see the book come to fruition, as well as Diane Ganeles, James Peltz, and Anne Valentine. Gratitude for the editorial assistance kindly provided by Johanna Knutzen and Maria Montenegro in the final stages. Many thanks to the talented Eva Natanya (University of Virginia) who assisted by doing the primary work on translating the Foreword by Ven. Pencho Rabgey, M.S.C.

Finally, my warmest gratitude to my mother, Gila Cupchik, and father, Will Cupchik, and my grandmother, Miriam Holtzman, who supported this project with kindness and patience.

I welcome feedback and interest from Tibetologists, anthropologists, religious studies scholars, Buddhologists and, of course, ethnomusicologists and musicologists who may wish to examine together the Chöd Traditions across lineages, and other tantric ritual traditions, as they are realized in practice—indeed, as living traditions.

Portions of chapters 1 through 3. modified here, were previously published as an article in the inaugural issue of the Yale Journal of Music & Religion, as "Buddhism as Performing Art: Visualizing Music in the Tibetan Sacred Ritual Music Liturgies." *Yale Journal of Music & Religion*. Vol. 1, No. 1 (February 2015): 61–91. DOI: https://doi.org/10.17132/2377-231X.1010

Chapter 4, with some minor modifications, was previously published in the Journal for the Society for Asian Music as: "The Tibetan gCod *Ḍamaru*—a Reprise: Symbolism, Function, and Difference in a Tibetan Adept's Interpretive Community." *Asian Music*, 44:1 (Winter/Spring 2013): 113–139.

# Introduction

## Approaching Chöd Ritual Studies

*If the perfection of generosity*
*were the alleviation of the world's poverty,*
*Then since beings are still starving now*
*In what manner did the previous Buddhas perfect it?*

*The perfection of generosity is said to be*
*The thought to give all beings everything,*
*Together with the fruit of such a thought;*
*Hence it is simply a state of mind.*[1]

*****

*At the beginning, the Guide of the World encourages*
*The giving of such things as food.*
*Later, when accustomed to this,*
*One may progressively start to give away even one's flesh.*[2]

—Śāntideva, 8th-century Buddhist Master,
Nālandā Monastic University, India

This book maps the Tibetan Chöd Ritual Practice—its internally performed meditative visualizations and externally performed musical gestures—revealing the ways in which they are mutually interdependent, enacted in practice, and designed to cohere during the ritual process in order to create effective meditative experiences.[3]

Throughout this book, a transmission and translation of the Chöd ritual practice with ritual masters of the Chöd Tradition is recorded and analytically explored. A guiding question throughout this project was to identify the aspects of music that assist in the meditation practice and ritual process. There were four distinct stages to investigating this question: an initial extended period of apprenticeship in which the music, meditation techniques, and meaning were transmitted from teacher to disciple; a subsequent longer period of practice and performance with the Chöd lamas; an analytical period of music transcription and analysis; and finally, a series of ethnographic interviews which discussed the findings of the analysis.

A fifth stage was the writing of this book, which itself was an interpretive process. Yet, the question at the end of the project remained the same initial query and guiding force that continually energized my commitment to seek answers: What are the functions of music in the Chöd ritual meditation practice? Although the word "function" hearkens back to an earlier era of structural-functionalist scholarship, in this project looking for answers concerning musical functions was inspired by a great paradox. As important as it was during the pedagogical process to learn to perform the music of Chöd according to traditional expectations, the music was de-emphasized as a site of meaning in favor of the linguistic text of the liturgy. The linguistic text, too, was de-emphasized as a site of meaning—no matter how fascinating the poetic allusions, metaphors, alliterations, and how well-crafted the song-poems' mnemonic devices appeared—in favor of the inculcation of a change in the heart-mind (Skt. *citta*) of the practitioner. The purpose of Chöd is not primarily to perform music. Yet, to the extent that music is the vehicle through which transformation occurs, its study within the context of tantric ritual meditation practice may be of value to students and scholars alike.

## The Tibetan Chöd Ritual Practice

Chöd is one of the most well-known Buddhist rituals across Central Asia. Chöd literally means "to cut" (*gCod*) in Tibetan. Machik Labdrön (Ma gcig Lab sgron, 1055–1153), a Tibetan female ascetic, developed and then taught the Chöd ritual to hundreds of thousands of disciples during her lifetime. Machik Labdrön's oral and textual instructions were disseminated extensively throughout the Central Asian Plateau and Himalayan regions to Mongolia, Nepal, India, Ladakh, Sikkim, Buryatia, and Bhutan. Several translators from these various regions would attend her public teachings, along with thousands of disciples. Her Chöd ritual—a Vajrayāna (tantric) practice founded on *bodhicitta*, the altruistic motivation of Mahāyāna Buddhism—was continually tested and found to be one of the most efficacious means for rapidly attaining Buddhist enlightenment.[4]

During several Chöd rituals, the practitioner goes to a solitary place and conducts an outward performance of playing the *ḍamaru* drum and Tibetan bell, and singing prescribed beautiful melodies composed by Machik Labdrön and her best disciples, while simultaneously conducting an inner performance of powerful visualizations. Founded upon Buddhist notions of compassion and wisdom, consciousness and rebirth, the Chöd practitioner learns how to transform her experiences of suffering, as well as the suffering of others, into the path to enlightenment. The practitioner visualizes transforming her body into all things beneficial and desirable to others (such as medicines, food, clothes, wealth, etc.) and then giving these to others; at the same time, she visualizes taking into her own heart others' sufferings, sins, and negative karma. While the Chöd practitioner visualizes "cutting" and offering her body, she also "cuts" the way she habitually clings to the notion of "self" or "I." Thereby, she can realize the impermanent and contingent nature of the relationships between her mind, body, and "self." As Chöd is a highest yoga tantra (Skt. *anuttarayoga tantra*; Tib. *bla na med pa'i rgyud*)[5] practice, aspects of Machik Labdrön's teachings were taught only in secret, between teacher and disciple—an intimate bond with profound results and religious significance in terms of continuity of a lineage transmission and personal transformation through the practice. Some of the lineage practices were transmitted only orally, and teachers were forbidden to divulge some teachings except to certain disciples.

It is presently a critical historical moment in the history of the Tibetan Diaspora. Tibetan exiles with lived memory of Buddhist traditions inside pre-1959 Tibet are now sexa-, septua-, and octogenarians. While some of the nearly 7,000 monasteries destroyed in Tibet between the 1950s and 1970s have been rebuilt in exile (in India, Nepal, or in the West),[6] in the case of the Chöd ritual—which has traditionally been practiced outside monastic institutions—the process of lineage transmission has undergone significant challenges and transcultural transformations. Much responsibility lies at the juncture between Tibetan teachers and their Tibetan and non-Tibetan disciples.

Today, Tibetan elders who are themselves disciples in the Chöd lineages, now living outside Tibet in India and the West, have sought new ways and means to transmit their knowledge and preserve the continuity and integrity of the Chöd Tradition and its lineages. I have been receiving a transmission of the Chöd lineage teachings through the normative traditional transmission process from recognized lineage holders since 1995. My main teacher of Chöd, Ven. Pencho Rabgey, whom I call "Pala," is one of the last and eldest lineage holders in the Tibetan Ganden Chöd Tradition who retains a memory of how the tradition was practiced inside pre-1959 Tibet, and he selected me to learn in the close, one-to-one, *guru-śiṣya paramparā* (master-disciple relationship) context of musical and spiritual transmission.[7] This raises important questions about my own hybridic identity as a Western Buddhist and my insider-outsider status vis-à-vis the Buddhist tradition. As well, since I am inscribing my understandings and experience of Chöd within Western academic discourse, I am always implicated in the process of transcultural translation and its attendant responsibilities.

## Ways of Approaching Chöd Ritual Practice

Chöd practice has different functions on the individual and social level. On the individual level and setting, the practice can be used as a tool for achieving enlightenment. On the social level, Chöd rituals are often used to heal others and to prevent calamities and disease. Traditionally, the Chödpa (Chöd practitioner)[8] was requested to come out of their retreat place in the mountains down to the village to perform rituals that would remove disease and sickness from individuals and communities. At this point, it must be made clear that "suffering" within Buddhist epistemology is understood in terms of causality. That is, as the direct result of living in "cyclic existence" (Skt. *saṃsāra*, Tib. *'khor ba*), one is constantly driven by "the three poisons" (Tib. *dug gsum*)—"attachment," "anger," and their root, "ignorant self-grasping" mind—to act in negative ways through the doors of body, speech, or mind which could manifest as karmic illness or injury.[9] According to tradition, Chöd practitioners are not allowed to seek healing from doctors, but must utilize the practice to heal themselves, though it must always be performed with the compassionate motivation to improve one's own condition in order to ultimately benefit others. The Chöd practitioner patiently accepts the results of bodily suffering from previous karmic causes—yet attempts to purify that karma. The Chöd practitioner experiencing physical illness can transform her own suffering into the path to Buddhist enlightenment by thinking compassionately that her illness is the suffering of others ripening upon herself. The most advanced practitioner, if actually contracting an illness, would rejoice that her desire and efforts to relieve others of their suffering actually came to fruition.

Furthermore, if we were to theorize the Chöd ritual in terms of reciprocity in the healer-patient relationship, or perhaps in terms of "sacrifice," our analysis would reveal a unique conceptualization of reciprocity in the exchange between the Chödpa and others. From the perspective of Mahāyāna Buddhism, when the Chödpa gives her body (mentally transformed into all things desirable) to others, she is not enacting the initial stage of the exchange; rather, she is repaying her debts to other beings. According to Buddhist conceptions of the continuity of consciousness and rebirth, we took rebirth countless times before this life, and for each of these lives we must have had a mother and father. By logical extrapolation, every being in the universe has been our mother and father countless times before. In each of our lives, our mother and father took care of us compassionately. While today most of us do not recognize our former mothers and fathers due to an absence in powers of clairvoyance, Mahāyāna Buddhists nevertheless endeavor to visualize others as such, and are therefore *always already* indebted to the kindness of all "mother sentient beings." A component of the Chöd practice, then, is the paying off of our karmic debt to those whom we have harmed (knowingly or inadvertently) and to those from whom we have received kindness. From the tantric perspective, Machik's Chöd Tradition is radical and could be dangerous. She not only pays off her karmic debt, she pays the most needy beings first. They are needy because of their marked malevolence and ill intentions from which *they*, the harmdoers (Tib. *gdug pa can*), will further suffer as a result of their negative karmic imprints. These needy beings are potentially the most harmful. Moreover, the site of practice is a major catalyst for rethinking the relationship of phenomena and beings to one's "self." It suggests exercising a constructive giving through imaginal self-destruction at the site of habitation of those dangerous and destructive beings. It is counterintuitive because at the moment the practitioner is most vulnerable and exposed to harm, and would normally seek self-protection, she gives the body away and then searches for the "self" that seeks protection. Finding none, she works toward cutting identification with, and attachment to, the body as the site of the "self."

While Chöd has been mistakenly theorized as a shamanic rite, a sacrificial offering, and even a barbaric feast, I discuss the practice in terms closer to its Buddhist epistemological underpinnings. According to His Eminence Kyabje Zong Rinpoché (1905–1984), the renowned twentieth-century Chöd practitioner and former head of the Ganden Chöd Tradition's lineage, Chöd is the practice of *bodhicitta*.[10] *Bodhicitta* is the altruistic mind devoted to the alleviation of suffering for all sentient beings—the compassionate mind that is a prerequisite to attaining buddhahood.

## Approaching Chöd from Buddhist Studies

Although the last three decades have seen a gradual increase in the amount of Western scholarship produced on Chöd, the ritual has captured the interest of Buddhist studies scholars more so than ethnomusicologists.[11] Scholars of Buddhist studies and Tibetology have been fascinated and loquacious in their enthusiastic entrance into the academic study of the Chöd ritual, and a number of Western scholars of Tibetan Buddhism have produced works dealing exclusively with Chöd (Harding 2003; Edou 1996; Savvas 1990; Gyatso 1985).[12]

These philological explorations have examined aspects of Chöd from various perspectives, including: historiographical research on tradition and lineage (Sorensen 2013; Gyatso 1985); Chöd theory, doctrine, and sādhana translation (Orofino 2000; Savvas 1990); goals of the practice (Tucci 1980); hagiography (Harding 2003); and a combination of all of the above (Edou 1996). Taken together, these illuminate several aspects of the Chöd rite. Thus, a great deal is now known about the life and history of the Tibetan saint Machik Labdrön, such as the advent and dissemination of her tradition's lineages. Yet Western students and scholars of the Chöd Tradition are interested to know more about the significance of the Chöd ritual as a Tibetan tantric practice.

### Tantric Studies and Ritual Theory

Studies of Tibetan tantric ritual have sometimes proceeded without locating the research within the larger discourse of ritual studies in ethnomusicology, anthropology, and religious studies, as was discussed at a conference on Tibetan tantric ritual.[13] After nearly two days of presentations, Donald Lopez concluded that dualistic categories of sacred/profane typically encountered in works authored by E. B. Tylor and Emile Durkheim were unknowingly woven into the narrative of the majority of papers. He argued that categorical differentiations were often unconsciously embedded in the work of scholars emerging from Western European approaches to the study of ritual. In particular, he suggested more critical probing into the ongoing and problematic distinction in academic studies between that which constitutes a *bona fide religious practice* on the one hand, and a *folk belief* or *attitude* on the other. The legacy of this differentiation in the social sciences and humanities, with its history of attaching greater value to the importance of conducting studies in one subject area over another, needs to be more critically addressed in Tibetan ritual music studies.[14]

This is necessary because in the Tibetan context what scholars name "ritual" (Tib. *cho ga*) occupies a social and cognitive space in which religious belief and ritual practice are intertwined for Tibetan lay and ordained practitioners as well as for householders and itinerant nuns and monks, elders and youth, clerics and ascetics, females and males. Tantric ritual performances attract practitioners and participants from these social domains, building a bridge across the deep crevasse of what is considered relevant and superfluous in Durkheim's categories. The dyadic categories of religion/magic or religious worship/superstition are doctrinally defined; but, in practice, blurring is evident in many Tibetan social contexts (which makes writing about Tibetan ritual practices a very delicate enterprise). Moreover, the categorical definitions of magic, belief, religion, and worship are not universally understood across all Tibetan social contexts. An additional confusion about worship has to do with the notion in Vajrayāna practice that buddhas are not solely external beings. The identity of individuals is shaped through the tantric practice of guru-deity yoga,[15] which is coextensive with the worship of deities.

Many Tibetans receive their name from a lama, not from their parents; and, from a lama they may also receive and recognize a personal *yidam*, or "meditational deity," which functions literally as a "mind" (*yi*) "protector" (*dam*). The *yidam* is the meditational deity with whom a practitioner personally identifies and in whose form she or he seeks to become enlightened, recognizing that the deity is not an inherently existing form, but manifests as a consequence of the dependent arising of karmic causes and conditions.[16] This is a very different tack than deification and worship in the Abrahamic and other theistic based traditions in which a conventional subject (worshiper) is interminably separate from a theistic source (God). Early Western writers of Tibetological literature focusing on Tibetan Buddhist ritual sought to recognize the integrated practice of religious ritual and belief in daily life. They worked at building a vocabulary to describe the Buddhists' worship of an omniscient being (buddha) who may also be coextensive with the practitioner. Tibetologists' first approaches to research on ritual often, however, treated religious subject matter in the language of Orientalist superiority and exotica, and attended primarily to the clerical role of monks who occupy the office of monastery ritual performers.[17]

## On Tibetan Lifeways

One barrier to a deeper understanding of Tibetan Buddhism may be overcome by recognizing the ways in which Tibetans are taught to listen to Buddhist teachings from a lama. From a doctrinal perspective, buddhas can teach other beings how to reach higher levels of knowledge on the path to omniscience so that they may know the causes and conditions that lead to suffering in order to stop themselves from creating the conditions for further suffering, and instead transcend "cyclic existence." Thus, it is important to understand that, according to Buddha's teachings, the onus is on the individual practitioner to put the teachings into practice.

At the same time that people worship the buddhas (by making offerings, confessions, etc.), many Western Buddhists become confused about basic points. If it is up to the individual to become enlightened, then why worship another being? In conversations between Buddhists and non-Buddhists, I have heard a great deal of confusion on this point. For example:

> I thought Buddhists were atheists. If they are, then why do they place such strong emphasis on ritual worship and meditation practice? Do they believe in gods, or not? If they are *worshipping* buddhas, then the buddhas might as well be gods—they are just gods by another name. What are they praying for anyway?[18]

Tibetan lamas maintain that for many this confusion persists. The dividing line between those who understand the nature of buddhas and those who worship buddhas *as if they are gods* (believing that buddhas can *save* them from environmental calamities, minor misfortunes of thieves, and great misfortunes such as a rebirth in hell or as an animal) has primarily to do with education level.

Pala (Ven. Pencho Rabgey), born in the mid-1930's in rural Tibet, recalled that while growing up, most of the lay population had very limited access to formal education, whereas becoming ordained as a monk or nun was the main route affording one that opportunity. This relates to early Western Tibetological writings, which conveyed a sense that, among lay practitioners (householders, farmers, nomads, and semi-nomads)—who gained some education by attending periodic traditional spiritual teachings given by lamas—many appeared to be worshipping buddhas in a manner that seemed theistic. However, the rituals of worship, in essence, express reverence for the realized human potential of the Buddha as well as the great accomplishments of highly realized lamas and practitioners. The key distinctive aspect rests in the ways in which Vajrayāna practitioners engage in guru-deity yoga. After having received a tantric initiation from a qualified lama, thus being blessed and empowered, one can visualize oneself as a buddha deity—whether one is a nun, monk, or lay practitioner. Yet, among lay Tibetans, who comprise the majority of the community of worshippers, many tend to weave belief, superstition, faith, and practice in everyday life (as do educated people who consult astrological charts). Similarly, blurred lines are evident in the social reception of the Chödpa. For example, in some Tibetan Buddhist communities, Chöd practitioners live in hermitages in the forest or in caves. They are widely regarded as unconventional ascetics; and because Chöd practitioners train to develop non-attachment to their own body, typically they are the ones called upon to remove a deceased person's body from a family home and carry it to the funerary site. Some Tibetans exercise caution about the disease they feel they could contract merely by touching the Chödpa. Thus, a Chöd practitioner may engage in retreat, living apart from a community to take nightly meditation and train extensively in the practices, only to later be called upon to perform spiritual and social services.

## Approaching Chöd from Ethnomusicology

### Ethnomusicology and Tibetan Ritual Music Studies

Without Tibetologist-ethnomusicologist Ter Ellingson's "road map" to the study of Tibetan ritual music, this exploration into the genre of the Chöd ritual meditation practice and the performance tradition would have been significantly hindered.[19] To assist the reader with expertise in *either* music *or* Buddhist ritual practices *but with* minimal knowledge in the other would require a treatise-length exposition which, thankfully, Ellingson (1979) has already undertaken.[20] Ellingson showed that a close ethnographic study and treatment of the music within the intimacy of ritual could reveal the intricacies of symbolic levels of Tibetan culture and Buddhist practice.

Historically speaking, however, the Chöd practice did not emerge within, or exclusive to, the performance genres of Tibetan ritual music that have already been studied: ensemble based monastic chant (Kaufmann 1978), monastic orchestral ensemble performance (Ellingson 1979; Canzio 1978), and ritual dance (Schrempf 2001; Calkowsky 1992; Nebesky-Wojkowitz 1975). From an historical perspective, such a view mistakenly overlooks the fact that the Chöd Tradition's melodious dharmic poetry is derived from the Tibetan *mgur* tradition ("songs of meditative realization"), which itself may stem from the Indian *dohā* tradition of meditative poetry composed by mahāsdiddhas; and, from a ritual perspective, Chöd is associated with ascetic meditation traditions due to the site and context of its intended practice.

Given the particular differences in the Chöd ritual music's historical origin and performance context, we may wonder to what extent Ellingson's "mandala" concept should be prioritized in analyses of Tibetan ritual music. Ellingson himself admits that the "mandala of sound" perspective is but one possible conceptual paradigm, and writes that indigenous Tibetan interpretations may be grounded in different viewpoints. Ellingson qualifies his focused attention on the "mandala" concept as follows:

> Tibetan interpretations of music present several alternatives to the 'mandala' concept, which might equally well have been chosen for primary emphasis: the poetic quantitative 'ocean of melody' image, Atiśa's 'sensually pleasing offering,' and Sa skya Paṇḍita's 'for the benefit of others' concepts, to mention only a few. Generally, in both writing and speaking, Tibetans cite these concepts of music far more often than the 'mandala of sound' concept.[21]

Ellingson's treatise includes a survey of the various alternative perspectives to which a comprehensive description, analysis, or interpretation of a Tibetan ritual music tradition may be subject. He openly disavows singular representations as insufficient, finding them to be no more than footholds for explanatory theory. However, he takes the position of the "mandala" concept quite far and his doctoral thesis has remained arguably the most important treatise in the English language on Tibetan ritual music, correcting and advancing the work of earlier researchers Ivan Vandoor and Walter Kaufmann.[22]

In sum, the scholarship on Chöd has up until now focused on the written ritual text and visualizations, but minimally on the integrally related sounds, rhythms, vocalizations, gestures, and mantric utterances to name but a few performative aspects.

## Native/Indigenous Perspectives

Since Chöd is a tantric ritual music tradition in which visualization of a *maṇḍala* is not the guiding concept for sound production or musical gesture in performance, my research necessarily involves an alternative focus to that of Ellingson's work. In this book I attempt, as much as possible, to illuminate normative conceptions within Chöd pedagogy, ritual meditation practice, and ritual music performance. By doing so, I hope to provide a fuller understanding of the multifaceted nature of Tibetan tantric ritual.

There are certain culturally internal interpretations of Chöd practice and performance that a Tibetan Chöd lama (Skt. *guru*; Tib. *bla ma*) imparts to student practitioners for them to put into practice. Due to a cultural relativist perspective inherited from sociocultural anthropology, learning the "native-perspective" or "indigenous perspective" as much as possible is one of the main aims of ethnomusicologists. As one ethnomusicologist points out, "The notion of 'native perspective' is fundamental for most recent humanistic research in ethnomusicology."[23] Likewise, learning the indigenous perspective provided a basis for the ways in which I studied Chöd ritual meditation practices and attempt to explain my findings here.

## Methods of Inquiry

My approach toward learning and explaining the Chöd ritual practice relied on the combined methodologies of participant-observation in cultural anthropology, and a musical apprenticeship in the *guru-śiṣya paramparā* paradigm familiar to the Classical Hindustani and Carnatic forms of music transmission within Indian traditions (in which there is also often a spiritual transmission, as there is in the Chöd transmission process). In addition to these dialogic and performative methods, I also employed the research approach of Buddhist studies scholars,[24] working with my Chöd teachers in translating Chöd ritual texts while receiving commentary into their meaning.

My overall approach, much aligned with James Spradley (1979), yielded an important methodological insight about the value of seeking indigenous interpretations.[25] I attended to Tibetan interpretations of what is important about the music and its performance in the Chöd meditation tradition.[26] I also sought out advice from Tibetan scholars and lamas about what would be potentially useful to Tibetan scholars and practitioners following an immersive ethnomusicological study of Chöd. I was advised to (1) endeavor to receive as full a transmission as possible, and (2) to transcribe the music.

## Ethnographic Field Research on Chöd: Context of Study

Currently, it is a crucially important moment in the Tibetan Chöd Tradition. With few leading exponents remaining who carry a living memory of practices as they were in Tibet, students face serious challenges to receiving the full explanation of the Chöd traditional practices. Despite the challenges, I have been fortunate to have studied with several Tibetan ritual masters in the context of transmission of teacher to disciple within the Chöd Tradition, receiving an initiation and then studying chiefly two areas: the musical practices and meditation practices on a one-on-one basis.[27] My studies of these two areas are woven throughout this book. In particular, I was exceptionally fortunate to work most closely with Ven. Pencho Rabgey (hereafter also "Pala"[28]), a leading expert in the Chöd system, with whom I made initial word-for-word translations of Chöd liturgical texts (Skt. sādhanas). I received, in tandem with the translation, commentarial instructions into each aspect of the meditation practice and musical performance initially over the course of several months. I am grateful to have continued to translate and receive transmissions in the tradition for more than twenty years with Pala.

An ethnomusicological perspective on Buddhist ritual music can offer insights into at least three areas to a study on the Chöd ritual for both Buddhist Studies scholars and ethnomusicologists engaged in research on liturgical ritual practices.[29] First, an ethnomusicological perspective may be valued for the extent to which an intimate ethnographic context offers a "truly participatory participant-observation" experience that helps to bring the ethnographer closer to the "lived experience" of those who practice a ritual.[30] Second, the framework of learning an instrument (or several instruments as is the case with Chöd) offers insights through the pedagogical process to understand such important facets of a ritual as symbolism, ethical principles, and standards specific to the teacher(s) and by extension to those in the same sociocultural milieu. Lastly, as is often the case with ethnomusicological studies, a multisite ethnography allows one to reconstruct internal lines of connection between different masters' traditions across a global Diaspora, which in the Tibetan context is understood in terms of lineage. By participating in the study of Chöd in six different pedagogical contexts,[31] in several communities, in four countries, and over the course of several years, my study of this single tradition has helped me gain a clearer understanding of the transmission of oral tradition, the permissible variations in Chöd ritual music performance, and the challenges related to the continuity and change of ritual traditions.

## Efficacy of Chöd Practice

Empirical claims about the efficacy of Chöd practice abound in the informal discourse among Tibetan ritual masters and their disciples. Efficacy here refers to the effectiveness of Chöd as a Buddhist tantric rite in comparison with other tantric rites. Thus, efficacy denotes the power and effectiveness of a ritual as a basis for producing the result of changing one's perspective about the nature of "self" and reality. According to Chöd theory as well as practice, this involves testing out the effectiveness of the Chöd method for gradually reducing the mental attitude of "grasping" to one's "self" and phenomena as "self-existent," and moving toward what the tradition considers a more realistic conception of reality and one's own nature. The Chöd practitioner's goal is to work toward eliminating all latent mental clinging to the notion that there is any intrinsic reality, or inherent existence, to the "I" that is perceived to be located at the center of one's experience.

In discussing efficacy with respect to Chöd ritual performance elements, our concern is with the function of musically associated performance aspects—all physical and sonic gestures, including mantric utterances, which occur in the context of Chöd ritual performances—as in some way helping to bring about the desired results of the meditation practice. In this book, we investigate various ways in which aspects of music such as vocal performance (of melody as well as mantra) in the Chöd ritual practice function in the meditation process. To frame this study in terms of efficacy, we ask: "How does the musical performance assist with the meditation?" "How do the speech and bodily aspects of the ritual (the vocal/oral and physical performance aspects) help to enhance the mental visualization aspects?" "To what extent are certain sounds necessary (or peripheral) to the (proper/successful) execution of the ritual performance (within the particular context of the occasion of performance)?" Attending to these questions, we will attempt to gauge the contingencies of meaning *in situ*.

### *Ritual Studies: "Flow" and Efficacy*

Ritual theorist Catherine Bell notes that there has been significant debate among scholars as to which aspects of ritual are most efficacious. She juxtaposes two interpretations: on the one hand there are the physical, kinesthetic "sensations experienced by the body in movement"; and, on the other hand, there is the synesthetic "total, unified and overwhelming sensory experience."[32]

> Most performance theorists imply that an effective or successful ritual performance is one in which a type of transformation is achieved. Some have described it as a transformation of being and consciousness achieved through an intensity of "flow."[33]

The concept of "flow" developed by Mihaly Csikszentmihalyi[34] places emphasis on the efficacy of the kinesthetic aspect of performance. He attempts to illustrate a major goal of performance theory:

> [To s]how that ritual does what it does by virtue of its dynamic, diachronic, and physical characteristics, in contrast to those interpretations that cast ritual performances as the secondary realization or acting out of synchronic structures, tradition or cognitive maps.[35]

Bell maintains that the kinesthetic aspects of rituals are those that "grasp more of the distinctive physical reality of ritual so easily overlooked by more intellectual approaches."[36] In contrast, other scholars "have debated whether the efficacy of ritual performance resides in the transformation of the meanings of symbols [chapters 3, 4, and 5] or in the non-discursive, dramaturgical and rhetorical levels of performance [chapters 2, 6, and 8]."[37] The processual and dramaturgical aspects of the latter are what performance studies theorists point to as the emergent qualities of a ritual event.[38]

In this book, we explore both physical and intellectual aspects of ritual, the musical performance, and the simultaneously produced visualizations. I suggest a need to provide a model for how to "map" ritual in order to see where concordances might exist between the intellectual/cognitive and the bodily/somatic aspects of ritual performances in the tantric ritual context. This may be useful more generally beyond Buddhist Studies for those engaging in studies of ritual through the disciplines of ethnomusicology, performance studies, and cultural anthropology in different geographic regions. In chapters 1 through 5, we look at examples of how such "ritual mapping" may be used in ritual analyses.

From an ethnomusicological perspective, the study of ritual involves exploring questions about the significance of physical and sonic gestures as well as the symbolic and cognitive visualizations that occur during ritual performances. To approach such questions, one of the important methodological tools is the ethnomusicologist's study of, and participation in, ritual music performances. Formally, the ethnographic method of inquiry in cultural anthropology does not necessitate incorporating participation and performance. In other words, according to the conventional understanding of what many anthropologist fieldwork-oriented researchers refer to as the participant-observation mode of ethnographic research, a less performative approach is the norm—but this is not so in ethnomusicology.

## "Emic"-"Etic" Ethic

As an example, for the majority of cultural anthropologists, the ethnographer attempts to adopt the role of "participant-observer" in so far as it is culturally acceptable in a given community, setting, and occasion. The *participant* side of the ethnographer's hyphenated identity is the "emic," or cultural "insider's" perspective, which is a highly negotiated status and may be gained in some cases by learning a trade, craft, or performance skill, as would a native student of the tradition. On the other side of the hyphen is the *observer* identity, the "etic" or "outsider's" perspective. In this capacity, the ethnographer assumes a social and intellectual distance from the cultural context of the ritual despite their participatory involvement. Many ethnographers working in the discipline of cultural anthropology since the mid-1980s have maintained a reflexive dialogue about this methodology, periodically revisiting the issues, problems, and difficulties in attempting to maintain an "emic" and "etic" perspective at the same time while in the context of studying a ritual tradition.[39] More recently, several ethnomusicologists (Barz and Cooley et al. 1997) joined their voices in this chorus of questioning how this can be done.[40] The collection of articles in *Shadows in the Field* seem to suggest the question: How can one truly get "inside" a ritual performance if one is also somehow "outside" it and watching it all happen from a "bird's-eye view" at the same time? Barz and Cooley note the uniqueness of the experiential aspects of the ethnomusicological approach as opposed to the often more theoretically charged investments of the cultural anthropologists.[41] Additionally, as Catherine Bell notes, eminent cultural anthropologist Victor Turner suggested late in his career that the ethnographic study of ritual "should be supplemented with performances of it, by the theorists themselves, in order for them to grasp its meanings. His suggestions were picked up by others who have interwoven the study and the practice of ritual in various ways."[42]

### *Level of Ritual Involvement: The Difference Participation Makes*

Indeed, it may be asked, "How is it possible for an ethnographer *who is not involved in performance* to understand the various symbolic referents cued by instruments, vocalizations, poetry, and movement in a ritual?" For example, by spending one year living in Vietnamese-American Buddhist Diaspora communities across the United States and Canada while volunteering as the translator/coordinator and cultural broker for a delegation of Tibetan monks from Sera Monastic University, I observed the Tibetan abbot, an elder ritual master, engage daily in leading Tibetan tantric ritual performances. In this case, I saw how a skilled ritual officiant could alter a ritual performance due to contingencies such as: weather conditions, size and shape of venue, context of venue (home, temple, hospital, or another site), available materials for offering, participant knowledge of ritual protocols, participants' fear or excitement, and an officiant's ritual assistants' levels of skills and experience among other numerous aspects related to performance practice. By assisting and watching the abbot, translating the ritual sādhanas, and even observing the same translated sādhanas being enacted in ritual performances, I did not acquire a full understanding of how to perform all the rituals myself—though I gained a strong appreciation for the abbot's ritual knowledge and artistic skill. My understanding of the symbolic referents in the Chöd practice rituals exceeds my understanding of many other rituals because I have experienced learning to practice Chöd myself. That being said, my somewhat more "emic" perspective vis-à-vis Chöd ritual performances has been informed and strengthened by the relatively "etic" involvement I have had with the abbot's ritual performances.[43]

### *Combining "Emic" and "Etic" Approaches*

I argue that both "emic" and "etic" perspectives are not easily balanced, but my experience studying the Chöd Tradition for several years informs me that the "emic" perspective yields particular kinds of useful data, while an "etic" viewpoint provides other sorts of insights. To be sure, an ethnographer is by definition never completely "emic," though there is a strand of ethnomusicological theory and practice that prescribes one strives toward achieving bi-musicality.[44]

This book indicates the ways in which three ethnomusicological methodologies respectively yield complementary "emic" and "etic" perspectives of a Tibetan tantric ritual: (a) studying the ritual through the traditional master-disciple context with different lamas and practitioners in the same lineage tradition and across traditions; (b) creating musical transcriptions of the melodies; and, (c) graphing characteristics of the ritual performance for analysis. I hope to show that bringing all these research methodologies together has an important value. The first-person accounts given by lama practitioners who have performed the ritual and gained insights through meditational experiences are certainly valuable as an "emic" perspective. As well, since the students of the tradition who attempt these same techniques and paths of meditation may gain insight through practice experiences, their first-person accounts may also inform the tradition from an "insider" or "emic" standpoint.[45] Moreover, transcribing the Chöd melodies and "ritual mapping" all the performative aspects of the tradition (methodologies b and c, above), a largely "etic" endeavor, may refer back to and inform what the analyst has gleaned from an "emic" viewpoint. In a practical way, music analysis endows the ethnomusicologist with a deeper understanding of the relationship between the performative and linguistic aspects of the ritual and the associated visualizations. The results of musical analysis may also have a positive valence for practitioners who can observe the mechanics of ritual design underlying the practice.

Drawing upon Buddhist studies, I also employed a textual research methodology, developing a word-for-word translation of the Chöd sādhana's liturgical poetry by receiving a close commentary on each section from a qualified ritual practitioner who has expert knowledge in that ritual. The commentary involved a deep process of oral transmission (Tib. *lung*) ensuring that the disciple understood the meaning of the practice. Thus, one aim of the translation/transmission process—to use the formal language of ethnography—was *to bring* the disciple/apprentice *to the tradition*, shifting from an "etic" perspective toward an "emic" perspective.

## Ethnomusicological Approaches to Chöd Studies

In Western secondary literature on Chöd, almost none of the studies to date have dealt comprehensively with the music of the tradition, its transmission, pedagogy, and performance, which has resulted in a serious gap in the literature.[46] Previous studies concerned with Tibetan ritual music have given cursory attention to the Chöd ritual (Canzio 1978; Kaufmann 1978; Ellingson 1979), and only one work discusses the music of Chöd or its performance in any detail (Dorjé and Ellingson 1979). That said, in the literature on the enacted musical aspects of the Chöd ritual—besides Dorjé and Ellingson's article on the *ḍamaru* drum, which I revisit and expand upon with ethnographic detail and analysis in chapter 4—ethnomusicological research had not yet adequately addressed the specific role of musical performance in Chöd. Yet such a role seems vital to our gaining a more complete understanding of Buddhist ritual practice. How does a particular tune relate to a certain section of the liturgy? Does a particular melody and rhythm make meaningful the specific section of the textual liturgy to which it has been composed? Is it mere accompaniment and decorative art, or is something integral to the meditation practice embedded in the music and/or occurring through musical performance?

Although I had learned to practice, and then taught musical aspects of the Chöd ritual for several years, when I posed these questions to my teachers, they often redirected my attention to the *meaning* of Chöd practice: (1) the analytical meditation on the relationship of the corporeal body to the "self;" and, (2) the analysis of the connection between the mind's "grasping" to the corporeal body and all other phenomena as if they were self-existent and intrinsically good or bad, and the experience of suffering as a result of regarding phenomena uncritically as such. The music of the ritual performance was largely de-emphasized as a site of meaning beyond the notion that, in performing the melodies exactly as one's teacher had, the practitioner could obtain both (i) the lineage lamas' blessings, and (ii) the realizations imbued within the melodies. Indeed, the melodies are believed to contain the blessings and realizations of the lineage lamas since exceptional adepts who composed the melodies were practitioners of the tradition.[47] Yet, from the Mahāyāna point of view, the most important aspect underlying Chöd practice is the essential inculcation of the correct motivation for the practice: the attitude of renunciation (weariness with cyclic existence), and *bodhicitta* (altruistic wish to attain enlightenment for the sake of all beings, who are subject physically, cognitively, and emotionally to suffer due to various causes and conditions in cyclic existence), and combining both with the view of "emptiness." These three are known as the "three principal paths" (Tib. *lam gyi gtso bo rnam gsum*), and form the foundation of the Chöd Tradition. According to my teachers, when engaging in Chöd practice, it was to be an exercise of my understanding of these three principal paths. In a sense, then, I was performing philosophy—turning theory into practice.

Even while engaged in interdisciplinary ethnomusicological research, I understood my role was to follow the prescribed indigenous method of learning the tradition, particularly given the rarefied context and privilege of having a one-to-one individualized teacher-student transmission of the ritual. I was taught that the meaning of Chöd was important insofar as I could learn not only to perform the sādhana, but also to practice the values of the tradition throughout my life. I would therefore likely not need to transcribe the melodies to gain more access to the meaning, but rather could draw upon my own meditation experience and the oral testimonies of recognized practitioners regarding the music and its importance to aspects of the tradition. The indigenous informants' interpretations of the significance of the music were primarily to inform my understanding, and I was merely to act as a conduit in assisting the tradition to survive some generations longer by preserving this valuable information. Initially, it was understood that musical transcription could later serve as a prescriptive tool in assisting in the preservation of the tradition, but it would not be needed for analytical purposes.

An earlier era of ethnological inquiry would have had me mask my "emic" position in favor of a more "objective" accounting of the ritual and significance of its performance.[48] What is an ideal position within ethnomusicological discourse today? For the past twenty years, ethnomusicologists have followed cultural anthropologists in situating ethnographic studies by making positionality (personal identities and biases) explicit such that the lens through which a musical ritual is filtered is made known to the reader. As a specific disciplinary program, ethnomusicologists attempt to gain as close a perspective on a tradition as possible. When appropriate, while studying oral traditions of South and Central Asia,[49] for example, they learn to perform a tradition through an apprenticeship. Yet, they are cautioned not to retain an insider's perspective and "go native" to such an extent that they would lack the critical distance needed to view the tradition from an outsider's perspective.

The legacy of this approach, with its complicated tension in balancing emic-etic concerns, is historically drawn from an ethical code underlying anthropological inquiry. This code works in concert with an earlier anthropological paradigm of preferably leaving undisturbed that which, and those whom, the ethnographer encounters.[50] This code has since changed, such that the idea of engaging in research without meaningful involvement beyond one's own project is no longer expected or advisable. With the instituting of a new ethical code in favor of greater reciprocity, there is an expectation that a researcher will attempt to maintain ongoing relationships with the individual consultants and community where the ethnographer studied. Steven Feld has made several return visits to the community of the Kaluli in Papua New Guinea and is among the best-known exemplars of this ethnographic practice of "return."

## A Shift in Research Analysis: An End to "Disciplinary Blinders"

During the final stage of my research I learned that my methodology was limiting me from seeing deeper connections between performance elements of the ritual (rhythm and melody), music and liturgical elements (melody and poetry), and all three together (poetry, melody, and rhythm). Because I followed the disciplinary swing away from musical analysis and toward the ethnographic, I had explored the Chöd meditation practice and musical performance as separate elements that combined only in the process of performing the ritual. What ethnomusicologist Udo Will calls the "intradisciplinary imperialism" during the initial period of my research, was corroborated by other ethnomusicologists whose critical approaches to examining recent trends in the methodology of the discipline confirmed my understanding that much in the Chöd ritual music performance had yet to be researched.[51] It seems that I had on "disciplinary blinders" and was metaphorically walking along a path unaware of the scope of interesting material in the forest around me. To disclose what my research process had been before reaching this point: I had attempted to approach scholarship through a method that was faithful both: (1) to the traditional process of transmission of the Chöd Tradition (learning by rote as close to one's teacher's understanding, instruction, and performance technique as possible), and (2) to the then current of ethnomusicological thought.

Udo Will critiques the "emic-etic distinction" at the height of the turn away from nonverbal data in the ethnoscientific encounter:

> Since the unfortunate introduction of K. Pikes' emic-etic distinction into the ethno sciences, there has been a tendency of *intradisciplinary imperialism* whereby the emic strategy deliberately denies the validity of alternative research options. There is the insistence of many ethnoscientists that inquiries into the field of human culture is only definable in emic terms, and that means, only with reference to the way people talk about it . . . Emic commitments have become blatant, insistent and parochial and there is an air of scholasticism or of arm chair detachment about much of the formal analysis of the new ethnography including ethnomusicology . . . not denying the scientific credentials ethnolinguistics has brought to certain domains of the ethno sciences . . . due to their fixation on verbal behaviour, they are unable to see the importance of other, non-verbal behaviour and its structural manifestations.[52]

Other scholars have expressed an undercurrent of apprehension about the direction of the new musicology. Jane Sugarman reached the same critical perspective toward the dominant interpretive paradigm of privileging "ethnoaesthetics" that describes the initial research approach I undertook in my musical apprenticeship.[53] Furthermore, like myself, she finds that "ethnoaesthetics" is a "necessary but not sufficient" interpretive methodological approach. Sugarman writes:

> The interpretive paradigm has transformed the work of Western ethnomusicologists in several crucial ways. We have learned to give serious attention to the ideas and interpretations of musicians and their constituencies, to carefully render the terminology that they use to convey their ideas and the collective meanings that music is said to generate, and to recognize the importance of individual agency in the formulation of musical practices. Together with a number of scholars, however, I have come to view this paradigm as "necessary but not sufficient": as in need of refinement and expansion, in part because of shortcomings that became evident to me in the course of my fieldwork.[54]

To be clear, I did not modify my approach because of Udo Will's and Sugarman's statements and those of other scholars expressing an undercurrent of apprehension about the direction of the new musicology.[55] Rather, I came to uncover these after I understood what was lacking through doing the work of transcribing the music.[56] The transcriptions immediately revealed the compositional skill of Chöd lamas who created melodies and poetic verses with a general structural coherence and yet a mood suited specifically to each section of the sādhana (ritual liturgical text).[57] Their expressive numinosity combined with artistic craftsmanship and aesthetic continuity had yet to be formally recognized.

It was subsequent to these discoveries that I returned to ethnomusicological theory and uncovered these warning signs in the critical ethnomusicological discourse. I learned of Kofi Agawu's attack on the new musicology, and became even more secure in my conviction that my earlier approach was unnecessarily limiting. Also, having read Knopoff, I saw clearly that I had been merely doing what *was* believed to be the correct procedure in the then-current trend. Even though my research methodology was drawn from my intuitive sense of being a student-disciple to a master musician and meditator, and it was correct in so far as this is considered the proper way to learn the tradition, I was resistant to applying the West-writing-East paradigm[58] with its power-laden textualization of what was heretofore an oral/aural tradition in a near secret musical transmission. I also understood that, in part, my role—both as disciple in the cross-cultural translation, and as researcher—was to be forward-looking to the issues surrounding the Chöd Tradition's continuity and change.

While my study of Chöd (as much coincidentally as practically) involved learning in the mode of an apprentice, there are logical reasons to suggest the merits of the concomitant approach that I adopted during the final stage of my analyses. As Sugarman's findings suggest, a two-pronged approach may be more appropriate for subsequent research into Buddhist tantric ritual music studies. This would entail: (1) an initial apprenticeship (in the *guru-śiṣya paramparā* mode of musical transmission) followed by (2) a period of musicological transcription and analysis.[59] Having intuitively applied such an approach in this study, these two research periods resulted in mutually enhanced understanding of the tradition and its musical expression. There was the benefit of gaining knowledge as to how the musical and meditation aspects of the tradition have been transmitted traditionally. As well, musical analysis revealed insights into the design and craftsmanship of the sādhana's music and poetic liturgy. Perhaps this dual understanding will prove useful as I work to articulate the coherence of the Chöd genre of ritual music as a unique expression in Tibetan ritual studies.

## An Integrated Approach to Chöd Studies

Remarkably, when I began this project, virtually none of the previous research on Chöd had focused in depth on the ritual meditation as a performed event and living practice. Consequently, factors integral to the practice of Chöd remained unexamined. These included: the performance practices of specific instruments and mantric utterances, the relationships between the musical, poetic, and visualized elements, and the permissible variations in performance due to alterations of practice context such as the different expectations for solo and group Chöd performance. Other than a single anomalous and excellent ethnomusicological study detailing the symbolic aspects of one of the musical instruments employed in the Chöd ritual,[60] essentially there was a dearth of exploratory and critical discussion on the Chöd ritual performances.

Yet today, perhaps more than ever before, ritual practice and performance have become germane to the interests of Buddhist studies. Amid what appears to be a current shift in the academic interest toward (1) the combined ethnographic and philological study of living Buddhist practices; and, (2) the inclusion of socioeconomic and environmental factors affecting ritual performances, such a gap in Chöd studies is more noticeable now than in previous eras of scholarship.[61]

The corpus of sādhanas and commentaries in Machik's Chöd Tradition is quite vast, and therefore I do not attempt to address all of the various types of ritual that are performed.[62] Rather, this research explores primarily the functions of music in the most frequently practiced rituals in the Ganden Chöd Tradition. Some of the rituals that may be studied further include the following nonexhaustive list: the 108 Spring Wilderness Retreat (Tib. *chu mig rgya rtsa*), the Five Ḍākinī Retreat (Tib. *mkha' 'gro sde lnga*), fire puja, the four hundred meat offerings (Tib. *sha brgya zan brgya*), and several rituals with Troma Nagmo (Khro ma rnag mo) as the central meditational deity.

To summarize, while Ellingson's dissertation research focused on the "mandala" concept as a cohesive organizing framework during the era of the interpretive anthropological paradigm, I attend to the current disciplinary trend in ethnomusicological scholarship which follows more closely to the indigenous values and interpretations rather than seeking to subsume all musical events within a single overarching sociomusical paradigm. In any event, the Chöd Tradition's song-poetry is not musically or socially organized according to the "mandala" concept. Moreover, attending to the "native-perspective" in recent scholarship involves working to understand the valuation of certain notions of musical and spiritual practice in this unique ascetic tradition. I entered into a musical and spiritual apprenticeship as a disciple of a recognized Chöd practitioner, and learned native values in the intimacy of this context. Inspired by the work of James Spradley, I wanted to ensure this research project would be of use to the practitioners who had expressed concerns with lineage transmission and cultural survival, so I asked my Tibetan Chöd teachers and other Tibetan scholars their opinion of what they felt a useful contribution would be to Tibetan scholarship on the Chöd ritual from an ethnomusicological perspective. This Spradlean approach was partly an effort to engage in reciprocity not after the fact, but rather have it built into the study. I wanted to ensure I was engaging in an endeavor with further reaching benefits than the limited horizon of one person's research project.

## Six Integrated Concepts

This book provides six new concepts that illuminate, in different ways, the meaningful connections between the meditation practice and musical performance elements in Chöd ritual practices. These are: (1) Graduated Skill, (2) Transcription as Analysis, (3) "Ritual Mapping" Layers of Symbolic Meaning in Performance, (4) "Interpretive Community" of Symbolic Attributions, (5) The Confluence of Dissemination and Transmission with Preservation; and, (6) Giving, Reciprocity, and the Possibility of Altruism.

The concept of "Graduated Skill" explores the notion that Chöd students' experience of the ritual practice varies with their progressive advancement in both musical ability and meditation skills. Initially, while students are learning how to play the ritual instruments, read liturgical texts, and perform meditative visualizations, they are engaged in a beginner's level "*performance*-centered practice." For disciples to develop into advanced Chöd practitioners, these novices and beginners need to embody the performance elements so that they can become immersed in a "*practice*-centered performance."[63] By drawing upon the Chöd masters' oral traditional pedagogical discourse, I formalize this terminology into a sliding scale of progressively increasing ability. As Chöd masters note, the practice functions differently for, and expectations vary in accordance with, practitioners at these different levels (see chapter 1). Monitoring their students' levels in ritual skills inspires maximizing the meaningful articulation of performed elements, which become integral to the efficacy of the practice.

The concept underlying "Transcription as Analysis" follows from the specialized transcription work ethnomusicologists engage in of notating the musical performance elements. This inherently analytical work reveals the special relationship between the text and melody in Chöd. Like the process of making a close reading of a literary text to uncover how an author constructs her narrative with a careful and deliberate mixture of literary devices, so too, musical analysis deconstructs ritual performance to reveal how compositional devices are variously intertwined. Transcribing a multilayered performance in order to look at how one element moves with another is a logical step toward achieving a critical understanding of an artistic Buddhist practice. Even within the Chöd rituals' austerely textured, bell- and drum-accompanied melodies, so much that occurs externally maps internally—in musically symbolic performative gestures—that it deserves our analytical attention.

A third conceptual approach—"Ritual Mapping" the Layers of Symbolic Meaning in Practice—centers on all physical, imaginal, and sonic gestures *as they are performed* and the ways in which they contribute to meaning. Ritual analysts can use graphic depictions, or "mappings," to observe how the aural and visualized elements work in concert with one another. These mappings reveal what I call the "internal intertextuality" within a Vajrayāna ritual. In one subritual, the melody—composed by Machik Labdrön herself—is visualized as an instance of "sonic iconography," depicting vultures' wings through the music composition technique of "tone painting." The practitioner is to experience this melody as either terrifying vulnerability or empowered confidence during a scene in which the poetic visualizations describe the deconstruction of the "self." It appears expert craftspersons designed the ritual to enhance meditative contemplations through either perspective. If melodic symbolism through "tone painting" conveys ritual meaning and action, melody would be considered a "primary text." Music would not be mere accompaniment, but an expressive *rasa* shaping the meditative experience.

The fourth concept—"Interpretive Community" of Symbolic Attributions—concerns the different interpretations of symbolism recognized by various exponents of the Chöd practice and the extent to which these interpretations are meaningful to practitioners. Empirical research led me to gain a nuanced understanding of variation in the individual attribution of symbolism. There are detailed variations in the precise gestures used as meditational aids, such as the meaning of kinetic movement in the rotation of the *ḍamaru* drum.

The fifth concept centers on the issue of what I call "The Confluence of Dissemination and Transmission with Preservation" that is affecting the continuity of the Chöd ritual. I suggest that traditional modes of pedagogical transmission (i.e., the mode of teacher-disciple apprenticeship that promotes inquiry and correction, and thereby facilitates deeper understanding and fuller transmission) might be challenged through new practices of dissemination and encouraged through the productive capacity of new consumer recording technology.

The sixth concept focuses on the broader literature in anthropology and philosophy on "gift and exchange theory and practices." We first examine the feeling underlying the obligation to reciprocate a gift that is suggested by Marcel Mauss's notion of the gift, with its power to compel the flow of exchange. We then look cross-culturally at studies of giving blood (blood donations) in the USA and UK which illustrate starkly contrasting motivations for donors: economic exchange and social altruism, respectively. Drawing upon Levinasian ethics and Mahāyāna *bodhicitta* practice, we suggest the possibility of altruism that involves giving (of/from) the body in an analogous contemporary context.

## Chapter Outlines

I have maintained an overall organizational approach that addresses these concepts in a logical progression. The book moves broadly in stages, through history, practice, instrumentation, symbolism, mantric utterances, and interpretation. It begins with the historical context of the inception of the tradition (chapter 1), followed by, in chapter 2, a detailed description of the practice and musical performance of one key Chöd ritual. Chapter 3 moves through a discussion of aspects of each of the musical elements (rhythm, form, etc.), beginning with vocal melody, and introducing "ritual mapping." Then chapter 4 moves to focus on the main instrument used in the practice besides the voice, the *ḍamaru*, and various interpretations of its symbolic meaning. Chapter 5 turns to the mantric syllables "*phaṭ*" and "*Āḥ*," the mantra of the Perfection of Wisdom, the thighbone trumpet, and the bell, and their functions in the Chöd ritual. Chapter 6 concerns the four ritual actions in Tibetan ritual music, and chapter 7 explores the Buddhist philosophical terminology and concepts regarding sound enacted and performed through the Chöd ritual practice. Chapter 8 discusses transmission, pedagogy, and the role of the practice in transforming the practitioner from being self-focused to being other-focused in daily life. Finally, chapter 9 offers an interpretive approach through an interdisciplinary and intercultural study of the Chöd bodily sacrifice in terms of gift and exchange theory, a field pioneered by social anthropologist Marcel Mauss, which leads into a discussion of the possibility of altruism.

# Part I

# Chöd Ritual Practice in Context

# 1

# Ritual Efficacy

## Music Performance in Chöd Practice

### Introduction

An interest in studying the efficacy[1] of meditation ritual practices is shared across the boundaries of the behavioral sciences, social sciences, and humanities, though disciplinary approaches and goals of inquiry differ. Grounded in the interdisciplinary perspective of ethnomusicology, this book centers on questions about the roles of musical practices and performance in the Chöd ritual, a Tibetan tantric meditation tradition that is meant to be practiced in fearful contexts, and which uses terrifying imagery[2] and unconventional thinking to bring about the mental transformation of the adept.

Two interrelated questions are relevant to the notions of function and efficacy with respect to the musical performance components of the Chöd ritual: "What are the functions of the musical aspects of the Chöd ritual?" and "How does the traditional discourse on skill and ability in music and meditation, as revealed within the Chöd oral transmission process, have an impact on one's experience of the ritual practices?"

Based on these two questions, this book's research findings indicate: (1) the level at which music functions for a given Chöd practitioner in the ritual context is related to both their individual level of skill in meditation and their experience with the musical aspects of the practice; and, (2) the relationship between the music and text in the ritual is highly significant: composers of the Chöd melodies used melodic movement and rhythmic gestures to meaningfully enhance the prosody and textual symbolism in several ways, deepening the meditator's experience.

Both findings reveal the important connections between the "outer" musical performance elements and the "inner" mentally performed visualizations. This suggests that ritual music performance offers a space for meditation that strengthens the efficacy of the Chöd ritual, and allows the meditation practice to proceed in the context of fear. Each of these findings will be discussed in this chapter, but first I will provide a general description of the ritual.

## Chöd: A Multifaceted Ritual

From a phenomenological perspective, Chöd is perhaps the most multifaceted ritual music tradition practiced and performed by Tibetan Buddhists today. The practitioner performs song-poems vocally while accompanying herself or himself with Vajrayāna ritual musical instruments: the large hourglass-shaped drum (Skt. *ḍamaru*), ritual bell (Tib. *dril bu*), and thighbone trumpet or *kangling* (Tib. *rkang gling*). The practitioner must play these instruments and sing, all the while maintaining a cognitive attentiveness to the inward performance of detailed visualizations described in each syllable during an hour-long musical-meditation practice session. The Chöd practitioner follows a ritual text or sādhana ("meditation manual," Tib. *sgrub thabs*), which functions as a liturgy that is to be musically performed. The sādhana is at once a guide to, and a structured sequence of, mentally performed visualizations that are said to lead one to buddhahood.[3] The ritual process of the Chöd meditation practice occurs in the rapid, moment-by-moment flux and flow of physical and mental performance. The successful completion of a Chöd ritual sādhana does not involve improvisation, but proper execution of the performance instructions given in the text, imparted to the initiated disciple in a formal oral transmission (Tib. *lung*) by a qualified teacher or "lama" (Skt. *guru*, Tib. *bla ma*), and then carefully explained through oral commentary.

### The Chöd Ritual Practice: "Setting the Stage" of the Event

Here, to "set the stage" of the Chöd ritual, one may imagine a Chöd practitioner who walks alone at night to a cemetery with the intention of inviting spirits and all other beings, but particularly those hostile to her, to pay the debt she owes them. She meditates that she welcomes her worst enemies, visualized as demons (Tib. *bdud*) and harmful beings (Tib. *gdug pa can*), to partake of a feast of her psychophysical aggregates,[4] most obviously her body, mentally transformed into all things desirable to others. At a central moment of the ritual practice, she performs the "transference of consciousness" or *phowa* (Tib. *'pho ba*)[5] practice, sending her mind into space where it mixes with her guru's heart. She then instantly exits from the guru's heart as a female buddha ḍākinī[6] (Tib. *mkha' 'gro ma*, Eng. "sky-goer") pictured in a dancing posture and playing ritual music instruments. The beautifully radiant ḍākinī sings poetic verses which detail giving to these imagined harmdoers her mentally transformed "psychophysical aggregates" (Skt. *skandha*, Tib. *phung po*).

With her old body visualized as given away, and her mind mixed with space, she is confronted by the paradox of the still strongly felt sense of "I." She may search desperately for it, or skillfully conduct an analytical meditation: Upon what basis is there a felt sense of "self": the body or the mind? Who is the "I" who notices this paradox? Who is the "I" who notices, period? Applying analytical techniques to this meditation, she may not find the object of self-grasping ignorance after all; and thereby cut her attachment to the false notion of a self-existent "I"—the root delusion from which it is said all 84,000 delusions arise.

In fact, there is no self-existent "demon" (Skt. *māra*, Tib. *bdud*) poised to harm her; all fears and harms originate in her mind. However, as an ingenious psychological tool, the mind, which needs an object to work with, is used for its propensity to habitually attribute self-existence to an object (to uncritically see phenomena as real, lasting, and self-sufficiently existent). The Chöd ritual provides a means to critically analyze the seemingly intrinsic, self-existent "I" (the root of the mistaken identity of a "self") and then to cut off grasping onto this inherently existent "self" with the wisdom mind realizing emptiness.

## Utilizing Fear on the Path

Chöd is translated from Tibetan language as either "cutting" or "severance," and refers to the ritual of "cutting off" one's "self-grasping ignorance" (*bdag 'dzin ma rig pa*), the misconception about the way in which material and mental phenomena, including oneself, exist. Within the context of a Chöd ritual, the practitioner cuts her attachment to the notion of "self," enacting a concept of intersubjectivity[7] and compassion powerfully central to the essence of Buddhism by emphasizing the mutually interdependent nature of phenomena, and dissolving the egotistical framework that separates "self" and "other." The purpose of the Chöd ritual is to destroy the demon of "self-grasping ignorance" by "cutting it off" (*gCod*) at its root. To do so, the

Chöd practitioner is instructed to perform the ritual in frightening sites where spirits are said to live (cemeteries, haunted places, temple ruins, ramshackle dwellings, the meeting of two paths in a forest, etc.). The practice is also considered a personal test of her or his level of *bodhicitta* (Tib. *byang chub kyi sems*), which is the altruistic resolve to achieve enlightenment for the benefit of all beings in order to relieve their suffering.

Confronted with a fearful situation, having invited harmful beings (spirits) to the place of practice using music—by singing compelling melodies, drumming in steady rhythms, and playing other "calling" instruments such as the thighbone trumpet—practitioners utilize the situational fear and their instinct for self-preservation to clearly elicit the innate notion of "self," a "self" that the practitioner feels must be protected from harm. The purpose of the rite is to then "cut" through that notion. The self appears to exist from its own side, in an independent substantive way, yet upon deeper examination it is discovered to be empty and merely relational. The Chöd ritual is a synesthetic, performative method for realizing this philosophical truth.

During the practice, the Chöd practitioner sends her consciousness into space and offers the "old" body—mentally transformed into all desirable things (food, clothes, materials, etc.)—to the invited spirit guests. When a harmful spirit appears, the practitioner's habitual tendency to protect herself is to be thwarted by realizing that there is no "self" left to protect. Her mind has already been sent into space, and her body has already been given away and has been consumed by the spirits. At this point, "when fear arises, one must then thoroughly search for the self that is threatened and, at the same time, let go of the body that is threatened."[8]

In the middle of this frightening scenario, a profound insight and transformation are said to occur for the most advanced practitioners, who can perceive themselves (mind, body, and identity) as relationally existent, and not as inherently existing beings. Thus, they will have "cut" the "root" of delusions, which is the erroneous belief in the truly existent substantial self. They can then altruistically give to all spirits, gods and ghosts (Tib. *lha 'dre*), peaceful and harmful beings alike, that which they have held most precious all their lives—the body, which they no longer identify uncritically as "I," "me," or "mine."

The main question this book seeks to answer is: "How does ritual music performance function in the context of the experience of fear to help bring about this profound transformation?" We will turn to this question shortly, but first some historical background on the tradition would be appropriate.

## Chöd Philosophy, Lineage, and Transmission

Philosophically, Chöd is founded upon the *Perfection of Wisdom* (*Prajñā-pāramitā*) sūtras.[9] Traditional historiography claims that these texts were revealed and systematized by the Indian Buddhist mahāsiddha Nāgārjuna (c. 150–c. 250 CE), and later clarified by Candrakīrti (7th century CE).[10] Chöd is the tantric embodiment of the *Prajñāpāramitā Sūtra*[11] which, in its longest form, contains 100,000 lines. There are also versions of middling length at 20,000 lines and one shorter still at 8,000 lines.[12] In Tibet the *Perfection of Wisdom* texts were frequently recited as a form of merit-making. Machik Labdrön (Ma gcig lab kyi sgron ma, 1055–1153) was a recitation specialist of the *Prajñāpāramitā Sūtras* and from an early age would stay in lay benefactors' homes. She was known for both the speed with which she read and her comprehension of the sūtras[13] that describe how to realize the essence of "wisdom," or the "emptiness" of all phenomena.[14] These scriptures are embodied as "The Great Mother" or Yum Chenmo, the anthropomorphization of the wisdom realizing emptiness. The Great Mother is a central meditational deity (*yidam*) in Chöd ritual practices. Indeed, Machik Labdrön herself, due to her level of realization, is generally said to be an emanation of the Great Mother.[15]

Figure 1.1. Machik Labdrön (Ma gcig lab sgron, 1055–1153), Tibetan female ascetic, founder of the Chöd Tradition. She is depicted white in color, in a dancing posture atop a lotus flower and moon disc. She is playing two of the main Chöd musical instruments, the double-sided, hourglass-shaped ritual drum (*ḍamaru*) in her raised right hand, and Tibetan bell (*dril bu*) in her left hand. Detail of a *thangka* from the author's collection.

Figure 1.2. Machik Labdrön, Central Figure, Merit Field of the Chöd Tradition. Machik is the central figure surrounded by the merit field (*tshogs zhing*) of the main buddha deities and teachers of the Chöd Tradition—in whom practitioners go for refuge (*skyabs 'gro*) as they engage in the practice. Directly above Machik is Green Tārā, with Yum Chenmo (The Great Mother) above her. Immediately below Machik are her two sons who became the main lineage holders of the Chöd Tradition; below her to her right, wearing monastic robes, playing a *ḍamaru* and bell, is her son Tönyön Samdrup (Thod smyon bsam 'grub), and below her to her left, wearing clothes of a yogi lay practitioner, with long dark hair, playing a *ḍamaru* and bell, is Gyalwa Döndrup (rGyal ba don grub). Above and to the right of Machik, at the center of a cloudbank is her teacher, the Indian mahāsiddha Padampa Sangyé, surrounded by lineage practitioners. Above Machik and to her left is the buddha deity Varjayoginī in the aspect of the wrathful red ḍākinī, Vajravārāhī, surrounded by female deities. Closeup images featuring aspects of this *thangka* may be seen in Figures 1.3 and 1.4, respectively; from a *thangka* in the author's collection.

Indian Mahāyāna Buddhism provides the cultural and religious background for the Tibetan Buddhist Chöd ritual. The Indian mahāsiddha Padampa Sangyé (Pha dam pa sangs rgyas, d. 1117) is said to have traveled five times to Tibet, where he taught his "pacification" (*zhi byed*) practice that contains the essence of the Chöd teachings to Kyotön Sönam Lama (sKyo ston bsod nams bla ma) who, in turn, transmitted it to Machik Labdrön. On a subsequent visit, Padampa Sangyé transmitted his teachings directly to Machik Labdrön. In her spiritual biography she is said to have also received transmissions of Chöd teachings directly from the female Buddha Tāra.[16] Machik Labdrön remains arguably Tibet's most renowned female adept and is credited with developing the Chöd Tradition in Tibet and surrounding areas.

## Machik Labdrön (1055–1153)

It is said that all buddhas who appear to attain enlightenment on Earth have reached buddhahood many lifetimes before; they merely manifest progressive levels of realization following concentrated periods of training in meditation. This training is performed for the benefit of ordinary human witnesses who might become inspired to study the Dharma, gain strong faith, and follow their example. According to traditional historical and hagiographical accounts, Machik Labdrön attained a high level of realization as a young woman while reciting the *Prajñāpāramitā Sūtra* at the home of a sponsor. Very soon thereafter, she is said to have achieved complete enlightenment.[17] Her biography recounts how her fame spread to India where three Indian yogis were dispatched to verify her claims of enlightenment. When they arrived, as proof of her realization, Machik Labdrön greeted them in Sanskrit language, and recounted her memory of previous lifetimes to over 500,000 witnesses. Although she had never left Tibet, she described the location in India of a sealed cave inside of which still remained the body of her previous life. She explained that, if cremated, the body would produce special substances.[18] Her teacher, Padampa Sangyé, was asked to oversee the cremation proceedings. He returned with the three Indian yogis to India and all transpired exactly as she had prophesied. Thereafter, she was publicly vindicated and revered throughout India and Central Asia. While all other tantras traveled from India to Tibet, Machik Labdrön's Chöd tantra is said to be the only one that went from Tibet to India.[19]

Figure 1.3. Padampa Sangyé (Pha dam pa sang rgyas, d.1117), teacher of Machik Labdrön, the Indian mahāsiddha who founded the *shi jé* (Tib. *zhi byed*) or "pacification" tradition. In his right hand he holds a *ḍamaru* drum, and in his left, a thighbone trumpet (*rkang gling*). He is seated on a cloudbank to Machik Labdrön's right, and is surrounded by male lineage masters who are depicted actively practicing or teaching Chöd. He wears a loincloth and a red meditation belt around his right shoulder and left leg. He wears his long white hair in a topknot, and has a white beard; detail of a *thangka* from the author's collection.

## Inception of the Chöd Lineage: *Dohā, Gur*, and Chöd

Since the inception of the Chöd ritual tradition in the eleventh century as a tantric yoga—a meditation sādhana that effectively combines a musical tradition with a meditation practice—it has yet to be studied in relation to the Chöd performance tradition itself, into its most salient characteristics and social practices. Such an examination now reveals that the pedagogical method of Chöd transmission draws from the *guru-śiṣyā paramparā* oral transmission method most commonly associated today with the Hindustani and Carnatic (North and South Indian Classical) music traditions; while the expectations incumbent upon the practitioner are best understood within the meditation traditions and lifestyle of Buddhist tantric yogis and ascetics.

From an historical perspective, Chöd song-poetry likely stems from the Indian *dohā* tradition of Sanskrit poetry composed by mahāsiddhas. The melodies of the Chöd ritual fall within the *gur* (Tib. *mgur*, "songs of meditative experience") tradition of Tibetan poetry writing and sung recitation.[20] *Gur* spiritual song poetry is said to be derived from the Sanskrit tradition of poetic literature, the Indian mystic writings of the *dohā* tradition that fostered such compositions as Saraha's "Royal Song."[21] Following *The Blue Annals*,[22] Herbert Guenther traces the history of the Indian tradition and lineage of *dohā* poetry and the manner in which it was taught to Tibetans.[23]

Even though Padampa Sangyé knew the *dohās* well, he emphasized the internal practice and transformation rather than the external poetic structure. As Karma Trinley (Kar ma phrin las pa) explains: "The followers of the *zhi byed* system, which derives from Padampa Sangyé, emphasized the inner experience of what the *dohās* suggested rather than the dissemination of the teaching itself."[24] It is necessary to point out, for the purpose of reconstructing the history of the transmission of the textual aspects of the Chöd Tradition, that "Padampa Sangyé was less concerned with the teaching and promulgation of his 'pacification' system (*zhi byed*) than with the realization and teaching of the meaning of the *dohās*."[25] This could account for the continuity of this emphasis on practice through the last millennium, wherein sometimes Chöd meditation texts have been written in prose rather than in the formal metric strictures of *dohā* poetics, such as in the Chöd sādhana and commentary written by Tsongkhapa.[26] In contrast, the sādhana discussed in more detail below is written in a strict meter of nine syllables per line.

Figure 1.4. Varjayoginī (Tib. *rDo rje rnal 'byor ma*) appearing in the form of Vajravārāhī (Tib. *rDo rje phag mo*), a wrathful female buddha deity with one face and two hands, standing in a dancing posture, holding a curved flaying knife and a skull cup. She is red in color, wearing bone ornaments, situated on a cloudbank surrounded by female tutelary deities; detail of a *thangka* from the author's private collection.

These Dharma song-poems are meant to serve as instructional guides for their disciples and to any others who would benefit from hearing them.[27] Thupten Jinpa notes that the manner of heightened expression in this sacred Tibetan poetry genre is inherited from the Sanskrit tradition of the nine "*rasas*" (Skt., Eng. "moods" or "sentiments") of poetic expression.[28] This genre is therefore highly significant for Tibetan Buddhist practitioners who believe that by hearing or singing, but especially by understanding (and subsequently taking to heart and practicing), the dharmic-imbued advice in such *gur*, they can receive the blessings of the practitioner who composed the poetic verse (and melody, if still extant). They regard the song poems as originating from a pure source, a realized lama or mahāsiddha; and hear the poetic song texts as an act of meditation, imparting skillful instructions on a personal level about how to remove obstacles to achieving realizations.

## *Gur* and Chöd: Similarities and Differences

The difference between the liturgical song-poems of Chöd and *gur* concerns their respective scope and length. By performing a Chöd sādhana, one practices the entire path to complete enlightenment. One does so through a sequence of progressive meditations, composed as subrituals of a liturgy, each with its own melody of a particular quality and emotional tenor.

Chöd draws from several *gur* melodies for one liturgy, which is quite unlike the majority of song-poems in the *gur* tradition that consist of only one musical tune on a single Buddhist theme such as "impermanence" (Tib. *mi rtag pa*). Each of the *gur*-styled melodies is sung to a particular section of a Chöd liturgy, and functions as a meditation process that eventually completes the ritual. In other words, each melody is composed as a component of the larger meditation, and is but one movement, a part of the larger ritual process. Yet, in both poetic forms, the music is an evocative complement to the poetry. The music enhances the experience of meditation in that particular section of the ritual through performance. Thus, stylistically, the song-poetry of *gur* and Chöd are similar, while structurally the Chöd ritual is dramaturgically more extensive than the *gur*.

The Chöd ritual is akin to the Catholic Mass in that it exists formally as a multisectioned liturgical ritual that leads to a climactic section, with musically appropriate settings for the liturgical text in each subritual section. Moreover, the melodies for the subrituals are not interchangeable; rather, each is part of a deliberate compositional strategy to enliven the liturgy for the worshiper at particular moments—on specific words, syllables, and key melodic phrases in certain sections within an emotional arc that is architecturally appropriate to the dramaturgical narrative and weight of particular themes—musical and dramatic—woven throughout. It is the climactic section of a widely practiced Chöd ritual sādhana to which Chapter Three of this book attends. First, however, some further contextualization about the ritual may be helpful.

As a point of clarification, it would be prudent to mention here something about the inopportune discursive practice of adhering to inaccurate labelling of Chöd. It would seem that due to sloppiness in everyday parlance when referring either to a particular Chöd sādhana text, or to one's own daily sādhana practice of Chöd, as "the Chöd ritual," the many and varied rituals practiced in the Chöd Tradition are semantically glossed together. It is probably time to offer the corrective that there are numerous Chöd rituals, including: initiations, retreats, fire pujas, and rituals involving dough effigies. The more advanced an adept becomes in the Chöd meditation practice, the more complex are the rituals their lamas will advise them to practice.

## Tibetan Chöd Lineages

Chöd rituals are practiced in each of the four main schools of Tibetan Buddhism: Nyingma, Sakya, Kagyü, and Gelug as well as in Bön.[29] Each of these schools has its own collection of sādhana texts, melodies, and ritual objects. One of the most important ritual objects is the traditional meditational aid of a *thangka* painting,[30] which features the iconography of Machik Labdrön with Padampa Sangyé and Vajravārāhī performing the Chöd practice. They are depicted on either side of Machik Labdrön, holding the Chöd ritual instruments and are surrounded by the Chöd lamas from the specific lineage (See figure 1.3).[31] With the inception of Chöd in the eleventh century, the ritual was transmitted to all four schools and lineages. This book focuses on the performative architecture in Chöd rituals, exploring the artistic underpinnings of this Buddhist ritual music and how this performing art functions in practice.

### The Ganden Chöd Tradition

To some extent, this book centers on the Chöd sādhana and ritual practice traditions of the Gelugpa (dGe lugs pa) School[32] as carried by lineage masters from the Ganden tradition.[33] From among these four schools, the liturgically based melodies of the Ganden Chöd Tradition's main sādhana practices are widely known to be the most melodically ornamented and rhythmically complex.[34] The characteristically ornate melodies require more time to train in how to reproduce them precisely. This is necessary, according to the oral tradition, so that the practitioner can receive blessings from the Chöd lineage lamas and purify obstacles to accomplishing the goal of the practice. That it takes so much time to learn has been seen as presenting an obstacle to transmission. The Ganden Chöd Tradition's lineages are, therefore, relatively rare today—and there is yet another specific reason for this.

Rhythmically, Ven. Pencho Rabgey maintains that only the Ganden Chöd Tradition has the complex *ostinato* rhythmic figure "*ma dang, lha yi, khan dro*" (Tib. *ma dang, lha yi, mkha' 'gro*) played on the drum. The rhythm may be rendered as follows: [(quarter note—quarter note), (eighth note—dotted quarter note), (half note—half note)]. It is played on the large *ḍamaru*, the hourglass-shaped pellet drum, throughout most of the sādhana. The words of this rhythmic phrase have important meaning with direct significance to the practice. In translation from the Tibetan, "*ma*" refers to the female buddha deities Machik Labdrön, Vajravārāhī as well as Yum Chenmo; "*dang*" means "and;" "*lha*" refers to the visualized meditational deities; "*yi*" is a connective grammatical particle and "*kha[n] dro*" (Tib. *mkha' 'gro*) refers to the enlightened feminine form, which again refers to Machik Labdrön. Other Chöd Traditions primarily have a recurring quarter note rhythm—with occasional eighths and sixteenths—played by a back-and-forth rotating motion of bringing the drum to and fro. The Ganden Tradition's practitioners also employ these micro-beat patterns, but primarily use the aforementioned six-beat pattern.

Historically, in terms of transmission, practitioners passed on Chöd teachings in secret between teacher and disciple for the first four hundred years after Machik Labdrön passed. The Ganden Chöd Tradition is traced to the moment when the disciples of Tsongkhapa (1357–1419) asked their teacher to receive the teachings in Chöd in order to instruct them. After studying with several lamas, yet finding no one completely qualified, Tsongkhapa consulted with Mañjuśri through Lama Umapa Pawo Dorjé (dBu ma pa dpa' bo rdo rje) who acted as a medium.[35] The lineage was called the "Ganden Hearing Lineage" or "Ganden Ear-Whispered Lineage" (dGa ldan snyan brgyud)[36] since the Chöd meditation manuals had never been written down. The tradition tells us that later, in the mid-sixteenth century, one prescient Chöd adept, Gyalwa Ensapa Lobsang Döndrup (rGyal ba dben sa pa blo bzang don grub, 1505–1566)—by some reckonings, the third in the lineage of the Panchen Lamas—saw that the Ganden Chöd was in danger of disappearing. Finding no one else besides himself who could remember all the words of the poetic texts, the Chöd melodies, and the details of the performance instructions, he asked for, and received, permission from his lama to write down the sādhanas and commentaries. This effort to pen all the liturgical texts is understood to have saved the Ganden Chöd Tradition from extinction. The name of the tradition at this point was changed to the "Ensa Ear-Whispered Lineage" (dBen sa snyan brgyud) to honor this lama's contribution.[37]

The Ganden Chöd Tradition is a combination of two lineages: the "near lineage" or *nye gyü* (Tib. *nye brgyud*), which begins with Tsongkhapa's visionary communication with Mañjuśrī, as mentioned above, and the "long lineage" or *ring gyü* (*ring brgyud*) which extends back through Machik Labdrön to her teacher Padampa Sangyé and to his teacher and so on. According to Tsongkhapa's disciple Jampel Shenyen ('Jam dpal bshes gnyen), Je Tsongkhapa received the long lineage of Chöd from his disciple Khedrup Chojé (mKhas grub chos kyi rdo rje)"[38] who inherited the Gelugpa throne at Ganden (dGa ldan) Monastery. The *nye gyü* proceeds from Je Tsongkhapa to his disciple Togden Jampel Gyatso (rTogs ldan 'jam dpal rgya mtsho, 1356–1428) by means of secret transmission. Savvas writes, "Je Tsongkhapa did teach the Chöd secretly, passing it on to his disciple rTogs ldan 'jam dpal rgya mtsho."[39] From that point onward, Togden Jampel Gyatso passed along both the *nye gyü* visionary lineage from Mañjuśrī as well as the *ring gyü*.[40]

In practice, both the *nye gyü* and the *ring gyü* are invoked in each Chöd sādhana performance. During the meditation section of the sādhana ritual called "Request for blessings from the lineage lamas" the practitioner sings the names of each of the lineage lamas individually, in succession, beginning with the most ancient. The names of the *ring gyü* are sung first followed by those of the *nye gyü*. It takes about twenty minutes while practicing the *Chöd Tsog* (Tib. *gCod Tshogs*) sādhana to sing all the names in both lineages until the present-day head of the lineage.

Today, the lineage lamas or *la gyü* (*bla brgyud*) and disciples of the Ganden Chöd music tradition use several methods of transmission and dissemination, including: oral, aural, and most recently electronic media (audio and video cassette, CD, DVD, and Internet). With the advent of improved consumer technology and the increasing availability of digital recording and playing devices, many Chöd melodies are more accessible than ever, making it easier for disciples to learn the melodic ornamentations of the Ganden Chöd Tradition themselves. This could be seen as meeting the challenges to the continuity of the Ganden Chöd Tradition, while also raising complex issues regarding transmission and preservation.[41] At the same time, it brings up questions about how to effectively address similar concerns about the continuity of oral traditions globally.[42] The implications of the use of these new media for the transmission and dissemination of oral traditions are explored further in chapter 8.

## Outer and Inner Chöd: Levels of Sādhana Practice

Machik Labdrön taught that there are four levels of Chöd: "outer" (*phyi*), "inner" (*nang*), "secret" (*gsang*), and "thatness" or "suchness" (*de kho na nyid*).[43]

At the outer level, the Chöd ritual involves the practitioner engaging simultaneously in several performance tasks. One is the vocal work of chanting, singing pitched melodies, and performing mantric utterances. The practitioner is also engaged in the physical work of the right arm rotating, wrist turning, and finger/thumb twisting to play the two-sided drum as well as the periodic diaphragmatic and oral muscular work of blowing through loosely pursed vibrating lips to play the thighbone trumpet. The practitioner must also finesse the gentle falling of one's left wrist so that the ritual bell (*dril bu*), held with the left thumb and middle finger, can be lightly stopped with the fourth (ring) finger to properly time the sounding of the *dril bu* with the struck beats of the *ḍamaru*. It is altogether a highly coordinated performance event; but this is only one component of the outer, or external, level of Chöd. There are other subrituals such as dances associated with going to the place of practice that are referred to as the "four modes of going" and the subritual of the "three rounds of subduing" (Tib. *zil gnon skor gsum*) which are to be performed as one approaches and arrives at the place of practice.

At the inner level, during Chöd practice one works toward reducing attachment to one's body and material possessions. The aim is to increase the level of *bodhicitta* along with the level of realization of "emptiness" (Skt. *śūnyatā*). One does this by first developing greater equanimity toward all beings (one method of which is to recognize all as one's mothers and fathers from former lives) and augmenting one's compassionate resolve to relieve all beings of suffering. Ven. Pencho Rabgey points out that at a more advanced stage, "if you are doing Chöd practice, you are actually practicing the 'equalizing and exchanging oneself with others'" or *dag shen nyam jé* (Tib. *bdag gzhan mnyam brje*), which does not require the recognition that all beings were one's mothers and fathers in order to develop the infinite altruism of working for the welfare of all beings. Here, regardless of others' specific relationship to oneself, you develop *bodhicitta* based on identifying the three types of suffering that beings experience, and, motivated by wishing to relieve that existential threat, you practice Chöd.

Since Chöd is a tantric ritual practice, the final goal of the practice is the attainment of enlightenment in this very lifetime through the meditative combination of "method" (development of the altruistic intentionality of *bodhicitta*) and "wisdom" (the direct realization of "emptiness"), which masters say need to be kept in balance, like the two wings of a bird. Balancing in this way, one proceeds toward transforming one's consciousness and sense of identity through the Chöd method of guru-deity yoga.[44] In the Ganden Tradition, developing the inner Chöd also involves extensive preliminary meditation on the "three principal paths" (*lam gtso rnam gsum*), which can be studied in the system of the "Stages of the Path" (*lam rim*) discourses.

> In order to practice Chöd, we must gain realization of the three principal paths: renunciation, *bodhicitta*, and the correct view of emptiness, as explained by Je Tsongkhapa. Chöd practice is like an ornament to the three principal paths. Je Rinpoché [Tsongkhapa] said that the three principal paths are the roots. Without them, we cannot sustain the branches of tantric practice that deal with the channels, winds and drops of the completion stage. With firm roots, such advanced practices will be fruitful.
>
> Whenever we practice Chöd, we need *bodhicitta* motivation at the very least. We must contemplate very carefully why we are practicing Chöd before we start to engage in the practice. Following that contemplation, we engage in "internal Chöd," or "internal cutting." This is another name for generating *bodhicitta* in the Chöd system. In general, it should be done before beginning the sādhana itself and should be recollected during the inner mandala offering and during the requests to the gurus for blessings.[45]

To practice Chöd on the secret level, one must have received the initiation. In the Ganden Tradition, the first initiation ritual one receives is called "The Common Initiation of Opening the Door to the Sky" (*Nam mkha' sgo 'byed thun mong yin pa'i dbang*).[46] Having received the initiation from a qualified lama, the practitioner must keep tantric vows and any commitments given. As a tantric yogic practice, guru-deity yoga forms a major component of the practice, with the central meditational deity (*yidam*)[47] seen as both the lama and Machik, who is understood in this context to be an emanation of Yum Chenmo and visualized in the aspect of Vajrayoginī.[48]

Guru-yoga refers to seeing the lama and the other buddha deities as being of the same essence, since they are all meant to be seen as fully enlightened buddhas. This sort of visualization, where two, three, or four buddha deities are "seen" as simultaneously present in the image of only one buddha deity is among the essential requirements for practitioners on the tantric path. The example of the sameness and simultaneity of buddhas—no matter their outer appearances—is traditionally given as follows: the many reflections of the moon one can see in several buckets of water does not mean that there are several moons. Each one is a reflection of the same essence. Another traditional visualization involves the image of the Dalai Lama, for example, since Tibetans view him as the Buddha of Compassion. The two are seen as inseparable or *yer mé* (Tib. *dbyer med*) from one another. This concept can be further exemplified by the traditional example of milk and water mixing which results in an inseparable combination.

## Graduated Skills in Chöd

### "Beginner" to "Advanced" Chöd: Toward a "*Practice*-Centered Performance"

The functions of music in the Chöd ritual may be seen as linked to an individual practitioner's level of achievement in both musical performance and meditation practice.[49] Although, as noted above, the liturgical text and music work together to enhance the visualizations, learning to perform the musical instruments, to sing the highly ornamented melodies, and to coordinate all these tasks together with the prescribed visualizations can be more than a slight encumbrance before one is able to engage fully in meditative experiences. Contemporary Tibetan Chöd pedagogues maintain that music functions in a graduated manner. Both musical and meditational ability are enhanced with practice, as adepts progress from what may be referred to as a "*performance*-centered practice" toward a "*practice*-centered performance."[50] The discursive dynamic of the Chöd pedagogy, learned while undergoing the traditional training process, is drawn out here as an analytical framework. Making this discursive training process known can help us to see how and why traditional Chöd pedagogues regard music as functioning in accordance with the stage of meditation ability achieved by the Chöd practitioner as they gradually improve in level from "beginner" to "intermediate" to "advanced" and beyond. By attending to an indigenous perspective,[51] the various functions of music in the Chöd ritual may be gleaned from the normative context of Chöd pedagogy. Here, function implicitly ties together the notion of musical ability with the level of practice achieved.

"Beginners" are generally preoccupied with the performance of the musical instruments even while benefiting from the meditation. During the period of study when the text has not yet been memorized, and the drumming patterns and melodies have not yet been learned, "beginner" Chöd practitioners are instructed to follow along by reading the text.[52] If practicing in a group setting, one follows the "chant leader" or *umdzé* (Tib. *dbu mdzad*) while also matching one's partners. Coordinating all these activities can be rather daunting, and some may see it as an obstacle to engaging in the meditation visualizations. At this stage of study, the beginner is engaging in what may be called "*performance*-centered practice." In other words, one's practice is so centered on *performance* that one cannot yet be fully immersed in the meditation *practice*.[53] It may be recommended that during this stage of the learning process, in addition to practicing the musical performance aspects of the ritual, students should read the ritual text (silently, or chanting softly) while drumming or learning the melodies. "With the melodies or the drum solid, the other can be learned more easily."[54]

"Intermediate" level practitioners are those who have learned the musical practice well enough that they can begin to use the music as an aid to concentration. "Music serves to keep one's mind on the practice, like two canes function for an elderly person as aids to walking."[55] The highly physical musical performance assists in keeping focused attention on the visualizations. In other words, at this level, musical performance has the opposite effect from that which it has on the "beginners": instead of being somewhat cumbersome and distracting, it enriches the meditation experience through the flow of attention to the different visualizations, guided in performance. Although "intermediate" level practitioners are engaged in a "*practice*-centered performance," they are, as yet, unable to willfully transfer their consciousness out of the body.[56] The Chöd ritual may still be engaged in through visualization, as a way to increase the practitioner's level of *bodhicitta* and produce the realization of emptiness. Indeed, it is said that merely visualizing the consciousness being transferred out of the body is effective modeling for *'pho ba* meditation practice.[57]

"Advanced" practitioners of Chöd can perform the "transfer of consciousness" or "*phowa*" (*'pho ba*) practice, separating the mind from the body at will.[58] At this stage of the Chöd ritual, "beginners" who wish to focus on their inner potential for enlightenment are instructed to *at least visualize* that, like "advanced" practitioners, immediately upon ejection from the body the consciousness enters into the guru-deity's heart. From that state, by correctly uttering the mantra syllable *phaṭ* the practitioner emerges spontaneously out from the lama-deity's heart in the form of a ḍākinī holding a curved knife (Tib. *gri gug*). Then, the practitioner visualizes having the identity of a ḍākinī and, looking down at the old discarded body below, swoops down and ceremoniously cuts this old body and prepares it for offering and giving away.[59]

The ability to actually separate consciousness from the body distinguishes the practitioner who can advance in stages toward buddhahood. The Chöd practitioner who has reached this level of expertise may perform a number of advanced rituals. Some of these rituals are described in a commentarial text on Chöd composed by Je Tsongkhapa, one of the greatest masters of sūtra and tantra in Tibet. Tsongkhapa composed this Chöd sādhana and commentary in which he provides a short description of seven such rituals. Each ritual is designed for a specific situation, or set of environmental conditions, as follows:[60]

- If one is suffering from leprosy caused by *nāgas* and earth owners.
- For those attacked by illness caused by Rahula.
- If one's body becomes like a nest for spirits.
- How to avert harmful spells or black magic.
- The way to transform omens and change them into good fortune.
- Removing obstacles of disturbed elements which cause illness: [a] suffering from heat [b] suffering from cold.
- How to influence weather conditions: [a] to bring about a rainfall and [b] how to stop a hailstorm.[61]

Tsongkhapa does not give full and elaborate accounts, but rather brief synopses of how to engage in these rituals. The section also works to illustrate the effectiveness of the Chöd ritual method for "advanced" practitioners. It is said that one of the signs of success of "advanced" Chöd practitioners is that they might become unconscious while performing, and, when they come to, not recognize who or where they are or the body they inhabit.[62]

## Scientific Perspectives on "Long-Term Meditators" and "Novices"

Scientists at the Mind and Life Institute (MLI),[63] partnering with an advisory committee of Buddhist studies scholars led by the Dalai Lama,[64] have utilized a categorical framework that registers gradated levels of meditation experience as a central variable in the empirical measuring of a meditator's ability. In a widely cited paper, *Neural Correlates of Attentional Expertise in Long-Term Meditation Practitioners*, MLI scientist Richard Davidson and colleagues have fostered the inclusion of this categorical distinction in such a way that it strikes the right chord with both parties.[65] First, it satisfies the criteria of the hard scientists' experimental paradigm; and second, it resonates with the values held by Buddhist contemplatives who recognize differences in experience and ability, at least in part, by the criterion of time spent doing meditation practices. In the study, a person's *experience* meditating, expressed as a "*time* variable," was used not only as a criterion to demarcate the groups of meditators, but also as the basis of scientific hypotheses and experimental methodology. Thus, so-called "long-term meditators" or "advanced meditators" with an estimated 44,000 hours of meditation practice were compared with those who had spent 19,000 hours, and "novice meditators" who had only a week of training.

It may be useful to include the opening of the study abstract here: "Meditation refers to a family of mental training practices that are designed to familiarize the practitioner with specific types of mental processes." Note that the meaning of the Tibetan word *gom* (Tib. *sgom*) is "to familiarize," which has been often mistakenly translated in English as, "to meditate." To "familiarize" oneself implies gradual progression through practice. Such a corrective is useful to consider in terms of Buddhist practices generally. The notion of "familiarization" is significant here in its association with the development in meditation ability expected of Chöd practitioners as they gradually progress toward advanced levels of "*practice*-centered performance."

## Preparing for Nightly Ritual Practice: Performing Chöd *in Situ*

Although Chöd practitioners should ideally practice Chöd at night, alone and in fearful places, Chöd pedagogy typically involves warnings, admonitions, and cautionary tales about legendary practitioners who lost their drum in a graveyard due to being overcome with fear, such as thinking a spirit was grabbing them when it was actually a tree branch, and so on. In terms of preparedness, Zong Rinpoché cautions the "beginner" practitioner:

> [Although] in order to practice Chöd, we should go to a cemetery, or wherever there are spirits . . . we should seek fearful places only in accordance with our experience and bravery. As

> our strength of mind develops, we should definitely seek more terrifying places such as graveyards and mountaintops, but to begin with, we should practice in our rooms until we are accustomed to the sādhana, and then we can begin to practice without a candle. Also a good place to begin is anywhere that has been blessed by earlier great teachers. Only when a practitioner is highly realized should he or she go alone to cemeteries.[66]

Here, Zong Rinpoché points to the graduated increase in ability, which results from personal meditational experience. For "beginner" meditators, Chöd could be said to have the nature of a rehearsal. Chöd lamas guide the student who is not yet ready to face a fearful situation alone in a cemetery at night, instead enabling the student to practice with others inside a dwelling during the daytime.[67] This protective advice notwithstanding, an idealized notion of Chöd practice is important for "beginners" to have in mind as a goal so that they may gauge their current level with respect.

It is additionally interesting to note the terms used in this statement of cautionary advice. Zong Rinpoché merges the practitioner's level of being "accustomed with the sādhana" and "experience" together with "bravery" and "strength of mind." We might investigate what it suggests about the practice that these last two traits ultimately have to do with character development.

By now the reader should understand that the Chödpa's goal is not to seek out "more terrifying places," which require, as a prerequisite that the practitioner become more "highly realized." Such a flawed interpretation would be a reversal of priorities. Rather, what is key here is how the practitioner's level of familiarity with the sādhana (having already memorized the liturgy so that singing in the darkness is possible), and character development ("bravery . . . strength of mind") are connected with the context of performance. The context of performance refers at once to the practice place, time of day or night, and the number of participants (whether it would be psychologically/spiritually/physically safe to go alone). The framing of cautionary advice in this way suggests that Chöd practice is conceived in terms of gradual improvement on a number of fronts, including a gradual increase in such character traits. Several character traits that one develops as a result from engaging in Chöd practice are discussed further in chapter 8.

## Efficacy of Chöd as a "Beginner" and "Advanced" Practice

Yutang Lin,[68] an interpreter of Chöd, writes of the effectiveness of the practice for "beginners"[69] and "advanced" level practitioners:

> Why is Chöd a practice that can be taught to novices as a preliminary practice and yet is also characterized as a practice aiming at the highest achievement of Enlightenment? In the light of Limitless-Oneness the answer is forthcoming. In Chöd there is a tangible object to work with, namely the body in visualization. Hence it can be taught to novices as a preliminary practice, and as such its main function is 1) the accumulation of merits through almsgiving and 2) the reduction of bad karma through paying back to creditors and enemies.
>
> As a Chödpa *gradually* understands *better and better* the philosophy of Limitless-Oneness and *gains more and more* insight and realization through accumulation of practices, Chöd *gradually* displays its intended function and power as a direct attack to the self-clinging rooted in attachment to the body. In other words, as a Chödpa expands *gradually* into Limitless-Oneness through Chöd practices, Chöd is simultaneously sublimated from a superficial enactment of imagined activities into an experience of Limitless-Oneness in action [emphases added].[70]

Lin's question provides an opportunity to clarify the reasons why I have suggested that the Chöd practice can be effective both when employed by a "novice" ("beginner") and by the "highest achieved" ("advanced") Chödpa. Note this distinction in how he formulates his question: he allows for a "both/and" rather than an "either/or" appraisal of the significance for Chöd practitioners at differing levels. Lin explains here the distinction between *how* the practice operates for each on the basis of function, which dovetails precisely with a major theme of this chapter and the book as a whole. He maintains that both for the "novice" and "experienced" practitioner, Chöd practice is working with a "tangible object . . . the body in visualization."[71]

Contrasting the two, Lin finds that for "novices," Chöd practice functions as an effective means to accumulate merit by "almsgiving," giving the body away, and "reducing bad karma" by paying down karmic debt. Conversely, for "experienced" practitioners, the "intended function and power" of Chöd practice is to make a "direct attack to the self-clinging rooted in attachment to the body." Thus, when the practitioner realizes "emptiness" ("Limitless-Oneness") they will no longer be working with the body merely on the level of "imagined" giving, and will be "sublimated from a superficial enactment of imagined activities into an experience of Limitless-Oneness in action."

Lin maintains the ritual functions in a different way but nevertheless still effectively for Chödpas who are at various stages in terms of their level of experience in meditation and level of realization. His interpretation strongly resonates with the traditional perspective of Chöd lamas on a main point: that these different functions of the same ritual practice refer to earlier and later stages along the same graduated path. As will be noted, Ganden lineage pedagogues of the Chöd ritual mention the practice will function differently for those at an earlier and later stage of acquiring performance skills and experience with the meditation practices. Mainly, the combination of the outer musical performance and inner meditative performance develop into the complementary and necessary parts of one vehicle that work together to steer the practitioner on the path toward the projected transcendent goal of the practice.

Yet, even these categorical assignments of expectations accorded with musical skill and level of meditational achievement could engender the troublesome problem of inadvertently establishing a reified notion about "what a beginner Chöd practitioner should think about." Clearly, these levels of Chöd practice should not be taken in the sense of being reified absolutes because of the false importance that mere labels can impress upon one's mind. To do so would be contrary to the point of Chöd practice.[72] The purpose of recognizing some as "beginners" and others as "advanced" and so forth, is not to establish new lines of categorical distinction. Rather, it is to recognize both the terminology and concepts used in Chöd theory and pedagogical discourse. A large part of the weave in the fabric of lessons is focused on the importance of improvement, achieving successively greater levels of ability through genuine engagement in meditation practice. Certainly, it should be remembered that these are traditional categories of distinction, and placing them here for consideration offers an important look into the Chöd pedagogical discursive method.[73]

Alexandra David-Néel, who traveled to Tibet five times early in the twentieth century from her native France, provides one of the earliest written observations by a European of the Chöd rite. She notes the distinction between "beginners" and those more "advanced." She writes:

> Those who have obtained the fruit of Chöd may dispense with the theatrical side of the rite. Its different phases are, then, called to mind only, in the course of silent meditation, and soon even this exercise becomes unnecessary.
>
> Nevertheless, either because they enjoy remembering through that performance, the exertions of their novitiate days

> or for other reasons known to themselves alone certain *gomchens* sometimes meet to celebrate Chöd together.[74]

She discloses this analysis to the reader, having secretly observed monks from a distance engaging in the "theatrical side" of the Chöd rite.[75] David-Néel suggests, by implication, that the "theatrical side" is the first of three stages of graduated ability in the practice.

The first stage refers to those still engaged with the theatrical side who have not yet obtained the inner results of the Chöd rite. Next are those who have "obtained the fruit of Chöd" and can "dispense" with the "theatrical side," and instead "silently meditate" on recalling the "phases" (the subritual stages) of the rite. Finally, there are practitioners who, although they achieve the latter level, a *practice*-centered performance, gather to "celebrate Chöd together" recalling the arduous training as a "novitiate." These three stages describe the indigenous notion of graduated ability.[76]

## Ethnomusicology in Buddhist Ritual Contexts: Approaches to Performance Practice

Research on Chöd provides a space for the conceptualization of "performance practice" as the integrated study of sound and context. As Gerard Béhague writes of the musical occasion taken as an object of study, "[I]t becomes imperative to document the total and often multiple contextual dimensions of that occasion."[77] Thus, this project represents a contribution to the study of Tibetan tantric ritual performance practices as ritual performance events that take place in social, cultural, environmental, and physical contexts as well as within the mental life of their practicing participants.

### The Ritual Experience

Several functions of music in a Chöd ritual are related to the musical instruments that shape the experience. I will give a short introduction here, followed by a more elaborate exposition regarding melody, text, and rhythm in chapters 2 through 6 respectively. The reader may recall that all of the following functions operate as a continuous musical performance amid the experience of fear.

*Ritual Instruments/Implements*

Along with the voice, three important musical ritual instruments are used in Chöd practice.

- The large *ḍamaru* (hand held, hour-glass-shaped drum): An "advanced" Chöd practitioner understands the *ḍamaru* to be not merely symbolizing but producing the sound of emptiness. Because sound is produced, it is impermanent and therefore "empty" of self-existence.[78] For the "beginner," the two sides of the drum symbolize the conventional and ultimate truths, and the clappers (or pellets) striking them simultaneously symbolize the ultimate nature of mind.[79]
- The Tibetan bell (*dril bu*): symbolizes wisdom, which is the realization of emptiness. It is played as a rhythmically ornamented accompaniment to the drum in the same basic rhythmic figures and tempo, though the texture is far more ornamented. An "advanced" practitioner experiences the sound of the bell in the same way as they experience the *ḍamaru.*
- The thighbone trumpet, or *kangling* (*rkang gling*), calls all beings to the offering feast periodically throughout the ritual, and reminds the practitioner of impermanence.

*Melody, Mantra, and Rhythmic Flow*

The vocal melody, mantric utterance, and rhythmic flow also play important symbolic functions within the context of sādhana performance practice.

- Singing the melody (*rta*) is an act of performing guru-yoga, because one is invoking the blessings of the lineage lamas. The melodies were composed by lamas who achieved realizations while engaging in Chöd practice. Their melodies are said to embody their insights and convey blessings. Correct performance of their melodies brings merit and blessings, as the melodies are said to be the "actual wisdom of the Buddhas."[80]
- Singing produces a joyful feeling.[81] While singing, one is anchored to the melodic movement, even as the eerie sounds of one's singing in a haunted place bring strange echoes and

acoustical reverberations that elicit emotional tendencies of insecurity due to feeling exposed or threatened. This is meant to enhance the vivid appearance of the habitual self that the adept ordinarily seeks to protect.

- Rhythmically, the constancy of the *ḍamaru* anchors one to the ongoing practice despite any perceived outer or inner mental distraction. The flow of drum, bell, and melody in rhythmic unison keeps the mind focused on the task without wandering.[82]
- The rhythm may also function as a mnemonic referent to textual poetry in sections such as the seven-branch practice, in which the "*chom den de*" (Tib. *bcom ldan 'das*) anapest pattern offers a performative complement to the verse.
- The mantric utterance *phaṭ* has several functions: spoken softly, it clears away obstacles and hindrances, pacifies harmdoers, and so forth.[83] As well, the "*Gaté*" mantra of the *Prajñāpāramitā Sūtra* is recited during Chöd practice in rhythmic concordance with the *ḍamaru* at the same time that the *kangling* is blown to invite all beings to the site.
- At a macro level, each melody is composed as a two-, three-, or four-phrase verse that is sung to each two-line or four-line stanza of meditative poetry in a subritual. While the musical verses have the same musical content, the poetic stanzas have changing content of visualizations related with the subritual in question.
- Each melody evokes a mood appropriate to the meditation. Assigned purposefully to a particular meditation section, it sustains the mood for the duration of the meditation subritual section.

## Convergence of Layers in Chöd Ritual Practice

Since Chöd training involves study of these various aspects of ritual separately prior to combining them together, it is prudent to consider a theoretical approach that can accommodate multilayered study and performance. Furthermore, analysis of the ritual is made possible by considering the various layers both separately and together. The Chöd ritual performance may be investigated more deeply through the ethnomusicological technique of transcription. This is a technique that sets down, in a visual medium, the layers of performance in the ritual. A layer in the performance here refers to one layer within the whole ritual, such as: the poetic text (describing the mental visualizations), the sung melodies (which have discernible accordant patterns that complement the text), the performed rhythms (constantly interwoven with the performed text, sometimes as a mnemonic), the blown "calling" forth of spirits through the thighbone trumpet and the use of the bell and other musical implements, and all intentionally performed utterances and gestures, such as the powerful pacifying mantra "*phaṭ*."

In this respect, the Chöd ritual can be thought of as having an internal intertextuality, and of being an intertextual performance event, requiring layered study of each of the "textual" elements.[84] Each of the ritual's layers, or textual elements, demands a separate type of training on the part of the adept, such as the vocal production, the study of the rhythmic sway of the two-sided drum, the playing of the Tibetan bell, and the intentional meditation in the blowing of the thighbone trumpet and performing the mantric utterance "*phaṭ*."

The practitioner's study of melodies alone requires periods of intense concentration while trying to reproduce the manner of vocal production. These highly ornamented melodies require special use of vibrato in the glottal area of the trachea. It takes tremendous effort to achieve a level at which this stylized vocal production can become so seamless, like the playing of the *ḍamaru*, that the manner of singing ornately comes as second nature. In any event, the musical performance is significant as a multilayered, intertextual energizing of the poetic text, which brings the liturgy to life in the mind-space of visualization.

## Case Study I: Music-Poetry Correspondences in a Chöd Ritual

The sādhana focused on here is entitled *Dedicating the Illusory Body as a Heaped Offering* (*sGyu lus tshogs su sngo ba*) and is arguably the most common Chöd ritual sādhana performed in the Ganden Chöd lineage tradition.[85] As a skillfully executed ritual performance by a knowledgeable and experienced Chöd meditation practitioner, it becomes a powerful ritual for the development of *bodhicitta* and an antidote to self-grasping ignorance.[86]

In terms of structure, there are seventy-six stanzas, each having four lines, and each line having nine syllables. There are four preliminary sections, and five sections of the actual practice. The actual practice begins with the "transference of consciousness" (*phowa*) practice and is followed by all the distributions ("white," "red," and "variegated") of offering and giving,[87] meditations on emptiness and on the "three spheres of giving," and finally, the "dedication." There are extensive pre- and post-meditation ritual practices, but limited space prevents discussion here.

## Transcription of a Chöd Ritual Performance

At the inception of this research project, several Tibetan scholars and practitioners were consulted about the manner in which to study the Chöd ritual while working from the perspective of ethnomusicology that could also be useful to scholars in Tibetan studies and Buddhist studies. A prominent Tibetan anthropologist suggested trying "to receive as full a transmission as possible"[88] with Pala, which I have attempted. Further advice came from Tibetan scholars and Chöd lamas, interested in preserving the Ganden Chöd Tradition lineages' melodies, to transcribe the melodies with musical notation. It must be pointed out that Tibetans developed musical notation long ago for their multi-phonic "tone-contour" chanting and accompanying instrumental ensemble performances in local monasteries. However, the Chöd music and performance practice instructions have been passed on through oral tradition alone without such graphic aid. According to Ellingson:

> While all Tibetan song texts exist in written form, melodies are notated only in the tone-contour *dbyangs* style. Since *mgur* are usually set in the discrete-pitch *'debs* melodic format, responsibility for their correct transmission rests with the oral transmission lineage of the *dbu mdzad* (music leader/directors).[89]

It seems that to undertake such an enterprise several issues need to be considered. For over sixty years, since the official inception of the discipline, ethnomusicologists have debated the limitations of Western music notation as a viable means for the accurate transmission of sonic data and performance practice. It is certainly the case that Western "staff" notation has limited usefulness even for Western art music, let alone traditional music rituals of non-Western cultures.[90] The challenge is to develop a notation that is neither wholly prescriptive nor descriptive. It should not be so Eurocentric that Tibetans formerly unschooled in Western musical "staff" notation would be uninterested because of the time it would take to learn to read the symbols of a foreign system that denotes the intervallic relationships of tones, semi-tones, etc., nor so simplistic and vague that it would not be of use.[91] By working together with Tibetan musicians and Chöd lamas, it may be possible to develop a notation that has cross-cultural legibility, and thereby be retained as a visual aid to help students to reproduce the intricate vocal ornamentations. In the meantime, at the current stage of research, Western staff notation provides an expedient means to transcribe melodies due to its familiarity and the purposes of my analysis. One Chöd lama, Zasep Tulku Rinpoché, encouraged me to continue using Western staff notation because he would like the transcriptions to serve as a pedagogical aid, in a prescriptive capacity, for his non-Tibetan disciples, many of whom can read sheet music.

### *Music Enhancing Text in Chöd: Observations through Transcription*

By producing graphic representations of the Chöd ritual in the conventional textual apparatus of the musicologist (Western music "staff" notation), it may be seen how the music enhances the text in numerous ways. Historically, this finding is potentially significant as it provides evidence, in addition to that of Kyabje Zong Rinpoché's advice cited above, that composers set music to the poetry in ways to enhance the meditative experience of the Chöd practitioner. The composers of melodies used a number of compositional devices to set the music to the text. Three specific areas of establishing text-music concordances include harmonic implications of melodies as associated with references to the guru-deity in the written liturgy, phraseology, melodic contour, and rhythmic complements to the mnemonic prosody.[92]

### *Musical Text-Setting in the Chöd Liturgy*

The present analysis attempts to illuminate the ways in which melodies appear to have been composed to enhance the text. I contend that the melodies function artistically as a "sonic iconography," an efficacious meditational aid for the Chöd ritual practitioner. The point should be made at the outset that each section of the liturgy is designed for meditation purposes, and is part of a longer series of meditations that work in succession to complete one Chöd sādhana. While the dramatic narrative of the overall practice is produced from this logical series of meditations, the structure of the ritual event is also a musically progressive process. Each melody is designed to function as a meditational aid into a section of the drama, in part, by highlighting certain aspects of the text. In this way, each melody can assist in procuring realizations into the given meditation of a section of liturgy *while one is practicing.*

Looking at two lines of the liturgical text that are representative of the compositional devices used throughout the entire sādhana, several "melody-text" and "melody-text-rhythm" relationships may be illustrated. As a method of analysis we will proceed linearly through the text, taking each of the features in turn, followed by a summary.

| | | | | | | | |
|---|---|---|---|---|---|---|---|
| Tibetan: original sādhana liturgy | ༄༅། །མདུན་གྱི་ནམ་མཁར་སེང་ཁྲི་པད་ཟླའི་སྟེང་། | | | | | | |
| Transliteration in Wylie | ***mDun*** | ***gyi*** | ***nam mkhar*** | ***seng khri*** | ***pad*** | ***zla'i*** | ***steng*** |
| Phonetic Romanization | Dun | gyi | nam kar | seng tri | pe | dé | teng |
| English: Translation | **In front** | **of** | **space** | **lion-throne** | **lotus** | **moon** | **upon** |
| English: Correct Grammar | In space before me, upon lion-throne, lotus, and moon-disc | | | | | | |

Figure 1.5. Tibetan Liturgy: Transliteration, Phonetic Romanization, and Translation (line 1).

| | | | | |
|---|---|---|---|---|
| Tibetan: sādhana liturgical text | །བླ་མ་ཡུམ་ཆེན་ལབ་ཀྱི་སྒྲོན་མ་ལ། | | | |
| Transliteration in Wylie | ***bLa ma*** | ***yum chen*** | ***lab kyi*** | ***sgron ma la*** |
| Phonetic Romanization | La ma | Yum chen | Lab chi | drön ma la |
| English: Translation | **Teacher** | **Great Mother** | **Lab chi** | **drön ma la** |
| English: Correct Grammar | [Sits my] Lama, Great Mother, [Machik] Lab drön ma la | | | |

Figure 1.6. Tibetan Liturgy: Transliteration, Phonetic Romanization, and Translation (line 2).

**Going For Refuge**

*Dedicating the Illusory Body*

Figure 1.7. "Going for Refuge": Musical Transcription.

This transcription is a faithful rendering of Ven. Pencho Rabgey's voice and *ḍamaru* performance. It features the notation of the melody on the upper stave, with melodic phrase markings indicating where the practitioner is to take a breath, the undergirding pattern of drum accompaniment on the lower stave, and liturgical text-setting to the ornamented melody in-between the staves. E-flat is the opening pitch Pencho Rabgey most commonly sings. Practitioners will attest that this portion of the liturgy does not always begin on his note. In practice, this musical system is organized according to a relative tuning and variable tonic pitch, which can be transposed. While practitioners do not tune to a particular instrument or another external pitch source, the voice, as a bodily instrument, is considered sacrosanct. He enters the first phrase singing the lowest comfortable pitch for himself when he is performing as a solo practitioner; and, when leading a group, he sings the most comfortable lowest pitch agreeable to all. While there is not a vote, testing the agreeability of a starting pitch, after meeting regularly in a group of between 2 to 30 practitioners (approximately), the *umdzé* knows which pitches will be accommodating to the vocal range of most and transposes accordingly.

## *Melodic Movement: Defining Characteristics*

In the Chöd corpus of melodies, the strength of the first (1) and fifth (5) degrees of the scale relative to the other scale degrees is a notable feature. Generally, the movement of phrases retains a sense of moving from "home" to "away" and then "home" again. This sense refers musically to the directionality of the musical phrase and its temporary destinations, which allows for a meditative musical ebb and flow. Specifically, the opening musical phrase of most two-line Chöd melodies moves initially from the first to the fifth degree of the scale; this is immediately followed in the second musical phrase (sung to the second line of poetry) by a return of the melody from the fifth degree (5) back to the first (1). Here, in this first example, the movement of 1 to 5 and the return to 1 occurs in the opening phrase of a three-phrase melody. In this case, it is the second musical phrase that moves from 1 and ends on 5, and the third phrase that shifts from 5 back to 1. However, as has just been mentioned, most Chöd melodies consist of two phrases of a two-line poetic stanza sung to two melodic lines.

While the term "tonal area" denotes the relative strength of scale degrees, I do not use it to refer to the equal temperament scale of twelve tones and the sense of consonance and dissonance in Western diatonicism. More precisely, a given pitch and the perfect fifth above it are naturally occurring overtones in the harmonic series, which contributes to their frequency and prominence in many melodies of various musical cultures around the world. I submit that I am extremely reluctant to use any terms or concepts in Western tonality to understand or describe a non-Western musical genre. However, given the regularity with which these patterns in melodies in Chöd occur, emerging as they do from the *gur* genre of song poetry, the observation of phraseology and directionality and "tonal area" prominence is a characteristic and defining feature of the genre, and is thus important to mention.

*First Phrase*

The first melodic phrase of the sādhana travels only a short distance; it begins on the e-flat, ascends a perfect fifth to b-flat, and descends back to the e-flat, creating an arc-like contour that completes the first phrase [figure 1.7: "Going for Refuge"]. This first phrase establishes the "tonal area" of e-flat. The melody passes through the minor third both on its ascent and descent, setting up a pensive and contemplative feel that is appropriate to the meditation expected of the practitioner at this moment. The meaning of these first four syllables, *mDun gyi nam mkhar*, which is translated as "in the space before me," relates to the meditation required in this section. The first section is referred to in the liturgy as the "merit field" (*tshogs zhing*) visualization. It involves mentally imagining the "merit field"—which includes all the lineage lamas, buddhas, meditational deities, and protectors surrounding the central *yidam* figure. They sit luminously in space in front of the meditator, floating in the sky, in an ethereal stasis with texts in front of them emitting the sound of Dharma. These visualized enlightened beings are the "objects of refuge" (*skyab yul*).

Each sādhana of a meditational deity (*yidam*) has its own merit field. Prior to practicing Chöd, the meditator will have already received extensive teachings on the merit field, and will know the meaning and purpose of visualizing. Even though there are many details that can be visualized in the merit field, here in the poetic text only the essential elements are given. One may read about the fine points of the merit field in commentarial texts of Chöd and other practices, or receive instructions from a qualified lama. The details include such features as the exact position and posture in which each of the buddha deities sits, what kind of clothing they wear, the nature of their facial expression, the hand positions (*mudras*) they hold, any special hand implements they use, and the symbolism thereof.

### *Second Phrase*

Rhythmically, this first phrase *dun gyi nam kar* (Tib. *mdun gyi nam mkhar*, "in the space before me") falls completely within one cycle of the *ostinato* rhythm "*ma dang, lha yi, mkha' 'gro.*"[93] The second time this rhythmic cycle[94] is played, the first of the paired *lha-yi*[95] beats of the drum are sounded at the same time as the practitioner sings the syllable *seng*. The syllable *seng* begins the phrase *seng khri pad zla'i steng*, which means, in order of the appearance of words in the text, "lion-throne, lotus, moon-disc, upon." When reordered grammatically in English, the first line is rendered as: (first phrase) "in the space before me" and (second phrase) "upon a lion-throne, lotus and moon-disc." Again, the second phrase rhythmically falls nearly within one complete cycle. However, the word denoting "upon" (*steng*) is the only syllable that remains outside the second rhythmic cycle: this important word falls upon the first of the *lha-yi* beats and begins the next, and third, time we hear the *ostinato* cycle.[96]

Melodically, the second phrase is more elaborate than the first. Although it starts on the e-flat, and ascends in the same way as did the first phrase, the melody rises through ornamented pitches on the syllables *pad* and *zla'i*, and reaches all the way up through the d-flat to the e-flat an octave above. The leap upward of a perfect-fourth to the syllable *pad* from the a-flat on the syllable for "throne," (*khri*) of "lion-throne," is dramatic and noticeable given the staid contour of the nearly stepwise movement of the melody thus far. The syllable *pad* denotes "lotus" (from the Sanskrit word *padma*), and the leap upward to this syllable may be symbolically significant in so far as this flower has important meaning within the Buddhist tradition as something unsullied that has grown from mud, but rests above it. It symbolically represents renunciation (*nges 'byung*), a whole-hearted wish for liberation from suffering. To elaborate, the lotus flower grew in dependence on having its roots in the earthen mud at the bottom of a pond; yet, it transcends this domain and now floats atop the pond. It must be emphasized here how ubiquitous this image is. Every depiction of a buddha deity—whether in Thailand or Tibet, male or female, in standing or sitting posture, with multiple limbs or only two arms and two legs—is iconographically represented in statues and paintings *on top of the stamen of a lotus flower*. Since the lama-buddha-deity will be visualized (in the third phrase) sitting upon the moon-disc on the stamen of the lotus, which is itself situated on the lion-throne (a throne held up by eight lions, two on each corner), it may be suggested that what can be heard in this leap upward is the lotus's freedom from the mud. Symbolically, the lama-buddha-deity's genuine freedom from cyclic-existence is symbolized by the lotus flower, "upon" which the buddha-deity sits.

### *Third Phrase*

With the syllable *steng* ("upon") falling on the first beat of the third rhythmic cycle, and being held for one half note and one quarter note followed by a whole note rest, it allows time for the meditator to visualize a space in front of them to be occupied with the "lion throne, lotus and moon disc." Temporally, this is a pregnant pause, of only rhythmic drumming, which functions as a preparatory moment to concentrate upon the next line of text, which is as follows: *bLa ma yum chen labs kyi sgron ma la*. The syllable *steng* falls on the fifth degree of the scale, which is b-flat. Spending time—one full rhythmic cycle—on this pitch helps to shift the focus from the tonal area of e-flat to the tonal area of b-flat,[97] and the b-flat becomes the starting pitch of the third phrase.

Thus, while the first and second phrases commenced on e-flat, the third phrase starts in the tonal area of b-flat and reaches up to the tonal area of f-natural (which is a perfect fifth "above" the tonal area of b-flat), and descends to the low e-flat again. Interestingly, the third phrase requires the span of three rhythmic cycles, and it operates exactly the same way as did the rhythm and text of the second phrase insofar as the last syllable of the third phrase, "*la*," falls on the *lha-yi*, which is the beginning of the sixth rhythmic cycle. Structurally, this provides one rhythmic cycle of time for the meditator to visualize the buddha deities in the refuge visualization, just as time was employed on the syllable *steng* at the end of the second phrase.

What is the most important feature to point out in the transcription and analysis? I propose it is the way in which the melody is written to highlight the most important words and ideas of the poetry. The most important visualization in this section of poetry is the assembly of enlightened beings, the "object of refuge." These are necessary for successful meditation in the Chöd meditation practice. Their centrality is musically and poetically illustrated in several ways, as the following analysis indicates.

We may observe the repetition of the scale pitches used for the sung names of the buddha deities. Each of the two syllables of the named buddha deities is repeated on the same pitch: *bla ma* (lama) on b-flat; *Yum Chen* (The Great Mother) on e-flat; and *Labs sgron* (Machik Labdrön) on b-flat again. First, what is the identity of these three buddha figures? *Lama* is the Tibetan translation of the Sanskrit word *guru*, which means "teacher" or "spiritual guide." There is a special practice of guru-devotion in Buddhist tantric ritual where the meditator aims to see (as close as possible) their teacher as inseparable from the buddha. The symbolic importance of this visualization at the tantric level need not be discussed extensively here, since other scholars have discussed this elsewhere.[98] In sum, the practitioner visualizes the central figure of the "object of refuge"—who sits atop the moon-disc, lotus and lion-throne—as an inseparable mix of three buddhas: one's lama, The Great Mother (Yum Chenmo), and Machik Labdrön.[99]

The first line of text sets the meditational ground for the Chöd practitioner to visualize the "object of refuge" in the space before her or him. The buddha deity will sit upon the "lion-throne, lotus and moon disc" imagined in the sky, and the meditator is poised to sing the name of the first buddha deity that will appear "upon" (*steng*) the moon disc. It is interesting to attend to which sung pitches are emphasized in the second line of text, because they are completely consistent with the prominence given to the particular buddha deities visualized in the Chöd practice. As the third musical phrase commences, the first sung pitch is *bla* ("la"), the first syllable of the name *bla ma* (lama), on b-flat. The second syllable "*ma*" is also sung on b-flat. The name "*Yum Chen*" is sung up a perfect fourth on e-flat, at the octave. Each of the two syllables of the names—*Yum* and *Chen* as well as *Lab* and *Drön*—is sung on the strongest beat of the measure. Finally, the historical founder and female buddha deity Machik Labdrön, has both syllables of her family name, *lab* (Lab) and *sgron* (drön), sung down a perfect fourth on b-flat.

This repeating of the pitches that sound the names of the figures most essential to the Chöd practice would otherwise seem to be only a remarkable coincidence if not for the fact that there are other syllables that are not given such melodic prominence by being situated on notes other than those marking the two main tonal areas—e-flat (the starting pitch, or primary tonal area, which would be considered the "tonic") and b-flat (or secondary tonal area, a fifth above the e-flat, which would be considered the "dominant"). Indeed, the names of these three buddha figures are given prominence in four ways in this context: (1) through note repetition; (2) through being sung on the most important pitches of the scale; (3) through rhythmic emphasis; and (4) through note value (the length of time that the note is held).

The singing of *Yum Chen*, referring to the name of Yum Chenmo, is given the highest priority in terms of pitch, sounding at the octave (e-flat) above the starting pitch of the first and second phrases. It is climactic in a visceral sense since the Chöd practitioner is physically exerting herself to reach those higher notes and then descend the octave. As well, the second part of Yum Chenmo's sung name, *Chen*, which translates as "great" or "supreme," has increased prominence when sung: the pitch extends upwards to the structurally important neighbor note, the f-natural (which Western music analysts would consider to be the "supertonic"), before descending back to the e-flat. In terms of range, this is the highest pitch reached during the singing of this verse, which has a total of five phrases and thirty-six syllables.[100]

These findings are interesting because an important compositional device used for emphasis is repetition. And when the most important notes in the scale are emphasized in ways such as they are here, this is good evidence to suggest that deliberate attempts have been made to highlight a pitch, or in this case, a word, the name of the guru-deity. To be clear, the emphasis of the two-syllable name of both the guru (*bla ma*) and deity (*Yum Chenmo*), each having two syllables, are both repeated at the same pitch. Furthermore, each of the note values for the name-related syllable is longer than for other pitches on other syllables. What is even more compelling for the music analyst is the implication of the melody here, because in this instance the pitch that has the second most importance is the b-flat, the tonal area on the fifth degree (what would be considered the "dominant"), reserved for the lama. The most important pitch is the e-flat, the tonal area on the first degree, an octave above the first iteration (in the first phrase) on which the name Yum Chenmo is sung, the deity considered to be the mother of all the buddhas. The resolution of the distance traveled occurs when the melody falls back to the tonic an octave below (which may be heard in this instance as implying the referential distance between the buddha deity and the practitioner herself, who visualizes the buddha deity floating directly in front of her). Now, the next meditation section (on taking refuge and generating *bodhicitta,* the altruistic intentionality) may ensue, once the presence and proximity of the divinity has been mentally, melodically, rhythmically, sonorously, and textually established. As in numerous moments throughout the Chöd liturgy, composition techniques may allow the singer-practitioner to move deeper into the experience of guru-yoga through the deliberate musical setting of the text.

## Chöd Healing Rituals: Why Attend to Music Performance?

In recent decades, several scholars have explored various aspects of the Chöd ritual practice (Gyatso 1985; Savvas 1990; Edou 1996; Harding 2003); but, previously, none had analyzed or discussed its musical and compositional architecture, or performance characteristics. It is understandable that this gap in the literature has persisted, however, because of a paradoxical discourse around the importance of the musical and performative components of the meditation practice. A Chöd lama may frequently assert that music is "not the essence of Chöd." Yet, at some point in the transmission, the same Chöd lama may impress upon the student the fact that to perform the music correctly is *vital* in order to retain the blessings. Given this seeming contradiction in Chöd pedagogy, it may be asked: (1) "In what ways is music necessary to complete the ritual successfully?" and (2) "Through which manner of performance does Chöd become productive of, or efficacious in bringing about, the results promised in Tibetan Chöd commentaries?"

We do not begin with the baseline question "If music were not needed, why would it be there?" However, sometimes a naïve question is best for teasing out the relative distance in implicit beliefs between learner and teacher in the context of studying an indigenous (Tibetan) tradition, and it may evoke varied responses, interesting dialogue, and an exchange of values in the context of ethnographic inquiry. Instead, we have started by looking at the textual aspects of the liturgy, of which the closest parallel poetic Tibetan tradition are the "songs of meditative realization" or *mgur* genre. Certainly, the song-poems of Milarepa—even with most of the melodies lost to historical time—remain highly inspirational instructional works.[101] Furthermore, the poetry and melodies of Chöd and *mgur* are based upon the same literary-music genre from India, the *dohā* tradition.[102]

Next, we will look at the musical aspects of the *mgur* genre, and again ask why music would be valued in Chöd beyond that of an "epiphenomenon." Ethnomusicologist Steven Friedson's monograph *Dancing Prophets: Musical Experience in Tumbuka Healing* recounts his revisiting of the Ndembu ritual site where anthropologist and ritual theorist Victor Turner did most of his fieldwork decades earlier, armed with the conceptual framework of medical anthropologist Arthur Kleinman. In his critical review of *The Performance of Healing*,[103] a collection of papers on ritual healing by medical anthropologists and ethnomusicologists, Friedson explains that:

> [M]usical experiences are treated here and elsewhere in the book as epiphenomena—things that enhance or intensify other performative happenings. Though music no doubt enhances moods and intensifies experience (Laderman, Hoskins, Kendall), musical performance first and foremost constructs a clinical reality.[104]

For Friedson, "a clinical reality is saturated with the musical . . . experience that penetrates into bodily existence."[105] Although we are glancing cross-culturally, here perhaps lies the answer to why music is not simply an "epiphenomenon" of the Chöd practice. Geshé Thupten Jinpa recounts that when his teacher Geshé Zemey Rinpoché, a leading scholar and poet-adept in the *mgur* style, would on rare occasions sing one of his own *mgur*, it made listeners in attendance weep[106]—such has the power of music to allow one to experience embodied emotion along with the taste of realization through sung poetic verse.

The question may be posed more directly: Why is it important to learn the music of Chöd? According to Zasep Tulku Rinpoché's oral transmissions on the practice of the Chöd Tradition:

"It is important to learn the melodies well. They have healing power. They go deep in the mind and body. Drumming and chanting make you go into trance faster than any other method."[107]

The lesson is not so different from what is known of studies of the music of shamanic traditions.

## Chöd Ritual Practice as a Healing Performance: Some Theoretical Considerations

Medical anthropologists draw upon the work in ritual studies and performance studies to explain the transformative healing power of ritual based performances that regard the mind and body in specifically holistic ways. Ethnomusicologists, too, have also been called upon to think about the role of music and dance in the performance context of healing rituals (Laderman and Roseman 1996; Friedson 1996). In recent years, performance studies and ritual studies have become increasingly dialogic and mutually productive, drawing on the ethnographic work of anthropologists. Initially, Victor Turner's theories about ritual as social drama influenced Richard Schechner's approaches to performance studies.[108] Schechner sought to combine an interest in the physical and sonic space of performance with the notion that organized *ritualized* experience, through dramaturgy and performance utterance, induces a psychological reframing of the self. Interested in shifting notions of identity, achieved through transformative states of heightened affective experience, Schechner borrowed Victor Turner's concept of "liminality" to explicate the dramatic process in formal, experimental, and indigenous cultural theatre.

With respect to Chöd, while certainly there is a "liminal" space upon exiting the body through which a transformation of identity occurs, the audience in the Chöd ritual remains at once unseen (invisible, visualized for the beginner) and all encompassing (all beings throughout the universe). Such an expansive mental visualization process is required even when the practitioner is seemingly "alone" in the wilderness at a haunted place, or *nyen sa* (Tib. *gnyan sa*). In contradistinction to the notion of "alone," the Chöd practitioner is blessed by the continual presence of the proximity of the guru-deity. The constancy of the close relationship between the lama and the practitioner in the tantric Buddhist context may allow a distance into the spirit world to be traveled through which one seeks to enrich an already strong sense of "communitas" with one's lama and lineage lamas.

Perhaps, in Chöd, one needs deep embodiment in order to achieve disembodiment. Although it has been shown here that melody-text relationships have been designed carefully, it is unknown until one studies the connections oneself, and then practices the ritual meditation performance *in situ*, whether such knowledge of the music-text connections assists one in performing the guru-yoga meditation more ably or profoundly. One needs not only to know and understand the meaning of Chöd, but also to experience every aspect of Chöd performance many times, such that the entire ritual is like the "autopilot" sought for by Ven. Pencho Rabgey before one can transcend the body and self-based concerns.[109]

The suggestion of some scholars that Chöd is shamanic misses the practice's strong epistemological and ontological roots in Buddhist practice. The notion of exorcism or sacrifice using the body as a scapegoat or ransom (*glud*)[110] does not quite capture the essence of what is being aimed at in the Chöd ritual. While it is true that one's old body is made the object which is to be transformed and offered, and one's karmic debts are being paid down through the cutting, offering, and giving with conventional and ultimate *bodhicitta* (to the extent one can combine these during practice), there remains an epistemological difference in terms of extent.

In chapter 9, I discuss this issue of extensiveness with respect to Marcel Mauss's theory of "the Gift." I posit that the departure point for looking into the theory of "the Gift," and the common ground shared with Mauss's position, is that there is "no free gift," and therefore always an attendant "obligation to repay" a gift, and a "debt owed" to one's creditors. As a result, initially Mauss's gift theory seems to provide a compelling framework. After some investigation, however, the Mahāyāna Buddhist perspective completely obviates the possibility for a closed system of exchange. From the Mahāyāna viewpoint (in which Chöd and all Buddhist tantric ritual is couched), one is always already indebted to all (m)Other sentient beings for their kindness. Therefore, the exchange can never be closed as one must always be completing the exchange by both paying back the kindness of one's mothers, and paying off the debts one owes to one's creditors from having committed (knowingly and unknowingly) negative karma. Chöd is unique among most Buddhist practices, in that the more difficult of these two "exchanges," the latter, is done first; and there is good reason for this within the Mahāyāna distinction of the altruistic *bodhicitta* motivation.

## Chöd: A Radical Counter-Intuitive Practice

The imagined harmdoers (Tib. *dug pa can*) are understood to be causing harm not only to the Chöd practitioners and others besides, but also *to themselves through harming others*. They do not understand the negative mental imprints they are accumulating through committing sinful actions.[111] They do not even realize how destructive their thoughts, actions, and spoken words have been in the past, and continue to be even now. They think they are doing well, and believe they have been acting and speaking correctly; but, in fact, they are engaged in just the sort of thinking, doing, and speaking that will cause them to reap the opposite effect of bringing themselves, let alone others, real happiness.[112] This is why Machik Labdrön taught that the Chöd practitioner needs to *give to these harmdoers first*, because by harming others *they themselves* will definitely take rebirth in a hell realm,[113] and experience terrible suffering there. As Machik Labdrön writes of her tradition:

> My Dharma system does not have even one-hundredth of a hair's worth of self-serving concern—it is not stained by any such idea. And though it does have the concern to serve others, it does not have even one-hundredth of a hair's worth of partiality. Nevertheless, powerful, hostile (*gdug pa can*), frightening, savage spirits, both embodied and unembodied, can cause harm at some point to many sentient beings. [Not only that], the hostile spirits themselves have a very difficult time escaping the reaches of cyclic existence. I cannot bear to see their suffering. So I have made the powerful hostile spirits my particular focus. Sending out the messengers of love, compassion, and *bodhicitta*, I draw in those powerful spirits. Then I give the spirits and their retinues my own body, life, wealth, and whatever is in my domain, so that they are completely satisfied, and I lead them to the stages and paths to enlightenment. That is the Dharma system of this beggar woman.[114]

## Ritual Mastery: Prerequisites for Going to the *Nyen sa*

Chöd lamas ask "beginners" to exercise patience and refrain from going to practice at a frightening site (*nyen sa*), such as a cemetery, alone before they have sufficiently acquired some experience with cultivating realization of method and wisdom. Within the context of giving cautionary advice, some Chöd commentators say that while inviting beings to a terrifying place and giving away to them one's dearest attachments, it is most important to maintain a perspective that is at least imbued with an understanding of emptiness. By seeing the selflessness of (attributing a lack of inherent existence to) all perceived phenomena, one "cuts off" attachment to that which is being given and obviates one's conceptual imputation upon the receivers of such labels as "enemy" and "friend."

Another view, also expressed by Chöd lamas, emphasizes that, as a minimum, it is more important to cultivate the altruistic motivation of *bodhicitta* prior to going to the site of offering, and to maintain this compassionate resolve while willingly giving away the body to whomsoever the practitioner might encounter there. I find the latter to be rather powerful precisely because of the counter-intuitive nature of not removing oneself from a difficult situation, or expelling others, but openly presenting the opportunity for contact while pacifying all (mis)conceptions that would incite conflict. Indeed, in order to perform the radical act of summoning one's creditors (who may have malevolent intentions toward oneself and others) and pacify this atmosphere of potential tension (and to not withhold any reservations while giving to one's perceived enemies, willingly parting with all that the practitioner has cherished up until now) *bodhicitta* is a necessary and powerful antidote. It activates and transforms the desire for peace of mind into being desirous of actualizing others' beneficence—even at the expense of the practitioner's own seeming loss or peril. Ironically, there is no peril so long as the practitioner is authentically engaged in the altruistic mind of enlightenment (*bodhicitta*); but if jealously guarded, ambivalent, or otherwise experiencing reluctance, it is said to foster a disposition in some of these guests that would not be called friendly. In sum, the practitioner must have the prerequisites of method and wisdom, but primarily method, prior to going to the *nyen sa*.[115]

As Durkheim's student Hertz said, the body, "is good to think with."[116] Machik Labdrön, dealing with the stark reality of the impermanence of the body, taught the Chöd method of "cutting" through appearances, misconceptions, and both latent and overt attachments. She once asked her teacher, Padampa Sangyé, "How can I help sentient beings?"

Padampa Sangyé replied:

Confess all your hidden faults.
Approach that which you find repulsive.
Whomever you think you cannot help, help them.
Anything that you are attached to, let go of it.
Go to places that scare you.
Sentient beings are limitless as the sky.
Be aware.
Find the Buddha inside yourself.[117]

## Contextualized Performance: Themes in Chöd Musical-Meditation

This chapter discusses the common history of the Tibetan schools' Chöd lineages, several aspects of pedagogy and transmission, and brings a tight focus on a single ritual in the Ganden Chöd Tradition for which there are extant poetic texts and a living practice tradition. This study is based upon research conducted through discipleships with recognized and accomplished exponents and masters of the Chöd Tradition. The Tibetan literature on Chöd contains several types of specialized rituals, taught by Machik Labdrön, and passed down in unbroken lineages from teacher to disciple that are designed both: (a) to increase one's level of *bodhicitta*; and (b) to produce the realization and transformation that results from cutting grasping to the erroneous conception of an intrinsic, self-existent "I."[118]

The musical practice is traditionally transmitted through an orally/aurally transmitted musical performance pedagogical tradition. Attendant with the musical performance tradition—and considered to be of substantially greater importance than its aesthetic strictures and well-developed performance practices—is a meditation practice tradition. The *guru-śiṣyā paramparā* ("master-disciple tradition") involves a musical transmission of performance practices as well as a spiritual transmission (Tib. *lung*) of the meaning of Chöd and its meditation techniques. These two aspects of musical performance and meditation practice are framed as the "outer" and "inner" layers of Chöd respectively.

There are numerous functions of the ritual instruments/implements and melodies, and even the musical element of rhythm is involved in several ways. The multilayered musical elements overlap in ways that suggest a close reading of ritual elements is possible and necessary for a full analysis of the functions of music in Chöd.

Extracted from the indigenous pedagogical discourse, the differentiated notion of "beginner" and "advanced" practitioners relates to a significant aspect of transmission. Drawn from this discursive tract, I formalize a graduated scheme between these designations of practice level in terms of skill and experience. I discuss how Chöd practitioners aim to progress from a *performance*-centered practice to a *practice*-centered performance. This discursive framework applies to the performances of both "inner" meditative and "outer" musical practices. Likewise, the notion of progressive advancement is referred to in terms of "preparedness" to practice in the "more terrifying sites" which relates to strength of character: thus, there is a notion of graduated development of bravery based on one's altruistic motivation to be able to accommodate environmental and spiritual challenges.

The Mind and Life Institute has also recognized Tibetan Buddhist contemplatives' indigenous categories of practice levels "beginners" and "advanced," and scientific investigators are actively using these distinctions as variables in behavioral science experiments on questions pertaining to the efficacy of meditation. For example, once distracted by a sound (as an external stimulus), how quickly can the meditator reroute his/her (internal) mental pathways back to the intended subject of meditation? To put this another way, having quantified "experience" in temporal terms (the approximate hours of meditation practice an individual has accumulated over a lifetime), scientists measure a meditator's skill level by timing his/her ability to effectively re-implement the mindfulness meditation practice technique, once distracted by a sound.

## Fear Beyond the Three Scopes: Preparing for Chöd Practice

In terms of transmission and advancement from a doctrinal perspective, Ganden Chöd lamas often exhort disciples to study the *Lamrim* or *Stages of the Path* discourses more deeply. They maintain that all the instructions on the "three principal paths"—"renunciation," "*bodhicitta*," and the "view of emptiness"—serve as the basis for Chöd practice. Zong Rinpoché said, "In general we should follow the path of the past, present, and future buddhas. In particular, we must meditate on *Lamrim* thoroughly and continuously."[119] The *Lamrim* instructions are divided into three scopes which differentiate the three types of practitioner according to their motivation.

A practitioner of the lower scope pursues the goal of taking rebirth next life in one of the three upper realms. A practitioner of the medium scope seeks the goal of liberating herself or himself from *saṃsāra*, while a practitioner of the greater scope generates *bodhicitta* and pursues the goal of reaching buddhahood in order to benefit all sentient beings. According to the *Lamrim*, the development of renunciation—a meditation section common to the practitioners of small scope (*skyes bu chung ba*), medium scope (*skyes bu 'bring ba*), and greater scope (*skyes bu chen po*) of the Buddhist path[120]—begins with thinking over the causes for taking refuge. It emphasizes that one should have fear in order to cultivate faith in the objects of refuge: the guru (teacher), buddha (founder teacher), Dharma (teachings), and sangha (community of practitioners). Thus, fear is *operationalized* in the earliest meditations on the path. One takes refuge out of fear and faith: fear about the place of one's next rebirth due to karma (felt by lower scope practitioners), fear for one's future rebirths in *saṃsāra* (known to practitioners of the medium scope) and fear and compassion for the suffering others will have to undergo in their future rebirths (experienced by practitioners of the greater scope).

In the context of the Chöd ritual, however, it is one's deep-seated fear that acts as a catalyst. What is different about the thought meditation in Chöd is that *one uses fear to notice the way in which one grasps onto the "self,"* one's body being the apparent source, however impermanent and illusory, for the conceptual designations of "I," "me," and "mine." There is no basis for attributing permanence to the "self" other than a habitual and conceptual imputation since the feeling "I" is said to persist even after one passes on.

# 2

# Musical Character of the Chöd Genre

## Buddhism as Performing Art: A Brief Historiography of Tibetan Ritual Studies

From an historiographical perspective, Stephan Beyer's monograph *The Cult of Tārā: Magic and Ritual in Tibet*[1] follows in a tradition of Western scholars attempting to address the voluminous number and kinds of rituals practiced in Tibetan tantric Buddhism as well as the intricacy and multivalent aspects of their performance. Beyer locates his as the fourth major attempt to accomplish this task. At the top of this list, in order of historical appearance, he places Ferdinand Lessing's study of Yung-ho-kung, the magnificent Tibetan Buddhist temple complex in Beijing. Lessing sought to deal with an unwieldy mass of material in discussing all the rituals that took place in the various spaces within this temple complex.[2] Tibetologist David Snellgrove similarly attempted to discuss all the rituals that he had seen take place at Chiwang Monastery in his book *Buddhist Himalaya*.[3] René de Nebesky-Wojkowitz honed his project *Oracles and Demons of Tibet* according to a different category of interest: away from the idea of describing the totality of rituals in a given place, and instead focusing on the Tibetan protective deities and their associated rituals.[4]

Beyer acknowledges these three treatises in the nostalgic language of the ardent folklorist interested in the survival of traditions: "All three authors clearly felt deep bonds of affection for and sympathy with the Tibetans, and their works are important in their attempt to capture the spirit of a living tradition and to describe a practice of Buddhism which is still a vital force among an entire people."[5]

However, Beyer's experience in observing a living tradition *in situ*—a Tibetan refugee community in Dalhousie, Himachal Pradesh, India—inspired him to take a different approach. None of the above-mentioned works, with their focuses on historical lineage (Snellgrove) or on place and iconography (the concerns of Lessing and Nebesky-Wojkowitz), take precedence over Beyer's fascination with the "detailed analyses of the complexities of Tibetan ritual."[6] Lessing writes, "A book could well be written describing in detail these rites alone, with the ritual books translated, annotated, and illustrated by sketches, drawings, and photographs."[7]

Beyer's insight, which changed the direction of his dissertation project to examine in detail the "processes and presuppositions" underlying the performative content of rituals associated with the deity Tārā, is similar to that which guided my approach to the analysis of the Chöd ritual practice. Beyer explains why he came to focus on ritual practice *as* performance:

> The paper began originally as a history of the goddess Tārā, but once in the field, I found myself growing more and more engrossed in the "actual practice" of Buddhist ritual as a study in itself; a scholar from our secular society, I discovered, may too easily ignore the fact that *Buddhism is basically a performing art* [emphasis added].[8]

Likewise, this book is motivated by a need to address how extremely performative the Chöd ritual is in all of its sādhana and ritual manifestations—essentially, to investigate how much it is like a performing art, both in its performance in ritual practice contexts and in the unusual life path of the Chöd adept. The literary focus of Western scholars of Buddhism—who clearly have great affinity with the tradition and are informally effusive in their regard for the music and sung verses—has produced scholarship on Chöd that mostly leaves the performance dimension aside.

As a corrective, I value Beyer's (ethnographic and textual, mixed-methods) approach in trying to understand all that occurs in a Tibetan ritual liturgy in terms of both music performance and meditation practice. This study of the role of music in the meditation practices of the Chöd rite closes a gap left by previous ethnomusicological work on Tibetan ritual music by discussing the ways in which Chöd is performatively dissimilar to the Tibetan tantric ritual performance genres concerned with monastic orchestral instrumental ensembles. I henceforth explore the specific performance elements in Chöd ritual practices, which such a study of its musical functions demands.

## Contrasting Tibetan Ritual Music Genres

There is a substantive difference between the music this study examines and the type of ritual music that has already been looked at in some depth by Western-trained ethnomusicologists. The Chöd ritual is somewhat of a maverick among Buddhist rituals generally, yet it is necessary to contextualize it in conversation with other Tibetan tantric ritual practices. Thus, to broach Chöd ritual performance as an area of scholarly interest, a general comparison of Tibetan ritual music genres will be made. Through this comparison, we may observe the differences between the much-studied monastic ensemble performance and the less well-known Chöd ritual performance in Tibetan religious contexts. While both performance genres may be understood in their capacity as tantric rituals to share essentially the same soteriological goals, divergences in the specific manner of execution of each will be noted.

Following this comparison, I provide evidence that tantric rituals may be productively conceptualized as performed liturgies with layers of textual meaning that may be peeled away and reassembled in an analytical process that uses performance as a key paradigm. Within the broadening purview of recent scholarship on Tibetan tantric ritual, this close examination of Chöd ritual sādhanas illustrates why such a perspective may be important to consider. Focusing specifically on the relationship between the music and the written liturgy reveals a host of associations between tune, poetry, rhythm, and prescribed meditative visualizations. Moreover, by juxtaposing the layers of meaning in a given Chöd ritual sādhana, there is compelling evidence to suggest that recognized Chöd adepts, the composers of these liturgical works, have designed the "outer" ritual performance to assist subsequent Chöd meditators with their "inner" meditative practices by developing concordant musical elements across the written liturgies.

### Monastic Ensemble Rituals and Chöd Rituals

A broad study of the Buddhist musicological literature on Tibetan ritual indicates that there are considerable differences between monastic ensemble ritual performances and Chöd ritual performances. Previous work on Tibetan tantric ritual music has focused primarily on: (1) the vocal chant (*dbyangs*), which is (2) often performed in large, instrumentally accompanied ensembles (3) within monastic institutions, (4) where specially trained monk musicians occupy the role of ritual performers.[9]

In contrast, the Chöd rite primarily involves (1) singing melodies (*rta*) in the soprano, alto, tenor, and baritone ranges, rather than chanting in the deep bass range; (2) solo performance (ideally), rather than in an ensemble setting;[10] (3) performances that often take place outside in nature (at prescribed sites), rather than within monastic institutions;[11] and (4) both lay and ordained individuals are allowed to practice Chöd. The ritual is particularly cherished by lay individuals; among the ordained, the majority are not exclusively males (monks), as many nuns practice as well.[12] There is no evidence of restrictions based on gender with respect to gaining access to Chöd initiations and permissions. Both male and female initiates receive approval to thereafter attend teachings and take music lessons in how to play and use the ritual instruments[13] (see table 2.1, opposite).

### Musical Instruments in Chöd Ritual Practice

Following these categorical distinctions, further contrast can be made between the musical instruments used in these practices.[14] Chöd practitioners play the highly symbolic instruments: the large hourglass-shaped drum (*ḍamaru*, or *cang te'u*),[15] the Tibetan bell (*dril bu*),[16] and the thighbone trumpet (*rkang gling*).[17] When compared with the variety of instruments sounded by Tibetan monastic ensembles—which include aerophones[18] (long horns, conch shell, oboes, and trumpets), metallophones (cymbals and bells), and membranophones (double-sided frame drums of numerous sizes, and the small hourglass-drum, or *ḍamaru*[19])—Chöd may seem to have a limited range of expression. Yet among its three instruments/implements, Chöd incorporates a membranophone (*ḍamaru*), metallophone (*dril bu*), and aerophone (*rkang rgling*). Thus, according to the Sachs-Hornbostel system for the classification of musical instruments, the Chöd ritual instruments are at least categorically representative of the instruments used in other Tibetan monastic ensemble ritual performance traditions. Similarly, all these performance traditions deliberately lack a chordophone (stringed instrument), as it is considered too worldly for religious ceremonial contexts.[20]

## Chöd Studies: Through an Ethnomusicological Lens

As an additional point of orientation it might be mentioned here that ethnomusicology, as a discipline, maintains that ethnographic fieldwork approaches

Table 2.1. Contrasting Tibetan Ritual Music: Monastic Ensemble vs. Chöd Ritual

**A. ELEMENTS OF CONTRAST**

| **Music Performance Aspect** | **Monastic Ensemble Ritual** | **Chöd Ritual** |
|---|---|---|
| **1. Melodic Style** | deep bass tone-contour vocal chant (*dbyangs*) | higher range baritone/tenor and alto/soprano (*rta*) |
| **2. Ensemble/Solo** | ensemble performances | solo or group |
| **3. Site/Context** | monastic institutions | outside institutions, prescribed |
| **4. Performers** | monks or nuns (trained specialists) | ordained and lay practitioners |
| **5. Gender** | women previously excluded | female adepts common |
| **6. Instrumentation** | Various instruments: cymbals (*sbug chal, sil snyan*) | Specific *Chöd* ritual instruments: |
| | long horns (*dung chen*)<br>oboes (*rgya gling*)<br>drums (*rnga*) | hourglass-drum (*ḍamaru*)<br>Tibetan bell (*dril bu*)<br>thighbone trumpet (*rkang gling*) |
| **7. Musical Roles** | musical division of labour | adept plays all instruments |
| **8. Music Notation** | widespread | passed on orally |
| **9. Pedagogy** | literacy and aural training | aural training |

**B. ELEMENTS OF SIMILARITY**

| **Music Performance Aspect** | **Monastic Ensemble Ritual** | **Chöd Ritual** |
|---|---|---|
| **Liturgy** | precomposed (not through, or improvised) | precomposed |
| **Pedagogy** | extensive training required, with instrument experts | extensive training required, *guru-śiṣyā paramparā* |
| **Instruments** | no stringed instruments | no stringed instruments |

can reveal crucial factors in the understanding of how music and ritual are (re)created and (re)produced in the context of performance. Ethnomusicologists studying the performance of ritual generally retain the notion that the social, economic, cultural, and political factors that affect the context of a performance also influence its content. My perspective on Chöd provides a space for the conceptualization of *performance practice* as the integrated study of sound and context.[21] As Béhague writes of the musical occasion taken as an object of study, "it becomes imperative to document the total and often multiple contextual dimensions of that occasion."[22] This project also contributes to the study of Tibetan tantric ritual practices the notion that ritual performance events take place not only in social, cultural, environmental, and physical contexts, but also within the mental life of its participants.

## Group vs. Solo Performance Practice

In terms of Chöd performance practice, it is necessary for each practitioner to learn to play all the instruments since Chöd does not have the musical "division of labor" common to the more extensive ritual music ensembles found in monastic settings. The reason for this emphasis on solo performance has to do with the social context in which practitioners aim to perform the ritual. Chöd is an ascetic tradition with prescribed performance locations for the solitary yogin/yoginī retreatant. The Chöd practitioner must know how to perform all the instruments by oneself while practicing alone in isolated locales.[23]

### Group Performance Practice

Within the context of group performance (whenever two or more practitioners are present) a music director or "*umdzé*" (Tib. *dbu mdzad*) leads the Chöd ritual performance. In this setting, a hierarchy familiar in some respects to that of the monastic ritual ensemble is retained in group Chöd performance. The person in this musical role leads off both the drumming and singing and determines the musical pitch at which each of the melodies for the different subritual sections should begin in a given Chöd sādhana. She or he adjusts the pitch level and tempo of each meditation section, gauging the range of the melody (highest and lowest pitches to be sung) as well as the incremental rise in pitch that is expected in ritual performances.[24] Often the *umdzé* will perform the *kangling* along with the *ḍamaru* at the appointed moments in the liturgical text. However, this instrumental role may be shared with all or some of the other practitioners. There may be one person designated as the individual whose role it is to blow the *kangling*, or several participants may play together. Even when lacking the physical presence of a *kangling* at the ritual performance, the sound of "calling" is to be mentally imagined and all beings summoned forth are visualized assembling around the practitioner, like geese in a lotus pond. There are some advanced rituals in the Chöd corpus, such as the 108-spring wilderness retreat (*chu mig rgya rtsa*), in which group practice is typically the protocol for Chöd trainees since it is considered safer than solo practice. This ritual involves the consecutive performance of a Chöd sādhana at 108 different sites in as many days and nights, and the practitioner should have received special initiations and permissions before embarking on this extended stay in the wilderness.

## Solo Performance Practice

As a general rule, throughout the Chöd liturgy, if practicing alone, the Chöd practitioner can soak in the experience generated by meditating on the meaning of a verse while playing the *ḍamaru*. When proceeding in a group context, however, it is important that all participants at the practice session adhere to an agreed upon standard external performance, lest there be an unattractive musical result or mental confusion. The *umdzé* and other practitioners will decide beforehand how many rhythmic cycles (of "*ma dang, lha yi, khan dro*") to play between each section's melody to allow everyone ample time for meditation. Usually, three rhythmic cycles is considered sufficient; but one, seven, or nine cycles may also be set as the standard. This can be decided upon collectively by all the participants. Yet, when practicing alone, the adept may choose—if there is enough time for deeper meditation—to insert one rhythmic cycle of unaccompanied drumming between each sung line of text in a particular meditation subritual section, or for the duration of the entire sādhana.[25]

It is important to point out that Chöd is not the sole tantric practice that can be performed by one person. Tantric adepts learn to do by themselves what they were trained to do as monks or nuns when they played instruments in the large monastic ensembles. When they engage in retreat or perform their daily practice, they use the cymbal (*sbug chal*) and frame drum (*rnga*) as well as the bell (*dril bu*), the handheld small *ḍamaru*, and the thunderbolt scepter (*rdo rje*). In the setup of ritual practice instruments I have observed, the drum is positioned in front of them at face height, hanging within a frame, and raised about one foot (30 cm) above the floor. They hold the top half of the cymbal pair in the right hand with their three smaller fingers while the thumb and index finger together hold the lower end of the drumstick loosely. They play the cymbals by simultaneously lowering the right wrist, which supports the upper half of the cymbals, and raising the left hand, which holds the bottom portion of the cymbals. The thumb and index finger of the right hand are slightly closed and guide the drumstick forward and play the drum in rhythm at the moment the cymbals meet.

Above all, despite its unique social and musical configurations, Chöd is a liturgically based vocal performance tradition. In this respect, there is no difference at all between Chöd and other tantric rituals across Tibetan religious society.

## Musical Structures: Style and Character of Melodies and Rhythms

There are two continuously overlapping musical themes that characterize the predominantly austere sound texture of a Chöd sādhana: a repeating rhythm played on the *ḍamaru* drum and repeating melodies sung atop this patterned underlay. The melodies occur in stanzas of visualized drama, which manifest poetically as thematic verses. The melodies function like the melodic (non-percussion accompanied) *mgur* in the repetition of the melody over several verses with different poetic content. The sweet high-pitched ringing of the steadily ornamented bell is played in synchronicity with the *ḍamaru* rhythm, and props up the periodic calls from the thighbone trumpet. As well, the mantric utterance "*phaṭ*" inflects the performance at key intervals, particularly at sectional transitions between two melodies and their respective meditation subjects.[26]

Most noticeably, a rhythmic *ostinato* underpins nearly the entire sādhana, *Dedicating the Illusory Body*, and links all the meditation sections. In Western music terminology an *ostinato* is defined as a recurring rhythmic or melodic pattern that pervades a section of a piece, or, in this case, an entire work. The *ostinato* rhythm in this sādhana is comprised of a rhythmic phrase of six beats played on the *ḍamaru*, and is named for its pattern "*ma dang, lha yi, khan dro*" (Tib. "*ma dang, lha yi, mkha' 'gro*"), and performed as follows: two beats of medium duration ("*ma dang*"), immediately followed by two shorter beats ("*lha yi*"), and then two longer beats ("*khan dro*"). Upon listening to (or performing) Chöd, it is apparent that nearly every syllable of the poetic text is sounded at the same time as is a rhythmic beat on the *ḍamaru*. Depending upon the length (and phrasing) of the melody, a corresponding stanza of two lines will receive the rhythmic "support" of as many as six *ostinato* cycles; and a four-line stanza will need double that number.

Melody and rhythm are intertwined, and balance each other. With nine syllables per line, and every syllable receiving the rhythmic complement of the *ḍamaru*, the melodic refrain recurs at slower intervals than does the rhythmic cycle. While singing "over" the continuous rhythmic *ostinato* pattern, the practitioner need not keep track of the number of cycles being played on the *ḍamaru*.[27] Instead, the adept is completely focused on performing the mental visualizations described in the text. As the Chöd practitioner performs the melodically phrased text, the melody of the stanza is repeated until all the stanzas are sung in a meditation subritual. Thus, it is not a dull or insistent rhythm that compels the music onward, but the overlapping *ostinati* of rhythm and melody. These allow for the practitioner's depth of experience to grow deeper while focusing on the sādhana ritual text and the meditative visualizations invoked by the melody and the poetic liturgy.[28]

To reach this level of competence in the context of performance, however, requires some time spent in training. The study of melodies alone can lead one to spend periods of intensive concentration on trying to reproduce the manner of vocal production. The highly ornamented melodies require making special use of vibrato in the glottal area of the trachea. Like the playing of the *ḍamaru*, it takes tremendous effort to achieve a level at which this stylized vocal production can become so seamless that singing ornately comes easily to the practitioner.[29]

The use of aural training has changed over the past thirty years with the advent of consumer recording technology, which provides students of Chöd with the ability to study the Chöd melodies on their own. Ven. Pencho Rabgey (Pala) remarked how privileged my experience was compared with his. I was able to study through both personal training and recordings. His experience involved listening repeatedly to his "root lama" (*rtsa ba'i bla ma*) train a student in the melodies. While cooking and preparing dinner, serving his teacher, he was able to pick up all the melodies faster than the student in training. Pala recounts that years later, while staying in Buxa Duar refugee camp in the early 1960s, Kyabje Zong Rinpoché would teach Chöd. He would introduce a new melody by repeating it only twice, and expect the students to have it memorized by the next day.[30]

## Musical Reflections: Chöd Performance

During the Chöd sādhana ritual practice, *Dedicating the Illusory Body* (*sGyu lus tshogs su sngo ba*), all meditative events are experienced performatively, with the constancy of the rhythmic drumming pattern underlying nearly all thirteen melodies.

### Body Mandala Offering

The rhythmic continuity of the *ostinato* is temporarily interrupted during the *a capella* melody for offering the mandala, but the *ḍamaru* is still functionally important, since its very structure and material makeup operate symbolically.

To explain this further, during the "mandala offering" the *ḍamaru* is held horizontally above one's lap with the handle, the drum's tail of symbolically ornamented brocade and the bell (if used) are placed on top of the drum. The skin of the *ḍamaru* represents one's visualized skin spread out across the universes. The first words of the mandala offering are *pags pa dbang chen*, meaning, "great expansive skin." One's spine is visualized as Mount Meru and one's severed four limbs represent the four continents, with one's intestines forming a mountain chain surrounding them. Furthermore, one's right and left eyes become the sun and moon, respectively. One's head becomes the mandala palace, and one's heart is transformed into a wish-fulfilling jewel. One's ears become the victory banner and the umbrella, while one's internal and external flesh, muscles, and tendons become perfect enjoyments, and so on. One offers this body mandala to the ocean of gurus, meditational deities, buddhas, *bodhisattvas*, and Dharma protectors, and requests their blessings and attainments to be able to accomplish the practice.

In contrast to this momentary stillness, the rhythmic *ostinato* drum pattern ("*ma dang, lha yi, khan dro*") grounds most visualized events because it links all the melodies of the sections together. Each melody, adhering to a particular meditation section, is thereby rhythmically connected to the broader arc of the drama. Each section appears to play a dramatic role through the progression of meditative experiences and emotional states. Similar to the *Offering to the Spiritual Guide* (Tib. *bLa ma mChod pa*) liturgy,[31] this Chöd sādhana (*Dedicating the Illusory Body*) is characterized by (a) melodic continuities, (b) sectionally-defined transitions,[32] and (c) demarcated shifts from one melody to the next as required by the structure of the subritual meditations.

## Music and Trance in Chöd: A Shamanic Rite?

The ritual analyst might intuit that there is possibly a trance-inducing quality to the performance because of the intertwined repeating cycles of both the *ostinato* rhythm and melodic refrain. At some level, the presentation of the Chöd ritual in academic research requires discussion of its trance elements, as previous scholars have done; however, several considerations must be taken into account regarding the musical aspects before the notion of trance is introduced fully.[33]

First, each melody has a distinctive character and pulls slightly and differently at the rhythm: stretching some beats, shrinking others, playing with the integrity of the established rhythmic lilt in one direction or another. (For example, one two-line stanza has a note of long duration on the fourth syllable of its second line, while another melody has a long note on the sixth syllable of its first line. In each case, the rhythmic pattern is subtly drawn to and fro.) Second, the tempo of the overall performance will often speed up gradually during the course of the performance of one sādhana practice, which usually lasts about one hour.[34] These minor variations notwithstanding, the rhythmic *ostinato* cycle still remains relatively constant. Third, after the practitioner sings several repetitions of any given Chöd melody, a "groove" is established which could be felt as inducing a state of embodied rhythmic flow, and which may be affectively experienced as joyful. Joy also comes in being aware, at some level, that the melody the practitioner is singing was composed by a Chöd lineage lama who gained insight through the practice by way of singing it. Fourth, there are "interruptions" at each transition between meditation subrituals. For example, once all the stanzas of a section of the liturgy have been sung (i.e., once the subritual is complete), the practitioner recites *phaṭ* softly and begins to sing the next melody and meditate upon the next subritual. Fifth, although the melody is repeating, the text is always changing, requiring careful attention to the different visualizations described. The Chöd meditation is therefore a highly involved activity on both cognitive and somatic levels. The fact that there are complex mental visualizations that the practitioner performs during every moment of the Chöd ritual is not an extraordinary event, for this is the standard domain of the yogi's/yoginī's tantric practice. Whether or not we consider these continuous visualizations in Chöd "shamanic," the ideation must be situated in some detail before the Chöd ritual's trance-like elements or so-called shamanic aspects are taken into account.[35]

Several Western scholars have already pointed out the shamanic aspects of Chöd: the patterned drumming that underlies a meditative melodic chant; the separation of consciousness from the body; the transformation of the body as the practitioner interacts with unseen beings (spirits), pacifying them with precious gifts and sacrifice, and affecting a healing of an individual from sickness and/or a community from calamity. Yet, the difficulty with labeling Chöd a "shamanic" tradition involves the problem of definitions that Samten Karmay pointed out at a conference on Tibetan ritual. Karmay was concerned that the label "shamanic ritual" had been variously appropriated to explain elements that appear outwardly to reference the same experience.[36] But what occurs in ritual experiences among cultures as non-filial as Caribbean voodun and Buriatian shamanism, where "shamans" do their respective healing work, may or may not be as similar as they outwardly appear.[37] In the Tibetan context, a better term than "shaman" would be "ritual master" as this more accurately describes their functional role.

## Case Study II: A Sādhana in the Ganden Chöd Tradition

### *Dedicating the Illusory Body*: "Thick Description" of a Chöd Ritual

The sādhana focused on here is titled *Dedicating the Illusory Body as a Heaped Offering* (*sGyu lus tshogs su sngo ba*, pronounced "Gyu lü tshog su ngo wa") and is arguably the most common Chöd ritual sādhana performed in the Ganden Chöd lineage tradition.[38] This meditation text is favored, in part, because all four of the main meditation sections on offering and giving that can comprise a Chöd sādhana, are included:

white distribution (*dkar 'gyed*)
red distribution (*dmar 'gyed*)
manifold distribution (*sna tshogs 'gyed*)
meditation section on the "giving of Dharma" (*chos kyi sbyin pa*).

Table 2.2. Stages of the Actual Practice

| **Four Stages of Distribution** | **Offering: Contents and Recipients** |
|---|---|
| White distribution (*dkar 'gyed*) | Offering to the lamas, meditational deities, buddhas, *bodhisattvas*, etc. the refined parts of the body transformed into nectar. |
| Red distribution (*dmar 'gyed*) | Giving the remaining flesh, blood, and bones. |
| Manifold distribution (*sna tshogs 'gyed*) | Giving the skin, having mentally transformed it into all things needed and desired by all beings. |
| Meditation on the "giving of Dharma" (*chos kyi sbyin pa*) | Giving of Dharma by teaching how to eliminate suffering by contemplating the verses on the "four seals of Buddhism" and mind-training. |

This is regarded as the most complete Chöd sādhana in the Ganden Tradition lineage's corpus of liturgical practices because the practitioner must exercise their ability to visualize and meditate on:

- Giving to all possible guests, which includes lamas, meditational deities, buddhas (white distribution) as well as malevolent beings (red and manifold distributions, and giving of Dharma) who are the so-called "enemies"—labeled as such habitually by practitioners who adopt an uncritical stance about their relationship to all others, and have fear of experiencing harm to their "self";
- Giving away all materials imaginable, to satisfy all beings' needs and wants, with the practitioner's own (mentally transformed) body as the most precious of these[39]; and,
- Giving dharmic advice, teaching Dharma to all sentient beings.

While distributing and giving, according to these four meditation sections, the practitioner must recall the emptiness of the "three spheres of giving," that is, the complete interdependence of giver, given, and recipients.

The second most commonly practiced liturgical ritual in the Ganden Chöd Tradition is the *Chöd Tshogs* sādhana based upon the *Offering to the Spiritual Guide* or "Lama Chöpa" (*Bla ma mchod pa*) ritual text. It includes the body, along with the other material offerings, mentally transformed into nectar and offered to the buddha deities, exercising the practitioner's ability to practice guru devotion.[40] This ritual contains only the "white distribution" and therefore is considered far easier for the practitioner to visualize than the "red" and "manifold" distributions, which involve giving to malevolent beings. The third most popular sādhana in the Ganden Chöd lineage is *Cutting-off Self-Grasping through the Red Distribution*, which is specifically a *dmar 'gyed* related rite and has only the "red distribution."[41] With only malevolent beings invited to the feast, it directly challenges the practitioner's ability to give away what is most precious while feeling vulnerable and exposed. Though less well-known currently, it was very popular in Tibet, and it appears to be undergoing somewhat of a revival at certain sites in India.

## Formal Structure of a Chöd Sādhana (Abridged)

In terms of the formal structure of this sādhana, there are five meditation sections on "preliminary practices" (*sngon 'gro*), six sections of the "actual practice" (*nyams len gyi dngos gzhi*), a dedication section, and a final dedication prayer sealing one's aspiration (See table 2.3, Ritual Structure of the Chöd sādhana: *Dedicating the Illusory Body*). For each of these thirteen sections, a specific melody is assigned which, it will be shown, purposively enhances the character of the requisite meditation. The three sections may be described as follows. The (A) "preliminary practices" are meant to train the mind by: (A1) visualizing the object of refuge (the merit field; *tshogs zhing*), taking refuge and generating *bodhicitta*; (A2) performing guru yoga; (A3) collecting merit through performing the seven-branch offering practice; (A4) making the body mandala offering; and (A5) requesting blessings from the Chöd lineage lamas in order to be able to accomplish the Chöd sādhana successfully. In response to these requests, the Sanskrit syallble "*Āḥ*," which is considered to be the essence of the *Prajñāpāramitā Sūtra*, is then visualized as descending from the heart of the personified *sūtra*, Yum Chenmo, with nectar lights and purifying body, speech, and mind. This concludes the section on the preliminaries. The (B) "actual practice" begins with (B6) the "transference of consciousness" (*'pho ba*), guru-deity yoga, and preparing the body for giving away. This is followed by the three distributions—(B7) white, (B8) red, and (B9) manifold—and a fourth, (B10) of giving Dharma.[42]

## Description of the "Actual Practice" of a Chöd Sādhana (Elaborated)

To elaborate, the (B6–B7) "white distribution" in the sādhana *Dedicating the Illusory Body* involves offering the purified and transformed substances to all buddha deities and beings in succession: the root and lineage gurus (*rtsa brgyud bla ma*), the meditational deities (*yidam*), the Three Jewels (*dkon mchog gsum*), and Dharma protectors (*bstan bsrung*), as well as the "guests" who are harmdoers, interferers, and creditors (*gdon bgegs lan chags mgron*), and all sentient beings who transmigrate among the six realms (*'gro ba rigs drug sems can kun*). The (B8) "red distribution" involves giving the remaining flesh and blood to all beings, with those harboring harmful intentions as the main invited "guests." The (B9) "manifold distribution" involves visualizing the transformation of the remaining skin into materials desirable to all beings, satisfying their needs and wants. The meditation on the "giving of Dharma" immediately follows these three material-based distributions; and, in this text, involves meditating upon the *bodhicitta* mind training (*blo sbyong*) practice of "giving and taking" (*gtong len*).[43] Once these four meditations, or "distributions," are completed, the practitioner invites all beings to return to their respective abodes. The

Table 2.3. Ritual Structure of the Chöd Sādhana, *Dedicating the Illusory Body*

| Meditation Section: | | Ritual Action | Verses (Lines) | Melody |
|---|---|---|---|---|
| **A. PRELIMINARIES: Training and purifying one's mindstream through the four great commentaries** | | | | |
| 1. Going for Refuge and Generating *Bodhicitta* to make one's mind a suitable receptacle | ^^^[1] | Peaceful (*zhi wa*) | 3(4)[2] | 4 A |
| 2. Guru Yoga to be able to receive blessings | | Peaceful | 4(4) | 4 B |
| 3. Seven Branch Offering Practice, and 4. Mandala Offering to accumulate merit | ^^^ | Increasing (*rje pa*) | 1(4) + 3(2) | 2 C/D |
| 5. Requesting Blessings from Lamas, flowing of nectar from "*Āḥ*" to purify sins/obscurations. | | Increasing | 13(4) | 2 E |
| **B. ACTUAL PRACTICE: Accumulating the two collections of merit to lay imprints for the two divine bodies.** | | | | |
| ***Offering the illusory body to accumulate the collection of merit.*** | | | | |
| 6. Stages of the White Distribution: 1st melody: "Cutting the Body" Offering the refined parts of one's body by transforming them into nectar | | Powerful (*wang po*) | 3(2) + 2(2) + 2(2) + 3(2) | 2 F |
| 7. 2nd melody: Offering/Distributing | | Increasing | 1(4) + 5(2) | 2 G |
| 8. Stages of the Red Distribution: offering the remaining flesh and blood | ^^^ | Powerful | 1(4) + 1(4) + 3(4) | 2 |

*continued on next page*

Table 2.3. Continued.

| Meditation Section: | | Ritual Action | Verses (Lines) | Melody |
|---|---|---|---|---|
| 9. The Manifold Distribution: offering the skin by transforming it into desired materials | ^^^ | Powerful | 1(4) | 2 H |
| 10. Giving Dharma and Meditating on "Giving and Taking" (*tong len*) | | Powerful | 5(4) [+ 1(4) invite back] | 2 |
| ***Meditating on the lack of intrinsic existence to accumulate the collection of wisdom.*** | | | | |
| 11. Meditating on Emptiness, the three spheres of giving | | Peaceful | 1(4) | 4 I |
| **C. DEDICATION: Dedicating the accumulated root virtues** | | | | |
| 12. Dedicating the accumulated root virtues to the unsurpassable great enlightenment | | Peaceful | 4(4) + 3(4) | 2 J |
| 13. Thought Training Prayer to make fervent sealing of merit | ^^^ | Increasing | 9(4) + 3(4) + 3(4) | 2 K |

1. The symbol "^^^" refers to the meditative interlude during the practice, at which time the practitioner rhythmically depicts *The Heart Sutra* "Gaté" mantra played on the *ḍamaru drum*. At the same time the thighbone trumpet (*rkang gling*) is blown to call forth beings.
2. In the expression "#(#)" the first digit refers to the number of stanzas in a section; the second, in parentheses, refers to the number of lines in a stanza. The stanzas are generally two or four lines in length, and each line is composed of nine syllables.

"actual practice" proceeds with meditations on emptiness (B11) to recognize the true nature of gift, giver, and recipients. Finally, the practitioner dedicates (C12, C13) any accumulated merit and wisdom to achieve the two buddha bodies, completing the liturgical portion of the sādhana.

## Detailed Description: Formal Structure of a Chöd Sādhana

Since musical analysis will follow, the reader will find here a detailed description of the ritual dramaturgy, which includes the meditation activities described in one Chöd sādhana. The reader can compare the detailed description below with the brief description above. While reading the subsequent analyses, table 2.3 will be a useful guide. As has been noted, *Dedicating the Illusory Body* is divided into three main sections. The formal structure within these three main sections—(A) the "preliminary practices," (B) the "actual practice," and (C) the "dedications"—retains five meditation subritual sections of "preliminary practices," six meditation subritual sections of the "actual practice," a dedication meditation section, and a final meditative dedication prayer that seals the practitioner's aspirations. For each of these thirteen sections a specific melody is assigned which, it may be shown, purposively enhances the character of the requisite meditation.

### Preliminary Practices

The (A) "preliminary practices" begin with visualizing the "merit field," (A1) "taking refuge" and "generating *bodhicitta*." In the "preliminary practices," the (A2) "guru yoga" in Chöd is practiced with Vajravārāhī (Tib. Rdo rje phag mo) as the visualized aspect of the central meditational deity.[44] She is to be regarded as indivisible, in essence, from Machik Labdrön, Yum Chenmo, and the lama. After the "wisdom beings" (actual buddhas and their retinues) are invited to melt inseparably with the "concentration beings" (the meditatively generated visualization of buddhas and their retinues), hooked rays of light emanate a second time from the letter *Hūṃ* at Vajravārāhī's heart, this time calling forth all beings with harmful intent and debt-owners to gather and settle around the practitioner "like geese gather in a pond."[45] The presence of the summoned beings laying-in-wait is reminiscent of the attendance of vultures that gather around the mortician who does the work of flaying and chopping the body for distribution at a "sky burial" (Tib. *bya gtor*) site awaiting their chance to partake. The practitioner actively invites these beings to attend.

This is followed by (A3) the "seven branch offering practice," and (A4) the "mandala offering." Next is the "request to the lineage lamas" (A5)—the father, mother, union, and near lineages—to purify and bless the mindstream of the practitioner and all sentient beings. This is the last of the "preliminary practices," and it concludes with a visualization of purification: countless "*Āḥ*" syllables pour out from the heart of The Great Mother (*Yum Chenmo*), who is imagined at the heart of the endowed transcendent subduer, Vajravārāhī, seen as inseparable from the lama and Machik Labdrön. These letters are imagined overflowing and melting into the body, speech, and mind of the practitioner and all beings, purifying their negativities, sins, obscurations, diseases, and hindrances. The letter "*Āḥ*" represents the *Prajñāpāramitā Sūtra* in its most condensed mantric form, and is understood to embody the wisdom of all the buddhas.

## Actual Practice

As a cautionary note to the reader, the following description of the offering of the body could be viewed initially as gruesome and graphic, as has been the case in early Western literature on Chöd. Yet, I urge the reader unfamiliar with tantra to consult the explanations of symbolic meaning of the transformed body in chapters 3 through 7 to avoid any such misapprehension.

The (B) "actual practice" portion of the sādhana consists of two main parts: (B6 through B10) offering and giving away the body to collect the "accumulation of merit" (Tib. *bsod nams kyi tshogs*), and (B11) meditating on emptiness to build up the "accumulation of wisdom" (Tib. *ye shes kyi tshogs*). Both merit and wisdom accumulations are necessary to lay karmic imprints for the two buddha bodies: the form body (Skt. *rūpakāya*, Tib. *gzugs sku*) and the truth body (Skt. *dharmakāya*, Tib. *chos sku*) respectively.

The (B6) "white distribution" (*dkar 'gyed*) begins with the "transference of consciousness" or "*phowa*" (*'pho ba*) up and out of the practitioner's crown aperture and into the heart of the lama. From the lama's heart, the consciousness emerges again in the form of a ḍākinī holding the ritual implements of the "curved knife" (*gri gug*) and "skull cup" (*thod pa*), the implements used to prepare the body for offering and giving away. The practitioner identifies with the ḍākinī (meditating upon the divine pride of the deity), having now disassociated from the old body that lies on the ground. She circles above, like a vulture, and swoops down, making five main incisions with the ritual flaying knife: from the crown to the groin, from the heart out to the tips of the right and left hands, and from the groin to the tips of the right and left feet. With the skin spread out, three human heads are visualized upright forming a tripod-like stove; and the top part of the skull from the old body, once touched by the end of the curved knife's handle, becomes the vessel of offering. Various secret substances (brains, semen, and bone marrow) are brought into the vessel, become purified by the letters "*Ōṃ Āḥ Hūṃ*" and (B7) are offered to all guests in turn: the root and lineage gurus, the *yidams*, the Three Jewels, the protectors, the debt collectors (creditors) with harmful intentions, and beings of the six realms. Each two-line stanza includes an offering to the named guest and a request for them to bestow a specific blessing.[46]

The (B8) red distribution (*dmar 'gyed*) consists of giving away all the remaining flesh, blood, and bones, which are so immense in quantity that they fill up a billion worlds.[47] All sentient beings, regarded as one's mothers from countless former lives, are invited to the feast. The larger and stronger beings are urged to kindly allow everyone, especially the weaker and smaller spirits, to collect their share. Those who like to eat meat, drink blood, and chew marrow are all encouraged to partake, enjoy, and fill their stomachs. The poetry is quite colloquial in this stanza and provides the practitioner with the impression of the discourse that takes place at a meal in a social context in which there is an absence of need for honorific language.[48] The ḍākinī, in her role as host, urges the guests to have their fill of food and drink, and to take with them whatever they cannot finish at the one sitting.

During (B9), the "manifold distribution" stage (*sna tshogs 'gyed*), the skin is visualized as vast as possible, cut into billions of tiny pieces, and given to all sentient beings individually. Each piece of skin is to be visualized transforming into any and all material things that others need or desire (e.g., gold, silver, mansions, clothes, etc.). The fourth and last section, (B10) "giving Dharma" (*chos kyi sbyin pa*), begins by acknowledging that while all beings may have been satisfied *materially*, they still lack the possibility of achieving lasting happiness due to not understanding what causes themselves and others suffering. This is the experience of sentient beings living through the cycle of conditioned existence: our self-cherishing leads to a greed for our self-satisfaction alone, which causes us to seek our personal "fill" of desirable conditions. Yet, even when this temporary goal has been "achieved," we are still unhappy and do not know why. The answer is provided in the following verse. The practitioner, as the ḍākinī, sings the four-line stanza known as "the four seals" (Tib. *phyag rgya bzhi*), which the historical Buddha gave as his last teaching before passing into *mahāparinirvāṇa* (Tib. *mya ngan las 'das pa chen po*):

Like this, all composite phenomena are impermanent.
All contaminated things are in the nature of suffering.
All phenomena are selfless and merely dependent-arisings,
By meditating on these, the true peace of nirvana [is known].[49]

In the next stanza, the practitioner instructs beings in an imperative fashion, imploring them to stop their negative actions of body, speech, and mind, and perform only virtuous actions by subduing their minds. During the two stanzas that follow, the practitioner engages in (B10) "giving and taking" practice. Finally, all the beings are requested to return to their respective abodes and maintain a benevolent state of mind. This concludes the meditations on the four distributions to accumulate merit, and "the actual practice."

At this point, a crucial section of the ritual remains, which is for the practitioner to meditate upon "emptiness" in order to collect the accumulation of wisdom. In this sādhana, the practitioner's initial meditation on emptiness is based on a stanza written by the Seventh Dalai Lama, Kelsang Gyatso (Bskal bzang rgya mtsho, 1708–1757).

Looking at this side, neither the body nor the mind exists as objects to be harmed.
Looking at that side, the harmdoer is also like a snake projected onto a multi-colored rope.
May I realize decisively that holding merely labeled dependent-arisings to be truly existent is the projection of my hallucinating mind.
With strong and definite understanding of the view as it is thus taught.[50]

This, the first of two meditations on emptiness, is unlike any other section in this liturgy in that it is not sung, but mentally performed. It is a thought meditation while the *ḍamaru* rhythmic cycle continues on unabated. In fact, the *ḍamaru* has been ongoing, gradually speeding up since section (A5) the "requests for blessings from the lineage lamas," which was the last of the "preliminary practices." While there may be an absence of melody here, in this initial meditation on emptiness, the sound of the *ḍamaru* symbolizes the wisdom of realizing emptiness, so that playing the *ḍamaru* helps the meditator and is a completely appropriate musical accompaniment to the thought meditation.[51]

The second meditation on emptiness (B11) is also meant to procure the "wisdom accumulation" (*ye shes kyi tshogs*). It is known as the "three spheres of giving" (*sbyin pa'i 'khor gsum*). Here, the adept sings a stanza of logical reasoning applied to how the three—giver, gift, and recipient—are each devoid of even an atom of independent existence.[52] The melody is a combination of the first half of the refuge visualization melody and the second half of the guru yoga melody, and seems to operate formally as a recapitulation of the opening musical statements.

### Dedications

The sādhana concludes with four dedicatory stanzas of meditations (C12), which suffuse one's contemplations on how phenomena lack any self-existent properties. These stanzas also instill the essential point that both method and wisdom are needed to cross the ocean of cyclic existence and accomplish the path to enlightenment. The analogy of the bird's two wings, both necessary for flight across this great ocean, recalls the need for the two accumulations toward the fully combined realizations of *bodhicitta* and emptiness. A final dedicatory sealing prayer (C13) is optional, though it is generally practiced either as a chant or sung to a melody.

## Ritual Mapping: Musical Transcription and Analysis

### On Transcription

There has been much discussion in ethnomusicological literature about whether the traditional method of transcription and analysis is an appropriate analytical tool for the study of the musics of indigenous peoples.[53] The criticism stems from a theoretical leaning toward cultural relativism, which resists the attempt to apply Western techniques of musicological analysis to indigenous musics. Some might view transcription as an application or imposition of "Western-values" upon indigenous lived experience—an unconscious, but somehow violent, concretizing reduction of what has been heretofore a centuries old, organically evolving, and changing tradition. Hobsbawm and Ranger[54] undid the reification of traditionalism in their explanation that all "traditions" were at one time "inventions" and many of those traditions dearly held to with staunch pride, exceptionalism, and patriotism (at the regional, ethnic, or national level) were far more recent than many practitioners of traditions might realize. Hobsbawn and Ranger's analysis, of course, was conducted in the European cultural context. In conversations among Tibetan intellectuals involved in cultural productions, the considerations of which aspects of traditional Tibetan music should be open to change and which should ideally be preserved "as they were" is a meaningful and ongoing dialogue.[55]

The important question of whether Western musicological analysis could or should be applied to the analysis of an indigenous musical tradition is vexing, and in devising an analytical methodology, I wrestled with this for some time. I consulted with Tibetan scholars and musicians about what sort of research approach they felt would be appropriate. Although the Dalai Lama's Principal English Translator, Geshé Thupten Jinpa (PhD)—an expert in Buddhist philosophy, textual translation, and tantric ritual—advised me to transcribe the melodies of the Chöd Tradition, I initially resisted the suggestion. Having been theoretically committed to learning the Chöd ritual through the traditional transmission process, and gaining as deep an understanding as possible by learning, thinking, and performing within the culturally internal logic of its lineage carriers, it appeared that transcribing the oral tradition and detailing the performance practices might assist in its preservation—using transcription as a prescriptive tool, but not as a basis for analysis.[56]

A critical evaluation of my ethnographic methodology may question the correctness of my initial theoretically committed position, finding it to be a dogmatic adoption of the cultural relativist position. However, I would debate the point that my initial effort to work within the traditional expectations of the Chöd tradition in order to receive "as complete a transmission as possible" could only be facilitated through learning the Chöd Tradition in the expected pedagogical framework established by my teachers. That said, I agree that it is expected the ethnomusicologist will depart the ethnographic fieldwork site and work with their field notes, journals, musical experiences, and music recordings, and make music transcriptions in order to analyze the musical tradition.

### *How Transcription Can Yield Unexpected Insights*

The *musical text* in Chöd is one of many layers of a multilayered performance, and I had initially thought it was not connected in so many ways to the *written liturgical text* even though I had sung the melodies and performed the Chöd ritual for nine years. It was only after transcribing the melodies that the music-text correspondences "leapt off the page" and the expertise in the architecture of text-setting became apparent to me.

At first, my Chöd teachers led me to understand that the music would not need to comprise a significant component of my analysis. They insisted that the meaning of the Chöd Tradition *when properly conceived of as a meditation practice* is to be found in the "three principal paths" (*Lam gyi gtso bo rnam gsum*). These three undergird the written liturgical text at the sūtra level and manifest at the tantric level through guru-deity yoga meditation practices. The liturgical music is performed as but one component of the multivalent meditation yogic practice.

Finally, I came to better understand the traditional philosophical pedagogy of Tibetan experts who are charged with transmitting the Highest Yoga Tantric practices. They must remind students constantly of the foundational principles of the sūtra-based meditations lest they become entranced and distracted by the more esoteric aspects of the tantric ritual process such as visualizing the transformation of symbolic ritual implements into deities, or the dissolving of deities into "emptiness."

## Ritual Mapping

I propose that an analytical approach that allows for the possibility of slowing down a given ritual—slow enough to "map" the simultaneously occurring events—could be a useful investigative device. By creating a "story board" of a number of snapshots of layers in succession (since interwoven layers of a single practice event are moving together through time), ritual analysts may be able to observe connections previously undisclosed, or at least, unobserved. These connections could be helpful in a number of ways. These storyboards or "ritual maps," as we might call them, may be useful as both descriptive and prescriptive tools.

### *Transcription as a Descriptive Tool*

As a descriptive tool, setting into relief the various elements of practice as they occur during performance may assist in making transparent relationships previously unnoticed. To set elements into relief requires a notation that graphically represents simultaneously occurring social and musical events, such as: (1) imaginatively cognized (visualized) meditations, e.g., all beings gathering and guru-deities filling the sky above the practitioner; (2) orally delivered expressive utterances, such as the mantric syllable *phaṭ* and sung melodies; and (3) sound textures of the combined drum, melody, bell, and thighbone trumpet. My analytical interest in exploring the Chöd ritual through this graphic mapping method was animated by my unexpected "discovery" of noticing coordinated composition of text, melody, and rhythm.

*Transcription as a Prescriptive Tool*

Tibetan ritual music in monastic settings is one of the largest notated liturgical repertoires in the world.[57] Tibetan monastic chant notation, "*yang yig*" (*dbyangs yig*), is comprised of sequences of undulating lines illustrating the arc of melodic gesture and ornamentation of the liturgical chant (*dbyangs*) that is to be sung. There are notated musical texts with the "tone-contour *dbyangs* style" for Highest Yoga Tantric rituals concerning the practices of buddha deities, such as Guhyasamāja, Cakrasaṃvara, Yamāntaka, and so forth.[58] In contrast, while the Chöd ritual is a somewhat complex musical event with rich textures and sonorities, its melodies (*rta*) have recognizable fixed pitches (*'debs*) rather than the (*dbyangs*) contours of the overtone chant. Yet, it has not received any notation designed for the performance or transmission of its melodies, rhythmic structures, or performance utterances.

As ethnomusicologists have done in other contexts, it would be a useful project to develop a notation that would assist in both the analytical and pedagogical processes.[59] Transcriptions help teachers, students, and researchers alike to observe connections (cognize visually the relationships) between melody and text. This, in turn, allows for improved speed in learning, transmission, and study. As a prescriptive tool, an ethnomusicologist can utilize transcriptions as a pedagogical method for re-establishing traditional ritual where it has fallen out of the repertoire and memory of its hosts. Catherine J. Ellis (1935–1996), an Australian ethnomusicologist, used the transcriptions of Australian Aboriginal songs as a means to teach Aboriginal children their own cultural media rather than have them spend hours watching conventional television and becoming absorbed into the vortex of mainstream cultural influences.[60]

## Musical Analysis as an Intervention

Catherine Ellis focused on Aboriginal women's songs and utilized transcription and description for a larger intercultural legal project. Textualizing the sound, and contextualizing the cultural process, Ellis published ethnographic accounts and musical transcriptions as part of an advocacy project of explaining to a wider Australian public how the Aboriginals' (re)enacting, performing, and practicing of meaningful ritual could renew their communal ties to the land. Moreover, she explained that practicing their lifeways and performing their ritually embedded cultural knowledge coaxed individuals toward recognition of their interrelationship with, and stewardship of, the ancient land.[61] She pointed out the ways in which music and song texts cue culturally meaningful and ancient connections to their local environment. By transcribing these ritual events and analyzing their music, Ellis offered specific evidence that bolstered the humanist perspective she delivered to the Australian scholarly community, politicians, and public. Her transcriptions indicated Aboriginals' sophisticated artistic craftsmanship and performance consistencies. Their conscious creative effort directed through the medium of music and ritual performance, Ellis argued, was a clear indication of intelligence. Therefore, they were a people who could not be ignored. Once recognized within the human family, their human rights, legal rights, and entitlements had to be honored. Thus, rituals, which connected Aboriginals to their land through socially enacted music and dance, were literally the key to their cultural survival.

## Ritual Analysis: Mapping the Chöd Ritual

### *Inner and Outer Chöd*

The primary and secondary layers of a multilayered performance may be revealed through such a transcription device as figure 2.1, "General Ritual Structure of a Moment." We learn that the liturgy of a Chöd sādhana is foremost in the ritual, with the music nearly always at the behest of the text. From another perspective, however, it may be argued that the transcriptions reveal that the outer and inner levels of Chöd are interwoven and complementary, as depicted in figure 2.2, "Ritual Elements Experienced During a Moment of Chöd Performance." To put this another way, the *outer* musical performance—continuous

Visualization
↑
Written Liturgical Text
↑
performance gesture → Melody ← mantric utterance
↑
Rhythm (drum and bell played together)

Figure 2.1. General structure of a moment within Chöd performance.

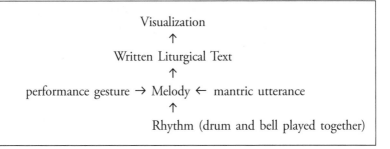

Visualization
↑
performance gesture → Melody / Written Liturgical Text ← mantric utterance
↑
Rhythm

Figure 2.2. Ritual elements experienced during a moment of Chöd performance. As a percussive introduction into the flow of singing, the rhythmic *ostinato* commences with the accompaniment of vocable syllables (akin to the use of *bols* in South Asian Classical music) to the drum beats, such as "*ma dang, lha yi, khan dro*." These vocables are chanted aloud or silently to oneself at certain introductory sections. Gilbert Rouget notes that some scholars suggest that the constancy of a rhythm may also provide the physiological ground for a trance-like experience.[64] Biofeedback experts reveal that hearing repeated tones at certain speeds can put the brain into an alpha state, and a subject may be neurologically induced to go into trance. Although the rhythm in Chöd begins at a pace far slower than this, there is a trance-like effect experienced by the practitioner as the tempo gradually increases over the course of this one-hour-long performance. As the "ground," or basis, for both an aural and physical sense of continuity, rhythm is an ephemeral but constant element of the ritual. The sound and rhythm are, at the ultimate level of Buddhist philosophy, without intrinsic reality or substance; while, on the conventional level, sound is a substantively powerful constant with individual and social meaning in the ritual context and in the silence in-between ritual practices. At the most esoteric level of Chöd practice, advanced practitioners may experience a "falling away" such that "they may no longer hear the drum."[65] The most advanced practitioners, if they decide to eject the consciousness from the body, may drop the drum completely. This is because there is no longer a physically embodied form (ritual practitioner) to do the work of instrumental performance. The adept's consciousness has already been ejected out of the old body, traveling up through the crown aperture of the skull out into space, and into the guru-deity's heart.

rhythmic underlay of drum and bell instruments in a meter synchronous with its overlay of vocal melody and performed-utterance—maps not onto, but *within*, the *inner* liturgically guided meditations.

Figure 2.1 is a schematic representation of Buddhist tantric ritual performance. Are musical elements (percussion effects, sung melody, etc.) experienced differentially, even hierarchically, with melody closer to the rhythm than to the visualization? In this schema, melody cannot interface with visualization directly since it is mediated through the poetry. In other words, the written poetry (because of the seemingly greater salience of language to invoke specific meaning) would be the interface between the music and the visualization.

An alternative perspective—from the point of view of the practitioner's experience—may furnish a more accurate graphic representation. The written liturgical text is experienced *through* music; and the semiotic referents *embedded in* musical gestures/utterances are capable of conjuring up meaningful visualizations. The "hierarchical mapping" [figure 2.1] showing the separation of elements (musical and poetic) may not accurately reflect the practitioner's experience of those elements in a single gesture of sung poetry. Thus, just as the combination of colors, shapes, figures, images, and facial expressions in a Tibetan *thangka* painting conveys a single holistic iconographic image in a viewer's experience, so the combination of ritual elements (rhythm, melody, poetry, vocal ornamentation, and imagery) creates a single holistic musical experience of "Visualization" while practicing the ritual.

As we see in figure 2.2, "Melody" (as well as mantric utterance) is the expressive medium through which the liturgical text carries the visualization material. Therefore, the placement of melody (graphically) is much closer to "Visualization." Yet these levels are misleading, for "Melody" can be experienced concurrently with "Visualization." In fact, a melody is directly capable of generating visualizations through the meaningful referents that are invoked by the music.

To assist in describing how these layers are related and function within the context of the Chöd ritual performance, each of these layers will be described in turn. In the Chöd ritual, the "Written Liturgical Text," describes an ongoing continuous set of "Visualizations," poetically depicted *instructions* of what to imagine as the meditation practice proceeds. The liturgical text has been written in poetic verse form[62] to which "Melodies" have been composed such that the text is sung as the ritual proceeds. Since melody has pitch and is also intrinsically rhythmic, "Rhythm" inheres in the melodic-poetic structure. Rhythm undergirds the poetic text and visualizations and is steadily maintained by the flow of the drum and bell.

### *Musical Layer and Function: Rhythm*

The drum's "rhythm" is depicted in figures 2.1 and 2.2 as underlying the entire ritual. It is drawn like this to suggest that it is heard acoustically "under" the melody while enhancing it; the rhythmic *ostinato* supports the melody but in quite different ways than the latter supports the text. The rhythm establishes the greatest constraint on the form, invariant in its insistent *ostinato*. Amid the negotiated space of our Chöd lessons—part traditional transmission, part ethnographic interview—I often asked Pala whether the rhythmic *ostinato* is all-important to the efficacy of the accomplishment of the practice. Silence was given as an answer to suggest that it is a matter that can only be learned/known through the practitioner's engaging in the practice.[63] After some time, the rhythmic pattern becomes a deeply embodied continuous motion that entrances the practitioner as it punctuates the text regularly at certain syllables in the metered verse.

## Performance, Competence, and Transcendence

We might return briefly to consider the stages of training in text and music performance in the Chöd transmission process. Let us take the example of a pianist working toward the performance of an étude or "study" (akin to a "method of accomplishment," such as the word sādhana translates). A musician still learning the notes on the page cannot perform an étude by Frédéric Chopin well enough to express what the composer intended. Once the notes are learned, the larger gestures of meaningful expressive content may be articulated. After the piece is memorized and "well under the fingers," the three-minute piece becomes a single flow: one musical gesture, one thought. That gesture resonates as the performer's interpretation of the composer's intention; and, as the performer matures, the performance approach to the work will change along with the changed understanding of the composer's intention. Where a performing artist's own experience resonates with a composer's, they may embody more easily the perspective of the composer. Likewise, an actor works to embody a character not to "become" another person, but to search out elements of that character within the actor themselves and then articulate those elements. An excellent "performance" convinces an audience that the actor *is* the character.

To follow Richard Schechner's insight, the dramaturgical narrative of a ritual operates like a script, as does the musical score. But meaningful inner transformation depends on the performer's authentic engagement with the material. The artistic process is not substantially different from the Chöd practitioner's initial artistic work—the mechanical skill-building of playing ritual instruments, learning the performance-utterances and vocal singing style—before reaching beyond the level of competence in musical ability to enter the art of meditation work.

MUSICAL ANALYSIS: THE TIBETAN RITUAL CONTEXT

In Tibetan tantric rituals, the reconfiguring of space as a sacred environment is an essential element of the practice. Tibetan sand mandala art and associated rituals, for example, are performed in various sites.[66] The popular advertisement billing of mandala construction as a "spiritual healing" event is adequate and serves to attract a more mainstream audience, although it is more correct to promise that the construction of the mandala will "purify the environment." The sacred ceremonies surrounding the construction of the mandala include: (a) requesting the local spirits who feel that the site is their own, literally the "earth owners" (*sa bdag*), for permission to use the site; (b) the consecration of the mandala and visualized entrance of initiated monks or nuns into the completed mandala to pay homage, make offerings, and receive empowerment from the buddha deity (e.g., Yamāntaka) within the purified environment through musically accompanied meditative visualization; and (c) the final dissolution ceremony where the completed mandala is ceremoniously "destroyed." Cultural interpreters who explain to the visiting public the symbolic significance of the ceremonies and mandala architecture often host these events. I was asked to occupy this role of cultural broker eight times between 1999 and 2011. The main roles in this context are twofold: first, to instruct how the Tibetan sand paintings are architectural maps of the buddha's celestial abode (a purified divine palace) designed to serve as an aid in tantric meditative visualization. Second, it requires some explanation about how to visualize the colored sand painting as a three-dimensional structure, since the architecture initially appears not to be a relief plan drawing of an ornately ornamented palace but a flat series of colorful intricate designs. Similarly, musically guided tantric rituals such as Chöd appear as colorful song-poetry in their initial presentation, but the layers of performance, text, melody, and meditative visualization may be skillfully revealed through the lama's instructions, and also, as we will illustrate, through graphic representation.

## Consciousness and Lifeways of the Chöd Practitioner

All elements of the Chöd practice, musical and cognitive (aurally/orally and mentally performed), assist in the practitioner's transformation. This meditation "performance" can continue, and in fact should do so, beyond one's engagement with the conventional parameters of the ritual text. Between meditation sessions—that is, outside of the structured sādhana practice—the essential meaning of Chöd can inform one's experiences. In terms of mind training, the practitioner ought to cultivate renunciation (emphasizing the strong wish be free of the "eight worldly dharmas" Tib. *'jig rten chos brgyad*), the motivation of *bodhicitta*, and the realization of emptiness. To accomplish the third of these, there are two recommended mental attitudes. First, the Chöd practitioner should go through life as if in a dream. In a dream, one reacts to external and internal phenomena with the sense that they are "real"—until one wakes up and understands otherwise. The awareness that life is like a dream can help overcome the experience of fear. Second, the practitioner can visualize mixing the mind with space. There is no need to be fixated on one's body. Knowing that the mind is not confined to the body, but can travel outside the body through the "transference of consciousness" practice helps in this regard, and forms one component of the advanced training in Chöd.

These two strategies for the Chöd practitioner's mental attitude are suggested according to the meditation instructions of how to act in-between meditation sessions.[67] The mental life of the Chöd practitioner has primacy. The practitioner observes thoughts arise, and views them dispassionately with the wisdom eye of emptiness. Since the goal is to overcome all "demons" (Skt. *māras*, Tib. *bdud*), primarily the internal "demon" of arrogance, the practitioner is continually working with the mind. In terms of the practitioner's lifestyle, the Chöd meditation practice is focused less on that which is heard than on transcending one's habitual egoic relationship to sensorial experiences and emotions. The adept's *internal* performance is more important than the *external* melodies and drumming. In the two tables below (2.4 and 2.5), the upper table fits into the lower one, denoting how the lifestyle of the Chöd practitioner is being shaped by continued practice in-between meditation sessions (Tib. *rjes thob*).

It is important to make the distinction that the practitioner may mentally augment the sounds audible during ritual practice through mental visualization.[68] Whereas in-between practice sessions, the audible soundscape can be regarded as ephemeral causal relations that remind one of the panoplies of everchanging *saṃsāric* displays, which typically entrance and confound.

## Mental Disposition In-Between Chöd Practice Sessions

Following a sādhana practice, during the post-meditation period, the mental attitude of the practitioner is still given primacy; for, after this period of contemplation, sensory perceptions and daily activities can be distracting. Thus, irrespective of external circumstances, if one's life experiences are

Table 2.4. During Meditation Practice Session: Actual and Mentally Performed Ritual

| Outer / Inner Performance | Written Liturgy | Music (Melody / Rhythm) |
|---|---|---|
| **Actually Performed** | Oral/Aural performance of the liturgical poetry | Performance of melody (*rta*), trumpet (*rkang gling*), and rhythm instruments (*ḍamaru* and bell) |
| **Mentally Performed** | Poetically articulated meditation instructions on the content of visualizations | All oral/aural sounds that may be given or offered appropriately in this context |

Table 2.5. Post-Meditation Periods: Disposition of Mind In-between Sessions

<table>
<tr><th>Practice Occasion</th><th>Outer / Inner Performance</th><th>Written Liturgy</th><th>Music (Melody / Rhythm)</th></tr>
<tr><td rowspan="2">During Ritual Practice Sessions</td><td>Actually Performed</td><td>Oral/Aural performance of the liturgical poetry</td><td>Performance of melody (rta), trumpet (rkang gling), and rhythm instruments (ḍamaru and bell)</td></tr>
<tr><td>Mentally Performed</td><td>Poetically articulated meditation instructions on the content of visualizations</td><td>All oral/aural sounds that may be given or offered appropriately in this context</td></tr>
<tr><td>During the Post-Meditation Periods</td><td colspan="2">Whatever experiences occur in-between ritual sādhana practice sessions during the post-meditation periods should be regarded with the “wisdom eye of emptiness”; the altruistic bodhicitta motivation combined with one’s level of realization into śūnyatā or emptiness.<br>Frightening appearances are to be “seen” and “heard” as if appearing in a dream.</td><td>All aural phenomena, sounds and music</td></tr>
</table>

Table 2.5 contains all of Table 2.4 (within its upper right section), indicating the temporal continuity of meditation in *Chöd*. From the perspective of the transformative goal of this Vajrayāna tradition, it is said that a practitioner’s mental disposition during the “post-meditation periods” (*rjes thob*) is ultimately just as important as during the ritual practice sādhana sessions.

thought to be like those in a dream, there is no great loss or gain to be had since one's status in a dreamt milieu is necessarily temporary (see tables 2.4 and 2.5). This is a practice that is best articulated socially and cognitively by the most advanced Chödpa—to be put into practice rather than merely written about. But, to the extent that it may give the reader an idea of the approach to Chöd practice, and its wider role in a practitioner's life as well as life in her/his community, some notion of the foremost importance of mental attitude during and in-between sessions may be useful.[69]

## Informing Chöd: Ritual in Ethnomusicological Theory and Practice

Curiously, ethnomusicologists, as the rather cumbersome disciplinary title suggests, have not historically been interested in merely "musical" or "cultural" questions (those that may be answered in the sonic or social dimension alone). Yet, some scholars in related disciplines, such as cultural anthropologists, have been surprised to learn that ethnomusicologists consider all features that contribute to a music/sonic performance as being potentially significant, insofar as they are socially relevant and personally meaningful. For example, ethnomusicologists consider: the pre-planning stages of a ritual, the selecting of performers, the instruments and implements used, the size of the performing ensemble, the duration of the performance, and the positioning of musicians and other participants to name but a few factors. An ethnomusicological study of a given ritual is informed by understanding all the permutations—in all domains social, cultural, political, economic, physical, and spiritual—to which a performance may be adjusted and nuanced in a given circumstance.

An ethnomusicological perspective can assist in effectively mapping and analyzing the Tibetan Buddhist Tantric Chöd ritual because it draws upon: participant-observation (an ethnographic-based methodology of cultural anthropology), the tradition of interpretive anthropology begun in the 1970s, ritual studies theory, performance studies innovations, and the analytical work of critical musicology. Moreover, it can involve the specialized and intimate transmission process of apprenticeship, often with the best recognized local masters of the tradition.

### Issues in Transcription and Analysis

A common area of concern among ethnomusicologists is the graphic transcription of oral tradition. Such analytical efforts, if uncritically engaged in, would otherwise be seen as hearkening back to colonial practices. Ethnomusicologist Kofi Agawu suggests instead that ethnomusicologists can analyze music without losing sight of the importance of its relevant cultural and social meaning to local actors, performers, chiefs, and participants.[70] A second issue that arises is the question of whether recording a traditional culture's ritual performance may also, in some sense, "museumify" it; that is, to effectively "freeze" a living tradition at a particular moment may inhibit the creative growth of that tradition.[71] A third concern relates to the issue of subjectivity in transcription and analysis. The transcriber might be culturally predisposed to hear in certain ways that are different from the indigenous musician or listener.[72] Notwithstanding these important issues related to musical transcription, "ritual mapping" might help to produce graphic representations that value both the immediacy and variability of performance and the scripted dramaturgical process of ritual. For example, ethnomusicologist Regula Qureshi developed a unique method of notation for her videographic documentation following her ethnographic study of the performances of *qawwali* spiritual songs of Sufi masters by contemporary exponents.[73] Using a multilayered transcription, Qureshi mapped the calls of the main performer against the responses of the congregation, and explained the activities in diachronic juxtaposition.

## Design in Milarepa's mGur Song-Poems

Through musical transcription and "ritual mapping," we find the key to the *gur* (*mGur*) genre is its musical and liturgical design. Milarepa (Mi la ras pa), Tibet's most renowned yogi and poet-saint, is believed to have spontaneously composed didactic song-poems in the *gur* style as dharmic advice—to counsel, warn, or admonish, but always to teach—to those whom he encountered. Ethnomusicologists working with Tibetan ritual music have not yet fully investigated the melodic or rhythmic movement of these songs. While the meditative poetry remains extant and is popularly read and practiced, the majority of the original music is said to have been lost. Many of the musical characteristics of the *gur* genre are arguably retained in the Chöd ritual. Thus, it is a tenable hypothesis that clues as to the musical craftsmanship of the song poems of Milarepa may be studied in the design of the Chöd melodies.[74]

## Resistance to Musical Analysis

The extra-musical concern that has inhibited musicological analysis may have been due to the sensitivity around the matter of cultural appropriation, and the discovery of overt differences in the cultural cosmologies of non-native ethnographers, ethnologists, and other cultural workers. Some cultural workers might be seen as attempting to abstract from the sociocultural, political, and economic "native" context a music that, as an entity, could be considered a commodity and be manipulated by unbridled curiosity and unethical creativity. As a result, musical-spiritual ritual music has increasingly been seen as cultural property to be protected, regulated, contested, and paid for. The case of the popular music group Enigma appropriating Ami-Taiwanese Aboriginal singers' music from a track they "discovered" in a UNESCO-published music collection sparked an important debate about not only indigenous ownership but also the license on creativity.[75]

During the past decade, musicologists and ethnomusicologists have been separated by what amounts to an intradisciplinary conflict of doctrinal differences. Certainly, the time of critical sensitivity has passed such that musicologists (who might have wished to look at the music alone) can work with culture in ways ethnomusicologists have. A 2003 publication authored by musicologists and some ethnomusicologists appears to be an effort to exercise and reenergize the concomitant study of culture and music among the communities of musicologists.[76] Still, ethnomusicologists studying sacred ritual may be involved with a musical culture in a number of ways that are not within the scope of interest to musicologists.[77] Yet, what if musicologists and ethnomusicologists seek to reconcile their methodological differences by attending to both culture and music as analytical domains with equal potential in bearing the fruit of cultural and artistic insights? As a start, attending to the musical features in an ethnographic study of a musical tradition may be done in a way that allows for incorporating both kinds of data: (1) data from musical analysis through exploring musical patterns and gestures, and (2) "ethnoaesthetic" data, as evidenced by recent work in collaborative ethnography.[78]

Amid this crucial and critical transformation back toward the use of music analysis, bringing the musical analytical skills to the table might seem to some in ethnomusicology to be anathema to the work of getting to understand the meaning of the tradition as the exponents themselves interpret it. My dissertation was going to do just this sort of limited cultural work—focusing on the informant's reportage and oral history alone—prior to my unexpected discovery of artistic skill in musical text-setting in what were previously understood to be "spontaneous" compositions.[79] This finding was revealed through transcribing the music and seeing "writ-large" the musical craftsmanship. I realize that my enthusiastic use of a label like "expert text-setting" or "craftsmanship" needs also to be recognized as fraught with values originating in Western musicological discourse. But, be that as it may, is it important to report fully on the musical craftsmanship that transcription and analysis reveals?[80] Would it mean the musicologist is a predator of aboriginal songs if they find in the musical structures patterns that suggest that a wealth of creativity is retained in the musical repertoire of Chöd composers' ritual liturgies? With attention to this case here (and without any embellishment on the researcher's part), there is a clear use of musical structures and compositional principles to cue a succession of affective states for each subsection of the ritual with a different melody. Moreover, within this overall dramaturgically orchestrated emotional scheme, text-setting is observed at the micro-level to enhance meditative visualizations. I have not worked backwards from the need to find something of significance, nor did I attempt to approach an analysis of the Chöd melodies with Western-values of composition. I merely wrote down the melodies as I heard them, and looked at the transcriptions dispassionately as I was taught.[81]

Would not the inscription of the musical materials sustaining a heretofore oral tradition be the work and office of someone skilled, such as Gyalwa Ensapa (rgyal ba dben sa pa blo bzang don grub, 1504–1566), who had the foresight to write down the poetic liturgy before it was lost? I certainly did not believe I had the authority or calling to exercise such a role. And yet, when I consulted with living exponents of the Chöd practice in Canada, the United States, and India, asking how they felt about myself, or anyone, writing down the music, all stated without exception that it would be a good or *very* good idea. There was also less enthusiasm than I expected for my suggestion to develop a notation that combined the graphics of Tibetan monastic notation with Western staff notation since most felt, in a practical sense, that they were already familiar with, or could learn to read, Western staff notation. One Chöd lama asked if, by having a transcribed melody, an initiate could read and sing it. He wanted to find a way to easily transmit the music to his Western disciples. I explained that writing it down would not automatically convey how the music is to be performed, adding that all music notation is but a template that has performance practices and aural and oral traditions associated with it. He also asked if the notes could be entered into a computer that would "play" the melodies for the practitioner such that they could sing along, as he wished for a prescriptive notation that could be operationalized.[82]

With Chöd study and transmission, however, the newly available consumer-level recording technology and Internet-based transmission platforms are highly significant. For example, on the most popular video-sharing site, we find a videotaped performance of a gathering of thousands of Bhutanese Chöd practitioners that took place in Bodh Gaya, India, the site of Śākyamuni Buddha's attaining of enlightenment.[83]

In sum, I had entered the field of ethnomusicology at a time when, as Knopoff writes, such a theoretical orientation was frowned upon.[84] The problematic nature of applying Western music theory and analysis techniques to aboriginal music was foremost in my mind for a long time, particularly when it seemed likely that the indigenous tradition carriers themselves would not be in a position to derive any benefits from it. Yet, the indigenous exponents with whom I have consulted now wish to see more of the music transcriptions I have shown them, and are interested in this research continuing. In sum, historically the Chöd adepts and practitioners are laudable for their artistic skill and aesthetic command in creating the Chöd song-poems, as are the living exponents for encouraging in several ways the recording, transmission, and preservation of the Chöd Tradition.

# Part II

# Elements of Chöd Practice

ཕཊ༔ སྡུག་བསྔལ་རྒྱ་མཚོར་བྱིང་བའི་འགྲོ་བ་རྣམས།
།བསྒྲལ་ཕྱིར་བྱང་ཆུབ་མཆོག་ཏུ་སེམས་བསྐྱེད་ནས།
།དུས་གསུམ་བདེ་གཤེགས་སྲས་ཀྱི་སྤྱོད་པ་ལ།
།ཞུམ་མེད་བསམ་པ་ཐག་པས་བསླབ་པར་བགྱི།

*Phaṭ! In order to liberate transmigrators who are drowning in the ocean of suffering, I will generate the sublime mind of enlightenment, and will practice sincerely and without discouragement the deeds of those gone to bliss, and their children of the three times.*

—sung passage of generating *bodhicitta*, in *Dedicating the Illusory Body*

# 3

# The Sound of Vultures' Wings

## Ritual Mapping the Chöd Practice

### The Role of Music in Chöd: Paradoxical Claims?

During the oral transmission of a Chöd ritual, the lama might adopt a strong rhetorical stance, insisting that music is not the central point of the practice. Instead, the lama will gently affirm that one should, in contrast, place the mind's focus on increasing one's level of *bodhicitta*, and attaining a deeper level of realizing the nature of mutual interdependence and emptiness. According to a preeminent twentieth-century exponent of the ritual practice, Kyabje Zong Rinpoché, former head of the Ganden Chöd Tradition, one does not need the music in order to practice Chöd. Pala (Ven. Pencho Rabgey) echoes this sentiment when he tells me legends of Chöd adepts (including his own teacher, Geshé Trinley) who found it just as effective to sit in a cemetery (a "sky burial" site in Tibet) at night to perform a silent meditation, thinking through the process of a sādhana, mentally performing all the visualizations in each step, and in this way reaching attainments.

Yet, it is also the case that every Chöd lama implores their students to learn the melodies and instruments correctly, and some lamas may quietly display disappointment when this has not been sufficiently achieved.[1] Although seemingly paradoxical, both positions have their validity. My interest in the musical aspects of Chöd stems, at least partly, from this apparent contradiction. Since musical performance is a constant and complex feature of the ritual practices, we may ask: "What *are* the functions of music in the Chöd ritual?" Or, to put it differently: "How do the various aspects of the music ritual performance assist one in the meditation practice?" Zong Rinpoché notes that the study and practice of Chöd involve cultivated musical training and an appreciation of musical symbolism, style, and execution.[2]

Zong Rinpoché's pedagogical advice given to practitioners during a Chöd transmission is highly instructive in several ways. He states:

> It is important to remember that the Chöd melodies are not the compositions of chanting beggars, but the wisdom of Buddha in actuality. For that reason, reciting Chöd authentically, to the original melodies, creates great merit. In the same way, the *Guru Puja* must be kept pure. If the melodies degenerate, the authenticity and blessings will be lost. Some of the melodies used in this Chöd system are those composed by Machik Labdrön herself, particularly the section on the body being cut up. *This melody was inspired by the sound of the flapping wings of vultures arriving at a "sky burial"* [emphasis added].[3]

*Sound Images of Vultures and Tone Painting*

The last point is arguably the most important from an ethnomusicological perspective, implying, as it does, that one of the composition techniques used in Chöd meditation practice rituals is tone painting.[4] Tone painting is the name given to a technique of composition whereby culturally relevant musical gestures are combined—in melody, instrumentation, and rhythm—to conjure up an image in the mind of the listener. To put this another way, a composer evokes an image musically through culturally understood semiotic gestures. Often naturalistic imagery is depicted, such as the elements and forces of nature.

*Musical Depictions, Literary Concordances*

Machik Labdrön's melody was composed for the section of the "actual practice" of the ritual, in which there is the vivid visualization of separating consciousness from the body and then preparing the body for transformation and distribution. This enables the practitioner to visualize the pulling-up and flapping of vultures' wings more effectively with each rising two-note gesture displaying a short-long rhythm (see figure 3.1). The transcription indicates an initial upward moving sequence of successively higher starting pitches of a two-note ascending melodic gesture, characterizing the first half of the melody. This is answered by the "gliding" and "settling down" of the vultures characterized by the pitch contour in the second half of the melody. The palpable mental image that Machik Labdrön evokes through

Figure 3.1. "The White Distribution" (Tib. *dkar 'gyed*) melody is said to have been composed by Machik Labdrön herself. Using the composition technique of "tone painting," the melody depicts the sound of vultures' wings flapping as they arrive at a sky burial. Subsequently, the practitioner visualizes transforming and offering refined parts of the body to the lineage lamas, meditational deities, buddhas, *bodhisattvas*, and so forth.

musical gesture enhances the mood that the practitioner cultivates in the process of visualization. There is a dramatic transformation taking place as she prepares first to separate her consciousness from the body, and then to distribute the old body to all invited guests. The practitioner will utilize this image in meditation when the ḍākinī, whose identity is the practitioner's own transformed consciousness, is visualized flaying the old body.

*Melodic Parameters*

The melody has to obey the conventions of the genre (it must match the musical language and syntax of the other melodies in the sādhana) and also uniquely mark the imagined event with culturally appropriate musical gestures. It demands artistic skill to distill the essence of an abstract idea into a concrete image, that is, to evoke an image, or scene, with a single melodic line, just as it requires skill to condense the essence of a large written work into a précis, abstract, or sound bite.

In a Chöd sādhana, the musical texture is largely homophonic: one main melodic line is dominant, while other musical parts (played by instruments or sung) enhance, accompany, or support it.[5] There is, however, an important caveat with respect to this categorical designation. Although a Chöd sādhana requires only one sung melodic part in each meditation section, either in unison or at the octave, the musical texture *in toto* retains the melodic dominance of the voice—singing or chanting the liturgical poetry—and pitched instruments that influence the melodic texture.[6] Moreover, a melody is always rhythmic and has directionality, phrase structure, and certain pitches of importance, as well as shifting centers of pitch importance. In Chöd performance, the two-line stanza refrain is usually comprised of two sung musical phrases: a first phrase that departs from the home tonal area to a related tonal area, and a second phrase that returns from this related tonal area to the home tonal area.[7] A Chöd sādhana is usually designed so that a musical phrase can be expressed within one exhaling breath.

### *Performing Sonic Iconography: Visualizing Music in Chöd Practice*

When the composer has such restricted room for the creative realization of visualization, a limited palette with which to paint a portrait of the meditative event, it requires single brush strokes in an austerely constructed sequence. With the melody aptly evoking the ascribed symbolic image, the repetitions of the melodic refrain act as the ideal canvas for the specific details of the poetic text-based meditative visualizations.

Machik Labdrön's melody aids the practitioner's meditation because it depicts the vultures' actions through musical imagery. The sophistication of the composer's technique should be remarked upon here. The composer attempts to depict the psychology of fear associated with the onset of violent thunderstorms (in the case of Vivaldi[8]); and, in the case of Chöd, fear and vulnerability along with the feeling of attachment to the body as vultures arrive and circle above. The Chöd composer paints a scene that evokes an emotional response in the adept. Vultures fly confidently and prepare to land with four or five graceful flaps of their wings. Correspondingly, the melody depicts this confidence with a soaring sequence of melodic leaps and a rapidly reached melodic climax on the sixth syllable of the first line of the two-line melody, with the rest of the melody heard as a dénouement. The music has five melodic leaps in an ascending sequence, followed by a descending contour. Each melodic leap sounds like a flapping of wings; altogether, it sounds like an arc of determined, focused action.

Remarkably, there is but one literal reference to "vultures" (*rgod po*) in this sādhana.[9] The reference is found, in fact, during the meditation section where this melody of "cutting the body" is sung. This makes sense in terms of the logical structure of the ritual, as this is the precise moment when the Chöd practitioner's consciousness is transferred up and into the lama's heart and the body is left on the ground.[10] While the practitioner's consciousness has subsequently emerged from the lama's heart as a ḍākinī, vultures would arrive to attend to the body at this moment and no other. The sādhana's liturgical text proceeds as follows, in translation:

> v.3 From the pathway of the supreme channel,
> I eject [my mind] into the guru-deity's heart [above].
> *phaṭ! phaṭ! phaṭ! phaṭ! phaṭ!*
>
> v.4 My old body falls down, abandoned,
> Appearing whitish and oily, it covers a billion worlds.
>
> v.5 *phaṭ!*
> My mind emerges from the heart of the guru-deity,
> in the aspect of a ḍākinī holding a curved knife.
>
> v.6 Like a vulture circling above meat, holding the curved knife,
> [I swoop down and] from the crown to the groin, I cut.[11]

The poetic structure of this subritual in the sādhana should be noted. The two-line musical refrain recurs ten times. Thus, there are ten verses (each two-lines in length) to which this melody is sung. Five verses precede the cutting of the body, while five are sung to the cutting, transforming, and preparing of the body for distribution. The end of the third verse is the commencement of the "transference of consciousness" practice, while the fifth verse concerns the consciousness emerging from the heart of the lama. Clearly, this melody traverses several transformative experiences. From the beginning of the "actual practice" (the first three verses), when the subtle consciousness is recognized and is brought upward through the central channel (beginning from the navel chakra up through to the heart, throat, head, and crown chakras) and ejected out of the body through the crown aperture, until the moment after the tenth and final verse of the same sub-ritual (when the "white offering" substances are purified and prepared for distribution), the same melodic refrain sustains the practitioner's meditations by depicting the image of vultures arriving and awaiting the ḍākinī's work to be completed.

It is consistent with the need to go to scary places that the "tone painting" refers to the manner of vultures arriving at a sky burial site where they await the disposal of a carcass (the practitioner's own freshly dead body). While this may be gruesome and even terrifying to imagine, both this Chöd sādhana's poetry and its musical liturgy require the practitioner to think along these lines with respect to the predicament of the body. The idea is to work with the ego's normatively strongly felt association of the "I" with the body. By working with this habitual tendency to protect the self, observing the way in which the "self-grasping" occurs with respect to the body, it exposes the sense of relationship with this body as "self." Because the sādhana's written liturgy and melody have both been composed by adepts in the Chöd Tradition to assist the practitioner in gaining realization through the meditative process, it is instructive to consider what they wish the practitioner to experience through visualization in the context of music performance.

The melody and written liturgy together conjure up an entire scene for the practitioner, the moment when her consciousness exits the old body and she returns to it as a ḍākinī in order to actualize the practice of generosity (*sbyin pa*), first of the six perfections (*pāramitās*) in the *Prajñāpāramitā Sūtra* (*Perfection of Wisdom Sūtra*), by distributing the old body she formerly identified with as her "self." This melody is meant to evoke a scene that makes her feel vulnerable during the arrival of the vultures and other scavengers, and she is faced more profoundly with her own attachment to the body which she has not completely been able to let go of.

This is the moment for which the Chöd ritual is created.

## *Image Selection and Association*

The aesthetic image that is conjured up in written and musical liturgy is *anticipatory*, not gruesome. A few comments should be made about this. First, from among all the images that could be depicted musically during this scene of the ritual drama, Machik Labdrön selects an image that is relatively peaceful and benign.[12] The scene is constructed not with musical gestures that portray a vulture's hooked beak and sharp talons ripping into the flesh. We do not hear musical themes that evoke the ḍākinī slicing the body with a ritual flaying knife. The selection of images that Machik calls to mind is itself a clue to the sort of psychological work that is being performed.[13] Through musical imagery, the scene recalls the immediate and habitual fear related to the vulnerability of the body when it is identified with *as* the "self." The image depicted in the written liturgy, and in the music, conjures up the moments before the vultures partake of the flesh. It is anticipatory. This is consistent with the tradition. The parts of the body have not yet been distributed to vultures and other beings. In the Chöd ritual, this is the job of the ḍākinīs.

The mere mention of vultures, let alone seeing or visualizing their presence, is fear-provoking and practically forces the practitioner to recall impermanence and death and to think self-protective thoughts. This challenges the practitioner not to become distracted from doing the ritual work of the ḍākinī who is *to be "like"* vultures in their actions. The ḍākinī flying above the body is here *acting like a vulture*, portraying the expert mortician in its preferred domain prior to flaying the flesh to distribute to others.[14] The practitioner recalls the ordinariness of the scene as far as the vultures are concerned, and sees a body that has been left at the "sky burial" site. Yet, the powerful disconnect between the perspectives of an aerial scavenger who seeks nourishment, and the (beginner) practitioner who may not feel ready to die, is telling. The real enemy is neither "vultures" nor death itself, but the belief that there is a "self" that is simultaneously perishable with the body, the thought that there is an inherently existing "self" there at all.

## *Musical and Liturgical Repercussions*

A Chöd lama's oral commentarial discourse about music and imagery, which makes a clear connection between performed liturgical music and its ritual poetic text, is a very important convergence of data for research purposes into Chöd, and tantric ritual more generally. This is evidence from the "native perspective" about the prescribed *performance practices*, a domain of concerns that is often passed through oral tradition alone, and which ethnomusicological research typically seeks to explore (see chapter 2). It is highly significant that a melody is known to depict a particular visual image at all—be it an image of a ḍākinī, a vulture, either, or both. Because of the level of specificity in the *outer* depiction, and its reference to an *inner* transformative practice, I think of the "tone painting" of naturalistic imagery in this context as "sonic iconography" that is devised *by* Chöd adepts *for* other adepts and carried though the oral tradition as such. It may be wondered, given the vicissitudes of historical change, whether it could be the case, as forwarded by Kyabje Zong Rinpoché, that the first exponent of the Chöd Tradition: (a) composed this melody one thousand years ago; (b) intended to depict vultures arriving at the sky burial site; and (c) did so in order to evoke the fear due to vulnerability in the practitioner's mind as an aid to realizing the contingencies of the "self."

Given the degree of intimacy in the music pedagogy and tantric ritual pedagogical process, it does not seem a far-fetched possibility either that the melody could have survived or that such information about musical meaning in relation to practice has been retained successfully.[15] Alice Egyed finds that from generation to generation, the melodies of Tibetan liturgical chant (*dbyangs*) in some locales and circumstances are transmitted very much intact. She tells a story from her research in the Mustang region of Nepal of a music director (*umdzé*) who stayed in solitary, closed retreat for twenty years. When he emerged, Egyed observed that his disciple's disciple reproduced his melodies nearly exactly to his own. This provides evidence of the relative stability and continuity of the Tibetan monastic-based music traditions between three generations.

In addition, this raises two questions that require further critical investigation. Does the tone painting image, a type of *sonic iconography*, refer to the sounds of an actual vulture's wings as the oral tradition claims? Or, since the sādhana refers to the ḍākinī's actions at this moment with the phrase "like vultures circling above meat," does it refer instead to the ḍākinī's actions? If the latter is the case, then since the written liturgy uses the Tibetan word "*bzhin*" meaning "like" (or "similar to") are we meant to visualize the ḍākinī mimicking the vulture's actions of flapping? Given the sophistication in the use of homonyms and the adroit use of other poetic devices in this written liturgy, it is reasonable to conclude that there is not a perplexing ambiguity here, but rather a deliberate double entendre.

The word "vultures," where it emerges in the written liturgy, appears to evoke two meanings. The mention of "vultures" in the Chöd sādhana seems at first glance to be a literal indication about the ḍākinī's actions. Yet, with the insight provided from the oral tradition about the image of vultures being musically depicted *in the very same scene*, it may require further analysis. By placing these two "texts"—(a) the poetic image instructing the ḍākinī (to mimic the vulture's confident deliberate circling) and (b) the sonic image of actual vultures arriving (to elicit the practitioner's fear)—into intertextual relief, mapping their ritual functions, it is possible to study the ways in which they have been mutually designed to enhance the practitioner's meditative experience. The written liturgy refers to the image of the ḍākinī circling above ("like vultures"), while the aural/oral melody refers to the image of vultures arriving at the site. Thus, at this moment in the ritual, the "tone painting" musical imagery complexifies the poetic smile. On the one hand the *sonic iconography* of vultures arriving cues the practitioner to feel the impending act—in a sense, to *feel impermanence*—recognizing the continuity of the life-cycle. But the liturgical text's reference to vultures cues the practitioner to attend to a poetic analogy that instructs how to visualize initially circling above, acting like vultures, before swooping down and performing the role of a wisdom ḍākinī who is to cut and distribute the body to all beings, pacifying and satisfying them, while paying down karmic debt.

With the exposure of the old body to the aerial scavengers and/or ḍākinī, the practitioner is faced simultaneously with the possibility of two perspectives: the written liturgy instructs the practitioner to dispassionately disassociate from the old body and take up the vantage point of the self-assured ḍākinī. She first compassionately regards the old body (the body down below that is freshly discarded and possessing warm flesh for those who prefer to consume it as such) as the basis of food, drink, and satisfaction of others; and then quickly descends to "cut" the body and prepare the feast for all beings to partake. On the other hand, the melody, in depicting the vultures' willful reconnaissance over the freshly decomposing corpse, suggests the practitioner continues to identify with the vulnerability of the exposed body and remains in some way attached to the vantage point of the old body. Since only the most expert practitioner is able to transcend visualizing the "transfer of consciousness" and actually accomplish this level of the practice, by exercising the play between these two possible vantage points—maintaining an experience of either vulnerability or confidence—the meditator may choose whichever way is found to be most helpful to procuring realizations.

Thus, at one level, the practitioner imagines their own dead body amidst the scene of vultures arriving to feast off of it. While, at another level, instructed by way of the written liturgy, the practitioner visualizes themselves as the ḍākinī acting like a vulture: flying in circles above the old body and then swooping down to cut it with the ritual knife. By utilizing the normally terrifying image of being picked away at by vultures, the Chöd practitioner turns the situation of death into something with which to gain merit. For, while visualizing oneself as the ḍākinī, the practitioner does this work of cutting, flaying, and intentionally distributing. The adept gives away what can no longer be used: the old body—which will be consumed in any event—and transforms this potentially traumatic moment into an opportunity for liberation of both self and others from cyclic existence.

*Implications*

A working hypothesis may be constructed on the basis of information accumulated thus far:

1. Chöd melodies are meant to be evocative of imagery.
2. Imagery is evoked musically when a melody is crafted through combining structural elements in accordance with the aesthetic logic of the tradition.
3. The imagery is appropriate to Chöd theory in general.
4. The image-encoded melody is sung to a section of the written liturgy in which it enhances the affect and goal of that particular meditation section (e.g., vultures are mentioned only in the section that the ḍākinī, the practitioner in visualization, sings of her actions being like them).

To summarize the findings:

1. This is the only section of the sādhana in which vultures are mentioned in the written liturgy.
2. Vultures are mentioned in the only section where vultures *would assemble*: during the meditation on "cutting the body" prior to the first distribution.
3. The ḍākinī is visualized as mimicking the vulture's actions "circling like vultures above meat" (according to the written liturgy).
4. The ḍākinī is the practitioner herself (visualized as an enlightened form of a buddha, having left the old body on the ground).

5. The melody is meant to depict an actual vulture's wings flapping as it arrives at a sky burial site (according to the oral tradition).

6. The imagery employed is consistent with the notion that in this tradition fear is aroused through terrifying imagery for the purpose of spiritual realization.

## Ritual Mapping: Analysis of Tantric Ritual

Looking across these "texts" at multiple references to the image of vultures (which takes place during the practitioner's most profound psychophysical transformation in the sādhana), provides a bridge across domains of meaning production and suggests the usefulness of "ritual mapping" as a way of conducting ritual analysis. "Ritual mapping" is the process of separating simultaneously occurring layers in a sādhana liturgy, such as the pre-composed melodies and poetry that are performed during ritual practice. The evidence uncovered through ethnographic interview and musical analysis indicates that it is not words alone that cue the mind's performance of visualization. The ritual analyst must layer the "text" of written liturgy against the structure and aesthetic design of the melody, and each of these against the intended musical imagery—as explained in the oral tradition's commentary.

### Melodic Layer

The melody depicts a scene of flapping wings of vultures at a sky burial, which recalls impermanence and evokes a mood of fear and renunciation. The mood is a textured backdrop of an entire scene, like that depicted in the outer layers of a Tibetan thangka painting, which is why we can refer to it as *sonic iconography*. To put it another way, the melody elicits a mental image that is less specific than a thangka painting's central figure, yet its aesthetic qualities and meditative function are analogous to the complementary imagery in a painting's surrounding landscape and sky.

### Written Liturgical Layer

The written liturgy specifies how to visualize the ḍākinī's actions. At this point, the central figure in the drama is the practitioner-as-ḍākinī who orchestrates the giving (distributing the mentally transformed body) in four allotments. In the first mentally conjured scene after the transfer of consciousness, the practitioner's *old body* is the raw material for visualizing transforming and giving away. The practitioner's *consciousness* is transformed into the wisdom ḍākinī who works as a mortician in preparing the old body, and the practitioner's *field of giving* are the countless visualized beings who are in need of material and spiritual nourishment and fulfillment.

## Integrating Performance

The performative aspects of the Chöd ritual are included in this analytical process. With that said, we neither wish to *center* the ritual analysis on performance, nor privilege the performance event *over* the written liturgy in the sādhana. Either strategy would be a mistake and produce confusion. Similarly, it would be a mistake to de-link melody and poetry in the *mgur* genre-derived Chöd sādhana (except for the purposes of pedagogy, training, and "ritual mapping"). Within the context of performance, melody and poetry are integral "texts." One is not subordinate to the other. The written liturgy describes what the adept meditates upon in each moment of the ritual, whereas the melody enhances and supports the overall meditative experience with specific melodic gestures and *rasa.* The third option in ritual analysis is to privilege the written liturgy wherein music becomes peripheral. However, as has been suggested, music is neither an arbitrary assignment, nor a mere perfunctory association to fulfill traditional expectations.

## The Primacy of Performance?

Describing the performance process within an analytical framework presents a fascinating challenge because we are attempting to shift the focus of attention *away from a center* to look instead *across* the "texts" of musical and poetic liturgy as complementary domains of (inner and outer) practice. Initially, it seemed to be vitally important to recenter Chöd studies to a performance orientation—since a great deal of valuable information that is integral to the meditation practice is imparted through musical pedagogy, and the oral transmission regarding performance practices had yet to be studied closely.

On the one hand, there seems to be a primacy to the music when the sādhana is manifested in performance. The melody "carries" the written liturgy and sets the *rasa,* mood, or atmosphere. The music has a precedence that defies easy analogy. Although the music is not central, the poetic liturgy is "carried" through it, and thus meaning is conveyed simultaneously in at least two ways.

The musical liturgy creates one mood-image, or *rasa* (taste), during each subritual meditation, while the written liturgy is (1) enveloped within the broader *sonic iconography* and (2) describes specific meditations in the foreground.

On the other hand, the written liturgy of the sādhana is the most important tool for the meditation practitioner. It serves as (1) a meditation guide and (2) as a set of liturgical poetry that must be chanted or sung. These two aspects are integrated together in one document (the "practice manual" or sādhana), often with an accompanying written commentary. However the center is determined, the musical and literary aspects of the liturgy seem to both be integral to the visualization. Since the primary goal of this analytical process is to investigate how musical performance functions within Chöd meditation practice, following these preliminary findings a more specific question may be asked. How does each performance element or "text" appear to be *designed* to contribute to the practitioner's experience in the context of meditating upon a sādhana that is meant to facilitate cutting-off "self-grasping"? To assume that each performance element in the Chöd ritual is meaningful, and some or perhaps all of the performance elements are collectively significant, may seem to be a highly intuitive position.[16] Therefore, to investigate how these performance elements are meaningful both separately and together may enrich an understanding of the role of musical performance in tantric ritual practice while also developing a body of knowledge for ritual analysis.

In other words, ritual analysis can be approached from one of two basic theoretical stances with regard to tantric sādhana and performance: *either* it is maintained that the performance elements (including melody, poetic design, structure, *rasa*, etc.) are all randomly culled and assembled from disparate sources and assigned with minimal care to the written liturgy *or* one adheres to the notion that there is a purposeful, creative (and purportedly divinely inspired) process involved in the assignment of aesthetic complements to enhance the experience of the adept. In the case of the Indian *dohā* and the Tibetan Chöd, practitioners apparently "hear" a melody in a dream or it comes to them during meditation practice (and then they sing it until they remember it), and seek to incorporate it into their practice, offer it to their lama, teach it to their students, and so forth.[17]

## Incorporation of New Melodies in the Tradition

Following either of these options, there is a culturally internal and sanctioned process of recognition and incorporation (or rejection) of new melodies and verses by the Chöd lineage holder who serves as gatekeeper.[18] The composers of Chöd were mystics and skilled musical craftspeople who may have known how to compose a melody to suit a text, and, contrafactum, how to write poetry to complement an existing melody.[19] Both composition techniques are probably not accomplished with equal difficulty. Given the rules of Tibetan poetics, it must be assumed that devising a melody for an existing text would be comparatively simpler than composing the poetry to suit an existing melody. There is little to no written Tibetan record of the actual composition process,[20] nor is it clear within the Chöd oral tradition what part has been done by which lama in what chronological order. In the case of Pabongka's composed poetry in the sādhana, he created a text that, as he writes in the colophon, "is written in metered verse so as to be easy to chant."[21] To what melodies did he first compose the text?[22] Was there a previous model upon which his text relied? Some melodies in *Dedicating the Illusory Body* were likely based upon those in the *Bdag 'dzin tshar gcod* texts, but it is unclear at present which ones.[23]

More research needs to be done into which lama composed which Chöd melody. However, there is a great deal we can infer about the process by cross-referencing written details and the oral traditional knowledge of living exponents. Ven. Pencho Rabgey recalls a story as relayed to him by Kyabje Zong Rinpoché about Purchog Ngawang Champa Rinpoché (Phur mchog ngag dbang byams pa rin po che), the senior tutor of the Thirteenth Dalai Lama. Purchog Ngawang Champa Rinpoché composed a melody for his teacher's Chöd sādhana (Pabonkha Rinpoché's Chöd text, *Dedicating the Illusory Body as a Heaped Offering*). He composed this Chöd melody and then sang it, offering it as such to his lama by performing it for him. Pabongka Dechen Nyingpo liked it and said "Yes, that's good." Thereafter it became incorporated into the sādhana ritual practice. This approval indicates one process by which the tradition accommodates innovation and incorporates changes. The tradition is open to the creativity of its exponents, yet the type and extent of change permissible is defined very narrowly. Clearly, there are strictures and hierarchical levels of possibility in terms of acceptance. In another account, a Ganden Chöd lama, Drupwang Lobsang Namgyal (Grub dbang blo bzang rnam gyal, 1670–1741),[24] spent time in meditation in a place near Gompo in Tsang, the central Tibetan province. Some passing pilgrims were singing beautiful melodies as they walked, which the lama overheard and was pleased by. In return, he sang Chöd melodies he had composed which greatly pleased them. It is suggested that he then incorporated some of the pilgrims' melodies he heard on that occasion into the Chöd liturgical corpus.[25]

Reading backwards historically and aesthetically into the creative process may be a useful project for scholars and students engaged in tantric ritual studies. Here, rather by chance, in the esoteric Chöd ritual we have found evidence that suggests the ways in which correspondences that connect at the level of melody, visualization, and written liturgy derive from a thoughtful, deliberate, and intentional creative act. Just as the tip of an iceberg suggests there is a much larger mass under the surface, this finding raises questions about the extensiveness of such examples across Chöd sādhanas in the Ganden Tradition and across other Chöd Traditions in the other Tibetan religious schools and lineages, as well as across other tantric rituals.

## Ritual Analysis in Context

What is being attempted in "ritual mapping" is akin to the thick description process that Clifford Geertz forwarded in his "interpretive anthropology" insofar as it is intended to privilege the context of ritual performance.[26] "Ritual mapping" does not ignore matters of belief. Rather it *brackets* the faith component concerning the matter of divinely inspired melodies—which are said to carry and invoke the buddhas' wisdom—in order to examine the compositional design of the sādhana with the analytical tools available. Why is it important to consider the sādhana's design? Because in doing so we may get closer to what was originally intended for the Chöd meditator to experience. Moreover, we may learn the value of formal design in this "performing art" and the linked aspects of melody, visualization, written liturgy, and performative gesture in tantric ritual performance.

Stephan Beyer's insight that Buddhism is a "performing art" is relevant to this analysis. The gateway to fully understanding the design of a Chöd sādhana is through performance. Transcribing (i.e., "mapping") the performance "texts" can illuminate correspondences internal to the ritual. As a caveat, it should be noted that while this is an initial prescription for how to analyze Tibetan tantric ritual, it is not meant to be conclusive. "Ritual mapping," as considered here, is a formalized way of making transparent the methodology and the analytical process undertaken that yields the findings described. This process involved the following stages: learning to practice a Chöd sādhana under the tutelage of a qualified master, receiving oral traditional instructions into the meaning of Chöd, learning how to adjust performance style and content according to various practice contexts, studying Chöd commentaries written by Chöd lineage lamas, translating Tibetan sādhana texts, transcribing the musical liturgical "texts," and finally, looking across poetry and melody and noticing correspondences. Other researchers will no doubt follow different paths and uncover new insights.

This approach suggests the possibility of removing the latent assumption that it is *only* the written liturgical portion of the sādhana that contains the meditative techniques and instructions that are meaningful for the practitioner's meditation practices. In other words, the finding of literary-music correspondences indicates that the exclusive locus of meaning production is *not* in the words of the sādhana's poetry alone. Rather, interlinked "texts" reference the same meditative imagery in the context of performance. That the melodies of the sādhana complement the written liturgy in *some* functional capacity is practically unquestioned.[27] What may be instructive for future research into Chöd, and by extension the *mgur* and *Vajra Gīti* (Tib. *Rdo rje'i glu*) song genres,[28] is understanding the degree to which Tibetan tantric ritual analysis draws from several primary sources to learn the sum of the sādhana's assigned meanings for the Chöd adept. It draws from: (a) the sādhana's written liturgy, (b) the sādhana's musical tradition, (c) the written commentarial tradition, and (d) the oral commentarial tradition. By cross-referencing between these primary sources, it is possible to learn the sādhana's assigned meanings for the Chöd adept. That is to say, by looking across the "texts" of music and written liturgy, it could be advantageous to read backwards historically through the performance artifact (i.e., sādhana) to learn the scriptural and aural sources for the resultant tradition.

## Motivations

The findings here emerge not from a Boasian program of seeking out cultural instances that prove a universalizing theory about culture or mind and body, music and ritual, nurture vs. nature,[29] or ritual text against ritual performance. Rather, these insights emerged gradually while spending time training in Chöd practice under Tibetan exponents. Despite nine years of training in Chöd practice, the correspondences between the written liturgy and music became noticeable once I started transcribing the ritual. Thus, the suggested analytical process of mapping ritual "texts" to note correspondences should ideally involve transcription of all layers that have been transmitted to ritual practitioners, including musical and meditation performance practices. A Western musical score includes room for melody, words, and rhythm. All the performance layers can be written in this format initially, though elsewhere other graphic methods could be equally or more instructive.

It may be wondered whether musical tone painting is the primary symbolic way in which the melodies are to be understood as significant—that is, by virtue of the fact that they enhance a mood through the evocation of images. In fact, there are numerous additional ways in which the melody enhances and complements the text. Musical transcription reveals several music composition techniques that have been employed, many of which assist the adept in gaining realizations while engaging in the meditative experience of practicing Chöd. Here, we will take up one more such technique, rhythmic mnemonic functions: prosodic references to the number three, and how lists of three correspond with anapest rhythms and melodic ornamentations.

### (2) Rhythmic and Mnemonic Prosody: The "Seven Branch Offering Practice"

Among the diverse instances of melody-poetry-rhythm correspondence in the sādhana, *Dedicating the Illusory Body*, let us examine in detail the careful composition design of the "Seven Branch Offering Practice" subritual. In this case, a rhythmic pattern played on the *ḍamaru* matches prosodic and melodic elements. It also functions as a mnemonic for the practitioner. Specifically, the relatively quick three beat anapest rhythm (two short, followed by one long beat) is played by the *ḍamaru* and bell as a complement to the ornamented vocal line of the verse. It is accompanied (silently) by the three *bol* syllables *bcom ldan 'das* (pronounced: "chom den dé") meaning "the conquerer."[30] The rhythm of the *ḍamaru* aligns skillfully with the prosody in this subritual, illustrating how precisely the music can complement the sādhana's poetic structure and words [figure 3.2].

First, it is important to consider the context of this subritual. The "Seven Branch Offering Practice" is an *essential* component of the preliminary practices of all Tibetan Buddhist tantric rituals. Presented in the order in which they are recited, with a brief description of their meaning, the seven branches are listed as follows:

(1st) Prostrating, paying homage to the buddhas.

(2nd) Offering to the buddhas.

(3rd) Confession of sins before the buddhas as witnesses.

(4th) Rejoicing in the buddhas' accomplishments.

(5th) Requesting the buddhas to teach.

(6th) Requesting the buddhas not to pass away, but remain to help sentient beings.

(7th) Dedicating the accumulated merit from the six previous branches to gaining enlightenment for the benefit of all sentient beings.

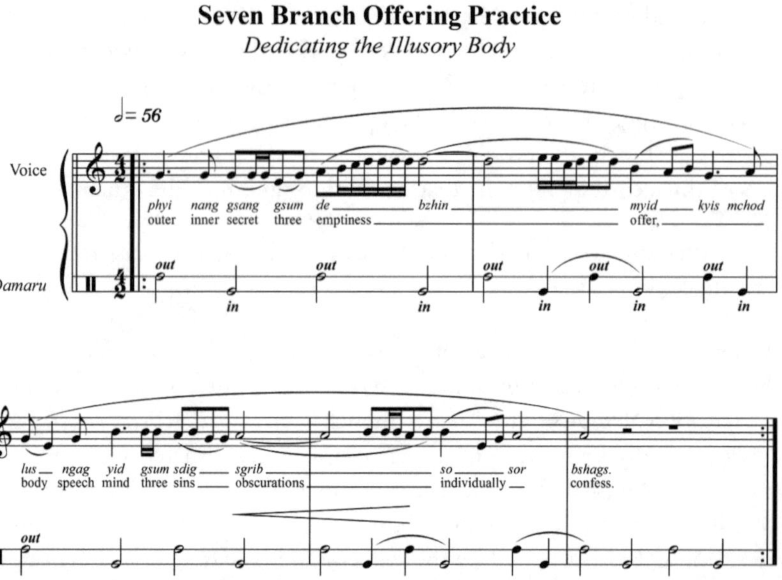


Figure 3.2. The "Seven Branch Offering Practice" is among the most powerful subrituals at the level of sūtra and tantra with which to build up an accumulation of merit. This liturgical portion is sung as one of the preliminary practices in a Chöd ritual, and is often followed by the body mandala offering.

There are short, middling, and extensive versions of this practice.[31] This sādhana features one of the short versions. The first four lines of this melody are devoted to the first of the branches, that of paying homage to the central deity figure, the female buddha and *yidam*, Vajrayoginī.

Thereafter, each of the six remaining branches (of the seven-branch practice) is set to one line of poetry. Each of these six lines of poetry is structured around the number "three." In every line of poetry the fourth syllable is the Tibetan word for "three" (*gsum*, pronounced: "soom"), while the first three syllables of each line are an enumeration of qualities related with the practice of Buddhadharma (figure 3.3).

The melody for this subritual takes two lines to complete; in other words, it is a two-line melody comprised of two one-line phrases, each of one branch of the practice. Thus, the two-line melody is set to the last six branches of the practice, allocated in paired order, as follows:

(2nd & 3rd branches) offering + confessing,
(4th & 5th) rejoicing + requesting buddhas to teach,
(6th & 7th) requesting buddhas to remain + dedicating all merits.

Within each of the seven branches (i.e., depicted within the poetry of every line), three aspects of Buddhist practice concerning traversing the path to enlightenment are listed in a pithy, concise manner. How is the music composed to correspond with the poetry? Or, to put it another way: How is the poetic structure enhanced by the music? During each two-line melody, which itself becomes a strophic refrain, anapest rhythms are sounded on the *ḍamaru*, evoking the sense of "three" that is stated in the text, but in a rhythmically synaesthetic way (see the lower stave in Figure 3.2). It is a nonverbal, gestural punctuation of text. This is a different kind of *sonic iconography*; it is mnemonic rather than painting a visual image.

The triplet (or, more properly, anapest) beats sonically (re)present the three aspects of practice referred to in the text, which themselves are *literally punctuated* with the very word "three" (*gsum*). The rhythm reinforces the poetry with a gentle playful three-beat gesture in a light melodic lilt. Thus, with considerable composition skills in poetry, melody, and rhythm, the musical punctuation of the poetry is *heard* in the Seven-Branch ritual *as a mnemonic.*

The Tibetan transliteration is given here with the English translation underneath. The English translation follows the logic of Tibetan grammar rather than that of grammatically correct English sentences. We do so in order to illustrate the placement of the word "three" and the three aspects of Buddhist tantric practice as special prosodic structural features. Note that both the transliterated Tibetan and English word for the number "three" are underlined in Figure 3.3 "The Seven Branch Offering Practice."[32]

## (3) *Rasa*

After much investigation, thus far I have found scriptural evidence in the voluminous written Chöd commentaries that describes the particular *rasa* or emotional taste each melody is meant to have in the Ganden Chöd Tradition lineages' sādhana practices. It seems this sort of information is accessible through the sādhanas but is lost to the oral tradition. For example, in the long sādhana of the Troma Nagmo (Khro ma nag mo) practice in the Ḍākinī lineage there are indications as to the *rasa* of the melody. With melodies composed for certain sections of the liturgy it is highly desirable to know which precise *rasa* or action, individual or in combination, is being invoked.

Each of the melodies may be ascribed a ritual action according to the "four ritual actions" (Tib. *'phrin las zhi*), as seen in the descriptive diagram, table 2.3. During an ethnographic interview with Ven. Pencho Rabgey, I

## Seven Branch Offering Practice

ཕྱི་ནང་གསང་གསུམ་དེ་བཞིན་ཉིད་ཀྱིས་མཆོད།
ལུས་ངག་ཡིད་གསུམ་སྡིག་སྒྲིབ་སོ་སོར་བཤགས།

*Phyi nang gsang gsum de bzhin nyid kyis mchod /* [Offering]
*Lus ngag yid gsum sdig sgrib so sor bshags.* [Confessing]

Outer, inner, secret, three; [and] the offering of suchness, I offer /
Body, speech, mind, three; each sin and obscuration, I confess.

I offer the three: outer, inner, secret, as well as suchness /
I confess each sin and obscuration of the three: body, speech, and mind.

རྣམ་དཀར་དུས་གསུམ་དགེ་ལ་རྗེ་ཡི་རང་།
འགྲོ་ལ་ཐེག་གསུམ་ཆོས་འཁོར་བསྐོར་དུ་གསོལ།

*rNam dkar dus gsum dge la rje yi rang /* [Rejoicing in virtues]
*'gro la theg gsum chos 'khor bskor du gsol* [Requesting Buddhas to teach]

Perfectly pure virtues [of the] three times; I rejoice [in the] /
Transmigrators for, the vehicles three; please turn the Dharma wheel.

I rejoice in the perfectly pure virtues of the three times /
Please turn the dharma wheel of the three "vehicles" for transmigrators.

རྟག་པའི་ཆོས་གསུམ་ངོ་བོར་བཞུགས་གསོལ་འདེབས།
དགེ་ཀུན་སྐུ་གསུམ་གོ་འཕང་ཐོབ་ཕྱིར་བསྔོ།

*rTag pa'i chos gsum ngo bor bzhugs gsol 'debs /* [Requesting buddhas to not pass away]
*dGe kun sku gsum go 'phang thob phyir bsngo* [Dedicating the accumulated virtue]

Permanence of Dharmas three; in the nature of, please stay /
Virtues all, [buddha] bodies three; [their] state, to attain, I dedicate.

Please remain permanently in the nature of the three /
I dedicate all virtues to attain the three buddha bodies.

Figure 3.3. The "Seven Branch Offering Practice."

asked whether he would, using these labels of the four ritual actions, ascribe to each melody what he felt was the most appropriate label. He first mentioned that in other tantric rituals commonly performed in monasteries (e.g., Mahākāla, Guhyasamāja, Yamāntaka and others in the pantheon of buddha deities) it was clear which sections of the ritual require wrathful or peaceful sounding music. But he had never heard of the melodies in the Chöd ritual being discussed in those terms. As an analytical exercise, I encouraged Pala to think about which ritual actions he would choose to ascribe to each melody and subritual (assuring him I would not ascribe these ritual actions to the melodies without explaining this process by which I arrived at them). He kindly agreed and applied the designations that I have placed in the table. The exercise yielded interesting results.

Noticing only three of the four categorical designations, I asked if any of the Chöd melodies were, in his view, "wrathful." Without hesitation, he replied softly, "none of the melodies in Chöd are supposed to be wrathful." The tone in his voice as he said this so gently reminded me that the purpose of the practice is to deal peacefully with all beings regardless of whether or not they appear as enemies at the moment, and whether or not there appears to be a threat to oneself.

Also observed in table 2.3, and this is important to consider, is a pronounced dramatic arc. In terms of dramaturgy, the ritual begins and ends with peaceful sections. These peaceful subritual sections effectively function as poignant bookends within the overall temperament of pacification. As the practitioner is gaining blessings through performing guru-yoga, making offerings of the "Seven Branch Practice" and the mandala, and supplicating the lineage lamas, she feels increasingly empowered to accomplish the "actual practice." During the "actual practice" she visualizes herself as a ḍākinī empowered with a great sense of purpose. First, she powerfully summons all the gods (*lha*) and ghosts (*'dre*)[33] throughout the universe. Second, she distributes to them all they need and desire. Third, she gives them pith instruction in the Dharma so that they may pacify their own minds, imploring them, "Do not perform any sinful or non-virtuous karma / diligently perform only perfectly virtuous karma."[34] Finally, she bids them to return to their homes and natural abodes. While singing her first dedication prayer, mixed as it is with meditation on emptiness and reminders of the fundamentals of the practice, she can experience a sense of peacefulness, having given away all she possesses or imagines she *could* possess. With the final dedication prayer, there is a great sense of inspiration from the sādhana practice and a growing confidence to accomplish the uncommonly compassionate tasks performed by former buddhas and *bodhisattvas.*

To summarize, preliminary research reveals which of the four ritual activities—peaceful, increasing,[35] powerful, or wrathful—is germane to each meditation subritual throughout the sādhana *Dedicating the Illusory Body.* However, there is one interesting point that must be mentioned at this juncture. In the sādhana practices, it is forbidden to bear a wrathful disposition mentally or in performance, at least at the outset. Therefore, only peaceful (*zhi ba*), increasing (*rgyas pa*) and powerful (*dbang ba*) are acceptable ritual actions for this sādhana. This led me logically to question: When, and in what circumstance, might a wrathful disposition be permitted? In Je Tsongkhapa's Chöd commentary, we find subrituals whereby, if the practitioner finds the malevolent beings have not yet been pacified, a more stringent method could be required.[36]

In observing how the melodies function to enhance the text on the more subtle level, we may pose the question: Whether it is possible that these subtle music-text relationships found in the liturgical text-setting of melodies to the Chöd sādhana enhance the practitioner's experience of guru-deity yoga? The nine moods or "tastes" (Skt. *rasa*) of Indian music theory tradition were imported to Tibet along with other musical traditions, and were condensed to "four ritual actions": peaceful (*zhi ba*), increasing (*rgyas pa*), powerful (*dbang ba*), and wrathful (*drag po*). Transcribing the music slows down visualizations and performance elements and allows one to see a complex set of events.

### (4) Naturalistic Imagery

Zasep Tulku Rinpoché concurs that the melody and text correspond in mutually enhancing ways. However, he has a somewhat different interpretation. He finds that the melodies imitate nature, evoking the character of the elements: earth, wind/air, water, fire, and even depicting thunderstorms. According to him, the first melody, which is set to the verses for taking refuge and generating *bodhicitta*, depicts the element of water.[37] He maintains it flows and undulates forth like waves. It can also, he relates, depict powerful rains, and can be heard as nectar-like rains pouring down to purify and bless the adept while they seek inspiration at the outset of the Chöd meditation practice. The guru-yoga melody sounds like earth,[38] and conjures for him the image of undulating, rolling hills, going up and down, like a mountain-side hike that proceeds to move the practitioner up and down on a rising and falling path through the woods.

### (5) Rhythmic Structures and Alterations: *Chöd Tshogs* Sādhana

The structure of Kyabje Zong Rinpoché's *Chöd Tshogs* sādhana is fascinating to observe. We will first examine the changed rhythmic patterns for the *ḍamaru* from the preliminary practice; and, second, we will look at the slowing down of a melody to aid in meditation. When Zong Rinpoché transplanted the "preliminary practices" and dedications from Pabongka Rinpoché's Chöd sādhana *Dedicating the Illusory Body*, he retained some of the subritual meditation sections—in text and melody—but not in rhythm. It is important to mention that he changed some of the drumming rhythms to the "*dram dram*" rhythm from the "*ma dang, lha yi, mkha' 'gro*" rhythmic *ostinato*.[39] Turning the drum back and forth in an even tempo whereby the pellets strike the drum with the same amount of force each time produces the "*dram dram*" rhythm. The performance of these melodies takes on a different character in the latter sādhana, as the melodic phrases are adjusted to match a staid rhythm of straight quarter beats at an even tempo. It is likely that Kyabje Zong Rinpoché decided to use the "*dram dram*" rhythm because it allows for a quicker performance, which could be an advantage when performing Rinpoché's longer *Chöd Tshogs* sādhana.[40]

Most noticeably, in the "preliminary practices," there are two lengthy meditation sections to be sung—paying homage by singing the names of the venerated lamas in the long lineage and the near lineage of the Chöd practice and requesting blessings in order to accomplish the practice. These two lineage sections are themselves followed by three melodies of special supplications to the lama to suffuse the practitioner's guru devotion. Each of these three melodies is heard and experienced aesthetically as increasing in beauty with growing opportunity for the heartfelt involvement of the adept. The last of these three melodies occurs in a subritual that explains the result of having made heartfelt requests directly to the lama. The practitioner visualizes that from the hearts of all the lamas in the Chöd lineages (father lineage, mother lineage, near lineage and long lineage), blissful nectar light rays emanate purifying the environment and all beings. The Chödpa and all beings imaginable become rejuvenated and the qualities of *bodhicitta* are restored. The text of this section is as follows:

Through the power of having single-pointedly requested in this way,
From the heart of the guru-deity nectar light rays flow down,
The body is washed, and the place, spirits, sins and obscurations and especially self-grasping and self-cherishing are purified.
The body is filled, all virtuous qualities are rejuvenated and especially the altruistic mind of *bodhicitta* is generated.[41]

## (6) Poetic Meter and "The Slowing Down" of Melody

Several literary devices employed in the poetry of Chöd liturgies are drawn from the *Lamrim* discourses and retain the *Lamrim* lineage scholar-practitioners' use of allegory, simile, metaphor, aphorism, and irony,[42] among other devices. The *Lamrim* teachings are meant to serve as powerful reminders to those attempting the tantric path to recall their foundational meditations that focus on realization of the three principal paths. Having been potentially drawn from the Indian *dohā* tradition—the likely antecedent of the *mgur* and the "varja songs" (Skt. *vajra gīti*, Tib. *rdo rje'i glu*)"[43]—the poetic text of this *mgur* styled Chöd liturgy is accordingly composed in strophic form. Usually, there are nine syllables per line, treated in the poetic meter 2+2+2+3 or "// // // ///."[44] Occasionally, when there are seven syllables per line, the poetic meter takes the common configuration 2+2+3 or "// // ///." Although the number of lines per stanza can vary, the liturgical texts of the Ganden Chöd Tradition are generally composed in two-line or four-line stanzas. This can be observed in the transcription of this subritual's melody and its recorded example.

A special exception to the rule of stanza length is a marvelous melody for the subritual section expressing devotion to the spiritual guide in Kyabje Zong Rinpoché's *Chöd Tshogs* sādhana. Following the normative request to the temporally distant and near lineage lamas for their blessing to accomplish the practice, this third section is a deeply moving guru devotional meditation in which each stanza is comprised of *only one line of text.* With expert skill in melodic composition, the melody set to this one-line stanza of nine syllables has *three musical phrases*, is highly melismatic, requires the same number of rhythmic beats—and consequently takes the same amount of time (approximately eighteen seconds) to perform—as the two-line stanzas. (Two-line stanzas usually have but two musical phrases per two lines, and are sung with somewhat less ornamentation and pauses.) The reason for this stretched length of musical execution is thought to provide a greater amount of time, which allows the adept more intensive immersion

Figure 3.4. "Devotion to the Spiritual Guide" (*bshes gnyen tshul bzhin*) from the sādhana, *Offering the Body as Gaṇacakra*, is among the most melismatic of melodies in the Chöd corpus.

into the mood of this unequalled pinnacle of meditation subjects.[45] In this same subritual, we find another instance of rhythmic concordance in the Chöd liturgy together with an option for the practitioner to perform it in two different ways. In the third phrase of this melody, the option is given of using a musical gesture to rhythmically punctuate the text and melody in a way that assists with the sense of supplication: three quick "*ma-dang*" beats on each of the syllables "*byin gyis rlobs*," which finish each line of request for blessing. This is referred to as "sum gya" (*gsum gya*) within the tradition. Alternatively, Zong Rinpoché advises that the six-beat rhythmic *ostinato* cycle can continue without specifically articulating the syllables on the three beats with the *ḍamaru*. Thus, it is up to the practitioner to use whichever rhythm they prefer.

## Composition Skills

Sakya Paṇḍita Kunga Gyeltsen (sa skya pan di ta kun dga' rgyal mtshan, 1182–1251), the thirteenth-century Tibetan music theorist, wrote in his treatise on music that the prized skills of poetic composition were showing evidence of decline.

> The singers of yore were masters of words.
> Those of today learn just the music.
> I fear that in the future, singers [being]
> Inept and of weak intelligence
> Will merely sing happy songs (i.e., without content).[46]

Tibetologist-Ethnomusicologist Ricardo Canzio comments further on Sakya Paṇḍita's passage:

> This is consistent with the belief [according to Buddhist cosmology] in the deterioration of the times, where the Buddha's doctrine as well as all man's moral standards and capabilities gradually decline until the world is pervaded by the three poisons of greed, hatred, and ignorance. It seems that formerly the experts could put words together artistically and sing them to beautiful music. Already in his time, Sakya Pandita noticed that singers just learned the chants, but could not compose good poetry. He foretells that in the future, when decay sets in, singers will only be able to render simple songs of little content.[47]

Canzio notes "curiously this section does not refer to actual changes occurring in any aspects of the language but rather to the diminishing standards of musical composition and performance as time passes by."[48] Sakya Paṇḍita does not provide any specifics about whether it is the poetry of religious or secular song that exhibits the trend of decline. As such, we do not know whether the Chöd liturgical poetry would be included in his lament.

# 4

# The Chöd *Ḍamaru* Drum

## Symbolism, Function, and Variation in an Interpretive Community

### Introduction

In this chapter, we explore the function of music in Chöd ritual practices by investigating how meaningful functions are assigned to symbols and enacted in performance. Specifically, we examine the conceptualization of symbols as assigned to an important musical instrument (and ritual implement) used in the Chöd ritual, the *ḍamaru* drum. It will further the progression of the study of Chöd and the role of the *ḍamaru* to learn how the drum is symbolic, and how the symbolism is performatively enacted, that is, how the symbolism is produced in this tantric meditation practice. Furthermore, we revisit an important notion in Ellingson's seminal discussion of the Chöd *ḍamaru* (Dorjé and Ellingson 1979) that a variety of interpretations may be attributed to a single instrument in the same tantric practice by different scholar-practitioners. Taking Ellingson's discussion of the *ḍamaru* commentary by Gyürmé Losel ('gyur med blo gsal) a step further, we look at specific differences between individual lamas' interpretations of the *ḍamaru* symbolism in the same tradition, examining areas of agreement and variation. This highlights the ethnographic encounter with living traditions whereby a closer level of engagement with tantric ritual practices (than Buddhologists have been expected to undertake) allows scholars to focus on the contingencies of difference and sameness. We examine the incorporation of difference and doctrine and the balancing of personal performance style with meditation practice. By studying the performance practices that lamas and musical directors or *umdzé* (*dbu mdzad*) employ in one tantric ritual tradition, such as the way the Chöd *ḍamaru* is played (its tempo, articulation, and directionality, etc.), we will offer a finer level of specific detail to *ḍamaru* symbolism and performance.

We will first revisit a unique article in the 1979 special "Tibet Issue" of the journal, *Asian Music*, which featured a traditional Tibetan Chöd master's written commentary on the symbolic elements and attributes of the ritual drum that is almost exclusively associated with the Tibetan Chöd musical-meditation practices.[1] Thirty-five years later, we pay homage to Rinjing Dorjé and Ter Ellingson's original work by expanding upon it following a multisite ethnographic study to see how practitioners link the Chöd *ḍamaru* drum's "outer" musical performance with its "inner" meditational practice through symbolic meaning, and how practitioners' meditative experiences and insights about symbolism are shared dynamically within an interpretive community.

## Symbolism and Interpretation in a Chöd Adept's Interpretive Community

In the Tibetan tantric ritual context, an individual adept's insights gained by engaging in meditation are considered to be a significant foundation for offering a unique expression or new interpretation of symbolism in a ritual practice. The lifestyle of the ascetic meditator in held in high esteem by Tibetan Buddhist practitioners, which may account for the high valuation granted to an individual practitioner's insights and interpretations within a given "interpretive community."[2] This is evidenced in the Chöd lineages' interpretive communities in which adepts will often contribute to the corpus of explanatory literature through written commentaries and oral discourses after meditating for extended periods on their own. A specific example of this process will be considered here with respect to the interpretation of the symbolism of one of the main instruments used almost exclusively in Chöd practice, the large *ḍamaru*[3] or hourglass-shaped drum, in a Tibetan author's written commentary and in the oral commentaries of living practitioners.

Ellingson finds that the interpretation of the symbolism of the Chöd *ḍamaru*, as offered by Gyürmé Losel, provides but one reading of many:[4]

> [W]e can see Blo gsal's treatise on the *ḍamaru* . . . as a brilliant individual contribution towards increasing the depth and mean-

> ingfulness of the experience of the Chöd practitioner through contemplation of one of the characteristic Chöd instruments. As such it is a valid "explanation" of the *ḍamaru* for those with the interests, abilities, and training to follow his approach. It is *not an explanation of the symbolism of the instrument which says the last word on the subject* and *admits of no alternative interpretations.* Like all Tibetan writings on music and other aspects of Buddhist practice, it represents *both* the "official" explanations received by the author through his lineage of teachers, which are valid for followers of that lineage's tradition, *and* the insights of the individual author [emphasis mine].[5]

An individual exponent of a ritual practice will interpret and creatively infuse a practice with insights from personal meditative experiences. Ellingson observes this in his study of the Chöd *ḍamaru* treatise by the Tibetan Chöd practitioner Gyürmé Losel, writing:

> None of these alternative symbolic meanings of the *ḍamaru* would be accepted as a simple statement of fact by all Tibetan Buddhists. *Someone studying 'Gyur med Blo gsal's special viewpoint* would disregard the other interpretations as irrelevantly simplistic . . . however, the interpretations are not mutually exclusive, for *a follower . . . might accept and use the other interpretations at different stages in his religious practice* [emphasis mine].[6]

Tibetologist Janet Gyatso similarly observes that an individual adept's meditative experiences are creatively articulated by the meditator themselves through the reflexive literary genre of the "spiritual autobiography" (*rnam thar*) in Tibetan Buddhism (Gyatso 1998).

## Context of the Chöd Interpretive Community

Through making this observation about the receptivity of difference among Tibetan practitioners themselves, it is possible to provide a more accurate portrayal of the social nexus between an individual adept's experience and that of their interpretive community.[7] To show how unrealistic it is to articulate a single monolithic reading of all the symbolic aspects of a ritual tradition such as Chöd, or any tantric tradition in the religious and social context of Tibetan Buddhism, it is not necessary to invoke postmodern theory with its attention to the constructed nature of traditions. Instead, the indigenous historical setting in which Buddhist monastic institutions and non-monastic ascetic traditions flourished across the Tibetan Plateau provides sufficient context for a consideration of the variations in the interpretations of symbolism in meditation ritual performance practices. Prior to 1959, Tibetan regions comprised an area roughly comparable to the size of Western Europe[8] and were sparsely populated with only six million inhabitants, about one-sixth of whom were ordained and among the literate and educated (predominantly male) elite. A huge number of monastic traditions were thriving in approximately six thousand monasteries across the Tibetan Plateau prior to the Cultural Revolution.[9] Along with monastic traditions were ascetic traditions such as Chöd that were practiced in hermitages, forests, caves, and modest dwellings.

## The Function of Symbols at Different Levels of Understanding

That there are different levels of interpretation attributable to a single symbolic implement or action is an inescapable fact that Ellingson is correct to highlight in his microstudy of the Tibetan Chöd *ḍamaru*. Ellingson asserts that symbolism functions on different levels as a ritual practitioner "reaches new levels" of "understanding":

> If, as Tibetan Buddhists maintain, the Buddhist teaching itself was *taught in different forms to suit the needs, abilities and inclinations of different persons*, so that each person will necessarily interpret the same things differently as his understanding reaches new levels, *then there must necessarily be different levels of interpretation for any particular symbol* [emphasis mine].[10]

The research finding from the present study shares with Ellingson's the insight that music *functions differently*, and is *experienced differently*, depending upon a practitioner's level of knowledge, ability, and understanding in meditation practice. Even when the Chöd practitioner reaches a level beyond the stage of the "beginner"—when musical competency is no longer an issue and the drumming performance and melodies are known and memorized—there is a protracted path toward reaching an "advanced" level, should an adept choose to spend the time and energy focusing on the practice to that end.

It is not only a far more realistic perspective to conceive of techniques in *ritual meditation practice* and *ritual musical performance* as graduated and acquired skills, but it is also the indigenous perspective on practice maintained by lamas in the various Chöd lineages of Tibetan Buddhism. Through the notion of differentiation (at the individual level)—whereby meditation practice *and* musical performance in a ritualized context may be considered in terms of skill level—the research problem ethnomusicologist Ricardo Canzio admitted to having may be heretofore avoided. The effect of Canzio's dissertation analysis was diluted by a substandard performance of a ritual because he had not yet accounted for the important notion of individual difference with respect to performance. Canzio writes,

> At the time of recording the ceremony and procuring the text and scores here presented, I had not developed a critical attitude towards its performance. Now, in retrospect, applying the knowledge acquired from a thorough analysis of the piece, I can see that the performance of the ceremony I recorded was not very polished or carefully rehearsed.[11]

Canzio notes in his conclusions that he did not realize early enough in his research process the significance of the extent of variations in skill between ritual performers. Canzio admits to his oversight, which necessarily affected his subsequent analysis. In sum, he apparently recorded ritual performances by individuals who were not the best exemplars of the tradition available.[12]

## Symbolism in Tibetan Buddhism

Robert Beer, an interdisciplinary scholar-artist who studies Tibetan Buddhist symbolism and iconography as employed in tantric rituals, explains that his use of the term "symbol" has a particular inflected meaning in terms of Tibetan Buddhist iconography:

> I have used the term "symbol" to refer to the intrinsic meanings ascribed to a particular object or attribute. A more accurate interpretation of this term should perhaps be "purity" as these

> attributes essentially represent the enlightened qualities or "purities" of the deities.[13]

Thupten Jinpa explains that the term "deity" itself requires qualification because it is "symbolic" in various ways. It can refer to a buddha, and is also

> used as a generic term to refer to "divine" representations visualized in a meditator's transformed states of consciousness. In a strict sense, a deity is nothing but the archetypal *symbol* of the perfected state of the meditator's own mind. In Tibetan Buddhism, the concept of the meditation deity is an essential element of the religious practice as the identification of one's own mind with the guru *and* one's meditation deity constitutes the core of a daily meditation [emphasis mine].[14]

Beer adds that in the Highest Yoga Tantras the meanings of symbols are multivalent at three levels such that the one visualized deity (e.g., Machik Labdrön), which represents all deities together (e.g., Machik Labdrön, Vajrayoginī, and Yum Chenmo as inseparably mixed), has yet another three levels of depth.

> In Vajrayāna [tantric] iconography the three levels of an outer, inner, and secret *symbolism* are sometimes given, particularly within the practices of the Highest Yoga Tantras. The depths of meaning concealed within these teachings are extremely profound and multifaceted. Like a wish-granting gem that refracts myriad rays of rainbow light, the nature of this light is one, although its aspects of illumination appear to be many [emphasis mine].

Ellingson observes that symbolic objects and meaningful actions are "synthesized" and layered in Chöd performance:

> The uniqueness of Chöd and the genius of Machik Labdrön and her followers is shown not so much in the individual elements of ideology, dramatization or use of ferocious imagery, as in the complex and powerful way in which all of these elements are synthesized in the Chöd ritual. In Chöd, every philosophical teaching is vividly dramatized, and every object and action of the ritual expresses both surface and deep meanings.[15]

Figure 4.1. Machik Labdrön (Ma gcig lab sgron, 1055–1153) holding two of the main Chöd instruments, the drum (*ḍamaru*) and Tibetan bell (*dril bu*); detail of a *thangka* from the author's private collection.

## Living Traditions, Living with Variations

Although some workers in religious studies, whose primary interest is the translation and interpretation of ritual texts, often adhere to a disciplinary practice of providing singular readings of rituals,[16] Beer claims that the variations of interpretation in symbolic meaning are *de rigueur* for a living tradition with multiple lineages. He writes,

> [t]hroughout the texts, I have also used the terms "often, usually, frequently, generally, and traditionally" to refer to particular symbolic definitions or descriptions. The use of these terms does not stem from an uncertainty about a symbol's meaning or depiction, but from the fact that these symbols often have iconographical *variations* according to *different* traditions or lineages.[17]

Anthropologists are well aware of such differences but are only "slowly" coming to deal with the fact that "people [are] employing multiple, contradictory symbolic classifications at the same time." They maintain that this leads some anthropologists who investigate deeply into a single tradition to admit, "it is with cognitive-symbolic contradictions of this kind (not either/or, but both/and) that anthropology has come slowly to recognize it must deal."[18]

Before considering some specific examples of differentiation in the Chöd ritual, we will turn first to the concept of symbolic meaning in anthropology.

## Symbolic Anthropology: Some Historical Considerations in Ritual Interpretation

An historical trend of examining the variation of meaning in symbols and practices has long existed in anthropological thought. Whereas in the French school of anthropology Durkheim, and Mauss after him, fostered the cross-cultural comparative method as "armchair ethnographers" (and therefore did not focus upon internal cultural differences). In the British school of anthropology, Max Gluckman sought to understand the forces that create social stability versus those that generate social change. Gluckman's work built upon Radcliff-Brown's notion of social structure, but turned away from the idea that such structures were static and atemporal, focusing instead on the dynamics of social control and change in South Africa. He focused on ritual performances because of their ability to sublimate and minimize conflict, and called them rituals of "rebellion." He said these were "release valves" for any social order observing that they became so within the context of ritual performance.[19]

Victor Turner, one of Gluckman's best-known students, also pursued process-oriented ethnographic research on social organization among the Ndembu of Zambia. Turner focused on the social role of symbols and the ways in which material culture and belief practices were (re)established or negotiated in the ritual process.[20] Following Gluckman, Turner became the top figure in British symbolic anthropology and therefore his work and his insights are unavoidable when engaged in the study of ritual as a locus of interpretation.

## Indigenous Variation in the Interpretation of Symbols

The examination of difference in the interpretation of ritual symbols within a given dominant cultural framework inspired Victor Turner's ethnographic monograph *The Forest of Symbols: Aspects of Ndembu Ritual* (1967). In this study, he inscribes his ethnographic exploration of the white *mudyi* tree, a multivalent symbol for the Ndembu. Depending on the ritual, the tree symbolically evokes (1) milk, (2) the kinship bonds between mothers and their children, (3) the continuity of kin relations between generations, or (4) the gendered difference between females and males. Turner writes,

> [w]e can see how the same dominant symbol, which in one kind of ritual stands for one kind of social group or for one principle of organization, in another kind of ritual stands for another kind of group or principle, and its aggregate of meanings stands for unity and continuity of the widest Ndembu society, embracing its contradictions.[21]

Turner notes that the meaning of ritual symbols may vary "between the normative elements in social life and the individual." These differences in interpretations of symbols may be collected for analytical purposes "from widest to narrowest significant action context."[22] As an interpretive anthropologist centering on ritual analysis, Turner writes that to conduct his analysis he will "[D]iscuss the semantic structure and properties of some of the principal symbols found in Ndembu ritual" (ibid.). Turner further suggests that "Each kind of ritual may be regarded as a configuration of symbols, a sort of 'score' in which the symbols are the notes. The symbol is the smallest unit of specific structure in Ndembu ritual."[23]

## Some Variations: The Symbolic "Notes" in Chöd

Turner's analogy of reading a "configuration of symbols" in a ritual as a musical "score" is helpful to consider with respect to musical symbolism in the Chöd ritual. Regarding the symbols as "notes" suggests that intentional thought inflects symbolic meaning. The melodies of the Chöd rituals have strong harmonic implications, which means every note and its attendant performance gesture in this genre has a meaningful inflection associated with a tonal area, and this can be felt in the process of singing. Moreover, each note sung is heard in relation to its neighboring notes within a musical phrase, and each phrase is heard in relation to the whole verse. Symbolic movements in the melodies—ascending and descending contours, sequences, repeated and elongated pitches, and climactic phrase breaks—are shown to have significant meaning in the context of the written liturgy. Nearly every one of the syllables in the poetically symbolic melody is punctuated with the rhythmically supportive Tibetan bell and *ḍamaru*. As such, the melody and rhythm have a quasi-trance-inducing *ostinato* flow.

## Symbolism in Tibetan Ritual

Ellingson made an important contribution to studies of Tibetan ritual music by explaining that the total symbolic meaning of music is greater than the sum of all audible parts. He claims that practitioners may concurrently experience *actual performed* music on the one hand together with *imagined* music on the other.

> This inclusion in the concept of ritual music, of music that is mentally produced but not physically present, implies that, from a performer's perspective, the whole of the music offered in a given performance is always more than the sum of its audible parts. Furthermore, not only is the "music" substantially different from the sounds heard, it is also *different in different ways for each individual performer!* Such concepts pose a special kind of problem for external observers who center their attention on physical observation and measurements [emphasis mine].[24]

There may be variations between Chöd lamas' interpretations in the same lineage, each possessing a wide range of abilities and training in the interpretations of symbolism of musical instruments and musical gestures as well as sung melodies. Through the Chöd initiation, disciples receive an initial lineage transmission of the tradition from a qualified lama. Following this, there may be tens or hundreds (or even thousands) of disciples whose insights are specific and personal. In an interpretive community, several respected exponents may be reading different written commentaries on Chöd practice and having different meditative experiences at the same time. Since they may share these experiences with their disciples, telling them what occurred, there is a repertoire of symbolic meanings that an individual apprentice exponent will "inherit" from her personal lama and the lineage lamas whose commentaries she reads. Each will select from these to meaningfully enhance her own meditation practices in accordance with her level and disposition.

One Chöd lama described an experience in which a melody came to him while reciting a mantra. He attributed this insight to the blessing of the ḍākinīs. He had this experience during a retreat focused on a meditation deity in preparation for giving his disciples the initiation that gives them permission to engage in the practice. Later, in the setting of the initiation ritual, he told his disciples how the melody came to him, and transmitted the melody orally/aurally so his disciples could sing and take part in the experience of this blessing gift of the ḍākinīs through the medium of the lama. Advanced practitioners recognize such experiences of lamas as significant and find them to be personally transformative. For beginner lay practitioners, such experiences that occur during practice may be very inspiring, although there is a caveat. Most students would not know whether to acknowledge such "signs" as the blessings of the ḍākinīs, or to attribute them to the play of *nāgas* or malevolent spirits.[25] This is why students new to Chöd are instructed to consult with their lama if "signs" occur. In this respect, an important textual source to consult is Machik Labdrön's commentary on the interpretation of "signs."

## Chöd Performance Traditions: Variation and Stability

To what extent is the core meaning of Chöd stable? Is there a sliding scale between those aspects of the Chöd ritual that have stability and those that are negotiated? My approach to this issue is informed by my dialogic ethnographic encounter involving interactions with lamas in the Chöd Tradition as well as students who are Tibetan monks, lay Tibetans, and lay non-Tibetans.

## Relative Stability of the Chöd Tradition

Which aspects of the Chöd performance tradition are considered stable, and which are subject to variance and may be negotiated? Is there a core stable belief about what the purpose of Chöd practice is supposed to obtain for the adept? There are differences in three main categories that are drawn here as concentric circles (though they might be best understood in three dimensions as spheres)[26] with increasing opportunity for varied interpretation as the circles of variance emanate from the core beliefs (see figure 4.2):

A. Core meaning of Chöd

Across all Tibetan Buddhist traditions and lineages, Chöd means "cutting off" the mental habit of *bdag 'dzin ma rig pa* (self-grasping ignorance) to attain the mind state of *bdag med rtogs pa'i shes rab* (wisdom of realizing selflessness, or identitylessness).

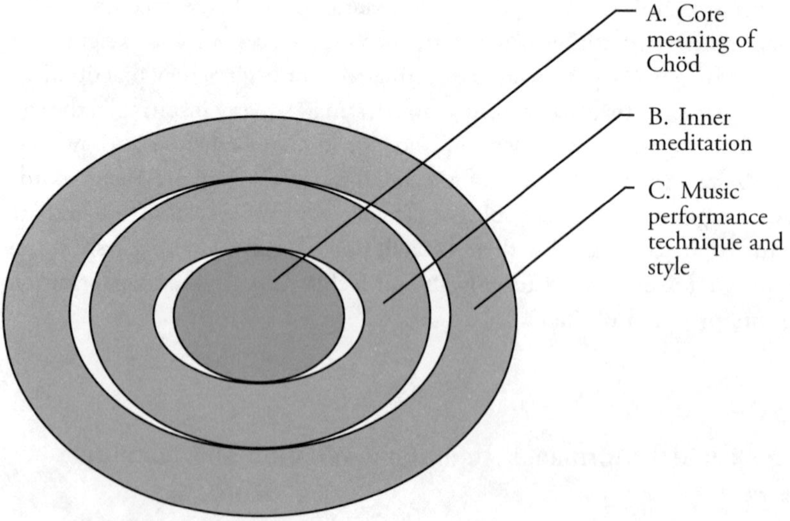


Figure 4.2. Relative stability of tradition: Core beliefs and the extent of variation.

B. Inner meditation

All Tibetan Buddhist traditions maintain that the "inner method" is practicing Chöd with an attitude of renunciation conjoined with the altruistic intentionality of the Mahāyāna path and the insight of "emptiness," the realization of the truth of mutual interdependence (lack of self-existence) of all phenomena.[27]

C. Music performance technique and style

Performance techniques and styles are taught according to a Chöd sādhana liturgy. In addition, factors such as pedagogy, transmission, an adept's interpretation of the symbolism, and the size and shape of the instruments may affect performance.

## Sources of Symbolic Interpretation: Oral Testimony and Texts

Practitioners place a high value on the cultural sameness and cohesiveness of the core meaning of Chöd across the four schools of Tibetan Buddhism (and Bön), each of which maintain Chöd practice lineages. However, individual exponents vary to some extent in their personal approaches to practice, pedagogy, and musical performance. Within the Chöd lineage that I studied most closely (Ganden Chöd lineage), there are slight variances between lamas' symbolic interpretations, even among those who share the same Chöd teachers. That is, even within one tradition of initiates in the same lineage of teachings there are some differences! It is through investigating multiple voices and subjectivities that a holistic picture of a musical tradition takes shape. An ethnographic study of a ritual music tradition can include the experiences of multiple exponents, their various talents and preferences, interpretative insights, and other internal diversities germane to establishing a complete portrait of a tradition. As well, the ethnographic methodology helps to debunk the misshapen notion that a particular ritual music tradition stands as a monolithic or static feature of Tibetan Buddhist culture coupled with a definitive interpretation of symbolic meaning and performance style merely because (1) there is a written liturgy, and (2) recordings of the performance of that liturgical text are in circulation.

With respect to the author's personal experience, it would be appropriate here to disclose my background of study into the Chöd Tradition as it might illuminate some of the benefits of the kind of anthropological approach (which implies participant observation and fieldwork) I undertook, particularly as it manifests in an ethnomusicological project of teacher–disciple transmission, quite similar to the *guru-śiṣyā paramparā* method of transmission in many South Asian classical music *gharānā* traditions. In my case, I was fortunate to apprentice for over twelve years to Ven. Pencho Rabgey, a Tibetan-Canadian elder and former monk of twenty-seven years who taught me both the meditative visualization instructions and musical practices. My research/study method of apprenticeship afforded me several opportunities to see and experience such variances up close.

I had received the Chöd initiation from the head of the Ganden Chöd lineage, His Eminence Khalkha Jetsun Dampa Rinpoché[28] (hereafter Khalkha Rinpoché) in 1995, and my close apprenticeship with Ven. Pencho Rabgey began in 1997. The *ḍamaru* instructions and music training I received from Pala were singularly valuable since he was previously a music director (*dbu mdzad*) and an experienced pedagogue (see figures 4.4, 4.5, and 8.1).

## Performance Practice: Training in the *Ḍamaru* Drum

Khalkha Rinpoché's oral instructions to Chöd initiates on the *ḍamaru* were pointed, and clearly connect *ḍamaru* performance to the "proper" singing of melodies. "It is important to learn how to use the *ḍamaru*; and it will help you to sing and produce proper melodies."[29] At an initiation and teaching of 36 beginner students, many of whom had not had prior training in the *ḍamaru* and melodies, Khalkha Rinpoché illustrated the importance of learning the instruments and singing by performing one verse (verse 50) from the Chöd sādhana, "Dedicating the Illusory Body" (Tib. *sGyu lus tshogs su sngo ba*).[30] After providing this example, he then said:

> The verse I just sang concerns "the four seals of phenomena." When you sing this you can contemplate the meaning; otherwise, if you do not know how to use the *ḍamaru* or to sing, it is difficult to have the realizations while chanting . . . When you sing, meditate on it at the same time like this, line by line. The first line of verse 51 says, "I will not create non-virtues." The second line of the verse says, "I will only have virtuous thoughts." These verses are profound, and once you have learned them you can really concentrate upon them.[31]

With a reasoned approach to learning the *ḍamaru* in order to have realizations "at the same time" as one is performing, Khalkha Rinpoché insists upon building a solid musical foundation that can support meditative experiences. Rinpoché advocates concentrating on the verses in order to have realizations "while chanting." But being able to do so begins with knowing how to use the *ḍamaru* and how to sing. Echoing Rinpoché's explicit reference to having "realizations" *while performing*, Ven. Pencho Rabgey has said that the visualizations are the most important part of the Chöd practice, and the primary avenue for transforming the mind from an egotistical, self-centered engagement with one's environment to being other-focused.

Figure 4.3. His Eminence the Ninth Khalkha Jetsun Dampa Rinpoché, Jampel Namdröl Chökyi Gyaltsen (1932–2012), head of the Ganden Chöd lineage.

## Musical Priorities: The Order in Which to Learn Musical Aspects

Khalkha Rinpoché prioritized learning the *ḍamaru* as a key element of the ritual practice. "It is important to learn the *ḍamaru* first, before the tunes. This is not the fast method, but we have a different purpose, and we do it slowly."[32] Like Khalkha Rinpoché, Ven. Pencho Rabgey emphasized the primacy of the *ḍamaru* in the context of performance. To gain competency in the instrument, I spent between three to four hours per day for one month practicing the *ḍamaru* in order to get it solidly in my hand, wrist, and arm. Pala said, "You have to make friends with your *ḍamaru*." He explained that each *ḍamaru* is different in its weight, shape, diameter, width, tautness of skins, beater string length, and adornments. We often traded *ḍamarus* during my training so that I learned how to adapt my performance technique to a drum of a different size and weight, beater string length, width and torque, and so forth. He reskinned the *ḍamaru* and sewed new beaters on the drums of several students in the "Chöd Club" of a Tibetan Buddhist Center in Toronto, Canada, for which I served as volunteer music director for 10 years (2000–2010). One student found that Pala's work on her *ḍamaru* skin and beaters markedly improved the way she played. Her performance on the instrument thereafter was seamless, and she was arguably one of the best performers of the *ḍamaru* I have taught.

### *Tempo*

Music performance practice is tied to the practitioner's effort in meditation. To meditate most effectively and "soak up" the practice, Rinpoché advises to maintain a slow tempo:

> When you learn to sing properly it will help you to meditate properly on the subject. If you go slowly, you can contemplate and focus upon the meaning more than is possible if you go very quickly through the words.[33]

Pala would start the sādhana at an extremely slow pace, such that I could learn to rotate the *ḍamaru* slowly enough to make the beaters sound. Initially, the beaters often flopped awkwardly beside my wrist. I noticed that the combined gestures of the arm, wrist, and fingers have to be carefully articulated in order to perform the *ḍamaru* slowly. To play slowly I had to rotate my wrist all the way in and out, and swing my arm out away from my body and back toward my chest. Otherwise the beaters would not swing upward properly and strike the skins.[34]

Pala also incorporated a technique by which he would sing using a moderate tempo but pause after each sung line of poetry while continuing to play several rhythmic cycles. He explained:

> This allows time to think about every meditative visualization described in the text. The words come too quickly. As soon as you are saying one meditation instruction, another one is coming along right away before you have a chance to think of the previous one. Most practitioners do not take this time, but my teacher did this and I do as well. This is the best way for me, because I can think carefully about the meditation and practice more deeply. Maybe you can go quickly through, but I need to go slowly and think about it. Of course, when you are performing in a group, you have to match everyone else, so that requires a different approach.[35]

*Group Performance Aesthetics*

All the Ganden Chöd lamas I have studied with, and groups I have practiced with, agree that the ideal aesthetic result of group performance is to sound as if one *ḍamaru* is playing. Khalkha Rinpoché prescribes the performance ideal for group Chöd practice as follows:

> If all of you learn the *ḍamaru* and melodies, then although there are thirty people playing, it will sound like one. Otherwise there are some people not keeping time, swinging the *ḍamarus* in different ways and so forth. (Khalkha Rinpoché 1996, 8)

Another reason for playing all the instruments in synchronicity, swinging the *ḍamarus* in the same way and keeping time, is its potential to inspire faith and interest in the practice among its observers. Conversely, if the instruments are swinging in various directions, this serves as a distraction from the spiritual experience, potentially discrediting the teacher and the effectiveness of the Dharma.[36]

*Purpose*

Khalkha Rinpoché spoke about the importance of singing in Chöd meditation practice:

> The purpose is to make one's mind peaceful; when you sing these verses to gods and ghosts you are giving the gift of Dharma. You need to know that the essence of Chöd practice is how to subdue the mind, and how to practice conventional *bodhicitta* and then ultimate *bodhicitta*.[37]

The former head of the Ganden Chöd Tradition, Kyabje Zong Rinpoché, said, "When we play the *ḍamaru* it should be played softly." Zong Rinpoché's performance ideal is closer to that of the aesthetic principle outlined by Atiśa for Dharma music. It should be "beautiful sounding instrumental music that overpowers the mind . . . and melodies . . . that are beautiful, and yet have a meaning."[38]

*Symbolism of Sound and Material*

Zong Rinpoché's oral commentary on the sound production of the *ḍamaru* is important to consider:

> The sound of the *ḍamaru*, being a product, should remind us of impermanence, and therefore emptiness, whereas the two sides of the drum and the two pellets should remind us of the inseparability of conventional and ultimate truth.[39]

This authoritative commentary by the former head of the Ganden Chöd Tradition is extremely valuable, although it is highly condensed. Some elucidation may be useful. Rinpoché connects the musical instrument's sound production with the adept's meditations on the impermanence not only of sound, but also of all physical and psychophysical phenomena. Meditations on impermanence, in turn, help the practitioner recall their meditations on the selflessness (lack of inherent existence) of phenomena, and the fact that a *produced* phenomenon is necessarily interdependent. Rinpoché associates a sacred instrument's material construction, its musical performance, and the practicing adept's meditative visualizations at a deeper level than mere surface symbolism. By declaring the aspects of meditative practice that the *ḍamaru's* (1) sound production and (2) mechanical parts "should remind us of," he is, in effect, explaining the functional purpose of symbolism in the ritual context: the direct applicability of various aspects of experience to personal transformation. The "two sides of the drum and the two pellets" are to be seen as reminders of their conventional purpose and their ultimate nature as interdependent causal links in sound production. Eventually the practitioner can associate this single instance of interdependence with the pervasiveness of mutual interdependence of all phenomena, and thereby understand the causes and conditions that produce suffering in order to eradicate it from one's experience. By "cutting" the grasping onto the "self" of any and all phenomena as "truly existent," one's exaggerated projections upon things that are actually in a process of changing, becoming, and deteriorating will vanish. This is why an understanding of the three root delusions—attachment, anger, and ignorance—is so important for the practitioner to develop. Buddhist teachings instruct that so long as we remain without a depth of knowledge of the way things actually exist, we are driven habitually to mentally grasp onto phenomena as if they were permanent and attainable. We are impelled by this ignorance to shift from one obsession to another, without pause to consider the underlying reasons for our dissatisfaction.[40] In summary, playing the *ḍamaru* in accordance with Rinpoché's instructions on what its sound and construction "should remind us of," as explained here, provides a great depth of meaning to Chöd practice.

### *Treatment of Instruments*

On the question of where and how to keep the Chöd *ḍamaru*, Khalkha Rinpoché was clear: "We keep the Chöd drum in a case and only use it at night." In Gelugpa Tibetan Buddhist monasteries *ḍamarus* are kept very secret and are never exhibited. It is believed that calling attention to a sacred spiritual practice invites the possibility of obstacles arising. When I visited Kusho Kundeling in Bylakuppe, Karnataka, South India, despite his fame with the Chöd Tradition, and his frequent teaching, he had kept his drum wrapped in its cloth case and hidden in a corner of a lower cabinet in his bedroom, which he had his assistant retrieve due to his restricted hip and leg movement resulting from his diabetic condition. In fact, I saw this protocol of concealing adhered to by every Chöd lama I encountered, and it is likewise expected of disciples, such that the drum not be exhibited except when it is brought out to practice. One modification to the care and concealment of the *ḍamaru* is illustrated by an innovation started by the community of Chöd practitioners in Canada with whom I spent time studying and practicing. They use empty cylindrical metal tins of Danish butter cookies as an extra protective environment for the *ḍamaru*, lest it be accidentally dropped. I was gifted such a metal tin, and it provides the ideal protective shield for my drum.

*Instrument Construction*

Variations in instrument construction constitute a discussion of nuances for different possibilities with respect to performance and meditation practice. The instrument's

> striking-pellets or "suspended strikers" (*rgyag btags*) are roughly egg-shaped pellets . . . suspended by cords long enough to reach the center of either drumskin from diametrically opposite points on the waistband.[41]

An innovation by Ven. Pencho Rabgey in his construction of the *ḍamaru* has the holes for the suspended cloth cords emerge not at "diametrically opposite points on the waistband" that bisects the two halves of the hourglass drum, using clockface coordinates at 9:00 and 3:00, but rather closer to 9:30 and 2:30 (the handle at 6:00). An additional innovation is to ensure that the length of cord can "reach the center of either drumskin" from the point at which the pellet emerges from the suspending cord (see figure 4.4). Given that pellets may be between one and two centimeters in width and

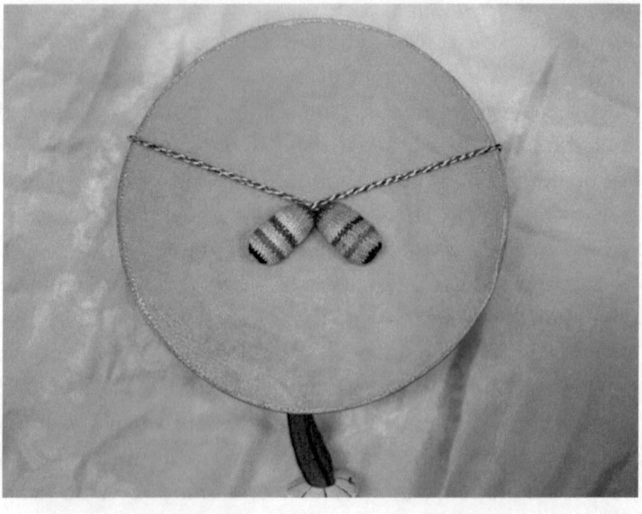

Figure 4.4. Position of the Chöd *ḍamaru's* suspended pellets and length of the strings, as modified by Ven. Pencho Rabgey.

two to five centimeters in length, the measurement of string length is an important consideration. Ven. Pencho Rabgey has experimented and finds that measuring the string length in this way provides a slightly longer string, which maximizes the possibility of playing the *ḍamaru* with slow rotation; and, as many recipients of his improved *ḍamaru* drums have noticed, the slower the rotation the slower can be the singing, which allows more time for meditation. Of course, the converse is also true. If the "suspended cords" are too short, then the rotation of the *ḍamaru* must be faster in order to make them sound. It follows that if the tempo of the *ḍamaru* is faster, so must be the melody; and therefore the experience of meditating upon the meanings of the liturgical poetry is more rushed.

Thus, the details of the *ḍamaru* construction and its performance affect the quality of meditation practice. The place from which the suspended cords emerge from the waistband, the length of the cords, and the size of the pellets affect not only the ease of *ḍamaru* performance (a slower rotation), and a softer sound (the beaters ideally strike the drum about halfway between the center and the rim, rather than at the center), but also the tempo of meditation.[42]

### *Hand Position and Performing Technique*

Pala instructed me to balance the drum vertically in such a way that as I turned my arm away from my body, I could turn my wrist, and twist my fingers, balancing both sides perpendicular to the floor. I found that I was holding the drum in five places with (1) the index finger's outer side (as if pointing ahead), (2) the inner pad of the thumb, and (3) the middle finger folded with the flat area of the digit between the first and second knuckle all touching the wood at the bottom of the drum. To hold the handle, (4) the right side of the right hand below the pinky finger pushes against an ornament fastened to the brocade, giving a tighter fit between the base of the drum and the ornament, and (5) the ring finger and pinky lightly squeeze the handle.

Yet this manner of holding the *ḍamaru* may be changed in dependence upon another drum of a different shape and size. As Ellingson observes, "performing traditions ordinarily play the [small] *ḍamaru* by movement only of the thumb and forefinger. However, since the *ḍamaru* used in Chöd is so large, it is usually played by oscillating the whole hand."[43]

With a larger drum and a wider girth between the two hemisphere halves of the drum, a different grip is possible—with two fingers (the index and middle finger) used to balance the weight of the drum against the thumb on the other side of the handle. Special modifications may be made to some instruments since the practicality of comfort in playing is prioritized. One student practitioner with a wide hand, and playing a *ḍamaru* with a narrow space between the two hemispheres, was assisted by a fellow practitioner who is an engineer with a woodshop. She widened the waist of the *ḍamaru* for him to increase his comfort. Some students who have been gifted a *ḍamaru* by their lama, or acquired their instruments through unique circumstances, may be reluctant to alter the instrument in any way, lest it lose the blessing from the original custodian with respect to the manner in which it was kept.

The rhythmic patterns associated with the Ganden Chöd performance ritual liturgy require a mellifluous arm movement. Ideally, this is generated by a lower back-originated arm movement that proceeds as follows: The elbow's position begins at a 45-degree angle to the torso, at 1:00 (if the body is visualized from overhead with 12:00 as the performer's position facing forward). The shoulder swings the arm outward to 3:00 at its side. As the arm is turning outward, the wrist turns out, and the thumb and index "forefinger" twist outward. On the way back in toward the torso, the shoulder leads the elbow first, with the wrist twisting inward, and so on, in reverse. If these micro-movements occur in succession, led by the arm, it allows a greater amount of time for the suspended beaters (pellets) to stay aloft. As discussed above, the slower tempo positively benefits the depth of the meditation.

## Case Study III: Manner of Performing the *Ḍamaru*— Four Contrasting Interpretations

It may not be surprising to the reader that Chöd *ḍamaru* performance practices vary among Ganden lineage lamas. With several widely accepted aspects of *ḍamaru* performance already touched upon, it will be instructive to also consider four contrastive interpretations of the symbolism attributed to the physical motion of the *ḍamaru*. First, Khalkha Rinpoché maintains that when performing the sādhana of the Ḍākinī lineage you must begin by swinging the *ḍamaru* in toward the body. And, according to the Ganden Ear-Whispered lineage, you begin by swinging away.[44]

Kusho Kundeling, the *umdzé* chosen by Zong Rinpoché to lead practices at *Kyirong* (*sKyid grong*) or "Happy Valley" in Tibet, appeared visibly pleased when, during our first interaction, I echoed Khalkha Rinpoché's interpretation, demonstrating that I understood that the Ḍākinī lineage drumming pattern is "out-in" and the Ganden Ear-Whispered lineage pattern is "in-out."[45]

Zong Rinpoché provides a third interpretation of the *ḍamaru's* motion in the Ganden Ear-Whispered lineage, saying, "[T]he *ḍamaru* should be played toward the body. This was suggested by a Drepung Monastery Geshé,[46] and Je Pha bong kha approved of this."[47] This is a fascinating statement, chiefly because the information about the direction of rotation is given in the form of an "approval" from an authoritative source. This suggests that the direction of the swinging motion of the *ḍamaru* had already been a matter of symbolic interpretation, and perhaps contention, by the time Zong Rinpoché allowed himself to be recorded when mentioning this in 1984.

A fourth interpretation of rotation of the *ḍamaru* is provided by Geshé Trinley (dGe bshes 'phrin las), Pala's first Chöd lama. He advised that in the Ganden "Ear-Whispered" lineage sādhana, *Dedicating the Illusory Body*, one could play the drum by swinging the arm "inward" (or "out-in," meaning the first beat and note of the melody is played furthest from the practitioner's torso) during the six preliminary practices until the end of the lineage prayer, all the while thinking that we are "taking in and receiving" blessings from the lineage lamas. During the second half of the ritual practice, while we are meditating upon giving our mentally transformed bodies away, we should be playing by swinging our arm "outward" (or "in-out" on the first beat and note of the melody) and feeling we are sending away to others all the good qualities and merits we possess.[48] Fellow student Chöd practitioners to whom I have relayed Geshé Trinley's symbolic interpretation of the swinging motion of the *ḍamaru* have expressed much enthusiasm upon hearing this, possibly adopting this symbolism into their own practice.

Thus, rather than thinking of the Chöd *ḍamaru* as a ritual implement that has solely sonic and material symbolic attributes, Geshé Trinley's interpretation adds a kinetic dimension. He offers another way to think symbolically that connects the physical action and gestures of the practitioner's drumming motion directly with the meditation practice. This is yet one more level of conceptualization that is provided to the adept to enhance their meditation experience while performing the ritual.

It is important to note that this symbolic aspect of drumming performance practice (i.e., its swinging motion)—not the instrument *itself*—is an aspect that goes without mention by Gyürmé Losel in his written commentary on the *ḍamaru* (as translated by Ellingson; Dorjé and Ellingson 1979). In fact, in all the Tibetan commentarial literature read for this project, I have not seen attention given to the direction of rotation of the *ḍamaru*. It seems that only the more fundamentally agreed upon aspects of performance are written about in the Tibetan commentaries, such as the two sides of the drum symbolizing conventional and ultimate *bodhicitta*.

Figure 4.5. Venerable Pencho Rabgey ("Pala") at his home in Canada, demonstrating how to practice with the *ḍamaru,* and the manner and role of drum performance at an introductory section of a Chöd liturgy when the rhythm "*ma dang, lha yi, kang dro*" is first sounded.

Figure 4.6. Ven. Pencho Rabgey practicing the Chöd sādhana, *Dedicating the Illusory Body.* While playing the *ḍamaru,* Pala subtly adjusts the drum's rotation with his right shoulder, wrist, hand, and fingers to make the two pellets meet the drum skins on specific sung syllables. Note the blurred motion of the pellets.

## Variations in Pedagogy

Learning to play the *ḍamaru* is a matter of significance in Chöd training and pedagogy. Pala revealed his method for teaching the *ḍamaru* some years after he began to train me. Sitting in his study, Pala told me:

> I taught you to play with the *ḍamaru* going 'out-in' first because it is harder. Now it will be much easier for you to play it going

> the other way." In genuine appreciation for his pedagogical technique, I thanked him and asked, "How did you know to do that?" He replied, "If no one tells you it is harder, then you don't know the difference. You try just as hard. If someone says, 'It's harder,' then you feel that is so." (Ven. Pencho Rabgey, personal communication, 1998)

Lama Thubten Yeshe (1935–1984), who was also a Chöd practitioner and a disciple of Kyabje Zong Rinpoché at Buxa Duar in Assam, India, said, "What your mind believes becomes reality for you, whether it is reality or not."[49] In a similar vein, Robert Beer writes,

> These teachings are perfectly integrated as they are . . . can be apprehended and understood by the human mind . . . wherein one ultimately realizes that the *Dharma* exists nowhere except in one's own mind, and that what one has been looking for is in reality what is actually looking.[50]

We may thus note the connection between imputed thought and symbolism, and how musical-meditation pedagogy proceeds in the practice of Chöd.

## *Valuing Difference* in a Tibetan Buddhist "Interpretive Community"

It must be emphasized here that recognizing this differential between individual exponents is an important step toward an advanced type of reading of Tibetan ritual that incorporates differentiation into the analytical research process. Thus, rather than providing an idealized version of the Chöd rite that glosses over divergences, nuances in an individual's practice may be recognized. Moreover, instead of presenting a monolithic reading of symbolically attributed aspects of performance, variations in internal and external aspects of Chöd practice may be validated. Variances may be noted and catalogued with respect to the symbolic attribution of music-related aspects of ritual such as individual instrument performance styles, ascribed symbolism of instruments and their component parts, ritual hand gestures (*mudras*), *mantras*, dance steps, and the vocalized chanting (*dbyangs*) and singing (*rta*). Through such a perspective, additional areas of research may be opened up in the ethnomusicological study of Tibetan tantric ritual. A comparative study could investigate, in a complementary fashion, individual adepts who have quite varied approaches to ritual performance and yet who may be students of the same "root lama," or have been trained in the same village monastery, residence house, or monastic college or dratsang (*grwa tshang*).[51] Particularized studies enhance the overview organological research already done by such scholars as Helffer (1989, 1994).[52]

## *Valuing Expertise*: The Music Director (*umdzé*)

The most helpful Western scholarship on Tibetan ritual music has been done by scholars working closely with the best-trained indigenous ritual masters who serve as "music director" or *umdzé* (*dbu mdzad*). Ellingson takes to task ethnomusicologists and Tibetologists working in Tibetan ritual music when they have failed to disclose the name of the *umdzé* with whom they studied and from whom they gleaned interpretive data. In a review essay of recordings of Tibetan ritual music, including performances of a song attributed to the poet-saint Milarepa, Ellingson writes, "We are glad to see—for the first time in any Tibetan recording—the name of an *dbu mdzad* 'Omzela' identified here" (Ellingson 1981, 139).[53] This is a sarcastic remark because the actual name of the *umdzé* is, in fact, *not* given; "Omzela" is only the phonetically rendered Tibetan title *umdzé* with which everyone is to address the "music director" (with the honorific suffix "-la") due to his official monastic appointment.[54]

In contrast to the negligent ethnographic practice that Ellingson highlights, Yael Bentor dedicates her published dissertation to the *umdzé* who assisted her most.[55] Yet, while her study provides a comprehensive outline of the structure of rituals, she does not delve deeply into issues surrounding the performance of ritual music. Unfortunately, to date, most studies of Buddhist tantric ritual, like Bentor's, have been conducted without ethnomusicological analysis. They also overlook that which may be garnered through musical analysis and a performance perspective. Because of this persistent gap in the literature on Tibetan ritual, it is hoped that the present work, although focused primarily on the Chöd ritual, can outline some of the important matters, such as (1) the high valuation of an individual adept's experiences and interpretations within an interpretive community of Buddhist practitioners, and (2) the differing levels of interpretation of symbolic meaning that may serve as meditation tools depending on an individual practitioner's level of understanding. These are issues that may be brought into the light and considered by Buddhist Studies scholars in subsequent research.

# 5

# Mantric Utterance in Chöd

Scholars generally agree that mantras are sacred syllables, transmitted from master to disciple, often ostensibly unintelligible, which are recited in a strictly controlled ritual context from which they derive their esoteric meaning.[1]

—Donald S. Lopez Jr., Professor of Buddhist and Tibetan Studies

## Symbolic Utterance: Significance of Mantra in Chöd

Mantra recitation, a key component of guru-deity yoga in Highest Yoga Tantra practices such as Chöd, has several functions; one of which is that it establishes the karmic imprints for the attainment (*siddhi*) of enlightened speech. In the sādhana, *Dedicating the Illusory Body*, the syllable *phaṭ* is one of only three mantras sounded in this ritual, though each is derived from the *Prajñāpāramitā Sūtra*.[2] The mantric syllable *phaṭ* is used in various ways. Mainly, it is recited in order to clear away obstacles, but it is also uttered to move the adept's consciousness upward through the body's central channel (Skt. *avadhūtī*, Tib. *rtsa dbu ma*). Furthermore, it is common for each of the meditation subritual sections of a Chöd sādhana to begin with the utterance of a single, soft "*phaṭ*." As such, recitation of this single-syllable mantra precedes singing each new melody. When uttered in this context, it is referred to as "*tsam chöd phaṭ*" (Tib. *tsam gcod phaṭ*). In terms of the manner of performance, "*tsam chöd phaṭ*" is meant to be said calmly and without intentional force, and it is considered to be an effective way of clearing away obstacles before beginning a new subritual section within the sādhana. Depending on the circumstances the practitioner encounters during the practice, there are other ways in which to perform this mantric utterance. Chöd commentators warn against reciting *phaṭ* with undue bravado, brashness, suddenness, or too loudly. It is meant to be uttered softly, and to trail away after the initial expression of the aspirated "*phaṭ*," which is generally pronounced "pé," or "pay" with an aspirated "p," as in "pay down karmic debt." It is said that reciting the mantra with excessive vigor may harm or even kill weak and fragile beings.

## The Mantric Syllable *Phaṭ*

In order to illustrate the importance of the functions of the mantric syllable *phaṭ* in Chöd meditation practice, let us first outline its role in the "transfer of consciousness," a practice that is situated at the structural center of the sādhana and the Chöd ritual experience. Table 2.3 illustrates that, structurally, the link between the preliminary practices and the actual ritual of the Chöd sādhana, *Dedicating the Illusory Body*, is the "transference of consciousness" or "*phowa*" (Tib. *'pho ba*) practice, during which this mantric syllable is uttered. Preceding this is the descending of nectar from the mantric syllable *Āḥ* from Yum Chenmo's heart, which purifies the practitioner's body, speech, and mind, and thus prepares the body for offering and giving away. As Zong Rinpoché says, "The descent of nectar from *Āḥ* marks the end of the preliminaries to Chöd practice."[3] The "transference of consciousness" section of Chöd practice is performatively guided by the recitation of the mantric syllable *phaṭ*. Additionally, this syllable is significant in other ways throughout a Chöd sādhana liturgy and ritual process, as will be demonstrated below.

### *Moving the Subtle Consciousness: Tantric Meditation on the Dying Process*

Practitioners of the Highest Yoga Tantras learn, as one of their main techniques, how to control their mind's activities during the dying process. By guiding the mind through death, the "intermediate state" (*bar do*) and rebirth, practitioners can mentally determine the manner of their subsequent rebirth.[4]

> It is said that the best practitioner of Highest Yoga Tantra is one who can attain complete enlightenment within this lifetime; the intermediate level practitioner attains complete enlightenment in the intermediate state; the inferior level practitioner attains complete enlightenment in a future life. Practitioners in the

two latter categories are taught the practice of transference of consciousness.[5]

It is vital to debunk the notion that "reincarnation" is an ability, experience, or "mystical" process reserved for Tibetan yogis alone. Quite the contrary, Buddhists maintain that all sentient beings reincarnate. That is, just as it is certain that all beings must eventually pass from this life, it is certain that they will take rebirth. Advanced practitioners can control this process of rebirth in order to be born where and when they discern they can be of most benefit to others. Thus, for example, the Indian yogi who passed in India and was reborn in Tibet as Machik Labdrön had the ability to control his rebirth, as well as the clairvoyance to see the benefit that would accrue if he transferred his consciousness from his body at that time and took rebirth in Tibet.[6]

It is important to note that "beings" (*sems can*)[7] are also referred to in Tibetan language as "transmigrators" (*'gro ba*). According to Tibetan Buddhist tradition, following the demise of the current life's body, a being will be reborn, but may—depending upon their karma—"transmigrate" between the six realms of existence when they take rebirth. Those with a net accumulation of positive karmic merit may ensure a rebirth in one of the three upper realms, while those with an accumulation of negative karma greater than their positive karmic imprints will take rebirth in one of the three lower realms.[8] One of the meditations leading to appreciating the fortune of a human birth,[9] which is considered to be the most opportune realm in which to take rebirth, is thinking over what one's life would be like in the eighteen hot or cold hells.[10]

Controlling the dying process involves meditating on the dissolution of the body's elements, which successively dissolve into one another, beginning with earth, which dissolves into water, then fire, wind and, finally, space.[11] Familiarizing oneself over many years with the experience of these elements dissipating and draining from the body is said to be essential in order to be prepared for the moment of one's actual death. Tibetan Buddhist adepts maintain that "clinical death" is the ceasing of the gross mind which includes the gross level of sensorial consciousness. However, the deepest subtle mind remains with the body in such a way as to enable the practitioner to continue in meditation.[12]

Tibetan Buddhist practitioners claim that some advanced yogic practitioners are able to maintain a very fine manipulation of the deepest, most subtle level of consciousness in a state of meditation during the "clear light" experience in death. It is documented that the Fourteenth Dalai Lama's Senior Tutor, Kyabje Yongzin Ling Rinpoché (1903–1983), was in such a state for thirteen days following what Western medical science refers to as "clinical death." The body remained fresh and did not begin to decompose or smell. As the Fourteenth Dalai Lama explains,

> [B]efore you go through the first stage of subtle dissolution, white appearance, the karmic links between your physical body and the gross levels of mind have already been severed. Your physical body can no longer function as the basis for your gross levels of mind. So clinically speaking, the person is dead at the point when the air dissolves into consciousness, just before the white appearance. Until then, although the karmic link between the body and the mind has been severed, the *self* of the person is still within that old body.
>
> The body may not decompose when the person is in the clear light. Some people can remain in that stage for a week, or some, twenty-two days. This has actually happened in India. For example, the late Kyabje Ling Rinpoché, my tutor, remained for thirteen days in the state of clear light. His body remained very fresh. This consciousness, the very subtle consciousness, is the *self* or consciousness and carries on into the next life. Consciousness is already completely independent of the body. Therefore, it can move . . . This explanation has been based on the system of the Highest Yoga Tantra.[13] [emphasis mine]

Cases such as this are rare, as a high level of practice and extensive training are required to achieve this level of control of one's own mind. However, some cases of a controlled dying process are reported each year. In 2004, Sermey Khensur Lobsang Tharchin (Ser med mkhan zur blo bzang mthar phyin) was observed remaining in such a state for five days.[14]

According to the Indian mahāsiddhas, for the Highest Yoga Tantra practitioners, death is a valuable opportunity for meditation.

> Nāgārjuna and Āryadeva in their commentaries on tantra and in their quintessential instructions, elucidate the techniques by which the practitioner can utilize these natural stages of death, intermediate state, and rebirth for higher purposes. Rather than experiencing these states with no control, one can control and utilize them to achieve the three resultant bodies of buddha-

> hood—the Truth Body [*dharmakāya*], the Complete Enjoyment Body [*saṃbhogakāya*] and the Emanation Body [*nirmāṇakāya*]—which, respectively, have features similar to death, intermediate state and rebirth.[15]

The most advanced tantric adepts mentally prepare for these "natural stages of death" by meditating upon the experience of achieving the three bodies of buddhahood. The key here is using the otherwise ordinary process of death for meditation by mentally controlling the process through which the consciousness departs the body. Advanced Chöd practitioners can learn to manipulate and utilize the "very subtle consciousness" during the "actual practice" stage of Chöd meditation. They mentally control the exit of the very subtle consciousness from the body. The recitation of the syllable *phaṭ* aids the exit of consciousness.

The Dalai Lama notes that the meditation technique for dissolving the gross levels of consciousness may be also employed in deep states of meditation outside the context of death. He writes, "In Highest Yoga Tantra, a special meditative technique is explained by which we are able to dissolve and withdraw the gross levels of mind; we bring the mind to its subtlest level where there is no possibility of distraction arising."[16]

*Utilizing the Subtle Consciousness at Death*

Due to accidents and other unexpected happenings, a skilled tantric practitioner is not always able to fully proceed through the dying process in this manner. A story from the Cultural Revolution tells of a prisoner march in which Tibetan monks were led on foot in a procession. At that time,

> [o]ne elder monk said to the young armed troop that he had to urinate. He was given permission to do so. He walked several yards away a little bit over a hill. He had been there some time when the guard started shouting for him to come back. The elder monk did not move. Frustrated, the soldier yelled again. There was still no response from the elder monk. The soldier went over and nudged him on the shoulder with the blunt end of his rifle. The old monk's body just fell over on its side, limp. He had taken his consciousness out of his body already.[17]

Stories like this are not uncommon within Tibetan Buddhist society because of the emphasis placed upon the development of inner abilities of both conquering the mental delusions (Skt. *kleśas*, Tib. *nyon mongs*) and advancing in mental ability using meditative techniques of subtle consciousness movement.[18] Robert Thurman describes Tibet's spiritual project of devoting the intellectual energy of its most talented scholars to exploring the internal universe and technology of mind, rather than the outer material world. Thurman holds that Tibetan Buddhist adepts may be thought of as "psychonauts [who have] personally voyaged to the furthest frontiers of that universe which their society deemed vital to explore: the inner frontiers of consciousness itself, in all its transformations of life and beyond death."[19] That Tibetan society lagged behind other societies in the greater geocultural region of Central Asia and South Asia is a critique launched by noted cultural critics within Tibetan society,[20] as well as those outside with political agendas. The importance of this critique should not be understated. Yet, to the extent that it has followed a recognizable socioreligious project, Tibetan religious society can be recognized for producing expert tantric adepts who train in using subtle levels of consciousness for higher purposes, passing from life to life in a controlled manner and returning with the intention of serving or benefiting other beings: a humanly possible but clearly uncommon feat of accomplishment.

## *Phaṭ* in Chöd Rituals

His Eminence Kalu Rinpoché (1905–1989), a renowned senior practitioner of the Kagyü lineage of Tibetan Buddhism said, "Chöd is one hundred times more powerful than *phowa* practice."[21] Still, a significant moment in Chöd practice involves the "transference of consciousness" (*phowa*) meditation technique.[22] During Chöd practice, the practitioner visualizes the manner in which to separate the consciousness from the body, transferring the mind directly into the heart of one's lama. Exiting from the lama's heart, as a green karma action ḍākinī, the practitioner's mind returns to cut and distribute the old body thereby practicing the "perfection of generosity" (Skt. *dānapāramitā*, Tib. *sbyin pa'i pha rol tu phyin pa*). However, even if a practitioner has not been able to successfully transfer consciousness out of the body during the Chöd meditation in one's lifetime, it is said that having gained familiarity with the *phowa* aspect of the Chöd practice could have the effect of ensuring one's next rebirth takes place in one of the "upper realms" as a god (*lha*) or human (*mi*).[23]

In the "transference of consciousness" practice in both *phowa* and Chöd meditations, the mantric syllable *phaṭ* assists this separation of mind from matter—of subtle consciousness separating from the coarse physical body. In each Chöd ritual sādhana, *phaṭ* is recited (1) a specified number of times and (2) in a certain manner—which brings the subtle consciousness upwards through the body's central channel from one chakra (Skt. *cakra*) to the next through the navel, heart, throat, and crown, and exiting from the crown up and immediately into the visualized lama's heart.[24]

*Phaṭ* should be recited a certain number of times, depending on which sādhana one is practicing, and as instructed by the Chöd lama, who imparts oral instruction on the visualizations of chakras. Secondly, according to the Chöd commentarial literature, the manner of recitation of this single-syllable mantra is highly specific, requiring instruction from a qualified lama. The ritual officiant requires great sensitivity, since reciting too loudly or too brashly may have undesired consequences. These consequences and the meaning and manner of recitation of this syllable are discussed in the following section.

## Commentary on *Phaṭ* in Chöd

### Translation: Commentary on the Meaning of *Phaṭ*

The following offers our translation of the commentary on the syllable *phaṭ* by Kachen Lobsang Zopa (dKa' chen blo bzang bzod pa). Here, he inscribes quotations drawn from other texts to outline the importance of this mantric syllable and its specific use in Chöd practice. This short commentary is organized into two sections. Initially, Kachen Lobsang Zopa comments upon the meaning and power of the *phaṭ* syllable, addressing those functions served by the utterance "*phaṭ*." In the second part of the commentary, he discusses the various ways the adept should say "*phaṭ*" and the respective results of doing so. Thus, he is concerned in the second part with aspects related to performance practice. Kachen Lobsang Zopa writes:

> Now then, I will explain the meaning of the syllable *phaṭ* [ཕཊ]: the syllable "*pha*" [ཕ] represents the causal *Prajñāpāramitā Sūtra* vehicle, while the syllable "*ṭ*" [ཊ] represents the resultant Vajrayāna, or tantra, vehicle. Together, the syllable *phaṭ* [which is made up of these two letters, "*pha*" and "*ṭ*"] incorporates the condensed meaning of both sūtra and tantra. As explained in [Machik's] *gCod rNam*,[25] "My tradition of Mahāmudrā Chöd is, at the outer level, the practice of the *Prajñāpāramitā Sūtra*; while, at the inner level, it is the practice of Highest Secret Yoga Tantra. The one practising both [sūtra and tantra] together

> is practicing Mahāmudrā Chöd. Therefore, the syllable *phaṭ* is equal to [the practices of] these two [levels: inner and outer]."[26]

Clearly, parallels may be drawn between the combining of the two practices into one and the combining of the two letters into the syllable *phaṭ*. Kachen Lobsang Zopa continues:

> Futhermore, in the root text *Dorjé Tsemo* (*rDo rje tse mo*),[27] it is written, " 'What is the meaning of saying *phaṭ*?' It completely pacifies harmful beings and destroys all suffering; as well, it brings all bliss.[28] By [utterance of] the sound of '*phaṭ*' it pacifies and destroys the 'black side enemies' [or 'enemy, which is the side of darkness' (*nag phyogs*)] and harmful interferences, undesirable causes and conditions, and all suffering. And it brings in the 'white side' (*dkar phyogs*) gods and ghosts, desirable things, and all happiness."[29]
>
> Again, from the same text, "*Phaṭ* is the sound of destruction because it destroys [all the negativities] together with their retinues [and accompanying obstacles], as mentioned in the text."[30] By merely hearing the sound of "*phaṭ*," it pacifies and overwhelms 'the force of harmful thoughts' (*gdug sems kyi ngar*) of 'those with destructive mental attitudes' (*gdug pa can*) together with their retinues, and the harmful thoughts are destroyed within their mental continuum.[31]
>
> The commentary by Khedrup Rinpoché (mkhas grub rje dge legs dpal bzang po) on *Tag Nyis* (*brTag gnyis*, or Two Chapters) says, "*Phaṭ* itself destroys the harmdoers.[32] If you say '*phaṭ*' wrathfully, without a specific need, it will break [burst/explode] the hearts of lesser ghosts.[33] If you repeat '*phaṭ*' in a wrathful manner 108 times on a single occasion, it can destroy any harm present. Therefore, you should not do so without purpose.[34] The spontaneous sound of '*phaṭ*' breaks the head of self-grasping," as stated in the *Ngags rim chen mo*,[35] which says, " '*Phaṭ*,' itself, breaks."[36]

*Summary of First Section*

Kachen Lobsang Zopa's commentary on both the symbolism and manner of performance of the *phaṭ* syllable during specific moments in Chöd ritual practice draws from written Tibetan commentaries by two preeminent exponents in the Ganden Chöd Tradition lineage: Je Tsongkhapa and his close disciple, Khedrup Je, or Khedrup Gelek Palzang (mkhas grub dge legs dpal bzang, 1385–1438), as well as the tradition's founder, Machik Labdrön. He has assembled these interpretations of the powerful effects of the utterance of "*phaṭ*," and warns of the dangers from misusing this power through excessive repetition or saying it in an unnecessarily wrathful manner.

He goes on to describe the various ways in which a practitioner must recite "*phaṭ*" during a single sādhana of the Chöd ritual. It is highly instructive for the practitioner to be introduced to these differentiated performance gestures, particularly if it is the case that saying "*phaṭ*" incorrectly or too forcefully might have powerful effects such as those described in the above commentary. Kachen Lobsang Zopa explains the manner of performance in the following passages.

## Translation: Manner of Utterance of the Syllable "*Phaṭ*"

Kachen Lobsang Zopa's commentary continues:

> How is one to say "*phaṭ*"? Machik's text *gCod rNam* states that when offering and giving, you have to say "*phaṭ*" in a way that is 'naturally at ease' (*lhug par*). [With respect to spirits,[37]] if you are inviting them, or if you need to 'send them away' or 'expel' them (*bskrad*), then you have to say a '*phaṭ*' of slightly longer duration. Say a shorter '*phaṭ*' (*tsam gcod phaṭ*) between melodies of the liturgy.[38] When during earlier and later practices, when you are offering and giving away, you should say "*phaṭ*" loudly and deeply like [the shape of] a wild yak's tail which is large and flanges out slowly and then tapers to a point.[39] While summoning gods and ghosts, say it longer like [the shape of] a rhinoceros's horn, the root [base] of which is fat and narrows to a tip.[40] At the time of separating the mind and matter, and on similar occasions, say a short "*phaṭ*," like the grain of a good crop year.[41]

### *Summary of Second Section*

Introduced above, the Tibetan term "*tsam gcod phaṭ*" is understood to mean the "*phaṭ*" that is to be uttered before each new melody. Thus, it may also be translated as the 'boundary *phaṭ*' or "between melodies *phaṭ*." Usually, each "*tsam gcod phaṭ*" is written into the Chöd sādhana. Often in Tibetan Chöd and *Gur* (Tib. *mgur*) song-poetry, naturalistic images are used to associate sound with visualization and performance gesture, as with the above descriptions of the manner for performing the mantric utterance "*phaṭ*." This is not unlike the image-association attributed to a Chöd melody composed by Machik Labdrön, as discussed above in Chapter Three.

## Intentionally Produced Sound

Throughout the performance of a Chöd ritual, there is a structured presentation of conceptual symbolism. This is a series of meditative visualizations and intentional thought that produce, in succession, a progressive advancement in mental states. It requires conviction and confidence in the ritual on the part of the adept who must know the intentionality underlying each visualization and how it is conjoined with specific performed utterances during every moment of the ritual sādhana practice.

### Heart Sūtra Mantra and Thighbone Trumpet Refrain

An instrumentally accompanied silent recitation of mantra, a sort of refrain-interlude, occurs five times during the Chöd sādhana practice *Dedicating the Illusory Body*. This part of the Chöd ritual is denoted by the graphic "^^^" as displayed in table 2.3. Each of the five times it recurs, two meditative visualizations are performed simultaneously along with instrumental performances of the *ḍamaru* and *kangling*.

There is no melody sung during this refrain. When practicing alone, the adept can play both the *ḍamaru* and the *kangling* at the same time, holding them in the right and left hands, respectively. When practicing in a group, the *umdzé* will typically play the *ḍamaru* while one designated person will blow the *kangling* to summon forth beings. Alternatively, several people can blow the *kangling* while several others play the *ḍamaru*. There are two silent meditations going on at the same time: one on emptiness at the drum-accompanied recitation of the mantra, another on calling forth beings, which may elicit fear. These complement each other.

Tables 5.1 and 5.2 are provided as a form of performance notation, a kind of musical score, and may also be read as a style of ritual mapping. The vertical lines separating columns may be understood to be "bar lines," and the spaces they delineate can be referred to as "measures." Reading from left to right, horizontally, these lines represent a steady tempo or rhythmic pulse, though the width of the column may vary. Horizontally, as if along

Table 5.1. Perfection of Wisdom Mantra with *Ḍamaru*: Variation 1

Sanskrit: *tadyathā oṃ gate gate pāragate pārasaṃgate bodhi svāhā*
Phonetic rendering: tayatā oṃ gaté gaté paragaté parasamgaté bodhi soha

| | | | | | | | | | | | | |
|---|---|---|---|---|---|---|---|---|---|---|---|---|
| 1 | ta ya tā | oṃ - | ga té | ga té | pā ra | ga té | pā ra saṃ | ga té | bo - | dhi - | so - | ha - |
| 2 | x o | x o | x o | x o | x o | x o | x o | x o | x o | x - | o - | x o |
| 3 | "one | two | three | four | five | six | seven | eight | nine | dram | dram | dram dram" |
| 4 | "*gcig* | *gnyis* | *gsum* | *bzhi* | *lnga* | *drug* | *bdun* | *brgyad* | *dgu la* | *dram* | *dram* | *dram dram*" |
| 5 | "chik | nyi | sum | shi | nga | drook | dun | gye | gu la | dram | dram | dram dram" |

Line 1: meditative visualization while reciting the mantra of the Perfection of Wisdom.
Line 2: *ḍamaru* drumming pattern; "x" = play away from one's body, "o" = play toward one's body.
Line 3: quietly counted beats in the language most familiar (e.g., English); used during training.
Line 4: as in line 3 above, beats counted in Tibetan language (rendered in Wylie transliteration).
Line 5: as in line 4, counted in Tibetan language (rendered in English Romanization).

Table 5.2. Mantra of the Perfection of Wisdom with *Ḍamaru*: Variation 2

| | | | | | | | | | | | | |
|---|---|---|---|---|---|---|---|---|---|---|---|---|
| 1 | ta ya | tā - | oṃ - | ga té | ga té | pā ra ga té | pā ra saṃ | ga té | bo dhi | so - | ha - | - - |
| 2 | x o | x o | x o | x o | x o | x o | x o | x o | x o | x - | o - | x o |
| 3 | "one | two | three | four | five | six | seven | eight | nine la | dram | dram | dram dram" |
| 4 | "*gcig* | *gnyis* | *gsum* | *bzhi* | *lnga* | *drug* | *bdun* | *brgyad* | *dgu la* | *dram* | *dram* | *dram dram*" |
| 5 | "chik | nyi | sum | shi | nga | drook | dun | gye | gu la | dram | dram | dram dram" |

Line 1: meditative visualization while reciting the mantra of the Perfection of Wisdom.
Line 2: *ḍamaru* drumming pattern; "x" = play away from one's body, "o" = play toward one's body.
Line 3: quietly counted beats in the most familiar language (e.g., English); used during training.
Line 4: as in line 3 above, beats counted in Tibetan language (rendered in Wylie transliteration).
Line 5: as in line 4, counted in Tibetan language (rendered in English Romanization).

a time axis, we can read the drum-accompanied recitation of this mantra occurring in rhythmic time, wherein each measure requires approximately one second in real time. Vertically, all events occurring simultaneously are illustrated within the measure as follows: the first syllable appearing to the right of each bar line, within each column or "measure," is to be uttered at the same time that the two *ḍamaru* pellets are heard striking the drum skins, represented by "x."

Ven. Pencho Rabgey recommends that whenever practicing in a group, beginners softly recite the numbers "one" through "nine" (as indicated in lines 3, 4, and 5), rather than the mantra—either in Tibetan language or English, or the language with which they are most familiar. He maintains that beginners can become confused if they endeavor to recite the mantra right away, as there are two ways to do this recitation in accordance with the rhythmic pattern of *ḍamaru* beats. Given these two subtly different renderings of the mantra recitation (noting variations 1 and 2 here), such a pedagogical strategy avoids confusion. Yet, even while practitioners recite numbers, they are nevertheless advised to think about the essential meaning of the mantra: "emptiness" (Skt. *śūnyatā*; Tib. *stong pa nyid*). Whichever way beginners practice, "x" denotes the playing of the *ḍamaru* beat at the same moment that a number increment is uttered; which is spoken, not sung, like a *bol* or mnemonic aid. Each number refers to the beat of the drum that is played in a certain direction. Some sādhana practices require that one first play the beat that is counted on the "outside" (away from the torso), and others require that the initial beat be played on the "inside" (toward the torso).

The Chöd practitioner blows the thighbone trumpet to invite the spirits to the place of practice. Each time the *kangling* is played to summon forth the spirits, the action is accompanied by a specific intentional thought, increasing from a gentle request with peaceful demeanor, to an urgent call, to insistence. The first time, one has a gentle manner while playing, thinking "Please come here." The second time, one thinks with a slight increase in urgency, "All beings come here." The third time, the practitioner displays the strongest intent, more than an earnest intensity and much closer to an insistence, thinking, "All beings *must* come here now!"

The gradual augmentation of urgency in thought is reflected in the musical performance practice. The first *kangling* call is played without an ornament, the second with one ornament in the middle caused by the forcing of less air through the trumpet for a moment, and then increasing again, and the third time with two of such neighbor-note ornaments. In a conical instrument without valves, the pitch falls or rises as one blows less or more forcefully through the air passage. Traditionally, the practitioner's performance of the *kangling* should emulate the shape of a grain of rice with each call, slowly building to a louder sound by forcing more air through it, and then decreasing in equal measure.

Just prior to blowing the *kangling,* it is necessary to hold the stem of the thighbone trumpet in the left hand while tapping the end that is to be blown three times with the flat open palm of the right hand. The practitioner does this in order to warn the beings so as not to frighten the weaker spirits who, lacking fortitude, might be scared by the sudden blowing of the instrument.

At the same time the *kangling* is blown, the mantra of the Perfection of Wisdom Sūtra, which itself is a condensed version of the *Prajñāpāramitā Sūtra,* is recited quietly or silently by the practitioners playing the *ḍamaru* in accordance with the syllables: "*tayatā (oṃ) gate gate pāragate pārasaṃgate bodhi sohā.*" Thus, each beat of the *ḍamaru* is marked by one of the syllables of the mantra. The silent mantra recitation "Tayatā . . ." accompanied by the *ḍamaru* is performed twice followed by (a) two repetitions of six beats, "*ma dang, lha yi, khan dro,*" (b) two repetitions of four beats, "*ma dang, khan dro,*" and (c) two repetitions of two beats, "*ma dang*"—all in the *dram-dram* (quarter note-quarter note) rhythm. Thus, the syllables to be played and uttered phonetically are: "*ma dang, lha yi, khan dro*" (2x), "*ma dang, khan dro*" (2x) and "*ma dang*" (2x). This whole sequence is executed as a refrain between certain subritual sections; and, at the end of the second repetition of "ma dang," the practitioner recites "*phaṭ*" to begin the next subritual section. If one is practicing in a group it is not necessary to say the *bol* syllables of the *ḍamaru* ("*ma dang, lha yi, khan dro*") out loud unless the *umdzé* thinks that it might be helpful to do so for the beginners who are present so as to ensure that they do not lose their place in the drum beats. It can effectively enhance one's visualizations to speak the syllables audibly and softly while one plays the *ḍamaru* beats, because each syllable attends to and cues guru-deity yoga, the foundational practice of this Vajrayāna tradition, as follows: *ma* = great mother, *dang* = and, *lha yi* = divine/celestial, *khan dro* = ḍākinī or sky goer. This subtle performance supports the meditative dramaturgy of the sādhana and its subritual sections. Here, in table 5.3, the structure, content, and meaning of the refrain is graphically represented as a "ritual mapping" of the ritual event.

Table 5.3. Calling Forth Beings with the Thighbone Trumpet (*Kangling*)

| **Structural placement in sādhana liturgy** | **Musical Element** | **Instruments** | **Ritual Function** | **Meditation** |
|---|---|---|---|---|
| (*before*) Going for Refuge<br><br>(*before*) Seven Branch Offering<br><br>(*before and after*) Red Distribution<br><br>(*after*) Dedication | Melody (trumpet *glissandi*) | *kangling* (thighbone trumpet) | Calling forth beings to the ritual feast. | Calling peacefully, then progressively more urgent.<br><br>e.g., "All beings please come here"<br><br>"All beings come here now!" |
| *The Heart Sūtra "Gaté" Mantra*<br><br>(refrain: nine beats, x2) | Rhythm "*ma dang lha yi, khan dro*"<br><br>Voice (non-melodic mantric recitation) | *ḍamaru* (drum)<br><br>*dril bu* (bell) | Meditative focus on "emptiness," the lack of intrinsic, independent, self-existence of all phenomena and the five aggregates. | *The Heart Sūtra "Gaté" Mantra*<br><br>(*ḍamaru* drum accentuates mentally recited syllables.) |

We can see how the ritual aspects are purposefully demarcated, and associate the meditation practice with the design of the performance. During the refrain-interlude, the practitioner is engaged in two mental activities interchangeably. While meditating upon emptiness, and recalling the significance of the practice, one is calling all beings with the thighbone trumpet. Thinking of emptiness helps the practitioner stave off fear and maintain a balanced mental disposition no matter what frightening appearances may arise. Thus, it is important while blowing the *kangling* to meditate upon the emptiness of the beings, oneself, and all phenomena. If all lack inherent existence, then malevolent thoughts and fears arise only due to habits in the mindstream of the beings and practitioners. When thinking critically in this way about appearances, the practitioner is less likely to react out of fear while calling forth beings and is more likely to be able to complete the practice.

## Levels of Depth, Layers of Meaning: "*Oṃ Ma Ṇi Pad Me Hūṃ*"

There are many levels of depth to each ritual act in Chöd, since it combines the *Perfection of Wisdom Sūtra* (*Prajñāpāramitā Sūtra*) within a tantric method. Another articulation of the sūtra is the six-syllable mantra "*Oṃ Ma Ṇi Pad Me Hūṃ*" of the Buddha of Compassion (Skt. *Avalokiteśvara*, Tib. *spyan ras gzigs*), which requires a tantric method of recitation. There are numerous visualizations that can be mentally performed during its recitation. According to one interpretation from the Ganden Oral Tradition, each syllable in the six syllable mantra is representative of one of the six perfections (*pāramitās*) from the *Perfection of Wisdom Sūtra*: generosity, ethical discipline, forbearance, effort, meditative concentration, and wisdom (emptiness). To practice this, the adept can say or chant each of the syllables of the mantra, with each recitation being actively imbued with the qualities of "generosity," "ethics," "patience," and so forth. Thus, as can be seen (table 5.4), as one recites "*Oṃ*," one may think about "generosity," and while reciting "*Ma*" one may meditate upon "ethical discipline," and so on with the other perfections as indicated.

An alternative meditative visualization for the same mantra may be practiced in the following way. One recites the mantra with the same oral

Table 5.4. Layers of Depth in Mantric Visualization: Interpreting Symbolism

| Mantra | Six Perfections (*pāramitās*) | Six Realms of Existence |
|---|---|---|
| *Oṃ* | Generosity | Gods |
| *Ma* | Ethical Discipline | Demi-gods |
| *Ṇi* | Patience | Humans |
| *Pad* | Effort | Animals |
| *Me* | Concentration | Hungry ghosts |
| *Hūṃ* | Wisdom[1] | Hell beings |

1. Realization of emptiness (*stong pa nyid*), the ultimate nature of phenomena as mutually dependent and not self-existent.

gesture, but focuses on generating compassion by thinking of the plight and conditions of living for beings in each of the six realms of existence. Thus, while the practitioner recites *Oṃ Ma Ṇi Pad Me Hūṃ*, each syllable can receive the attentive thought of regarding all beings in a realm with compassion. Alternatively, if one is counting the mantra on a rosary (usually of 109 beads), one rosary length can be allotted for each of the six perfections, until all six perfections have been meditated upon. Similarly, one rosary length can be used to recite the mantra while thinking over the suffering of each of the six realms of beings in turn. Intentional sound and thought are directed during each part of the meditation.

Various symbolic interpretations guided by intentional thought may be attributed to a particular mantra or ritual instrument. The function and power of mantra is given by Ani Choying Drolma, a Tibetan Buddhist nun from Nepal. She sings the Chöd melodies internationally to fundraise for her nunnery in Nepal, and spoke in 2007 about the significance of this mantra:

> The mantra of [the] compassion Buddha . . . We strongly believe that the power of this mantra is *very* strong to bless us with an ability to develop one's own compassionate qualities through which we will not only be able to heal [ourselves], but we will be able to heal others too.[42]

The Chöd practitioner can use the lived experience of symbolic practice to discern the meaning of compassionate intentionality, thereby allowing for a deep connection with the guru and spirit beings.

## Visualization of the Mantric Syllable "*Āḥ*"

The syllable "*Āḥ*" is the mantric expression of the essence of the *Prajñāpāramitā Sūtra*, and is vital in Chöd rituals.[43] Its symbolic meaning and function concerns the purification of sins and obscurations through visualization and utterance. The focus is on receiving the blessings of all Chöd lineage lamas through the guru-deity at Yum Chenmo's heart. As in previous examples, the practitioner can select a visualization from among those practiced within an interpretive community, as taught by Chöd lamas. Although the different visualizations pertaining to the mantric syllable "*Āḥ*" are similar, slight differences may be observed. One interpretation involves visualizing all the lineage lamas dissolving into Yum Chenmo at whose heart a lotus flower is visualized, on top of which sits another Yum Chenmo. At the center of the second Yum Chenmo's heart, standing upright on a lotus, is the mantric syllable "*Āḥ*."[44] The practitioner visualizes that from the yellow "*Āḥ*" letter, light rays of nectar flow to the practitioner and all beings, purifying their three doors: body, speech, and mind. Another interpretation involves visualizing the main buddha deity Yum Chenmo with the mantric syllable "*Āḥ*" at the center of her heart (without the second Yum Chenmo). As well, instead of visualizing white light rays of purifying nectar emanating from "*Āḥ*," it is possible to imagine that millions of mantric "*Āḥ*" letters emanate from the original letter at Yum Chenmo's heart, overflow and melt into the practitioner's body and that of all other beings in the universe, purifying everyone and everything.

## Utterance of the Mantric Syllable "*Āḥ*"

The utterance of the purifying mantric syllable "*Āḥ*" a total of twenty-one times prior to giving the body away accompanies the visualizations described above. And, as with the examples above, there is more than one way in which to perform this utterance. The mantric syllable "*Āḥ*" can be said very quietly to oneself even while visualizing nectar light rays raining down, or millions of syllable "*Āḥ*" mantras overflowing. The enunciation of the syllable is produced at the glottal stop, and is only slightly vocalized; it is very subtle and quiet.

There is rhythmic accompaniment to this mantric utterance with the *ḍamaru*. Each "*ma dang, lha yi, khan dro*" accommodates one run of seven "*Āḥ*" syllables, and doing so three times sufficiently encompasses the twenty-one required utterances.[45] Another method of enunciating the twenty-one "*Āḥ*" syllables utilizes the "*ma dang, lha yi, khan dro*" beat cycle in a more markedly rhythmic fashion.[46] The following two tables, 5.5 and 5.6, illustrate a comparison of these patterns of enunciation, in the order in which they have been presented here.

The bold text indicates that these syllables are produced with more vocalization, are stronger, and give the rhythmic sense of "short-long" where "***Āḥ*** *Āḥ*" recurs in the second example, Variation 2. The final exclamation marked "***Āḥ!***" indicates that this syllable is the strongest utterance of the seven "*Āḥ*" syllables. The ritual function here is the purification of the body, speech, and mind of the practitioner, and all beings surrounding the practitioner, following the request to the lineage lamas for their blessing to accomplish the practice.

The importance of the symbolism and function of these mantras that are specific to the *Prajñāpāramitā Sūtra* and employed throughout Chöd ritual meditation practice sādhanas should not be underestimated.

Table 5.5. Utterance of the Mantric Syllable "*Āḥ*" (21x): Variation 1

| **Musical Element** | **Enunciation Pattern** | | | | **Repetition** |
|---|---|---|---|---|---|
| Mantric Utterance (vocal enunciation) | "***Āḥ*** *Āḥ Āḥ Āḥ Āḥ Āḥ Āḥ*" | | | | repeat 3x |
| *Ḍamaru* drum | x o | x | o | x o | |
| Tibetan Transliteration | "*lha yi* | *mkha'* | *'gro* | *ma dang*" | |
| English Romanization | "lha yi | khan | dro | ma dang" | |

Table 5.6. Utterance of the Mantric Syllable "*Āḥ*" (21x): Variation 2

| **Musical Element** | **Enunciation Pattern** | | | | **Repetition** |
|---|---|---|---|---|---|
| Mantric Utterance (vocal enunciation) | "***Āḥ*** *Āḥ* | ***Āḥ*** *Āḥ* | ***Āḥ*** *Āḥ* | ***Āḥ**!*" | repeat 3x |
| *Ḍamaru* drum | x o | x | o | x o | |
| Tibetan Transliteration | "*lha yi* | *mkha'* | *'gro* | *ma dang*" | |
| English Romanization | "lha yi | khan | dro | ma dang" | |

Within the subject of mantra—sounding sacred syllables that invoke the essence of a buddha—a key purpose is to suffuse the mind of the practitioner with the seed of transformation so that one can eventually become enlightened as that buddha. One of the most recognizable properties of mantric utterance is its vocalized repetition. In Tsongkhapa's commentary on Chöd practice, we find that besides the mantric syllables *phaṭ* and "*Āḥ*," and the mantra, *Tayatā (Ōṃ) gaté gaté pāragaté pārasaṃgaté bodhi soha*, the only phrase he advises we repeat a great many times is a special sentence for "taking refuge." This sentence helps the practitioner develop both renunciation and *bodhicitta*, as well as the resolve to pursue Chöd meditation practice to these pronounced liberative ends. Je Tsongkhapa writes that the practitioner should recite the following "at least 100 times since it is so very important":

> I and all living beings as extensive as the sky, especially those living beings who are intent on doing harm to me due to the debts I owe them from beginningless time, and the owners of the place and the local gods, all of us take refuge in the guru.[47]

Je Tsongkhapa adds that of utmost importance here is the intentionality, the generation of the altruistic awakening mind (*bodhicitta*) in the practitioner's heart while reciting these words.

# 6

# The Four Ritual Activities

## Peaceful, Increasing, Powerful, and Wrathful (*shi, jé, wang, dra*)

In Tibetan Buddhist Vajrayāna practices, there are generally "four ritual activities," or "modes" (Tib. *phrin las rnam bzhi*), differentiated by their expressive disposition in terms of both appearance and sound. These four actions are known as "peaceful" (*zhi ba*), "increasing" (*rgyas pa*), "powerful" (*dbang*), and "wrathful" (*drag po*). In many contexts, these are commonly referred to, and phoenetically rendered here, as "shi", "jé", "wang", and "dra." In terms of their varied sonic referents, this chapter offers a translation and exploration of an instruction from the Tibetan oral tradition on the contrastive ways of playing the drum that accord with the four ritual actions. Each of these four short poetic descriptions characterizes a natural phenomenon as an aural analogy to sound production on the ritual instrument. Moreover, each poetic expression of a ritual action inscribes with it the respective external and internal benefits of playing the ritual drum in said manner in terms of Buddhadharma. Just as poetic numinosity in analogies to different types of rain may be made in relation to sound, and embody a specific inner or outer characteristic or aspect of the Buddhist path, these ritual actions can also be considered with respect to the varied manifestations of buddha deities.

### Peaceful and Wrathful Manifestations

Buddhas can manifest in various ways; each may appear in peaceful, wrathful, as well as semi-wrathful (Tib. *zhi ma khro*), and other forms. Machik

Labdrön, for example, is often depicted with a semi-wrathful facial expression conveyed by smiling while baring fangs, like Vajravāhārī, a related female deity in thangka paintings and internal meditative visualizations. She is often visualized standing in a dancing pose while playing the Chöd ritual instruments, as described in the sādhana *Dedicating the Illusory Body.*

Let us also take the example of the Buddha of Compassion (Skt. Avalokiteśvara, Tib. *spyan ras gzigs*), pronounced "Chenrezig" in Tibetan language. Chenrezig is widely understood to manifest in different forms, and is depicted artistically in several distinctive ways. The Buddhas Chenrezig and Hayagrīva manifest respectively as peaceful and wrathful forms of the Buddha of Compassion. Mahākāla is yet another wrathful manifestation of Chenrezig. The most common depictions of Chenrezig in Tibetan iconography are shown having two-arms, four-arms, or one-thousand-arms. They are all buddhas that primarily focus compassionate energy, but are said to appear in different forms to attract beings with different mental dispositions.

In addition, there are several different Buddhist traditions and cultures in which the Buddha of Compassion is a centrally important deity for public and personal propitiation not only across Tibet and Mongolia but throughout all of Asia. One of the most common forms of Chenrezig in the Tibetan tradition has one face and two arms. Practitioners of Buddhism in East and Southeast Asia propitiate the female Buddha of Compassion, Kwan Yin, who generally appears as a young female emitting radiant white light in all directions.[1] The Indian Buddhist nun Gelongma Palmo (Dge slong ma dpal mo), had a vision of an eleven-faced, one-thousand-arm, and one-thousand-eye[2] form of Chenrezig, which is still popularly propitiated by Tibetans today.

Both Kwan Yin and the thousand-arm Chenrezig are peaceful manifestations of the Buddha of Compassion. The Tibetan *yidam* of Chenrezig has a peaceful expression, bears a benevolent smile, has a pale-ish white color and is often portrayed sitting in the posture of meditative equipoise—with both hands on his lap, palms facing upward, the right palm resting gently atop the left and the tips of the thumbs touching lightly just in front and below the navel.

Across the Tibetan Plateau, and in the Diaspora, His Holiness the Dalai Lama is traditionally believed to be an emanation of the Buddha of Compassion in this form.[3] In rather dramatic contrast, Hayagrīva is a wrathful form of Chenrezig and is depicted with three heads, each having three eyes, wide open mouths, bared fangs, a red-colored body, and six arms—each of which holds an implement: a lasso, spear, ritual axe, and so forth. The wrathful facial expression shown by Buddhist deities who assume an outer expression of anger and disgust is never directed toward beings, but rather against the delusive mental states (Skt. *kleśa*, Tib. *nyon mongs*) in beings' mindstreams which cause them to think and act in ways that are harmful for both themselves and others. These afflicted mental states are impermanent rather than intrinsically rooted in a person's mindstream, and through practices of purification, and accumulations of merit and wisdom, these destructive mind states can gradually become lessened in their potency, and eventually eliminated. Every being is understood to have "buddha-nature" (Skt. *tathāgatagarbha*, Tib. *de bzhin gshegs pa'i snying po*), which is literally the embryo or "essence of the tathāgata."[4] The mind of any being is clear and pure in a way that is analogous to a clear blue sky that has clouds, even storms, that pass through it, but the nature of the sky as an open expanse is unchanged. It is clear and pure as before—the weather does not alter the vast pristine nature of the sky. Similarly, the buddha-nature of all beings refers to their having the embryonic essence of a buddha. An individual's realization of buddhahood is the fulfillment of their cultivating the appropriate karmic causes while following the path set by a qualified teacher. There are several schools and paths that may lead a practitioner to buddhahood. The gradual path school was taught by Dīpaṃkāra Śrījñāna Atiśa (982–1054), first in India and subsequently in Tibet during the "the later dissemination of Buddhism in Tibet" (*phyi dar*), and was revitalized by Lama Tsongkhapa (1357–1419) who is regarded as founder of the Gelugpa school.

## Karmic Imprints, Delusive Mental States

Several questions arise from the epistemological convention whereby Buddhist practitioners do not regard beings who *perform* negative actions *equivalently as* negative beings. That is to say, there is an epistemologically located disconnect between the *root causes of* harmful actions and *the actions* themselves. They understand that the karmic disposition that produces these actions is based on previous mental imprints. What are the delusive mental states or kleśas? Where are these delusive mental states located? What is their origin? How can they be rooted out and eliminated? Here, the answers might follow best from the Four Noble Truths, the first teaching given by Buddha Śākyamuni at Sarnath some forty-nine days after his having eliminated all the delusive mental states. Buddha taught the: (1) truth of suffering, (2) truth of origin of suffering, (3) truth of cessation, and (4) truth of the path. To summarize, the teaching on the Four Noble Truths instructs how the origin of suffering is caused by the negative karmic imprints and delusive mental states that yield harmful actions of body, speech, and mind, which in turn cause the experience of suffering. As these are studied in the treatises on Buddhist Psychology, the mind and its categories (*blo rig*), through logical reasoning, the practitioner learns to reduce habitual negative mental states and consequently engage in positive actions of body, speech, and mind, following a path with specific meditation and ritual practices by which these negative karmic imprints and mental states may be eliminated. Buddha Śākyamuni tested methods of meditation and taught that by gradually lessening the influence of negative mental states, and by applying the appropriate antidotes to counteract a particular negative mental state with a positive one, it is eminently possible for a being to cultivate positive mental states in their mindstream and eventually reach buddhahood. As Machik Labdrön pointed out: under the Bodhi Tree, the Buddha was doing nothing other than finally "cutting off" the root of suffering, "self-grasping" (*bdag 'dzin*), having gradually attained that level.

## Ritual Action: Internal and External Distinctions

While the four actions of enlightened actvity (*phrin las bzhis*) have been introduced elsewhere, primarily external aspects have been addressed. An important addition to this research drawn from the Tibetan oral tradition offers an emphasis on, and shows the important distinctions between, the external and internal goals, which the four actions of enlightened actvity are meant to address.

The distinction between the external and internal goals, or functions, of the four kinds of ritual actvity will be discussed below. While these four actions may have been explained by Ellingson with respect to the musical context of large monastic ensembles, we might add to this by accounting for the possibilities of these actions in single drum performances outside of a large ensemble performance situation. Furthermore, we may add to the notion of subrituals that within a wrathful deity propitiation ritual, there may be space for all four activities to find expression in various parts of subrituals in accordance with expected levels of mind training and practice.

### *Peaceful* (*zhi ba*)

According to the oral tradition of Geshé Trinley of Chungba Valley near Litang, Kham, Tibet, as passed down to Ven. Pencho Rabgey, in the "peaceful" mode, the drum should be played in a manner similar to a spring shower: "rain which falls gently"; it descends tranquilly, is "evenly diffused and amply covers everything."

Ven. Pencho Rabgey indicated this musically with the example of a gentle drum roll in which two mallets, at middling speed, fall softly on a drum skin from a height distance of between 6 to 8 cm above the drum surface. He created a gentle rumble that would accompany an ensemble of ritual instruments during a section of the ritual, such as the prostration section following invocation of a buddha deity and his or her retinue. The analogy of the sound of "rain" resulting from a played instrument to that of the naturally occurring phenomena of rain provides a useful "measurement" or gauge here.

The sort of rainfall employed in the analogy is that which may be experienced in such climes as Vancouver where, typically, the tiny rain droplets gradually dampen the air and materials. When I inquired with Pala, "Could this 'peaceful' manner of rainfall be described aptly as the type of rain you often experience in the coastal mountains of Vancouver?" He gave an enthusiastic response, "Exactly! This type of rain, or light drizzle, can be very good for the healthy growth of certain kinds of crop."

Peaceful-directed meditation practices, and the activities which follow in accordance with a peaceful attitude, have two respective goals: "quick pacification at both the external and internal levels." The following explains in more detail the distinction between these external and internal levels of pacification according to the oral tradition:

At the external level, the pacification of the fear from harms/harmdoers illnesses (*nad*),

> demons (*bdud*), interferers/interferences (*bgegs*), obstacles or inhibitors (*bar chad*); in sum, the complete pacification of all of these. At the internal level, the goal is the peaceful overcoming of harms/harmdoers that result from having the 84,000 delusions in one's mindstream,"[5] primarily, the three poisons—attachment, anger, and specifically, ignorance, which is the root cause of these.[6]

### *Increasing* (*rgyas pa*)

According to the oral tradition, playing the drum in a manner of "increasing" is said to sound similar to "rain which falls heavily and continuously." At the external level, such practices may be the cause of an increase in both the quality and quantity of the necessary conditions for success. Specifically, these include the following: being surrounded (*'khor*) with a retinue of supporters and support networks (e.g., fine colleagues, excellent associates, good family, and friends); having the necessary supporting materials and facilities (*longs spyod*) to accomplish meritorious tasks (*mnga' thang*), and practice companions. Thus, an abundance of helpful materials and dharma companions.

At the internal level, increase-directed meditation rituals and practices will lead to an augmentation of the following: (a) "lifespan" (*tshe ring po*)—to have a long life as a human being since the human form is considered most beneficial; (b) "merit" (*bsod nams*), whereby more merit is accumulated through practices of the "six perfections" (*phar phyin drug*);[7] and, (c) "knowledge through transmissions of Buddha's teachings" (*yon tan rten pa'i lung*). This refers to the increasing of knowledge conferred by qualified teachers as well as gaining "realization of attributes" (*yon tan gyi rtogs pa*) into the teachings by engaging in meditation practice on these teachings. Knowledge also refers to gaining "realization" (*rtogs*) of any of the Buddha's main teachings such as: (A) the "three principal paths"—"renunciation" (*nges 'byung*), *bodhicitta* (*byang chub kyi sems*), and the "correct view" (*yang dag pa'i lta ba*) common to the sūtra and tantra Mahāyāna paths; and (B) the "two stages" or "generation and completion stages" common to the Highest Secret Yoga Tantra practices.[8]

### *Powerful (dbang)*

Playing drum in a "powerful" manner sounds like a torrential downpour, such as "rain falling amid gusty winds," strong rains that have speed and force. Just as in the above cases of peaceful and increasing meditation practices and rituals, what can become positively affected by power-directed playing and meditation rituals is traditionally distinguished at the level of external and internal benefits. Externally, the aim of directing one's *bodhicitta* imbued practice with power can bring: "good-minded people (*mi*)," "jewels" (*nor*) which here signifies wealth, food "what to eat" (*zas*), and clothing "what to wear" (*gos*) as well as the power to use "whatever I have" (*phyi 'byor ba*) to enable all sentient beings to become peaceful (*zhi ba*) and have blissful (*bde ba*) mindstreams. Power-directed meditation practices can be used to positively transform circumstances for other beings and/or for the practitioners themselves. At the internal level, the power-directed meditation ritual practices are aimed at achieving both the "common and supreme attainments" (*mchog dang thun mong gi dngos grub*).[9]

Using power to gain "ordinary attainments" (*thun mong gi dngos grub*) can be understood as the power to reach the highest levels of attainment within the small and medium scopes of the Buddhist path, common to the Theravāda School of "Individual Liberation." These levels of attainment are respectively as follows: according to the "small scope" path, the goal is to avoid rebirth in the three lower realms (the hell realms, the realm of hungry ghosts or the animal realm), and rather, to attain rebirth in one of the three higher realms (of humans, gods or demi-gods). The aim of the "medium scope" practitioners is to liberate themselves from the cycle of existence (*saṃsāra*, *'khor ba*).

In contrast to the practitioners of the small and medium scope paths, "great scope" practitioners who follow the path of "Universal Salvation" seek both the "ordinary" (*thun mong*) and "supreme attainment" (*mchog gi dngos grub*). They seek full awakening—which means liberation from cyclic existence for the benefit of all beings. Their motivation relies on *bodhicitta*, the compassionate state of enactive altruism to benefit all beings without discrimination.

### *Wrathful* (*drag po*)

A wrathful mode of playing destroys both outer and inner enemies. What are the enemies for Buddhist practitioners of the Mahāyāna path? This is a subtle and crucial point. Practitioners of the Mahāyāna do not regard sentient beings as enemies; and, in any case, it is considered unethical for such practitioners to harbor the intention to harm any being. They regard anything that harms beings as their enemy. According to the oral tradition:

> "Wrathful practice is like a tremendously powerful lightning bolt. At the outer level, wrathful practice destroys all external enemies and interferers. At the internal level it destroys the enemy, self-grasping ignorance."[10]

The "outer enemy" is that which harms any and all sentient beings. Wrathful practice liberates beings from all harmful enemies including interferers/interferences, hindrances, and obstacles. The "inner enemy" is 'self-grasping ignorance' (*bdag 'dzin ma rig pa*). Thus, wrathful practice, at the internal level, is aimed at eliminating the self-grasping ignorance.

## Transformation through the Four Actions

1. This teaching from the oral tradition divides the four ritual actions into internal and external goals.[11] Thinking in this way helps the practitioner recall the goal of inner and outer transformation that is effected through the ritual.

2. Although the four ritual actions are usually associated with Tibetan monastic ensemble ritual music, in the Ganden Chöd Tradition, the Chöd practice requires a peaceful performance mode rather than a wrathful mode.[12] However, the visualizations performed during different sections of the ritual may be categorized as peaceful, peaceful-increasing, or powerful-increasing. For example, in the sādhana *Dedicating the Illusory Body* there is a complete absence of wrathful activity.

3. The aesthetic of Chöd ritual performance is shaped by the mood or *rasa* of certain Chöd melodies; however, the *rasa* is not always explicitly indicated in the sādhana text, or in the oral tradition. However, some melodies' *rasa* is clearly marked by name in the long sādhana text of the Troma Nagmo (Tib. Khro ma nag mo) practice of the Ḍākinī Chöd Lineage.

# Part III

# Meaning and Application of Chöd Ritual Practice

# 7

# Mind and Sound in Chöd

## Introduction

As noted in the Preface, the interdisciplinary audience for this work is is primarily fourfold: (1) Buddhist Studies scholars and Indo-Tibetan and Himalayan Studies specialists; (2) practitioners of Chöd, as well as contemplatives informed by other Buddhist tantric rituals; and (3) ethnomusicologists, music theorists, and musicologists wishing to explore the role of music where liturgical ritual texts are performed in Buddhist practice traditions. In addition, (4) scholars in the fields of anthropology of religion, medical anthropology, ritual studies and performance studies, may find it helpful to have an introductory grounding in some of the fundamental philosophical concepts and terminology undergirding a Chöd liturgy when unpacking performative meanings, which is the main focus of this chapter.

Recognizing that each of these audiences approaches Chöd in their own ways, seeing through their respective lenses, each will be addressed slightly differently here. Every section speaks to at least two of these audiences at a time. Both the Buddhist studies scholars and practitioners will be familiar with the philosophical terminology, though perhaps less acquainted with an approach to liturgical music that explores these terms in the context of sound/music experiences when performed/practiced during a ritual. By the same reasoning, anthropologists and ethnomusicologists of Buddhist communities and ritual events may find these terms and concepts useful when investigating the role of musical elements in Chöd practice, and other Buddhist tantric practices more generally. Finally, Buddhist practitioners who are deeply engaged in Chöd, and those emerging into the depth of its practice, may find here a consideration of the contingencies of sound production and the nature of mutual interdependence that connect with their intuitive experience.

In essence, researchers require a lexicon to serve in a cross-disciplinary commentarial approach to a multi-modal and multi-faceted Buddhist ritual. By the same token, practitioners may also find useful this exercise, which takes an analytical approach to the language of the ineffable. Ultimately, we may consider Chöd in all its layered epistemological and performative aspects. Furthermore, performative elements can help us to visualize the liturgical vibrancy and textured numinosity that practitioners of the Chöd tradition experience.

## Sounding Out Chöd Concepts in Context

Since the Chöd practice directly concerns "the disidentification with the egoic self,"[1] it would be useful to introduce the concepts and terminology from Buddhist philosophy that the adept learning to practice a Chöd sādhana encounters. The beginner Chöd adept is involved in:

a) hearing oral instruction on Chöd practice from their lama;

b) reading the commentaries on Chöd practice written by Tibetan lamas who are recognized practitioners;

c) singing the Chöd sādhana's poetry; and,

d) performing the meditative visualizations that the poetry describes.

There are conceptual tools that we, as beginner Chöd practitioners-in-training, need to use to begin to recognize the egoistic ways in which we understand, and engage in, the world. Subsequently, we can work to disidentify with the egoic "self" within the fields of thought and experience. Just as the four noble truths involve recognizing the origin of suffering before learning how to eradicate it, there is a logic to identifying the "self" that we must cut before being able to cut it.

Advanced tantric adepts can enter into a state of perceiving reality that is radically different from that of the ordinary perspective of reality held by persons without such training. As Ven. Pencho Rabgey says of advanced practitioners, "They see what we see, but they do not perceive and understand it in the same way that we do."[2]

The point here is that the protracted path toward this state of realization involves initial stages of training, and putting into practice what has been learned in situations of every moment of life rather than merely in the comparatively easier context of ritual performance experiences in a retreat hut or in the cloistered settings of monastic halls and chambers. The terms presented below denote the kind and level of misunderstanding (of ordinary perception) that the Chöd practitioner seeks to undo through this spiritual practice and lifestyle. The Chöd adept gradually learns to exploit the immediacy of experience in compromising or terrifying situations where the "I" (the egoic self) typically looms large. The adept uses the mind's habitual tendencies for self-protection—for protection against impingement upon it (the "self")—from others, to monitor the mind's fear and attachment and "cut through" that self-grasping mind, the mind which grasps mistakenly onto a seemingly solid, self-existent "I." The adept is advised to utilize the encounter with difficult circumstances by putting into practice what has been learned. As Kyabje Zong Rinpoché instructs,

> "Right there! Put the 'correct view' on that experience."[3]

Certain conceptual terms correspond to the work the adept will do to challenge their deeply set sense of identity, of a capital "S" "Self." I was taught that these conceptual terms are necessary to understand in order to be able to fully engage in this practice of "severance" (Chöd) and undo the habits that keep the individual "trapped" in cyclic existence (Skt. *saṃsāra*; Tib. *'khor ba*). The adept utilizes these terms in the contexts of philosophical contemplation, ritual practice, and a lifestyle based on purposeful renunciation.

Philosophical contemplation and lifestyle refer to the practitioner's meditative engagement with these philosophical concepts both during and in-between meditation sessions (the Chöd ritual practice sessions). Buddhist scholar-practitioners emphasize the period of time spent between sessions as a valuable opportunity for practice. A Chöd sādhana is meant to be a life practice rather than merely a ritualized meditation rite. Practicing a sādhana in the tantric context actually means adopting a way of ceasing ordinary involvement in circumstances and instead accomplishing a path to enlightenment.[4] One is reminded of the spontaneous dharmic songs of realization that Milarepa was inspired to compose and sing aloud to *saṃsāric* beings who he encountered occasionally during his years of meditative contemplation and retreat in West Tibet.

## Conceptual Terminology

The following conceptual terms from Buddhist philosophy will assist in an understanding of Chöd practice:

- "holding two" or "dualistic-grasping" or "duality" (Tib. *gnyis 'dzin*);
- "deceptive truth" or "conventional truth" or "relative truth" (Tib. *kun rdzob bden pa*);
- "ultimate truth" (Tib. *don dam bden pa*);
- the "correct view" or "emptiness" (Skt. *śūnyatā*, Tib. *stong nyid*);
- "self-grasping" (Tib. *bdag 'dzin*);
- "grasping at true-existence" (Tib. *bden 'dzin*).

The "cutting" of "self-grasping" (*bdag 'dzin*) and "grasping at true existence (*bden 'dzin*) concerns what is known as "cutting off" the truly-existent "I," which is essentially the goal of Chöd practice.

### Dualistic Grasping (Tib. *gnyis 'dzin*)

"Holding two" (*gnyis 'dzin*) is a literal translation of "two" (*gnyis*) "*holding*" (*'dzin*).

Lama Thubten Yeshe refers often in his oral discourses to the problem of the ordinary mental activity of "dualistic grasping." By this, he means the mistaken habit of thinking of subject and object as independent and separate, which he identifies as the root of suffering. Herbert Guenther explains "dualistic grasping" as "the belief in subject and object as ultimate entities."[5]

Ven. Pencho Rabgey explains the philosophical perspective of those who retain this mental state as follows:

> The mind that [uncritically] apprehends the outside object and object perceiver/subject as being separate and having no relationship; and, in seeing this, [apprehending in this way], understands this to be the true mode of existence of that self and object.[6]

He adds that "a high practitioner sees the object but understands it in a different way."

Thus, *gnyis 'dzin* is the dualistic view that regards subject and object as separate and unrelated. It is also explained with respect to only external objects (leaving the subject perceiver out of it for the moment). In this case, *gnyis 'dzin* is the mind that mistakenly sees objects as possessing one of two possible realities: either an outside object is "truly-existent" (arising from its own side, self-existent and permanent, unaffected by causes and conditions) or it is "nonexistent." The opposite of either of these two extremes—of substantialism (the former view) and nihilism (the latter view)—is not the other, but the Middle Way view between these two poles. The Middle Way was the view of Nāgārjuna, who is said to have received the *Perfection of Wisdom Sūtra* (*Prajñāpāramitā Sūtra*) from the nāgas, and whose interpretation of "emptiness" forms the basis of thought undergirding Chöd practice.

There are two levels or "two truths" to every object: the "conventional or deceptive truth" and the "ultimate truth." Every phenomenon exists, functions, and has meaning on a "conventional" level. We can see an outside object, use it, and work with it. But, on the "ultimate" level, it has no intrinsic existence other than that which is imputed upon it. Consider, for example, the label of "president" given to a person. She was not born "president," but later she was elected, given the title, and treated according to the conventions of that office. However, "president" is not the essence of who she is. She will not always be "president." Her status is impermanent. And when she passes away and takes rebirth, again, she will not be reborn as "president."[7]

## Identifying Emptiness

In Buddhist teachings I have attended over the past decades, Tibetan scholar-practitioners explain that "emptiness" does not mean "nothingness;" it means "empty" of, or lacking in, "self-existence." In other words, when a lama states that "all phenomena are lacking 'self-existence,'" it means phenomena do not come into being on their own. Seeing the total mutual interdependence of all phenomena is understood in relation to the view of "emptiness."[8] Moreover, to refer to emptiness and to discuss emptiness is different than having a nonconceptual realization of emptiness. The experience of having a nonconceptual realization of "emptiness" is said to be ineffable.[9] This is the goal of Chöd meditation practice and, in particular, its rituals, in which recurring rhythms in patterned flow are conjoined with melodic refrains to aid the practitioner in achieving a contemplative state of meaningful depth and transcendence.

As Pala reminded me, "That is why Buddha said, '*ma sam jö mé*' (Tib. *smra bsam brjod med*), meaning 'inconceivable, inexpressible' when describing the essence of emptiness," quoting the first four syllables of a well-known liturgical verse of homage to Yum Chenmo.[10] On the one hand, the wisdom experienced from the realization of "emptiness" cannot be described. On the other hand, the experience in tantric practices, like Chöd, where one visualizes oneself as the buddha deity Machik Labdrön, and at the same time contemplates one's emptiness, contains the experience of emptiness in the same moment of consciousness. The Dalai Lama explains that this is the special value of tantric practice:

> In the tantric practice of deity yoga . . . a single moment of consciousness apprehends the divine form of a deity while, at the same time, being clearly aware of its empty nature. So, in this case, both meditation on the deity and an apprehension of emptiness coexist in complete form within a single cognitive moment.[11]

## Two Truths: "Conventional"/"Ultimate"

Acharya Thupten Champa maintains that while the presentation of the four noble truths may be difficult at first for someone to grasp, those of higher capacity of intelligence may find it easier to understand all of Buddhadharma within the teaching on the "two truths." The "conventional truth" is the apparent mode of existence of any object, entity, or phenomenon which we can see, hear, smell, taste, touch, or think about. The "ultimate truth" is the insight into the actual way in which it exists, the actual nature of any object, entity, or phenomenon. Due to our conditioned perception, our initial apprehension of objects is misleading. We do not differentiate the "conventional truth" and "ultimate truth" of every object we encounter, even though every object is able to possess both "truths." According to Acharya Thupten Champa, the "conventional" and "ultimate truths" are perhaps most clearly explained in the concise poetic verses of Je Tsongkhapa:

> When with respect to all phenomena of samsara and nirvana,
> You see that cause and effects never deceive their laws,

And when you have dismantled the focus of objectification,
At that point you have entered the path that pleases the Buddhas.

So long as the two understandings—of appearance,
Which is undeceiving dependent origination,
And emptiness devoid of all theses—remain separate,
So long you have not realized the intent of the Sage.

However at some point when, without alternation but at once,
The instant you see that dependent origination is undeceiving,
If the entire object of grasping at certitude is dismantled,
At that point your analysis of the view has culminated.

Furthermore when appearance dispels the extreme of existence,
And when emptiness dispels the extreme of non-existence,
And if you understand how emptiness arises as cause and effect,
You will never be captivated by views grasping at extremes.[12]

We experience a referential point, a "self," identifying strongly with our name, body, and our accomplishments when we hear our favorite music, hear our dearest ones' voices, and think about our most prized material objects. These strong experiences (of "self") are not to be denied as "nonexistent," just as our visual perception of a mountain on the horizon as a reference point to where we sit is not "nonexistent." Other examples may illustrate the strong sense of "self": when someone insults me and I feel "he hurt 'me' " or " 'I' have been hurt." Or when my perception of "self" clouds my ability to see another person's perspective clearly. Or when "my position" requires defending in the midst of a conversation with a colleague/friend/loved one who disagrees strongly with my point of view. In all these situations, the "self" seems to be "truly-existent," very real and large; in fact, it seems *not* "nonexistent." Yet, if even the opaque objects we perceive are not "truly-existent," if they are contingent, dependently arising, interdependent phenomena, then how could the "self" and its referents "I," "me," "mine" be "truly existent"? When we differentiate between the egoic sense of "self" and the psychophysical aggregates (which include the body and the mind) we can gradually come to see that there actually is no "self" to harm. Yet, while this disidentification with the egoic "self" requires effort channeled through a powerful practice such as Chöd, the corollary is that we entertain an absurdity: we accept all phenomena as they appear and believe in what we perceive with our senses uncritically. The root of all suffering stems from a person's habitual identification with a "self" that is "truly-existent." We may extrapolate from the philosophical theory to a practical example of the experience of sound/music.

## The Relativity of Sound

### Cultural Relativity

Music is culturally relative, meaning that any given piece of music is not intrinsically beautiful. Conversely, if a collection of sounds or musical performance were intrinsically beautiful to everyone, then no matter the society, culture, or time period, that sound/music would be regarded equally by everyone as beautiful. However, this is not the case. Certainly, there is strong interdependence between sociocultural milieu, cultural identity, and musical aesthetics; and this connection makes possible and credible sociomusical homologies.[13] Sound and music provide a basis for meditation upon emptiness and mutual dependence.

### Physical-Cognitive Relativity

Our experience of sound, of say, a plucked lute, is dependent on the vibration of air molecules reaching our ear drums. Our sense faculties, neurological pathways, and mental factors help us understand that the occurrence of the pluck is a contributing cause to our experience of the lute sound. Every sound is completely "empty" of self-existent properties. It is interrelated with all phenomena around it, including:

a) the space or media through which it vibrates;

b) our physiology which allows us to experience sound vibrations as tones;

c) our aesthetically charged cultural values (positive or negative) and subjective scales of acceptance or rejection attributed to it in terms of listening enjoyment; and,

d) societally based measures of commercial worth, social use, political function, and economic value.

Meditating upon sound/music at this level of analysis can help one to reach an experiential realization of dependent-arising or emptiness. This same insight can be useful at the level of interpersonal interaction.

## Emptiness in Practice

When we refer to a person as "enemy," whether in thought or by spoken word, it is a label merely imputed upon that person and has little basis in reality. The extent to which there appears to be a person who seems to think of ways to harm us or say hurtful things to us has much to do with the perceivers' own sense of reality. As practitioners-in-training, we are instructed to endeavor to regard the label of "enemy" as being given by ourselves to a person who is empty of "self-existent" properties. Furthermore, that "enemy" may be driven to harm us due to his or her own misapprehension of what kind of karmic effect harming us will have on him or herself.[14]

If, on the one hand, someone thinks that something does not exist because it could not exist, or could never exist, then that is considered to be a wrong view as it does not obey the law of karma. Things and events are brought into effect because of causes and conditions. If a phenomenon existed prior to causes and conditions, it must be a permanent phenomenon. If a phenomenon exists independent of causes and conditions, then there is no way it could be destroyed or embellished (it could not subsequently change and become something else or disappear). Take space, for example, which appears to be a permanent phenomenon relative to the transitory nature of clouds. Clouds, rain, and lightning are objects that appear in space but do not obliterate space.[15] One meditation that forms the basis of the preliminary training for practicing the Chöd ritual (in addition to other tantric practices) involves considering the clouds, rain, and such as symbolic of negative thoughts arising in one's mind whereas the true nature of mind is symbolically like the sky: clear and pure.

## Chöd Practice as Antidote to Ignorance (*ma rig pa*)

Ignorance here is defined as the mental state of not understanding the way in which "self" and "phenomena" actually exist. In Buddhist philosophy the way in which "self" and "phenomena" exist is considered according to the two truths, the "conventional" and "ultimate truth." Within this perspective, the conventional truth is understood to refer to the way in which your self and other people's selves appear to you to exist at the present moment before any critical examination into their true nature. The "ultimate truth" refers to the way in which self and phenomena actually exist, beyond their natural appearance. This requires some further explanation. It is traditionally held that one can only understand the "ultimate truth" of "emptiness" when it is realized through extensive and protracted meditation on the *Prajñāpāramitā Sūtra* and by engaging in tantric sādhanas such as those for practicing Mañjuśrī, Yamāntaka, and Chöd, among others. One purpose of these meditations is to investigate and realize the true nature of reality, the way in which phenomena actually exist. Beginner practitioners work with investigating the "self of persons" (*gang zag gi bdag*) to search for the truly-existent "I." Chöd ritual practictioners work with this in the intimate site of their own body.

Furthermore, practitioners work with each individual phenomenon during their training.[16] They attempt to discern whether there is any essential reality to it, any intrinsic quality to a phenomenon that can be identified as self-existent, independent of any causes or conditions outside of its immediate self-sufficient appearance. When all phenomena, including space, time, ideas, concepts, and so forth are each seen equally through the meditator's perspective as being impossibly "self-existent," they are understood to be merely dependent-arisings and their immediate appearance is considered to be like an apparition as if conjured by a magician. They are seen as real, or "conventionally true," insofar as they are appearing to the mind and senses, but their actual reality—their mode of existence—is not independent of other phenomena, including the perceiver's mind.

## Tibetan Buddhist Doctrine and Practice

Tibetan Buddhists practice the tantric or Vajrayāna (Adamantine Vehicle) form of Buddhism, which is itself based upon the Mahāyāna (Universal Vehicle) ethic of *bodhicitta*, seeking liberation from cyclic existence with the motivation to do so for the benefit of all sentient beings. Both these vehicles encompass the Hinayāna, also called Theravāda (Vehicle of Individual Liberation) in which seeking liberation from cyclic existence for oneself is the primary goal.

> The general structure of the Buddhist path is outlined in the first turning of the wheel of Dharma in terms of the thirty-seven aspects of the path to enlightenment. They are divided into seven categories. First are the four mindfulnesses, referring to mindful-

> ness of body, feelings, mind, and phenomena. Mindfulness here refers to contemplative practices that focus on the fundamentally unsatisfactory nature of samsara and on the transitoriness of this conditioned existence, the perpetual cycles of our habitual patterns of thought and behaviour. It is by means of such reflections that the practitioner develops a true determination to become free from the cycle of conditioned existence.[17]

Thus, seeking liberation from the "cycle of conditioned existence" or "cyclic existence" for one's own benefit is the chief goal of the Theravādan Buddhist path. Seeking liberation for oneself is also known as the mind of renunciation. Wishing to seek liberation from *saṃsāra* is absolutely necessary before one can become a Mahāyānist, who has the wish to liberate others. The defining characteristic of a Mahāyānist is one in whom the thought is born, having already determined to liberate oneself from *saṃsāra* that, since all other sentient beings are likewise suffering in *saṃsāra* like oneself, their fate uncertain like one's own, one will decide to liberate all sentient beings from *saṃsāra*. By comparison, liberating one being would be severely limiting since so many other beings would be left behind. Thus the Mahāyānists resolve from the start to practice Dharma for the purpose of gaining enlightenment, a state in which they can help other beings by teaching or engaging in other beneficient activities. The Vajrayāna or tantric path is the swifter path to enlightenment, and is based upon the Mahāyānist ethic. It is important for the practitioners to know what they are supposed to think and do in Chöd meditation practice since it is different from other tantric meditation practices, as well as to understand the purpose of performance practices in the various kinds of Chöd rituals.

## Guru-Deity Yoga in Chöd

Guru-deity yoga is an essential part of the Chöd practice whether on the beginner level of merely visualizing the process of separation or the advanced level of actually separating consciousness from the body. There is some confusion about the extent and nature of guru-deity yoga in the Chöd ritual. Students often have questions about the point in the sādhana during which the practitioner should perform deity yoga[18] and which deity to visualize oneself as: Machik Labdrön (in a peaceful aspect), or her wrathful aspect Troma Nagmo (Tib. Khro ma nag mo), Vajrayoginī, or Yum Chenmo? This suggests the complexity of visualizations in Chöd and the versatility in attitude required in tantric practices. Any puzzlement around when to perform deity yoga in the Chöd ritual sādhana, *Dedicating the Illusory Body*, is due to the ordinariness and vulnerability the Chöd practitioner is supposed to feel during the main section of "preparatory practices."[19] The practitioner feels vulnerable due to his or her willful exposure of the body to malevolent spirits. This is the antithesis of the sensibility derived from performing deity yoga meditations, in which the practitioner regards the "self" as enlightened, and the deity's environment as obtaining purified qualities. Early in the practice, during the seventh verse when the practitioner visualizes *the body as a corpse, and the mind as a corpse-bearer* the practitioner does not have to be concerned about the "self" since, as Zong Rinpoché says, there is no body or mind left to be harmed.

In the other Highest Yoga Tantric practices, the deity yoga visualization that is generated at the outset is maintained and embellished throughout the sādhana. In contrast to this, when first going to the place of practice, the Chöd practitioner cultivates the "divine pride"[20] of the deity and goes according to the "four ways." As the practitioner travels to the site, each "way" expresses a different dance-like movement of a ḍākinī who chants that she is surrounded by a cloud of gurus and deities above, while hosts of gods and ghosts surround her on the ground as she "goes to lead all beings to enlightenment."[21] Je Tsongkhapa suggests walking first in the opposite direction to the intended destination, or putting one's shoes on backward to throw off the spirits who may not be expecting the practitioner.[22] This is done so as not to surprise the spirits, and to ensure that they do not suffer from experiencing fear. Many of the spirits are weak, fragile beings who would flee if frightened.

Another method of "going" explained in the Ganden Chöd Tradition's sādhana, *Cutting the Root of Self-Grasping* (*bdag 'dzin tsar gcod*) is that of visualizing a huge Vajrayoginī above the designated place of practice (*gnyan sa*) when setting out from one's home to the site. The practitioner visualizes that Vajrayoginī powerfully invites all harmdoers and spirits throughout the universe, calling them to the site in a manner they cannot disobey, gently but firmly hooking their hearts with her mentally produced ritual hooked weapons, such that they cannot leave or harm the practitioner. This rather confrontational mode protects some of the weaker beings from being trampled and harmed by the larger more powerful and aggressive spirits who await the practitioner's distribution (*bkye*). It ensures that all beings will receive the gift of the body, materials, and Dharma teaching. All the preparations must be made by the practitioner before the beings and spirits can partake.

The notion that one would not cultivate "divine pride" throughout a Highest Yoga Tantric practice, such as Chöd, is corrected here. Generally, divine pride is an essential component of tantric practice. The Fourteenth Dalai Lama maintains that "[i]n all four tantras—Action, Performance, Yoga, and Highest Yoga—it is established that a practitioner must view his or her body as a divine one."[23] The chief difference between the four classes of tantra is with respect to the generation and completion stages, which is thoroughly explained and practiced in Highest Yoga Tantras but not explicitly dealt with in Chöd. As Jérôme Edou explains, it is assumed that the practitioner would know at which points in a given Chöd sādhana to do generation stage and completion stage practices.[24] Lama Tsongkhapa also provides one line in his Chöd practice commentary that mentions those with knowledge of how to do so may, at that point, engage in completion stage practices.[25]

Now that the groundwork has been laid, it is possible to address the question posed at the outset: which buddha deity should the practitioner visualize becoming? In fact, generally speaking it does not matter whether the practitioner visualizes themselves as Machik Labdrön or Vajrayoginī since they all have the exact same nature: they are regarded as fully enlightened buddhas.[26] On a personal level, it is advised that the practitioner receive instructions from their lama about which deity to visualize generating at which point in a given Chöd sādhana.

Having made these qualifications, the visualizations of deity yoga in the Ganden Chöd Tradition sādhana, *Dedicating the Illusory Body*, proceed as follows. In the first stages, when heading to the site of practice, the practitioner generates in visualization the appearance of Machik Labdrön. During the preparatory practices while the practitioner is visualized as an ordinary being, Vajrayoginī is visualized just above and in front of the crown of the practitioner's head—she is magnificent in appearance and regarded as completely inseparable from the lama, Machik Labdrön, and Yum Chenmo. After the transfer of consciousness out of the old body and into the lama's heart, the practitioner visualizes emerging out of the heart of the lama as a green karma action ḍākinī who has the power to cut and transform the old body into purified substances and distribute it to all beings throughout the universe. Lamas have various interpretations and I did not understand this for some years,[27] but to the extent that it will be helpful for subsequent students of the Chöd practice and other readers, I place my understanding here.

It must be made clear that all tantric adepts would say that it is possible to "cut through" the mental grasping onto the notion of a truly-existent "I"—the mistaken notion that there is an intrinsic, self-substantiated "self" existing apart from the conditioned existence of possessing a body and mind. Advanced practitioners maintain that cutting through this "self-grasping ignorance" (*bdag 'dzin ma rig pa*) produces nothing less than realization of the ultimate truth through the experience of a dramatically (quite literally, in the ritual context) altered state of being.[28] Emptiness—the insight allowing cutting through the egoic identification with the "self"—is realized by reaching beyond ordinary perceptions of conventional reality, and seeing ultimate reality *through* the conventional. This is an ineffable quality, inexpressible, and beyond discursive thought. Although emptiness has been written about extensively by Indian mahāsiddhas and Tibetan scholar-adepts in the well-developed literary tradition of spiritual biography (*rnam thar*), through which an adept reflexively recounts the method he or she practiced to attain states of realization, there is said to be no literary or musical substitute for experiencing transcendence.

By considering this sādhana within this wider lens of tantric ritual studies, it shifts interest onto the *performance* of the meditation practice without recentering it, and without "over-correcting" for the literary textual focus of earlier analyses. Scholars working in an earlier era during which analytical work prioritized philologically based evidence were less engaged in the analyses of the phenomenological aspects of performance.

## The Goal of "Cutting"

Therefore, what is to be "cut" is the mind's grasping to any phenomenon as if it has self-existence. This includes the appearance to the mind of a melody that one identifies as "my music," or a voice one recognizes as "my friend" or "my enemy"—or, for that matter, any sound or phenomenon that appears to the senses as having reference to an "I" that is independently existent. With the "self" symbolically associated with the body, the notion of independence is too easily assimilated with the "I." This is what the practice of Chöd seeks to lay bare within the instance of a dramatic fearful appearance of a threat to the "self."

To put it in a logical formulation regarding death and rebirth: either the "self," the mind, or consciousness, ceases to exist when the body dies, or the "self," mind, or consciousness continues after the demise of the body. This is the first point of consideration. If the "self," the feeling "I," passes out of existence immediately upon the clinical death of the body, then there is—Tibetan lamas say—no point in even practicing Dharma. If the opposite is the case, that the body is temporary and the relationship of the mind, consciousness, and feeling of "I" continues afterward, then there is a strong reason to practice Dharma. If a person can recognize this impermanence of the body, and the relative continuity of the mind/consciousness/"I," then an important decision can be made about whether this is a good enough reason to follow a spiritual path. (It does not have to be thought of as a spiritual path. In fact, it could be an ethical path.) The question remains, where does a person's mind/consciousness go after death? Does it disappear from the universe, travel to another plane, or go directly into another body? Can a mind be body-less? What determines where a mind goes after death? The answers, according to experienced Buddhist practitioners, may be explored through study of karma. Based on the law of karma, the causes and conditions that affect one's life everyday continue to affect life after the demise and passing away of this life's body. That is to say, one's habitual propensities and mental attitude (positive/negative) determine where one takes birth and what one may experience in the next life. If one is happy with all of one's experiences in this life and has no desire for any change of circumstance then there would be no reason to practice Dharma. There would be no purpose in seeking a different behavior, in seeking renunciation of *saṃsāra*. However, if one is disappointed with one's mental life, one's feelings, and one's mental activities, there would be a good logical rationale to seek a different attitude and different mental habits that will produce more positive behavior which in turn will produce positive results.

Some practitioners express confusion around the matter of one's identity during the Chöd ritual; perhaps this is because the notion of "self" is so sacrosanct. They wonder at what point during the ritual should they perform deity yoga, and whether they should see themselves as the deity or as ordinary. According to lineage Chöd masters, the deity yoga (visualizing oneself as Buddha Vajrayoginī, or Machik Labdrön) is performed prior to arriving at the place of practice, and immediately following the "transference of consciousness" ritual. Otherwise, during the Chöd practice one should view oneself as an ordinary person, and vulnerable to the outside elements.

Monks and nuns engaging in Chöd practices are instructed to visualize themselves as they were prior to the time they took ordination vows, wearing their previous garments rather than their sacred robes, because they would otherwise be breaking a vow by "cutting" their body. Lay people need not do this, but the notion of cultivating an attitude of being exposed and vulnerable to the invited spirits and malevolent beings is important. Exercising one's response to fear in relation to "self" leads to both introspective analysis and ritualized action: "cutting off" the symbolic "body" from the attachments of the mind assists in "cutting off" the misconceptions of the way in which the "self" appears to exist. The ritual act as a performed event is based on relationships: (1) it is in response to other *saṃsāric* beings' apparent malevolence, and suffering that ensues from this; (2) it takes place in the blessed soundscape of sung and performed melodies that intone the power of the lineage lamas, ḍākinīs, and buddhas; and (3) it is one's previous karmic relationship with the beings who one has wronged that needs attentive healing and repair through the paying down of karmic debts, with the compassionate giving away of the mentally transformed body.

8

# Transmission and Transformation

## Approaching the Chöd Practice

A Vignette

5:00 pm, late August, Tibetan Settlement, Karnataka, South India

As the evening draws closer, a breath-like breeze searches the roadside Tibetan café where I'm quickly finishing an early dinner of *momo* (dumpling) soup. The wind lifts the sand and dust off the rolling hills of India's gifted-farmland—ground on which the group of elder lay Tibetan Chöd practitioners I'm to meet again have tilled the soil for some fifty years—and moves along the reddened muddy road that leads to the nearby monastery up at one end. Down at the other end of the road is the "Tibetan Camp," as they still call the refugee settlements, where they practice Chöd nightly. They ritually gather at 5:30 p.m. and practice Chöd until 9:45 p.m. They wake up early at 3:30 a.m. and work all day in the fields and then return to practice Chöd together every evening.

One of the elders told me last night that they now wish, in their last years, to make their lives meaningful by devoting themselves to meditation practice. Shopping for a bag in the practically empty market during the afternoon, I overheard some of the resident shopkeepers gossiping about matters of little consequence. That atmosphere of wasted breath, in itself, seemed to be an incentive for the elder Tibetans to learn to sing the Chöd melodies with their hearty lungs. Such a seachange in lifeways is not particular to Tibetan Buddhist society. Across Asia, elders who were not necessarily devout practitioners during their youth or middle age seek retreat in a hermitage, or an older monastery building, and live out their twilight years piously among a community of fellow lay retirees, parents and grandparents, while ordained monks and nuns come to visit. They perform daily prayer rituals and devote their remaining days and nights to the accumulation of Buddhist merit or "sonam" (Tib. *bsod nams*) and the purification of "sins and obscurations" (Tib. *sdig sgrib*). Generally speaking, elder lay Tibetans will meditate, if they have learned how to, and perform mantra recitations, prostrations, and make offerings. Above all, they carefully avoid harming any living being.

Walking by me on the pathway to the Chöd practice site is one of the elder women who knows English well and wants to chat. She's jolly and does not mince her words. Her sentences are punctuated with a smile and a little laughter, amused at my presence though not in a way that makes me feel uncomfortable, quite the contrary. From the questions she poses, she seems pleased that we are so similarly interested despite the cultural and continental gulf between us. When we reach the courtyard, I see that I am the only Westerner, and the dogs and strangers need to be introduced to me formally.

> *"Di Jeff re, Jampel re," she says. "Khorang Canada ne re. Chöd shing gi yo re. Khorang gi, 'Khyerangtsho nyamdo Chöd nyamlen che gi yin na, di gi re bes?' ke cha tri song."*
>
> ("This is Jeff, or Jampel. He is from Canada. He knows some Chöd, and asks if it is okay if he practices with us.")
>
> *"Oh, Di gi re!"*
>
> ("Yes, it's ok!")

While we await the move to the practice place, there is an awareness of the heightened hesitation and anticipation prior to gathering to practice Chöd that transcends age and any social barrier. We are in a transition space, chatting about Chöd, and we will soon enter the room where we will practice the ritual. I feel the sense of penultimate loss of social context and identity as my previous world falls away from me. I lose my sense of identity as "ethnographer," and my role as "academic"; I am not even "performer"; there among many ascetics-in-training, I am but one. In this moment, it is a recognition of renunciation, the powerful sense that "my mind is carrying a corpse." As the sādhana recitation goes: *lu po ro dang sem nyi ro kur tshul* (trans: "[my] mind, a corpse bearer, carries a corpse, the body").[1] Loose and giddy, two of the men joke around while four of the women spend these few minutes together practicing a new melody. The woman leading them holds a piece of paper on which is a numbered notation that is typically used in the transmission of folksongs from the secular tradition, where a line may be sung as "6, 1 2 3" or "la, do re me." Since the melodies in the Chöd ritual are highly melismatic,[2] it is expedient to use this type of notation together with the leadership of one person who already knows the melody.[3] She repeats the melody in short phrases for the three newcomers while some dogs begin to mill around. Later, while we are inside the room practicing and reach the sections where the *kangling* (thighbone trumpet)[4] is blown to call forth all the spirits and other beings, the dogs outside howl together; it has the sense of a gathering in a haunted place and it certainly augmented the soundscape of an already eerie preliminary practice.

I did not expect them to be so expert in their performance, but they were so unified in their drumbeats, and so accomplished in their singing that I was greatly moved. The *umdzé* (Tib. *dbu mdzad*) or "chanting master," an elder Tibetan who is also an expert in Tibetan opera, led each melody with subdued volume but perfectly pitched entrances. (Perhaps his frequent travels throughout the Tibetan exile community in India, where he sings in various opera productions, keep him looking like he is fifty years old while he is actually seventy years old).

A less sprightly man, a warrior who now wishes to repent for his years of more questionable behavior, wobbles from side to side and has a smooth lurch forward due to sitting for extended periods of time and arthritic muscle tension. His spoken voice is less sure than that of the *umdzé*, but there is something pleasantly sincere in his approach. He swings the *ḍamaru* drum hesitatingly, unsure as yet about the rhythm, his muscular right arm holds it high above his head without the least sign of tiring, while others use their left forearms as an armrest with their drums swinging at shoulder height (their left forearms are folded across their stomach as a support for the drumming right arm).

Afterward, simple biscuits and hot black tea are distributed by two of the women practitioners who carry in large trays from a side kitchen. Other members of the group stay in place, sitting cross-legged around the circle, now with *ḍamaru* drums resting vertically by their right thighs, as is the protocol. Each helps to distribute the biscuits and tea by twisting torsos and leaning side to side. Our throats are parched from singing for over an hour and we gently embrace the wetness of tea, the teacup edges lingering on our lips. The dryness of the biscuits turning wet brings an ironic charge, our transformed bodies having just been fed to others, the ultimate dissolution of the "I." Our corporeal identity has shifted somewhat, and is now in transition. Playful humor in quieter, more relaxed, tones ricochets off the walls in this space of reconstructing identities through laughter and community.

## Musical and Spiritual Transmission of Chöd

In the first part of this chapter, we explore factors affecting the transmission of the Chöd ritual practices. We discuss pedagogical techniques, practice sessions, the ethnomusicological modes of transmission and the expected results. We also explore the roles in the relationship between the ethnographer/disciple and consultant/teacher in ethnomusicological research when studying in the apprentice situation of a lineage transmission of Chöd. At times, the narrative is reflexive and personal since this is an accurate reflection of the context of transmission.

In addition, we address the concerns Chöd lamas have expressed about the continuity of the Ganden Chöd Tradition, focusing on what I call "the confluence of transmission with dissemination and preservation." Since Chöd is a musical-spiritual ritual practice tradition, its transmission effectively requires two types of transmission: a musical transmission and a spiritual transmission (Tib. *lung*). These two are distinct, but related, aspects of the Chöd Tradition; both are required for successful continuity of the Chöd lineage and its blessings. With very few Chöd lamas in the Ganden Chöd Tradition, the lineage may be in danger of extinction.

I suggest that the ways in which digital recording technology is used as a means of Chöd transmission requires some rethinking and restrategizing if the tradition is to survive to the next generation.

Where the use of a recording of a Chöd ritual performance has conflated purposes—of transmission and dissemination (as well as preservation)—it is likely not effectively serving the originally intended goals of the recording project. I suggest that digital technology and affordable consumer-level recording and playback devices make possible a retooling of Chöd recordings toward a pedagogical paradigm, such that they may more appropriately suit the present context of Chöd lineage transmission—a context in which Chöd lamas and disciples are spread throughout a transnational Diaspora and can only meet infrequently.

## Confluence of Transmission with Dissemination and Preservation

Perhaps never before has less contact with a Chöd teacher been compensated for, or matched by, as many or more teachings available online, on video, audio mp3, or other formats. There seem to be more minutes of digital files on Chöd music and training available than there are minutes available with a teacher. The logical conclusion that might be drawn from this is that it is therefore easier, more efficient, and ultimately more beneficial to utilize the technologically available teachings. However, it is essential to consider the ramifications of this changed process in the "transmission" (in the musical sense) of the Chöd Tradition and the extent to which this might affect the "transmission" (in the Buddhist sense) of this meditation ritual practice.

The meaning of the term "transmission" in ethnomusicology differs in essence from its use in Buddhist studies. A detailed explanation of the differences in interpretation of this term in each discipline may be helpful. In Buddhist studies, the "transmission" (Tib. *lung*) of a given teaching is understood to carry with it the blessings of the lineage lamas who have come before and practiced that particular teaching. Since Tibetan Buddhists practice guru-deity yoga, the lama's teachings—conducted through the "door of speech"[5]—are given credence as the oral blessing of a buddha. Thus, whether the lama is reading aloud a written text, reciting a mantra, or singing a melody, each act of speech is considered to have a blessing-imbued result for the listeners because the lama's realization of the ultimate nature is transmitted through their sacred speech. However, the extent to which the transmission will have a positive result is said to be dependent upon the disciples' faith in the lama.

In contrast, "transmission" in ethnomusicology has a different connotation. Some scholars maintain that "music transmission" has to do with pedagogy: that "music transmission" of oral traditions concerns the musical training and passing on of the skills, techniques, and repertoire that build a foundation for performance expertise. Harvard ethnomusicologist, Kay Kaufman Shelemay, forwards the following definition:

> By musical transmission I refer to any communication of musical materials from one person to another whether by oral, aural, or written forms without regard for the time depth of materials transmitted. But for the sake of discussion here, I will focus

> primarily on the role of live musical performance in the process, and secondarily on musical materials mediated and conveyed by technologies such as the LP, cassette, or compact disc.[6]

I will pursue the following line of thought with respect to Shelemay's definition of transmission.

The Chöd ritual has moved from being a secret tradition that was passed down carefully by teacher to disciple over several centuries to a tradition that one can pay $115.00 for a seven DVD set and have it shipped to one's home.[7] One never has to leave one's computer desk or laptop, and can watch the teachings online or on a private disc set. Traditionally, many of the main lamas in the Ganden Chöd lineage would receive teachings only after traveling great distances to seek out a teacher at risk to themselves, or be instructed to meditate for years alone in a sealed cave before being given sacred instructions in Chöd meditation practice.[8] The transmission that I received involved traveling to and living in India; and, whilst in Canada, traveling by car the 133 kilometer (82 mile) journey, sometimes in challenging weather conditions, on a weekly basis.[9] Yet whatever Chöd disciples undergo today is said to be nothing compared to the hardship endured by the main lineage lamas whose hard-won teachings into the Chöd method were acquired only after arduous struggle with physical austerities (often said to be for the purpose of purification).

## Ethnomusicology and Emptiness: From Learner to Teacher

Music is highly intimate and personal, and is not "heard" in the same way by each person on each performance occasion. Ethnomusicologists have an opportunity to bridge the gap between how the ethnographic fieldworker seeks to understand a musical system and the musical system itself. As they write about musical experience, performance, the meaning of sound, and the social significance of shared singing and performing from the perspective of a student disciple (Skt. *śiṣya*), ethnomusicologists are perhaps less refined and more unmasked than their social and cultural anthropologist colleagues. They think about the music-making practices of their teachers through the lens of their own experiences during their apprenticeship. They are often humbled recipients of musical knowledge because they themselves become a student or an apprentice, as opposed to being merely a participant-observer.[10]

### Rules and Limits on the Apprenticeship

While the teacher may establish rules and limits on the apprenticeship, the ethnomusicologist may be encouraged to be working toward Mantle Hood's methodological practice model of "bi-musicality"—gaining a level of musical competency such that the "native consultant" and expert practitioners recognize them as being a proficient trainee, and perhaps later an exponent or medium of the indigenous expressive art. Thus, once entrusted as an apprentice of the tradition, the ethnomusicologist is usually given parameters that prescribe their involvement as an exponent. For instance, at a certain point in my training, my main Tibetan-Canadian Chöd teacher, Ven. Pencho Rabgey, initially said that I could take his place at a Toronto temple where he was invited to teach Chöd, since it was too far for him to travel on a weekly basis. He initially said I could teach the music of Chöd and performance practices to others, but not the meaning of the Chöd practice. Publicly, he called me a "professional" in terms of the musical abilities I had acquired. However, being able to gauge my level of understanding in my responses to everyday events, observing my changed demeanor and character (reduced anger, increased patience, an ability to get along with so-called "enemies," willingness to accept a loss, fear of accumulating negative karma, a wish to help and work for others' welfare, etc.), he still initially assessed me as being inadequately prepared to teach the meditational practice aspects of Chöd.

After some years, I asked again what to do in the context of the weekly ritual practice sessions at the "Chöd Club" when fellow Chöd "practitioners-in-training" asked me philosophical or religious questions related to the practice. I was instructed to respond if I knew the answer, particularly when I could give a reference to the source of my information. But, I was not allowed to teach new things, come up with new melodies, or divert from the traditional lineage practices . . . unless I wanted to accumulate large amounts of negative karma and send both myself and my lama to the lower realms together.[11]

## Chöd Pedagogy

### Group Practice

While musical performance in Chöd practice can be somewhat individualized, during group practice sessions it is highly social and involving. Music can summarize (in a national anthem, for example,) a collective identity that interns the self within the prism of a larger identity, where performance, expression, and gesture (hand over the heart, standing up tall, chin up, facing forward, head still, eyes looking straight ahead) is meant to display collective unity and a humbling of the self-as-hearer and self-as-performer before self-as-one-of-a-collective. We hear and perform differently when practicing in group contexts. Our priorities change as we seek to match our performing colleagues in sound, volume, linguistic articulation, and dynamic modulations. Thus, the music of a single yogin can be a clue to the expressive artistry of one exponent of a tradition; while in an ensemble, music can be a cohesive and collectivising expression, unifying the experience of discipleship.

### *Interaction between Musicians in Chöd Ensembles*

The Chöd ritual involves a meditation practice throughout a musical performance that lasts for between one to four hours—depending on the sādhana, and purpose for which it is practiced—during which the meditator engages in extensive musical and cognitive work. A music director, or *umdzé* (Tib. *dbu mdzad*), provides musical guidance for the ensemble. There are traditional protocols for following the *umdzé* that are subtly evident when exploring the interaction between practitioners/musicians in the ensemble. The signals between musicians while practicing are subtle, yet meaningful, as moments of shared agreement, adjustment, and sometimes "communion."[12] During discursive sessions preceding and following a ritual practice, the subject and tone of conversations can shift in emotional tenor. Before practice, sometimes expressions of anxiety and concern are present; while afterward, feelings of euphoria, and/or exhilaration may be shared over a cup of tea.

## Music Training and Transmission

While I was being trained in Chöd music performance practices by Ven. Pencho Rabgey ("Pala"), I was introduced to the Chöd pedagogical method for the transmission of melody. I later found out—through listening to the cassette recordings of Kyabje Zong Rinpoché made in 1983 and 1984 during his visits to Los Angeles, California and Lindsay, Ontario—that Pala's pedagogical method is quite similar to that of one of his main Chöd teachers. Zong Rinpoché transmitted the Chöd melodies in particular ways, for which we presently have recordings. While in Lindsay, Zong Rinpoché transmitted a Chöd sādhana to a group of disciples. On the audio cassette, we hear not only his singing, but can also attend to his pedagogical method. He sings the melody twice or three times *a capella*, and then follows by singing the same melody with the accompaniment of the *ḍamaru*. The bell's harmonics are too "live" and drown out some pitches in the melody, so it is not usually played during recordings (unless it can be dampened with a piece of duct tape on its inside[13]). In Los Angeles, there was a Chöd student to whom Rinpoché gave performance practice instructions as he proceeded through the sādhana liturgy. He gave alternative ways of performing the rhythm and melody in a couple of cases, describing the advantages of each when practicing in different contexts.

A videotape recording made in 1984 in the UK shows Zong Rinpoché practicing the *Chöd Tshogs* (Tib. *gcod tshogs*), the sādhana that he compiled by combining the Chöd practice with the *Guru Puja*, also known as the *Lama Chöpa* (Tib. *bla ma mchod pa*) or "Offering to the Spiritual Guide" practice. We see Rinpoché in the role of *umdzé*, leading a group practice of about seventy-five lay and ordained students through the ritual performance, from beginning to end. This was a videotaped performance of the ritual, not a pedagogical aid in the sense of his aforementioned audio cassettes. That being said, since Rinpoché was the only practitioner with a *ḍamaru*, the recording can function as a pedagogical aid as it illustrates certain aspects of the practice, including: the posture, at what height to hold the *ḍamaru*, the arm's position relative to the body, and how to rotate the *ḍamaru* with the wrist and hand. Although elderly at that time, he plays the large *ḍamaru* slowly and fluidly, holding it in his right arm as if it is made of light cotton material, rather than wood, indicating the strength of that arm's muscles from decades of Chöd practice. He leads the group practice calmly and steadily. Ven. Pencho Rabgey led group practice sessions through the *Chöd Tshogs* sādhana in Canada, having been requested to do so by Zong Rinpoché.

His Eminence Khalkha Jetsun Dampa Rinpoché produced cassettes and CDs of the sādhana, *Dedicating the Illusory Body*, together with his disciples Andrew and Nathalie (an English and French Canadian respectively) as a pedagogical aid to learn his melodies. Several Mongolian students visited Takten House, his residence and center in Dharamsala, for extended periods of time to study Chöd with Khalkha Rinpoché, and listened to his recordings to practice their melodies when absent from him. The earliest videorecording of Khalkha Rinpoché practicing Chöd that I saw was made in 1995, when his disciples in Vancouver recorded a VHS cassette of him performing the practice *Dedicating the Illusory Body*. Later, his students from Buriat produced a DVD featuring not only segments of this practice but also his return to Buriat and sites in Mongolia. Ven. Pencho Rabgey and I also made recordings of ourselves practicing the sādhana, *Dedicating the Illusory Body*. Zasep Tulku Rinpoché has also allowed audio and video recordings of his melodies, teachings, and practice of Chöd to be circulated among his students. Both Zasep Tulku Rinpoché and Ven. Pencho Rabgey were disciples of Khalkha Jetsun Dampa Rinpoché and Kyabje Zong Rinpoché, the two former heads of the lineage. As well, both are attempting to pass on the tradition with personal instruction, allowing students to use these recordings as teaching aids.

## Methods of Training

When learning a new melody, if one repeats the first stanza over and over again until the rhythm of the drum and its placement with the melody are suffused, one will understand where certain syllables land on the beat and which syllables are sung in-between the beats. This approach is similar to drilling a passage of a guitar-accompanied folk song. Since the guitar rhythm and the melodic pattern rarely changes from verse to verse, instead of singing the entire song through, the first verse can be sung repeatedly until it is close to perfect, with the logic being that if the melody of the initial verse syncs up with the rhythm perfectly, then the other verses will similarly follow. Conversely, if one tries to sing all verses (each with different poetry) at one time, that is, in immediate succession, some messiness and sloppiness is bound to occur. Concentrating on the new words in each line will distract the beginner, who needs to focus solely on the melody at first. The beginner practitioner is still feeling out where the drumbeats touch the melodic notes, and at which words. Moreover, while still learning the liturgical text, the Chöd practitioner-in-training has to attend to diction in addition to melodic movement and phrasing.

According to the traditional Tibetan pedagogical method, one first memorizes a sādhana's poetry, after which, one may receive an oral commentary explaining its meaning. In this way the commentary can be mentally absorbed more quickly because the main text is already familiar. The word-for-word translation and commentary into the poetry's meaning that I received illuminated the text on profound levels, deepening my practice.

Sometimes I was introduced to a new melody for the first time by my teachers singing through the poetry, which is not uncommon. Singing it through with one's guru when first encountering a melody and subritual is said to plant seeds for the text and melody to take root in one's mindstream. The expectation is that immediately after first being introduced to the melody and subritual, the student is to train carefully step-by-step to learn and memorize it.[14]

In sum, the method of training in a new melody under Zong Rinpoché and Ven. Pencho Rabgey is a process that usually proceeds as follows:

1) The melody is sung *a capella* to the first stanza with full ornamentation.

2) Then the melody is sung with the *ḍamaru*, leaving out some melodic ornaments in order to maintain the rhythmic structure within the tempo.

3) Finally, after the teacher's approval of the first stanza, the subsequent stanzas are sung.

Ven. Pencho Rabgey ensures that his students train by making multiple repetitions of reciting and singing each section. His pedagogical philosophy is not for the faint-hearted. He advises that the best way to learn is by trying, making mistakes, and then trying again. "If you try 1,000 times and get one right, still, you have learned *something*. It is much better than never having tried at all," he is fond of saying. Under his tutelage, I was encouraged to try repeatedly until the musical performance was as close to perfect as possible. Competency in musical performance is seen as but a gateway into practicing a Chöd sādhana in a deeper way.

Sometimes, in learning a new melody, Pala would insist that I study the smaller phrase fragments and vocal ornamentations. He would repeat these, prompting me to listen more closely in order to reproduce them. He often gently pushed me to sing a passage perfectly. Several times he would have us double back to practice the fully ornamented melody *a capella* even after learning to sing with the *ḍamaru*. As well, when I was unsure of the vocal ornamentation in a passage, I would ask him to repeat it. He did so several times, trying to produce the ideal model for me to emulate, which was very useful. He encouraged me to listen, and sing immediately after him. Whenever I asked him to repeat a phrase, he would kindly do so.

## Melody and Drum Together: Dropping Ornaments

According to my analyses of the recordings of Chöd performances, there are noticeably fewer melodic ornaments when the *ḍamaru* is being played, such that a drum-accompanied performance needs to drop several *melismas* in order to keep pace with the rhythm. I noticed this during my lessons, and remarked on it to Pala. His response was a matter-of-fact, "Of course, we have to drop some of these ornaments. The next drumbeat is coming too fast to sing all the notes. But you must know how to perform it both ways." In other words, it is important to know the fully ornamented version of the melody when singing unaccompanied, as well as the basic tune version that is used when accompanying oneself with the *ḍamaru*.

### *Chöd Ḍamaru Training Techniques*

I noticed that when playing the *ḍamaru* it can be difficult, depending on the construction of the particular Chöd *ḍamaru*, to be keep the drum in a vertical plane when twisting it to and fro with one's hand and wrist, while also turning it inward and outward with one's arm. The practitioner has to test the *ḍamaru* for comfort in his or her hand due to its particular shape and weight. Furthermore, it is important to feel the extent to which the pellets are attached to strings that are of a length such that rotating the *ḍamaru* slowly allows them to strike the two opposite-faced drum skins simultaneously. The *ḍamaru* should be held aloft vertically, perpendicular to the floor, with the skins at a 90-degree angle to the ground. It should not lean to either side at any point in its rotation, but feel merely as a constant weight on one's arm, which one is continually shifting due to the centripetal force of the swinging pellets.[15]

### *Physical Exertion in Ḍamaru Training*

Some drums are extremely light, such as those made from acacia (*seng deng*) wood that are now produced in Nepal and distributed to individual shops and suppliers worldwide. According to Chöd commentaries, ideally the *ḍamaru* should be made of red sandalwood, which is quite a heavy wood and produces a mellow but spirited tone, but the tree is now a protected species and other types of wood need to be used. Each *ḍamaru* can also be of varying thickness. The space between the two concave (bowl-shaped) drum halves may be wider or narrower, allowing for a larger or smaller hand, and the diameter of the drum may be large or small. These variables directly affect the sound of the instrument and the overall performance.

Pala revitalized a few students' Chöd drums; he reskinned their *ḍamaru*, sewed new beaters, and, in doing so, helped them to overcome their sometimes disgruntled relationship with their drum. The two pellets are each attached by string to the cloth band that circumscribes the two halves of the drum as it turns. He modified the string length of the pellets, making them slightly longer. He also thickened the cloth band reducing the narrowness of the space connecting the two wooden halves of the "hour-glass," so that the thumb, index finger, and folded middle finger would not become lodged in the narrow gap, thus allowing the hand and wrist to be able to rotate more freely. Everyone expressed appreciation for these micro adjustments, which allowed for an improved holistic relationship between hand and drum, in accordance with each ritual instrument's weight and size. The wrist and arm became less fatigued from twisting and turning. Likewise, students also noted that the weight felt more evenly distributed over the drum and they had greater control. My own sense while playing Pala's modified *ḍamaru* drums is gratitude for the greater ease with which the Chöd ritual may be practiced.

After having acquired a drum that one can play, one must, as Pala says, "Make it your friend . . . you have to make friends with your *ḍamaru* through practice." He maintains that once the drum is comfortable in one's hand and arm, one can go on "autopilot" and sing and play the bell and drum without needing to think much about performance. One reaches a natural state of "flow" with repetitive gestures of slow, rotating motion.

## Pedagogy of Testing: Incorporating Technology

As a test of my progress, Pala would record us practicing one or more sections of a Chöd sādhana together and then listen back to it on the audiotape cassette machine right in front of us on his desk. He was listening closely to how well we matched. He was sparing with his complements, but when pleased with a section he would say, "That's not bad." Whenever it was a well-performed section he would not be effusive, but rather even-keeled about it and then return our attention to the point of the practice. "Playing music means nothing. It *sounds good*, but *what kind of mind* do you have!? Chöd is *not easy*, Jeff!"[16]

He was listening to all aspects of the performance: whether we were in sync, whether I was singing on top of him and anticipating, or following slightly behind him as is the protocol. As a rule, the leader sings the first four syllables of a new melody, while the others remain silent. The congregation enters on the fifth syllable at the unison pitch or at the octave. Usually women will sing an octave above the men. Those following the *umdzé* have to listen closely and sing a fraction of a second behind him or her. They should never sing on top of, or anticipate, what the leader will sing, as it is possible that the *umdzé* may decide to slightly adjust the tempo or pitch in-between discrete sections of a liturgy or during a phrase.

## Intensive Immersion

I found the pedagogical process to be an incredibly intense and rewarding experience. Dharma teachings were combined with music pedagogy, translation work, secret descriptions of elements of practice, and discussion about what was meaningful in life for the Chöd practitioner as against what was meaningful for ordinary people. The contrast was always a very important component to the lessons since it seemed fundamental to the Chöd lama to instruct how to integrate the practice into daily life. Pala would sometimes look around our Chöd practice area in his office and his surroundings with a detached disdain:

> If you take away everything here tomorrow, I would be very happy. I need this house because everybody in this society has to have somewhere to live. If I don't have this the society will judge me and not accept me. But I have no attachment to this house. It does not do very good for me. It is not kind to me. It gives me a lot of problems. Because of it, I have to pay all kinds of bills: heating, water, electricity, cable, internet, and phone. That's why we do not use the hot water heater here unless we have guests. Most of the time, we heat water on the wood stove inside, and use the propane stove outside on the deck to cook. It's much cheaper. You know, all those big companies take money away from people. One University of Toronto Professor, he understands us. He does the same thing. Both he and his wife: they have no cable, no hot water. They live very simply, and they survive. He bicycles everywhere, too. Leaves the car at home, so he doesn't burn fuel in the city. He's happy; he survives.

We stayed beside his cast-iron wood-burning stove practicing, translating, and discussing long into the snowy afternoon until his wife, Tsering (called "Amala" by the community), arrived home from work at a nearby factory. It was a little chilly in some areas of the house, but never cold. The house was built over one hundred years ago. It is incredibly well insulated, cool in the summer months and warm in the winter: a highly temperate environment. But I did like it toasty by the stove. However, that is just the kind of discrimination between places that the Chöd practitioner seeks to undo. The mental attachment to some places and aversion to others needs to be undone.

## Reflexivity: A Dedication to Learning

During the initial stages of learning Chöd, training was a full-time obsession for me. Learning the drumming, melodies, and meaning of every word in the ritual text was my main priority. Every week I was invited to spend one day in training with Pala, receiving the transmission. I would return to Toronto, thrilled to have learned meditation techniques to control my mind, and the performance techniques of the tradition. I felt like I was the luckiest person alive. I would practice the music for four to five hours per day, and translate the sādhana text for another four to five hours. I spent the day after each lesson transcribing fieldnotes, and recalling the oral instructions and advice on the practice.

In my enthusiasm, I applied for the Commonwealth Scholarship to undertake my doctorate at the School of Oriental and African Studies (SOAS) in London (UK). I was accepted on a full scholarship, which I eventually declined so that I could continue receiving the Chöd transmission with Pala. Some thought me ill-advised to have passed up such an opportunity. However, I could anticipate that I would be restricted from continuing with the Chöd transmission and be shifted to another topic once in London. To receive a transmission in Chöd requires tremendous dedication of time and energy: personal resources, financial, temporal, and physical resources need to be diverted to the task.[17]

## Public Performance vs. Spiritual Practice

When Pala and I have prepared for a public performance-demonstration of the Chöd ritual on occasion, such as we did for a York University Graduate

Colloquium, and at the Royal Ontario Museum exhibit,[18] we would meet in Lindsay or Toronto to practice and briefly go over details prior to the event. Together, we would calculate by the time length given us: (a) how many subrituals/melodies to sing, (b) how many stanzas (repetitions of a given melody) would be sufficient to give a sense of the distinctive character of the melody for each subritual, and (c) how many *ostinato* rhythm cycles of "*ma dang, lha yi, khan dro*" we would play in-between each of the different melodies.

It is important to note the traditional protocol around the public performance of sacred tantric practice—specifically the performance of the Chöd ritual in a public space of non-initiates. First, the potential karmic imprint, positive or negative, depends upon the motivation of the Chöd performer/practitioner. I once saw a videotape of Pala performing Chöd publicly with the "*dram dram, chom den de*" (quarter-quarter, eighth-eighth, quarter) anapest rhythm of the *ḍamaru* as the accompaniment to a melody for which the standard rhythmic accompaniment is always "*ma dang, lha yi, khan dro.*" This could be interpreted as negotiating the public/private space of cultural display and practice of meditation, guarding the privacy of one's own practice and not fully revealing what used to be a much more secret tradition.

Second, the melodies of the "preliminary practices" or "*ngön dro*" (Tib. *sngon 'gro*) and "dedication" or "*ngo wa*" (Tib. *bsngo ba*) subrituals, which respectively open and close a Chöd sādhana ritual liturgy in every tradition, may be sung publicly because the accompanying parts of the practice are common to all tantric rituals. With respect to the former, the sequence of subrituals is: visualizing the merit field, taking refuge, generating *bodhicitta*, practicing guru-deity yoga, practicing the seven-branch offering, making a mandala offering, and requesting blessings from the lineage lamas; and, with respect to the latter, dedicating the accumulated merit and wisdom. The melodies of the "actual" or "main body of the practice" or "*ngo shi*" (Tib. *dngos gzhi*) subritual sections of a sādhana are restricted to practice by initiates, and ought not to be revealed to non-initiates.

Today, these two related concerns, (1) negotiating the public/private spaces with performances of Chöd and (2) selecting carefully which melodies will be publicly featured, come to the fore perhaps most prominently in the recording projects and public performances of the Tibetan nun, Ani Choying Drolma and guitarist-composer Steve Tibbetts.[19] Their CD albums have received wide popular acclaim, and in negotiating this public/private boundary with respect to Chöd performances/practices, they have reached

Figure 8.1. Ven. Pencho Rabgey, "Pala," giving an invited lecture in the Interfaith Chapel, University of Rochester, New York at the event "Music, Healing, and Ritual in Tibetan Cultural Contexts."

an international audience.[20] While Tibbetts plays the chord changes he hears around the melodies (illustrating the incredible potential for hearing harmonic implications in the melodies), Ani Choying Drolma acts as gatekeeper to the tradition. As a student of the Chöd lama Tulku Urgyen Rinpoché, she does not sing publicly those parts of the "actual practice" which are considered secret (i.e., known to be restricted only to those empowered with a Chöd initiation). Moreover, she gives away whatever profits she makes to the nunnery for which she is responsible, an action considered to be living the practice of generosity rather than merely preaching about it. In Buddhist terminology this is considered an aspect of "skillful means" (Skt. *upāya,* Tib. *thabs*) and "right livelihood" (Skt. *samyagājīva,* Tib. *yang dag pa'i 'tsho ba*).

## "Beggar's Chöd"

Historically, in Tibetan society, there have long been two kinds of Chöd: (1) the ascetic tradition of itinerant monks, nuns, and yogis, and (2) a performance busking tradition of wandering beggars (thus the moniker "beggar's Chöd"). The latter is referred to by Zong Rinpoché when he says of the Ganden Chöd melodies, "This is not a beggar's Chöd!' "[21] With respect to this label, "beggar's Chöd," it seems that the lines between public and private have been blurred. The beggar performs sacred melodies in exchange for food and alms. Coming to a village and traveling to each home, and sitting in front of the door or gateway and singing (out of reach of the canines and incisors of the family mastiff, a guard dog commonly kept by Tibetan families who are farmers and nomads), they would busk and accept donations offered. Thus, intraculturally it appears that Chöd melodies have long been performed to "please the ears" (after Atiśa[22]). However, as is often said in conversation among Tibetans, one cannot judge another person's mind. The busker could be enlightened, and masquerading as a beggar to test one's practice of generosity, and teach how near or far one is from the compassionate ideal at present.

In various locations along the outer circumambulation circuit of the Mahābodhī Temple complex in Bodh Gaya, India—a major pilgrimage site for Buddhists globally as this is where the Bodhi Tree sits under which Buddha Śākyamuni meditated and achieved enlightenment—I have seen Tibetan Buddhist practitioners from various Chöd Traditions and lineages perform rituals and accept donations. Between one to three groups position themselves along the temple pathway every day in the winter months, apparently enacting the "beggar's Chöd." Notably, an exception seemed to be one elder Chöd practitioner who came to the temple every evening at around dusk, and would sit on a steep grassy hill facing away from the main pathway, but toward the Mahābodhī stupa, where he began a Chöd ritual under the cloak of nightfall that lasted more than two hours. Usually between thirty to fifty people gathered behind him to listen as he practiced his lineage's stunning melodies. His voice, *ḍamaru*, and *kangling* rang out from under the shady boughs of trees and were heard across the dimly lit temple grounds. One night, a devotee gave the Chödpa a little portable battery-powered lamp so he could see his sādhana in the darkness. After finishing his dedication prayers, he accepted donations in a slightly different way. As he was perched on a hill with a steep incline, patrons could only make an offering to him while he was putting his *ḍamaru* into its case to leave the temple grounds, or they would push some bill notes into his hands while he was quickly walking out. I shared my appreciation as well, remarking that his melodies were beautiful sounding. "*Allé. Ngö ne re wé?*"

("Oh, really?"), he responded softly in a voice made a little hoarse from his singing for much of the evening.

## Urgent Transmission for Cultural Survival

It is a vitally important moment in the Ganden Chöd Tradition. The most revered Chöd lamas are in their 50s, 60s, 70s, and 80s. The main lineage holder, His Eminence Khalkha Jetsun Dampa Rinpoché, was in his 80s when he passed away in 2012. He had recently received a kidney transplant donated by his son, Choepel la. With strong concern to facilitate the transmission of Chöd, Khalkha Jetsun Dampa Rinpoché as well as other lamas utilized the available consumer technology and recorded their musical traditions in video and audio formats. These recordings have been disseminated by his disciples and are now in circulation around the world.

Although there is an urgent purpose to record the tradition before the melodies are lost, it is important to take a critical perspective toward these recordings in relation to the Buddhist notion of transmission. The practice of disseminating Chöd sādhanas and teachings in audio and video formats could be of questionable benefit since, from a more traditional viewpoint, the disciple's character and skill may not have been tested. Although the Chöd lamas I have studied under all preface their practice instructions by emphasizing the importance of the prerequisite of an initiation before studying the practice (let alone engaging in the practice of visualizing giving the body away or going to the cemetery), there are minimal guarantees that ensure students are actually doing so. Without the full transmission of meditation techniques, teachings that are unavailable to the uninitiated, the musical pursuits have limited meaning. Using digital media as a tool for musical transmission in the absence of the lama's presence can be a positive use of this technology, as one can sing along with the recording to retain the memory and integrity of the melodies. However, this should not supplant the intimacy of the *lung*. Training in Chöd meditation should ideally be buttressed with periodic consultation with the lama about the results of the student's practice.

### Preservation Efforts: A Critical Evaluation

From conversations I had with Chöd practitioners in India and elsewhere, I gained a strong sense that Kyabje Zong Rinpoché's effort at recording the

Chöd melodies produced quite effective pedagogical aids for the musical transmission of melodies—and also, in part, for the transmission (*lung*) of the lineage blessing—even in the lama's absence. However, the recording of the complete performance of the whole sādhana made by Khalkha Jetsun Dampa Rinpoché's students seems to have been used for three purposes: preservation, dissemination, and musical transmission. There has been a confluence of purposes in these projects whereby the recordings meant to keep the tradition, and spread the tradition, were also being used as pedagogical aids by those learning at a great distance from the lama.[23]

The confluence of transmission with dissemination and preservation as it relates to making recordings in recent years has, to an extent, shaped the traditional transmission process in conventional Chöd pedagogy. The question arises whether this change implies that the efficacy of the transmission is reduced? After all, what is the necessary prerequisite to be able to practice Chöd effectively?[24] It requires receiving the blessings from the lineage lamas' direct transmission of the tradition. The blessings are said to be inherent in the melodies, and the practitioner's proper vocal reproduction of the melodies allows them to invoke the blessings of the buddha deities. The converse is also true, if the melodies are not sung properly, with all the melodic ornamentations, the blessings may be lost to the practitioner. Thus, it is vital that in order for the Chöd practitioner to engage successfully in the practice, they must receive the full transmission of the melodies through the personal interaction of teacher-disciple. As mentioned above, Ven. Pencho Rabgey says, following Zong Rinpoché, that it is important to know both the ornamented *a capella* version and the drum accompanied version of the melodies. If a practitioner employs the contemporary tools of the Internet and recording technologies, not merely as a resource or aid/tool for study of melodies, but as the main source of instruction, it is wondered what will happen to the Chöd lineages. The student practitioner who learns from the CD of a full performance is exposed only to a version of the melodies in which the drum accompanies the Chöd lama's singing. Thus, the more complex version of the transmitted ornamented melodies will not be learned. Indeed, this might be a matter of concern for those practicing the Ganden Chöd Tradition's melodies.

During Khalkha Rinpoché's teachings in Toronto and Vancouver he asked his disciples to try to preserve the Chöd Tradition since the lineage was in danger of dying out. One of his disciples in the Toronto Chöd Club relayed to me that Rinpoché's heartfelt sentiment so moved her that she decided to devote time and energy she initially did not think she had to learning the tradition. This explicit mention of the endangered status of the tradition, spoken by the lama in such an earnest way, has energized the commitment of several of his students to attempt to find ways to preserve the tradition.[25]

What is clear in making this demarcation between the musical transmission of Chöd and the transmission (*lung*) of the blessings of the lineage lamas is that the full Chöd transmission involves both. In other words, Chöd pedagogy requires training in both music and meditation from qualified instructors. Moreover, the training is ideally situated in the intimate context of one disciple, or a few disciples, and their teacher. Historically, this was the case.

> Chöd was passed only to one disciple at a time in Gelugpa. It was considered very secret, and not to be practiced by everyone. Je Tsongkhapa criticized its being practiced by those who did not have the proper foundation of Guru Yoga, the necessary fundamental yoga essential for all further practice of the Buddhist Tantras, i.e., those who did not see the Guru and meditational deity (*yidam*) as inseparable.[26]

In traveling throughout the United States, Canada, Nepal, and India for the past several years to find Chöd practitioners who might add other dimensions to the understanding I received through studies with Ven. Pencho Rabgey, I have discovered how rarefied and precious the type of individualized personal training I received truly is. This book in so many ways owes the deepest gratitude to Ven. Pencho Rabgey for his musical skill, his depth of knowledge of the tradition, and especially his patience and time spent teaching me. It is my deep hope that some of what is conveyed in these pages may be useful to other disciples studying Chöd, whether in the Ganden Tradition or other lineages. As well, I hope this study will be helpful to other ethnomusicologists and ritual studies workers who, like myself, have the privilege and honor to study with genuine practitioners of a musical-spiritual tradition.

The first Chöd initiation I received from Khalkha Jetsun Dampa Rinpoché in Vancouver in 1995, which was translated by Ven. Zasep Tulku Rinpoché, formulated one of my strongest impressions about the practice. Khalkha Rinpoché gave a long introductory exposition on Chöd with respect to its foundation in Mahāyāna practice and the need for one's unequivocal reliance upon generating *bodhicitta* as the underlying motivation with which to engage in the ritual practices of giving away one's mentally transformed body.

In the initiation ritual ceremony, each ritual instrument/implement is first played by the lama conferring the initiation and then passed around to every disciple present who must then play it briefly. The *ḍamaru* and *kangling* are passed from student to student amid an atmosphere of playful delight. If someone could not blow effectively to make a sound from the *kangling*, for example, the lama would gently laugh to assuage the egoic state that arises. It is a somewhat scrutinizing and yet joyful atmosphere while watching fellow initiates engage in what is their first earnest performance attempt at the art of Chöd practice.

Over the past several years, I have also received Chöd instructions from Venerable Zasep Tulku Rinpoché. He encouraged my research into Chöd. He welcomed Ven. Pencho Rabgey's version of melodies to be taught at the Chöd Club at Gaden Choling Mahāyāna Buddhist Meditation Centre, where I helped some of his students to learn aspects of the practice, thereby strengthening my own practice and teaching abilities.

## Various Lamas' Chöd Traditions

It is interesting to note that, over the past few decades, Chöd lamas and practitioners alike in the Ganden Chöd Tradition have received initiations, oral transmissions, and musical transmissions from different lamas. Ven. Pencho Rabgey began studying Chöd as a boy at fourteen years of age with his root lama, Gen Trinley, in Chungba Valley in Eastern Tibet. Yet it was at sixty-two years of age that he received initiation into the Gelugpa Chöd Ḍākinī lineage through Khalkha Jetsun Dampa Rinpoché who visited Toronto in 1995. In the 1960s, Ven. Pencho Rabgey spent six years studying the Ganden Chöd Tradition directly with Kyabje Zong Rinpoché in Buxa Duar refugee camp in Assam, India. Over many decades in Canada, Ven. Pencho Rabgey has taught Chöd to Tibetan monks, lay people, and most recently myself and a number of non-Tibetans.

An oral history of every lama's lineage ties, the initiations they received and from whom, and the extent of their training and teachings may be compiled as a component of a Ganden Chöd Tradition lineage preservation project.[27] Due to limited space I will not do so here. However, it will be useful to give a summary of the points mentioned thus far.

## Chöd Transmission: Key Issues

The issues related to the transmission of the Chöd Tradition may be summarized as follows:

(1) Group Chöd practice is unifying and comforting in its collective discipleship. At once, group members engage in a consciously directed meditation practice to accomplish the goal of the practice and make a mutual effort to preserve the tradition.

(2) The preservation of the tradition is a chief concern of the few remaining Ganden Chöd lamas and their disciples. They understand the role entrusted to them, and are attempting to transmit, sustain, and revitalize both the musical performance and meditation practice traditions in ways relevant to their communities. Some Tibetan monks as well as lay practitioners and Western disciples have engaged in periods of immersion with their Chöd lamas after which they have produced audio and video recordings of their lama's Chöd practices.

(3) It is important to identify two different but related processes of transmission in the Chöd tradition: the "musical transmission" and the sacred or spiritual "transmission" (Tib. *lung*) between a lama and disciples. The training context of the close intimate pedagogy between the lama and one disciple, or a few disciples, involves not only the transmission of musical materials, which are necessarily sacred, but also meditation instructions—a component of *lung*, since these involve the master's realization attained through practicing Chöd rituals. During lessons, there can be a continual pendulum swing between training in music and being reminded of the foundation and goals of the practice with illustrative stories and warnings. This dynamic characterizes the importance of detailing the qualitative aspects of Chöd pedagogy and transmission that relate musical functions, skills, and understanding, to spiritual practice.

(4) In the transcultural translation of the Chöd practice into Western Buddhist communities (in Canada, United States, South America, Australia, and Europe) and more recently, into Mongolia and Sothern Russian Federation States with Buddhist populations, such as Buryatia, as well as other places where lamas have taught (e.g., Taiwan), the use of the recorded Chöd materials has been varied and possibly confused. Different types of recorded Chöd materials have periodically been made available to disciples, most recently on the web. Initially, Kyabje Zong Rinpoché who was the head of the Ganden Chöd lineage until he passed away in 1984, made two types of recordings in the year before he passed away: (A) practice cassettes of melodies for his disciples studying Chöd who wanted to learn the melodies more closely; and (B) complete performances of his melodies on (i) video and (ii) audio cassette.

(5) His Eminence Khalkha Jetsun Dampa Rinpoché became the subsequent head of the Ganden Chöd lineage. Beginning in the mid-1990s, video and audio recordings of Rinpoché's Chöd practices have been made, packaged, and distributed. These recordings were used to fulfil multiple purposes: musical transmission (an aid to disciples for learning their Chöd practice), dissemination (for reaching students far away in Mongolia, Canada, the USA, and elsewhere, who are unable to visit India), and preservation (in the sense of making an historical record of Khalkha Rinpoché's voice).[28] With respect to performance practice, the recordings sound out how to make the transitions between melodies/subrituals in ways that Kyabje Zong Rinpoché's pedagogical guides to the melodies on audio cassette do not.

(6) The enabling use of ubiquitous consumer-affordable recording technology has led to what I have called a "confluence of transmission with dissemination and preservation." Following anthropologist Maurice Godelier's insight, there may be reason for concern about the extent to which technology allows for an increased tendency toward isolation and, in this case, isolated practice outside the experience of the concomitant transmission of the musical practice and meditation tradition. It should be noted that the trend observed in the past two

decades may affect the ongoing transmission not only of Buddhist tantric Chöd music rituals but also music ritual practice traditions of other faiths and spiritual traditions in which transmission in the sense of *lung* is necessary.

(7) Historically, in Tibetan society, the public/private distinction has been represented by what is referred to as the "beggar's Chöd." This is a busking tradition of spiritual bards who sing for donations and offerings of food and alms. These talented individuals learn the melodies to make a living. However, since it is impossible to read the mind of another person, the embodiment of Machik Labdrön's melodies showing up on a farmer's front yard might be considered a venerated sign for a householder. The fact that on Tibetan soil there was a social space for the indigenous public display of the music of this secret tantric tradition ought to illustrate the many ways Chöd occupies a blurred category as both a tradition of meditation practice and musical performance. International tours of monk and nun delegations to the West and East from Tibetan monasteries and nunneries based in India and Nepal have increasingly incorporated a Chöd performance segment into their stage repertoire. This is a fascinating example of a spiritual tradition on public display. Negotiating the public/private space of Chöd practice specifically concerns which aspects of the practice are being performed publicly. Most of the preliminary practices in a Chöd liturgy do not contain scripture or information restricted to non-initiates, thereby enabling occasions for public performance.

# Transformation

## What Results from Practicing Chöd?

### *Bodhicitta* Motivation: Equanimity, Love, Compassion and Labeling

Chöd practice is fundamentally based on *bodhicitta*; the altruistic intention to practice and reach enlightenment in order to free all beings in the universe from suffering. The Ganden Chöd Tradition's lineage lamas instruct disciples that it is possible to develop *bodhicitta*.[29] They explain that the first step is to cultivate "equanimity" (Tib. *btang snyoms*) toward all beings in the universe, followed by generating love and compassion for their situations in *saṃsāra*. A way of meditating on equanimity that is particularly revealing of how our mental habits work to hinder a universalist compassionate ethic begins as follows. One can visualize inviting in front of oneself three "categories" of persons: one's enemies on one's left side, one's friends on one's right side, and directly before oneself are those whom one regards neutrally as neither "friend" nor "enemy," for example, a complete stranger. The analysis of the ontological verity of the "friend" proceeds by conducting an honest, careful check in which one asks oneself whether this person or being has *always* been one's "friend." In other words, have they ever been seen by oneself as a "stranger" or otherwise. One proceeds logically from one "category" of person to the next and learns that the beings external to oneself become designated either as "friend," or "stranger," or as "enemy" largely as a result of one's *own* mental perceptions, and attribution of labels upon the object of one's perceptions. And it is one's *own* perception and labeling that cause one suffering. There is nothing inherent in Pema or Jack that is (was, has been, and will always be) "enemy" or "friend." These attributions are due to one's projections and imputations of permanent qualities onto persons who are interdependently existent, just as all persons and phenomena exist as such. So, whether one is engaged in Chöd practice, another Mahāyāna Buddhist practice, or between practice sessions in so-called normal everyday life, the meditation on equanimity reveals that the accuracy of one's perceptions of who and what is "good" and "bad" for oneself is questionable at best and terribly mistaken at worst.

## So-called "Enemies": Loosening the Grasp on Mere Conceptual Designations

The category of "enemy" and also "friend" derives from our exaggerated attribution of solid nature to impermanent and conditioned phenomena.[30] When today's "friend" becomes tomorrow's "enemy," the Tibetan Chöd masters ask us to examine not what was wrong with *that person*, but rather, what is wrong with *our perceptions* of that person—our exaggerated projections of who that person is in relation to ourselves. Is there any relationship we experience for which we did not create the conditions? According to the law of karma, if there is an effect, there is necessarily a (direct, secondary, or tertiary) cause. The point of this meditation must not be misunderstood: it does not mean that we have no *real* friends, but that to a large extent we are *constantly* in a creative mode of developing relationships through our actions, beliefs, desires, feelings, and cravings, that lead us to spend time with those whom we wish to get close to and stay away from those about whom we feel quite the opposite.

## Chöd Practice in Everyday Life: The Yogi's Perspective

According to Buddhist doctrine, our relationships with others encompass not only the present life's encounters with acquaintances and strangers and "friends" and "enemies," but also all previous lives' relationships. Every being has been a *real friend* and even one's own *mother* and *father* countless times throughout all of one's previous lives. The karmic relationships between ourselves and others are an ongoing feature of our lives, which leaves us with much confusion when they change if we do not analyze our situation carefully. Despite our creative mode of developing relationships of all kinds, there is the underlying fact of our Being. With the understanding that we have either knowingly or unknowingly wronged others in the past during this life or past lives, we might wish to apologize, to make amends, to pacify any hurt feelings, to compassionately take away others' suffering, and to make others happy. Such a disposition would lead to the genuine forgiveness of others for their wrongdoings, and a sincere wish to pay back others for the wrongs one has done instead of carrying these debts on into the future of this life and future lives. Chöd practitioners make this radical gesture of compassionate reparation: embodying an ethic not dissimilar to that of Jesus who forgives all beings' sins, no matter the size of the sin, and loves all no matter their appearance or identity.

## Social Image

At the social level, when considered within the scope of Tibetan Buddhist ritual music performances, Chöd practice is regarded among Tibetans as occupying a unique space and role. The heroic feat of imposing self-exile in order to defeat one's "demons" for the benefit of all is seen to be on the same path as that of Buddha Śākyamuni 2,500 years ago. Prince Siddhārtha Gautama escaped the royal inheritance of fame, land, wealth, and subjects in order to seek the causes of suffering and eliminate them for the benefit of all beings. At some point, he realized that he would have to test for himself whether his methods worked, and so instead of teaching after gaining only a few insights and realizations, he continued meditating until he was able to overcome the last of his mental delusions and attain full awakening.[31]

Similarly, Chöd practitioners aim to cut the root from which all other delusions arise. They practice in circumstances that cause them to feel terrified and even afraid for their lives.

By doing so in psychologically and physically exposed circumstances, they create an optimal opportunity to realize selflessness by investigating the actual nature of their "self" at the very moment they fear for their own lives. It is then that they discover the insubstantial basis of the "I" which provides the causal link for that fear to arise, and note in what they have mistakenly placed their trust (perhaps the longevity of their body).

In the hermitage, forest, cave, or other appropriate sites of practice a Chödpa usually lacks the context of the social scrutiny to bear upon her performance techniques, musical skill, and capacity to remove obstacles and harms from other beings.[32] However, this does not mean that they are forever social recluses.

## Suffering seen as a "Positive Result" of Practicing Chöd

In Tibetan areas across the Plateau, in the Himalayas, as well as in Diaspora locales, Chöd practitioners are often called upon to remove a deceased person's body from a home or to go into communities where there is a disease or an epidemic to practice healing rituals. It is also common for Chödpas to be requested to practice at the bedside of a person who is dying. Chöd practitioners' lack of concern for the "self" is related to their compassionate regard for "others," and is said to prevent them from contracting the illness if they venture into a community or household where there is a disease.[33] Moreover, if Chöd practitioners ever do become ill, they are not permitted to seek the help of a physician or take medicine in order to cure the illness. Rather, they are to meditate on the "emptiness" of the illness, and generate compassion and *bodhicitta* while praying for those who suffer from the same sickness or worse illnesses. The most advanced practitioners can accept their illness gladly. Chöd practitioners interpret an illness and the suffering it causes as being the ripening of negative karmic imprints that they would have experienced in the future in this life or in future lives. In these ways, Chöd can be seen as a radical and counter-intuitive method for engaging with life and its challenges.

As far as the suffering that results from the visualization practices in Chöd is concerned, one of the most interesting, albeit seemingly contradictory, effects of engaging in Chöd practice is the advent of frightening images and appearances that practitioners might see, or of actual sickness they might contract.[34] The "Chöd practitioners-in-training" can consult the instructional texts written by Machik Labdrön and her lineage disciples which provide both general and specific descriptions on how to regard frightening appearances, and how to incorporate them into their meditation practices while retaining the view of emptiness and a completely compassionate frame of mind. What Chöd practitioners *should* be doing—if they are honest about engaging in Chöd practice and its associated rituals for altruistically motivated reasons, and not for purposes of financial gain—is wishing that all other beings' sufferings would ripen on themselves. Thus, if Chöd practitioners *do* experience suffering, it would be absurd for them to feel the practice is somehow not working the way it should.

Once frightening images appear, the commentarial texts in the Chöd corpus and one's teacher's oral instructions provide a basis for helping to discern how one should think about and/or engage them. Ultimately, the frightening appearances (such as ghosts, malevolent spirits, terrifying visions, and nightmares) are lacking any intrinsic existence from their own side. They are empty. However, their *apparent* malevolence is the result of one's own negative karmic imprints (accumulated during this life and countless previous lifetimes) that *make one see these appearances as malevolent*. Thus, whatever negative experiences one reaps are the results of the karmic causes and imprints one has sown. There is no place for assigning blame here other than the habitual propensities for self-grasping and self-cherishing in one's mindstream.[35]

Geshé Rabten, one of Ven. Pencho Rabgey's early instructors, maintains:

> Whenever any difficulty or trouble arises we usually blame it on some other person or object. Whether it is an individual or a large group, someone else is always accused. Nations accuse other nations of causing conflict and even dogs blame their troubles on other dogs. However, it is entirely incorrect to blame

> someone else since the true enemy deserving this blame is the self-cherishing attitude (Tib. *bdag gces 'dzin*) which we have always had within us.[36]

*Understanding the Causes of Suffering*

Here I would like to make a general comment that in the Western "culture of blame," Chöd might not be such an easy practice to undertake. Many Tibetan teachers, particularly elders born in Tibet, feel that Westerners can be too fad-driven. I have heard it said, "They like something today, but discard it tomorrow." In our contemporary disposable culture where basic recycling seems like a chore, one is perhaps unequipped to see suffering as anything but unwanted.[37] Normally, one endeavors to be removed from suffering, to fight suffering, to be in conflict with it—to oppose it, as one opposes one's "enemies." Engaging with suffering in order to relieve others from *their* suffering is not a widely expected practice.[38]

For the practitioner who has obtained higher levels of the Buddhist path, the Mahāyāna motivation of *bodhicitta* may be exercised even through seemingly destructive acts, the Indian Buddhist sages have said, to liberate others from suffering. Thus, in Mahāyāna Buddhism, primacy is given to intentionality; desires, emotions, fears, and actions are investigated for their alignment with what would be, or would not be, beneficial for others. Upon reflection, if suffering is completely undesirable to someone, then she or he should not become a Chöd practitioner![39]

In terms of this notion of blame, I draw from the insights of Lama Thubten Yeshe (1935–1984) of Kopan Monastery in Kathmandu, Nepal (an esteemed conveyer of Buddhadharma to Westerners and a Ganden Chöd practitioner), in finding that "blame" is a concept that perhaps best describes the lack of sense of ownership over our perceptions of reality. There is a lax sense through which our superstitious (unscientific) mental approach to difficulties conceives of the source of our experiences as being determined by external causes. Either that, or we possess a reified notion of an internal source of "blame" in self-destructive thoughts, such as, "I am deserving of deep feelings of guilt and to have these bad things happen to me." However, it may be observed that within one family, individuals respond very differently to the same external circumstances. Our responses to external stimuli are not determined from without, but can be controlled from within. This is not to say that habitual responses do not lead us to certain tendencies that appear automatic and authentic to our "self." Yet, the possibility to change our response is ours. It is a sign of genuine renunciation (Tib. *nges 'byung*), for example, if instead of responding to a situation that would normally otherwise elicit anger, a person decides of their own volition to respond differently, and maybe even make a joke to ease tensions. Establishing an innovative response alters neural pathways, making it easier to respond positively again on subsequent occasions.[40]

### How Chöd Practice Impacts Upon Everyday Experience

It is important to mention here that Chöd lamas—like other enlightenment oriented Buddhist teachers—do not abstract the Chöd practices from everyday reality. They always bring the teaching back to its direct application in life and the "time period in-between meditations" (Tib. *rjes thob*). It is such an important question in every social context: our identity, and how we deal with our subjectivity in the communities we live in. Is it, as Tibetan lamas maintain, that the world's problems arise from this misapprehension of reality? Do the world's problems arise from this misconception of our actual nature based on our habitual "self-grasping"?

The following sections shift the attention from theoretical to practical teachings based on the understandings wrought by Chöd practice.

## The Chödpa's Practice: Taking a Loss and Accepting Bad Conditions

### Forbearance: A Characteristic of the Chödpa

Ven. Pencho Rabgey explained in incisive ways the radical disposition of the Chödpa.

> Chöd practitioners are happy if they encounter obstacles. They are not looking for good things. Then they can sit there and think, "Good, I had that big obstacle." That's excellent. Let more obstacles rain down on me! Not tomorrow, not the next day, but now. Right now! Then, after waiting a few minutes they look around to see if any further obstacles are arising. If not, then they say, "What? That's all? No more?"

The Chödpa might need to adopt a brazen attitude at times as she tries to defeat her *real* "enemy," which is her negative karmic imprints and egoic attachment, *not* other living beings! The lessening of these karmic imprints is seen/realized in the transpiring of obstacles. Thus, the difficulties *themselves* indicate the ripening of this karma. As Pala instructed me, "Once the difficulty has arisen, there is no reason to worry any more about it because it has *already* come and gone. It is now in the past."[41]

*Happiness in Paying Down Karmic Debt*

Here, Pala is alluding to the happiness Chöd practitioners are said to feel when their karmic debt is being paid down by encountering difficult circumstances.

> Chöd practitioners are happy when bad things happen to them. Most people in Toronto do "good," want "good," and expect "good." But Chöd practitioners are the opposite. If they are having bad things happen to them as a result of every good effort, then they could feel their practice is working.

Paying off debt successfully can be signified by encountering obstacles in life. The debt that needs to be paid is whatever is owed to embodied (and disembodied) beings from one's actions in the present life or during previous lives when, knowingly or unknowingly, harm has come to others through one's thoughts, words, and deeds (i.e., one's actions through the "three doors": mind, speech, and body).

*Dealing Honestly With People*

Pala also emphasizes the need for any authentically engaged Dharma practitioner, like the Chödpa, to deal honestly with people:

> Honest people and crooked people don't match. Some people spend their whole life looking at how to beat and cheat others. They are experts at it. Honest people are sometimes surprised. They wonder, "How can that happen, how can they do that?" But honest people say things directly and stay truthful no matter the consequence. We [honest people] lose a little financially, but in the end we're ok. We can make our own way. We cannot beat the powerful liars, but we can control ourselves.

Although this is a relatively oppositional framework of representing the various types of people, it offers a perspective that makes sense within the logic of the tradition.

### *Lack of Attachments*

The Chödpa's poverty and lack of attachments may result in their unconventional appearance. This was certainly the case in Tibet, as Pala explained, "Chöd practitioners can stay in a very bad place because they don't need anything. They can go naked, or wear very poor clothes, and handle very poor conditions."[42]

Pala speaks of their fearlessness and fortitude amid difficult physical conditions and complex situations. Where others are afraid of bad conditions, Chöd practitioners can go toward such situations and places. They say, "OK, I'm here. Let's deal with it!" They use these poor conditions on the path, to test their *bodhicitta* and increase it, and conversely to decrease, lessen, and finally destroy their "self-cherishing" and "self-grasping."

## At Cost to Herself: The Chödpa's Acceptance of Good and Bad

The image of the Chödpa courageously sitting at night in a forest, attempting to confront her demons is unsettling even for the beginner (let alone the non-initiate). The attitude of altruism fortifies her resolve to try to stay and continue practicing. The strength of her belief in the lama's blessings imbued within the ritual instruments/implements she uses protect her, and singing the melodies which embody her lamas' blessings further empower her while anchoring her to the visualizations. The drum's continuous rhythmic flow helps her all the more by allowing her to focus closely on the melody and liturgical text. Before each new subritual section, she softly utters the mantric syllable *phaṭ* to pacify obstacles. If she senses any particular fear arising within, or external danger such as the approach of wild animals, she might utter *phaṭ* in a slightly different way as instructed by her lama.

The vivid recollection of all her lama's instructions in-between practices reinvigorates her practice sessions. Her living memory of the tradition that she now draws upon in the ways her lama instructed can bring her closer to the goal even when she feels it escaping from her grasp. This, too—her fear of failure—is a negative karmic imprint she attempts to see nakedly;

and, pacifying her habitual response to fight it, by accepting it, she might well overcome that fear.

At times, she will likely be drawn in by one of the four main *māras* every Chödpa seeks to defeat; her overexcitement or arrogance at experiencing "success" through the practice, symbolized in positive signs. Her egoic relationship to the practice due to her seeming success is like a false summit to the mountaineer, a delusive distraction that must be recognized in its raw "empty" nature. This recognition that obstacles and enjoyments must both be transformed is vital, as is her vigilance not to succumb to the play of ego during and in-between meditation sessions. In these ways, the Chödpa becomes an unconventional warrior with determined courage, ready to confront obstacles on the front line of the battle against the innermost delusive thoughts her mind can harbor.

## Applying Patience (I): Reasoning Out Conflict

The following example presents a contemporary setting for exercising the practice of patience. This is a discourse between a Chöd practitioner educated in this tradition of thought and some school children at an assembly in a middle school in Boston, Massachusetts. The former teaches how to apply these ethical principles in the situation of the grade school playground. I include this to illustrate the usefulness and functionality of the logic applied to analytical meditation within the same tradition that the Chöd ritual is inculcated.

Pala recounted an occasion in Boston when he was invited by Maya, the daughter of a friend, to visit her grade seven class. Maya said she had never seen her classmates act as peacefully. On this occasion, an intellectual approach toward considering the options for responding to schoolyard violence was proffered. The following is the account of the students' response to the new notion in dialogic form:

> Pala asked, "What do you do if someone hits you?"
>
> One student responded, "You hit them back."
>
> Pala offered an alternative response, "How about if you stay there, and do nothing? Wait ten minutes. That person is going to go away. Then you will not have to fight with them."

The students were initially unimpressed with this pacific approach. Pala came at the problem from a different angle,

> "Think about it . . . if one person cuts off your ear, you're going to be mad, right?"
>
> The students excitedly jumped up and agreed, "Yeah!"
>
> Pala said, "Yeah. Then, if you have the same weapon, you are going to want to cut off that guy's ear too, right?"
>
> The students chimed in unison, "Yeah!"
>
> "Okay, now sit down and think about it. If you do *nothing* . . . then what happens . . . ?"
>
> Pala paused, allowing them time to analyze the situation. Then, he posed a thought experiment: "One guy still has an ear, another guy doesn't have one. But the other way around, if you retaliate, *two* guys would *each* be missing an ear. So, which is better? Everybody, just stop and think."
>
> The students collectively paused and exclaimed, "Wow!"
>
> He smiled at their response in awakening to the critical logic applied to the familiar situation, perhaps for the first time in their lives.
>
> Then one student asked him, "What do *you* do?"
>
> Pala said, "I keep patient and stay quiet. Wait ten minutes. For sure, that person is going to go away."[43]

### Applying Patience (II): Parable of the Monk Meditating on Patience

Another example to illustrate both the rationale and correct method of the cultivation of patience is recounted from the *Lamrim* discourses.

> One day, a monk was walking in the forest when he came upon another monk who was meditating, sitting in quiet repose, his spine vertical, in the correct meditation posture.
>
> The first monk asked him, "What are you doing?"
>
> The meditator replied softly, "I am meditating on patience."
>
> The first monk said, "Oh really? Oh good!" He paused, and then suddenly cursed at the meditator, "*Chak pa zo!*" (which translates from Tibetan as, "*Eat shit!*")
>
> The meditator immediately turned to look up at the accuser, losing his meditation posture, his face red with anger for having been disturbed at the insulting words. In a thoughtless rejoinder, he retorted, "*You* eat shit!"

I have heard several retellings of this story by various respected teachers in the Ganden Oral lineage tradition. Most often, at this point in the narration, the storyteller laughs (usually along with the listeners) since the point has already been illustrated. When the parable has been told to me, the storyteller animates these characters by imitating both roles, in particular the swift turning of the neck to the side and upward of the meditator, breaking his posture to look angrily at the "accusing" monk who is, in fact, testing his mettle. Then, to reiterate the point made, the lesson of this moral play may be variously given in summation: "Right there, in that fraction of a second when he retaliated, the meditator's patience was lost."

This parable tells us about the importance of the cultivation of patience in the company of others, rather than in the confines of a meditative retreat of solitude. It illustrates the reason why the seed of patience is ideally cultivated in the "field" of sentient beings, not merely in the "merit field" of visualizations. Patience is, emphatically, not a quality of mind or an ethical disposition that can be developed and perfected by practicing on one's own. A practitioner must train in patience amidst difficult situations. As Pala said to me, "If you remain alone, in solitude, who is there to be patient with? A wall, a book, or pen?"

A second, and related, point in this moral play is the importance of maintaining vigilance over one's thoughts, lest one's speech and actions be committed without a hint of *bodhicitta* motivation. The Indian mahāsiddha Śāntideva writes of keeping close watch over his own thoughts like a sentry at the door of the mind in order to immediately catch negative thoughts that would lead him to commit negative karmic actions.[44]

*Responding with Patience*

Both of these stories concern insults to a person from the doorway of mind that are intended to hook the ego and raise the sense of "I." These challenges to the ego may be theoretically analyzed as performative utterances in social discourse that contain moments of intersubjective disjuncture to illustrate ethical principles that ground the tradition and serve as moral plays. Such an analytical summary, however, would likely miss the very crux of the point being made, if it stops there. Thus, what is important to note in both examples is the primacy of an individual's own application of an analytical meditation to a situation, maintaining a clear spacious mind in order to offer a cogent response in the immediacy of the interaction. A philosophical and dispassionate analysis of potential outcomes, given the range of responses, is what is ideally required. When some intellectual distance from habitual emotions is acquired, the individual's choice of action in a situation may be selected from a number of possible responses. Outcomes, in terms of establishing positive karmic imprints that reduce harm, are traditionally said to be due to three stages: the motivation, the actions (Skt. *karma,* Tib. *las*) and the final step, the dedication of merit, providing the feelings following the actions are free of pride or regret. This is, in a practical sense, a basis for "renunciation," which is the first of the three principal paths.

The Chöd practitioner maintains what may initially seem to be a counter-intuitive disposition: intending to give that which is most precious to those who have harmed her in the past, not only those who have been kind to her. The philosophical underpinning of this thought is the Mahāyāna *bodhicitta* motivation, but at the Vajrayāna (tantric) level it is practicably a yogic form of giving: performing *corporeal generosity* to accumulate merit and actively dedicating this merit from the practitioner's heart to gaining attainments and finally the state of enlightenment for the benefit of all sentient beings. But again, the practitioner ought not recite, "I dedicate this merit I have accumulated from giving" before contemplating deeply upon the emptiness—the lack of inherent existence (i.e., the absence of even an atom of self-existence)—of every aspect of the *giving event* (including both the intentioned thought to give and the merit accumulated from giving). This is especially so during the subritual section known as meditation on "the three spheres of giving" (Tib. *sbyin pa'i 'khor gsum*) toward the conclusion of the Chöd sādhana (see B11 in Table 2.3).[45]

The meditation upon emptiness within the framework of the "three spheres" (*'khor gsum*) can also be applied to each of the first five perfections.[46] For example, the practitioner can meditate upon the "emptiness" of each element of the "three spheres of patience" (Tib. *bzod pa'i 'khor gsum*):

1. the one who is being patient (the practitioner);
2. the object of patience (some harmful words spoken by someone toward the practitioner); and,
3. the recipient of that patience (the person with whom one exercises patience, i.e., by the practitioner not becoming angry with them).

Like the "perfection of generosity," the "perfection of patience" is similarly approached in terms of cause and effect, and as a mental disposition with which one can become familiar. From the side of the practitioner who possesses the understanding that, by her retaliation, two persons would then have insults hurled at them instead of one person; and, moreover, that the total sum of the negative karma in the world would be twice the amount of what would otherwise be accrued, there is a way to stop the cycle: by remaining patient. The Vajrayāna practitioner who is urgently on track toward buddhahood makes a logical calculation and tries to avoid accumulating any negative karma.

## The Chödpa's Actions: Conveying The Unconventional

### Sacrifice

I think we can find meaning in both broad and subtle gestures. If we look at the paradigm of giving and reciprocity, a number of works suggest that Chöd presents as a "sacrifice." To think of Chöd in terms of sacrifice, as some have suggested, may be quite limiting when the sacrifice of the body is understood as one component of a multifaceted practice. I find that assigning this label subsumes Chöd theory under a category in which bodies of all kinds—goats, chickens, as well as statues—are given to the gods, offered up and killed for spiritual profit. This is a highly reductive category for the Chöd ritual, not because there is a lack of sacrifice, for certainly there is a deeply *felt* sense of personal sacrifice, but because the sacrifice in Chöd practice occurs as a prelude to the intellectual incongruence experienced through the investigation of the constructed concept of "self." As against the very real experience of being-in-the-world, when confronted with the absence of the body as the adept's main sensorial referent, one experiences a loss of the normative concept of "self."

Sacrifice incorporates loss for the righting of balance, whereas in Chöd the loss not only rights a social balance, but also reveals—in the peeling away of the structures of the mind's deepest adherences to "self"—the conventional attachments to being and form. While Chöd is emphatically a ritual practice involving the paying down of debts the practitioner owes from previous negative karmic imprints and actions, the philosophical depth of Chöd for the adept suggests that this ritual is not an appeasing of spirits alone. As an ascetic practice, Chöd presents a path to full enlightenment through direct confrontation with the mental habits of attachment and "grasping" that bind one to *saṃsāra*. "Cutting off" the seemingly truly-existent "I" at its root, eliminating any mental grasping, leads one to the ultimate insight of transcendent awareness: buddhahood.

## Inviting *All* Beings: The Need for Interdisciplinary Discourse

A colleague who was generously proofreading one of the sections of this book, asked for clarification on an important point, for which she had little context.

> "Are you sure you mean blowing the thighbone trumpet invites *all* beings?"
>
> When a Chöd practitioner out there is blowing their trumpet are they also calling *me*? Am *I* invited to eat *their* flesh?"

This was her first encounter with Chöd or perhaps any Vajrayāna Buddhist tradition. However, in answering her question, we arrived at a reconciliation that alerted me once again to the importance of employing an interdisciplinary perspective. I think it could help the reader to consider Chöd in comparison with other, perhaps more familiar, cultural traditions (that happen, in fact, to bear striking similarity to their doctrines). In so doing, I suggest that (by coming from a cultural relativist perspective) it may be helpful to adopt a comparative religion/ritual viewpoint to elucidate what is meant by *all* beings. By comparing Chöd doctrine with other strongly ethics-based religious doctrines, the Chöd practice tradition can become not only better appreciated but also seen to have contemporary social relevance. In this section I will consider some of the ways in which the perceived perspectival "gap" between traditions may be bridged.

The same reader then asked, "Does the thighbone trumpet *symbolize* the calling of spirits, or does it *actually* call spirits?" For a practitioner of any level, the ritual instrument/implement symbolizes impermanence because it is unmistakably a human thighbone. For those who believe the tradition's practitioners' claims that the sound of the thighbone trumpet *calls forth* spirits, that is precisely what they feel happens. "Beginners" who call with the trumpet *visualize* that beings come (in the three ways described in chapter 5); and practitioners—"advanced and upward"—may report *actually seeing* spirits arriving. The point here is the sonic association with intentional thought, and belief in the notion that what one is doing is *actually calling* in order to develop a way out of the emotional relationship of fear with the beings who are responding to the call. The point of calling beings with the *kangling* is to invite them effectively with its compelling sound. The internal practice aims at trying to exercise love and compassion for all beings, to be able to love and give to even those beings who have an unusual appearance or frightening demeanor.

I began by assuaging my reader's most prevalent concern: "This ritual is not dealing with cannibalism or actual flesh eating. It is about developing an expansive heart of loving compassion for all beings, being able to imagine giving others that to which one is most attached and feels is most precious to oneself: the body. The practitioner-in-training is developing an expansive heart of non-discriminating loving-kindness and compassion toward *all beings*." As I was still referring to the doctrine supporting the basis of Chöd theory, I was still not connecting fully with my reader friend.

By taking a comparative religion approach, I found I was better able to convey the meaning of Chöd, and reduce the very tendency of "othering" (the ritual) that the ritual practice itself seeks to destroy. I asked her, "From a Christian perspective (her background), is anyone excluded from those whom Jesus wishes to save? Were the Romans who crucified him excluded from his intentions? Were the merchants in the temple's marketplace excluded?

Was Judas excluded? Is anyone excluded from Jesus' wish to save everyone?" The answers should be clear within our Judeo-Christian society.

"Of course, *everyone* is included," she replied.

Therefore, I suggested, I would be putting the cart before the horse if I ask, "Does that mean Jesus wants to save *me*, too? Am *I* included within the *everyone* whom Jesus loves, forgives, and wishes to save?" Within that scope, *I* am included in Jesus' work; *my* soul can indeed be saved.

Chödpas exercise the same totalizing and expansive heart, loving all, especially the meek, and work to save them by teaching how to avoid further suffering. Chöd lamas have said, in teaching about the rite of giving the body, that what Jesus did was no different.[47]

In Chöd practice, inviting *all beings* is a visualization that does not exclude any being. "*All beings*" includes the icky, sticky, poisonous, venomous, wretched, and ugly creatures, as well as the beautiful ones. At the higher stages of practice the Chödpa has to open herself to the harm of others. "Beginners" might "not be willing to part with even the tip of their fingernail if asked by another to give it up."[48] Furthermore, if beings come forth, one imagines that they are provided with exactly what they need and desire, rather than something they would find disgusting. The idea of the Chöd practice is to please all beings: giving them that which they need and desire; and taking away from them that which they no longer want (i.e., suffering, longing). After satisfying beings materially, the Chöd practitioner "gives Dharma" to nourish their minds by singing a well-known verse of a pithy spiritual instruction on the "four seals."[49] Then the Chödpa engages in *tong len* (Tib. *gtong len*) practice, a meditation in which she first visualizes shaving off the last of other beings' sufferings and negative karmic imprints as if with a powerful razor, and taking these "into the center of her heart in the form of thunderstorms, hail, scorpions, and spiders." She then bequeaths to them her accumulated merit, singing that she "transforms her body, wealth, virtue, and the like into all desirable things that fulfill beings' wishes, and into the blessings of the Buddha's cessations and realizations."[50]

Since the time devoted to this meditation on *tong len* lasts but two four-line stanzas, one is meant to reflect upon the compassionate sensibility one had developed during previous meditations—if even for only a few moments—which enriches the ritual experience with meaning. This is how one's Chöd practice is to be met with the possibility for deepening; one's previous meditations on giving and taking become preparatory for this moment during this ritual.

## An Unconventional Warrior[51]

Akhu Jamyang, who Pala remembers from his childhood, was a Chödpa who had meditated for thirty-eight years. Akhu Jamyang had about forty cats, hundreds of birds, and twenty dogs, all around him every day. He lived at the village monastery, and was exceptionally kind. His setting, atop the rolling green grassy hills of wildflowers in summer, and forest patches of evergreens covered in snow in the winter, was only partially removed from human society. He had visitors coming every day, asking for divinations and advice. When people visited him, they saw cats, birds, dogs, and humans all living together in the same surroundings, and even eating together. "Everyone shared the daily meals together. No one was first or last. Cats ate with humans. Sometimes he had to separate two cats who were fighting for their share," said Pala, in recounting what he called "unusual living conditions that Westerners might not believe or like very much, or appreciate." He continued recounting the story,

> On the day Akhu Jamyang passed away, people reported unusual events. The birds disappeared completely and never came around again. Of course, that's not a surprise; they can fly away. But all the dogs and cats also disappeared. No one knows where they went. Some people got one or two cats (they were considered a blessing since they were in that Great Lama's presence and received his almsgiving everyday). But suddenly, after that day, none of the many cats or dogs were to be found on the mountain. It was very strange. No one could explain it.

As I gleaned from the effect of the story's mysterious ending (after two retellings over the years) the purity of this practitioner might have emanated kindness such that, like Saint Francis of Assisi, he was continually surrounded by birds, animals, and the needy and hungry.

### *Everyday Social Role of the Chödpa*

In Tibetan communities, the role of the Chödpa is widely acknowledged. He or she is seen as a trusted person, a practitioner who looks beyond designations of "friend" or "enemy," who aids others while risking loss or peril to him- or herself. The social role of a Chödpa does not contradict the practice's ascetic roots. Rather, it confirms the need for the practitioner to engage in a period of retreat to practice deeply so that he or she may be better able to help others later when situations arise.

## Transformation Within Transmission

While training in Chöd, Pala initially instructed me to study the *Lamrim* ("Stages of the Path") discourses, which describe in full the meditation on equanimity and subsequent stages for the development of altruism through "equalizing and exchanging self with others." I found that these discourses are both preliminary to, and interwoven within, training in Chöd practice because the meditation sections are structurally set in the same sequence as in a Chöd sādhana, and similarly aimed at developing both conventional and ultimate *bodhicitta*. Just as both method and wisdom need to be balanced in training at the Mahāyāna level, so conventional and ultimate *bodhicitta* are both cultivated through the Chöd method and sādhana practices at the Vajrayāna level. In this way, transmission and transformation are combined in the pedagogical and training process. Then, when practicing a Chöd sādhana in a ritual context, transmission and transformation are again related parts of the process, especially when the lineage lamas' names are invoked to inspire and empower with blessings the transformations that the Chödpa aims to bring about.

## Two Wings: Method and Wisdom

The meditation on emptiness based upon the "three spheres of giving" establishes the causes for the "accumulation of wisdom" (Tib. *ye shes kyi tshogs*) together with the "accumulation of merit" (Tib. *bsod nams kyi tshogs*), which are built up through the altruistically intentioned act of "generosity," the first of the six perfections. Each of the perfections *actualizes* the *bodhicitta* motivation, and is part of how transformation occurs. It is said that the two accumulations, of merit and wisdom, are needed to attain buddhahood. Traditionally, they are regarded as analogous to two wings of a bird, the left wing symbolizing the accumulation of wisdom, and the right wing symbolizing the accumulation of merit.

The presentation here is reflective of how the entire sādhana is structured around this penultimate meditation on emptiness. The sound of the *ḍamaru* in rhythmic flow symbolizes emptiness because "sound is a produced phenomenon" (as discussed in chapter 7). After the four distributions (white, red, manifold, and the giving of Dharma), the adept is instructed to meditate on the emptiness of giving in this unique way—looking at the causal dependencies of each of the three spheres of giving.[52] The sequential order of meditations makes sense holistically, as a complete ritual experience. Just as in daily life, once a gift is received, is becomes an act of generosity; prior to that it is but a thought and intention. Not only during, but also after giving or receiving, one may reflect on its meaning. Thus, one's contemplation on the "emptiness" of the three spheres can be done effectively as part of the act of offering/giving, and then once again recalled in this special section after everything has been transformed completely and given away.

The very title of the sādhana is reflected in this culminating moment prior to the final dedications—where stanzas focus on the wisdom borne from the realization of "emptiness" as dependent arising, within the practice of the six perfections. The title is inscribed as, "This sādhana is known as '*Dedicating the Illusory Body to Accumulate Merit. Bringing Quick Results in the Practice of Method and Wisdom—the Shared Riches of the Ganden Lineage Practitioners.*' "[53] If one wishes to train in Vajrayāna, the swifter or "diamond" path, and achieve quick results through the practice of both method and wisdom, one can engage in the Chöd sādhana, *Dedicating the Illusory Body.*

9

# Gift of the Body in Chöd

## Healing the Suffering from "Self-Interest"

### Intentionality and the Reciprocated Gift

An exploration of the Chöd ritual with respect to Marcel Mauss's *Essai sur le don*,[1] and his concept of reciprocity, may be instructive as a metaphorical key to help us understand the motivation in the giving process involved in the Chöd ritual. It also suggests important aspects of an analysis of giving that can be applied to other exchange processes outside this ritual—such as the transcultural gifting of the Chöd practice itself between Tibetan lamas and their Western students. From a Buddhist perspective, one's motivation is ultimately the determining factor of whether acts such as those involving the processes of giving (offering, taking, and/or receiving) will become Dharma or non-Dharma.[2] Thus, from a Buddhist vantage point we can move from the study of systems of reciprocity to a study of intentionality underlying the form and functions of those systems, and closer to an understanding of the "reason" for exchange that Mauss sought. In Mauss's most renowned anthropological work, *The Gift: The Form and Reason for Exchange in Archaic Societies*, emphasis on a theory of obligation touches upon the aspect of intentionality in the giving process. Unfortunately, however, Mauss does not develop the concept of intentionality further—he remains preoccupied with exposing the relevance of his subject's themes to other cultural observers of the socioeconomic and political conditions of France in his day.

In this chapter, we will first see how an analysis of both the Chöd ritual and Mauss's gift concept's main theme, reciprocity, evokes the study of a "total system," a methodological triumph that Mauss successfully drove home with *The Gift*. Second, we will discuss the development of the compassionate motivation of *bodhicitta* that is the prerequisite to Chöd practice and how *bodhicitta* guides the ritualization of the concept of the gift in Chöd practice. Finally, we will explore the social implications of a study of the "emotional life of the gift," in light of intentionality, with respect to augmenting Mauss's conception of exchange practices outside of monetary values to include altruism.

## Mauss's "Gift Economy" vs. "Self-Interest"

*The Gift*, as a cross-cultural comparative study, is primarily a foil for launching a cultural critique of Mauss's own society. After numerous comparative studies based on thematic interests, Mauss devotes his concluding section to an analysis of the political economy of contemporary France through the social lens of interactions involving reciprocity. Specifically, Mauss unpacks the processes of gift giving and exchange. He suggests they are not wholly self-interested in purpose and presents a critique of the market economy as it had emerged in France. Mauss contends that, "Several times we have seen how far this whole economy of the exchange-through-gift lay outside the bounds of the so-called natural economy, that of utilitarianism . . . it is indeed something other than utility that circulates in societies of all kinds."[3] Mauss plays with the distance between the extremes of self-interest and disinterest, and the absurdities of inconsistencies in the discourse around giving in the then current anthropology. He recognizes the "individualistic and purely self-interested economy that our own societies" have experienced and critiques the current trend in "our Western societies who have recently made man an 'economic animal.'"[4] Yet Mauss immediately qualifies this, writing "But we are not yet all creatures of this genus," to indicate that there are other means and motives for exchange besides market calculations. Mauss's study concludes that the interrelationships between individuals and groups in society are paramount for an "optimum economy." He claims these need not be exclusively understood within, or calculated as part of, the market economy—but can instead be sustained by practices of exchange which are guided by morality and encouraged, if not enforced, by laws. Mauss gives several contemporary examples in French society where principles of social benefits had recently resulted in legislation, encouraging in him the feeling that a shift in economic relations at the level of political change was afoot. Moreover, he contends that among the various motivating factors for exchange, individualistic pursuits of needs within a "purely self-interested economy" will not ultimately satisfy all individual or social needs.

## Emotional Quotient of Obligatory Reciprocation in Mauss's Gift Economy

Underlying the act of giving and the concept of reciprocity in both the Vajrayāna Chöd ritual and *The Gift* is an *emotional quality* that calls us to look at the social phenomenon of any "gift," and specifically the act of reciprocity, in terms of *intentionality*. For the Chöd practitioner, the motivation behind giving is a generosity imbued with the compassionate intention to benefit others. For Mauss, the motivation is an obligation to reciprocate in order to establish or maintain peaceful relations and a mutually beneficial symbiotic coexistence, but both are arrived at from an intentionality that has a profoundly important *emotional quotient*. One purpose of this chapter is to demonstrate that in order to understand the "reason" for giving one must understand the emotionally imbued motivation, not merely the system one seeks to regulate.[5] A "theory of obligation," such as Mauss worked through in his cross-cultural essay, requires an examination of intention. Mauss attempts to formulate this theory but does not complete it. This chapter proposes to elaborate upon Mauss's theory.

The implications of Maussian economics are important and help to inform a change in understanding the prevalent self-interested Western model of economics. Exchange is based not on obligation *per se*, but on a *feeling* of obligation, and once recognized as such, reciprocity could be cognized differently. The basis for reciprocity would become understood as the previous gift that has been received and the emotional quality of obligation. However, if these were both nuanced differently, within a Buddhist cosmology, we might see an entirely new way of thinking about the motivational aspect of the giving process. Buddhist approaches to compassion, and the reduction of self-interest, place important emphasis on the power of emotion and provide very specific methods for its cultivation; in contrast, until recently compassion has been nearly ignored in the Western (rational choice-influenced) lexicon of emotion.[6]

According to Buddhist epistemology, the individual giver is *always already*—to borrow the Derridean construction—indebted to others because one recognizes that other beings (from the tiniest insects to the largest mammals, to one's best friends and worst enemies) were once one's mothers and fathers. Though it is difficult to prove it in a conventional manner, it does stand to reason that if one's consciousness continues after death to a next life, then in the previous life one must have had a mother and father. In addition, in one's previous life, whether by egg or womb, one was born from a mother who then cared for one lovingly.[7] "Remembering one's mother's kindnesses" is one of the main progenitors to the development of caring for others, which leads to having a compassionate regard for all others' welfare.[8] Once one has developed the emotional levels that form the basis of compassion, one's feeling moves from primarily an emotion characterized as a heartfelt aspiration (to do *something* for others' benefit) through progressive stages to an actualized intentionality as "great compassion." Nurtured, it then grows into the altruistic intention of *bodhicitta* to benefit others by reaching enlightenment and teaching them in turn. Then one engages in practices toward that end, known as the *bodhisattva* practices.

> "Great compassion" refers to the spontaneous wish to see others free of sufferings simply because they are suffering creatures. It is universal, non-discriminatory, and passionate to the point where the individual is capable of dedicating his or her entire being for the benefit of other sentient beings. Such noble beings are called *bodhisattvas*, individuals with heroic aspirations.[9]

Once one attains this compassionate motivation, again, through a protracted series of practices, such those found in Chöd rituals—which act as a training ground for the development of *bodhicitta*—one can engage in the *bodhisattva* practices known as the six perfections: the perfection of (1) generosity; (2) ethical discipline; (3) forbearance; (4) joyous effort; (5) concentration; and, (6) wisdom. It is in pursuit of the perfection of these six practices that *bodhisattvas* fulfill their aspiration to bring about the welfare of all sentient beings.[10] As the eighth-century Buddhist philosopher Śāntideva outlines, the perfection of generosity is a thought-imbued feeling:

> If the perfection of generosity
> Were the alleviation of the world's poverty,
> Then since beings are still starving now,
> In what manner did the previous Buddhas perfect it?
>
> The perfection of generosity is said to be
> The *thought* to give all beings everything,

> Together with the fruit of such a thought;
> Hence it is simply *a state of mind*
> [emphasis mine].[11]

## Gifting as an Antidote to Suffering

There are many ways in which to understand the concepts of healing and religion. In particular, in order to heal oneself, another person, one's kin, or even a nation, one must first know what is understood as "suffering" in a given physical, mental, social, economic, religious, or political context. Relative to that notion of suffering, one can determine the causes of that suffering and then decide on the hermeneutical approach most effective for analysis of the causes, and finally apply the antidotes to effect the necessary healing.[12] One of the objectives of this chapter is to examine suffering as it is understood in Buddhism as well as the particular individual and social suffering that Mauss seeks to remedy in his seminal treatise, *The Gift*. Mauss adopts the position of the Durkheimian school and other French philosophers who maintain that individualist self-interest is "brutish and harmful." His remedy is to analyze the gift economies that lie outside "icy, utilitarian calculations" for, as Mauss contends, "it is not in the calculation of individual needs that the method for an optimum economy is to be found . . . we must remain something other than pure financial experts, even in so far as we wish to increase our own wealth. . . ."[13]

## Obligatory Reciprocation in the Gift Economy

Considering the above, let us turn here to the feelings underlying obligation apparent in Mauss's text, *The Gift*. Just as we privileged feelings in the discussion of the development of compassion, so will we look for clues in Mauss's treatise for indications that the motivation of giving (or not) or reciprocating (or not) is revealed as an emotional quotient. There is an underlying aspect to any gift, what we might call the "emotional life of the gift,"[14] or, more precisely, the emotional quotient of the intentionality that impels or inspires the giver to give. Mauss writes of emotional tensions around reciprocity—feelings of gratitude and those of an attendant obligation to return—referencing cultural systems of reciprocity that are Western and non-Western, as well as those that are contemporaneous and ancient. He writes: "In ancient systems of morality of the most epicurean kind it is the good and pleasurable that is sought after, and not material utility."[15]

Again, Mauss does not diminish the importance of the emotional aspect of reciprocal acts—a subject for which, despite a host of research on gifting, there is still minimal vocabulary in the West. Instead, he returns from the culturally archaic to his contemporary France to make his case for how "the gift of himself" (interpreted as the "time and life of the wage labourer" in industrial capitalist economic systems) should be reciprocated. It should be reciprocated in equal or greater measure according to a conception of the "gift economy," and not merely calculated "fairly" in rational economic terms. Mauss writes:

> We sense that we cannot make men work well unless they are sure of being fairly paid throughout their life for work they have fairly carried out, both for others and for themselves. The producer who carries on an exchange *feels* once more—he has always *felt* it, but this time *he does so acutely*—that he is exchanging more than a product of hours of working time, but that he is *giving something of himself*—his time, his life. Thus he *wishes* to be rewarded, even if only moderately, for *this gift*. To refuse him this reward is to make him become idle or less productive [emphasis mine].[16]

Unlike his emotionally detached armchair ethnographic descriptions of other societies' rituals of exchange, this passage exhibits perhaps Mauss's clearest account (though there are other instances) of his own society in which he explains modern capitalist exchange in terms of a *feeling*. Here, Mauss is conceptualizing wage labor in terms of the theory of the gift with an attendant feeling, albeit an "acute" feeling. The desire a man has to be "fairly paid" after "*giving something of himself*" is expressed in terms of the market-economy vocabulary. The rest of the passage is expressed in the vocabulary of the "gift economy." Indeed, the passage has a modernist tone, evocative of a manifesto, beginning with an unambiguous pronouncement: "man is a *producer* who carries on an exchange." The "*producer* . . . feels once more" that since he gives "his time, his life" he should be "rewarded"—indeed, he *wishes* so. Mauss makes a rhetorical understatement that he only *wishes* this result, where *wishing* is a rather softened feeling. In fact, this calmly stated "wish" is an emotion so strongly felt that if the "reward . . . is . . . refused" it will "make him become idle or less productive," and that much less of a "producer." In other words, the social bond between working men as "producers" and their employers—who should see that the "men" are "fairly paid"—would break down if the worker's perpetual feelings (emotions "he has always felt" . . . [and now] . . . "acutely" so) about his end of the exchange were hurt. They would be hurt because the exchange—which in Mauss "gift economy" is based on obligation, and involves expectations of "fair" payment or "even moderate reward"—should be properly reciprocated.

In noting the vocabulary of the tenuous social fabric of the relationship between worker and employer, let us rephrase Mauss's ideas to highlight the inner tension, the "emotional life of the exchange," which Mauss himself glosses over. We might conclude from the above that the "emotional life of the gift"—seen in Mauss's example of the worker who has "given something of himself" and "feels" (as "always," but now "acutely") that he "wishes to be rewarded . . . even if only moderately"—is precisely in need of obligatory reciprocation that will either result in his being "fairly paid" or in his staging dramatic strikes. Thus, the socioeconomic equilibrium here depends largely on how the "men" who "work well" *feel.*

Any Wall Street market analyst is concerned with the emotional life of exchange. He or she analyzes the *mood* of the marketplace to determine when to sell or buy. In 2002, in the wake of scandals surrounding some of the top ten Fortune 500 companies, the market dropped dramatically because of a lack of confidence among American buyers. Confidence was "stolen" from shareholders by a handful of elites to whom the former group had entrusted their 401(k) and other personal holdings. The rules of exchange were broken and the emotional life of the market waned for nine months. Previous to that, U.S. President George W. Bush asked Americans to keep being "good consumers," to be model Americans and "Buy, buy, buy" following the attacks of September 11 in order to drive the economy forward. With that optimistic sentiment, the stock market rose for the last three months of 2001.

Although Mauss posits a social system of gift exchange as a total social fact, he does not pursue an analysis of the emotional quotient of the gift to capture the socioeconomic climate of his day more effectively. Certainly, one reason he avoids this could be found in the influence of positivism. "Emotion vs. reason" was still a valid dichotomy, particularly in anthropology, which lacked sufficient vocabulary to discuss feelings or intentionality but was rich in the discussion of observable processes and systems such as the exchanges of gifts.[17] Durkheim had secured the split between the sacred and profane—but, in both universes, emotional life regulates exchanges. I suggest that Mauss noted this, but did not develop it. Obligation is, in essence, a *feeling* or *felt understanding*. Mauss writes:

> No longer are we talking in legal terms: we are speaking of men and groups of men, because it is they, it is society, *it is the feelings of men, in their minds and in flesh and blood* that at all times spring into action and that have acted everywhere . . . Therefore, let us adopt as the principle of our life what has always been a principle of action and will always be so: *to emerge from self, to give, freely and obligatorily*. We run no risk of disappointment [emphasis mine].[18]

Mauss concludes the above statement with the word "obligatorily" which, for him, is the crux of the principle of the system of exchange. However, within Chöd practice rituals, and more generally the altruistic Mahāyāna motivation of *bodhicitta*, obligation is taken further—to its most positive social end—in a definitive unequivocal obligation to repay the kindness of all, even if one is involved in a more or less "closed system" of transaction of goods, services, or persons. The uncommonly generous attitude is liberating in its limitlessness—its extension to all is socially and politically engaged and expansive. If we think of the "emotional life of the gift" in terms of Buddhist practice, we can transcend the ordinary boundaries of self-interested motivation and the impossibility of a free gift.[19]

While Mauss seems to have missed an opportunity to explore the undergirding emotive qualities of giving and the "emotional life of the gift," these were not necessarily his central questions. He stated two questions at the outset of *The Gift*:

> *What rule of legality and self-interest, in societies of a backward or archaic type, compels the gift that has been received to be obligatorily reciprocated?*
> *What power resides in the object given that causes its recipient to pay it back?*[20]

If we are committed to logic, we might look at these related questions closely and ask: From what is the obligatory reciprocation being "compelled" of us? From the gift as an (inanimate) object? No, for that is material, and material things do not compel us, or do they?[21] If a gun is pointed at us, or insults are hurled at us, certainly the gun or words are not themselves threatening, but the emotional state of the wielder of the gun might feel threatening, just as the vehemence behind the slander is what disturbs us. From where else does the obligation to reciprocate come, if not from a *feeling* of indebtedness? To what else can the word "compel" (in Mauss's question) refer, if not a *feeling* of indebtedness?

Mauss is entreating the individual to think about the motivating factors for social, material, and labor exchange and to relate them to the systemic processes that can establish peace through a political economy based on a morally guided reciprocation. Mauss's theory differs from the understanding of giving in Buddhism insofar as it is not programmatic and does not aim to teach individuals or society how to develop the feeling of obligation in order to maintain those regulations. It only describes the observable facts and results from a series of unidentifiable and/or undisclosed preliminary causes.

On the other hand, from a Buddhist perspective, the current stasis is wholly inadequate, not at all peaceful, and fraught with suffering. We are, at present, seemingly bound to conditioned existence, due to previous karmic causes and mental afflictions, which lead us to our imminent suffering: our own aging, sickness, and death. Our negative emotions, delusive mental states, and bad habits, which are believed to have been caused by previously established karmic imprints, such as a tendency toward miserliness rather than generosity, stem from our habitual "self-grasping." We can transcend these sufferings however, and purify our negative karmic acts, through the development of compassion and wisdom. But, at present, seeking benefit only for ourselves based on a self-interested motivation, we are not yet equipped to do so. The very root of our "cyclic existence" is our belief in a "self"—an entity with which we identify wholeheartedly by first recognizing "I," and then by attempting to acquire what is good for "me," and forevermore attached to the notion of needing to keep what is "mine." To cut the root of self-grasping we need to recognize the cause of our attachment to objects we view as "mine," in particular our attachment to our erroneous notion of a "self." The notion of "self" is symbolized by our own body in Chöd practice. By visualizing the mind having been ejected into space, and the "cutting" and "offering" of the previous body to others, we can loosen and then "cut" (Chöd, Tib. *gCod*) our attachment to our sense of "self," a seemingly intrinsically existent "I." It is through meditations, investigating the location in the body of the feeling of "I" or "me," and the more advanced practices where we give away our body, mentally transformed into all things other beings need or desire, that we may cut the root of *saṃsāra* and cease suffering. In this non-"self-grasping" state, free of self reference, we are open, generous, and have forbearance with difficulties. Contemplative techniques within Chöd, which adhere to the Vajrayāna teachings, are powerful methods for effecting this inner transformation.

## Suffering in Mauss and Buddhism Compared

Maussian ideas of self-interest (and individualistic efforts at maximizing gain) dovetail with the Buddhist concept of self-cherishing. In Buddhism, this attitude is the cause of individual and social suffering. For Mauss and others following Durkheim's socialist program, self-interested calculations in the socioeconomic realm—such as France's growing industrial capitalist wage labor system, which sought to develop an "optimum economy" of maximizing profits by minimizing payments to workers for their productive labor—were seen as morally ill-founded in the short term and "harmful" in the long term. As Mauss writes, "The brutish pursuit of individualist ends is harmful to the ends and the peace of all."[22]

Central to Mahāyāna Buddhism, the antidote to self-cherishing is *bodhicitta*. This is a compassionate motivation to care for others unequivocally regardless of their present or perceived relationship to oneself as enemy, friend, stranger, ghost, or god. The Chöd ritual develops one's ability to actualize the altruistic motivation of generosity, through practice. It is considered by Tibetans and Western Buddhists alike as one of the most powerful Buddhist rituals for this task because the Chödpa gives away their body and all possessions they own, in visualization.

Mauss shows that individual joys and social relationships are maintained outside the "purely self-interested economy" espoused by utilitarianism not only in archaic societies but in his own. He provides examples to illustrate how means of exchange in the "gift economy," involving obligations to accept gifts and then to reciprocate them in kind, motivates social and individual actors on a moral basis and not solely on a rational basis. The constitution of this moral basis for gifting is not as thoroughly developed by Mauss as we might hope. For example, among the potlatch of the Haïda one must reciprocate the gift because one does not wish to become held as inferior: "one loses face forever if one does not reciprocate."[23] Does the obligation upon oneself and one's group/tribe/clan/society/nation hold *fear*? What *emotional* aspect does obligation entail? Perhaps this is the *power* which Mauss seeks to understand in his second theoretical question: "What power resides in the object given that causes its recipient to pay it back?"[24] In fact, Mauss's analysis of exchange practically assumes the impossibility of altruism. Indeed, he precludes the notion of giving out of compassion with his first theoretical question: "What rule of legality or self-interest, in societies . . . compels the gift that has been received to be obligatorily reciprocated?"[25] Mauss does not entertain another option here such as kindness, or ask in a more open-ended way, "What motivation . . . compels the gift?" Thus, in terms of intentionality, Mauss has already made up his mind that there must necessarily be self-interest at work in both the gift and the market economy. Mary Douglas confirms as much, noting that there is no such thing as a "free gift" whether given under the name of donation, charity, philanthropy, or another label.[26] Regardless of Mauss's narrowed focus, as we can see, for adherents to Buddhist doctrine as well as for Durkheim, Mauss, and others, suffering is founded upon a similar epistemological notion. Purely rational profiteering on an individualistic level is "harmful" and causes individual and social suffering. The remedy is not completely clear in Maussian economics, but it is clear in Vajrayāna Buddhism. Through rituals such as Chöd, one learns to cut the root of self-grasping leading to suffering—but this is effective only if the Chödpa is altruistically motivated to benefit others.

## Post-Maussian Research on Intentionality in Gift-Giving

With the popularity of gift and exchange as an area of anthropological research following Mauss's seminal treatise, many scholars researching social and ritual forms of gifting in recent years have looked more closely at intentionality than did Mauss.

### The Possibility of Altruism

Natalie Zemon Davis points out that "a revived hope for 'the possibility of altruism' has also called attention to the gratuitous end of the gift register."[27] She alerts us to research into the actualization of altruism in the productive area of medical anthropology and a study by Richard Titmuss, *The Gift Relationship: From Human Blood to Social Policy*.[28] This topic is related to the altruistically imagined giving of blood in the Chöd ritual. Titmuss compared the blood transfusion systems in the United States and Great Britain: the latter functions based on the generosity of voluntary donors and the former on the profiteering of blood as a commodity. In contrast to Great Britain's systemic superiority with "lower rates of contamination," "low cost to the patient," and "little wastage of blood," the United States system was "costly" to the patient, saw "high rates of contaminated blood," and excessive "wastage." That Titmuss shows the advantages of the gratuitous system of exchange in Great Britain over the profiteering one of the United States is not my main point here. Rather, I propose we follow Davis's lead in pointing out the reaction of skeptical critics who deny the possibility of altruism, citing the "finite reserve" of compassion available for human use. The economist Kenneth Arrow concluded that Titmuss's theory pointed to merely one of " 'a large class of unilateral transactions,' of which the donation of blood, philanthropy, and certain government expenditures were examples."[29] Arrow articulates a widespread mistaken view on the impossibility of altruism: "Wholesale usage of ethical standards is apt to have undesirable consequences. We do not wish to use up recklessly the *scarce resources* of altruistic motivation." By noting that Arrow frames "altruistic motivation" in economic terms—as "unilateral transaction"—we can understand why he would be concerned about "economic efficiency" if the system (based on an apparently limited emotional capacity) relies too much on "altruistic motivation."[30]

Emmanuel Levinas sees oneself as being "responsible to the other" and posits the notion of an "absolute gratuity" toward the other.[31] Levinas regards the self as obligated to the other, and the other who is the beneficiary of kindness need not be concerned about return.[32] His view is summarily described in the parable from the Old Testament about Cain and Abel. After Cain murders Abel, God asks him, "Where is your brother?" to which Cain retorts defiantly, "Am I my brother's keeper?" The point Levinas makes is that Cain's question is precisely backwards. In terms of Talmudic theory, Cain, as a brother, is responsible *first* to his brother Abel, even before he is responsible to himself.[33]

Taking an altogether different position, Jacques Derrida discusses the "impossibility of the gift." Let us follow Rosalyn Diprose's analysis of Derrida's approach to Mauss in her book *Corporeal Generosity* (2002).[34] In Derrida's opinion, Mauss treats the gift as a commodity, and "remains caught within the logic of exchange and contract . . . within this logic . . . the gift and giving are impossible."[35] Diprose explains Derrida's position as follows:

> *Generosity is impossible because*, under the logic of contract and exchange, the gift is recognized as a gift (it functions as a commodity) and, once recognized [as such], the gift bestows a debt on the recipient and is annulled through obligation, gratitude, or some other form of return (pp. 12–14) . . . Derrida's analysis suggests that it is precisely this economy of contract and exchange between self-present individuals that makes generosity impossible. *The gift is only possible* if it goes unrecognized, if it is not commoditized, if it is forgotten by the donor and done.[36]

Derrida's summation concurs with my earlier view that, for Mauss, the motivation behind the gift is neglected in the original analysis. Derrida writes that what is important for Mauss is the exchange, made effective by the commodification of the gift.

I would argue that Mauss's attention to the process of giving (of indebtedness, obligation, and reciprocation) and the system of exchange (with the three obligations: to give, to receive, and to reciprocate) led him to gloss over key aspects of generosity. Derrida's stance is based on reading the structure and argument of Mauss's analysis and thereby interpreting Mauss's text in an ahistorical dimension. However, an historically attuned anthropology sees Mauss's obvious failing. He skips over the rich material in the area of intentionality behind generosity because of his research methodology (armchair ethnography) and the consequent lack of epistemic privilege given to the voices of individual social actors, the indigene. Were Mauss alive today, we can speculate that he would return to the "feelings" of "working men" who are "giving something of [themselves]." And, perhaps, similar to Pierre Bourdieu's study, *The Weight of the World: Social Suffering in Contemporary Society*, he would align his theory with social analyses that receive the benefits of inter-social communication between researcher and consultant.[37] Derrida seems to be overly concerned with the phenomenological aspects of exchange and the essential properties and meaning of the gift. As a consequence, his analysis, as with Mauss's, loses sight of the possibility of the bountifully optimistic focus on the altruistic suggested by Levinas.

## Altruism as "Total System"

For Chöd practitioners, altruism is not a requirement for practice, it is the method itself by which a "total system" of generosity is enacted, and through which the gifting of body, material goods, and Dharma flows to others.[38] Having cultivated even the first level of the path toward attaining *bodhicitta*, giving is done as a practice of the "perfection of generosity," which stems from altruism. The *bodhicitta* motivation is not a "ticket to ride" on the Chöd train, like a prerequisite one can forget about once the ritual begins. It is the profound view of one's relationship with all other beings. Chöd practitioners seek to "cut" attachment to the body, and thus, to the notion of a solid self. Once attaining a highly realized state, practitioners have a constantly felt ethical responsibility to ease others' suffering and give what may lead to happiness.

The Chöd practitioner's training involves honing their faculties such that they become able to ward off pride and self-interest, even while advancing in skill. Though the rewards of giving altruistically are immense in terms of accumulating Buddhist merit, the practitioner must not give any thought to it. One Chöd lama teaches:

> You must practise giving without expecting anything in return, or any [karmic] ripening effects. If your generosity is motivated by *bodhicitta*, then your giving a morsel of food or a little clean barley flour to beggars, the poor, and so on—or even to worms and ants would be a [true] practice of generosity, and a deed of the Child of the Victorious Ones . . . If you exchange this [practice] for the gifts received for performing these rituals, you have sold the Dharma for material goods. This is like dragging a king off his throne and forcing him to sweep the floor.[39]

Some Western theorists, such as Rosalyn Diprose, touch upon similar intentional characteristics in the conceptualization of generosity to those that are valued in Buddhist epistemology concerning the altruistic *bodhicitta* motivation. She relies upon the body of scholarly work on the gift following Mauss, and relates such altruistic intentionality in a gift economy to theories of social and economic relations that produce social justice outcomes. She writes:

> [A] social economy based on generosity rather than revenge, where self-overcoming involves the noble gift-giving virtue, and intersubjective relations are no longer creditor-debtor relations; an economy where "gifts can be given without expectation of return, and debts can be forgiven without penalty or shame."[40]

For Diprose, Levinas's "other-directed sensibility" perspective on generosity is an important contribution to the "philosophy of the gift":

> Levinas, more explicitly than either Nietzsche or Merleau-Ponty, describes subjectivity in terms of generosity as I understand it. His work lends itself to a philosophy of the gift, insofar as he bases a sociality that does not absorb difference on giving to the other without expectation of return. Subjectivity, for Levinas, is the passivity of exposure to another, *a giving of oneself without choice*, a movement toward another arising from a disturbance

> of the self provoked by the others' alterity. Moreover, this being-given to another is sensibility, being affected, and this carnal offering to another is inspired by alterity . . . And so with this understanding of generosity provoked by alterity, Levinas puts *ethics, as "other-directed" sensibility*, at the foundation of social existence [emphasis mine].[41]

In Mahāyāna Buddhism, the "other-directed" sensibility describes intersubjectivity and generosity in terms of loving-compassion for all beings. In ritual practices, the emphasis is placed on initially cultivating genuine *bodhicitta* from one's heart in order to act to relieve the suffering of all sentient beings. Our very existence as beings who are subject to impermanence, old age, and death within the conditioned existence that is *saṃsāra* is the chief cause of suffering. Because of the primacy of a graduated path to enlightenment—training in generating a heartfelt compassion for all beings until it is spontaneous and universal—one is advised to practice in stages. Thus, sincerely making a gift of the body may be possible only for the more advanced practitioners. Accordingly, beginners are cautioned as follows: "It may not be right to give your body, for example. Do not give your body while you are still at the stage of undergoing the process of familiarization and merely increasing your thoughts of giving."[42]

Luce Irigaray romanticizes the relationship between training the giver and her perceived object of giving in her chapter "To love to the point of safeguarding you."[43] The most challenging relationship between subject and object, self and other, when giving—even if one is so advanced that one can give one's body—is that of the perception of the object of one's giving. This highlights one's intimate karmic relationship to enemies, spirits, harmdoers, and all those to whom one is karmically indebted. Irigaray posits that the way in which the intersubjective exchange of self with other, exchanging one's virtues with other's suffering in the Buddhist meditation practice technique of 'giving and taking' (Tib. *gtong len*), is affectively achieved through love first and then compassion. One takes on the suffering of others into the depths of the self-cherishing at one's heart, and loses the tendency to grasp at an inherently existent self—all through love of the (m)other. Borrowing again, seemingly from Buddhism, Irigaray writes:

> If I become the other—through love, for example—I abolish the two poles I-you, she-he . . . Reality becomes a dream . . .

> Becoming the other without returning within myself is part of such a dream . . . to becoming that loses the way back: to the self . . . to the other.[44]

## Healing the Suffering from Self-Interest: Adding Altruism to the Exchange

Now let us take Mauss's theory one step further to describe how altruism expands the boundaries of Derrida's notion of the continuum (table 9.1), where we see egocentric self-interested motivation on the one side, with the impossible purely disinterested gift on the other. To this, we can add another possibility, an other-oriented altruistic giving (table 9.2):

Table 9.1. Mauss' Gift Economy vs. Market Economy

| |
|---|
| self-interested exchange ↔ impossible purely disinterested gift |

Table 9.2. Gift Economy with the Mahāyāna Buddhist *Bodhicitta* Motivation

| |
|---|
| self-interested exchange ↔ impossible pure gift ↔ altruistic compassionate giving |

The double arrows signify a continuum and articulated emotions that motivate acts of giving and a range of responses. In table 9.2, on the left is egocentric self-interest, the most harmful motivation; at the other end of the spectrum, a compassionate other-interested motivation. The continuum encompasses the range of possible motivations in Maussian terms while adding in the possibility offered by the Levinasian and Mahāyāna Buddhist perspectives. In the middle we can place the notion of the impossibility of the pure gift, to show the relative distance in terms of inner warmth and feeling between the egocentric and other-interested caring outward motivation. We could have a continuum for the range of responses as well. This would illustrate where an obligation to reciprocate can consist emotionally of a fear of inferiority if one does not capitulate appropriately, or a genuine kindness to return another's kindness, etc. To maintain systems of exchange, it is not merely the act that is important, but the way in which the thought behind the act is set into motion.

### Investigating the Nature of Compassion

At the Mind and Life Institute, an interdisciplinary team of Western neuroscientists, psychologists, and medical researchers are engaged in an ongoing dialogue with Tibetan monks highly experienced in meditation to investigate the Western scientific and Buddhist views on the nature of compassion and its development by the individual through contemplative practices.[45] In this context, the Dalai Lama responded to questions on self-interest and other-interest:

> Perhaps there's a slight problem in language here. The Tibetan word for compassion is *tsewa*, which need not necessarily imply that it is directed to someone else. One can have that feeling toward oneself as well. When you say that someone should be compassionate, there is no connotation that you should totally disregard your self-interest.

This connects with Mauss's notion that completely disengaging from the market economy would not be advisable—a point with which he differed from Durkheim's version of socialism. For Mauss, having just returned from Moscow where he saw the results of the government's brutal controls in post-Revolution Russia before writing *The Gift*, he felt socialism in France should be built upon institutions from the ground up and not be devoid of some self-interest. However, that self-interest should maintain a harmonious balance of exchanges and social ties based on morality and/or laws that enforce moral principles. It is important to understand, in light of this closer reading of Mauss, how Buddhist compassion is developed. The Dalai Lama explains:

> Compassion, or *tsewa*, as it is understood in the Tibetan tradition, is a state of mind or way of being where *you extend how you relate to yourself toward others* as well. Whatever or whoever the object of your affection, you wish it to be free of suffering [emphasis mine].[46]

Anne Harrington, Professor of History of Science at Harvard, then confirms, "And that object may be yourself as well."[47] The Dalai Lama replies:

> Yourself first, and then in a more advanced way the aspiration will embrace others. In a way, high levels of compassion are nothing but an advanced state of that self-interest . . . there is *specific training* in Buddhist meditation aimed at enhancing the compassionate disposition. The meditator is encouraged to develop an outlook where he or she disregards his or her own self-interest and pursues the well-being of others. But here the aim is to develop a deep conviction of the negative consequences of excessive self-absorption or self-cherishing [emphasis mine].[48]

In sum, the above dialogue demonstrates some important elements of the argument in this chapter. First, this seems to reveal large differences between Levinas and Mahāyāna Buddhism, particularly the notion that in developing compassion "you extend how you relate to yourself toward others." Levinas begins with the other. He would perhaps say that the Mahāyāna (and all other except his own) versions of compassion are ultimately collective selfishness.

Second, one's compassion or *tsewa* (Tib. *brtse ba*), is the wishing for the object of one's concern to be free from suffering. At a rudimentary level, it should be directed toward oneself first, but in more "advanced states of self-interest" one extends the object of concern outward to be inclusive of all beings. The Dalai Lama highlights the potentiality of every being to attain a higher level of the "perfection of generosity" by training first in methods of developing compassion.

Third, *bodhicitta* is the emotionally imbued motivation to act compassionately—exemplified by a mother who sees her child drowning in a fast flowing river and, without a second thought, jumps in to save them. In the case of someone else's child, or even someone whom one does not know or does not like, if one had *bodhicitta* in one's mindstream, then one would likely not pause to make a calculation before jumping in the water.[49] Normally, cultivating compassion through Mahāyāna practices takes many lifetimes, but tantric methods like Chöd practice greatly speed up the process of the development of *bodhicitta*. This is due to a number of factors: the initiation and empowerment from the lama, the power of visualization that allows for the practice of guru-deity yoga, and identifying oneself as the deity in a single moment of consciousness.

The Vajrayāna Chöd method operates within a cultural framework in which a socially sanctioned possibility of altruism is prized as a precious saintly ideal. The musical tradition that embodies this meditation tradition is gifted to disciples with an expectation to reciprocate by helping to preserve the lineage tradition. Yet disciples are not expected to learn immediately how to perform the musical tradition, or to be able to imaginally give their bodies away. The notion of becoming incrementally familiar is again invoked here, moving from self-interest outward, referring to the Dalai Lama's explanation of the graduated development of compassion.

## Gifting to Heal the Suffering from Self-Interest

Mauss's study on gift and exchange practices allows for an exploration of the power of the gift, and the underlying movitations that compel a gift to be reciprocated through obligation. Mauss's tight focus on exchange practices enables him to examine this socioeconomic dynamic cross-culturally and historically. In examining his own society, there is clearly an emotional aspect to exchange practices embedded in Mauss's critical explorations, which he did not develop in more depth. By including "the possibility of altruism" in subsequent research on the gift, we look at later cross-cultural studies of gifting practices, chiefly those of Titmuss and Davis. Each author studies cultural practices shaped by national health care policy, investigating the notion that various cultures might be predisposed to certain motivations that shape blood donor practices. Tables 9.1 and 9.2 (above) help us to consider the spectrum on which organ donors and blood donors may be understood to function in emotional terms. The point being made is that underlying an act of giving may be a range of emotional responses and motivations: from giving without thought of expecting return, to being compelled to give out of obligation to reciprocate, to giving out of enlightened self-interest. Through this cross-cultural exploration of giving the body in contemporary settings (blood and organ donation), it is possible to debunk the notion that a "finite reserve" of compassion shapes gifting practices.[50] Rather, it is apparent that culture, economics, politics, and social expectations shape the emotional life of the gift.

Through Mauss's cross-cultural study of giving, we learn an anthropological "truth": that people may be predisposed to be motivated by one or another of the "possibilities of altruism," "collective-interest," or "self-interest"—leaning toward one side or another along a sliding scale. The notion that there is a hardwired (neurological) finite possibility to the capacity of a person to give is very likely nonsense. We are but human beings with obvious limitations. However, the heart can open expansively such that the love emanated and displayed by persons like the Reverend Dr. Martin Luther King Jr. and Mother Teresa are recognizable to the hearts of others. Perhaps to recognize another's quality, one needs to possess it partly in oneself? The ability to harm others as well as the ability to act compassionately toward others are human capabilities in so far as we are raised to be culturally predisposed to certain responses.

Understanding that an emotional life underlies the gift, and compels it, comes from a particular framework of thinking. As hinted at through the discussion of Levinas, another form of gift giving exists from the Talmudic perspective: that of the unrecognized gift whereby the donor's name is unknown. The highest form of giving is the anonymous, selfless gift whereby the recipients are not charged with the compelling need to reciprocate. Mauss himself, being raised in Jewish Talmudic thought, understood that dynamic. Levinas, too, draws from this. Derrida, in his inimitable linguistic use of cognitive limits, is strongly influenced by this notion. He coins the notion of the "impossibility of the gift"—meaning that if it is recognized as being a gift, then it cannot actually be a genuine gift.

## Incremental Familiarity: *The Jātaka Tales*

Thinking of giving the body away as a compassionate act of sacrifice for the benefit of others reminds one of the *Jātaka Tales*, the collection of life stories of the Buddha's previous incarnations in which he demonstrated such virtues. Some of these parables are recounted in the final section of the Chöd sādhana, *Dedicating the Illusory Body*. Each stanza recalls a compassionate action performed by Buddha during one of his previous lives, exhorting the practitioner to train in order be able to cultivate the same level of intentional purpose and embodied action. In one stanza, the Buddha sacrificed his body to a tigress too weak to feed her two starving cubs:

> When he was born as King Great and Powerful Compassion,
> he fed the tigress with his own flesh.
> In the same way, may I be able to give with joy
> this cherished illusory body to the hosts of flesh-eaters.[51]

Ven. Pencho Rabgey (Pala) alerted me to the distinction between those who are ready to give their bodies away, and those who are not. "We cannot even handle it when we see a little blood on the tip of our finger. How can we give our whole body? Don't lie! As beginners, we are just *imagining*, but we have to *feel as if* we are going to give our whole body away."[52] There is a process to this work, which he describes through an example of childhood development:

> A baby cannot get to the top of the stairs right away. They see it. But they cannot get there today, right away. They first have to try to stand up; then, slowly, they can walk. They're going to get there, for sure, but not today. Not right away. Likewise, if you say, "I'm going to drive my car a little," and then you think, fearfully, "But how can I ever fly that big plane?" That's not correct. You cannot fly that big plane. It's silly for you to be afraid of doing that *because you're not there, at that level. You haven't reached that stage as yet.*

## Incremental Stages of Advancement: Learning How to Give Altruistically

Cultivation and abandonment is the dialectic to meditate upon when applying antidotes. By cultivating spiritual qualities one is reducing worldly qualities. As Pala says, "You get one, and abandon one. You get one 'virtuous mind' and abandon a 'delusive mind.' " First a person cultivates an ability to give a penny; later, she can give a dollar. Pala's root lama, Gen Trinley, did not even use coins to begin with, but a handful of soil.[53] In one of my first lessons in Chöd, he shared with me Gen Trinley's training method:

> Gen Trinley taught us how to give. He said that we could learn easily in this way. The first lesson he gave us was to take a little bag of soil, and visualize it as something valuable. We were to take soil in one hand and give to the other hand, and to *feel* like we're giving to this one here, and *feel* you are doing that in order to get enlightenment for all sentient beings. Then, you dedicate the merit from giving and the happiness you *feel* to your getting enlightenment for the sake of all mother sentient beings. Then you take soil from the other hand, and you give back to the first hand, and think, "I give to this one," again dedicating any accumulated virtues to getting enlightenment for all sentient beings.

This technique, involving a retooling and tuning of a practitioner's motivation, is as far away from a stage performance as could be. This is a method of mind training (*blo sbyong*) from the Mahāyāna oral tradition in which the ultimate goal is to cherish others more than oneself. I spent one night in Gen Trinley's retreat house above the monastery in 2004; the chilly, damp clouds, rising up the Chungba Valley's grassy slopes, wafted in wisps through the open window of this sacred space. I recalled the stories of how Pala as a young monk, then Phuntsok Rabgey, would cook for Gen Trinley, perform chores, and run errands while learning Dharma.

Following Pala's advice led me to try a version of Gen Trinley's method. After receiving the advice the first time, I went to a beach at an Ontario Provincial Park on Georgian Bay, sat on the shore and held a small handful of sand in my hand imagining it to be gold. Then, thinking that with this tremendous resource I could cure others and benefit as many beings as possible, I meditated on this thought. In other words, no sooner did I have this incredible sum than I should imagine putting it to use in helping others. At first this meditation was successful, and I could feel the lessening of attachments. However, somehow, while performing this practice, I noticed that even though it was sand, my thoughts turned to fantasize about what I could do personally with such a sum. Observing how my mind gravitated toward that habitual mental attachment and fantasy, even with a hand full of sand, helped me to understand how I view myself in relation to others. That I would, *even at the imaginal level*, seek first to help *one person*—myself—rather than others, who are countless, made me blush. Pala explains the benefits of repeated practice:

> Then, later, when you have a thousand dollars, if you give away one penny, it is easy. It doesn't bother anybody. Furthermore, you're not going to miss that. You give that penny and feel "I give this, and any virtue created from giving this, I dedicate to my getting enlightenment as soon as possible to benefit all mother sentient beings."

Gradually the practitioner advances in skill level with respect to giving, from beginner to advanced. One first tries the exercise with sand or soil and moves to actual currency in the tiniest amounts.[54] Whether one is practicing with sand, or engaging in Chöd ritual practices, these stages are crucial for gradually accumulating karmic merit. As well, these stages may indeed be useful for completing an exchange in such a way that a *feeling* directs one in an intentionally compassionate act toward both others and oneself, correcting a social and socioeconomic imbalance. Mind training practices that involve both *feelings* and physical actions help to prepare one for, and enhance, meditating during Chöd practices. The incremental moments spent in a mind state of generosity support acts that reinforce that state, and accrue toward one's happiness. The rhythmic patterned musical groove of the *ḍamaru* and singing melodies likewise support the meditative process, such that the combined performance of outer and inner aspects of the liturgy within a ritual context can eventually lead to transformation at a practical level in everyday life.

# Conclusion

## Continuity of the Chöd Ritual Tradition

This book is intended to fill a gap in the research published to date on Chöd rituals and meditation practices. At first, the effort was designed to produce a work of ethnomusicological scholarship that would be in accordance with other works in the field of Buddhist studies while providing a comprehensive and integrated look at the performative aspects of this musical liturgical tradition—an oral tradition of song-poetry that also has a large body of written liturgical texts and accompanying oral and written commentaries.

Besides students and scholars of ethnomusicology and Buddhist ritual, this work has focused on serving two other communities. First is the community of Buddhist studies scholars who have invested tremendous effort in studying Chöd through its rich philological legacy—often at a distance from the musical performance of the practice, but up close with the written commentaries that describe, discuss, and advise on the practice. Second is the community of Buddhist practitioners new to the Chöd Tradition who, like myself, were initially encumbered with the musical performance aspects, and have had to be able to get *beyond* these performative features to delve *into* the meditation practice. I also observed that the participants in this community of new Chöd practitioners who were reading the Tibetan song-poetry in English phonetics sometimes became hampered by the language barrier. They had yet to find a way to get *beyond* the filter of singing in a foreign language in English phonetics to get *into* experiencing the meaningfully integrated visualizations *while* singing the meditative poetry.

For all of these communities, I wished to explore whether there were any meaningful connections—on a functional level—between the musical performance and meditation practice. The book's findings—based on answering the question, "What are the roles of music in the Chöd ritual practice?"—suggest that this integrated experience of performing the Chöd song-poetry while understanding its multilayered meaning may be essential to fully accomplishing the meditative goals of Chöd practice.

One of the insights that emerged from my fortunate experience of apprenticing in the Chöd Tradition under Ven. Pencho Rabgey (Pala) was the theme of "graduated skill" in both musical performance and meditation practice. Pala's teachings wove together the musical transmission and spiritual transmission into a blanket of well-worn understanding. The discursive tract of comparing "beginners" to "advanced" practitioners did not catch my analytical interest at first. But in reading the written transcript of the oral commentary on Chöd practice given in 1984 by Kyabje Zong Rinpoché (one of Pala's Chöd lamas), I observed that Zong Rinpoché took the same approach and made the same kinds of distinctions as did Pala. This notion of graduated ability and experience in meditation and performance is formulaic, and formalized in the Ganden tradition. It seemed logical to extrapolate from the normative discursive framework and develop a terminology that could be of help to new non-Tibetan and Tibetan practitioners of the Chöd ritual practice. In other words, I was not adding anything new to the tradition, but rearticulating what was already prevalent in the oral tradition for a contemporary audience of practitioners and scholars. Thus, I return to the question of who I had in mind as the audience(s) for this book.

This research project has been animated by the wish to fill in a gap reflected in the large amount of secondary scholarly literature on Chöd that emerges from studies of Buddhism, religion, and Tibetan culture, which have generally given less focus to the musical, performative, and aural aspects of the practice, and how these, in some cases, cue and affect the inner meditative practices. However, previous studies largely adhered to a particular disciplinary expectation of centering on the written liturgical poetry, the tantric sādhana text, rather than on the oral/aural musical tradition of meaningful symbolic referents that are heard in the sung expression of that poetry—as well as the varied practice techniques and deliberately symbolic ways of performing sādhanas by different practitioners. Significantly, the inner visualizations and profound meditations, shaped in part by the musical performance practices that enliven the pithy poetry, involve the practitioner in what are said to be some of the key transformative aspects of the practice.

To address this gap, it has been important to show how ethnomusicologists can bring a powerful corrective when looking into a liturgical song-poetry tradition such as Chöd. We might regard the written liturgical poetic text as but one of many "texts"; and thereafter understand the expressive pedagogy to be a "text"; the oral and written commentarial instructions given by the lama to disciples as other kinds of "texts"; and the musical expression—the melodies and rhythms and mantric utterances—as, again, "texts" in their own right. That is why I maintain that the Chöd practice tradition has an "intertextual layering" of interwoven symbolic elements. The layers are combined in meaningful ways to enhance a meditator's experience during the performative act of engaging in the ritual practice.

Thus, with respect to meditation, while performing the ritual practices, a more "advanced" Chödpa, who is working at the level of a "*practice*-centered performance" rather than a "*performance*-centered practice," can (1) meditate on "emptiness" through the "inner performance" of the visualized separation of the practitioner's consciousness from the body and dissolve into the guru-deity (the lama, who is understood to be essentially inseparable from Yum Chenmo and Machik Labdrön). As well, they can (2) meditate on *bodhicitta* by imagining altruistically giving all parts of the "old body," mentally transformed into all things needed and desirable, to all beings throughout the universe whether at that moment they appear friendly and dear or hostile and destructive. (3) They can meditate on renunciation as they travel to the site of practice with only ritual implements and their mind focused on visualizing a huge gathering of beings with an extraordinarily strong compassionate motivation to relieve all beings from *saṃsāra*. (4) At the conclusion of the ritual, they can meditate on "emptiness" (from a different perspective) by focusing on the "three spheres of giving": the complete mutual interdependence between the giver (practitioner), gift (mentally transformed body), and recipients (all buddhas, bodhisattvas, ḍākas, ḍākinīs, dharma protectors, and sentient beings). These meditations can be powerfully supported by the ritual performance.

For scholars engaged in studies of Chöd, attending to the expressive act of performance here in this book was not initially meant to debunk the notion that the written text is the only aspect of the practice necessary to engage with, that it is only the "literary" content of the sādhana that is worth studying, or possible to study. That said, I had no motivation or desire to claim that the musical "texts" (layers) are as important as, or more important than, the written poetic "text." However, during the course of this research I found an oral transmission given by the former head of the Ganden Chöd lineage in which he stated that one of the melodies, composed by the founder of the tradition, Machik Labdrön, was meant to powerfully assist the meditator in the visualization practice by symbolizing a scene through tone painting, a music composition technique with literary referents.

Previously it was understood that the visualizations in Chöd were primarily cued by the written text, and the music somewhat assisted in the visualization through a number of other ways, including: (1) instrumental sound production and symbolism, (2) mechanical and physiological aspects such as "flow" (produced through playing the *ḍamaru* in its rhythmic *ostinato*), (3) intentional thought (underlying, for example, the calling forth of beings through the blowing of the *kangling*), and (4) the general aesthetic aspect of the mood, *rasa* or "taste." However, when I discovered that melodic symbolism could be used to conjure up a contextually appropriate (terrifying) image—of vultures arriving in anticipation of the departure of one's consciousness from one's "old" body—it shifted the balance of relative importance between the liturgical text and melody. Now, the written liturgy and melody (as "textual" layers) could *both* be regarded as primary "texts" and perhaps *equally* powerful in terms of visualization and meditative experience.

I referred to the musical composition technique of tone painting employed in the Chöd context as "sonic iconography." This term reflects how the music is designed to assist in the practitioner's meditative visualization in a way that is analogous to the way in which a Tibetan *thangka* painting functions. In the Tibetan visual art form, each color combination, brush stroke, background image, and central deity figure are designed to operate as functional aids for the practitioner's meditation. Similarly, on both a practical and aesthetic level, the musical design of the *mgur*-styled Chöd melodies can determine the mood, symbolic image, rhythmic gesture, and sensibility required for integrating the written poetic liturgy and meditative performance.

Once I realized the importance of attending to these musical layers of the Chöd ritual, I suggested the broader merits of "ritual mapping" in order to investigate additional instances in which music-poetry-rhythm-visualization correspondences occur. By utilizing the graphic technique of "ritual mapping," the intertextual layers of a multilayered performance may be juxtaposed, which assists in exploring the music-text relationship as expressive gestures in a single moment of performance. This mapping is illustrated in Chapters 1 through 5.

In chapter 4, we revisited Ter Ellingson's study on the symbolism of the Chöd *ḍamaru* drum, published in the *Journal of the Society for Asian Music* (Ellingson 1979b), by working through a case study of various practitioners' interpretations. Published in the same journal thirty-four years later, my article (included as this chapter with minor revisions) reexamined Ellingson's work, providing evidence found during my research that supported what he had initially written about individual interpretation of *ḍamaru* symbolism (Cupchik 2013). Here I gave form to the notion that a community of practitioners is ever shaping the "text"—in this case, a symbolic "text"—through personal meditational experiences. This may be identified as an "interpretive community." I discussed various experiential readings of *ḍamaru* symbolism, as conveyed by Chöd lamas. The underlying motivation was to reflect the teaching given to Chöd practitioners that symbolism, too, is but an imputation. While it may be efficacious to visualize the symbolism imputed upon a ritual instrument/implement, it is nevertheless also important to recognize the tendency of the mind to reify symbols, and then to utilize the analysis of "dependent arising" (Skt. *pratītya-samutpāda*, Tib. *rten cing 'brel bar 'byung ba*) to see the "emptiness" of these imputed symbols.

Chapter 5 approached "intentional thought" as an important component that underlies the imputation of symbolism. We investigated the specific mantric utterances used in Chöd rituals to better understand and convey their power and roles. This section is quite uncritical in its approach, and follows a more staid tract of Buddhological translation of a Tibetan scholar's written commentary about the mantric utterance *phaṭ*. This chapter offers the first English translation of the section of the Chöd commentary by Kachen Lobsang Zopa, a scholar of Tashi Lhunpo monastery, on the functions of the mantric syllable *phaṭ* and its varied manner of utterance in the context of Chöd practices. In addition, the "ritual mapping" in this chapter, with several figures and charts, is meant to provide an exemplary model for future investigations into tantric ritual analyses. By breaking down the elements of performance into their "intertextual layers," and situating the context of their utterance, we illustrated their function and meaning in Chöd ritual practices.

We focused on the internal and external benefits of each of the four modes of ritual performance in chapter 6. These refer to both the solitary and social functions of tantric ritual practices. The Chöd practitioner, as a ritualist, is working through an indigenous theory of music aesthetics concerning articulations of intentionally produced sound. According to this aesthetic theory, these articulations can produce meaningful inner and outer transformation for all beings.

Chapter 7 is situated at a point in the book where Buddhist philosophical terms and concepts need to be further elucidated to help the reader/practitioner to probe more deeply into Chöd meditation practices. For example, in this chapter we discussed conceptions of sound in relation to "emptiness." The previous chapters introduced many notions about Chöd such that this chapter can take the reader a step further, providing more evidence that the musical-spiritual practice is both philosophically rooted and a performance tradition.

Chapter 8 is possibly the most important for ethnomusicologists, folklorists, cultural anthropologists, and other scholars interested in the cultural survival of Tibetan and Himalayan oral traditions. I clarified the (sometimes misunderstood) distinction between musical transmission and spiritual transmission, providing the groundwork for understanding why and how Chöd pedagogy involves both types of transmission. I discussed transmission and lineage in terms of continuity and change, and also took up the particular configuration of goals and projects around preserving the Chöd Tradition's melodies through recordings. I introduced the reader to the idea that (in recent recording projects) transmission appears to have been unfortunately conflated with the goals of preservation and dissemination, and suggested that recording technology could be used more effectively to achieve the Chöd lama's overall goal of preserving the lineage. Recordings could, I recommended, be retooled toward a pedagogical imperative. This could be done by not recording only complete performances of a Chöd sādhana (from beginning to end as a "performance"), which satisfies only the preservation ethic of having a complete record of the lama's sādhana practice for future generations. Rather, for "beginners" still training in Chöd, recordings ought to be made *first* of the unaccompanied melody *followed by* a drum-accompanied version. Zong Rinpoché (the former head of the Ganden Chöd Tradition) recorded pedagogically oriented cassettes in this manner in the mid-1980s, and these were distributed to his disciples. Pala transmitted the melodies to me in the same manner: by first singing the fully ornamented version of the melody slowly, and then singing the *ḍamaru*-accompanied version of the melody. In the latter case, he dropped the less essential ornamented notes in the melismatic passage but kept the important pitches.

If, as Zong Rinpoché asserted in his oral commentary,[1] the melodies embody the wisdom of the buddhas, and singing "correctly" by authentically reproducing the melodies vocally (as one's Chöd lama sings them) allows for the spiritual transmission (*lung*) of those wisdom blessings, then the complete musical transmission of *both* the fully ornamented version of the melody *and* the drum-accompanied version (if possible to obtain), would seem vital to the continuity of the spiritual lineage and the ultimate goal of preservation of the Ganden Chöd Tradition.

While the first part of chapter 8 concerns the types of transmission involved in the Chöd Tradition, the latter part concerns the transformation inculcated in the practitioner through Chöd practice (taking a loss for oneself, accepting bad conditions, maintaining patience, etc.). The counter-intuitive nature of the approach that the Chöd practitioner is encouraged to take toward life obstacles and suffering is instructive whether in the forms of stories, parables, or philosophical logic. Therefore, I included all three here as a didactic and ethnographic compilation of new possibilities the spiritual practitioner could consider when responding to life's challenges. Many of these possible responses to conflict were drawn from the *zhi byed* ("pacification") tradition taught by Padampa Sangyé, the Indian mahāsiddha who taught Machik Labdrön how to mentally give up that which was most precious to her in order to pacify external spirits and internal hindrances to enlightenment.

Finally, chapter 9 provides an interdisciplinary approach looking into Marcel Mauss's gifting and exchange studies with respect Chöd practices. I suggest that underlying what compels reciprocity is a "feeling," which manifests as a need or obligation to reciprocate. I propose that Mauss understood the power of this "feeling" but did not approach it explicitly. Paying down karmic debts emerges from a feeling as well. If it is one's altruistic resolve to lead all beings to buddhahood that underlies the paying down of karmic debts, then this may allow one to transcend the cycle of debts paid and further owings. I examine what I call the "possibility of altruism," which may be symbolized socially and ethically as a one-way engagement without expecting anything in return. An example that relates to Chöd, which helps to explain how real the possibility of altruistic giving may actually be, is to rely upon a comparative study of the social practice of individual blood donations. It seems that the cultural contexts of blood donations—whether done for payment (in the USA) or for altruistically cultural reasons of Victorian neighborly charity (in the UK)—shapes the motivation of donors. That we are culturally conditioned to act contextually in ways that may be altruistic, or otherwise, should inform us of the need for more comparative studies of giving across religious traditions and cultural spaces. We have much to learn from each other; and, I argue, from the Chöd Tradition. A change in social practices may be instituted such that what today is called altruism—helping a stranger in need without asking "what will happen to *me* if I stop to help"—becomes an act of ethical and moral responsibility asking "what will happen to *them* if I do *not* stop to help."[2]

## Continuity and Preservation

When Ganden Chöd lamas ask disciples to "help preserve the Chöd Tradition" it is important to reflect upon what preservation means. Preservation refers to the continuity of lineage. On one level, this means preserving the heart-to-heart transmission from teacher to student and inculcating a transformation in the heart-mind (Skt. *citta*) of the disciple. On another level, continuity of lineage refers to the musical tradition. There may be no better indicator of whether or not there is successful continuity of lineage, whether preservation is taking place effectively through both musical and spiritual transmission—transmission of *both* musical practice *and* meditation instructions—than by looking into (a) the context of transmission and (b) the pedagogical tools employed. More precisely, it is important to look *historically* at (a) the context of Chöd transmission: both in *previous centuries* and in the *present period* of transmission. As well, it is vital to look at (b) the pedagogical tools used in each period.

Historically, in the Ganden tradition, Chöd was transmitted secretly from one spiritual master to one spiritual disciple. In that one-to-one context, the Chöd transmission involved using the pedagogical tool of the *human ear*. It was necessary for the student to memorize quickly all the melodies, texts, and meditation instructions. For centuries, even the liturgical poetry was not written down; it, too, was memorized. The secrecy involved in this process of transmission partially led to the rarity of passing on the lineage and the current scarcity of practitioners in the Ganden Chöd Tradition.

In contrast, the present context of transmission involves challenges which necessarily invite solutions. Over more than fifty years, during what I have referred to as "the transcultural translation of Tibetan Buddhism into Western Buddhist communities" (Cupchik 2009), Chöd lamas have been advocating the use of new pedagogical tools to assist in the goal of transmission. They have sought ways to help their non-Tibetan speaking students who have not received training in how to use the tool of the *ear*. Most students, including myself, lack the ability to memorize a melody or meditation instructions on first or second hearing. (This is the opposite of what was the expected protocol in the Tibetan context when Ven. Pencho Rabgey was a Chöd disciple during the 1940s and 1950s in Kham, Tibet, and then in Assam, India, during the 1960s, only one-and-a-half generations ago.) Culturally, Chöd disciples in the current generation have been raised to be highly reliant on recording technology rather than to be expected to memorize a melody during an initial iteration. Although, as several Chöd pedagogues maintain, eventually memorization of the Chöd sādhana is essential before going to the site of practice. Thus, pedagogical tools now include recorded audio and video materials as aids for Chöd study and training. In addition to allowing recorded materials, I was asked to produce written music notation of the Chöd melodies on Western music staff paper. Together, these digital and paper notation aids are considered to be helpful for the transmission of the musical aspects of the tradition, which necessarily include transmission of the spiritual aspects of the tradition, since embedded in the melodies are said to be the blessings of the Chöd lineage lamas who are to be regarded as inseparable from the buddhas.

In this context, I developed what I call the "Teng word-for-word translation"[3] and "Teng word-for-word translation with musical score" to facilitate the Chöd transmission at the nexus of cross-cultural transmission between Chöd lamas and their Western disciples. The idea was to facilitate transmission despite the language gap for non-Tibetan speaking/reading disciples of Tibetan Chöd lamas. I developed this method organically for others after using the same method in my own study and memorization of the melody and text of the Ganden Ear-Whispered lineage Chöd sādhana, *Dedicating the Illusory Body*, in 1997.

The idea came from an honest reflexive critique of my own training and transmission process with Ven. Pencho Rabgey. By singing a line of Tibetan poetry in English phonetics written on the left side of the page, and then glancing at a full sentence translation on the right side of the page to know the *general meaning* (which has been the standard protocol of Tibetan-English sādhanas for decades), I had to admit to myself that I *did not know* what I was singing/chanting *as I was* singing/chanting. To put it another way, as a beginner Tibetan language learner I did not know what the meaning was of the phoneticized Tibetan word I was singing while singing it. Therefore, I developed the method of "word-for-word translation" and transcription so that I would know exactly what I needed to visualize/meditate upon while singing during each moment of practice. To gain a full transmission, I realized, visualizations should line up precisely with my experience of singing: my "outer" performance should line up with my "inner" performance. I reasoned that, if possible, there should be minimal obstruction to experiencing an integrated meditation practice. Just as with any secular or sacred song in my mother tongue (English), I understand the meaning of the word in the same moment that I am singing the word: so should it be with this sacred song-poetry of Chöd. I wished to sing in Tibetan language *and* understand the meaning. Thus, my study of Tibetan language was partly inspired by this translation effort.

Whether the features of the original Tibetan poetry such as assonance, rhyme, alliteration, vowel and consonant vibration, cue changes in the spiritual practitioner's physiology is presently unknown. However, one medical doctor with whom I have practiced Chöd suggests that the words themselves would have certain vibrations, and the arrangement of consonants and vowels would retain—due to their vibration—the blessings encoded in the (re-)performance or reproducing of the melody and words *as closely as possible to the way one's Chöd lama has done.* As well, a yoga practitioner who has been a Chöd practitioner for two decades, and with whom I have practiced, insists that the proper singing of Chöd melodies involves the technique of *prāṇāyāma* (yogic breathing), since each outgoing breath can fully support one line of sung text. These two important areas concerning vibration and breathing on the subtle and gross physical levels may be accurate, although I have not found written textual evidence in Tibetan sources to support these claims.

To summarize, if the poetry and melody have been designed and set together to assist the meditator in facilitating meditation into each subritual of the sādhana, then the question arises whether it might be beneficial for the Chödpa to know what to visualize at each moment of the melody, that is, *while singing* each word. This contrasts with the notion held by some that it might be sufficient, for the purpose of one's meditation practice, to know *generally* what the subject of the verse is about. For my own practice, I found it necessary to understand *specifically* each word just as I find Shakespeare's *words* effective rather than knowing *generally* about the subject matter.[4]

I have formalized this graphic aid/method and presented it to fellow Chöd disciples at Dharma centers in the West. They find it to be helpful and immediately understand the logic of this multilayered representation of the written and oral texts. The positive result of developing this cross-language music-text notation is that it assists the pedagogical process for Chöd initiates both for training in, and in the performing of, a Chöd sādhana as a meditation practice.

The basic template of the "Teng word-for-word" Tibetan phonetic and English translation in six lines may be rendered as follows:

| | **Layered Music and Text** | **Type of Script** |
|---|---|---|
| 1 | Melody transcribed in music score | Music notation<br>(Western staff, Tibetan *Yang yig*) |
| 2 | **Tibetan sādhana liturgy** | **Tibetan language script** (original) |
| 3 | Tibetan in transliteration | Wylie Transliteration |
| 4 | Phonetic Romanization | English language script |
| 5 | English translation<br>(word-for-word) | English, aligned vertically<br>below phonetic |
| 6 | Phrase, in English grammar | English, in grammatical order |

Figure 10.1. See Figures 1.5, 1.6, and 1.7 on pages 59–60 for examples of Teng in use.

As an example of Teng, while beginner Chöd adepts sing the Tibetan sādhana liturgy, usually by reading the phonetic Romanization (on line 4), they can peripherally see the meaning of each word underneath (on line 5) in "word-for-word" translation.

| | **Music & Text Layer** | **Type of Script** | | | |
|---|---|---|---|---|---|
| 1 | Music score | Music notation, illustrating sung liturgical melody | | | |
| 2 | Tibetan sādhana liturgy | །བླ་མ་ | ཡུམ་ཆེན་ | ལབ་ཀྱི་ | སྒྲོན་མ་ལ། |
| 3 | Transliteration in Wylie | ***bLa ma*** | ***yum chen*** | ***lab kyi*** | ***sgron ma la*** |
| 4 | Phonetic Romanization | La ma | Yum chen | Lab chi | drön ma la |
| 5 | English Translation (word-for-word) | Teacher | Great Mother | Lab chi | drön ma la |
| 6 | English phrase in grammatical order | Lama | Great Mother | [Machik] | Lab drön |

Figure 10.2

As well, lines four through six (4–6) can serve as the middling-length abbreviated version of this transcription method for the Chöd disciple, as shown:

| | | | | | | |
|---|---|---|---|---|---|---|
| 4 | Phonetic Romanization (Chöd sādhana) | ***rang gi*** | ***chi wor*** | ***pad ma*** | ***nyi kyi*** | ***teng*** |
| 5 | English Translation (word-for-word) | My | crown | lotus | sun disc | on |
| 6 | English phrase, in grammatical order | On my crown, [a] lotus [and] sun disc. | | | | |

Figure 10.3

Each of these versions of this word-for-word transcription method has its limited usefulness. For example, the first six-line version is so 'descriptively thick' with information as to require a large portion of room on the page, which necessitates the frequent flipping of pages, or a relatively small font.

These textual aids serve as the materialization of a transcription method and pedagogical technique that grew organically out of my experience in receiving the Chöd transmission. This pedagogical method is used for a specific and prevalent context of Chöd transmission. (But it could be used more widely in any cross-cultural spiritual transmission of musical-religious liturgies, or translation context.) Using the practitioner's peripheral vision to cue their understanding of *what* is being meditated upon *while* it is being sung (what to visualize while singing) could engender/produce the cognitive richness of the experience had by the original composers of the Chöd meditative poetry, and meant to be experienced by their lineage disciples.

With the customary focus on the efficacy of tantric meditation methods in the traditional Gelugpa discourse, it seems useful to mention that the lineage disciples to whom I have taught Chöd rituals using this transcription method have found it assists them in deepening their meditations. Comments from two Chöd practitioners may indicate their enthusiastic verbal responses:

> "For the first time, I know the meaning while I'm singing."

> "This is amazing. It works, and I felt the meditation much more deeply. Please make more of these."

This is but one small innovation at the language crossroads in the current transcultural translation of Tibetan Buddhism into Western Buddhist communities. It is clear that its usefulness could extend to other cross-cultural language and performance contexts. While singing a sacred liturgical text in an original language, knowing the text's meaning could provide a vital link for practitioners engaging in a potentially transformative practice experience.

# A Note on Chöd Research

The study of Chöd ritual solo or group performance benefits from studying under exponents who have a deep knowledge and understanding of the performance protocols of the monastic ritual ensemble, and the significance of the musical leadership of the *umdzé*. Ethnomusicologists approaching the study of Chöd as disciples should understand that *not all* music material and meditation instruction that needs to be transmitted has to come from the Chöd lama who is head of the lineage. Often high lamas are extremely busy and do not have time to impart all the instructions. Therefore, it may be sufficient to study with a sincere, experienced practitioner who has been recognized for expertise in the musical and meditation aspects and is qualified by possessing all the initiations. However, the teacher should have received permission to teach from the high lama who is the head of the lineage (as was the case with my teacher, Ven. Pencho Rabgey). Ideally, the Chöd teacher should have training in the tantric ritual arts in spiritual and musical aspects, and a level of realization and experience into the practice such that they can explain the relevance of the practice to daily life. The information here is drawn from instructions given primarily by high Chöd lamas in the Ganden Chöd Tradition as well as sincere and experienced elder practitioners. I express my heartfelt gratitude to them in the introduction, and here once again, for taking the time to share with me their time and insights.

# Notes

## Tibetan and Sanskrit Terminology

1. Turrell V. Wylie, "A Standard System of Tibetan Transcription," *Harvard Journal of Asiatic Studies* 22 (1959): 261–267.

## Introduction

1. Śāntideva, chapter 5, "Guarding Alertness," verses 9, 10, in *A Guide to the Bodhisattva's Way of Life*, trans. Stephan Batchelor (Dharamsala: Library of Tibetan Works and Archives, 1979), 40.

2. Śāntideva, chapter 7, "Enthusiasm," verse 25, *A Guide to the Bodhisattva's Way of Life*, 90.

3. "Ritual mapping" is a term and notion coined by Ronald Grimes, and has a number of manifestations. I explore this concept in terms of ritual design in Vajrayāna Buddhist music ritual, examining sacred liturgical ritual performance in a musical-meditation tradition. For his discussion on "mapping" in the field of ritual studies, see Ronald Grimes, *Beginnings in Ritual Studies* (Waterloo: Wilfred Laurier University, 2007 [3rd ed.]), 24–26.

4. Tantra (Tib. *rgyud*) literally means "thread" or "continuity." See Lama Thubten Yeshe, *The Tantric Path to Purification* (Boston: Wisdom Publications, 1995), 303. Similarly, Willis translates the term tantra as, "Literally, 'continuity,' the term is used to refer both to the texts that elaborate the views and practices of Vajrayāna Buddhism and to those practices themselves." See Janice D. Willis, *Enlightened Beings: Life Stories from the Ganden Oral Tradition* (Boston: Wisdom Publications, 1995), 241. As well, Geshé Thupten Jinpa explains that, "[T]he Tantric Vehicle, or Vajrayāna, which is considered by the Tibetan tradition to be the highest vehicle, is included within the Universal [or Mahāyāna] Vehicle." Tenzin Gyatso, *The World of Tibetan Buddhism: An Overview of Its Philosophy and Practice*, trans., ed., and ann., Geshé Thupten Jinpa (Boston: Wisdom Publications, 1995), 11.

5. See Daniel Cozort, *Highest Yoga Tantra: An Introduction to the Esoteric Buddhism of Tibet* (Ithaca, NY: Snow Lion Publications, 1986).

6. In recent decades, a significant policy redressing the value of monasteries and nunneries has been instituted. The Beijing government and several local officials have allowed many monastic institutions across the Tibetan Plateau to be rebuilt atop the ruins where former monastery and nunnery buildings stood. Expansion has been restricted, while replacement has been permitted.

7. Further explanation of this special relationship for fostering the transmission and inheritance of a musical/spiritual tradition may be studied in Dan Neuman, *The Life of Music in North India: The Organization of an Artistic Tradition* (Chicago: University of Chicago Press, 1990), 43–58.

8. The suffix "-pa" in Tibetan language denotes "one who does." A Chödpa is a practitioner of Chöd.

9. In Tibetan language, the three poisons (*dug gsum*) are rendered as "desirous-attachment" (*'dod chags*), "hatred-anger" (*zhe sdang*), and "ignorance" (*gti mug*). Here, ignorance is usually rendered more fully as "self-grasping ignorance" which is literally, (*bdag 'dzin ma rig pa*). Here, "ignorance" denotes one's lack of seeing the "emptiness" of all phenomena as understood to mean the lack of inherent existence despite seeming discrete appearances. According to the Madhyamaka-Prāsaṅgika view, "emptiness" is to be understood as "dependent origination", and the "self-grasping" mind—grasping mistakenly to the seemingly intrinsic self-existence—is said to result from this lack of realization into "mutual interdependence."

10. Kyabje Zong Rinpoché (1905–1984) See Zong Rinpoché, *Chöd in the Ganden Tradition: The Oral Instructions of Kyabje Zong Rinpoché,* ed., David Molk (Ithaca, NY: Snow Lion Publications, 2006), 82–85.

11. The Western Buddhist studies literature on Chöd conducted from the 1920s through the 1970s often discussed the ritual practice in terms of what were called its "mystical" aspects, with an overemphasis on the imagery of sacrifice and the macabre feast of the body. This has led to many misinterpretations about the practice. It should be made clear that Chöd meditation practice uses the strong imagery of transferring the consciousness out of the body and distributing the mentally transformed parts to beings in order to pay down karmic debt, and thereby overcome the four "demons" (Skt. *māras*, Tib. *bdud*). But it is not a sacrifice in the normative sense, since it takes place on the imaginary level. Not a single being is harmed during the ritual. Moreover, the term "demon" refers to attitudinal aspects of the mind (e.g., "self-grasping" and pride) rather than external monsters. For commentary on the four *māras*, see Kyabje Zong Rinpoché, *Chöd in the Ganden Tradition*, 133–138.

12. Sarah Harding, trans., *Machik's Complete Explanation: Clarifying the Meaning of Chöd: A Complete Explanation of Casting Out the Body as Food* (Ithaca, NY: Snow Lion Publications, 2003); Jérôme Edou, *Machig Labdrön and the Foundations of Chöd* (Ithaca, NY: Snow Lion Publications, 1996); Carol Savvas, "A Study of the Profound Path of gCod: The Mahāyāna Buddhist Meditation Tradition of Tibet's Great Woman Saint Machig Labdrön." PhD dissertation (Madison:

University of Wisconsin–Madison, 1990); Janet Gyatso, "The Development of the Gcod Tradition," in *Soundings in Tibetan Civilization*, eds., Barbara Nimri Aziz and Matthew Kapstein (New Delhi: Manohar Publications, 1985), 320–341; Michelle Janet Sorensen, "Making the Old New Again and Again: Legitimation and Innovation in the Tibetan Buddhist Chöd Tradition." PhD diss. (Columbia University, 2013).

13. José Cabezón, working toward recognizing the study of Tibetan tantric ritual as a substantive body of scholarship in Buddhist studies, convened an international conference, "Theory and Practice of Tibetan Ritual," at the University of California at Santa Barbara, May 10–12, 2007. The book that is a collection of the expanded papers delivered on that occasion is titled, *Tibetan Ritual* and is available through Oxford University Press.

14. Robert Orsi's discussion of "the gender of religious otherness" explains a common trope in religious studies scholarship in which "ritual worship" is gendered female and marginal, and "religious belief" is gendered male and given higher value. See Orsi, "The Gender of Religious Otherness," Conference keynote essay, in *ISAE Bulletin* 3 (Winter 1999), www.wheaton.edu/isae/Women/Orsiessay99.html [accessed March 2009]. In a similar vein, in early Tibetological scholarship, Orientalist readings of religious rituals performed by indigenous exponents of Himalayan cultures, and contemplatives across the Tibetan Plateau, resulted in framing Buddhist art and practice in an exotic light, whereas religious rituals in the Western European Church are discussed in a more normalizing tone.

15. Guru-deity yoga involves the tantric practice of visualizing oneself as a buddha deity. It is a method of "bringing the goal into the path."

16. The practitioner recognizes that the buddha deity embodies the perfection of body, speech, and mind. Every sentient being has "buddha-nature," (Skt. *tathāgatagarbha*, Tib. *de bzhin gshegs pa'i snying po*) which is the seed of potentially reaching the ultimate goal of buddhahood. Since the state of buddhahood is a product of karmic causes and conditions, the beginner practitioner is taught that through practice they can attain this state.

17. Some of the language used by Nebesky-Wojkowitz in his major work *Oracles and Demons of Tibet* is revealing of presuppositions about those occupying the ecclesiastical office of religion and the religious practice of the majority of Tibetans. There is also the case of the writings of the Jesuit missionary to Tibet, Ippolito Desideri, who attempted to convert to Catholicism the Tibetan monks lacking conviction in a theistic source, with whom he debated emptiness at Sera Monastic University in Lhasa. See René de Nebesky-Wojkowitz, *Oracles and Demons of Tibet: The Cult and Iconography of the Tibetan Protective Deities* (Graz, Austria: Akademische Druck-u. Verlagsanstalt, 1975). See also Ippolito Desideri, *An Account of Tibet: The Travels of Ippolito Desideri of Pistoia, 1712–1727*, Filippo de Filippi, ed. (Taipei Ch'eng Wen, 1971).

18. UL, personal communication, July 1, 1998.

19. Ter Ellingson, *The Mandala of Sound: Concepts and Sound Structures in Tibetan Ritual Music*. PhD diss. (Madison: University of Wisconsin–Madison, 1979).

20. A compelling reflexive account of what is involved in this transmission process has been penned by Prof. Donald Lopez whose diachronic analysis of the nature of scholarship in Tibetan Buddhist studies with refugee lamas during the 1970s and 1980s offers much material for consideration. Lopez's critical ethnography should be read and understood in context with the then contemporary conversation insofar as the time of his article concerns the history of the Tibetan Studies discipline amidst the reflexive turn in American cultural anthropology. See Donald S. Lopez, Jr., "Foreigner at the Lama's Feet," in *Curators of the Buddha: The Study of Buddhism Under Colonialism*, ed., Donald S. Lopez, Jr. (Chicago: University of Chicago Press, 1995), 251–296.

21. Ellingson, *The Mandala of Sound,* 764–765. The "mandala of sound" refers to sound structures and symbolism employed in the context of Tibetan ritual performances of Vajrayāna practices that assist in procuring complete transformation of oneself into a buddha deity.

22. Ivan Vandoor, *Bouddhisme Tibetain* (Paris: Buchet/Chastel, 1976); Walter Kaufmann, *Tibetan Buddhist Chant* (Bloomington: Indiana University Press, 1975).

23. Harris M. Berger, *Metal, Rock, and Jazz: Perception and the Phenomenology of Musical Experience* (Hanover, NH: Wesleyan University Press, 1999), 12.

24. Buddhist studies scholars have traditionally worked with textual materials, seeking out living exponents who can elucidate the essential meaning of a text. In such study contexts, it often seems the tantric sādhana has been treated as a written text more so than as a template for ritual practice. The philological research paradigm is extremely valuable for close readings of the meaning, but performance aspects are frequently considered peripheral.

25. James Spradley's ethnographic manual discussed the importance of listening to consultants' recommendations. He was instructed by local residents to study "what goes on in that jail" and this became the subject of his dissertation research project. Spradley writes, "one way to synchronize the needs of people and the goals of ethnography is to consult with informants to determine urgent research topics. Instead of beginning with theoretical problems, the ethnographer can begin with informant-expressed needs, then develop a research agenda." James Spradley, *The Ethnographic Interview* (New York: Holt, Rinehart and Winston, 1979), 14–15.

26. There are practical aspects to maintaining a ritual tradition in an exile context with a massively reduced indigenous population, and a growing population of Western initiates with an appetite for tantric teachings. This has meant a desire for cooperation between Tibetan scholars and non-Tibetan scholars who mutually seek to record, study, understand, and transmit rituals as they were meant to be practiced in the indigenous context.

27. I received the Chöd initiation "Opening the Door to the Sky" (Tib. *Nam mkha' sgo 'byed*) from the current head of the Ganden Chöd Tradition, His Eminence Khalkha Jetsun Dampa Rinpoché (Khal kha rje btsun dam pa rin po che), in December 1995, and thereafter received further teachings when he visited Toronto in 1998 and 1999 and when I visited India in 2006.

28. Pala is the name that his close friends, family, and students use to address him. Literally, it means "father" and is a title of respect although it also functions for him as an honorific nickname. I address Ven. Pencho Rabgey as "Pala" in some dialogue sessions when this is appropriate in the discursive context.

29. I thank experts in Tibetan studies and Buddhist studies—José I. Cabezón, David Germano, Marc des Jardins, Samten Karmay, Robert Meyer, Francoise Pommaret, and Vesna Wallace (among others at the Conference on Tibetan Tantric Ritual Studies, University of California at Santa Barbara, May 10–12, 2007)—for suggesting the necessity of providing the outline of the ethnomusicological approach for scholars coming to Chöd ritual studies from a traditionally philological perspective. An ethnomusicological perspective may also be useful for those thinking through the lens of ritual studies or performance studies with its emphasis on dramaturgical analysis. These fields have intersected with interpretive and symbolic anthropology, which have, in turn, influenced ethnomusicology; so, there are several observers at this intersection exploring the nexus of concerns about ritual performance.

30. See Kay Kaufman Shelemay in Gregory Barz and Timothy Cooley, *Shadows in the Field*, 191, 189–204.

31. Six different pedagogical contexts for Chöd transmission in which I participated included:

(1) Teacher-student one on one lessons on the music, performance and meaning lasting up to eight hours (supplemented with six days of 4- to 6-hour daily practice sessions);

(2) Present during the transmission from my main teacher to two young less-experienced monks;

(3) Present during the transmission of Chöd between my teacher and a forty-year-old experienced itinerant monk;

(4) Teacher-class—participated as one of the students and assistant as my teacher led a group of ten non-Tibetan Dharma students in a group at a Dharma center;

(5) Teacher-student one-on-one lessons in the musical practice of a sādhana with a monk junior to me in age (in terms of lineage he was a "first cousin four times removed"), receiving instruction in the meaning through commentary given prior, during and after an initiation/empowerment; and,

(6) Music Director or *umdzé* (Tib. *dbu mdzad*). In 2000, I had the privilege to begin training a group of Western students in Chöd performance practices in the "Chöd Club" at a Buddhist temple in Toronto.

The preceding list is arguably not exhaustive of the possibilities for pedagogy and transmission. However, it may give insight into the kinds of activities Chöd pegagogy can involve.

32. Bell, *Ritual: Perspectives and Dimensions*, 74.

33. Ibid., 74.

34. See Mihaly Csikszentmihalyi, *Optimal Experience: Psychological Studies of Flow in Consciousness* (New York: Cambridge University Press, 1988). The author provides scientific and empirical basis for the state of "flow" that is probably similar

in the resultant state to the notion of "groove" developed by Steve Feld. See Steven Feld, "Aesthetics as Iconicity of Style, or 'Lift-up-over Sounding': Getting into the *Kaluli* Groove," *Yearbook for Traditional Music* 20 (1988): 74–133. See also Feld's subsequent collaborative work, Charles Keil and Steven Feld, *Music Grooves: Essays and Dialogues* (Chicago: University of Chicago Press), 1994. A second edition was published by Fenestra in 2005.

35. Bell, *Ritual: Perspectives and Dimensions*, 75.

36. Ibid., 74.

37. Ibid., 74–75.

38. Ibid., 75.

39. The reflexive critique that was launched during the 1980s explored not only issues related to the program of ethnological and ethnographic studies but also examined European originated philological studies. Sheldon Pollock explores the focus on the study of Sanskrit in Germany. See Sheldon Pollock, "Deep Orientalism: Notes on Sanskrit and Power Beyond the Raj," in *Orientalism and the Postcolonial Predicament: Perspectives on South Asia*, eds., Carol Brekenridge and Peter van der Veer (Philadelphia: University of Pennsylvania Press, 1988), 76–133.

40. Gregory F. Barz and Timothy J. Cooley, eds., *Shadows in the Field: New Perspectives for Fieldwork in Ethnomusicology* (New York: Oxford University Press, 1997). A second edition was published in 2008.

41. See Barz and Cooley, *Shadows in the Field*, 3–4.

42. Victor Turner, *From Ritual to Theatre: The Human Seriousness of Play* (New York: Performing Arts Journal Publications, 1982), 89–101. Referenced in Catherine Bell, *Ritual: Perspectives and Dimensions* (New York: Oxford University Press, 1997), 75. Bell adds that Ronald Grimes's work on "ritology" asks the ritual performer to reflexively assess the efficacy of the ritual.

43. "Emic" and "etic" ultimately have to do with being inside a tradition while still being objective. Being able to claim experiential knowledge, to say "I was there" and to know the place and situation through "my own eyes" is a powerful literary tool. In writing ethnographic accounts of a place and people, situation, and a ritual musical performance, there is the important question of authority and knowledge to say something of significance about an "other" person or culture. And these "emic" and "etic" perspectives are conflated together when an author can tell you that he or she personally experienced or witnessed events. This powerful trope of literary authority came under unprecedented scrutiny in the postcolonial period when the so-called "native" came to the "West" and the Subaltern school launched its critique. Cultural anthropologists and ethnomusicologists alike had to provide evidence of how they came to experience what they purported to see and hear, and why they framed their experiences of the "Other," who had become a neighbor and colleague, in a particular light. Although more nuanced readings have ensued, due to implications associated with claims to power and privilege, there is always tension that needs to be calibrated between emic and etic perspectives in each ethnographic text.

44. Mantle Hood, "The Challenge of Bi-musicality," *Ethnomusicology* 4 (1960): 55–59. See also Mantle Hood, *The Ethnomusicologist* (New York: McGraw-Hill, 1971).

45. There are limitations on the possibility of a true "insider's" perspective. From a postmodernist perspective, there is an absence of an authentic original. This is an imagined ideal separated from the reality of the contingencies of tradition, individual ability, access, and human endeavor.

46. While having looked at the historical development of the Chöd Tradition (Gyatso 1985), autobiographical details and oral instructions of its founder (Harding 2003; Edou 1996), and made translations of sādhana ritual texts into English (Savvas 1990), these studies had not explored the musical performance aspects, or the role of music as potentially contributing to the efficacy of the ritual.

47. These melodies have been passed down carefully from practitioner to disciple for a thousand years. The liturgical poetry describes the precise meditations and visualizations the practitioner is to concentrate on. As the practitioner is singing the poetry, he or she meditates on the visualizations.

48. Some comparative musicology studies were empirically based projects but concealed the extent to which the ethnographer was involved in the construction of meaning besides the front material of the monograph where the researcher established their authority.

49. Of course, this may be said of oral traditions in other regions as well.

50. See the American Anthropological Association ethics guide on the following site: http://www.aaanet.org/committees/ethics/ethcode.htm [accessed July 12, 2007].

51. Kofi Agawu (1997) and Stephen Knopoff (2003). In an interview I conducted with George List at his home in February 1997, he lamented the direction of ethnomusicological analysis in its turn away from the music. He said that the discipline would turn back toward the music and again incorporate musical analysis, but he could not yet see the signs of the said return on the horizon.

52. Udo Will "Et quand ils n'en disent rien? (And what if they say nothing?)" In *Cahiers de Musiques Traditionelles* 12 (Georg: Geneve, 1998), 175.

53. Sugarman characterizes "ethnoaesthetics" as follows: "focus[ing] upon verbalized accounts of music making among communities whose members explicitly recognize links between musical and non-musical domains, and for whom music serves as a conscious metaphor of specific clusters of beliefs." See Jane C. Sugarman, *Engendering Song: Singing and Subjectivity at Prespa Albanian Weddings* (Chicago: University of Chicago Press, 1992), 25.

54. Jane Sugarman, *Prespa Albanian Weddings*, 25.

55. See Agawu, "Analyzing Music under the New Musicological Regime," 297–307, and Steven Knopoff, "What is Music Analysis?" 39–50.

56. Thanks is due to Prof. Rob Bowman for his suggestion to look further into the music.

57. Each section of the liturgy guides the meditator through the stages of preparation and the actual giving away of the old body.

58. See Edward Said, *Orientalism* (New York: Pantheon Books, 1978), 6.

59. Specifically, Agawu's work inspired me, together with some colleagues, to hail the return of music to ethnomusicology.

60. Rinjing Dorjé and Ter Ellingson, "'Explanation of the Secret *Gcod Ḍa ma ru*': An Exploration of Musical Instrument Symbolism," *Asian Music* 10, no. 2 Tibet Issue (1979): 63–91.

61. Specifically, within Tibetology and Buddhist Studies, the recent move toward incorporating the ethnographic is evidenced by: (1) an increasing number of dissertations involving ethnographic work, and (2) a change in requirements in doctoral programs such that prioritization is given to learning modern colloquial spoken Tibetan language, and/or Mandarin, in addition to the classical Tibetan language. Thus, in order to conduct an ethnographic study of Tibetan tantric ritual performance, one needs to be able to read a sādhana written in classical Tibetan language and to be able to discuss it in conversation with living exponents in colloquial language. This shift was discussed at the conference, *Whither Buddhist Studies: A Workshop on Buddhist Studies Doctoral Education in North America*, held at the University of Toronto, April 6–7, 2007.

62. The term "Hearing Only Lineage" is the literal translation, but the notion of a one-to-one secret oral transmission has been somewhat exoticized in Western Tibetological and Buddhological literature such that the term "Ear Whispered Lineage" is also commonly used.

63. These terms will be explained in chapter 1.

## Chapter 1

1. "Efficacy" here is considered within Mahāyāna Buddhist epistemology and the eschatological goals of tantric ritual practices. Efficacy refers to the extent to which ritual elements (including meditation and musical performance) are regarded as productive of attaining buddhahood.

2. Frightening situations arouse the adept's habitual identification with the body as "self." The Chöd practitioner seeks to "cut off" (*gcod*) this notion of "self" in order to realize the selflessness of persons and phenomena. The purpose of such active identification and transformation through meditative ritual is explained in more detail over the next several pages.

3. Sādhana may be translated as "means of achievement" and thus can refer to a method. See Daniel Cozort, "Sādhana (*sGrub thabs*): Means of Achievement for Deity Yoga," in *Tibetan Literature: Studies in Genre*, eds. José Ignacio Cabezón and Roger Jackson (Ithaca, NY: Snow Lion Publications, 1996), 331–343.

4. From the perspective of Buddhist cognition, a person is comprised of five "psychophysical aggregates" (Skt. *skandha*, Tib. *phung po*): form, feeling, discrimination, compositional factors, and consciousness. Although there is limited

space to describe these fully, a short description of each is provided here. The form aggregate (Tib. *gzugs kyi phung po*) refers not only to one's physical body, but all material objects; the feeling aggregate (Tib. *tshor wa'i phung po*) may be experientially regarded as pleasure, displeasure, or neutral; the aggregate of discrimination (Tib. *'du shes kyi phung po*) distinguishes the particular characteristic feature of an object (shape, color, etc.); compositional factors (Tib. *'du byed kyi phung po*) includes all aspects that constitute the experience which are not included in the other four aggregates (like belief, intellect, personality, habits); and consciousness (Tib. *rnam shes kyi phung po*) includes awareness, cognition, and the six senses of vision, sounds, smells, taste, touch, and mind.

5. The Tibetan term is pronounced "*phowa*" in English.

6. The Sanskrit term ḍākinī is in common use in academic publications and will be employed throughout rather than the Tibetan and English terms. See Judith Simmer-Brown, *Ḍākinī's Warm Breath: The Feminine Principle in Tibetan Buddhism* (Boston: Shambhala Publications, Inc., 2001).

7. For further elucidation, see Alan Wallace, "Intersubjectivity in Indo-Tibetan Buddhism," *Journal of Consciousness Studies* 8. nos. 5–7 (2001): 209–30

8. Kyabje Zong Rinpoché, ed., *Chöd in the Ganden Tradition: The Oral Instructions of Kyabje Zong Rinpoché* (Ithaca, NY: Snow Lion Publications, 2006), 59.

9. A *sūtra* is a discourse given by the buddha, or by one of his main disciples, that has been written down by the disciples. A *śastra* is a commentarial text, usually written to explicate the meaning of a *sūtra*. Buddhist tantra, or Vajrayāna, refers to the Diamond Vehicle of esoteric texts and practices transmitted in a lineage to initiates.

10. Being widely recognized as the father of Mahāyāna Buddhist philosophy, Nāgārjuna was the disciple of the "Great Brahmin" Saraha who is recognized as revitalizing tantric teachings after they had gone underground for many centuries following the Buddha Śākyamuni's passing in sixth century BCE.

11. The text discusses six perfections (Skt. *pāramitās*) that are to be practiced: "generosity," "ethical discipline," "patience," "joyful effort," "meditative concentration," and "wisdom." Chöd practice emphasizes all of these, but especially generosity and wisdom. In Mongolia the practice is named "giving the body" or "lu jin" (Tib. *lus byin*) rather than "cutting" (*gcod*).

12. The Sanskrit letter "*Āḥ*" is the most condensed essence of the *Prajñāpāramitā Sūtra*. Since there is a visualization of this letter as a synesthetic source of purifying wisdom nectar at a key moment of the Chöd practice, it may be helpful to recognize its philosophical, spiritual, and textual source. The *Perfection of Wisdom* scripture (Skt. *Prajñāpāramitā Sūtra*; Tib. *Shes rab kyi pha rol tu phyin pa'i mdo*) originates in India. As well, the essence of the meaning of "wisdom" or "emptiness" explained in the *Prajñāpāramitā Sūtra* is also described in the uniquely dialogic *Heart Sūtra*, which is only three pages in length. Typically, the Chöd practitioner recites either the *Heart Sūtra* or a verse paying homage to Yum Chenmo or *Prajñāpāramitā* (also a

name for the female deity of wisdom who is the embodiment of the *Prajñāpāramitā Sūtra*) prior to singing the Chöd practice as a foundational grounding in the wisdom eye of emptiness from which the practitioner can proceed unfettered.

13. The traditional recitation of texts in a sponsor's home is a practice still done today. It is said to be meritorious to have the texts read, and more so if the reciter has comprehension into the meaning.

14. Even though the highest philosophical view maintained by the Buddhist Madhyamaka Prāsaṅgika (Tib. *dbu ma thal 'gyur pa*) School proponents "speaks of phenomena as being empty and having an empty nature, this is not to be misinterpreted as implying that phenomena do not exist at all. Rather, phenomena do not exist by themselves, in and of themselves, in their own right, or inherently. Because phenomena possess the characteristics of existing and occurring and are dependent on other factors—causes, conditions, and so forth—they are, therefore, devoid of an independent nature." "Emptiness" is understood in terms of "dependent origination." See *Bstan 'dzin rgya mtsho* (Tenzin Gyatso), *The World of Tibetan Buddhism* (Boston: Wisdom Publications, 2005), 44–45.

15. Machik Labdrön is revered for her compassionate regard toward the poor and neglected beings, which may be considered analogous to the motivation and work of her near contemporary, Saint Francis of Assisi (1181–1226).

16. See Edou, *Machik Labdrön and the Foundations of Chöd*, 104, 120, 135, 150–153. See also Sarah Harding, trans., *Machik's Complete Explanation: Clarifying the Meaning of Chöd, a Complete Explanation of Casting Out the Body as Food* (Ithaca, NY: Snow Lion Publications, 2003), 70, 86–89, 98. Harding's work is in ten chapters and was originally compiled by Machik's own disciples and sons.

17. Harding, *Machik's Complete Explanation*, 30–31.

18. Considering she had never spent time in India, her fluency in Sanskrit is understood to be one of the signs of the *siddhi* (realization) of knowledge, and proof of the omniscience achieved upon attaining enlightenment. Recalling previous lifetimes, seeing places, and foretelling events and occurrences through exacting description are said to be additional signs that she had attained omniscience.

19. Sarah Harding, *Machik's Complete Explanation*, 93–98; See also *Phung po gzan bskyur kyi rnam bshad gcod kyi don gsal byed*, in Gcod kyi chos skor (New Delhi: Tibet House, 1978), 9–410. *Phung po gzan bskyur kyi rnam bshad gcod kyi don gsal byed*, in Gcod kyi chos skor, (New Delhi: Tibet House, 1978), 9–410. This is the most important hagiography on Machik Labdrön's life and teachings. It is abbreviated throughout as *rNam bshad chen mo*.

20. Geshé Thupten Jinpa, personal communication, April 2004. Jinpa notes that the song-poems of the Chöd ritual stem from the *gur* (Tib. *mgur*) genre. The Tibetan poet-saint Milarepa (Mi la ras pa, 1052–1135) was famously recognized across Asia and Himalayan regions for his inspiring, spontaneously sung dharmic expositions on any aspect of the Buddhist path to enlightenment. See Thupten Jinpa and Jaś Elsner, *Songs of Spiritual Experience: Tibetan Buddhist Poems of Insight and*

*Awakening* (Boston: Shambala, 2000). See also Garma C. C. Chang, ed. and trans., *The Hundred Thousand Songs of Milarepa* (New York: Oriental Studies Foundation, 1962), 2 vols.

21. Herbert V. Guenther, trans. and ed., *The Royal Song of Saraha: A Study in the History of Buddhist Thought* (Berkeley, CA: Shambala, 1968), 15. [1st paperback ed., 1973.]

22. 'Gos Lo tsa ba Gzhon nu dpal,' ed. and trans. George N. Roerich, *The Blue Annals* (Calcutta: Royal Asiatic Society of Bengal, 1949–53), vol. II, 843.

23. Herbert V. Guenther, *The Royal Song of Saraha*, 15. He states that "the tradition of the *dohās* in Tibet goes back to Mar-pa (1012–97), who had studied them in India under Maitripa and who transmitted his knowledge to his favorite disciple Mi la ras pa."

24. Karma Phrin las pa, *Do-ha skor gsum-kyi ti ka sems-kyi rnam-thar ston-pai' me long* cited in Herbert Guenther, *The Royal Song of Saraha*, 16.

25. Guenther, *The Royal Song of Saraha*, 15–16.

26. See Savvas, *A Study of the Profound Path of Chöd*, 308–398. Tsongkhapa, *Zab lam gcod kyi khrid yig*, (*A Commentary on the Profound path of Chöd*), in *Chöd Tshogs. The Collected Chöd Teaching of the Gelugpa Tradition by Ma ti bha dra Kirti, Blo bzang don ldan and others* (Dharamsala: Library of Tibetan Works and Archives, 1986).

27. Over the past several years, the texts of such song-poems have been popularized through Western translations of the works of Milarepa and others. More recently, *mgur* song texts and commentaries were published by a number of scholars. See also Victoria Sujata, *Tibetan Songs of Realization: Echoes from A Seventeenth-century Scholar and Siddha in Amdo* (Leiden: Brill Academic Pub., 2005). For a study on the adamantine, or vajra, songs (Skt. *vajragīti*, Tib. *rdo rje'i glu*), consult Lara Braitstein, *Saraha's Adamantine Songs: Texts, Contexts, Translations and Traditions of the Great Seal*, PhD diss. (Montreal: McGill University, 2006). Braitstein has transformed her dissertation into a book.

28. Jinpa and Elsner, *Songs of Spiritual Experience*, 5–6.

29. The names of these Tibetan sects, or schools, are rendered in Tibetan as follows: *sNying ma, Sa skya, bKa' brgyud* and *dGe lugs*. Bön is the animistic religion that was indigenous to Tibet prior to the advent of Buddhism on the Tibetan plateau in the seventh century CE. In many cases, Bönpo Lamas have incorporated the theory and practice of Tibetan Buddhism. Today, Bönpo Chöd lineage traditions are extant in the Trans-Himalayan region and the diaspora. The period from the seventh to the ninth centuries is referred to as "The Early Dissemination of Buddhism into Tibet" (*snga dar*) and is contrasted with the subsequent period of fragmentation which was itself followed by the Tibetan Renaissance in the tenth through thirteenth centuries known as "The Later Dissemination of Buddhism into Tibet" (*phyi dar*). It was during the *snga dar* period that the *sNying ma pa* school (literally, "old ones") was established by the Indian Buddhist tantric adept Padmasambhava and scholar

Śantarakśita. The two schools *Sa skya pa* and *bKa' brgyud pa* came to prominence during *phyi dar* while the *dGe lugs pa* school (literally, the "reformers,") founded by Lama Je Tsongkhapa rose in the late fourteenth and early fifteenth centuries and came to prominence in Tibet through the centralized institution of the Dalai Lama. For an historiography on the period during which Machik's Chöd Tradition first flourished, see Ronald Davidson, *Tibetan Renaissance: Tantric Buddhism in the Rebirth of Tibetan Culture* (New York: Columbia University Press, 2005).

30. See Giuseppe Tucci, *Tibetan Painted Scrolls* (Roma: Liberiea dello Stato, 1949).

31. For more information on all the Chöd lineages, see Janet Gyatso's (1985) article-length treatment of the subject, "The Development of the Gcod Tradition" and chapter 5 on lineage transmission in Jérôme Edou, *The Foundations of Chöd*, 79–94.

32. This is because of the lamas with whom I studied most closely. That said, my Chöd lamas insisted that the core meaning of Chöd practice was the same across all schools and lineages, while each sādhana ritual, its liturgical music, and performance style may differ slightly. Pala would recall and sing melodies he cherished from among the liturgical repertoire of different schools and lineages, which he had learned decades earlier. He maintains a non-sectarian approach. Likewise, I have in recent years begun studying melodies from Kagyü and Nyingma Chöd lineages.

33. Ganden here refers to Ganden (dGa ldan) monastery, the first of the three large monastic universities to be constructed in the early fifteenth century under the direction of Lama Tsongkhapa.

34. David Molk, personal interview, April 2004. Molk has translated Chöd sādhanas for communities of practitioners in each of the four schools of Tibetan Buddhism, and has observed that the Ganden Chöd Tradition's melodies are characteristically more ornamented, with more melismatic ornaments than in those of other lineages. Kusho Kundeling maintains it is most important to attempt to perform these ornaments correctly in order to retain the blessings of the Chöd lamas and the ḍākinīs (sic.).

35. See Pawo Dorjé's short Chöd commentary, *gcod kyi khrid rje btsun 'jam dbyangs kyi gsung bzhin*, in *gCod Tshogs*, 181–190.

36. This is pronounced, "Ganden Nyen Gyü."

37. For more on Gyalwa Ensapa, see Janice D. Willis, *Enlightened Beings: Life Stories from the Ganden Oral Tradition* (Boston: Wisdom Publications, 1995), 57–72.

38. sLo dpon 'jam dpal bshes gnyen gyis mdzad pa'i *gcod khrid skal ldan 'jug ngogs chung ba, in gCod Tshogs*, 108.

39. *Ruby Garland*, 40.

40. For more information on the Ganden (Gelugpa) Chöd lineage, with a complete list of the names of all the lineage lamas from the near lineage and long lineage, see Carol Savvas 1990, 285–304.

41. Jeffrey W. Cupchik, *(Dis)embodied Ethics: The Transcultural Translation of Tibetan Buddhist Tantric Chöd Ritual* (Presented at the York Centre for Asian Research, York University, 2005).

42. Several ethnomusicologists have dealt with the issue of transmission of oral tradition and performance through new forms of technology that allow for the private and public circulation of cultural media. See: Philip Bohlman, *The Study of Folk Music in the Modern World* (Bloomington, IN: Indiana University Press, 1988) and also Mark Slobin, *Subcultural Sounds: Micromusics of the West* (Hanover, NH: Wesleyan University Press, 1993).

43. See Harding, *Machik's Complete Explanation*, 133–135.

44. Throughout, I use the term "inner" to refer to the "inner meditation practice." Implicitly, this refers to the development of the heart-mind of the practitioner as she works to generate the genuine altruistic motivation of *bodhicitta*. In some instances, the term "inner performance" refers to the meditative visualization (which is arguably the most vital component of the Chöd and any tantric practice). Doing so helps to make the distinction between this "inner meditative practice" and the simultaneous "outer musical performance" of the ritual. I clarify this point at the outset since this book primarily concerns the instances in which these two "inner" and "outer" levels appear to cohere in meaningful ways.

45. Zong Rinpoché, *Chöd in the Ganden Tradition*, 82.

46. *Nam mkha' sgo 'byed kyi dbang byed tshul* (The Initiation Manual of the Opening the Door to the Sky) by Blo bzang chos kyi rgyal mtshan, Panchen I, 1570–1662. In *The Collected Works of Blo bzang chos kyi rgyal mtshan*, vol. V, 675–681. New Delhi: Mongolian Lama Gurudeva, 1973.

47. *Yi dam* is often translated as "meditational deity," but this Tibetan word literally means, "mind protector." It is made up of two words: *yi,* which means "mind" and *dam* which means "protector." The tantric practices protect the mind from "seeing" the world in terms of ordinary appearances, and reacting habitually to them; instead regarding experiences as extraordinary in the way a buddha encounters phenomena. To do so, the practitioner regards the *yidam* as inseparable in nature from the buddha and she attempts to transform into this buddha through initiations and meditative visualization practices. This process of meditation—through which she comes to see herself as an actual enlightened being, becoming the *yidam* as it were, prior to the time when she has actually attained the state of enlightenment—is particular to tantra, and is known as "bringing the result *into* the path" or "divine approximation."

48. Vajrayoginī is a centrally important female *yidam* in Tibetan Tantric Buddhism and, as with Machik Labdrön, her sādhana is practiced at the level of Highest Secret Yoga Tantra. She retains the most prominent position in visualizations within a Chöd sādhana. See Judith Simmer-Brown, *Ḍākinī's Warm Breath: The Feminine Principle in Tibetan Buddhism* (Boston: Shambhala Publications, Inc., 2001), 146.

See also Karenina Kollmar-Paulenz, "*Khros ma nag mo*, The 'Wrathful Black One' and the Deities Summoned to the Ritual Feast in the gCod-Tradition of Tibetan Buddhism: A Preliminary Survey of the gCod Demonology," *Zentralasiatische Studien* 34, 2005, 209–230.

49. The insight in this section concerns graduated levels of achievement in meditation practice and categorical differentiations as remarked upon by Tibetan Chöd ritual pedagogues in the context of lessons and oral commentaries during training in Chöd.

50. The musical studies and lineage instructions have been imparted to the author primarily by Ven. Pencho Rabgey ("Pala") a Tibetan-Canadian elder and former monk of Sera Mey Monastic College in Tibet. He began studying Chöd at the age of fourteen under his root lama, Geshé "Gen" Trinley (dge bshes 'phrin las dar rgyas), in his village in Kham (Eastern Tibet). He later studied under Kyabje Zong Rinpoché (Zong bLo bzang brTson 'grus thub bstan rgyal mtshan, 1904–1984) for six years in India. As a youth, he was chosen to serve as the chanting master of his monastery. With unusual expertise in remembering and singing lineage melodies, and his personal experience practicing the Chöd ritual, Pala's professional assistance in this research project has been invaluable. The author has also benefited from formal and informal instruction, teachings, and consultations with Khalkha Jetsun Dampa Rinpoché (The Ninth Khal kha rje bstun dam pa, 'Jam dpal rnam grol chos kyi rgyal mtshan, 1933–2012) at Takten House in Dharamsala, and Acharya Za sep Trul sku Rin po che (The Thirteenth Zacep, Blo bzang bstan 'dzin rgyal mtshan, b. 1948) in Toronto and Vancouver, Canada.

51. An "indigenous perspective," also known as an "insider-" or "*emic*-perspective," is a methodologically based ethnographic theory and practice in ethnomusicology that largely derives from the work and experience in fieldwork research of cultural anthropologists. The normative discursive tract within Chöd pedagogy, of progressive development, in both musical practice and meditation ability, informs my interpretations.

52. One of the most common pedagogical techniques for studying ritual music performance in the Tibetan context is memorizing the text. Zong Rinpoché insists unequivocally, as do Ven. Pencho Rabgey and other Chöd lamas, that it is essential to memorize the sādhana prior to going to the site of practice.

53. As an example of the novitiate's musical studies, when first training in Chöd in 1997, I spent one month practicing between three and four hours each day to reach a level of competency with the *ḍamaru* such that the drumming action became physically entrained and it was no longer necessary to think about its motion. At the same time, I was taught how to sing a new melody each week. I made a word-for-word translation of the text, receiving commentary into each line with my Chöd lama. It took me four and a half months practicing several hours each day to be able to perform the entire sādhana known as *Dedicating the*

*Illusory Body (sGyu lus Tshogs su)*, which requires a continuous musical performance of about one hour.

54. Ven. Pencho Rabgey, personal communication, November 1997.

55. Ven. Pencho Rabgey, personal communication, June 1998.

56. We can distinguish between three levels: "beginner," the stage of acquisition of the physical skills of instrumental and vocal performance utterance as well as inner mental visualization of the rite; "intermediate," which begins from the time that the latter happens up to the time that it is no longer a mere visualization and the consciousness is intentionally expelled from the body; and "advanced," from the time that consciousness can actually be expelled up until buddhahood.

57. It may be that the Chöd ritual, as a whole, is considered to be a good practice for beginners. It is easier to find the illusory self—the object to cut—with persons than with phenomena. It is more difficult to find the "object to cut" when meditating on the emptiness of phenomena. For example, when one perceives a book, its "conventional existence," that is, the mode in which it appears, seems natural and one cannot easily perceive the way in which one grasps onto its self-existence and our own (in relation to it)—that is, until someone tries to take one's favourite book away! Thus, the Chöd method provides a direct, naked, mode of finding the way in which one misapprehends the manner in which things and beings exist. Chöd is commonly said to be a useful practice for lay Buddhists because of its stark imagery and direct approach to increasing one's ability to develop *bodhicitta* and realize emptiness.

58. See chapter 5 for a fuller explanation of the "transference of consciousness" or "*phowa*" practice.

59. A proposed explanation of the origin of this aspect of the Chöd practice being the "sky burial" has been given by Dan Martin, "On the Cultural Ecology of Sky Burial on the Himalayan Plateau," *East and West*, vol. 46, nos. 3–4 (December 1996): 353–70.

60. Lama Tsongkhapa's original text is titled, *Zab lam gcod kyi khrid yig. A Commentary on the Profound Path of Chöd by Matibhadra Kirti bLo-bzang grags-pa'i dpal.* His sādhana is in prose form, not poetic verse, and extends in Savvas's dissertation for some ninety pages (it is twenty-four folios in the Tibetan text). See Savvas 1990, 308–98.

61. Ibid., 364–375.

62. Zong Rinpoché, *Chöd in the Ganden Tradition*, 118.

63. "MLI" refers to the Mind and Life Institute, which fosters collaborative interdisciplinary research partnerships between modern science and Buddhism. Beginning in 1987, the MLI was based in Boulder, Colorado, with researchers engaged in projects around the world, and it has since moved to Massachusetts, and recently Charlottesville, Virginia. The Institute's former Chair, Adam Engle, sponsors the ongoing annual conferences between psychologists, neuroscientists, and

cognitive scientists, Buddhist studies scholars, and Buddhist contemplatives with regular participation of its cofounder, His Holiness the Dalai Lama.

64. José Ignacio Cabezón, "On the Nature of the Dialogue," in *Buddhism and Science: Breaking New Ground*, ed., B. Alan Wallace (New York: Columbia University Press. 1997), 35–68.

65. Brefczynski-Leis, A. Lutz, H. S. Schaefer, D. B. Levinson, and R. J. Davidson. *Neural Correlates of Attentional Expertise in Long-Term Meditation Practitioners.* Edward E. Smith, ed. (New York, NY: Columbia University). http://www.pnas.org/content/104/27/11483.short [Accessed: August 15, 2015].

66. Zong Rinpoché, *Chöd in the Ganden Tradition*, 59.

67. Performance practices for solitary and group ritual performance are differentiated traditionally in fascinating ways. Discussed in more detail in chapter 2, there is far more flexibility with a solo performance as regards taking time in between sections, verses, or lines in order to meditate more deeply on the meaning of the sung verse. The practitioner maintains the ongoing flow of the drum's rhythm to retain an absorbed state into the experience.

68. Yutang Lin, *Chod in Limitless-Oneness* (El Cerito, CA: California, 1996), 39.

69. In Lin's terminology, those whom I refer to as "beginners" are given the label "novices" while "advanced" practitioners are called "experienced." As well, Lin substitutes his term "Limitless-Oneness" for that which is usually termed "emptiness."

70. I have made minor changes to Lin for the purpose of placing emphasis, such that italics denote *graduated change*; bold indicates function of the ritual.

71. Lin, ibid.

72. The point of training in Chöd practice involves the practitioner in investigating, through analytical meditation, the *ultimate* (empty) nature of *conventionally* imputed labels such as names and titles. The meditation work of analyzing one's own mental attitude, here and now, toward everything and everyone one encounters and thinks about has an important objective. One's analysis is purposefully directed toward liberating oneself and others from holding uncritically onto conceptual imputations. Analyzing one's mental attitude toward outer phenomena is meant to loosen one's mental grasping onto concepts and ideologies. With every conceptual designation of the qualities of an outside object the thought of how it relates to the "self" is implicitly present. In other words, one's normally uncritical attitude about anything in the world automatically reinforces the conception of one's "self" in relation to it. Therefore, for Chöd practice it is important to develop a relaxed mental attitude rather than holding something in one's mind with an exaggerated regard for its goodness or badness and relating to it with excessive attachment or aversion. The musical performance together with the dramaturgical stages of the Chöd ritual—requesting and receiving blessings and then giving everything away to others—creates an atmosphere that pacifies one's fear of the loss of "self" in the process of changing one's selfish attitude from "self-cherishing" to being other-focused. One comes to see that phenomena lack intrinsic existence, and the dependent nature of phenomena—how

they depend on causes and conditions for their existence. Whatever appears to have intrinsic independent existence is actually dependent on causes and conditions.

73. These are formalized categories drawn from Chöd pedagogy. Ven. Pencho Rabgey and Kyabje Zong Rinpoché both use the terms "beginners" and "advanced" practitioners with reference to the ability and experience of the individuals engaging in Chöd practice. The demarcation of the "intermediate" level practitioners is an addition I have made to connect the other two levels. I thank José Cabezón for this suggestion. Other aspects of Chöd pedagogy will be looked at in more detail in chapter 8.

74. David-Neel, *Magic and Mystery in Tibet*, 1932, 165. Here, "celebrate" should be taken to mean "practice."

75. Ibid., 149–165.

76. This also provides a compelling example of the notion that the art of Chöd performance may be dispensed with at a very advanced stage of realization,

77. Gerard Béhague, "Introduction." In *Performance Practice: Ethnomusicological Perspectives.* Gerard Béhague, ed. (Westport, CT: Praeger Publishers, 1984).

78. In Tibetan, this is rendered as *sgra chos can mi rtag te byas pa'i phyir* as follows: *sgra chos can* means "sound," *mi rtag te* refers to "impermanence," *byas pa'i phyir* means "because it is a product."

79. Rinjing Dorjé and Ter Ellingson, "'Explanation of the Secret *Gcod Ḍamaru*': An Exploration of Musical Instrument Symbolism," *Asian Music*, vol. 10, no. 2 Tibet Issue (1971): 63–91.

80. Molk, *Chöd in the Ganden Tradition*, 58–59.

81. Jackson discusses the celebratory tone in the singing of *mgur*, "songs of experience" (*nyams mgur*). Joy is also a component of the experience in Chöd ritual performance. Roger R. Jackson, "'Poetry' in Tibet: *Glu*, *mgur*, *sNyan ngag* and 'Songs of Experience,'" in José Ignacio Cabezón and Roger Jackson, eds., *Tibetan Literature: Studies in Genre* (Ithaca, NY: Snow Lion Publications, 1996), 384. Further, Ellingson notes that Tibetan and Indian authors express "joy at having overcome an obstacle [or] hopes for future success." See Ellingson, *Mandala of Sound*, 67.

82. This explanation is given by Ven. Pencho Rabgey, personal communication, October 1997.

83. The special functions of the mantric utterance *phaṭ* are explored in chapter 5.

84. Recognizing that the notion of intertextuality has to do with the study across different events and materials, I am employing it here in order to denote the differentiated training and study in Chöd ritual performance and meditation.

85. Lama Zopa and Kathleen McDonald, *Cutting Off the Truly-Existent "I": Dedicating the Illusory Body* (Boston: Wisdom Publications, 1983). The original Tibetan source is here: pha bong ka pa bde chen snying po, *sGyu lus tshogs su sngo ba*, "Dedicating the Illusory Body."

86. Janice D. Willis, *Enlightened Beings,* 1995, xiv. As Willis points out, the lineage holders of the Ganden Chöd Tradition were *siddhas*, "accomplished or perfected" enlightened beings.

87. Much of the offering and giving practice sections will be described in greater detail in terms of the "distributions" in chapter 2.

88. I thank Tashi Rabgey, PhD (Harvard University, 2011), Rhodes Scholar (1992) for this suggestion.

89. Ter Ellingson, "Review Essay: Four Tibetan Recordings." *Asian Music* 23, no. 2 (1981): 139.

90. Steven Knopoff, "What is Music Analysis? Problems and Prospects for Understanding Aboriginal Songs and Performance," *Australian Aboriginal Studies* No. 1 (Spring 2003): 39.

91. Charles Seeger, "Prescriptive and Descriptive Music-Writing." *The Musical Quarterly*, vol. 44, no. 2 (April 1958): 185–195.

92. Additional instances of text-music concordance and compositional design are discussed throughout the book.

93. Only the Ganden Chöd Tradition has this particular rhythmic cycle, which involves six beats: two medium length beats, two beats played short-long, and two long beats. The specific length of each of the beats may be observed in the lower stave of the musical transcription, in conventional rhythmic notation. As can be seen, they are arranged respectively as follows: *ma dang* (medium-medium length), *lha yi* (short-long) *mkha' 'gro* (long-long). The pronunciation of this rhythmic phrase, rendered phonetically, is "*ma dang, lha yi, khan dro.*" Other Chöd lineages use a "*dram-dram*" rhythm as the primary organizing rhythmic structure, which is a simpler rhythmic cycle played by rotating the *ḍamaru* back and forth, in and out, toward oneself and away, although the tempo may vary.

94. The concept of a rhythmic phrase of syllables that accords with beats played by a percussion instrument is likely derived from the Indian music pedagogical concept of *bol* (Hindi language). *Bols* are "vocables," syllables that function mnemonically as a pedagogical tool to aid percussionists when learning the various ways in which to strike the drum and to hear, in their mind, the resultant sounds that are made by a particular method of striking. As a foundational pedagogical technique, percussionists must first learn to perform the vocables, that is, to deliver the drumming patterns orally to their teacher, before they are allowed to play the pattern on the drum. This technique is in current use in both Hindustani and Carnatic traditions, the North and South Indian classical music traditions respectively. In the context of Chöd, the syllables are often uttered in pedagogical settings rather than during the practice sessions of advanced practitioners. Since the *ḍamaru* instrument (also called the *cang 'teu* in Tibetan language) originates from India, the tradition of pedagogy was likely transferred along with it. See Neuman, *The Life of Music in North India*, 271; see also James Kippen, *The Table of Lucknow: A Cultural Analysis of a Musical Tradition* (Cambridge, UK: Cambridge University Press, 1988).

95. *Lha-yi* is the rhythmic motive on which the singers' entrances are always to begin; it is the quickest rhythmic motive in the rhythmic cycle. "Beginners" may become confused about which rhythmic motive represents the beginning of

the rhythmic cycle, "*ma dang, lha yi, mkha' 'gro.*" In fact, the first drum beats of this cycle that the practitioner plays are the "*lha-yi*" beats, and one recites the *bol* syllables in accordance with the rhythm (e.g., *ma dang, lha yi, mkha' 'gro*). When singing a melody, the singer's entrance is always on the *lha-yi* beats. Once the rhythmic cycle is entrained, it feels "natural" to make this adjustment just as it does to stress the second and fourth beats in jazz. One can easily say/think "*ma-dang*" and begin singing on *lha-yi*. It is important to clarify that the practitioner learns to differentiate the beginning of the rhythmic cycle "*ma dang, lha yi, mkha' 'gro*" with the *lha-yi* beat at which the singer's entrance to the vocal line begins. For "beginners," the rhythmic cycle is taught first, separately from the singing, and is learned by accompanying a teacher (and others, if present) while they both play the *ḍamaru* drum and sing.

96. *Ostinato* refers to a continuously repeated musical pattern. The rhythmic and melodic pattern in Maurice Ravel's *Bolero* (1928) is an example of *ostinato*.

97. I employ the terminology "tonal areas" on scale degrees (e.g., 1 and 5) that demarcate the temporary destinations of melodic phrases that function as bookends for poetic phrases. It is valuable to highlight and document the commonality and frequency of this type of melodic movement between "tonal areas" across several Chöd melodies. As ethnomusicologist Sarah Weiss said during my presentation on this research at Yale University on February 5, 2008, "you are articulating a genre." I believe that in this first attempt to do so, it may assist by using familiar terminology to workers trained in Western music theory. These designations are in common use in musicological analyses of Western music. Although I wish to avoid using symbols and concepts associated with Western music, and attempt to be vigilant in avoiding representations that are ethnocentric, the Chöd melodies apparently occupy a category of melodic movement that is very much aligned with a sense of "modulation." Curiously, it is also a musical genre that enjoys high cross-cultural appeal. Scholars and artists from various disciplines and cultural backgrounds have expressed, with some regularity, strong subjective sentiments such as, "I love the Chöd melodies." Therefore, to the extent that there is this strong cross-cultural aesthetic appeal among Tibetans and non-Tibetans globally, this musicological analysis of melody construction is intended to be a useful endeavor. The Western musicological terminology merely provides an anchor for an initial foray into describing features widely shared between melodies that seem to be characteristic of the genre.

98. Donald S. Lopez, "A Prayer to the Lama," in *Religions of Tibet in Practice* (Princeton, NJ: Princeton University Press, 1997), 376–386.

99. It has been said that all buddhas, no matter their form or iconographic dissimilarities, are understood to be of the exact same nature. Thus, the most challenging aspect for beginner practitioners is to see their own lama as a buddha. Closeness with one's teacher presents the problem here, in a manner of speaking, because this close proximity allows students opportunities to see their teachers' apparent faults. Student practitioners must work to visualize their teacher as faultless

and consider whether, in fact, their own misperceptions are at the root of perceiving their teacher's apparently "faulty" actions.

100. The transcription presented here only covers the first two lines of text (the first three phrases), but the verse is four lines in length.

101. Garma G. C. Chang, "Forward," trans. and ann., *The Hundred Thousand Songs of Milarepa*, vol. 1 (New York: University Books, 1962 [Third Printing]), ix–xiv.

102. Among the many Dharma subjects treated in the *mgur* and Chöd genres, the "direct experience of emptiness" (Skt. *śūnyatā*) is ineffable and defies description even for highly realized Indian masters, though expression through *dohā* song poetry was attempted. Janice Willis notes this regarding the expressive explanatory power and purpose of the *dohās*. "[It was] such a difficult topic of discourse even for siddhas themselves . . . [that they] most often resorted to extemporaneous songs, or *dohās*, in their attempt to point to it." See Willis, *Enlightened Beings*, 111.

103. Carol Laderman and Marina Roseman, *The Performance of Healing* (New York: Routledge, 1996).

104. Steven Friedson, (Review) *The Performance of Healing* by Carol Laderman; Marina Roseman, *Asian Music*, vol. 28, no. 2 (Spring 1997): 137.

105. Steven Freidson, *Dancing Prophets: Musical Experiences in Tumbuka Healing* (Chicago: Chicago Studies in Ethnomusicology, 1996), 118.

106. Thupten Jinpa, *Songs of Spiritual Experience*, 3–4.

107. Zasep Tulku Rinpoché, Chöd transmission, Ganden Choling Mahayana Buddhist Centre. Toronto, November, 2003.

108. Richard Schechner, *The Future of Ritual: Writings on Culture and Performance* (New York: Routledge, 1993). Schechner, a pioneer in this field, drew many of his notions about dramatic process as ritual from Victor Turner who specialized in ritual of the Ndembu in Africa. Turner coined the important notions of "liminality" and "communitas" which were essential to the growth of ritual studies in the 1990s.

109. Paul Connerton's notion of "habit memory," as performative remembrances rooted in the body, is relevant here. See Paul Connerton, *How Societies Remember* (Cambridge, UK: Cambridge University Press, 1989).

110. See Samten Karmay, *The Arrow and the Spindle: Studies in History, Myths, Rituals and Beliefs in Tibet* (Nepal, Kathmandu: Mandala Book Print, 1998), 31 and 246.

111. This notion is based upon the law of cause and effect as understood in Buddhist epistemology, often referred to in Sanskrit as *karma* and in Tibetan as *las* (pronounced "lay"). The Buddhist word *karma* is not to be confused with the same word as conceived within Hinduism. For an explanation of how mental karmic imprints function, see Tenzin Gyatso, *Essence of the Heart Sutra: The Dalai Lama's Heart of Wisdom Teachings* (Boston: Wisdom Publications, 2005), 34.

112. Happiness refers to "worldly pleasures" that sooner or later lead to the experience of suffering. In contrast, "real happiness" occurs from deeds that are

contributing causes to buddhahood. The word "joy" provides another translation synonymous with real happiness. For a more extensive articulation of the contrast between real and worldly happiness see Sermey Khensur Lobsang Tharchin, *Treasury of Shunyata* (Howell, NJ: Mahayana Sutra and Tantra Press), 312–315.

113. According to Buddhist cosmology, there are six realms in which beings take rebirth within cyclic existence, three lower and three upper realms. From the most favorable to the least, the realms are listed here: god (*lha*), demi-god (*lha ma yin*), human (*mi*), animal (*dud 'gro*), hungry ghosts (*yi dwags*), and hell (*dmyal ba*).

114. Harding, *Machik's Complete Explanation*, 271. This is Harding's English translation of Machik's spiritual autobiography (*rnam thar*) and hagiographical material written by her sons and close disciples. Jacob Dalton analyzes compassionate acts of violence intentionally guided by Mahāyānist ethics to "subjugate demons"—those beings harboring harmful intention—and considers various approaches throughout the one thousand year historical and cultural scope of rituals in Tantric Buddhism. Dalton explores sūtra discourses on compassionate violence to consider the act of killing harmful beings from the Mahāyāna perspective, recalling Asanga's *Stages of the Bodhisattva Deeds*, where (with altruistic intention) *not* killing a harmful being could be considered a sin. Dalton recalls the tale of the ship's captain who, as is described in the *Upāyakauśalya Sūtra*, sees through his clairvoyance that a thief onboard intends to kill all five hundred traders aboard. By reasoning out the potential harmful karma that would be accumulated without any intervention to foil the thief's scheme, the captain, Mahākarunā ("Great Compassion," the buddha in a previous lifetime), decides upon killing the harmdoer himself; and in doing so he saves the lives of the merchants while also preventing the thief from suffering the karma that he would have accumulated from his going through with his heinous act. It is nothing other than the depth of the captain's altruistic intentionality that saves him from what would otherwise be a heavy negative sin in committing the act of killing, and he is later reborn as the buddha. Machik's Chöd method of direct engagement indicates a way to subjugate demons through pacification within a non-violent tantric ritual, founded on Mahāyāna doctrine. She commits herself to *imaginal* "self"-destruction through corporeal transformation, pacifying harmdoers' intentions with acts of generosity—preventing their suffering from negative karma while simultaneously cutting attachment to her egoic self. Tantric Buddhist rituals designed for engaging with "evil and ignorance in Tantric Buddhism"—the terms with which Dalton frames this discourse—may be distinguished by whether the act meshes doctrinally with the overall Mahāyānist project of compassionate ethical engagement. For more on Dalton's argument on how the doctrinal pieces are in place to rationalize compassionate violence within exoteric Mahāyāna Buddhism, see Jacob Dalton, *The Taming of the Demons: Violence and Liberation in Tibetan Buddhism* (New Haven: Yale University Press, 2011).

115. Zong Rinpoché advised, "For Chöd practitioners, all of our actions are meditations. Just as soldiers in war should be inseparable from their weapons, in

a similar way, Chöd practitioners should be inseparable from method—*bodhicitta*, the mind of enlightenment—and wisdom, the understanding of emptiness. Chöd practitioners are warriors, too. They are battling self-cherishing and self-grasping. They are not fighting spirits. Toward spirits we should always cultivate love and compassion . . . If we lack wisdom at any time during the practice of Chöd, we are like soldiers who have dropped our weapons on the field of battle. From refuge practice onwards, we should always keep emptiness in mind." See Kyabje Zong Rinpoché, *Chöd in the Ganden Tradition*, 130.

116. Robert Hertz, "The Pre-Eminence of the Right Hand: A Study in Religious Polarity." In *Right and Left: Essays on Dual Symbolic Classification*, ed. and trans. Rodney Needham (Chicago: University of Chicago Press, 1973), 3–31.

117. Padampa Sangyé, source unknown. Distributed at Zuru Ling Mahāyāna Buddhist Centre, Vancouver.

118. This is the Mādhyamaka-Prāsaṅgika interpretation of emptiness which the Indian mahāsiddha Nāgārjuna explicated.

119. Zong Rinpoché, *Chöd in the Ganden Tradition*, 131.

120. Pabongka Rinpoché, *Liberation in Our Hands Part Three: The Ultimate Goals* trans., Sermey Khensur Lobsang Tharchin and Artemus B. Engle (Howell, NJ: Mahayana Sutra and Tantra Press 2001), 44n–45n (Halifax: Snow Lion Publications, 2000). The *Lamrim* instructions are divided into three scopes which differentiate the three types of practitioner according to their motivation. A practitioner of the lower scope pursues the goal of taking rebirth next life in one of the upper realms. A practitioner of the medium scope seeks the goal of liberating himself or herself from *saṃsāra*, while a practitioner of the greater scope generates *bodhicitta* and pursues the goal of reaching buddhahood in order to benefit all sentient beings.

## Chapter 2

1. Stephan Beyer, *The Cult of Tārā: Magic and Ritual in Tibet* (Berkeley: University of California Press, 1973).

2. Ferdinand Lessing, *Yung-ho-kung: An Iconography of the Lamaist Cathedral in Peking*, vol. 18 of *Reports from the Scientific Expedition to the North-western Provinces of China under the Leadership of Dr. Sven Hedin* (Stockholm, 1942). I visited this large temple complex in August 2004. At that time the custodians appeared to be Buddhist monks of the Gelugpa School from Inner Mongolia.

3. David L. Snellgrove, *Buddhist Himalaya: Travels and Studies in Quest of the Origins and Nature of Tibetan Religion* (New York: Philosophical Library, 1957).

4. René de Nebesky-Wojkowitz, *Oracles and Demons of Tibet: The Cult and Iconography of the Tibetan Protective Deities* (Graz, Austria: Akademische Druck-u. Verlagsanstalt, 1975).

5. Beyer, *Cult of Tārā*, xi.

6. Ibid., xi.

7. Lessing, *Yung-ho-kung*, 139.

8. Beyer, *Cult of Tārā*, xii.

9. See Alice Egyed, "Theory and Practice of Music in a Tibetan Buddhist Monastic Tradition" (PhD diss., University of Washington–Seattle, 2000); Mireille Helffer, "An Overview of Western Work on Ritual Music of Tibetan Buddhism (1960–1990)," in Max Peter Baumann, Artur Simon, and Ulrich Wegner, eds., *European Studies in Ethnomusicology: Historical Developments and Recent Trends: Selected Papers Presented at the Seventh European Seminar in Ethnomusicology, Berlin, October 1–16, 1992* (Wilhelmshaven: Florian Noetzel, 1992), 87–101; Mireille Helffer, *Mchod-rol. Les instruments de la musique tibétaine* (Paris: CNRS Editions/ Editions de la Maison des Sciences de l'Homme, 1994); Daniel A. Scheidegger, *Tibetan Ritual Music: A General Survey with Special Reference to the Mindroling Tradition* (Zurich: Tibetan Institute, 1988); Peter Crossley-Holland, "The State of Research in Tibetan Folk Music," in Jamyang Norbu, ed., *Zlos Gar: Performing Traditions of Tibet* (Dharamsala, India: Library of Tibetan Works and Archives, 1986), 105–124; Ter Ellingson, "The Mandala of Sound: Concepts and Sound Structures in Tibetan Ritual Music" (PhD diss., University of Wisconsin–Madison, 1979); Ricardo Canzio, "The Place of Music and Chant in Tibetan Religious Culture," in P. Kvaerne and M. Brauen, eds., *Tibetan Studies* (Zurich: Volkerkunde Museum der Universität Zürich, 1978); Walter Kaufmann, *Tibetan Buddhist Chant: Musical Notations and Interpretations of a Song Book by the Bka' brgyud pa and Sa skya pa sect* (Bloomington: Indiana University Press, 1975); Mona Schrempf, "From 'Devil Dance' to 'World Healing': Some Representations, Perceptions, and Innovations of Contemporary Tibetan Ritual Dances," in Frank J. Korom and Ernst Steinkeller, *Proceedings of the Seventh Seminar of the International Association for Tibetan Studies: Graz 1995* (Vienna: Verlag der Österreichischen Akademie der Wissenschaften), 4 (995): 91–102; Ivan Vandor, "Aesthetics and Ritual Music: Some Remarks with Reference to Tibetan Music," *The World of Music* 18/2 (1976): 29–32; Yael Bentor, *Consecration of Images and Stupas in Indo-Tibetan Tantric Buddhism* (New York: Brill, 1996). Yael Bentor's research showed that ritual specialists are often not only expert musicians (instrumentalists and vocalists), but also sand or wood mandala artists, skilled architects of stupas and butter sculptures, and ritual cakes or *torma* (Tib. *gtor ma*) offerings. For an overview of Buddhist ethnomusicology on Tibet and Mongolia, see Paul D. Greene, Keith Howard, Terry E. Miller, Phong T. Nguyen, and Hwee-San Tan. "Buddhism and the Musical Cultures of Asia: A Critical Literature Survey," *The World of Music* 44/2 (2002): 138–141.

10. There are two caveats here. Chöd ensembles are utilized when there are several people learning the tradition (in which case students meet regularly to train in the ritual practices and meditation performances as a group) and the specific ritual and/or performance context (e.g., pilgrimage) calls for group participation.

11. In the Ganden Tradition, there has been far less institutional support of Chöd since a controversy in the 1930s resulted in the banning of the practice of the ritual in the Gelugpa School's three main monastic universities. For more

details, see Edou, *The Foundations of Chöd*, 92–93. In contrast, several monasteries of the Nyingma, Kagyü and Sakya traditions use Chöd ritual performance as part of their repertoire.

12. The founder of the tradition, Machik Labdrön, became a nun and later returned her robes, yet she still attained "full awakening" (buddhahood) in her lifetime. She taught her "cutting" (*gcod*) meditation method to her five children. In turn, two sons passed on her teachings to their own disciples.

13. Recently, there has been a shift in the traditional musical roles held by nuns. Some nuns are studying Tibetan ritual music instruments and are learning the associated performance practices under the tutelage of monk specialists. For an ethnographic study see cultural anthropologist Kim Gutschow, *Being a Buddhist Nun: The Struggle for Enlightenment in the Himalayas* (Cambridge, MA: Harvard University Press, 2004). For a critical analysis of women's roles in Buddhism see Rita Gross, *Buddhism after Patriarchy: A Feminist History, Analysis and Reconstruction of Buddhism* (Albany, NY: SUNY Press, 1993). For a theoretical and philosophical work examining the nature of the enlightened feminine form and emptiness with stress on the comparative applicability of this seeming dichotomous relation to work on the essentialism-constructivism debate in the early-mid 1990s, see Anne-Carolyn Klein, *Meeting the Great Bliss Queen: Buddhism, Feminism and the Art of the Self* (Boston: Beacon Press, 1995). For an essay on the nature of the ḍākinī see Janice Willis, *Feminine Ground: Essays on the Lives of Buddhist Women* (Ithaca, NY: Snow Lion Publications, 1990). Another important work on the ḍākinī is Judith Simmer-Brown, *Ḍākinī's Warm Breath: The Feminine Principle in Tibetan Buddhism* (Boston: Shambhala Publications, Inc., 2004). For an autobiographical account of one of the first American women to become ordained as a Tibetan Buddhist nun, see Tsultrim Allione, *Women of Wisdom* (London: Routledge and Kegan Paul, 1984). Importantly, Ven. Lama Tsultrim was recognized as an emanation of Machik Labdrön in 2007 while on pilgrimage in Tibet.

14. Tantric ritual music instruments are also referred to as "ritual implements" because of their function as important symbolic referents to aspects of the practice. For an overview of these ritual implements see Robert Beer, *The Handbook of Tibetan Buddhist Symbols* (Boston: Shambhala Publications Inc., 2003), 87–112. Beer's section on "The Main Ritual and Tantric Implements" (pp. 87–112) features ten such implements of which six are vital to Chöd practice: the *vajra*, bell, *ḍamaru*, thighbone trumpet, skull-cup and curved knife.

15. Some *ḍamaru* drums are made from bone, and referred to as skull-drums (Tib. *thod rnga*).

16. Mireille Helffer, "A Typology of the Tibetan Bell," in Barbara Nimri Aziz and Matthew Kapstein, eds., *Soundings in Tibetan Civilization* (New Delhi: Manohar, 1985). See also Mireille Helffer, *Mchod-rol: Les instruments de la musique tibétaine* (Paris: CNRS Editions/Editions de la Maison des Sciences de l'Homme, 1994).

17. The thighbone trumpet should be of particular shape and material. According to the oral tradition it should ideally be the left thigh bone of a girl who

was born in the year of the Tiger, and died of natural causes at the age of fourteen. There are numerous stipulations for the correct size and shape of thighbone, often expressed in terms of the way in which the person died.

18. See Curt Sachs, *The History of Musical Instruments* (New York: W. W. Norton & Company, inc., 2006 [1940]). Among Tibetan Buddhist ritual music instruments, according to the Sachs-Hornbostel classification system, there is strong representation of ritual instruments that are blown (aerophones), struck (metallophones), and have skin and are struck (membranophones). See Sachs, *The History of Musical Instruments*, 157.

19. The small *ḍamaru* is typically played in tandem with the *dril bu*. The practitioner holds the small *ḍamaru* with the right hand and the *dril bu* with the left. See Ellingson, *Mandala of Sound*, 642–643.

20. In Tibetan religious contexts, stringed instruments play a symbolic role in "mentally-produced music" and may be placed as offerings on an altar or carried in processions, "but their physical sound-production belongs to secular music." See Ellingson, *The Mandala of Sound*, 565.

21. In a tantric ritual sādhana, all the stages of practice must be present to complete a ritual satisfactorily, and there are usually extensive, middling, and abridged versions. In the case of Chöd, some truncations of longer sections are possible, such as the long and short lineage sections in the *Chöd Tshogs* sādhana.

22. The notion of "performance practice" is highly germane to tantric ritual studies. See Gerard Béhague, "Introduction," in *Performance Practice: Ethnomusicological Perspectives*, ed., G. Béhague (Westport, CT: Greenwood Press, 1984), 3–11.

23. Group Chöd practice with fellow initiates is seen as one of the main methods for the practice of Chöd. In the Ganden Tradition, there are Chöd centers where this occurs on a regular basis. For example, Takten House in Dharamsala, India, where practitioners from Mongolia, Russia, Tibet, North America, Europe and elsewhere have visited for extended periods of training to practice together with students of His Eminence Khalkha Jetsun Dampa Rinpoché. There is also a Chöd group in Zurich Switzerland studying under Ven. Lodrö Tulku Rinpoché. There are regular Chöd sādhana practice sessions held at Buddhist temples, monasteries, and nunneries around the world including Europe, Canada, Nepal, India, and the United States.

24. According to Ven. Pencho Rabgey, the pitch of nearly each melody is to rise gradually, such that the starting pitch of a stanza after a series of sung stanzas is to be higher than the first iteration of the stanza. Although this describes the performance practice within a given subritual section (of stanzas sung to the same melody), there may also be an overall pitch rise from the beginning of a sādhana to its concluding practices. As well, the ritual performance may gradually increase in tempo imperceptibly, or in a more pronounced way. This is the case in the sādhana, *Dedicating the Illusory Body* as practiced by Ven. Pencho Rabgey. A solo practitioner or *umdzé* (if practicing with two or more people) can articulate these

aesthetic parameters, incremental pitch rise and tempo acceleration, at her or his discretion. In consideration of the context of practice for "beginners" and "advanced" Chödpas, the incremental changes may be difficult to hear for those new to the practice, and the *umdzé* may maintain the same pitch for "beginners" so as to help them become familiar with the melody. The longest subritual in the Chöd sādhana is the request for blessings from the lineage lamas, and during this subritual, the incremental rise in pitch is most noticeable.

25. Ven. Pencho Rabgey, personal communication, January 1997.

26. This important mantric syllable *phaṭ* is discussed in chapter 5.

27. Ven. Pencho Rabgey maintains that the practitioner's drum should be on "automatic pilot" such that it is entrained to the extent that one does not have to think about it and may attend fully to the text and meditational visualizations.

28. During the practice of Chöd rituals, whether the practitioner is playing the triplet rhythm "*chom den dé*," (*bcom bden de*) or the back and forth "*dram-dram*" rhythm or the "*ma dang, lha yi, khan dro*" rhythmic *ostinato*, the repeated pattern establishes a recognizable "groove" that allows for an abiding sense of underlying continuity while the main poetic materials can vary above at the level of song text and visualization.

29. Ven. Pencho Rabgey's notion of comfort with the music suggests that playing the drum should be like driving a car on an open highway, or walking, or any task that one can do without thinking of it, such that one can perform other tasks easily: for example, talking while driving and singing while walking, and so forth.

30. For information on Buxa Duar refugee camp, see John F. Avedon, *In Exile from the Land of Snows* (New York: HarperPerennial, 1997 [1979]), 72.

31. The *Guru Puja* or *Lama Chöpa* (Tib. *bla ma mchod pa*) ritual is one of the most important bi-monthly practice rituals of guru devotion and guru-deity yoga in the Ganden Tradition. It is a liturgy of offering real and visualized offerings to the guru and assembly. The First Panchen Lama, Panchen Losang Chokyi Gyaltsen (Pan can blo bzang chos kyi rgyal mtshan, 1567–1662), compiled this ritual text from fifty-one other texts. From an historical state religion perspective, the Panchen Lama stands second in religious hierarchy after the Dalai Lama.

32. The mantric utterance *phaṭ* is recited at the beginning of each subritual section. This is discussed in chapter 5. Between some subritual sections, there are transitions that involve meditative visualizations with accompanying mantric utterances, such as the visualization of the absorption of the seed-syllable *Āḥ* coming from the heart of Yum Chenmo into the practitioner's body, speech, and mind at the conclusion of the request for blessings from the lineage lamas. Also, before starting each new melody, a moment of transition allows for brief reflection to reset the practitioner's motivation, and prepare for the next section. This is conducted without verbal recitation although the drum pattern is still being played.

33. Gilbert Rouget explores the relationship between trance and music. See Gilbert Rouget, *Music and Trance: A Theory of the Relations Between Music and Possession* (Chicago: University of Chicago, 1985).

34. The Chöd meditator may wish to take twice as long, or longer, in order to meditate more effectively on each visualization.

35. Samuel notes the ritual analyst's legacy in inheriting the creation of a shamanic and clerical division of labor. He maintains that it is in large part due to interpretive anthropologists' labeling, that these categories have been artificially divided according to person and not task. Samuel finds that in the Tibetan context, ritual masters with skills in "shamanic-like" practices such as exorcism, or Chöd, often also hold clerical offices, and have meritorious status in the monastic system as erudite scholars and teachers. Informally, a Tibetan community's valuation of a lama's skills in ritual mastery in Chöd are levied less in accordance with a lama's education level (whether they achieved their Geshé degree), than in their understanding of scripture and skills in ritual performance with respect to achieving desired results. Primarily, the ability to remain calm and face a problem head-on is the telling difference in discerning Chöd practitioners. See Geoffrey Samuel, *Civilized Shamans: Buddhism in Tibetan Societies* (Washington, DC: Smithsonian Institution Press, 1993).

36. Samten Karmay queries as to the correct denotation of the term shamanic in Tibetan tantric ritual contexts. Karmay finds the term overused, and perhaps misused. "Theory and Practice of Tibetan Ritual," an *International Conference Hosted by the XIV Dalai Lama Endowment,* University of California Santa Barbara, May 10–12, 2007.

37. Additionally, Zasep Rinpoché cautions that to label Chöd "shamanic" makes it sound too worldly as it misses the vital elements the practice treats, which are the development of the Mahāyāna Buddhist fundamentals, the three principal paths: renunciation, *bodhicitta*, and the wisdom understanding of reality, "emptiness" (sic, September, 2007).

38. Lama Zopa and Kathleen McDonald, *Cutting Off the Truly-Existent "I": Dedicating the Illusory Body* (Boston: Wisdom Publications, 1983). The original Tibetan source is: pa bong ka bde chen snying po, *sGyu lus tshogs su sngo ba*, "Dedicating the Illusory Body."

39. "All materials imaginable" includes what are considered to be the best parts of the practitioner's own body (brains, semen, and marrow mentally transformed into "life-prolonging wisdom nectars" as the most precious of these); and, the remaining parts of the body are not transformed into nectar, but rather given as ordinary body parts (internal organs, blood, flesh, tissues, muscles, etc.) to beings who desire them during the red distribution. Except for the skin, which is imaginally transformed during the manifold distribution into vast materials needed and desired by others.

40. The inclusion of the body as a *kusali*-like offering is similar to the Vajrayoginī Highest Yoga Tantra practice. Some rituals in other lineages are also referred to as "Kusali Chöd."

41. *Bdag 'dzin tshar gcod tshul gyi dmar 'gyed.* "Cutting-off Self-Grasping through the Red Distribution." Blo bzang don ldan, Bka' chen, ca. early twentieth century. In *Gcod Tshogs, The Collected Gcod Teaching of the Gelugpa Tradition by Ma ti bha dra Kirti, Blo bzang don ldan and others* (Dharamsala: Library of Tibetan Works and Archives, 1986), 29–54.

42. The melody for the manifold distribution lasts only two 2-line verses and then extends into the giving Dharma section.

43. The meditation on "giving and taking" involves the practitioner in a creative visualization of taking the suffering of all beings into her own heart, and giving away her merits and virtues to those beings in return. Several commentaries have been written about this mind training (*blo sbyong*) practice. See Tharchin, Sermey Geshé Lobsang, *Achieving Bodhicitta: Instructions of Two Great Lineages Combined into a Unique System of Eleven Categories* (Howell, NJ: Mahayana Sutra and Tantra Press, 1999), 86–98.

44. In other Chöd sādhanas, Vajrayoginī (Tib. *rJe btsun rdo rje rnal 'byor ma*) is visualized as the central *yidam*.

45. Three combined beings or *sattvas* in tantric guru-deity yoga practice include the "commitment being" (Skt. *samayasattva*, Tib. *dam tshig sems dpa'*), the "wisdom being" (Skt. *jñānasattva*, Tib. *ye shes sems pa*), and the "concentration being" (Skt. *samādisattva*, Tib. *ting nge 'dzin sems pa*), and are to be seen as inseparable.

46. Dan Martin has suggested that this aspect of the Chöd practice may have its origin in the tradition of the "sky burial." See Dan Martin, "On the Cultural Ecology of Sky Burial on the Himalayan Plateau," *East and West* 46 (1996): 353–370.

47. These bodily substances are not purified as in the white offering, but visualized in their ordinary state. This is a key distinction between the white and red distributions.

48. The original stanza of four lines is provided here in Wylie transliteration:

> *sha la dga' ba'i rigs ni sha rnams zo /*
> *khrag la dga' ba'i rigs ni khrag rnams 'thungs /*
> *rus pa la dga' lha 'dres rus pa mur /*
> *nang khrol sogs la ci bder longs spyod cig*

Note the parallelism in the setting of the nine syllables per line, particularly in the first three lines of this stanza. The stanza employs verbs in colloquial rather than their honorific form, which is further characterized by the usage of the imperative form of the verb. When translated into non-Tibetan languages, the rearranged grammar might not capture the sense of the giver's raw imperative insistence to consume all that is being given. In its original presentation, it is as if the great mother, Machik Labdrön herself, is exhorting verbally all those invited into her kitchen to partake of their fill of enjoyments. In English, the grammatically adjusted rendering could be:

"[You who] enjoy meat, eat meat!
[You who] like blood, drink blood!
[You] gods and demons who enjoy bones, have your complete fill!
[And as for] the rest of the internal organs, freely consume these complete enjoyments!"

Rather than beginning with the pronoun "you," Tibetan language utilizes an implied subject which may be understood and clarified by the context surrounding a given sentence or passage. In this instance, the grammatical form of the imperative allows a practitioner to directly apprehend the sensibility. Note the setting of the poetry—focused on informing the invited guests as to what is available for consumption (the transformed materials), and urging them to consume whatever might be their preference. Specifically, the first word of the top three lines in this stanza is the noun denoting which food and drink may be consumed—"meat," "blood," and "bones" respectively—and the last word of each line is the verb in imperative colloquial form. In a familiar setting, one could imagine this briefer rendering: "You enjoy meat? Eat!; Blood? Drink(!); Bones? Chew(!); Have as much as you like. Enjoy!" Understanding the ways in which the poetic character of this stanza is shaped by the colloquial imperative grammatical form illuminates how the musical setting complements the architecture of Tibetan language. The poetic language is treated with normalizing colloquial phrases, suggesting a relaxed familiarity at a mother's kitchen table. Here, as if invited to a matriarch's feast, the setting absent of the pleasantries of Tibetan language's mannered honorifics, suggests a return home to a mother's table—a context for the hospitality accentuated in kindness by giving to others all they could want. Musically, by utilizing a return to the opening musical motifs of (A1) and (A2) here, the sensibility for the red distribution is made all the more welcoming because it sounds like a return "home." Such a return to the opening melody evokes comfort through familiarity, and is perhaps made more affectively powerful because it comes after introducing six new melodies for the same number of subritual sections. Thus, the character of the "red distribution" (B3) is suggested *musically* by the refrain to the musical themes of the opening two melodies (A1 and A2), and *poetically* by the vernacular expressing a maternal insistence directed to guests to consume as much as they would like.

49. The four seals of Dharma are given in verse form, as follows:

*'di ltar 'dus byas chos rnams mi rtag cing /*
*zag bcas kun kyang sdug bsngal rang bzhin ste /*
*chos kun bdag med rten cing 'brel 'byung nyid /*
*bsgom pas zhi ba myang 'das thob par 'gyur.*

See Pha bong kha pa bde chen snying po, *sGyu lus tshogs su sngo ba*, folio 12b. For a general explanation of the meaning of this verse, see Gyatso, *The World of Tibetan*

*Buddhism*, 31–39. For an explanation of this verse with specific respect to the Chöd practice, see Kyabje Zong Rinpoché, *Chöd in the Ganden Tradition*, 111–117.

50. The practice directions of the sādhana instruct the Chödpa to meditate silently upon the four-line stanza. Note that in terms of the poetic architecture, each line is eleven syllables in length, rather than the nine syllables that has been the established norm throughout.

> *ji skad du rgyal mchod bdun pa chen po'i gsung las /*
> *tshur bltas lus sems gang yang gnod bya ru ma grub /*
> *phar bltas gnod byed de yang thag khra yi sbrul bzhin /*
> *rten 'brel ming rkyang tsam la bden pa ru bzung pa'i /*
> *rang sems 'khrul pa'i snang bar thag gcod du gyur cig*

See Pha bong kha pa bde chen snying po, sGyu lus tshogs su sngo ba, folio 13b.

51. During this first subritual section for meditating on emptiness, when practicing Chöd in a group, the music director or "*umdzé*" (*dbu mdzad*) determines how many cycles of the *ḍamaru* rhythm "*ma dang, lha yi, khan dro*" to perform. If some people new to Chöd practice have not yet built up their arm muscles they might feel tired from holding up the *ḍamaru*, in which case the *umdzé* will shorten the time allotted for the thought meditation. On the other hand, the adept practicing alone may choose to continue playing the rhythmic cycle until having achieved a deep experience from meditating upon the verse.

52. According to Zong Rinpoché's commentary on the "three spheres of giving": "We must realize that 'giving' is merely imputed by name or label. The 'substance given' is merely imputed by name, the 'giver' is merely imputed by name, and the 'recipient' is merely imputed by name. The 'giver' is merely labeled in dependence upon their collection of aggregates." If things existed inherently, giving would be impossible. See Zong Rinpoché, 2006, 120. For further elucidation of this philosophical standpoint of the Madhyamaka-Prāsaṅgika school, see Je Tsongkhapa, *In Praise of Dependent Origination* (*rten 'brel bstod pa*). Translated from the Tibetan by Geshé Thupten Jinpa. *Institute of Tibetan Classics.* https://tibetanclassics.org/wp-content/uploads/2020/09/In-Praise-of-Dependent-Origination.pdf [Accessed June 25, 2021].

53. See Ellingson's survey of transcription issues in Helen Myers' volume. Ter Ellingson, "Transcription" in Helen Myers, ed., *Ethnomusicology: An Introduction* (New York: W. W. Norton, 1992), 110–151.

54. Eric Hobsbawn and Terrance Ranger, *The Invention of Tradition* (New York: Cambridge University Press, 1984).

55. See Jamyang Norbu, "Introduction," in *Zlosgar: Performing Traditions of Tibet. Commemorative Issue on the Occassion of the 25th Anniversary of the Founding of Tibetan Institute of Performing Arts 1959–84* (Dharamsala, H.P., India: Library of Tibetan Works & Archives, 1986).

56. In such a case, the transcription would be an intervention into traditional practices of transmission. Where a Chöd lama finds the tradition is in danger of

extinction and wants to try different strategies, transcription may aid in cultural renewal.

57. See Ellingson, *Mandala of Sound*, x.

58. Ellingson refers to this as the "tone-contour *dbyangs* style." See Ter Ellingson, "Review Essay: Four Tibetan Recordings." *Asian Music* 23, no. 2 (1981): 139.

59. As Bruno Nettl notes, "Transcription is used to solve specialized problems, and for this, many kinds of techniques, mechanical and manual, have been developed, including notation based on a culture's own notation system, or simplifications such as solmization, or various sorts of graph arrangements. The point is that a transcription or notation system may be developed to solve a particular problem in the music of a specific culture." See Bruno Nettl, *The Study of Ethnomusicology: Thirty-One Issues and Concepts* (Chicago: University of Illinois Press, 2005 [1983]), 89.

60. Catherine J. Ellis, *Program of Training in Music for South Australian Aboriginal People* (Adelaide: University of Adelaide, 1971). Catherine J. Ellis, *Aboriginal Music, Education for Living: Cross-cultural Experiences from South Australia* (St. Lucia, Queensland: University of Queensland Press, 1985).

61. Knowledge of the songs ensures survival in the desert "outback." The songs encode the directions to the watering holes. Those who know the locations of the water sources are considered owners of the land. Dr. Helen Payne, an ethnomusicologist formerly at the University of Queensland in Brisbane (now in Adelaide) for whom I worked as a research assistant transcribing aboriginal women's songs, was a student of Catherine Ellis, and explained this musical-environmental connection.

62. Each line of each verse is written in the Tibetan poetic meter of nine syllables per line. Victoria Sujata discusses this metrical form with respect to *mgur*. Her study of the *mgur* composed by the Tibetan scholar-practitioner Amdo Shar Kalden Gyatso (A mdo shar skal ldan rgya mtsho, 1606–1677) concerns the literary aspect of his repertoire. The music has been left largely unexplored. See Sujata, *Tibetan Songs of Realization*, 2003.

63. Ven. Pencho Rabgey, personal communication, February 1999.

64. Rouget notes a host of spurious claims by scholars about the sorts of rhythms that induce a trance state. He takes Danielou to task for claiming that only odd-rhythm patterns of 5 or 7 beats and the like induce trance and that square rhythms like common time (4/4) do not. See Gilbert Rouget, *Music and Trance*, xviii.

65. Ven. Pencho Rabgey, personal communication, June 2000.

66. Contemporary sites where sand and wood mandalas are constructed include Buddhist temples, Dharma centers, as well as public spaces such as libraries, community centres, and art museums.

67. Kyabje Zong Rinpoché, *Chöd in the Ganden Tradition*, 128–131.

68. Ellingson, *Mandala of Sound*, 364–365. See discussion on this point in chapter 4.

69. Chapter 8 explores the transformational aspects of the Chöd ritual practice in greater detail.

70. Agawu, "Analyzing Music," 297–307.

71. In the case of the Tibetan exile community, the issue of retaining cultural memory through song and dance performance has been important at the policy level of the exiled Tibetan leadership. The Tibetan Institute of Performing Arts (TIPA) was the first cultural institution set up by the Dalai Lama when coming into exile in 1959. It was given a particular mission and it served the refugee community as part of the project of maintaining a living memory of traditions *as they were in 1959*, when the majority of the exiled Tibetan population fled to India. The music and dance repertoire was not expanded for a number of years. This was the subject of complaints of boredom from local Tibetans in Dharamsala who also explained away their own complaints by acknowledging the importance of keeping a living record of songs and dance performances—even if it was from a time and place to which they could not personally relate. Frozen in a "1959 moment" for many years, TIPA later expanded their repertoire and enjoyed greater public approval. At the same time, TIPA maintained standard performance repertoire pieces like the Yak Dance, Black Hat Dance, and Deer Dance, retaining a living cultural memory of these comedic, historical, and spiritual set pieces. In negotiating this accommodation, they preserved valuable products of intangible cultural heritage of the Tibetan experience in the cultural memory of subsequent generations.

72. See Ter Ellingson, "On Transcription," in Helen Myers, ed. *Ethnomusicology: An Introduction* (New York: W. W. Norton, 1990), 110–151.

73. Regula Burckhardt Qureshi, "Sufi Music and the Historicity of Oral Tradition," in *Ethnomusicology and Modern Music History*, eds., Stephen Blum, Philip V. Bohlman and Daniel M. Neuman (Urbana, IL: Universityy of Illinois Press, 1991), 103–120.

74. Thus, the musical analysis of the Chöd Tradition's melodies may reveal some of the features of compositional design in the *mgur* tradition.

75. See Rosemary J. Coombe, *The Cultural Life of Intellectual Properties: Authorship, Appropriation and the Law* (Durham, NC: Duke University Press, 1998). See also Rosemary J. Coombe, "Fear, Hope and Longing for the Future of Authorship and a Revised Public Domain of Global Regimes of Intellectual Property." *HeinOnline De Paul Law Review*, 2002–2003. https://papers.ssrn.com/sol3/papers.cfm?abstract_id=2463774 [accessed January 20, 2021].

76. See Martin Clayton, Trevor Herbert, and Richard Middleton, eds., *The Cultural Study of Music: A Critical Introduction* (London: Routledge, 2003).

77. Ethnomusicologists studying sacred ritual often receive traditional lineages from, perform along with, and can become adopted into musical families as musical-spiritual disciples where they are charged with the task of maintenance, preservation, and appropriate transmission, along with attendant and understandable restrictions and permissions associated with lineage continuity.

78. See Luke Eric Lassiter, *The Power of Kiowa Song: A Collaborative Ethnography* (Tuscon, AZ: University of Arizona Press, 1998). Also see Luke Eric Lassiter, *The Chicago Guide to Collaborative Ethnography* (Chicago: Chicago University Press, 2005), 35. The collaborative ethnographic approach—with its author incorporation, and explicit mentioning of informant involvement in the construction of the ideas in the text—is an important way in which imbalance in equality may be broached. Consider also Cathy Ellis's work with the Australian Aboriginals. See Steven Knopoff, 2003, who describes Ellis's interventionist role in championing the indigenous value of the music within both the Australian legal system and musicological journal publications.

79. Thupten Jinpa finds that the meditative song-poem compositions in the *mgur* genre are not as spontaneous as many have previously thought. The *mgur* compositions derive from a studied technique and are formally constructed, with their spontaneity constrained by form. Once competent in writing in this form, the writer-composer can produce aesthetically charged melodic poems (with the appropriate *rasa*) in perfect conformity to the stylistic requirements of the genre. Jinpa notes that "There was a price to the impact of Sanskrit poetics . . . a potential loss of spontaneity . . . to a degree, mastery of form was emphasized at the cost of immediacy of content." See Jinpa and Elsner, *Songs of Spiritual Experience*, 12–13.

80. While completing my undergraduate degree in Theory and Composition at the University of Toronto, I was immersed in the musical analysis of the works in the Western canon. I was also introduced to the Hindustani classical music tradition and Sub-Saharan music traditions by Prof. James Kippen and Tibetan secular folk music by Tashi and Losang Rabgey, members of Potala Tibetan Dance Troupe, based in Ontario, who led a one-year course at the Faculty of Music in which I participated.

81. During the years I was at the University of Toronto, my fellow students in the composition program were given tremendous latitude to discover in the music what was there to be found. We were not told to contest the Shenkerian model, but to try it on as an analytical tack (it was one of the theory majors' required courses). When I took the course in Shenkerian Analysis with Edward Lauffer, I quietly questioned the goal of applying a music theory globally to all music, even to all (Western) tonal music. Indeed, Schenker's work is suggestive of a commonality of underlying patterns, and without a doubt this must be lauded. However, if the underlying structure is so similar how can music be as different as it is in terms of being emotionally moving, spiritually uplifting, melancholic, triumphantly majestic, and so forth? Here we may bring into the conversation Adorno, who, like others in the Frankfurt School feared the culture industries that would make of the masses a dull sheep herd. He feared the sameness of popular music expression, especially the reproductive capacity of recording technology and the globalizing access to media proliferation. On the one hand, it may be argued that masses can be "duped" to an extent by certain associations and articulations. There is reasonable evidence for

the truth behind Adorno's prescient concerns. Today an industry of Muzak-related research conducted by music cognition and neuroscientists is examining the relationship between music and the brain with the goal of achieving greater "inner" reach to inspire increased "outer" consumerist activity. In sum, the notion that musical craftsmanship can be (re)articulated in creative ways for emotional effect and for particular spiritual goals is directly in line with what is known today of the effect of music. To find this relationship in the Chöd musical liturgy is confirmation that Tibetan yogis and Indian mahāsiddhas had an understanding about the sort of musical design that achieves particular affective states.

82. Sociology of religion scholar, Saroj Chawla, notes that there are millions of devotees from around the world logging in to webcasts emanating from India to participate in pujas and ceremonies taking place there. A graduate student who worked with Tibetologist Donald Lopez at University of Michigan on the Ganden Chöd Tradition, placed online the sādhana featuring Khalkha Rinpoché singing the ritual and juxtaposed the music with iconographic images related with the ritual. It has since been taken offline.

83. There is local and global relevance to performing the ritual at night, *en masse*, at Bodhgaya under the Bodhi Tree where Buddha attained enlightenment and "cut" the last of his delusions. As a holy pilgrimage site for Buddhists, the association of Chöd with the site may have an impact on the re-ascension of the popularity of the ritual. See https://www.youtube.com/watch?v=xGXZ4xYMM5g, posted Jan. 18, 2019 [accessed January 25, 2021].

84. Knopoff writes, "Music analysis has played a consistently important role in studies of traditional Aboriginal songs in Australia. Some musicologists, including Catherine Ellis . . . have matched their extensive use of music analysis with critical and introspective concerns over the ethics and usefulness of musical analysis for understanding Aboriginal songs and performance practices. These mirror concerns held by scholars working with other non-Western musics . . . Despite its inherent cultural trappings and other limitations, analysis can and does provide an invaluable means for understanding Aboriginal songs and performance, and that the subjective input of the music analyst—something which is recognized in analyses of Western art music—could be more accepted as a normal part of analysis of Aboriginal (and other non-Western) musics." Knopoff, "What is Music Analysis?," 39.

## Chapter 3

1. Khalkha Rinpoché returned to Canada in 1999, and was visibly teary-eyed looking down at us from his seat on the throne while he guided a Chod practice one evening during his visit from India. He stopped playing his *ḍamaru* and held it, asking all the students in a soft voice why we had not yet learned to play the *ḍamaru* and melodies, as he had requested, since his last visit to Canada. He said this in a

heartfelt tone, lamenting, "This tradition is dying. Please try to learn everything I taught you, and will teach you now, in order to keep this lineage from going all the way down." The regular students at Gaden Choling were moved at Jetsun Dampa Rinpoché's imploring them to learn the musical aspects of the practice, and reached out to Pala the next day by phone, asking him if he could come down from his home to Toronto to teach them. Pala replied the drive would be too far a trip to make on a weekly basis. Instead, he said Jeff (me) could help guide them "through learning the musical aspects of the practice because he trained with me." He said I could guide them in the basics of the *ḍamaru* and melodies, and he would also come down periodically to give more instruction and lead the group practice. That's when I began teaching in the Chod Club, often serving as the *umdzé*, at Pala's direction, which lasted for about ten years before I moved to take up a position at the Eastman School of Music at the University in Rochester. One of Rinpoché's students, Harriet, who was there that evening, said that "seeing Rinpoché cry did it for me." She told me that was the moment when she solidified her intention, dedicating herself to learning the music of Chöd "however much time it would take," so that she could benefit from practicing the meditation unhindered. As she is no longer with us, I can report, without any hesitation, that she achieved her goal.

2. Furthermore, he insists that the practitioner must memorize the sādhana's written liturgy. Otherwise, it is argued, how will he or she be able to perform in the complete darkness of night? Memorization is not a prerequisite for training, but it is necessary for the more advanced practice of going to the "nyen sa" *gnyan sa* (frightening places, rugged sites where spirits dwell) at night. For more details on Kyabje Zong Rinpoché's instructions on the manner of practice, see David Molk, ed., *Chöd in the Ganden Tradition: The Oral Instructions of Kyabje Zong Rinpoché* (Ithaca, NY: Snow Lion Publications, 2006).

3. Ibid., 58–62. "Sky burial" (Tib. *bya gtor*) is a traditional Tibetan funerary rite by which bodies of ordinary deceased persons are disposed. It follows the ritual services and prayers that guide the consciousness through the "in-between" or "intermediate" stage (*bar do*) of death and rebirth. Instead of subterranean burial, or cremation (which is done for holy persons, lamas, or in some cases, after there has been an accident), a deceased person's body is carried to a cemetery (charnel ground) near the top of a mountain. A mortician who knows how to flay a corpse will cut the four limbs off the main body first, and strip the flesh from the bone, chop up the limbs into smaller pieces at the joints, and crush those bones into fragments with a large stone or hammer. He might arrange the remains in two piles: one of flesh, the other of bone. These smaller pieces are necessary so that animals and birds that scavenge for such carrion, like vultures, will be able to consume the body completely. In some Tibetan locales, another method, known as "water burial" is practiced, where the remaining body of the deceased person is similarly broken into smaller pieces and then put in a river, providing a meal for fish to consume. Though some cultural commentators associate this ritual with barbarism, Tibetans

consider sky burial and water burial to be ecologically sound ways to dispose of the body. With the consciousness already departed from the body, there is no harm done to anyone. For further context, see Dan Martin, "On the Cultural Ecology of Sky Burial on the Himalayan Plateau," *East and West* 46 (1997): 353–370.

4. Tone painting is a composition technique that involves using musical gestures to depict, or embody, phenomena at the imaginal level. Music may evoke an image, and an associated emotional state, such as the fear of the advent and passage of the summer thundershower in Antonio Vivaldi's *Four Seasons* (1723–25). Perhaps two of the best-known examples from the European Art Music repertoire besides Vivaldi's work are: Petrovich Mussorgsky's *Pictures at an Exhibition* (1874) and Gustav Holst's *The Planets* (1914–16). These are large scale multi-part works portraying actual phenomena in an abstract way, which conjures up concrete images in the mind of the listener. The field of musical semiotics (semiology), as discussed by David Lidov, explores how sonic referents often hold social and cultural meaning. See David Lidov, *Elements of Semiotics: Semaphores and Signs* (Toronto: Palgrave MacMillan Press, 1999).

5. In some subritual sections, such as during the "body mandala offering," a monophonic texture occurs, as there is no instrumental accompaniment.

6. It could be argued that since the *ḍamaru* is a pitched instrument, and the bell (*dril bu*) has a definite pitch producing a "flood" of harmonic overtones, therefore a *polyphonic* texture is heard. Yet, since each of the main Chöd instruments acoustically retains its own fundamental pitch, it is probably more accurate to say that when the bell, *ḍamaru*, and voice are sounding simultaneously Chöd exhibits an example of a type of drone polyphony. It may be observed, nevertheless, that the melody is dominant in the musical texture and takes precedence over all other instrumentally produced "pitches" played by the other instruments. Sometimes Chöd can be practiced without the bell or the thighbone trumpet and the texture then is solely the result of the *ḍamaru* drumbeats and the melody sung in precise rhythmic complement. It should also be noted that in dry or damp conditions, the moisture of the *ḍamaru* drum skins cause the pitch sounded by the pellets striking to be altered (raising or lowering the pitch). Very damp conditions may result in the *ḍamaru* skins losing much of their elasticity, and it may not only sound "puck-puck" (as Chöd lamas say in humorous onomatopoeic characterization), but also be less responsive, more difficult to play, and require greater effort by the muscles in the Chöd practitioner's arm, wrist, thumb, and fingers.

7. When the melody is set to a four-line stanza, there can be three or four musical phrases.

8. Paul Everett, *Vivaldi: The Four Seasons and Other Concertos, Op. 8* (New York: Cambridge University Press, 1996), 82–85. According to Everett's translation, Antonio Vivaldi mentions fear of thunderstorms is in his sonnet on the summer's rain three times. It is based on Vivaldi's own sonnet that he composed for the concerto, depicting the season's characteristically powerful storms. He elicits this emotion in the musical drama by tone painting.

9. *rgod po sha la lding bzhin gri gug gis / spyi bo nas bzung sum phrag bar du gshags.*

This instance may be found below in verse six.

10. The moment the body "falls down" (*'gyel*) is given in Tibetan as: *rang gi phung po rnying pa lings te 'gyel / dkar zhing tsho la snum pas stong gsum khyab.*

11. The verses are given here in the original Tibetan, as follows:

> *rtsa mchog a ba dhu ti' rgyun lam nas / bla ma lhag pa'i lha yi thugs kar 'phangs*
> *phaṭ! phaṭ! phaṭ! phaṭ! phaṭ!*
> *rang gi phung po rnying pa lings te 'gyel / dkar zhing tsho la snum pas stong gsum khyab*
> *phaṭ! rang sems bla ma lha yi thugs ka nas / mkha' 'gro gri gug 'dzin pa'i rnam par thon*
> *rgod po sha la lding bzhin gri gug gis / spyi bo nas bzung sum phrag bar du gshags.*

See Pa bong ka bde chen snying po, *sGyu lus tshogs su sngo ba* (*Dedicating the Illusory Body*), folio 10a.

12. When I employ terminology from theatre here (i.e., "scene" and "drama") to describe one of the meditation subrituals in the sādhana practice, I am borrowing from Victor Turner and Richard Schechner whose work at the collaborative nexus of anthropology of ritual, ritual studies, and performance studies was preceded by Turner's conceiving of ritual as a "social drama." See Richard Schechner's "Preface" in Victor Turner, *The Anthropology of Performance* (New York: PAJ Publications, 1988).

13. Chinese Buddhist art historian Eugene Wang refers to the transformative Buddhist ritual process in expressive artistic formulae as a psychodrama. See Eugene Wang, *Shaping the Lotus Sutra: Buddhist Visual Culture in Medieval China* (Seattle: University of Washington Press, 2005).

14. One Chöd teaching from the oral tradition advises the practitioner to imagine not one ḍākinī, but herself as a main central deity surrounded by a large retinue of hundreds of thousands of ḍākinīs helping to do this work. The body, if we recall, is visualized as huge, so that no being will be left hungry. Thus, a large retinue of assistants who can distribute all the parts of this mentally transformed body to beings throughout the universe may be visualized.

15. See Alice Egyed, *Theory and Practice of Music in a Tibetan Buddhist Monastic Tradition*, PhD diss. (Seattle: University of Washington, 2000).

16. It may seem "intuitive" to philologists who are not accustomed to studying the meaning in musical performance, but who share an interest in exploring how a Chöd performance tradition aligns with the meditation practice.

17. Ven. Pencho Rabgey, personal communication, February 2000. See also Jinpa and Elsner, "Introduction," in *Songs of Spiritual Experience*, 2000.

18. To the extent that the Chöd ritual has been transmitted with the possibility of change effected by only the most highly qualified lamas, lineage holders have served as gatekeepers for permissions to allow changes to the sādhana such as the incorporation of new melodies. Therefore, the written liturgy and melody assignments are kept carefully, and safeguarded by musically accomplished and spiritually advanced practitioners.

19. See Ricardo Canzio, *Sakya Pandita's "Treatise on Music" and its Relevance to Present-day Tibetan Liturgy*, PhD book (London: University of London SOAS, 1978).

20. Sakya Paṇḍita's "Treatise on Music" presents only general principles for composing melody and words together.

21. See Lama Zopa Rinpoché, *Cutting off the Truly-Existent "I,"* 1986. A colophon is a short section at the end of a publication that gives details about the publisher, text, edition and/or author, as the case may be.

22. It may be also be that Chöd melodies were composed to fit an existing text.

23. Ven. Pencho Rabgey, personal communication, December 1997.

24. Drubwang Lobsang Namgyal is understood to be a previous incarnation of Kyabje Zong Rinpoché. See Zong Rinpoché, *Chöd in the Ganden Tradition*, 38, 211. Drubwang Lobsang Namgyal authored the written commentary that served as the basis for the oral commentary given by Zong Rinpoché in 1984. The title of this commentary is: *Lamp Illuminating the Ritual Practice of the Chöd Scripture: Guide for Those Seeking Liberation* (Tib. *gcod gzhung thar 'dod ded dpon ma'i cho ga don gsal bar ston pa'i nyams len gsal ba'i sgron me*).

25. Ven. Pencho Rabgey, personal communication, April 2004.

26. Clifford Geertz, "Thick Description: Toward an Interpretive Theory of Culture," in *The Interpretation of Cultures: Selected Essays* (New York: Basic Books, 1973), 3–30.

27. Previously, no analysis had recorded *how* music works to assist in enhancing (or not) the chöd practitioner's meditations.

28. See Braitstein, *Saraha's Adamantine Songs*, 2006.

29. Margaret Mead's advisor at Columbia University, Franz Boas, sent her to Samoa in the South Pacific with the idea that she would learn and provide evidence that the turmoil of adolescence in the United States was due to cultural factors and not biological ones. This was part of an effort to show through cross-cultural studies that the social engineering of American culture would be preferable to the eugenics programs and genetic engineering then at work in the United States. Mead's ethnographic monograph *Coming of Age in Samoa* helped Boas to influence and revise public policy about eugenics research because it gave evidence that in another society adolescence is experienced quite differently. Margaret Mead, *Coming of Age in Samoa: A Psychological Study of Primitive Youth for Western Civilization* (New York: W. Morrow & Company, 1928). Philip K. Bock, Review: "The Samoan Puberty Blues," in *Journal of Anthropological Research* 39, no. 3 (Autumn, 1983): 336.

30. The *bol* syllables *bcom ldan 'das* (pronounced "chom den dé") are not onomatopoeic in the sense of the *bol* of the *tabla* and other percussion instruments

in the Indian Classical music traditions. Rather, in the Chöd context, it serves two functions: (1) it is a pulse-oriented rhythmic mnemonic device for the three-figure (anapest) rhythmic gesture: quarter note, quarter note, half note. This is represented graphically in figure 3.2 where the rhythmic line under the melody depicts the *ḍamaru* drum's rhythm, "in out, in" and "out in, out." (2) It also serves as a mnemonic reference to the epithet describing Buddha as the "Blessed Conqueror." The syllables "chom den dé" refer to enlightened beings; it also denotes *The Heart Sutra* because in dependence upon its practice, beings can attain enlightenment.

31. The homage branch alone, for example, can be set to several verses and require several minutes.

32. In proper sentence form, the seven branches may be translated as follows:

1. I prostrate to venerable Vajravārāhī [rDo rje phag mo].
2. I offer the outer, inner and secret offerings as well as the offering of suchness.
3. I confess individually all sins and obscurations of body, speech and mind.
4. I rejoice in the perfectly pure virtues of the three times.
5. I request, please turn the Dharma wheel of the three vehicles for transmigrators.
6. I request, please remain in the nature of the three permanences.
7. I dedicate all virtues to attain the three bodies of a buddha.

See Pa bong ka bde chen snying po, *sGyu lus tshogs su sngo ba*, folios 6a–6b.

33. As observed by Dorjé and Ellingson, these "external threats" are symbolic attributes of internal mental grasping to a self. They write, "The participant comes to know all threatening "gods and demons" as *bdag 'dzin lha 'dre*—"gods and demons of holding to [the concept of] the Self." See Dorjé and Ellingson "Explanation of the Secret *Gcod Ḍamaru*," 1979, 68. It should be pointed out that *bdud* "demon" refers to the four internal and external demons, while *'dre* "ghost" often refers to external spirits. However, *lha 'dre* is generally employed by Chöd composers and poets (rather than *lha bdud*).

34. In Tibetan transliteration, these lines are: *sdig pa mi dge ci yang mi bya zhing / dge ba phun sum tshogs par 'bad pas spyad*. See Pha bong kha pa bde chen snying po, *sGyu lus tshogs su sngo ba*, "Dedicating the Illusory Body," n.d., folios 12b–13a.

35. As a ritual action, "increasing" refers to a number of possible variables: a crescendo in loudness, beats coming closer together on the drum, a graduated increase in cents of the pitch of each subsequent verse, more intensity in the overall execution, more ornamented and louder bell, etc. Ellingson developed a fascinating

chart of a sliding scale of aesthetic performance elements related with vocal music that show the interrelated performance elements along with increased beauty (*snyan pa*). These elements include "vocalization (*'don pa*), skilfulness (*mkhas pa*), effectiveness (*nus ldan*), pitch (*phra sbom*), speed (*dal mgyogs*), and drum/cymbal accompaniment (*tshig rnga*). See Ellingson, *The Mandala of Sound*, 414.

36. These methods can be found by consulting Carol Savvas's English translation of Je Tsongkhapa's commentary in her dissertation. See Savvas, *A Study of the Profound Path of gCod*, 308–398. Trans. Tsongkhapa, *Zab lam gcod kyi khrid yig* (*A Commentary on the Profound path of gCod*). However, Ven. Pencho Rabgey strongly emphasizes that these methods are only to be engaged in by powerful lamas, ritual masters who know how to perform them. Further, he warns that the Chöd practitioner must never have the intention to do harm. Rather, she or he should bravely be willing to take a loss. That said, if the practitioner feels the practice is not proceeding accordingly, and is qualified to do so, s/he might employ these aforementioned subrituals and visualizations.

37. Zasep Tulku Rinpoché, personal communication, November 2006.

38. Ibid.

39. This is according to the *yig chung* (performance notes in the sādhana in smaller Tibetan font).

40. Kyabje Zong Rinpoché's long-time student, Ven. Pencho Rabgey, remembers the comical complaint Zong Rinpoché made about preferring the "*dram-dram*" drumming pattern because the "*ma dang, lha yi, khan dro*" cycle requires considerably more time in order to conclude each musical phrase. By comparison with the *ostinato* cycle, playing the "*dram-dram*" rhythm is perhaps no less effective for the advanced practitioner's meditation, but it does move the ends of phrases and the beginning of the next closer together, allowing the beginner practitioner less time to meditate upon the visualization. Aesthetically the "*dram-dram*" rhythm provides a more "matter of fact," staid, sensibility.

41. *De ltar gdung shugs drag po yi / gsol ba rtse gcig btab pa'i mthus / bla ma lha yi thugs ka nas / bdud rtsi 'od zer dpag med babs / lus bkrus nad gdon sdig sgrib dang / khyad par bdag 'dzin gces 'dzin sbyangs / lus gang tse bsod yon tan dang / khyad par byang chub sems gnyis skye.*

Kyabje Zong Rinpoché Losang Tsundru (blo bzang brtson 'grus). "Offering Gaṇacakra in Connection with the Yoga of the Profound Path of Chöd," *Zab lam gcod kyi rnal 'byor ba'i tshogs mchod 'bul tshul nag 'gros su bkod pa*. Private collection of Ven. Pencho Rabgey, folio 12a.

42. The last device, irony, is found in the meditations on the correct view according to the Mādhyamaka-Prāsaṅgika school's interpretation. See Gyatso 2005, *The World of Tibetan Buddhism*, 43–45, 49–50.

43. See Lara Braitstein, *Saraha's Adamantine Songs*, 2006.

44. Thupten Jinpa maintains that the arrangement of the syllables is the most common for Tibetan *mgur* verses. He states, "In conventional Tibetan verse,

there are two principal meters, one of nine and one of seven syllables, with the accent always falling on the first syllable of each foot." Jinpa and Elsner, *Songs of Spiritual Experience*, 13.

45. *bzhes gnyen tshul bzhin bsten par byin gyis rlobs / dal 'byor rnyed dka' shes par byin gyis rlobs / don chen snying po len par byin gyis rlobs / nam 'chi des med dran par byin gyis rlobs* (and so forth). See Zong Rinpoché, *Gcod Tshogs*, folio 11a. Ven. Pencho Rabgey, personal communication, February 2004.

46. Sakya Paṇḍita, trans. by Canzio, in Ricardo Canzio, *Sakya Pandita's "Treatise on Music" and its Relevance to Present-day Tibetan Liturgy*. PhD diss. (London: University of London SOAS, 1978), 100–101. Canzio's dissertation project involved the translation of Sakya Paṇḍita's treatise.

47. Ibid., 101.

48. Ibid., 100.

## Chapter 4

1. Rinjing Dorjé and Ter Ellingson, " 'Explanation of the Secret *gCod Ḍamaru*': An Exploration of Musical Instrument Symbolism." *Asian Music* 10, no. 2 (1979): 63–91.

2. Stanley Fish (1980) coined the term "interpretive community" to indicate that readers of a work become part of the work through reading and shaping a text. This is a compelling notion in terms of the attribution of symbolism following a meditator's protracted engagement with a specific ritual practice. It is appropriate to consider this in the context of culturally specific ritual performance because, like Fish, I adhere to a staunch cultural relativist position. The interpretation will have meaning for cultural-insiders to the tradition and will not have meaning to those outside a particular cultural domain of readers (read: practitioners). Stanley Fish, *Is There a Text in This Class? The Authority of Interpretive Communities* (Cambridge, MA: Harvard University Press), 1980.

3. The smaller *ḍamaru* drum is frequently referred to in Tibetan language as a "chang teu" (*cang te'u*), and is used in various Buddhist Tantric rituals besides Chöd.

4. Dorjé and Ellingson translated 'Gyur med Blo gsal's commentary into English in their 1979 article. I continue to rely primarily on English and Tibetan language sources throughout the present chapter.

5. Dorjé and Ellingson 1979, 77.

6. Ibid., 77.

7. This is also a powerful corrective to the perspective given by Kaufmann who makes a blanket statement covering much of Tibetan ritual music by claiming that Tibetan ritual chordal chanting is "noise." His opinion over complicates the performative value of this music in context, disallowing for the aesthetic valuation and recognition of level of ability or readiness to enter into the musical culture. See Walter Kaufmann.

*Tibetan Buddhist Chant: Musical Notations and Interpretations of a Song Book by the Bkah brgyud pa and Sa skya pa sects* (Bloomington: Indiana University Press, 1975).

8. This is without accounting for the vertical aspect of the mountainous terrain. See Melvyn C. Goldstein and Matthew T. Kapstein, eds., *Buddhism in Contemporary Tibet: Religious Revival and Cultural Identity* (Berkeley: University of California Press, 1998), 183.

9. Peter Harvey, *An Introduction to Buddhism: Teachings, History and Practices* (Cambridge, UK: Cambridge University Press, 1990), 281.

10. Dorjé and Ellingson 1979, 77.

11. Canzio, *Sakya Pandita's "Treatise on Music,"* 178.

12. It suggests that a revisiting of his research program and re-recording the repertoire with qualified *dbu mdzad* would be a productive project for an ethnomusicologist to take up at some point.

13. Robert Beer, *The Handbook of Tibetan Buddhist Symbols* (Boston: Shambhala Publications, Inc., 2003), xiii.

14. Thupten Jinpa and Jas Elsner, *Songs of Spiritual Experience: Tibetan Buddhist Poems of Insight and Awakening* (Boston: Shambhala Publications, Inc., 2000), 197–198.

15. Dorjé and Ellingson, *The Secret gCod Ḍamaru*, 1979, 72.

16. A performance related example of singular reading of a ritual will be relayed here. There are often several different kinds of ways of performing the same ritual. These may be variations in instrumentation, tempo, and length (short, middling, and longer versions); as well, certain occasions demand that special sections of "offering" (Tib. *mchod pa*) may be inserted into the liturgy. This is by way of background for the following recent exchange I shared with a colleague, a Buddhist studies scholar, who was excited to inform me that she had recorded some rituals at a prominent monastery. I inquired with her how many different instances of each ritual she had observed and recorded, citing the importance of other variations that might be performed, which may yet inform us of the core performance practices associated with that buddha deity and accordant rituals. I mention this because it is useful and important to study the contextual basis of the different occasions of performance and related musical variations.

17. Beer, *The Handbook of Tibetan Buddhist Symbols*, 2003, xiii.

18. Nigel Rapport and Joanna Overing, *Social and Cultural Anthropology: The Key Concepts* (London: Routledge, 2000), 84.

19. It will be helpful to consider some differences between American and British schools of anthropology: American anthropologists understood culture to comprise economic, social, political, and religious thoughts and behavior, with both synchronic and diachronic dimensions. In contrast, British anthropologists focused more narrowly on the synchronic study of society. See Paul A. Erickson and Liam D. Murphy. *A History of Anthropological Theory* (Peterborough, Canada: Broadview Press, 2003), 100–101.

20. Nigel Rapport and Joanna Overing, 2000, 108.

21. Victor Turner, *The Forest of Symbols: Aspects of Ndembu Ritual* (Ithaca, NY: Cornell University Press. 1967), 47.

22. Turner, ibid., 47

23. Turner, ibid., 48.

24. Ellingson, *Mandala of Sound*, 1979, 364–365.

25. Malevolent spirits may inflate the ego of the practitioner rather than help to destroy it. This is why one of the four *māras* or "demons" (Tib. *bdud bzhi*) to cut during Chöd practice is the "demon of arrogance." See Molk, *Chöd in the Ganden Tradition*, 136–138; and Harding, *Machik's Complete Explanation*, 36–37, 117–120.

26. These would be best conceived in three dimensions, as spheres, for the reason that each exponent in the role of teacher and each student in the role of disciple will generally have multiple influences.

27. Note that the first two of these concentric circles already address the "three principal aspects of the path," which are considered basic and fundamental to Tibetan Buddhist tantric yogic practices.

28. According to the English Romanization and, in parentheses, the Wylie transliteration system, his full name is His Eminence Khalkha Jetsun Dampa Rinpoché, Jampel Namdröl Chökyi Gyaltsen (Khal kha rje btsun dam pa rin po che, 'jam dpal rnam grol chos kyi rgyal mtshan).

29. Khalkha Rinpoché, *Commentary to the Cycle of Initiations Given at Gaden Choling*. Transcribed by Julia and Keith Milton, Toronto, Canada. Unpublished manuscript, 70 pages, 1996, 8.

30. Lama Zopa and Kathleen McDonald, *Cutting Off the Truly-Existent "I": Dedicating the Illusory Body* (Boston: Wisdom Publications, 1983). The original Tibetan source is the sādhana written by Pa bong ka Bde chen snying po, *sGyu lus tshogs su sngo ba* (*Dedicating the Illusory Body*).

31. Khalkha Rinpoché 1996, 9.

32. From Khalkha Rinpoché (1996, 9).

33. From Khalkha Rinpoché (1966, 8) with minor changes.

34. I found that the same principle that applies to musical performance in other genres also applies here. If one learns to perform correctly at a slower tempo, one can always increase the tempo later. But if you begin quickly, it is awkward and much more difficult to slow down the tempo.

35. Ven. Pencho Rabgey, personal communication, 1998.

36. Ven. Pencho Rabgey, personal communication, 2004.

37. Khalkha Rinpoché 1996, 8.

38. Atiśa, 281b–282a, quoted in Ellingson (1979).

39. Zong Rinpoché, *Chöd in the Ganden Tradition: The Oral Instructions of Kyabje Zong Rinpoché* (Ithaca, NY: Snow Lion Publications 2006), 141.

40. Due to what is said to be a fundamental ignorance that leads to misapprehending the way that things actually exist (as mutually dependent), one becomes

desirously attached to certain phenomena that appear attractive to the senses or mind. Unable to obtain that object of desire, or unwilling to accept that at its most basic nature it is subject to change, the grasping mental attitude toward the desired object causes unrest, dis-ease, and suffering. Anger easily follows from attachment, since the object cannot be possessed in the exaggerated way in which one envisioned it. The absence of feeling pleasure as a result of having the object of desire is experienced as a loss.

41. Dorjé and Ellingson (1979, 73) note that "the *ḍamaru* consists of two identical halves . . . joined where a waistband of padded cloth . . . encircles the cylindrical wooden 'waist' between the two hemispherical resonating chambers of the drum." A handgrip is formed by sewing the waistband closed, and allowing the cloth to be extended.

42. While the main construction material of the *ḍamaru* body is traditionally meant to be red sandalwood, the source trees are now classified as endangered. Therefore, alternative hardwood trees more plentiful and affordable, such as pine (Tib. *thang shing*) or cutch (Tib. *seng sdeng*), are used by *ḍamaru* makers in Nepal, the chief site of the handmade production today.

43. Dorjé and Ellingson 1979, 86.

44. Khalkha Rinpoché, personal communication, 2002.

45. In his later years, Khalkha Jetsun Dampa had been studying with monks in Kusho Kundeling's style whereas he used to perform in Zong Rinpoché's style. As a Tibetan elder who taught Chöd widely, his opinion was/is valued by thousands of practitioners. Continuity as well as variation and openness much be both understood and appreciated.

46. Drepung (*'bras spung*) is one of the three large Monastic Universities built in Lhasa in the early fifteenth century, the others being Sera and Ganden. In the 1960s, these three monastic learning centers were rebuilt by exile Tibetans in Karnataka, South India. Geshé (*dge bshes*) is the degree title, equivalent to "Doctor of Divinity," conferred upon graduates of this rigorous Buddhist academic curriculum. The four levels of Geshé degree, in ascending order, are Lingse, Rigram, Tshogram, and Lharam.

47. Molk, *Chöd in the Ganden Tradition*, 2006, 141.

48. Ven. Pencho Rabgey, personal communication, Toronto, 1998.

49. Lama Thubten Yeshe, *The Tantric Path of Purification* (Boston: Wisdom Publications, 1995), 13.

50. Beer, *The Handbook of Tibetan Buddhist Symbols*, xii–xiii.

51. An example will serve here. Two of my teachers had similar backgrounds while their musical and ritual expertise varies greatly. Ven. Pencho Rabgey and His Eminence Khensur Rinpoché Lobsang Jamyang (sera med mkhan zur rin po che blo bzang 'jam dbyang, 1933– ) were both students of the same root lama. However, the former became a "ritual master" (*dbu mdzad*) at the local monastery in their mountain valley while the latter did not. The former studied the Chöd ritual intensively while the latter studied other rituals. Today the performance style of Ven. Pencho Rabgey has affinity with the Gyüme (*rgyud med*) Lower Tantric

College performance style, while Khensur Rinpoché was trained at Gyütü (*rgyud stod*) Upper Tantric College and now performs in its performance style.

52. See Mireille Helffer. "Organologie et symbolisme dans la tradition Tibétaine: Le cas de la clochette *dril-bu* et du tambour *ḍamaru/cang-te'u*" (Organology and symbolism in the Tibetan tradition: The case of the handbell *dril-bu* and the drum *ḍamaru/cang-te'u*). *Cahiers de musiques traditionnelles* 2 (1989): 33–50. See also Helffer. *Mchod-rol. les instruments de la musique Tibétaine* (The instruments of Tibetan music) (Paris: CNRS Editions/Editions de la Maison des Sciences de l'Homme, 1994).

53. Ter Ellingson, "Review Essay: Four Tibetan Recordings." *Asian Music* 12, no. 2 (1981): 133–153. Ellingson reviewed the first Western recording of a *Mi la ras pa'i bla sgrub*, a guru yoga meditation on the lama.

54. The Tibetan honorific suffix "-la" is appended to names and titles and functions like "-san" in Japanese language. I thank Ter Ellingson for pointing out that the music director's name is Umdzé Kusang Wangmo, dBu mdzad sKu bsang dBang mo (Ellingson, personal communication, April 2009).

55. Bentor notes the practiced skills of the *umdzé* (*dbu mdzad*) in the following passage of dedication: "*Dbu mdzad* Zur pa of Dga' ldan chos 'phel gling not only informed me on the annual reconsecration of Bodhanath Stupa, which is the basis for the present work, but also encouraged my investigation. Tirelessly he guided me throughout the ritual before and after its performance and even in the breaks during the long days of the actual performance. His experience as both chant leader (*dbu mdzad*) and ritual helper (*mchod gyog*) and his personal fondness for rituals significantly contributed to the present work." See Yael Bentor. *Consecration of Images and Stupas in Indo-Tibetan Tantric Buddhism* (New York: Brill, 1996), xiv.

## Chapter 5

1. Donald S. Lopez, Jr., "Inscribing the Bodhisattva's Speech: On the 'Heart Sūtra's' Mantra." In *History of Religions* 29, no. 4 (May, 1990): 352.

2. In practice, the convention exists whereby the four-line verse paying homage to Yum Chenmo is recited prior to commencement of the sādhana liturgy proper, as follows:

> *smra bsam brjod med shes rab pha rol phyin /*
> *ma skyes mi 'gag nam mkha'i ngo bo nyid /*
> *so so rang rig ye shes spyod yul ba /*
> *dus gsum rgyal ba'i yum la phyag 'tshal lo.*

The practitioner also says three repetitions of the mantra of the Perfection of Wisdom, "Tadyathā Ōṃ gaté gaté pāragaté pārasaṃgaté bodhi svāhā." This is to be recited at the outset following the "three rounds of subduing" and in-between sādhana practices sessions.

3. See Molk, *Chöd in the Ganden Tradition*, 94.

4. For a more comprehensive introduction to this subject, see Lati Rinbochay and Jeffrey Hopkins, *Death, Intermediate State, and Rebirth in Tibetan Buddhism* (Ithaca, NY: Snow Lion Publications, 1980). As well, a short description of the "transference of consciousness" practice is found here: Garma C. C. Chang, *Teachings of Tibetan Yoga*, 1963. Reprinted as *The Six Yogas of Naropa* (Ithaca, NY: Snow Lion Publications, 1986), 111–115. One may also consult the most recent translation of the *Bar do Tho del* or *Tibetan Book of the Dead.* See Gyurme Dorjé, *Tibetan Book of the Dead* (New York: Penguin Group, 2007). It should be noted that the title of the so-called *Tibetan Book of the Dead* is, in fact, a misnomer. The correct translation of *Bar do Tho del* is "Guide to Liberation by Hearing in the Intermediate."

5. Gyatso, *The World of Tibetan Buddhism*, 143.

6. See Jérôme Edou's account of Machik Labdrön's previous life as the yogin Arthasiddhi Bhadra, who was advised by deities and Tārā herself to go to Bhadra cave at Potari; and, from there, depart for Tibet by means of consciousness transference, which led to Machik Labdrön's birth in Tibet. Edou 1996, 119–122.

7. In Tibetan language, "being" (*sems can*) literally means sentient being or "consciousness-having."

8. The karmic basis for the type of realm in which a being will take rebirth is explained in verses by Tsongkhapa that conclude his sixteen-verse meditation on the three principal paths, entitled *Brief Stages of the Path* (Tib. *Lam rim bsdus don*), verses 15–16. "After one dies, there is no assurance of escaping a lower state birth / And yet the certain refuge from that peril is the Triple Gem . . . Moreover, this depends on contemplating well the white and black deeds [read: positive and negative karma]." See Pabongka Rinpoché, *Liberation in our Hands Part Two: The Fundamentals*, trans. by Sera Mey Geshé Lobsang Tharchin with Artemus B. Engle (Howell, NJ: Mahāyāna Sutra and Tantra Press, 1994), 227, note 1.

9. Vivid descriptions detailing such a rebirth are given in the *Lamrim* discourses.

10. For an explanation of the cold and hot hells, see Je Tsong-Kha-Pa, Joshua W. C. Cutler and Lamrim Chenmo Translation Committee. *The Great Treatise on the Stages of the Path to Enlightenment*; The Lamrim Chenmo. Vol. 1 (Ithaca, NY: Snow Lion Publications, 2000), 162–168.

11. Gyatso, *The World of Tibetan Buddhism*, 136.

12. A cursory description of these different levels and approaches to accessing these levels of more subtle consciousness is provided in Gyatso, *The World of Tibetan Buddhism*, 93–102.

13. Dissolution of the five elements is detailed in *Gentle Bridges: Conversations with the Dalai Lama on the Sciences of Mind,* Jeremy W. Hayward and Francisco J. Varela, eds. (Boston: Shambhala Publications, Inc., 1992), 160.

14. Reported by his students in New Jersey, MM personal communication.

15. Gyatso, *The World of Tibetan Buddhism*, 135.

16. Gyatso, *The World of Tibetan Buddhism*, 95. Futhermore, Thupten Jinpa recalls, "I remember once His Holiness stated at a public teaching in Dharamsala, India, that he bases this observation—that there are three distinct approaches in the Highest Yoga Tantra—on various comments found in the writings of the Gelug masters Khe drup Nor bzang rGya mtso (1423–1513) and Chang kya Rol pai rDo rje (1717–1786)." See *The World of Tibetan Buddhism*, 166.

17. Ven. Pencho Rabgey, personal communication, 1998.

18. This story has been told to me previously by Pala. It illustrates a key point about a high practitioner's level of knowledge of karma (causes of actions and their effects) and morality as well as the ability to utilize the subtle mind and levels of consciousness. Thus, emphasizing the need to contextualize the motivation the practitioner had for exiting the body at that time: it may be that he did not wish to be a cause dependent upon which the soldier would accumulate negative karma for killing him, or that he wanted to exit the body on his own rather than not be able to control the manner of exit if shot or wounded. Both of these motivations may be interpreted as stemming from the *bodhicitta* motivation.

19. Robert A. F. Thurman, *Essential Tibetan Buddhism* (San Francisco: HarperSanFrancisco, 1995), 10.

20. Gendun Chopel (1903–1951), for one, was an historian, translator, geographer, traveler, ethnographer, political commentator and a strong critic of the centrist religious oligarchy in Lhasa that kept Tibet materially and socially behind its advancing neighbors. Donald S. Lopez Jr., *The Madman's Middle Way: Reflections on Reality of the Tibetan Monk Gendun Chopel* (Chicago: Universtiy of Chicago Press, 2006).

21. Zasep Tulku Rinpoché, "Discourse on *phowa* practice," Gaden Choling Mahāyāna Buddhist Meditation Center, February 2006.

22. Ven. Pencho Rabgey states that, "It can be very useful to familiarize oneself with the 'transference of consciousness' practice through the Chöd ritual." The Dalai Lama says that everyday he practices the art of dying. He meditates on the process of the dissolution of the elements in the five aggregates.

23. Ven. Pencho Rabgey, personal communication, September, 2002.

24. Lama Tsongkhapa's commentary on Chöd describes how practitioners of different levels can bring the consciousness up from the secret chakra first, or even from the soles of the feet. An explanation of the three channels—central, right, and left as well as the 72,000 channels that carry the psychic winds and consciousness throughout the body may be found in Daniel Cozort, *Highest Yoga Tantra* (Ithaca, NY: Snow Lion Publications, 1986).

25. *Gcod rNam* refers to the *Nam sha Chen mo*, the Chöd commentary attributed to Ma gcig Lab sgron.

26. *'o na phaṭ kyi don ci yin snyam na / bshad par bya ste / pha ni rgyu pha rol tu phyin pa dang / ṭa ni 'bras bu rdo rje theg pa ste mdo sngags gnyis ka'i gnad bsdus pa'i don yin te / gcod rnam las / nga'i chos lugs phag rgya chen po'i gcod bya ba*

*'di yang phyi pha rol tu phyin pa mdo dang / nang gsang sngags bla na med pa'i rgyud dang gnyis kyi don phyogs gcig tu dril nas nyams su len pa la phyag rgya chen po'i gcod zer ba yin pas / yi gi phaṭ zhes pa dang mtshungs so / zhes gsungs.*

27. Tib. *Rdo rje rtse mo.*

28. *De yang rgyud rdo rje rtse mo las / yi gi phaṭ ni ci zhig brjod / gdug dang sdug bsngal 'joms byed cing / bde ba dag ni 'gugs par byed / ces gsungs pa ltar.*

29. *Phaṭ kyi sgras nag phyogs dgra bgegs gdug pa can dang / mi 'dod pa'i rkyen dang / sdug bsngal rnams zhi zhing 'joms par byed pa dang / dkar phyogs kyi lha dang / de min pa'i 'dre dang / 'dod pa'i don dang bde ba dag 'gugs par byed do.*

30. *Yang de nyid las / phaṭ ni 'joms byed sgra yin te / grogs dang bcas pa 'joms par byed / ces gsungs pa ltar.*

31. *Phaṭ kyi sgra thos pa tsam gyis mi ma yin gdug pa can 'khor dang bcas pa rnams kyi gdug sems kyi ngar zhi nas zil gyis non nus pa dang / de'i rgyud kyi dan sems 'joms par byed do.* Acharya Thupten Kalsang Champa commented on this passage, noting that: "first, it [*phaṭ*] destroys the force of harmful thoughts, and then it destroys the harmful thoughts in their mental continuum." Archarya Thupten Kalsang Champa, personal communication, Toronto, September, 2006.

32. *Mkhas grub rin po che'i brtag gnyis kyi 'grel pa las / phaṭ ni gdug pa can zlog par byed pa'o / zhes gsungs so.* The full title of Khedrup Je's commentary is: *brtag pa gnyis pa'i rnam par bshad rdo rje mkha' 'gro ma rnams kyi gsang ba'i mdzod.* According to this text's colophon, Khedrup Je's commentary on the Hevajra Tantra was written at the behest of *Legs pa mtshan rgyal ti*, at *ribo mdangs can*, in *nyang stod*, with *dkon mchog dpal sgron* as scribe.

33. And could thereby kill them.

34. *Dgos med du phaṭ drag po brjod na 'dre phran phal pa'i snying gas pa dang / phaṭ drag po brgya rtsa brgyad dus gcig la gdab na / gnod byed gang yin yang brlag par nus pas don med du mi bya.*

35. Tsongkhapa's text sNgags rim chen mo (Great Exposition of Secret Mantra).

36. *Phaṭ ces pa ni khos shig ces pa ste / bdag 'dzin kyi mgo khos shig ces pa'i rang sgra sgrog pa yin te / rje sngags rim chen mo las phaṭ ni khos shig ces pa'o / zhes gsungs pas so.*

37. "Harmful spirit" is generally understood to mean a disembodied being with malevolent intentions.

38. *Ji ltar brjod pa'i tshul ni ma gcig gi gcod rnam las / mchod sbyin phaṭ ni lhug par brjod / 'gugs bskrad phaṭ ni ring du brjod / mtshams gcod phaṭ ni thung ngur brjod / ces pa ltar.*

39. *Gong 'og kun tu mchod pa dang sbyin pa bgyis pa'i skabs su 'brong gyag gi rnga phung lta bu'i phaṭ khong shugs lhug cing sbom por brjod.*

40. *Lha 'dre sogs 'gugs pa dang bskrad pa'i skabs su bse ru'i rwa lta bu'i phaṭ rtsa ba sbom zhing rtse phra ba ring por brjod.*

41. *Bem rig phral ba sogs mtshams gcod kyi skabs su lo yags kyi nas 'bru lta bu'i phaṭ thung dur brjod dgos pa yin no.*

42. Ani Choying Drolma introduces the meaning of the mantra of compassion before singing her inspired new melody based on this mantra, "Namo Ratna Traya," https://youtu.be/zBQfUqd8pqI, posted December 5, 2007 [accessed: March 28, 2020].

43. "*Āḥ*" is the most condensed form of the *Prajñāpāramitā Sūtra*, embodying its meaning in one syllable.

44. Yum Chenmo is the embodiment of wisdom as taught in the *Prajñāpāramitā Sūtra*, and the syllable "*Āḥ*" embodies the essence of wisdom.

45. Ven. Pencho Rabgey generally used this method, and taught how to use it when practicing the sādhana, *Dedicating the Illusory Body*.

46. Zong Rinpoché used this method of performing the "*Āḥ*" syllables twenty-one times in practicing his *Chöd Tshogs* sādhana.

47. Savvas, *A Study of the Profound Path of Chöd*, 1990, 323.

## Chapter 6

1. Also spelled Kuan Yin, or Guanyin, in numerous writings; and referred to by different names in various languages. For example, in Vietnamese, she is named Quan Âm.

2. The iconographic depictions of Chenrezig, as with other buddhas, such as Tārā, feature one eye in the center of each hand.

3. In Tibetan Buddhist communities this belief is widely held. However, the notion of divinity attributed to His Holiness the Dalai Lama is not equivalent with theistic worship. The forms of worship that proceed from such faith-inspired belief are perhaps best understood in cross-cultural terms with the living practices and ritual worship of Jesus Christ in the Eucharist of the Catholic Mass. At the level of individual eschatological goals, however, there is a marked contrast; tantric practice, with its varied ritual actions, are designed to cultivate within the individual practitioner those qualities that eventually lead one to the end goal of Buddhism: full awakening or "enlightenment."

4. Literally referring to "one who has thus gone," or "one who has thus come," tathāgata is an epithet of a buddha. See Donald S. Lopez, Jr., ed., *A Modern Buddhist Bible: Essential Readings from East and West* (Boston: Beacon Press 2002), 263.

5. Playing the drum in a 'peaceful' (*zhi ba*) manner is as follows: *Zhi la sbrang char sil bu ltar brdung ba'i don / Phyi'i gnod pa nad gdon bgegs bar chad sogs kyi 'jigs pa las nye bar zhi ba dang / Nang gi nod pa nyon mongs pa brgyad khri bzhi stong gi gtso bo dug gsum dang ma rig zhi ba*

6. Each of the three poisons is, for its own part, the cause of 21,000 delusions. From the poison of attachment there are 21,000 delusions; from the poison of anger, 21,000 delusions; and from ignorance another 21,000. A further 21,000 delusions are the result of the three poisons combined together in

the mindstream. Thus, the root causes of the 84,000 delusions are the three poisons.

7. The six perfections are described in more detail elsewhere. In brief, they are: generosity, ethical discipline, patience, joyous effort, concentration, and the wisdom realizing emptiness.

8. Playing in a manner of "increasing" (*rgyas pa*) is as follows: *Rgyas la ji ltar dgos pa ltar / Phyi'i mthun rkyen 'khor dang longs spyod mnga' thang rgyas pa dang / Nang gi mthun rkyen tshe dang bsod nams lung rtogs kyi yon tan rgyas pa.*

9. Playing the drum in a "powerful" (*dbang*) manner is as follows: *Dbang la drag char 'babs pa ltar / Phyi'i bsgrub bya ni mi nor zas gos sogs phyi'i 'byor ba thams cad 'gro ba rnams zhi ba dang bde bar sbyor ba la dbang ba / Nang gi bsgrub bya mchog thun mong gi dngos grub 'grub pa la dbang ba.*

10. Playing in a "wrathful" (*drag po*) manner is to be done in the following way: *Drag la thog ser 'byin pa ltar / Phyi'i dgra sems can thams cad la 'tshe ba'i dgra bgegs thams cad grol ba dang / Nang gi dgra bdag 'dzin ma rig pa grol ba bcas so.*

11. Translation and explanation by Ven. Pencho Rabgey from the Oral Tradition, as recalled from memory. Personal communication, April 2006.

12. His Eminence Khalkha Jetsun Dampa Rinpoché, Chöd teaching at Gaden Choling, Toronto, 1998.

## Chapter 7

1. I thank Prof. David Mott for pointing out this poetic summation of the goal of Chöd practice.

2. Ven. Pencho Rabgey, personal communication, February, 1998.

3. See Zong Rinpoché, *Chöd in the Ganden Tradition*, 120–133.

4. The depth of the meaning of sādhana exceeds the commonly understood meaning of the term when it is used to refer perfunctorily to a ritual or a ritual practice text. Perhaps conceived of in this way, the *dohā* poetry of India, as well as the didactic *mgur* tradition of Tibetan contemplatives, should be taken as spiritual instructions of a sādhana.

5. Herbert Guenther explains the meaning of "dualistic grasping" in the context of translating the etymology of the name of Saraha. Saraha was the Indian mahāsiddha who was the teacher of Nāgārjuna who, according to legend, received the *Prajñāpāramitā Sūtra* from the nagas and explained them to his disciple Āryadeva.

In giving the etymology, Guenther writes:

> "Saraha" [means] (he who has shot the arrow). In India, *sara* means "arrow" and *ha(n)* "to have shot" and so he became known as "He who has short the arrow" (*mda' bsnun*) because he had sent the arrow of nonduality into the heart of duality." (Guenther 1973, 6)

Saraha had destroyed his misconception of subject and object as ultimate entities.

6. For more detailed explanation on the Middle Way view of the Mādhyamaka-Prāsaṅgika school espoused by the Indian mahāsiddha Nāgārjuna, see Jeffrey Hopkins, *Meditation on Emptiness*, assist. and ed., Elizabeth Napper (Boston: Wisdom Publications, Inc., 1992).

7. However, one might conjecture that the mind stream may carry presidential karma (i.e., The Dalai Lama and other lamas). Most beings take rebirth without their previous life's karmic role or position being recognized.

8. According to *The Heart Sutra*, "Form is emptiness, Emptiness is form."

9. See Jérôme Edou, *The Foundations of Chöd*, 42–47. He draws on teachings of other exponents to explain Chöd.

10. This is the first line in the verse paying homage to *Prajñāpāramitā* Yum Chenmo. This verse is often recited when commencing a Chöd sādhana.

11. See Gyatso, *The World of Tibetan Buddhism*, 98–99.

12. Tsongkhapa, *The Three Principal Aspects of the Path, lam gyi gtso bo rnam pa gsum*. Translated by Geshé Thupten Jinpa. Montreal: Institute of Tibetan Classics, 2003.

13. Some of these "sound structure" as "social structure" homologies have been explored by Steven Feld, Marina Roseman, and others. See Feld's article in *Ethnomusicology* 28 (3): 1984.

14. The effect of the karmic imprint resulting from the negative intentionality that stems from the desire to harm another person.

15. Under a microscope, obviously unavailable to Buddhist sages until recently, the evidence suggests that this view is correct: there is more space in material objects than "material objects" that appear to the naked human eye. Objects seem to be arrangements of atoms, which themselves are made up of tiny particles that are not static, but in motion. Material objects are anything but static and unchanging. The relative permanence of space allows for other phenomena to arise, whither, disintegrate and change within it. See Dalai Lama, *The Universe in a Single Atom: The Convergence of Science and Spirituality* (New York: Broadway Books, 2005).

16. Ven. Pencho Rabgey, personal communication, February, 2007.

17. Gyatso, *The World of Tibetan Buddhism*, 20.

18. The yoga of visualizing himself or herself as the deity.

19. Up until the transfer of consciousness into the heart of the lama-*yidam*.

20. "Divine pride" is the sensibility and confidence that obtains from embodying all the qualities of enlightened thought, speech, and physicality of a buddha deity. In the context of a Chöd ritual, divine pride may be cultivated at different moments of a given sādhana. As per one's lama's instructions, one could cultivate divine pride with respect to: Heruka or Vajrayoginī while going according to the "four ways," or at other times as Vajravārāhī, a wisdom ḍākinī, Yum Chenmo, Troma Nagmo, or Machik Labdrön.

21. See *Dedicating the Illusory Body as a Heaped Offering*, Folio 3a.

22. See Lama Tsongkhapa's Chöd commentary in Savvas, 309–398.

23. Jeffrey Hopkins, ed. and trans. *The Yoga of Tibet: The Great Exposition of Secret Mantra—2 and 3 by Tsong-ka-pa* (Boston: George Allen and Unwin, 1981), 9.

24. Jérôme Edou, *The Foundations of Chöd*, 85. Ven. Pencho Rabgey confirms this.

25. "One may also meditate on the profound completion stage or any other virtuous practice." Lama Tsongkhapa, as quoted in Savvas 1990, 349.

26. This is the position maintained by Ven. Pencho Rabgey.

27. Initially, beginners may find confusing the notion that the practitioner is still able to perform the instruments after having been chopped up and distributed to all beings. Ven. Pencho Rabgey insists that the dismembering process is performed in visualization only and no being is harmed in the process.

28. As pointed out in chapter 1, the Mind and Life Institute's recent work on meditative states frames meditation in terms of efficacy in scientifically measured comparative states, which account for the experience of the practitioner. Thus, the experimental design includes and thereby values the differentiation of "novice" and "advanced" meditators.

## Chapter 8

1. In Wylie transliteration the Tibetan text reads, *lus po ro dang sems nyid ro kur tshul.*

2. *Melismatic* refers to a style of liturgical music in which many notes are sung to one syllable of text, as opposed to *syllabic*, which denotes one sung pitch to each syllable of text. In this form of notation, the underline drawn below a numbered pitch indicates the octave below, while an underline above denotes the octave above. Double parallel lines, either above or below a number, indicate tempo: to perform these pitches at twice the set speed.

3. Although Chöd is known primarily as an oral music tradition, here the teacher uses number notation as both a memory and pedagogical aid to effectively enable music transmission. She sings a phrase alone first, and then together with her fellow Chöd practitioner "students" who follow in an imitative fashion while reading the notation. By instructing in this way, she combines oral with written transmission.

4. Thighbone trumpet or "*kangling*" (Tib. *rkang gling*).

5. The "three doors" are body, speech and mind through which pass either virtuous or non-virtuous actions, speech, and thoughts respectively.

6. Kay Kaufman Shelemay, "The Ethnomusicologist and the Transmission of Tradition" in *The Journal of Musicology*, vol. 14, no. 1 (1996), 35. Shelemay's

research has involved working with the Jewish Diasporic communities of the Falashas and Syrians on their respective sacred liturgical traditions.

7. Lama Zopa Rinpoché released such a CD/DVD set in March 2007. See the FPMT (The Foundation for the Preservation of the Mahayana Tradition) media website.

8. Machik Labdrön had her son Thönyön Samdrup sealed in a cave for extended periods of time before she transmitted to him the complete set of her teachings, entrusting him thereafter with her pith instructions. See translated portions of Machik's hagiography in Jérôme Edou, *The Foundations of* Chöd, 150–157 and also in Sarah Harding, *Machik's Complete Explanation*, 2003, 89–92.

9. Pala would watch the weather channel on television, and tell me "Don't come today," if it was indicating poor winter weather conditions. Being enthusiastic to not miss a day of the transmission, I would sometimes drive up anyhow (slowly, with snowtires).

10. Shelemay points out, I think correctly, that ethnomusicologists engage in a "truly participatory participant-observation" method, which demands and rewards their particular type of research that can occur through and with performance. See Shelemay 1996.

11. This is considered to be the danger of the tantric path. At the time of the initiation, the lama as "vajra master" and the students as "vajra disciples" make a mutual commitment. If the students or lama break this commitment, both are said to go to lower realms, even to hell. If an error is made, they may engage in purification practices. But as Ganden lineage lamas maintain, it is better to have not broken a vow in the first place rather than to break one and mend it. It is like breaking a leg that later heals. The leg is never as good as it was before it got broken.

12. Communion in the sense of "communitas," as forwarded by anthropologist and ritual theorist Victor Turner, is a changed feeling and awareness of belonging following participation in a ritual, often marked by a shift in collective and individual identity after a rite of passage ritual. The Chöd ritual can be experienced as a rite of passage on the group level at the initial initiation ceremony; as well, communitas may be experienced recurrently in the daily or weekly context of regular group ritual practices. For more discussion on this, see chapter 3, "Liminality and Communitas," in Victor Turner, *The Ritual Process: Structure and Anti-Structure.* Chicago: Aldine Pub. Co., 1969 (7th edition).

13. Taping a piece of duct tape to the inside of the bell to dampen the wash of harmonic overtones was an innovation Pala introduced when recording us, so he could hear our melody more clearly.

14. One of my teachers, a monk from Ganden Shartse Monastic College who prefers to remain anonymous, insisted that I not record our lessons. His view was that those who record become "lazy"; they rely on knowing they have

the recording rather than develop skills and knowledge through the processes of memorization and teacher-to-student transmission. After an immersive period of training with him, just before we parted ways, he allowed me to record him so I would not forget his melodies.

15. I instruct learners of the *ḍamaru* to turn it as slowly as possible while maintaining its verticality, bringing it (in) toward, and (out) away from, one's torso. At a slow tempo, the drum should not droop to either side (break beyond the vertical plane) since, if it does, the beaters will not strike the skins on opposite sides of the drum at the same time. My method of pedagogy is to breakdown every motion into its different micro-level component parts, as I did when learning from Pala.

16. These are vigorous reminders to attend to one's underlying motivation for any task, whether it appears to be worldly or spiritual; and, in this way, the music is to be driven by one's intentionality.

17. Through my research into the economic situation in the site of study, Toronto or London, UK, I learned that University of London (SOAS) Commonwealth Scholarship holders still struggled financially and it would have precluded me from making rare, let alone, periodic visits back to Canada to continue receiving the Chöd transmission. My weekly trips to Pala's home were funded in small part by York University's Fieldwork Costs Fund. I did not pay Pala for over 98 percent of the time he spent giving me lessons into Chöd because I could not secure funding on such a scale. Our arrangement was understood to be based on an ethical bond in which reciprocity is expected. To every lesson I would try to arrive with a small offering that was practical. Usually this consisted of fresh vegetables from Toronto's Asian food markets (those not available locally in his town's grocery), and phone cards (before apps like WeChat were developed) that had inexpensive long-distance rates to India and China (where Pala and his family were supporting monastic education at Sera Mey Monastic University by building a residence for monks from his village to live, followed afterward by building primary and middle schools for children in his home village of Chungba in Tibet). From both our sides, my offerings were not considered an equalizing exchange. But it made both sides a little happy as I arrived to continue our transmission process. In essence, beyond the financial obstacles, the most challenging factor once in London would be finding a qualified Chöd instructor who could devote such attention to the transmission process as had Pala (and as has traditionally been done for centuries in the Ganden Ear Whispered Chöd Tradition). It was precisely the nature of the Chöd transmission I was privy to that made my declining the opportunity a logically sound decision. Only an immersive study would lead to my being able to illuminate granular aspects of the musical artistry in the Chöd musical meditation practice for a wider audience—by experiencing this Vajrayāna Buddhist tradition that had not yet been explored to such an extent.

18. In Toronto, we have performed together at the Royal Ontario Museum on "Tibet Night," at Harbourfront's "Rhythms of the World Festival," during my

*Living Songs* benefit concert series, as well as other occasions. We also performed together at a fundraiser for Machik (<machik.org>) at Jam Tse Choling in 2016, the Buddhist temple headed by Neten Tulku Rinpoché, the head of the Gelugpa school in Canada (<jamtsecholing.org>).

19. Tibetan monk tours sent abroad by Buddhist monastic universities and temples based in India and Nepal, as well as international delegations of Tibetan nuns from Abbeys in Nepal and India, have also featured the Chöd ritual as a segment of their stage performances.

20. Choying Drolma and Steve Tibbetts, *Chö* (Hannibal: January 21, 1997) CD: ASIN# B00000063A.

21. Zong Rinpoché, *Chöd in the Ganden Tradition*, 58–59.

22. Atiśa Dīpāñkara Śrijñāna, attributed. *Lamp for the Path to Enlightenment.* (Skt. *Bodhipatha-pradīpa-vrtti.* Tib. *byang chub lam gyi sgron me'i bka' 'grel*). TTRI: Vol. Ki. Referenced in Ellingson, *The Mandala of Sound*, 814. Atiśa (982–1054) was the Indian Buddhist pandit who held the keys to Vikramaśila Monastic University in India as its Abbot, and was among the few scholar-practitioners chiefly responsible for the spread of Buddhism during the "Later Dissemination of Buddhism into Tibet" (Tib. *phyi dar*). His closest Tibetan disciple was the layperson Dromtönpa ('brom ston pa rgyal ba'i 'byung gnas, 1005–1064).

23. It is possible that Khalkha Rinpoché allowed these recordings to be made while being fully aware of the multiple and conflated purposes they would serve. He likely expected students to understand from his teachings (during which he openly expressed concerns about the Gelugpa Chöd Tradition being in danger of dying out) that those who wish to gain a full transmission of all the melodies and performance practices would make sacrifices in order to spend an extended period learning in India with the lama and experienced disciples. Therefore, it is important for students of Chöd to periodically spend time learning with a recognized Chöd lama, rather than depending solely on the aural/video transmission aids of cassettes and videos. The Chöd lama can give transmissions (both musical and *lung*), meditation instructions, and interpret visions or dreams that students might experience. Most importantly, by staying in close proximity to a teacher, it may be easier to develop a deeper understanding of Chöd, and learn how the practice can be helpful to oneself and others.

24. This is a matter that is addressed in all the Chöd commentaries as well as in the lineage guru sections of the sādhana root texts.

25. Several students from around the world have visited Rinpoché at Takten House in India to study Chöd with him and his students there toward this end.

26. Khe drup rje (mkhas grub thams cad mkhyen pa), rnam thar mkhas pa'i yid 'phrog ces bya ba, 5-31, in *Mkhas grub thams cad mkhyen pa dge legs dpal bzang po'i gsung 'bum*, vol. *ka*, 14. Quoted in Savvas, 1990, 302–3.

27. Recently, on an annual basis, there has been a two-week Chöd Monlam ("prayer festival") in Mongolia led by Lama Woser Rinpoché of Sera Mey Monastic University, who trained under Khalkha Jetsun Dampa Rinpoché. Students from

Switzerland and elsewhere around the world travel there to be able to attend and practice together.

28. They may have also been used for a fourth purpose: as music enjoyed by faithful non-Chöd practicing disciples who reverently listen to their lama's Chöd melodies.

29. The Chöd Tradition relies primarily of the method of developing *bodhicitta* through the practice of "equalizing and exchanging self with others" or "*dag shen nyam jé*" (Tib. *bdag gzhan mnyam brje*). See Sermey Geshé Lobsang Tharchin. *Achieving Bodhicitta: Instructions of Two Great Lineages Combined into a Unique System of Eleven Categories*. Howell, NJ: Mahayana Sutra and Tantra Press, 1999.

30. To put this another way: exaggerated projections, and attributing a solid nature to impermanent and conditioned phenomena, can lead to designations such as "enemies" and "friends."

31. Buddha literally means "Awakened One" in Sanskrit (Tib. *sangs rgyas*).

32. The last of these is considered possible only due to their level of realization, such as: (a) the extent to which they are able to genuinely communicate with the spirit world, and (b) the extent to which they are able to seek and destroy the false conceptual basis for establishing in their mind the notion of a self-sufficiently existing "I" or "me," such that designating even their own body as "mine" becomes a notion that may be falsified in but a few careful logical steps.

33. Since they discover it ("self") is an imputed concept—implying solidity and permanence upon an impermanent, interrelated object (the body)—it is bizarre to care for what is merely a conceptual designation, *especially* when doing so means retaining the false apprehension of one's apparent separateness from other beings. Yet, they must find a balance before they fall into the extreme view of nihilism.

34. Ven. Pencho Rabgey explained the foregoing and added that some people in Tibetan society are afraid of Chöd practitioners because they are fearless and will dare go where no one else would. It is believed that around them dwell spirits who know that, out of compassion, the Chöd practitioner will make offerings and give them what they need and desire.

35. This is why during the practice of developing altruism through "giving and taking" (*gtong len*) one is instructed to take the sins, misdeeds, negativities, and two obscurations of others, into the self-cherishing at the center of one's own heart in the form of black spiders, thunderstorms, and scorpions.

36. Geshé Rabten and Geshé Ngawang Dhargyey, "The Seven Point Thought Transformation" in ed., Brian Beresford, *Advice from a Spiritual Friend: Buddhist Thought Transformation* (New Delhi: Nepal Mahayana Gompa Centre, Inc., 1977), 50. The quote above is the first statement in an oral commentarial discourse on the phrase, "banish the one object of every blame" which is itself within the subsection called "generating the conventional awakening mind." This teaching is relevant within the lineage of Chöd teachings presented here.

37. Ven. Pencho Rabgey, personal communication, March 2001.

38. Tibetan teachers I have studied with have called some occupations "*bodhisattva* professions." Although often supported with a philosophical doctrine grounded in religion or ideology, not all workers and volunteers subscribe to these. "Humanitarian" workers/volunteers try to transport aid to others in peril at great risk to themselves. A known example is the nongovernmental organization MSF (Médecins Sans Frontières / Doctors Without Borders) whose nurses, physicians, and healthcare teams assist on the fringes of, or directly within, warzones, and in areas with public health crises. As well, the engagement of students, documentary filmmakers, and journalists who put themselves at risk to benefit others through onsite research and media reportage is not substantially different. Yet, in such arenas, a cost-benefit calculation often sees a negative net result for the workers/volunteers themselves, and benefit accruing to others. With a visual example in memory, then, it is perhaps unnecessary to imagine a Chödpa in a cemetery at night, and associate an act of courage with an esoteric tantric practice: very likely similar work is being done in broad daylight.

39. This is the case for any kind of Mahāyāna Buddhist practitioner who takes the "*bodhisattva* vow" to relieve all beings of suffering for their sake. Vajrayāna (tantric) practitioners are implicitly Mahāyāna practitioners, but they follow the swifter path, energizing the commitments of the *bodhisattva* vow with the tantric vows (taken at initiations), commitments, and practices such as Chöd in order to gain enlightenment as soon as possible.

40. For a discussion on alternative responses to the destructive habit of assigning self-blame, see Lama Thubten Yeshe, *The Tantric Path to Purification* (Boston: Wisdom Publications, 1995), 101–106.

41. Ven. Pencho Rabgey, personal communication, December 1997.

42. Ven. Pencho Rabgey, personal communication, March 1998.

43. In one of our first conversations, Pala gave me similar advice when I consulted with him about a personal issue involving conflict. His logical approach to the situation involved suggesting I make calculations that considered the total amount of harm and/or benefit that would accrue to each party whether I would remain calm and patient or retaliate. By considering an analysis of various possible outcomes within parameters demarcated by harm and/or benefit, I determined that it would be more reasonable for me to stay patient and not respond in anger. While this sounds simple, I found it most challenging, but effective. Remaining patient does not mean being a "doormat," but it does mean avoiding responding in anger. The point on which this logic pivots is the consideration that *after* one has *already* been hurt (with insulting words, or physical or material loss), the potential opportunity for greater loss can be substantially increased if one is drawn into a fight with others who clearly harbor malevolent intentions and/or are under the influence of anger. Therefore, one must pause and undertake a cogent analysis of the situation. Careful calculation is necessary lest more negative karma be added to that which has already been enacted.

44. See Śāntideva, "Chapter 5: Guarding Alertness," in *Bodhicaryāvatāra* or *A Guide to the Bodhisattva's Way of Life*, trans. Stephen Batchelor (Dharamsala: Library

of Tibetan Works and Archives, 1979), 39–60. Verse 29 reads: "Therefore I shall never let mindfulness depart / from the doorway of my mind."

45. Rather than "three spheres," it may also be translated as "three circles."

46. According to Zong Rinpoché's commentary on the "three spheres of giving," "It is also very important to meditate carefully upon the three spheres [circles] of ethical discipline, patience, effort, and so on." See David Molk, *Chöd in the Ganden Tradition*, 120. He is referring to the first five perfections (Skt. *pāramitās*), which are "generosity," "ethical discipline," "patience," "joyful effort," and "concentration."

47. Several lamas with whom I have studied in the Ganden Oral Tradition have said they regard Jesus as a *bodhisattva*.

48. Ven. Pencho Rabgey, personal communication, November 1997.

49. The stanza on "the four seals" may be found in chapter 2.

50. Selected phrases drawn from the English translation of the sādhana, *Dedicating the Illusory Body* prepared by Ven. Lama Thubten Zopa Rinpoché, and edited by Gelong Thubten Chödak and Kathleen McDonald, *Chöd—Cutting off the Truly-Existent "I."* (Boston: Wisdom Publications, 1983), 13.

51. Kyabje Zong Rinpoché terms the Chöd practitioner a "warrior" who must hold the weapons of *bodhicitta* and *śūnyatā* together at all times. The analogy seems to suit well the story from Ven. Pencho Rabgey's oral tradition, and the life experience of a Chödpa he met as a boy in his village of Chungba, Tibet.

52. In addition to this meditation on "emptiness" through causality, which helps to loosen one's grasp onto the seemingly solid appearance of phenomena, as well as to let go of the exaggerated excessive focus on one's "self" (which appears, at least initially, as objectively self-existent), there is a more subtle way one can focus on the lack of inherent independent self-existence of self and phenomena. And to approach that more subtle and profound way to contemplate on emptiness, one can consult the Buddha's teaching on "dependent arising" (Skt. *pratītyasamutpāda*, Tib. *rten cing 'brel par byung ba*) and the commentaries on "dependent arising" by Tsongkhapa and the great masters of the Nālandā tradition.

53. The original title, in Tibetan, is: *sGyu lus tshogs su bsngo ba thabs shes nyams kyi bogs 'don dga' ldan sgrub rgyud spyi nor shes bya ba bzhugs so.*

## Chapter 9

1. The full title (in English) of Marcel Mauss's treatise is as follows, *The Gift: The Form and Reason for Exchange in Archaic Societies* (New York: W. W. Norton & Company, 1990 [1924]). Marcel Mauss (1872–1950) was a French sociologist and was Émile Durkheim's nephew. Under Durkheim, Mauss studied philosophy and went on to study the history of religion, Sanskrit and Indian texts at the École Pratique des Hautes Études. In 1924, Mauss published *Essai sur le don* (*The Gift*); and in 1925, Mauss founded the Institut d'Ethnologie de l'Université de Paris to support young anthropologists in their research and writing.

2. If an act becomes Dharma it is necessarily an antidote to suffering for oneself at a minimum, but optimally for all beings. Dharma refers to a buddha's teachings and the realizations that are attained in dependence upon practicing them.

3. Mauss, *The Gift*, 72.

4. Ibid., 76.

5. Note the use of the word "reason" in Mauss's title for his essay: *The Gift: The Form and Reason for Exchange in Archaic Societies.*

6. An important review of Western approaches to philosophical concepts of compassion and emotion may be found in Thupten Jinpa Langri, *A Fearless Heart: How the Courage to be Compassionate can Transform Our Lives*. Avery: New York, 2015.

7. A critical perspective may offset this orthodox presentation of Buddhist epistemology, weighted as this is toward a doctrinal perspective. However, by placing philosophical positions into conversation, a close adherence to doctrinal perspectives may be helpful at first to draw lines of comparison.

8. According to Mahāyāna Buddhist epistemology, the altruistic intention to achieve enlightenment for the benefit of all sentient beings, known as *bodhicitta*, is taught through two lineages, both of which aim to gradually develop this intentionality. One lineage, extending from Maitreya through Asanga is known as the "seven step cause and effect method."

9. Thupten Jinpa, *Institute of Tibetan Classics*. Available at www.tibetanclassics.org/doctrines1.html [accessed June 4, 2013].

10. Note that the first of these practices is generosity, which highlights the importance of the action of giving by the *bodhisattva* as being intentionally guided by *bodhicitta*. For a more complete, and erudite description of Tibetan Buddhism see Thupten Jinpa, *Institute of Tibetan Classics*. Available at http://www.tibetanclassics.org/en/media-resources/text/background-educational-resources#letter-central-doctrines-of-tibetan-buddhism [accessed August 15, 2015]. Thupten Jinpa is the Dalai Lama's principal English translator. With having earned a doctorate degree from both the Tibetan academy of Ganden Shartse Monastic University and Cambridge University, UK, he is one of the foremost world authorities on this subject.

11. Śāntideva, *Bodhicaryāvatāra* or *A Guide to the Bodhisattva's Way of Life,* trans., Stephen Batchelor (Dharamsala: Library of Tibetan Works and Archives, 1979), 40.

12. This is an approximation of the Buddha's teaching of the Four Noble Truths, which Buddha gave to his five ascetic companions during his first turning of the Wheel of Dharma in Deer Park, Sarnath, India. This formulaic analysis could be applied to the study of suffering in any context, but its original usage was for the determination of the causes and results of suffering, according to Buddhist historiography.

13. Mauss, *The Gift*, 76–77.

14. I use this phrase to extend Mauss's theory of the gift, and to call on the observer to recognize the importance of what underlies and compels obligation in an exchange.

15. Mauss, *The Gift*, 76.

16. Ibid., 77. Kindly forgive the absence of gender parity here.

17. Classification was also a preoccupation of anthropologists at the time, including and especially Mauss, who co-authored the essay *Primitive Classification* with his uncle, the noted sociologist Émile Durkheim. See Durkheim, Émile and Marcel Mauss, *Primitive Classification*, trans., Rodney Needham (Chicago: University of Chicago Press, 1963).

18. Mauss, *The Gift*, 70–71.

19. Mahāyāna is characterized by the *bodhicitta* motivation and the *bodhisattva* ideal, and all Tibetan Buddhism is a form of Mahāyāna. Vajrayāna, or the "Diamond Path," refers to the faster tantric methods of practice that were developed to their highest level in Tibet relative to other Buddhist cultures. The Vajrayāna practice methods, such as Chöd, emphasize the development of the Mahāyāna motivation as a prerequisite for engaging in more metaphysical experiences for transcending suffering.

20. Mauss, *The Gift*, 3. Italics in original.

21. I deliberately avoid Marxist notions of commodity fetishization in order to continue a line of reasoning according to Buddhist logic and epistemology.

22. Mauss, *The Gift*, 77.

23. Mauss, *The Gift*, 42.

24. Ibid., 3.

25. Ibid.

26. Mary Douglas is the author of the foreword, "No Free Gifts," in the 1990 publication of *The Gift*. See Marcel Mauss, *The Gift*, trans., W. D. Halls, and foreword by Mary Douglas (Abingdon, Oxon: Routledge, 1990), ix–xxiii.

27. Natalie Zemon Davis, *The Gift in Sixteenth-Century France* (Madison: University of Wisconsin Press, 2000), 221.

28. Richard Titmuss, *The Gift Relationship: From Human Blood to Social Policy* (London: George Allyn & Unwin, 1971).

29. See Davis, *The Gift*, 131. For the original source, see Kenneth J. Arrow, "Gifts and Exchanges" in *Altruism, Morality, and Economic Theory*, ed., Edmund S. Phelps (New York: Russel Sage Foundation, 1975), 13–28.

30. On the notion of a finite physical and emotional reserve in need of self-regulation, see T. J. Jackson Lears, "Preface" and "Roots of Antimodernism: The Crisis of Cultural Authority During the Late Nineteenth Century," in *No Place of Grace: Antimodernism and the Transformation of American Culture, 1880–1920* (Chicago: University of Chicago Press, 1983). Lears shows that in the late nineteenth century through the early twentieth century the managing of physical and emotional being was tied to notions of regulation, but nowhere has it been proven that the cultivation of compassion is limited in resources, or finite. According to a Mahāyāna perspective, there is no wellspring of altruism that would dry up from over depletion.

31. For Levinas's theory on "Substitution" see, Emmanuel Levinas, *Otherwise Than Being or Beyond Essence*, translated by Alphonso Lingis (Pittsburgh, PA: Duzqesne University Press, 1998, 3rd ed. [1981]), 113–118.

32. At first the lack of need for return would appear to be contradictory. If the self is obligated to the other, the other, in turn, becomes a self who then is obligated to the other (who, among others, is the original self). The confusion is easily cleared up because upon deeper examination there is no paradox. For Levinas, the obligation is not circular: each person is obligated to another necessarily, as the subsequent example of Cain and Abel illustrates.

33. This is where Talmudic theory and Buddhism might converge. According to University of Toronto political philosopher Gad Horowitz–an expert on Levinas and Talmudic theory–Levinas draws from his Jewish background and Talmudic understanding, which sees the individual as responsible necessarily to the other. Gad Horowitz, University of Toronto, November, 2002, personal communication.

34. For Derrida's interpretation of Mauss's concept of the gift, see Rosalyn Diprose, *Corporeal Generosity: On Giving with Nietzsche, Merleau-Ponty, and Levinas* (Albany, NY: SUNY Press, 2002), 5–9, 55–56.

35. Jacques Derrida, *Given Time*, trans., Peggy Kamuf (Chicago: University of Chicago Press, 1992), 24. See also Diprose, *Corporeal Generosity*, 6.

36. Diprose, *Corporeal Generosity*, 6, 12–14, 60.

37. Pierre Bourdieu, *The Weight of the World: Social Suffering in Contemporary Society*, trans., Priscilla Parkhurst Ferguson (Redwood City, CA: Stanford University Press, 1999).

38. Here I make reference to the theoretical work on social anthropology that Mauss aims to put forward with the concept of the "total system." In essence, I believe Mahāyāna Buddhist epistemology could be interpreted as a "total system." In this system all actions and thoughts imbued with *bodhicitta* are affective in all dimensions and all social relations across seemingly discrete barriers of political, religious, economic, artistic, psychological, and social life.

39. Pabongha Rinpoché, *Liberation in the Palm of Your Hand*, ed., Trijang Rinpoché, trans., Michael Richards (Boston: Wisdom Publications, 1992), 628. The context of this advice is the *Lamrim* (*Stages of the Path*) discourses. The principles of giving are the same for building the foundation of altruistic intention, whether engaged in the *Stages of the Path* meditations or practicing the Highest Yoga Tantric Chöd Tradition.

40. Alan D. Schrift, "On the Gift-Giving Virtue: Nietzsche's Unacknowledged Feminism" in *International Studies in Philosophy*, trans., Hazel E. Barnes (New York: Routledge, 1994), vol. 26, no. 3, 33–44, 35. Barnes is quoted in Diprose, *Corporeal Generosity*, 11.

41. Ibid., 13–14.

42. Pabongka Rinpoché, 1992, 631.

43. Luce Irigaray, "To love to the point of safeguarding you." In *To Be Two* (New York: Routledge, 2000), 48–53.

44. Ibid., 52. Here, Diprose is drawing upon Merleau-Ponty and Levinas.

45. For a collection of papers by participants at a Mind and Life conference meeting see, Richard J. Davidson and Anne Harrington eds., *Visions of Compassion: Western Scientists and Tibetan Buddhists Examine Human Nature* (New York: Oxford University Press, 2002), 98.

46. Ibid., 97.

47. Ibid., 98.

48. Ibid.

49. There are generally two meditation methods for the development of a genuine altruistic aspiration, one of which is the "seven-step cause and effect" method. There is another way to generate compassion and *bodhicitta* known as the practice of "equalizing and exchanging self and others." See Sermey Geshé Lobsang Tharchin, *Achieving Bodhicitta: Instructions of Two Great Lineages Combined into a Unique System of Eleven Categories* (Howell, NJ: Mahayana Sutra and Tantra Press, 1999), 86–98.

50. Recognizing that a sizeable literature explores "compassion fatigue" experienced by caregivers and health care professionals, perspectival shifts can be inculcated by introducing contemplative practices in health care sites. For example, see Anne Bruce and Betty Davies, "Mindfulness in Hospice Care: Practicing Meditation-in-Action." *Qualitative Health Research* 15, no. 10: (2005), 1329–1344.

51. See Lama Zopa and Kathleen McDonald, *Cutting Off the Truly-Existent "I": Dedicating the Illusory Body* (Boston: Wisdom Publications, 1983), 33, stanza 64.

52. Ven. Pencho Rabgey, personal communication, November 2000.

53. Tibet had its own system of currency, with coins and notes, for many centuries before the mid-20th century. See Wolfgang Bertsch, *The Currency of Tibet: A Sourcebook for the Study of Tibetan Coins, Paper Money and other Forms of Currency*, Library of Tibetan Works & Archives: Dharamsala, 2002.

54. The giving process has three stages: (1) the setting of motivation, (2) the deed, and (3) the dedication. This three-step training is drawn straight from the *Lamrim* discourses. According to the oral lineage commentary on these stages: (1) the motivation should be based upon *bodhicitta* (or a close approximation of contrived altruism) of engaging in the action for the benefit of others; (2) the deed is giving to others without holding back or expecting anything in return; and, (3) the dedication is thinking that any virtue accrued from the act of giving to others is dedicated to gaining enlightenment for the benefit of all beings.

## Conclusion

1. See section Zong Rinpoché, *Chöd in the Ganden Tradition*, 58–59.

2. Martin Luther King, Jr.'s address on April 3, 1968, in Memphis, Tennessee, where he recalled the parable of the ailing Levant fallen on the road from Jerusalem to Jericho, a dangerous winding road where bandits famously led ambushes. The

lesson was that to not help support the sanitation workers by marching with them would be abdicating a moral responsibility since we are collectively responsible to and for each other. In short, Reverend King's message was, "we should help them, despite the feared outcome of what might happen to us."

3. I also refer to this as the "word-for-word translation" or just "word for word" translation.

4. This also contrasts sharply with some Chöd translators' approach of singing the originally composed melody to newly composed liturgical poetry in English or other languages. Where poetry has been rewritten in English to suit the meter of the Tibetan verse, words touch the melody at places with meaning that is different to what it was when originally composed.

# Glossary

| **English** | **Tibetan*** | **Sanskrit** |
|---|---|---|
| action | "las" can be pronounced "lay" | karma |
| adept (realized adept) | sgrub pa (drub pa) | siddha |
| aggregate | phung po (pung po) | skandha |
| altruism | lhag bsam (lag sam) | |
| altruistic intention | byang chub kyi sems (chang chub gi sem) | *bodhicitta* |
| anger | khong khro (khong tro) | praṭigha |
| attachment/desire | 'dod chags (dö chag) | rāga |
| being/transmigrator | 'gro ba (dro wa) | gati |
| blessing | byin labs (chin lab) | adhṣhṭhāna |
| body | lus (lü) | kaya |
| Buddhist | nang pa | |
| chanting master | dbu mdzad (umdzé) | |
| Chöd practitioner | Chödpa (*Chöpa*) | |
| community | gendun | saṅgha |
| compassion | snying rje (nying je) | karuṇā |

*English pronunciation is provided in parentheses of middle column.

| | | |
|---|---|---|
| consciousness | rnam shes (nam she)<br>shes pa (she pa) | vijñāna |
| conventional truth | kun rdzob bden pa (kun dzob den pa) | *saṃvṛtisatya* |
| cutting practice | *gCod* (Chöd / *Chö*) | |
| cyclic existence | ’khor ba (kor wa) | *saṃsāra* |
| death / dying | ’chi ba (chi wa) | *maraṇa* |
| dedication | bsngo ba (ngo wa) | *pariṇāma* |
| deity yoga | lha’i rnal ’byor (lha nä jor) | devayoga |
| delusion | nyon mongs (nyö mong) | kleśa |
| demon | bdud (dü) | māra |
| development of *bodhicitta* | sems bskyed (sem che) | |
| dualistic grasping | gnyis ’dzin (nyin dzin) | |
| emptiness | stong pa nyid (tong pa nyi) | śūnyatā |
| energy-wind | rlung | prāṇa |
| enlightenment | byang chub/sangs rgya (chang chub/sang gye) | bodhi |
| faith | dad pa (dä pa) | śraddhā |
| generosity/giving | sbyin pa (jinpa) | dāna |
| great realized one | drub chen pa | mahāsiddha |
| hand gesture, symbolic | phyag rgya (cha gya) | mudrā |
| haunted site of practice | nyen sa | |
| hermitage | ri khrod (ri trü) | parvata |
| Highest Yoga Tantra | bla med rnal ’byor kyi rgyud (la mä nel jor gi gyü) | mahānuttarayoga-tantra |
| hindering spirits | bgegs (geg) | vighna |

| | | |
|---|---|---|
| hourglass-shaped drum | cang t'eu (chang tü) | *ḍamaru* |
| ignorance | ma rig pa (ma rig pa) | avidyā |
| impermanence | mi rtag pa (mi tag pa) | anitya |
| intention | bsam pa (sam pa) | *saṃdhi* |
| dependent origination | rten cing 'brel par byung ba (ten jung) | *pratītya-samutpāda* |
| lama | bla ma (lama) | guru |
| lineage lama | bla brgyud (la gyü) | *gurusaṃpradāya* |
| love | byams pa (cham ba) | maitri |
| means of accomplishment | sgrub thabs (drub thab) | sādhana |
| meditational deity | yidam | |
| merit | bsod nams (sö nam) | *puṇya* |
| merit field | tshogs zhing (tsog shing) | |
| method/means | thabs | upāya |
| Middle Way | dbu ma'i lam (uma'i lam) | mādhyamika |
| mind | sems | citta |
| mindstream/mental continuum | rgyud (gyud) | *saṃtāna* |
| mind training | blo sbyong (lo jong) | |
| motivation | kun slong (kun long) | samutpāda |
| music instruments | rol cha | |
| Pacification Tradition | *Zhi byed* (*shi jé*) | |
| patience | bzod pa (zö pa) | *kṣānti* |
| perfection | phar rol tu phyin pa (pha rol tu chin pa) | pāramitā |
| Perfection of Wisdom Sūtra | shes rab kyi phar rol tu phyin pa'i mdo bcom ldan 'das ma'i mdo | Prajñāpāramitā Sūtra |

| | | |
|---|---|---|
| pride | nga rgyal (nga gya) | māna |
| realization | sgrub ba (drub wa) | siddhi |
| renunciation | nges 'byung (ngen jung) | *niḥsaraṇa* |
| ritual cake | *gtor ma* | *balingta* |
| sky burial | *bya gtor* (ja tor) | |
| self | bdag | ātman |
| self-grasping | bdag 'dzin (dag dzin) | ātmagrāha |
| selflessness | bdag med | nairātmya |
| selflessness of persons | gang zag gi bdag med | pudgalanairātmya |
| selflessness of phenomena | chos kyi bdag med pa | dharmanairātmya |
| sentient being | sems can (sem chen) | sattva |
| Stages of the Path Discourses | *Lamrim* | |
| sound | sgra (dra) | shabda |
| suffering | sdug bsngal (dug ngal) | *duḥkha* |
| sūtra discourses by Buddha & disciples | mdo | sūtra |
| three principal paths | lam gyi gtso bo rnam gsum (lam tso nam sum) | |
| transference of consciousness | 'pho ba (pho wa) | |
| transmission/oral transmission | lung | āgama |
| ultimate truth | don dam bden pa (don dam den pa) | paramārthasatya |
| wisdom | shes rab (sherab) | prajñā |

| Terminology | Definition/Explanation |
|---|---|
| "ritual mapping" | The graphic interlayering of "texts" to explore how a moment, or section, of a ritual is made meaningful to the performer/practitioner or listener. The term "texts" is interchangeable with "performance layers" and may refer both to the "inner performance" of mentally-produced visualizations and the "outer performance" of music (vocal melody, mantric utterance, rhythm and instrumentally produced sounds) as symbolic referents. |
| "sonic iconography" | The use of a melody and/or rhythm to conjure up an image that is a symbolically appropriate visualization to that subritual section of the overall ritual dramaturgy. |
| "Teng word-for-word translation" | This facilitates the meditation practice of Chöd for the non-Tibetan speaker across the language barrier because the singer knows what the meaning of each word is while s/he is singing it. |

# Bibliography


Abu-Lughod, Lila. "Writing Against Culture." In *Recapturing Anthropology*, edited by Richard G. Fox. Santa Fe, NM: School of American Research Press, 1991, 137–162.

Agawu, Kofi. "Analyzing Music Under the New Musicological Regime." *The Journal of Musicology* 15, no. 3 (Summer, 1997): 297–307.

Agawu, Kofi. "Tone and Tune: The Evidence for Northern Ewe Music." *Africa* 58, no. 2 (1988).

Allione, Tsultrim. *Women of Wisdom*. London: Routledge and Kegan Paul, 1984.

Arrow, Kenneth J. "Gifts and Exchanges." In *Altruism, Morality, and Economic Theory*, edited by Edmund S. Phelps. New York: Russel Sage Foundation, 1975, 13–28.

Avedon, John F. *In Exile from the Land of Snows*. New York: HarperPerennial, 1997 [1979].

Barthes, Roland. "The Death of the Author." In *Image, Music, Text*, translated by Stephan Heath. New York: Hill and Wang, 1978.

Baumann, Richard. "Verbal Art as Performance." *American Anthropologist* 77, no. 2 (June 1975): 290–311.

Beer, Robert. *The Handbook of Tibetan Buddhist Symbols*. Boston: Shambhala Publications Inc., 2003.

Béhague, Gerard. "Introduction." In *Performance Practice: Ethnomusicological Perspectives*, edited by Gerard Béhague. Westport, CT: Greenwood Press, 1984.

Bell, Catherine. *Ritual: Perspectives and Dimensions*. Oxford: Oxford University Press, 1997.

Bell, Catherine. *Ritual Theory, Ritual Practice*. Oxford: Oxford University Press, 1992.

Bentor, Yael. *Consecration of Images and Stupas in Indo-Tibetan Tantric Buddhsim*. New York: Brill, 1996.

Berger, Harris M. *Metal, Rock, and Jazz: Perception and the Phenomenology of Musical Experience*. Hanover, NH: Wesleyan University Press, 1999.

Bertsch, Wolfgang. 2002. *The Currency of Tibet. A Sourcebook for the Study of Tibetan Coins, Paper Money and other Forms of Currency*, Library of Tibetan Works & Archives: Dharamsala.

Beyer, Stephan V. *The Cult of Tārā: Magic and Ritual in Tibet*. Berkeley, CA: University of California Press, 1973.

Blum, Steven, Philip V. Bohlman, and Daniel M. Neuman, eds. *Ethnomusicology and Modern Music History*. Urbana, IL: University of Illinois Press, 1991, 103–120.

Bohlman, Philip V. *The Study of Folk Music in the Modern World.* Bloomington, IN: Indiana University Press, 1988.

Bock, Philip K. Review: "The Samoan Puberty Blues." In *Journal of Anthropological Research* 39, no. 3 (Autumn, 1983): 336–40.

Bourdieu, Pierre. *The Weight of the World: Social Suffering in Contemporary Society*. Translated by Priscilla Parkhurst Ferguson. Redwood City, CA: Stanford University Press, 1999.

Braitstein, Lara. *Saraha's Adamantine Songs: Texts, Contexts, Translations and Traditions of the Great Seal.* PhD diss. Montreal: McGill University, 2006.

Brefczynski-Leis, A. Lutz, H. S. Schaefer, D. B. Levinson, and R. J. Davidson. *Neural Correlates of Attentional Expertise in Long-Term Meditation Practitioners*, edited by Edward E. Smith. New York: Columbia University, May 29, 2007.

Brown, Gavin. "Theorizing Ritual as Performance: Explorations of Ritual Indeterminancy." *Journal of Ritual Studies* 17, no. 1 (2003): 3–17.

Cabezón, José Ignacio. "On the Nature of the Dialogue." In *Buddhism and Science: Breaking New Ground*, edited by B. Alan Wallace. New York: Columbia University Press, 1997, 35–68.

Canzio, Ricardo. "The Place of Music and Chant in Tibetan Religious Culture." In *Tibetan Studies*, edited by P. Kvaerne, and M. Brauen. Zurich: Volkerkunde Museum der Universitat Zurich, 1978.

Canzio, Ricardo. *Sakya Pandita's "Treatise on Music" and its Relevance to Present-day Tibetan Liturgy.* PhD diss. London: University of London, SOAS, 1978.

Chang, Garma C. C. *Teachings of Tibetan Yoga*, 1963. Reprinted as *The Six Yogas of Naropa.* Ithaca, NY: Snow Lion Publications, 1986, 111–15.

Chang, Garma C. C. *The Hundred Thousand Songs of Mi la ras pa*. New Hyde Park, NY: University Books, 1962.

Chernoff, John Miller. "A Fieldworker's Initiation: African Rhythm and African Sensibility." In *Art in Small-Scale Societies: Contemporary Readings*, edited by Richard L. Anderson, and Karen L. Field. Inglewood Cliffs, NJ: Prentice Hall, 1993, 9–27.

Chernoff, John Miller. *African Rhythm and African Sensibility: Aesthetics and Social Action in African Musical Idioms*. Chicago: University of Chicago Press, 1979.

Clayton, Martin, Trevor Herbert, and Richard Middleton, eds. *The Cultural Study of Music: A Critical Introduction*. London: Routledge, 2003.

Clifford, James, and George E. Marcus, eds. *Writing Culture: The Poetics and Politics of Ethnography*. Berkeley, CA: University of California Press, 1986.

Coombe, Rosemary J. "Fear, Hope and Longing for the Future of Authorship and a Revised Public Domain of Global Regimes of Intellectual Property." *Hein*

*Online De Paul Law Review*, 2002–2003. http://www.google.com/scholar?q=info: NPX73YjYY7AJ:scholar.google.com/&hl=en&lr=&output=viewport&shm=1 [accessed December 4, 2006].

Coombe, Rosemary J. *The Cultural Life of Intellectual Properties: Authorship, Appropriation and the Law*. Durham, NC: Duke University Press, 1998.

Conze, E., trans. *The Perfection of Wisdom in 8,000 Lines and its Verse Summary*. Bolinas, CA: Four Seasons, 1973.

Cozort, Daniel. "Sādhana (*sGrub thabs*): Means of Achievement for Deity Yoga." In *Tibetan Literature: Studies in Genre*, edited by José Ignacio Cabezón and Roger Jackson. Ithaca, NY: Snow Lion Publications, 1996, 331–43.

Cozort, Daniel. *Highest Yoga Tantra*. Ithaca, NY: Snow Lion Publications, 1986.

Crook, John, and James Low. "Practicing *Chöd* in the Cemeteries of Ladakh." In *The Yogins of Ladakh: A Pilgrimage Among the Hermits of the Buddhist Himalayas*, 292–333. Delhi, India: Motilal Banarsidass, 1997.

Crossley-Holland, Peter. *Musical Instruments in Tibetan Legend and Folklore*. Los Angeles: University of California at Los Angeles, 1986.

Crossley-Holland, Pete. "The State of Research in Tibetan Folk Music." In *Zlos Gar: Performing Traditions of Tibet*, edited by Jamyang Norbu. Dharamsala, H.P., India: Library of Tibetan Works & Archives, 1986, 105–24.

Csikszentmihalyi, Mihaly. *Optimal Experience: Psychological Studies of Flow in Consciousness*. New York: Cambridge University Press, 1988.

Cumming, Naomi. *The Sonic Self: Musical Subjectivity and Signification*. Bloomington, IN: Indiana University Press, 2001.

Cupchik, Jeffrey W. "Melodies for Dissolving the Self: Tibetan Songs of Meditative Experience. *Journal of Musicological Research*. (forthcoming).

Cupchik, Jeffrey W. "Buddhism As Performing Art: Visualizing Music in the Tibetan Buddhist Ritual Music Liturgies." *Yale Journal of Music & Religion*, vol. 1, no. 1, article 4 (2015), 31–62. DOI: https://doi.org/10.17132/2377-231X.1010

Cupchik, Jeffrey W. "The Tibetan *gCod Ḍamaru*—A Reprise: Symbolism, Function and Difference in a Tibetan Adept's Interpretive Community." *Asian Music* 44, no. 1 (Winter/Spring January 2013): 113–39.

Cupchik, Jeffrey W. *(Dis)embodied Ethics: The Transcultural Translation of Tibetan Buddhist Tantric Chöd Ritual*. Presented at the York Centre for Asian Research, York University, Toronto, Canada, 2005.

Dalton, Jacob P. *The Taming of the Demons: Violence and Liberation in Tibetan Buddhism*. New Haven: Yale University Press, 2011.

David-Neel, Alexandra. *Magic and Mystery in Tibet*. Baltimore, MD: Penguin Books, 1971 [1929].

Davidson, Richard J., and Anne Harrington, eds. *Visions of Compassion: Western Scientists and Tibetan Buddhists Examine Human Nature*. New York: Oxford University Press, 2002.

Davidson, Ronald M. *Tibetan Renaissance: Tantric Buddhism in the Rebirth of Tibetan Culture*. New York: Columbia University Press, 2005.

Davis, Natalie Zemon. *The Gift in Sixteenth-Century France*. Madison: University of Wisconsin Press, 2000.

Derrida, Jacques. *Given Time*. Translated by Peggy Kamuf. Chicago: University of Chicago Press, 1992.

Desideri, Ippolito. *An Account of Tibet: The Travels of Ippolito Desideri of Pistoia, 1712–1727*, edited by Filippo de Filippi. Taipei: Ch'eng Wen, 1971.

Devereux, George. *Some Uses of Anthropology: Theoretical and Applied*. Washington, DC: The Anthropological Society of Washington, 1956.

Diehl, Keila. *Echoes from Dharamsala: Music in the Life of a Refugee Community*. Berkeley, CA: University of California Press, 2002.

Diprose, Rosalyn. *Corporeal Generosity: On Giving with Nietzsche, Merleau-Ponty, and Levinas*. Albany, NY: SUNY Press, 2002.

Dorjé, Gyurme. *Tibetan Book of the Dead*. New York: Penguin Group, 2007.

Dorjé, Rinjing, and Ter Ellingson. " 'Explanation of the Secret *Gcod Ḍamaru*: An Exploration of Musical Instrument Symbolism." *Asian Music* Tibet Issue 10, no. 2 (1979): 63–91.

Douglas, Mary. "Foreword." In Marcel, Mauss, *Essai sur le don* or *The Gift: The Form and Reason for Exchange in Archaic Societies*. New York: W. W. Norton & Company, 1990 [First Published 1925], ix.

Durkheim, Emile. *The Elementary Forms of Religious Life*. Translated by Karen E. Fields. New York: The Free Press, 1995.

Egyed, Alice. *Theory and Practice of Music in a Tibetan Buddhist Monastic Tradition*. PhD diss. Seattle: University of Washington, 2000.

Eliade, Mircea. *Shamanism: Archaic Techniques of Ecstasy*. Translated by Willard R. Trask. Princeton, NJ: Princeton University Press, 1964.

Edou, Jérôme. *Machig Labdrön and the Foundations of Chöd*. Ithaca, NY: Snow Lion Publications, 1996.

Ellingson, Ter. "On Transcription." In *Ethnomusicology: An Introduction*, edited by Helen Myers. New York: W. W. Norton, 1992, 110–151.

Ellingson, Ter. "Indian Influences in Tibetan Music." In *Sacred Music, The World of Music: Journal of the International Institute for Comparative Music Studies and Documentation in Association with the International Music Council*. Amsterdam: Heinrichshofen's Verlag. *UNESCO* 24, no. 3 (1982): 85–90.

Ellingson, Ter. "Review Essay: Four Tibetan Recordings." *Asian Music* 23, no. 2 (1981): 133–151.

Ellingson, Ter. *The Mandala of Sound: Concepts and Sound Structures in Tibetan Ritual Music*. PhD diss. Madison: University of Wisconsin, 1979.

Ellis, Catherine J. *Aboriginal Music, Education for Living: Cross-cultural Experiences from South Australia*. St. Lucia, Qld: University of Queensland Press, 1985.

Ellis, Catherine J. *Program of Training in Music for South Australian Aboriginal People*. Adelaide: University of Adelaide, 1971.

Erickson, Paul A., and Liam D. Murphy. *A History of Anthropological Theory*. Peterborough, ONT: Broadview Press, 2003.

Evans-Wentz, W. Y. "The Path of Mystic Sacrifice: The *Yoga* of Subduing the Lower Self." In *Tibetan Yoga and Secret Doctrines* or, *Seven Books of Wisdom of the Great Path, According to the Late Lama Kazi Dawa-Samdup's English rendering.* London: Oxford University Press, 1958 [Republished by Donald S. Lopez, 2000]. 277–300.

Everett, Paul. *Vivaldi: The Four Seasons and Other Concertos, Op. 8.* New York: Cambridge University Press, 1996). 82–85.

Feld, Steven. "Aesthetics as Iconicity of Style, or 'Lift-up-over Sounding': Getting into the *Kaluli* Groove." *Yearbook for Traditional Music* 20 (1988): 74–133.

Feld, Steven. "Sound Structure as Social Structure." *Ethnomusicology* 28, no. 3 (September, 1984): 383–409.

Feld, Steven. *Sound and Sentiment: Birds, Weeping, Poetics and Song in Khaluli Expression*. Philadelphia: University of Pennsylvania Press, 1982.

Fish, Stanley. *Is There a Text in This Class?: The Authority of Interpretive Communities.* Cambridge, MA: Harvard University Press, 1980.

Freidson, Steven. (Review) *The Performance of Healing* by Carol Laderman and Marina Roseman. *Asian Music* 28, no. 2 (Spring, 1997): 137.

Freidson, Steven. *Dancing Prophets: Musical Experiences in Tumbuka Healing.* Chicago: Chicago Studies in Ethnomusicology, 1996.

Frith, Simon. *Performing Rites: On the Value of Popular Music.* Cambridge, MA: Harvard University Press, 1996.

Geertz, Clifford. "Thick Description: Toward an Interpretive Theory of Culture." In *The Interpretation of Cultures: Selected Essays.* New York: Basic Books, 1973, 3–30.

Goffman, Erving. *The Presentation of Self in Everyday Life.* New York: Doubleday, 1959.

Goldstein, Melvyn C., and Matthew T. Kapstein, eds. *Buddhism in Contemporary Tibet: Religious Revival and Cultural Identity.* Berkeley: University of California Press, 1998.

'Gos lo tsa ba Gzhon nu dpal. *Bod kyi yil du chos dang chos smra ba ji ltar byung ba'i rim pa deb ther sngon po*, "The Blue Annals." Translated by George N. Roerich. Calcutta: Royal Asiatic Society of Bengal Monograph Series, VII, 1953 [1949].

Grimes, Ronald. *Beginnings in Ritual Studies.* Waterloo, ONT: Wilfred Laurier University, 2007 [3rd ed.], 24–26. www.wlu.ca/documents/18751/grimes,_beginnings_in_ritual_studies,_3rd_edApril2007.pdf [accessed December 7, 2007].

Gross, Rita. *Buddhism After Patriarchy: a Feminist History, Analysis and Reconstruction of Buddhism.* Albany, NY: SUNY Press, 1993.

Guenther, Herbert V., trans., and ed. *The Royal Song of Saraha: A Study in the History of Buddhist Thought.* Berkeley, CA: Shambala Publications, Inc., 1968.

Gutschow, Kim. *Being a Buddhist Nun: The Struggle for Enlightenment in the Himalayas.* Cambridge, MA: Harvard University Press, 2004.

Gyatso, Janet. *Apparitions of the Self: The Secret Autobiographies of a Tibetan Visionary.* Princeton, NJ: Princeton University Press, 1998.

Gyatso, Janet. "The Development of the Gcod Tradition." In *Soundings in Tibetan Civilization*, edited by Barbara Nimri Aziz, and Matthew Kapstein. New Delhi: Manohar Publications, 1985, 320–41.

Gyatso, Tenzin. *Essence of the Heart Sutra: The Dalai Lama's Heart of Wisdom Teachings.* Boston: Wisdom Publications, 2005, 34.

Gyatso, Tenzin. *The Universe in a Single Atom: The Convergence of Science and Spirituality.* New York: Broadway Books, 2005.

Gyatso, Tenzin. *The World of Tibetan Buddhism: An Overview of Its Philosophy and Practice.* Translated, edited, and annotated by Geshé Thupten Jinpa. Boston: Wisdom Publications, 1995.

Harding, Sarah, trans. *Machik's Complete Explanation: Clarifying the Meaning of Chöd, a Complete Explanation of Casting Out the Body as Food.* Ithaca, NY: Snow Lion Publications, 2003.

Harvey, Peter. *An Introduction to Buddhism: Teachings, History and Practices.* Cambridge, MA: Cambridge University Press, 1990.

Hattan, Robert S. *Musical Meaning in Beethoven: Markedness, Correlation and Interpretation.* Bloomington: Indiana University Press, 2004.

Hayward, Jeremy W., and Francisco J. Varela, eds. *Gentle Bridges: Conversations with the Dalai Lama on the Sciences of Mind.* Boston: Shambhala Publications Inc., 1992.

Helffer, Mireille. *Mchod-rol: Les instruments de la musique tibétaine.* Paris: CNRS Editions/Editions de la Maison des Sciences de l'Homme de Paris, 1994.

Helffer, Mireille. "An Overview of Western Work on Ritual Music of Tibetan Buddhism (1960–1990)." In *European Studies in Ethnomusicology: Historical Developments and Recent Trends. Selected Papers Presented at the VIIth European Seminar in Ethnomusicolog, Berlin, October 1–6*, edited by Max Peter Baumann, Artur Simon, and Ulrich Wegner [ed. by International Institute for Traditional Music, Berlin]. Wilhelmshaven: Florian Noetzel Verlag, 1992, 87–101.

Helffer, Mireille. "A Typology of the Tibetan Bell." In *Soundings in Tibetan Civilization*, edited by Barbara Nimri Aziz, and Matthew Kapstein. New Delhi: Manohar Publications, 1985, 37–41.

Hobsbawn, Eric, and Terrance Ranger. *The Invention of Tradition.* New York: Cambridge University Press, 1984.

Hopkins, Jeffrey, ed., and trans. *The Yoga of Tibet: The Great Exposition of Secret Mantra—2 and 3 by Tsong-ka-pa.* Boston: George Allen and Unwin, 1981.

Hood, Mantle. *The Ethnomusicologist.* New York: McGraw-Hill, 1971.

Hood, Mantle, "The Challenge of Bi-musicality." *Ethnomusicology* 4 (1960): 55–59.

Hornbostel, Erich M. von, and Curt Sachs. *Classification of Musical Instruments: Translated from the Original German by Anthony Baines and Klauss P.* Wachsmann. Oxford: The Galpin Society Journal, 1961, 3–29.

Hyer, Brian. "Homophony." In *Grove Music Online. Oxford Music Online*, http://www.oxfordmusiconline.com/subscriber/article/grove/music/13291 [accessed April 27, 2009].

Irigaray, Luce. *To Be Two.* New York: Routledge, 2000.

Jackson, Roger R. " 'Poetry in Tibet: Glu, mgur, sNyan ngag and 'Songs of Experience.' " In *Tibetan Literature: Studies in Genre*, edited by José Ignacio Cabezón, and Roger Jackson. Ithaca, NY: Snow Lion Publications, 1996, 368–92.

Jinpa, Geshé Thupten. *Institute of Tibetan Classics.* http://www.tibetanclassics.org/doctrines1.html [accessed June 4, 2018].

Jinpa, Thupten. 2015. *A Fearless Heart: How the Courage to be Compassionate can Transform Our Lives.* Avery: New York.

Jinpa, Thupten. "Science as an Ally or a Rival Philosophy. Tibetan Buddhist Thinkers' Engagement with Modern Science." In *Buddhism and Science: Breaking New Ground.* New York: Columbia University Press, 2003, 71–86.

Jinpa, Thupten, and Jaś Elsner. *Songs of Spiritual Experience: Tibetan Buddhist Poems of Insight and Awakening.* Boston: Shambhala Publications Inc., 2000.

Juergensmeyer, Mark. "Home and Belonging: Meaning, Images, and Contexts." In *The Postnational Self: Belonging and Identity*, edited by Ulf Hedetoft and Mette Hjort. London: University of Minnesota Press, 2002.

Karmay, Samten. *The Arrow and the Spindle: Studies in History, Myths, Rituals and Beliefs in Tibet.* Kathmandu, Nepal: Mandala Book Print, 1998.

Kaufmann, Walter. *Tibetan Buddhist Chant: Musical Notations and Interpretations of a Song Book by the Bka' brgyud pa and Sa skya pa sects.* Bloomington: Indiana University Press, 1975.

Keil, Charles, and Steven Feld. *Music Grooves: Essays and Dialogues.* Chicago: University of Chicago Press, 1994. A second edition was published by Fenestra in 2005.

Kippen, James. *The Tabla of Lucknow: A Cultural Analysis of a Musical Tradition.* Cambridge, MA: Cambridge University Press, 1988.

Klein, Anne-Carolyn. *Meeting the Great Bliss Queen: Buddhism, Feminism and the Art of the Self.* Boston: Beacon Press, 1995.

Kleinman, Arthur. *Patients and Healers in the Context of Cutlure.* Berkeley: University of California Press, 1980.

Knopoff, Steven. "What is Music Analysis? Problems and Prospects for Understanding Aboriginal Songs and Performance." *Australian Aboriginal Studies*, no. 1 (Spring 2003): 39–58.

Kollmar-Paulenz, Karenina. "Khros ma nag mo, The 'Wrathful Black One' and the Deities Summoned to the Ritual Feast in the *Gcod* Tradition of Tibetan Buddhism: A Premliminary Survey of the *Gcod* Demonology." *Zentralasiatische Studien* 34 (2005): 209–30.

Kollmar-Paulenz, Karénina. "Ma gcig Lab sgron ma—The Life of a Tibetan Woman Mystic between Adaptation and Rebellion." *The Tibet Journal*, xxiii, no. 2, (Summer, 1998): 11–32.

Laderman, Carol, and Marina Roseman, eds. *The Performance of Healing.* New York: Routledge, 1996.

Lassiter, Luke Eric. *The Chicago Guide to Collaborative Ethnography.* Chicago: Chicago University Press, 2005.

Lassiter, Luke Eric. *The Power of Kiowa Song: A Collaborative Ethnography.* University of Arizona Press, 1998.

Lears, T. J. Jackson. "Preface" and "Roots of Antimodernism: The Crisis of Cultural Authority During the Late Nineteenth Century." In *No Place of Grace: Antimodernism and the Transformation of American Culture, 1880–1920.* Chicago: University of Chicago Press, 1983.

Lessing, Ferdinand. *Yung-ho-kung: An Iconography of the Lamaist Cathedral in Peking.* Stockholm: Reports from the Scientific Expedition to the North-western Provinces of China under the Leadership of Dr. Sven Hedin, XVIII, 1942.

Lévi-Strauss, Claude. *Structural Anthropology.* New York: Anchor Books, 1967.

Levinas, Emmanuel. *Otherwise Than Being or Beyond Essence*, translated by Alphonso Lingis. Pittsburgh, Pennsylvania: Duzqesne University Press 1998 [1981, 3rd ed.].

Lidov, David. "The Mind in the Body." *Semiotica* 66, no. 1 (1987): 70–97.

Lin, Yutang. *Chod in Limitless-Oneness.* El Cerito, CA: California, 1996. For private distribution only.

Lomax, Alan. *Folk Song Style and Culture.* New Brunswick, NJ: Transaction Books, 1968.

Lopez, Donald S., Jr. *The Madman's Middle Way: Reflections on Reality of the Tibetan Monk Gendun Chopel.* Chicago: Universtiy of Chicago Press, 2006.

Lopez, Donald S., Jr., ed. *A Modern Buddhist Bible: Essential Readings from East and West.* Boston: Beacon Press 2002.

Lopez, Donald S., Jr. "A Prayer to the Lama." In *Religions of Tibet in Practice*, edited by Donald S. Lopez, Jr. Princeton, NJ: Princeton University Press, 1997, 376–86.

Lopez, Donald S., Jr. "Foreigner at the Lama's Feet." In *Curators of the Buddha: The Study of Buddhism under Colonialism*, edited by Donald S. Lopez, Jr. Chicago: University of Chicago Press, 1995, 251–96.

Lopez, Donald S., Jr. "Inscribing the Bodhisattva's Speech: On the 'Heart Sūtra's' Mantra." *History of Religions* 29, no. 4 (May, 1990): 351–72.

Martin, Dan. "On the Cultural Ecology of Sky Burial on the Himalayan Plateau." *East and West* 46 (1997): 353–70.

Mauss, Marcel. *Essai sur le don* or *The Gift: The Form and Reason for Exchange in Archaic Societies*, translated by W. D. Halls and foreword by Mary Douglas. New York: W. W. Norton & Company, 1990 [First Published 1925].

Mead, Margaret. *Coming of Age in Samoa: A Psychological Study of Primitive Youth for Western Civilization.* New York: W. Morrow & Company, 1928.

Merriam, Alan. *The Anthropology of Music.* Evanston, IL: Northwestern University Press, 1964.

Mullin, Glenn. *The Seventh Dalai Lama's Songs of Spiritual Change*. Ithaca, NY: Gabriel/Snow Lion Publications, 1982 [Reprinted, 1985].

Myers, Helen, ed. *Ethnomusicology: An Introduction*. New York: W. W. Norton & Company, 1992.

Nebesky-Wojkowitz, René de. *Oracles and Demons of Tibet: The Cult and Iconography of the Tibetan Protective Deities*. Graz, Austria: Akademische Druck-u. Verlagsanstalt, 1975.

Nettl, Bruno. *The Study of Ethnomusicology: Thirty-One Issues and Concepts*. Chicago: University of Illinois Press, 2005 [1983].

Nettl, Bruno, and Philip V. Bohlman, eds. *Comparative Musicology and Anthropology of Music: Essays on the History of Ethnomusicology*. Chicago: University of Chicago Press, 1991.

Neuman, Daniel M. *The Life of Music in North India: The Organization of an Artistic Tradition*. Chicago: University of Chicago Press, 1990.

Norbu, Jamyang. "Introduction." In *Zlosgar: Performing Traditions of Tibet. Commemorative Issue on the Cccasion of the 25th Anniversary of the Founding of the Tibetan Institute of Performing Arts 1959–84*. Dharamsala, H.P., India: Library of Tibetan Works & Archives, c. 1986.

Orofino, Giacomella. "The Great Wisdom Mother and the Gcod Tradition." In *Tantra in Practice*, edited by David Gordon White. Princeton, NJ: Princeton University Press, 2000, 396–416.

Orsi, Robert A. "The Gender of Religious Otherness," keynote essay. *ISAE Bulletin* 3 (Winter 1999). www.wheaton.edu/isae/Women/Orsiessay99.html [accessed: June 12, 2008].

Orsi, Robert A. *Thank You, St. Jude: Women's Devotion to the Patron Saint of Hopeless Causes*. New Haven, CT: Yale University Press, 1998.

Pollock, Sheldon. "Deep Orientalism: Notes on Sanskrit and Power Beyond the Raj." In *Orientalism and the Postcolonial Predicament: Perspectives on South Asia*, edited by Carol Brekenridge, and Peter van der Veer. Philadelphia: University of Pennsylvania Press, 1988, 76–133.

Powers, John. *Introduction to Tibetan Buddhism*. Ithaca, NY: Snow Lion Publications, 1995.

Qureshi, Regula Burckhardt. "Sufi Music and the Historicity of Oral Tradition." In *Ethnomusicology and Modern Music History*, edited by Stephen Blum, Philip V. Bohlman, and Daniel M. Neuman. Urbana, IL: University of Illinois Press, 1991, 103–20.

Qureshi, Regula Burckhardt. *Sufi Music in India and Pakistan: Sound, Context and Meaning in Qawwali*. Oxford: Oxford University Press, 1996 [1987].

Rabten, Geshé, and Geshé Ngawang Dhargyey. "Changing Adverse Circumstances into the Path." In *Advice from a Spiritual Friend: Buddhist Thought Transformation*, edited by Brian Beresford. New Delhi: Nepal Mahayana Gompa Centre, Inc., 1977.

Rapport, Nigel, and Joanna Overing. *Social and Cultural Anthropology: The Key Concepts*. London: Routledge, 2000.

Rinbochay, Lati, and Jeffrey Hopkins. *Death Intermediate State, and Rebirth in Tibetan Buddhism*. Ithaca, NY: Snow Lion Publications, 1980.

Ringer, Alexander. "Melody," *Grove Music Online*, edited by L. Macy, http://www.grovemusic.com [accessed September 17, 2007].

Rinpoché, Zong. *Chöd in the Ganden Tradition: The Oral Instructions of Kyabje Zong Rinpoché*, edited by David Molk. Ithaca, NY: Snow Lion Publications, 2006.

Rinpoché, Pabongka. *Liberation in our Hands Part Two: The Fundamentals*, translated by Sera Mey Geshé Lobsang Tharchin with Artemus B. Engle. Howell, NJ: Mahayana Sutra and Tantra Press, 1994.

Roerich, George N. *The Blue Annals*. Calcutta: Royal Asiatic Society of Bengal, 1953 [1949], Vol. II, 843 ff.

Roseman, Marina. *Healing Sounds from the Malaysian Rainforest.* Berkeley, CA: University of California Press, 1991.

Roseman, Marina. "The Social Structuring of Sound: The Temiar of Peninsular Malaysia." *Ethnomusicology* 28, no. 3 (September, 1984): 411–45.

Rosen, Joseph. "From a Memory beyond Memory to a State beyond the State." In *Difficult Justice: Commentaries on Levinas and Politics*, edited by Asher Horowitz, and Gad Horowitz. Toronto: University of Toronto Press, 1996.

Rouget, Gilbert. *Music and Trance: A Theory of the Relations Between Music and Possession*. Chicago: University Of Chicago, 1985.

Sachs, Curt. *The History of Musical Instruments*. New York: Dover Publications, Inc. 2006 [1940], 158–59.

Said, Edward. *Orientalism*. New York: Pantheon Books, 1978.

Samuel, Geoffrey. *Civilized Shamans: Buddhism in Tibetan Societies*. Washington DC: Smithsonian Institution Press, 1993.

Samuel, Geoffrey. *Mind, Body and Culture: Anthropology and the Biological Interface*. Cambridge, MA: Cambridge University Press, 1990.

Savvas, Carol. *A Study of the Profound Path of Gcod: The Mahāyāna Buddhist Meditation Tradition of Tibet's Great Woman Saint Machig Labdrön*. PhD diss. Madison: University of Wisconsin–Madison, 1990.

Schechner, Richard. *The Future of Ritual: Writings on Culture and Performance.* New York: Routledge, 1993.

Schechner, Richard. "Preface." In Victor Turner, *The Anthropology of Performance.* New York: PAJ Publications, 1988.

Scheidegger, Daniel A. *Tibetan Ritual Music: A General Survey with Special Reference to the Mindroling Tradition*. Zurich: Tibetan Institute, 1988.

Schieffelin, Edward. "Problematizing Performance." In *Ritual, Performance, Media*, edited by F. Hughes-Freeland. London: Routledge, 1998, 194–207.

Schieffelin, Edward. "On Failure and Performance." In *The Performance of Healing*, edited by Carol Laderman, and Marina Roseman. London: Routledge, 1996, 59–89.

Schieffelin, Edward. "Performance and the Cultural Construction of Reality." *American Ethnologist* 12 (1985): 707–24.

Schrift, Alan D. "On the Gift-Giving Virtue: Nietzsche's Unacknowledged Feminism." Translated by Hazel E. Barnes. *International Studies in Philosophy* 26, no. 3 (1994): 33–44.

Seeger, Anthony. *Why Suyá Sing: A Musical Anthropology of an Amazonian People*. New York: Cambridge University Press, 1987.

Seeger, Charles. "Prescriptive and Descriptive Music-Writing." *The Musical Quarterly* 44, no. 2 (April 1958): 185–95.

Śāntideva. *Bodhicaryāvatāra* "Guide to the Bodhisattva's Way of Life" Byang chub sems pa'i spyod pa la 'jug pa, P5272, vol. 99. In *A Guide to the Bodhisattva's Way of Life*, translated by Stephen Batchelor. Dharamsala: Library of Tibetan Works and Archives, 1979.

Shelemay, Kay Kaufman. "The Ethnomusicologist, Ethnographic Method, and the Transmission of Tradition." In *Shadows in the Field: New Perspectives for Fieldwork in Ethnomusicology*, edited by Gregory F. Barz and Timothy J. Cooley. New York: Oxford University Press, 1997, 189–204.

Shelemay, Kay Kaufman. "The Ethnomusicologist and the Transmission of Tradition." *The Journal of Musicology* 14, no. 1 (Winter, 1996): 35–51.

Simmer-Brown, Judith. *Ḍākinī's Warm Breath: The Feminine Principle in Tibetan Buddhism*. Boston: Shambhala Publications, Inc., 2004.

Slobin, Mark. *Subcultural Sounds: Micromusics of the West*. Hanover, NH: Wesleyan University Press, 1993.

Snellgrove, David L. *Buddhist Himalaya: Travels and Studies in Quest of the Origins and Nature of Tibetan Religion*. New York: Philosophical Library, 1957.

Sorensen, Michelle Janet. "Making the Old New Again and Again: Legitimation and Innovation in the Tibetan Buddhist Chöd Tradition." PhD diss., Columbia University, 2013.

Spradley, James P. *The Ethnographic Interview*. New York: Holt, Rinehart and Winston, 1979.

Sugarman, Jane C. *Engendering Song: Singing and Subjectivity at Prespa Albanian Weddings*. Chicago: University of Chicago Press, 1992.

Sujata, Victoria. *Tibetan Songs of Realization: Echoes from a Seventeenth-Century Scholar and Siddha in Amdo*. Leiden: Brill Academic Publications, 2005.

Sullivan, Lawrence E., ed. *Enchanting Powers: Music in the World's Religions*. Cambridge, MA: Harvard Center for the Study of the World's Religions, 1997.

Taussig, Michael. *Shamanism, Colonialism and the Wild Man*. Chicago: University of Chicago Press, 1987.

Tharchin, Sermey Khensur Lobsang. *The Key to the Treasury of Shunyata: Dependent Arising and Emptiness*. Howell, NJ: Mahayana Sutra and Tantra Press, 2002, 312–15.

Tharchin, Sermey Geshé Lobsang. *Achieving Bodhicitta: Instructions of Two Great Lineages Combined into a Unique System of Eleven Categories*. Howell, NJ: Mahayana Sutra and Tantra Press, 1999, 86–98.

Thompson, Evan. "Empathy and Consciousness." In *Between Ourselves, Second Person Issues in the Study of Consciousness*, edited by Evan Thompson. Charlottesville, VA: Imprint Academic, 2001, 1–32.

Thurman, Robert A. F. *Essential Tibetan Buddhism*. San Francisco: Harper-San Francisco, 1995.

Titmuss, Richard. *The Gift Relationship: From Human Blood to Social Policy*. London: George Allyn & Unwin, 1971.

Tsong-Kha-Pa, Je, Joshua W. C. Cutler and Lamrim Chenmo Translation Committee. *The Great Treatise on the Stages of the Path to Enlightenment; The Lamrim Chenmo*, Vol. 1. Ithaca, NY: Snow Lion Publications, 2000.

Tsongkhapa, Je. *In Praise of Dependent Origination* (*rten 'brel bstod pa*). Translated from the Tibetan by Geshé Thupten Jinpa. *Institute of Tibetan Classics*. https://tibetanclassics.org/wp-content/uploads/2020/09/In-Praise-of-Dependent-Origination.pdf [Accessed June 25 2021].

Tsongkhapa. *The Three Principal Aspects of the Path, lam gyi gtso bo rnam pa gsum*. translated by Geshé Thupten Jinpa. Montreal: Institute of Tibetan Classics, 2003.

Tucci, Giuseppe. *The Religions of Tibet*. London: Routledge & Kegan Paul, Ltd., 1980, 87–92.

Tucci, Giuseppe. *Tibetan Painted Scrolls*. Roma: Liberiea dello Stato, 1949.

Turner, Victor. *The Anthropology of Performance*. Maryland: PAJ Productions, 1987.

Turner, Victor. *From Ritual to Theatre: The Human Seriousness of Play*. New York: Performing Arts Journal Publications, 1982, 89–101.

Turner, Victor. *Dramas Fields and Metaphors: Symbolic Action in Human Society*. Ithaca, NY: Cornell University Press, 1974.

Turner, Victor. *The Forest of Symbols: Aspects of Ndembu Ritual*. Ithaca, NY: Cornel University Press, 1967.

Tylor, Edward B. *Primitive Culture: Researches into the Development of Mythology, Philosophy, Religion, Art and Custom*. London: John Murray, 1871.

Van Dijk, Teun. "Principles of Critical Discourse Analysis." *Discourse and Society* 4, no. 2 (1993): 249–83.

Vandoor, Ivan. *Bouddhisme Tibetain*. Buchet/Chastel, 1976.

Van Maanen, John. *Tales of the Field: On Writing Ethnography*. Chicago: University of Chicago Press, 1988.

Wallace, Alan. "Intersubjectivity in Indo-Tibetan Buddhism." *Journal of Consciousness Studies* 8, no. 5–7 (2001): 209–30.

Wallace, Vesna A. "A Generation of Power Through Ritual Protection and Transformation of Identity in Indian Tantric Buddhism." *Journal of Ritual Studies* 19, no. 1 (2005): 115–28.

Wang, Eugene. *Shaping the Lotus Sutra: Buddhist Visual Culture in Medieval China.* Seattle: University of Washington Press, 2005.

Williams, Paul. *Mahāyāna Buddhism: The Doctrinal Foundations.* London: Routledge, 1991.

Will, Udo. "Et quand ils n'en disent rien?" ("And what if they say nothing?"). *Cahiers de Musiques Traditionelles* 12 (Georg: Geneve, 1998), 175–85.

Willis, Janice D. *Enlightened Beings: Life Stories from the Ganden Oral Tradition.* Boston: Wisdom Publications, 1995.

Willis, Janice. *Feminine Ground: Essays on the Lives of Buddhist Women.* Ithaca, NY: Snow Lion Publications, 1990.

Wylie, Turrell V. "A Standard System of Tibetan Transcription." *Harvard Journal of Asiatic Studies* 22 (1959): 261–67.

Yeshe, Lama Thubten. *The Tantric Path of Purification.* Boston: Wisdom Publications, 1995.

Yeshe, Lama Thubten. *Introduction to Tantra*, edited by Johathan Landaw. Boston: Wisdom Publications, 1987.

Zammito, John H. *Kant, Herder The Birth of Anthropology.* Chicago: University of Chicago Press, 2002.

Zopa, Lama, and Kathleen McDonald. *Cutting Off the Truly-Existent "I": Dedicating the Illusory Body.* Boston: Wisdom Publications, 1983) English translation of Pabongka Bde chen snying po, *sGyu lus tshogs su sngo ba*, "Dedicating the Illusory Body as a Heaped Offering." Private collection of Pencho Rabgey, Canada.

## Tibetan Sources

Blo bzang Skal bzang Rgya mtsho, *Chos rgyal chen po'i gsol kha lhun grub bde chen ma.* In *Gnas chung Chos spyod.* Gangtok: S.T. Kazi, n.d., 1969, 101. Quoted in Rinjing Dorjé and Ter Ellingson, " 'Explanation of the Secret *Gcod Ḍamaru*' an Exploration of Musical Instrument Symbolism," in *Asian Music*, 10, no. 2 Tibet Issue (1979): 76.

His Eminence Khalkha Jetsun Dampa Rinpoché, *Commnetary to the Cycle of Initiations Given at Gaden Choling*, December 26, 1995–January 2, 1996. Transcribed by Julia Milton. Private copy of Chuck Damov.

Khe grub rje (mgkhas grub thams cad mkhyen pa), rnam thar mkhas pa'i yid 'phrog ces bya ba, pp. 5–31 in *mkhas grub thams cad mkhyen pa dge legs dpal bzang po'I gsung 'bum*, vol. *ka*, p. 14. Quoted from Savvas, 1990, 302–303.

Pa' wo rdo rje, *gcod kyi khrid rje btsun 'jam dbyangs kyi gsung bzhin in Gcod Tshogs*, 181–90.

Śāntideva, *Bodhicaryāvatāra* "Guide to the Bodhisattva's Way of Life" Byang chub sems pa'i spyod pa la 'jug pa, P5272, vol. 99. In *A Guide to the Bodhisattva's Way of Life*, translated by Stephen Batchelor, Dharamsala: Library of Tibetan Works and Archives, 1979.

Slo dpon 'Jam dpal bshes gnyen gyis mdzad pa'i gcod khrid skal ldan 'jug ngogs chung ba, in gcod tshogs, 108.

Tsongkhapa, "*Great Exposition of Secret Mantra*" *Sngags rim chen mo*, Collected works, vol. ga (3). In *Tantra in Tibet*, English Translation of the first two sections by Jeffrey Hopkins. London: George Allen & Unwin, 1977.

## Commentaries

Blo bzang chos kyi rgyal mtshan (The First Panchen Lama), *Gcod kyi gdams pa thar 'dod ded dpon*, "The Guide to Those Who Wish for Liberation." In *Dga ldan snyan brgyud kyi gcod kyi gdams pa'i skor:* A Collection of texts of the Gelugpa tradition on the *Gcod* practice transmitted in the *Dben sa snyan brgyud* lineage of Bkra shri lhun po, by Bka' chen blo bzang bzod pa (The Collected Works of Bka' chen Blo bzang bzod pa), vol. IV. Delhi: Dorjée Tsering, 1985, 105–38.

Grup bang Blo bsang rnam rgyal, *gcod gzbung thar 'dod ded dpon ma'i cho ga don gsal bar ston pa'i nyams len gsal ba'i sgron me*. Lamp Illuminating the Ritual Practice of the *Gcod* Scripture: Guide for Those Seeking Liberation. (Manuscript in private collection of Ven. Zong Rinpoché Tenzin Wangdag, Zong Labrang, Mundgod, India.)

Kar ma phrin las pas, *Do-ha skor gsum-kyi ti ka sems-kyi rnam-thar ston-pai' me long* cited in Herbert Guenther, *The Royal Song of Saraha*, 16.

Ma gcig lab sgron, *Phung po gzan bskyur kyi rnam bshad gcod kyi don gsal*, in gcod kyi chos skor. New Delhi, Tibet House, 1974.

Tsong kha pa blo bzang grags pa, *Zab lam gcod kyi khrid yig ma ti bha dra kirti sbyar ba* "The Profound Path, A Textual Commentary on Gcod," in *Gcod Tshogs: The Collected Gcod Teachings of the Gelukpa Tradition.* Dharamsala: Library of Tibetan Works and Archives, 1986, 1–48. Translated by Carol Savvas. "A Study of the Profound Path of gCod: The Mahāyāna Buddhist Meditation Tradition of Tibet's Great Woman Saint Machig Labdrön." PhD diss. Madison: University of Wisconsin–Madison, 1990, 308–98.

Tsong kha pa blo bzang grags pa, *Zab lam gcod kyi khrid yig* (*A Commentary on the Profound path of Gcod*), in *Gcod Tshogs. The Collected Gcod Teaching of the Gelugpa Tradition by Ma ti bha dra Kirti, Blo bzang don ldan and others.* Dharamsala: Library of Tibetan Works and Archives, 1986.

Za sep trul sku rin po che, "Discourse on *'pho ba* practice," Gaden Choling Mahāyāna Buddhist Meditation Center, February 2006.

### Sādhana

Pha bong kha pa bde chen snying po, *sGyu lus tshogs su sngo ba*, "Dedicating the Illusory Body as a Heaped Offering." Manuscript in private collection of Ven. Pencho Rabgey, Kawartha Lakes, Ontario, Canada.

*Bdag 'dzin tshar gcod tshul gyi gcod dmar 'gyed.* "Cutting-off Self-Grasping through the Red Distribution." Blo bzang don ldan, Bka' chen, ca. early 20th century. In *Gcod Tshogs. The Collected Gcod Teaching of the Gelukpa Tradition by Ma ti bha dra Kirti, Blo bzang don ldan and others.* Dharamsala: Library of Tibetan Works and Archives, 1986, 29–54.

(First Panchen) bLo bzang cho kyi rgyal mtshan. *bLa ma mchod pa.* English trans., Alexander Berzin. *The Guru Puja.* Dharamsala: Library of Tibetan Works & Archives, 1979.

Zong Rinpoché blo bzang rtson 'grus. *Zab lam gcod kyi rnal 'byor ba'i tshogs mchod 'bul tshul nag 'gros su bkod pa.* "Offering Gaṇacakra in Connection with the Yoga of the Profound Path of *Gcod.*" In private collection of Ven. Pencho Rabgey, folio 12a.

## Initiation Texts

*Nam mkha' sgo 'byed kyi dbang byed tshul* (The Initiation Manual of "Opening the Door to the Sky") by Blo bzang chos kyi rgyal mtshan, First Panchen Rinpoché, in *The Collected Works of Blo bzang chos kyi rgyal mtshan*, vol. V. New Delhi: Mongolian Lama Gurudeva, 1973, 675–81.

## Conferences

Cabezón, José, Keynote Speaker. *Whither Buddhist Studies: A Workshop on Buddhist Studies Doctoral Education in North America.* Hosted by the Center for Studies in Religion, University of Toronto, April 6–7, 2007.

Cupchik, Jeffrey W. Conference Paper, "The Sound of Vultures' Wings Arriving at a 'Sky-Burial': Visualizing Music in the Tibetan Chöd Ritual Meditation Practice." *The Tung Lin Kok Yuen Conference: Visualizing and Performing Buddhist Worlds.* An International Conference at the University of Toronto Scarborough, Nov. 2–4, 2007.

Lopez, Donald S., Jr. Discussant, "Theory and Practice of Tibetan Ritual," an *International Conference Hosted by the XIV Dalai Lama Endowment*, University of California Santa Barbara, May 10–12, 2007.

## Discography

Beethoven, Ludvig Van, *Symphony No. 5 in C minor, Op. 67* (1804–1808).

Chöying Drolma and Steve Tibbetts. *Selwa.* San Francisco, CA: Six Degrees Records, Ltd., 2004. 657036 1104-2. Produced by Lee Townsend.

Choying Drolma and Steve Tibbetts. *Chö* (Rykodisc/Hannibal, 1997) CD: ASIN# B00000063A.

His Eminence Khalkha Jetsun Dampa Rinpoché. *Chöd Practice According to the Ganden Ear-Whispered Lineage.* Vancouver: Zuru Ling Tibetan Buddhist Society, 1996. Audio cassette produced by Brian Den Hertog.

His Eminence Khalkha Jetsun Dhampa Rinpoché with his Students. *Chöd Practice According to the Ganden Ear-Whisper Lineage,* dGa' ldan snyan brgyud kyi rim brgyud ltar gcod kyi nyams len. McLeod Ganj, H.P., India: Takten House Chöd Center, 2001. Audio cassette produced by Choephel Yonten.

Holst, Gustav. *The Planets* (1914–1916).

Lama Thubten Yeshe. Chöd *Sādhana*, "Cutting of the Truly-Existent 'I' " Recorded at Pomaia, Italy. 1983. (Archive #689, Last Updated June 17, 2008.)

Mussorgsky. *Pictures at an Exhibition* (1874).

Pachelbel, Johann. *Canon and Gigue in D major for three Violins and Basso Continuo* (*Kanon und Gigue in D-Dur für drei Violinen und Basso Continuo*), 1680.

Ravel, Maurice. *Bolero* (1928).

*Tibetan Buddhist Chants: The Ritual Orchestra and Chants.* New York: Nonesuch H-72071 Explorer Series, Reissue 1995 [1976]. CD recorded at Khampagar Monastery, Tashigong, H.P., India. Photograph on reverse of the late Drukpa Dhungsey Rinpoché, with *ḍamaru* (pellet drum) and *dril bu* (handbell).

*Tibetan Buddhist Rites from the Monasteries of Bhutan.* New York, Lyrichord Discs [1972]. Recordings, notes and photographs by John Levy. SR222.1

## Filmography

Choying Drolma, Ani. "(The Great Compassion Mantra) by Ani Choying Drolma" http://www.youtube.com/watch?v=7KGcspcLdO0, posted November 12, 2008 [accessed November 28, 2008]. Executive producer: Ven. Ann McNeil.

His Eminence Khalkha Jetsun Dampa Rinpoché. *Chod Practice According to the Ganden Ear-Whispered Lineage*, VHS. Videographer: Jane Foster. Vancouver: Zuru Ling Tibetan Buddhist Meditation Centre, December 8, 1995.

His Eminence The Ninth Khalkha Jetsun Dampa, Jampal Namdrol Choekyi Gyaltsan. "Dedicating the Illusory Body to Accumulate Merit," in *Ansanyengyu Chöd Tayang*, DVD. McLeod Ganj, H.P., India: Takten House, 2004.

Ven. Pencho Rabgey. "gCod Teaching," DVD. Kawartha Lakes, ON: Home Recording, 2004.

## Webmedia

"Chöd at the Stupa," http://youtube.com/watch?v=oHN21UqVe5E, posted November 5, 2007 [accessed January 05, 2008].

# Index

This Index is meant to be used as a reference guide. The reader will find that many terms are interrelated. Therefore, any discussion on Chöd pedagogy, for example, will weave perspectives in musical training and pedagogy with training in meditation practices; and how these mutually enhance one's progressive understanding of the multi-layered symbolism within a sādhana—in both senses, a ritual liturgical text to be experienced in practice, and the lifepath of the contemplative. As such, topics on musical practice will connect with related meditation practice topics, and the foundational Dharma subjects in sūtra as well as tantra within this Vajrayāna tradition. Bringing ethnomusicology and Buddhist studies into conversation in this way, it is hoped, will be useful to researchers and practitioners.


*a capella* (recited/sung chant)
  during body mandala, 84
  as musical transmission method, 219, 221
  Ven. Pencho Rabgey on, 230
Aboriginal Australian songs
  Catherine Ellis, 98–99, 325n78
  as cultural survival, 98–99
  issues around musical transcription of, 326n84
Aboriginal Ami-Taiwanese singers, 108
Abrahamic theistic traditions, 7, 40, 251
absolute gratuity, 266. *See* Emmanuel Levinas
acceptance
  of bad conditions, 241–243, 284
  of good or bad circumstances, 243–244
access, 43
  to formal education, 8
  to initations and permissions, 78
  insider's perspective, 299n45
  to recording technology, 325n81
accompaniment
  bell (*dril bu*) rhythmically ornamented, with *ḍamaru*, 53
  *ḍamaru* drumming pattern (music notation), *60*
  instrumental, to liturgy, 328n5
  to chanting, as aesthetic element, 332n36
  to mantric utterance *Āḥ*, 180–182
  public/private context of, 225–226
  role in Chöd ritual practice, 18, 25
  of sound of *ḍamaru* to meditation, 94
  to vocable syllables, 100
  vocal pedagogy on, 219

accumulation of merit (Tib. *bsod nams kyi tshogs*), 51, 92, 94, 130, 167, 212, 253
accumulation of wisdom (Tib. *ye shes kyi tshogs*), 92, 94, 187, 253
actual practice (Tib. *dngos gzhi*), 88, 226–227
 in Chöd rituals, 57, 88–95, 114–115, 117–118, 133
 stages of, 86–95
 symbolism in, 148–149
adept, 16, 29, 39, 41
Adorno, Theodor, 325n81
"advanced" practitioners, 46–54, 100, 106, 143, 149. *See also* practice-level, "beginner"
 accepting illness, 239
 *bodhicitta*, 44
 melodies from ḍākinīs, 149
 *phowa*, 104, 167–169
 rituals, 48, 143
 Ven. Pencho Rabgey on, 196–197
aerophone, 78, 317n18. *See also* Sachs-Hornbostel classification system, metallophone
aesthetics
 in Chöd ritual practices, 72, 192
 ethnoaesthetics, 20, 108, 299n53
 imagery conjured, 118–123
 logic of, xxix, 122
 meditative function and, 123
 solo and group performance practices, 80–82, 155, 217–219, 233
afflictions
 mental states, 187, 263
afflictive emotions (Skt. *kleśa*, Tib. *nyon mongs*). *See also* delusive mental states, three poisons
 as demons (Skt. *māra*, Tib. *bdud*), 104, 331n33
 freedom from, 247
 impermanence of, 187
 recognizing causes of, 263
Agawu, Kofi, 107, 300n59
 on the new musicology, 21
aggregates (Skt. *skandhas*, Tib. *phung po*)
 dissolution of, 339n22
 emptiness of, *178*
 the five (detailed), 300n4
 mentally transformed, 31
 merely labeled upon, 322n52
 person comprised of, 300n4
 psychophysical, 30–31, 156
*Āḥ* (mantric syllable)
 essence of *Prajñāpāramitā Sūtra*, 88, *89*, 92, 301n12
 manner of utterance, 181–183
 mantric utterance accompanied by *damaru*, 181
 visualization of, 180–181, 318n32
Akhu Jamyang, 252
almsgiving, 51, 252
altruism, 25, 285, 348n35
 as aspirational bodhicitta, awakening mind, 2–4, 18, 258, 272
 *bodhicitta*, 70–71, 258, 268
 Chödpas, 243
 compassion and, 44, 192, 236, 258
 cultivating, xxvi, 70, 236, 253
 Davis on, 265–266, 273
 developing infinite, 44
 in gift-giving practices, 265–267
 in giving Dharma, 86–87, 253, 267
 incremental advancement, 275–276
 intentionality and, 66, 151
 Levinasian alterity, compared with, 272
 in Mahāyāna Buddhism, 351n8
 meditation for development of, 354n49
 merit from, 268
 motivation for, 273–274

possibility of, 25–26, 265, 272, 273, 285
suffering from self-interest, healed by, 270
as total system, 267–270
in Vajrayāna, 272–273
without discrimination, 19
working for others' benefit, 44
*See also* bodhicitta
altruistic resolve, 32, 44, 70, 182, 205, 243
analogies and examples
bird's two wings, 45, 95, 253
lightning bolt, 191
lotus flower, 63
milk mixed with water, 46
moon's reflection, 46
musical "score" as symbols, 148
rain sounds in drumming, 188–191
rope apprehended as snake, 94
sand as gold, 276
sound of emptiness, *ḍamaru* produces, 54
sound of vultures' wings, 121
analytical meditation
on emptiness of the three spheres of giving, 57, 87, *90*, 94, 253–254
on grasping to phenomena as if they are "truly existent," 18
on imputed names and labels, 308n72
on patience, 244
on relationship of corporeal body to the "self," 18
on the three spheres of patience, 248
anapest (rhythm)
as mnemonic, function with liturgy, 55, *132*
in seven branch practice, 55, 129–131
three beat drumming pattern, *130*, 226, 331n30
anger (Tib. *zhe sdang*), 4. *See also* three poisons
arising from ignorance and attachment, 336n40
patience, as antidote to, 244–248
reduced through practice, 217
as root delusion, 157
in three poisons, 189, 294n9
toward delusive mental states, not persons 186–187
wrathful expression symbolizing, 187
animism, 303n29
Ani Choying Drolma. *See* Choying Drolma
anthropology, 353n38
American school of, 334n19
armchair, 146, 260, 267
British school of, 334n19
cultural, 14–15
economic, gift and exchange, 256, 267
influence on ethnomusicology, 11
interpretive, 106
medical, 68, 265
reflexivity in, 15, 296n20, 298n42
of religion, xxiv, 6, 146, 195
ritual theory and practice, 11, 14–15
symbolic, 146–148, 297n29
thought and inquiry, 19, 148
*See also* ethnography, research methods
*anuttarayoga* (Tib. *bla na med pa'i rgyud*). *See* Highest Yoga Tantra
antidotes
applying, Buddhist approach to, 188, 351n2
to ignorance, Chöd practice as, 203
to self-cherishing, 264
to self-grasping, realization of emptiness, xxiii, 204
to suffering, gifting as, 259
Pala's advice on, 275

apparition, 204. *See* self-existence
apprenticeship, xxiv, 19. *See also* transmission, ethnomusicology research methods
in both musical and meditation practices, 11, 47, 106
extended period of, 2, 24
goals of, 25
immersion prior to musical analysis, xxvi–xxvii, 22, 224–225, 233, 346n14
logic of approach, 20–21
as method of research in ethnomusicology, 19, 216
musical and spiritual transmission (Tib. *lung*), 23
promotes inquiry and correction, 25
rules and limits on, 217
shifting from etic to emic perspective, 17
with master Chödpa "Pala," 12, 152, 280
arrogance, 104
as demon (Skt. *māra*, Tib. *bdud*), 335n25
at experiencing success, 244
Arrow, Kenneth, 266
Arthasiddhi Bhadra, 338n6
Āryadeva (Tib. 'Phags pa lha), 168, 342n5
Asanga, 313n114, 351n8
ascetic, 7
Chödpa as, 9, 10, 23
interpretive community, 140
in-training, *212*
Machik Labdrön as, xxiii, 2, *34*, 38
non-monastic tradition, 142
solo v. group performance practices, 80
ascetic practice. *See* contemplative
Buddhist non-monastic tradition, 142
Chöd as, 10, 80, 249
social role of Chödpa does not contradict, 252
Atiśa, 187
Abbot, Vikramaśīla Monastic University, 347n22
gradual path, 187
on musical aesthetics, 156
attachment (Tib. *'dod chags*), 294n9
to the body viewed as the "self," xxiii, 51, 116, 118
cutting off (*gCod*), 5, 9, 121
ignorance, root cause of, 189, 336n40
to the notion of a self-existent "I," 31
to objects viewed as "mine," 44, 263
suffering from, experienced as a loss, 336n40
understanding, through Chöd practice, 9, 243
*See also* three poisons, self-grasping
attainments
common (*thun mong gi dngos grub*), 190
supreme (*mchog gi dngos grub*), 190–191
autobiography, spiritual, 141, 316n13. *See* hagiography
autopilot, 69, 223, 318n27
Avalokiteśvara (Chenrezig), 179, 186. *See* Buddha of Compassion
aversion
antidote to, 308n72
toward some places, undoing mental attitude of, 225

banquets. *See* distributions
*bar do*. *See* intermediate state
Barz, Gregory, 15
Beer, Robert, 146, 163, 316n14
"beggar's" Chöd, 70, 114, 227–229, 235. *See also* "mendicant's practice"

"beginners," 25, 46–54, 68, 72, 119, 142, 149, 196, 220. *See* practice-levels, "advanced"
becoming "intermediate," then "advanced," 46–48
cautioned to refrain from going to the *nyen sa* before ready, 70
*ḍamaru* and *gaté* mantra recitation, training in, 176–177
in giving away the body, 263, 269, 275
graduated skill development, in Chöd, 46
*kangling* visualizations for, 250–251
performance-*centered* practice, 46
singing a Chöd liturgy, 284, 287
Béhague, Gerard, 53, 80. *See* performance practice
Bell, Catherine, 13–15, 24, 298n42
bell (Skt. *ghanta*, Tib. *dril bu*), 30, 54–55, 78, *79*, 81, *178*
aural texture of overtones, 328n6
dampening overtones of, with duct tape, 219, 345n13
drone polyphony, texture with *ḍamaru*, 328n6
duct tape, as sound dampener, 219
iconography of, held by Machik Labdrön, *34*, *145*
manner of holding and playing
as ritual implement, 54–55
sounding with struck beats of *ḍamaru*, 44
symbolic meanings of, 54
Bentor, Yael, 164, 315n9, 337n55
Beyer, Stephan, 75–76
on Buddhism as performing art, 76, 127
Black Hat Dance, 324n71
blessings, *jin lab* (Tib. *byin labs*)
of the ḍākinīs, 149
by keeping melodies pure, 114
lineage, 230
request for, 137, 181
blood donations in UK and USA, compared 25, 265–266, 273
*Blue Annals* (Gö Lotsāwa), 38
Boas, Franz, 128, 330n29
Bodh Gaya, 110, 228, 326n83
Bodhi Tree, 188, 228, 326n83
*bodhicitta*, 18, 25, 32, 66, 69, 351n10. *See also* altruism
actualization of, 253
altruistic mindset of, 70–71, 183, 258, 268
as antidote, 71
aspirational, 3–4, 18
conventional and ultimate, 156, 253
Chöd ritual as practice of, 3, 6
in Chödpa's mindstream, 243, 253
development of level of, 44–47, 56, 72, 236, 348n29
engaged, 32, 264–265
generating, in the Chöd system, 45, 232
in Mahāyāna Buddhism, 204, 262, 264, 272, 352n19
meditation on, 281
motivation for, 255–256, 267–268
rejuvinated and restored, qualities of, 135–136
taking refuge and generation of, 66, 88, 112–114, 226
within "three principal paths," 73, 190
bodhisattva vow, 349n39
bodhisattva warrior, 244, 313n115, 350n51
Akhu Jamyang of Chungba, 252
Chödpa as unconventional, 213, 244
Kyabje Zong Rinpoché on, 313n115, 350n51

body
attachment to, 5, 31, 44, 51, 116
as corpse, 206
developing non-attachment to, 9, 243
final offering of this life, 16
gift of, 206, 254, 273
imaginal offering of one's, 124
mentally transformed (old body), 5, 86–87, 124
physical, 31
Ven. Pencho Rabgey on, 274–275
vulnerability of, 5, 17, 209
body mandala practice, 84, 88, *89*, 130
*bol*, 100, 129, 176–177, 311, 330n30. *See also* vocable
defined, 310n94
*Bolero* (Ravel), 311n96
Bönpo tradition, 41, 151, 303n29
boundaries
between altruism and self-interest, 270
disciplinary, 26, 29
traditional, 25
Bourdieu, Pierre, 267
bravery
develop, based on altruistic intentionality, 73
practice in accordance with our experience and, 49
willing to take a loss, 332n36
Zong Rinpoché (Kyabje) on, 49–50
breath
one exhale can support/encompass one melodic phrase, 116
musical staff notation mark illustrates when to, 60
*prāṇāyāma*, 288
wasted, 211
*Brief Stages of the Path* (Tib. *Lam rim bsdus don*), 338n8
buddhahood, 6, 36, 48, 73, 187
advance in stages toward, 48
*bodhicitta* (altruistic resolve) as prerequisite to, 6
Machik on leading beings to the stages and paths to, 70
Mahāyāna goal of leading all beings to, 30
two accumulations needed for, 253
Buddha of Compassion. *See* Avalokiteśvara, Chenrezig
Dalai Lama and, 46, 186–187
mantra, levels of depth of, 179–180
Buddha Śākyamuni, xv, 110, 238
achieving enlightenment at Bodh Gaya, 110
on cause and effect, 188
Four Noble Truths, teaching on 187, 196, 200, 351n12
second turning of Dharma wheel, xv
buddha-nature (Skt. *tathāgatagarbha,* Tib. *de bzhin gshegs pa'i snying po*), 187, 295n16
Buddhism. *See also specific topics*
Beyer, Stephan on, 75–76, 127
karma (cause and effect), 312n111
as performing art, 76, 127
reciprocity in, 257
suffering, 4, 264–265
Vulture Peak, Buddha's teaching on emptiness at, xv–xvi
women's roles in, 316n13
Buddhist epistemology, 4, 257, 268, 300n1, 312n111, 351n7, 353n38
*Buddhist Himalaya* (Snellgrove), 75
Buddhist practices
in everyday life, 7, 9, 26, 81–82, 104–106, 144, 262
Buddhist ritual music, xviii–xvvi, 12, 41, 317n18
composition techniques in, 114, 128–129

ethnomusicological approaches to studying, xxiv, 12, 9–23
instruments/implements, functions of, 53–55, 317n18
mapping of layers in, 123–127
melodic symbolism in, xviii
performative architecture of, 41, 66, 96
performance practices within, 53, 57, 80, 317n22, 317n24
ritual mapping of, 97–102, 123–125, 127–134
sonic iconography in, xviii, 116, 120, 121, 123
symbolism of tone painting in, 114, 120–123
Buddhist studies, 195
on Chöd practice, 6–9, 294n11
ethnography in, 300n61
ritual focus within, 6–8
transmission in, 215
*bzod pa'i 'khor gsum*. *See* three spheres of patience

Cabezón, José I., 295n13, 297n29, 309n73
*cakra* (Tib. *rtsa 'khor*). *See* chakra
Canzio, Ricardo, 9, 138, 143
Carnatic music, 11, 38, 310n94. *See also* Indian Classical music, Hindustani
Catholic Mass, 40–41, 341n3. *See also* Christianity
cause and effect / law of causality. *See* karma, 201, 203, 209, 237, 248
afflictions and, 263
dependent origination, 201, 302n14
emptiness arises as, 202
impermanence and, 237
in perfection of patience, 248
seven-step method to generate *bodhicitta*, 351n8, 354n49
causes (and conditions), 199, 203
of interferences, destroyed by mantric utterance *phaṭ*, 172
leading to suffering, 8
resulting in cyclic existence, 18
of suffering, eradicating by meditating on *ḍamaru* sound, 157
causes of suffering
Geshé Rabten on, 239–240
Lama Thubten Yeshe on, 240
recognizing the object to blame, 239–240, 348n36
cemetery as Chöd practice site, in India, 30, 50. *See also* sky burial
sky burial site, in Tibet and Mongolia, 113
central channel (Skt. *avadhūtī*, Tib. *rtsa dbu ma*), 117–118, 165, 171. *See* crown chakra
cessation (of suffering), 187, 251, 263. *See* Four Noble Truths
Candrakīrti, 33
chang teu (Skt. *ḍamaru*, Tib. *cang te'u*), 78, 333n3
chakra (Skt. *cakra*), 118, 171, 339n24
chant (Tib. *dbyangs*, *rta*). See also *mgur*, tone-contour overtone chant, melody
chant master (Tib. *umdzé*), 46, 337n35. *See* music director
Chawla, Saroj, 326n82
Chenrezig (Tib. *Spyan ras gzigs*), 179, 341n2. *See* Avalokiteśvara, Buddha of Compassion
Dalai Lama seen as, 46
forms of, 179, 341n2
meditational deity, 186
childhood development, as analogous to practice, 275
*cho ga*. *See* ritual
Chöd
role of music in, 30, 66–69

Chöd *(continued)*
theoretical considerations, 68–69
as Vajrayāna practice, 3
Chöd Club, 154, 217, 230–232, 326–327n1
Chöd lamas, xxvi, 2, 21, 41, 70, 149, 214
Chöd liturgy. *See also* written liturgy
image selection in sādhana, 118–119
musical repercussions, 119–122
text-setting in, 58–60
transliteration, *59*
Chöd Monlam, 347n27
Chöd ritual practice. *See also specific topics*
efficacy of, 29, 50–53
ensembles, 315n11
ethnomusicological approach to, 17–19
function in, 29
group performance practice aesthetics, 155
group performance practice, importance of, 317n23
*in situ* performance of, 49–50
Lin on, 50–53
literary concordances in, 114–115
mantra in, 53–54
melodic movement characteristics in, 60–66
melody in, 53–54, 82–83, 122
multifaceted nature of, 30–32
musical reflections on, 83–84
musical structures in, 82–83
musician interactions in, 218
oral tradition in, 30–31
paradoxical claims about, 113–122
resistance to musical analysis of, 107–108
rhythmic cycles in, 81
rhythmic flow in, 53–54
sādhanas in, 22–23
second phrase in, 62–63
shamanic elements in, 84–86
sonic iconography in, 116–118
themes in, 72–74
third phrase, 63–66
trance in, 84–86
treatment of instruments, 157–158
variation and sameness in, 149–160
Chöd pedagogy, 46–48, 66, 284–285. *See also* transmission
contexts, 297n31
*ḍamaru* drum, 162–163, 222
formalized categories drawn from, 309n73
group practice, 217–218
intensive immersion in, 224–225
melody teaching, 221
music training in, 218–220
musical transmission, 218–220
Rabgey on, 217, 221
reflexivity in, 225
technology in, 223–224
of testing, 223–224
training methods in, 220–223
variations in, 162–163
of Zasep Tulku Rinpoché, 231–232
of Zong Rinpoché, 113, 166, 218–219, 221
Chöd ritual practice
actual practice in, 88–95, 114–115, 117–118
advanced, 46–48
aesthetic of, 192
as antidote to ignorance, 203–204
approaching, 4–6, 211–214
beginners, 46–48
*bodhicitta* in, 6
Buddhist studies perspective on, 6–9, 294n11
concepts in context, 122–123
conceptual terminology, 198–202
convergence of layers in, 55–56
dedications in, 95
disembodiment in, 68

efficacy of, 12–14
embodiment in, 68
ethnomusicology perspective on, 9–22, 78–80
in everyday life, 237, 241
experience, 53–55
fear in, 31–32
flow in, 13–14
formal structure of, 87–88, *89*, *90*, 91
Graduated Skill in, 46–53
group, 80–81
*gur* compared with, 40–41
guru-deity yoga in, 205–206
healing rituals, 66–67
initiation ceremonies, 232
inner, 44–46, 72–73, 99–100, 305n44
intentionally produced sound in, 174–182
interpretive community, 140–149
intertextual performance event, 11, 309n84. *See* ritual mapping
liminality in, 68
lineage of, 41–46
mastery of, 70–71
meaning of, 18
monastic ensemble ritual compared with, *79*
musical instruments in, 78
musical transmission of, 214–217
music-poetry correspondences in, 56–71
*nyen sa* in, 70–71
oral transmission of, 72, 113
outer, 44–46, 72–73, 99–100
*phaṭ* in, 170–173
philosophy of, 33–46
physical illness in, 4–5
practice-centered performance in, 46–48
preliminary practices, 91
preparation for, 73–74
public performance of, 225–227
recordings of, 14
ritual mapping, 97–98, 99–102
the self in, 13, 31–32
semantic glossing together of, 41
six integrated concepts in, 23–25
solo, 81–82
as spiritual practice, 225–227
spiritual transmission of, 214–217
stage setting in, 30–31
stages of, *86*
structure of, *99*
subrituals, 226, 243
suffering as positive result of, 238–241
symbolism in, 140–149
tantric studies and, 6–9
text enhanced by music in, 58
textual elements of, 56
thick description of, 86–87
in Tibet, 1–4
tone painting in, 114
transcendence in, 102
transcription of, 57–66, 127
transcultural translation of, 234
transformation from, 236–241
transmission of, 33–46
visualization in, 281–282
Chöd Tradition, xiii, xvi. *See also specific topics*
core meaning of, 150–151
cutting in, 3
inner meditation in, 151
of lamas, 232
musical imagery in, xvii–xviii
oral tradition in, 3
relative stability of, 150–151
role of music in, 1–2
sādhanas in, 22–23
*Chöd Tshogs*, 87
poetic meter in, 136–137
preliminary practices in, 135
rhythmic structure in, 135–137

Chödpas, 5
attachments lacked by, 243
*bodhicitta* of, 243, 253
consciousness and lifeways of, 103–104
forbearance of, 241–243
hermitages of, 9
honesty of, 242–243
illness and, 238–239
obstacles faced by, 241
patience of, 244–248
*phaṭ* uttered by, 243
sacrifice of, 248–249
social role of, 252–253
suffering of, 238–239
as unconventional warriors, 252–253, 350n51
Ven Pencho Rabgey on attitude of, 241–242
wisdom of, 253–254
Zong Rinpoché on, 313n115
Chopin, Frédéric, 102
*chos kyi sbyin pa*. *See* giving Dharma
Choying Drolma (Ani), 180, 226–227, 341n42
fundraising for nunnery, 181
music collaborations with, Steve Tibbetts, 180–181
public performance of Chöd, 226–227
Christianity, 39, 250–251
Chungba Valley (Tibet), 188, 232, 276, 346n17, 350n51
*citta* (Tib. *sems*). *See* heart-mind
*Coming of Age in Samoa* (Mead), 330n29
Common Initiation of Opening the Door to the Sky, xxi, 45, 296n27
communitas, 68, 312n108. *See* liminality
Turner on, 345n12
comparative musicology, 299n48
comparative religion approach, 250
comparative cross-cultural studies of giving, 256, 285
compassion, 269
counterintuitive acts of, 5, 239
cultivation of, in Mahāyāna Buddhism, 3, 31, 74, 180, 236
Dalai Lama on, at MLI dialogue, 271–272
development of, 263–266
fatigue, 352n30, 354n50
great compassion, defined, 258
Machik Labdrön and, 302n15
reduction of self-interest, 257–258
concentration, 258
meditative concentration, perfection of, 179, 301n11
music as an aid to, 47
concentration being (Skt. *samādhisattva* Tib. *ting nge 'dzin sems pa*), 91, 320n45
conceptual terminology
in Buddhist philosophy 195–202
in ethnomusicology, 9–22, 106–107, 202–203
in ritual studies, 13–14
conditioned existence, 93, 204–205, 208, 263, 269. *See also* cyclic existence, *saṃsāra*
Connerton, Paul, 312n109
consciousness. *See* transference of consciousness, *phowa* (*pho 'ba*)
continuity of, 5
ejecting, 32, 47, 100, 118, 169
mentally performed imagery, 103
transformation of, 45, 144
contemplative practices, 205. *See* ascetic
continuity of Chöd tradition
and change, 12, 21, 284
successful, musical and spiritual transmission as, 214, 286

controlled dying process, 167–169, 170. *See* death and dying
conventional reality/truth (Skt. *saṁvṛti-satya*, Tib. *kun rdzob bden pa*) 54, 199, 200–202, 204
Cooley, Timothy, 15
corporeal body
  *Corporeal Generosity* (Diprose), 266
  generosity, 247, 313n114
  identity, 114
  relationship to the "self," 18, 214
corpse
  body as, visualization, 206, 212–213
  mortician's work, 327n3
  sky burial, 327n3
  vultures seeking, 121
crown chakra. *See* chakra, central channel
  aperture, 92, 100
  visualization, *117*, 118, 171, 289
Csikszentmihalyi, Mihaly, 14, 297n34
*The Cult of Tārā* (Beyer), 75
cultural relativity, 202
Cultural Revolution, 142, 169
cultural survival, 23, 99, 229–235, 284
"cutting" (Tib. *gCod*) method, 3, 31, 157, 197, 263. *See* severance
  finding object of, 307n57
  goal of, 208–210
  through self-grasping, 207–208
  visualization during, 209–210
*Cutting-off Self-Grasping through the Red Distribution*, 87, 206
cyclic existence, xiv, 4, 73, 197, 315n120. *See* conditioned existence, *saṃsāra*, *'khor ba*
  bound to, 249
  cross the ocean of, 95
  driven by the three poisons toward, 4
  freedom from, 63, 205, 236
  liberation of self and others from, as *bodhicitta* ethic, 8, 122, 204–205
  misconception of nature of "self," at the root of, 263
  undo habits that keep one trapped in, 197
  weariness with, 18
cymbals (Tib. *sbug chal*), 78, *79*, 81–82

daily practice, xxviii, 7, 26, 41, 81, 144, 297n30
  acts of generosity, 254
  of Chöd sadhana, 41
  deity-yoga, 144
  integrated ritual within, 7, 224
  other-focused, 26
  peacefully shared meals together, 252
  post-medtiation periods (Tib. *rjes thob*), 104–106
  prayer rituals, elders performing, 212
  relevance of Chöd to, 291
  of tantric adepts, 81
ḍākinī (Tib. *mkha' 'gro ma*), xiv, 31, 133
  action ḍākinī, identity of, 48, 124
  blessings of, 149, 304n34
  signs of, 149
  studies on, 316n13, 301n6
  visualization of, 329n14
  as vultures, 119–122
  wisdom ḍākinī, 121
Dalai Lama, 46, 48–49, 168, 304n29
  as Buddha of Compassion, 186–187
  on compassion, 271–273
  faith in, 341n3
  Fourteenth, xxvii, 168, 207
  on self-interest, 271
  Seventh, 94
  on tantric practices, 200, 207
  Thirteenth, 126
Dalhousie (India), 75–76
Dalton, Jacob, 313n114

*ḍamaru* (drum), 25, *34*, 54, *145*, 213, 346n15. *See* rhythm, bell (*dril bu*)
case study on, 160–164
*chang teu* (Tib. *cang te'u*), 78, 333n3
construction of, 156–159, 222, 336n40
Ellingson and Dorjé on, 17, 142, 282, 336n43
emptiness symbolized, 253–254
hour-glass shaped, interpretations of, 160–164
Khalkha Jetsun Dampa Rinpoché on, 152–153
manner of holding, 159–160
melody accompanying, 222–224
mnemonic function, 129–131
pedagogy, 162–163, 222
performing technique, 32, 159–160
physical exertion in training for, 222–223
polyphonic texture from, 328n6
rhythms for, 82–83, 94, 131, 135, 310n93
rhythms interwoven with sung text, 56
solo performance practice, 81–82
symbolism of, 140–141, 253, 282–283
tempo of, 154
training in, 152–153
(Ven.) Pencho Rabgey on, 153–155, *158*, 158–159, *162*, 223
wood sourced from, 336n42
Zong Rinpoché (Kyabje) on, 156–157, 161, 219
Dampa Sangyé. *See* Padampa Sangyé
dances. *See* four modes of going (Tib. *'gro tshul rnam bzhi*), 44
*Dancing Prophets* (Friedson), 67
David-Néel, Alexandra, 52–53
Davidson, Richard, 49
Davis, Natalie Zemon, 273
on the possibility of altruism, 265
*dbang ba*. *See* powerful activities
death and dying, 121–122. *See* transference of consciousness
clinical, gross level of physical appearances dissoving, 167–168
controlled dying (Tib. *thugs dam*), 167–168
mantric syllable *phaṭ*, 166
meditation on the dying process, 166–169
recalling impermanence and, 119
subtle consciousness at, 166–170
*Dedicating the Illusory Body as a Heaped Offering* (Tib. *sGyu lus tshogs su sngo ba* (sādhana liturgy), 56, 134, 152, 161, *162*, 192, 206
cassette recordings of, 219–220
*ḍamaru* drum in, 174
dedication of merit subritual, 88, 91, 95
description of, abridged, 87–88
detailed description of, 91–95
elaborated description of, 88–91
*Heart Sūtra* mantra in, 174–179
*kangling* (thighbone trumpet) in, 174–179
mantra in, 165, 170–174
melody in, 126
memorization of, 306n53
musical structure of, 82–84
pitch of subrituals, Ven. Pencho Rabgey on, 317n24
subrituals overview, *89–90*
sung passages in, 112
visualizations in, 207
Deer Dance, 324n71
deity yoga, 206. *See* guru-deity yoga
delusive mental states (Skt. *kleśa*, Tib. *nyon mongs*), 32, 170, 187–189. *See* afflictive emotions
Buddha overcame the last of his, 238
overcoming, 188, 203

self-grasping ignorance, as root of all, 31
demon (Skt. *māra,* Tib. *bdud*), 30, 335n25
of arrogance, 104
as attitudinal aspects of mind, 294n11
external and internal, 331n33
as not self-existent, 31
root, "self-grasping ignorance" (Tib. *bdag 'dzin ma rigs pa*), 31
dependent arising (Skt. *pratītya-samutpāda*, Tib. *rten cing 'brel bar 'byung ba*), 7, 39
of karmic causes and conditions, 7
merely labeled, 94, 322n52
realizing through practice, 254
sound/music as "empty" of inherent self-existence, 203
utilize analysis of, 283
Derrida, Jacques, 23, 266–267, *270*, 274
Desideri, Ippolito, 295n17
desirous-attachment (Tib. *'dod chags*), 294n9. *See* attachment
"Devotion to the Spiritual Guide," 136, *137*
*dGe lugs*, 41, 303n29. *See* Gelug
Dharamsala (India), 219
Dharma, 133–134, 209, 312n102
four seals of, *86*, 93–94, 152, 251, 321n49
song-poems as instructional, 40
Diamond Path, 352n19. *See* Vajrayāna
Diaspora, Vietnamese, 38. *See also* Tibetan Diaspora
Diprose, Rosalyn, 266–269
on generosity in Derrida, 266–267
on Levinas and "other-directed sensibility," 268
disciples. *See also* apprenticeship, transmission
advancing in stages, 24
emic and etic roles, 16–23
of Khalkha Jetsun Dampa, Western 109
mantra transmitted to, 165
master-disciple relationship, 4, 16
*mgur* sung as dharma instruction for, 40
musical and Buddhist traditional, 2
process of oral transmission, 17
role of, to a master musician, 21
thousands attending Chöd teachings, 2
transmission to, 12, 42
treatment of *ḍamaru* and sacred instruments, expected of, 157
of Tsongkhapa, 43
of *umdzé* in Mustang gonpa, 120
in unbroken lineages, 72
who read Western music staff notation, 58
disciplinary blinders, 19–22. *See* research methods
as metaphor for a limiting methodological paradigm, 19–20
disembodiment, in Chöd ritual practice, 68
dissemination conflated with transmission and preservation, 214, 284
distributions (Tib. *'gyed*) or banquets. *See* four distributions
divine pride, 92, 343n20
cultivation of, 206–207
*dkar 'gyed. See* white distribution
*dmar 'gyed. See* red distribution
*'dod chags. See* desirous-attachment
*dohā* tradition, 38–41, 125, 136
Guenther on, 38, 303n23
Dorjé, Rinjing, 140–142
on the *ḍamaru* drum, 17, 336n41
external/internal threats to "self," 331n33
*Dorjé Tsemo*, 172

Douglas, Mary, 265
*drag po*. *See* wrathful
*dranyen* (Tib. *sgra snyan*), Tibetan lute, xxvii
dramatic process in ritual
in Chöd practice, 41, 133
Victor Turner on, 68, 312n108. *See* communitas, liminality
Drepung Monastic University, 161, 336n46
*dril bu*. *See* bell
Dromtönpa, 347n22
drumming patterns
compared, as analogous to rainfall, 188–192
*dram-dram*, 135, 177, 310n93, 318n28
*ma dang*, *lha yi*, *kang dro*, 42, 62, 81–82, 177–178
*ostinato*, 42, 82–85, 100–102, 135, 137, 148
symbolizing the four ritual activities, 187
Drupwang Lobsang Namgyal, 126
dualistic categories
sacred/profane, 6
religion/superstition, 6
dualistic grasping (Tib. *gnyis 'dzin*)
defining, 198–199
Guenther on, 342n5
Lama Yeshe on, 198
Ven. Pencho Rabgey on, 198–199
*duḥkha* (Skt., Tib. *sdug bsngal*). *See* suffering
*dug gsum*. *See* three poisons
Durkheim, Emile, 71, 146, 259, 261, 264–265, 271, 350n1
on classification, 6, 352n17

earth owners/local deities (Tib. *sa bdag*), 48, 103
Early dissemination of Buddhism into Tibet (*snga dar*), 303n29. See also *phyi dar*
Ear-Whispered Lineage, 300n62, 346n17
Edou, Jérôme, 6, 207
efficacy. *See* functions
at beginner/intermediate/advanced levels, 50–53
of Chöd practice rituals, 12–14
in context of fear, 30
defining, 12, 300n1
of flow, 13
function, related with, 29
of meditation practices, 29–31
music as a cause of results, 66
of musical practices, 24, 29–31, 53–55
in scientific analysis, 344n28
ego, 31–32
disidentification with "self" 196, 201
habitual relationship to, 31, 104, 118, 153, 241
identity, 208
pride, 244
in terrifying situations, 197, 300n2
eight wordly dharmas (Tib. *'jig rten chos brgyad*), 104
gain and loss as, 106
Ellingson, Ter, 9–10, 164
on aesthetics, 331n35
on *ḍamaru* drum, 17, 139–142, 159
on external threats, 331n33
on mandala as organizing concept, 10, 23
on melody, 57
on symbolism, 140–141, 144–145, 148
Ellis, Catherine, 98–99, 323n61, 325n78
on musical analysis, 326n84

embodiment
of Chöd melodies, 68, 235
of *Prajñāpāramitā Sūtra*, Yum Chenmo as, 33, 302n12, 341n44
emic perspective, 19
defining, 298n43
distinction in the ethnosciences, 20
in ethnomusicology, 15, 306n51
etic perspective, combined with, 16–17, 298n43
Will on, 20
emotion, 116, 258, 351n6. See *rasa* (mood)
in dramaturgical narrative, 84, 109
elicited through "tone painting," 116, 328n4
evoked through *mgur*, 67
fear and insecurity, 55, 250
habitual, 247
melody appropriate to subritual, 40, 131
negative, 263
regulation, 352n30
tone painting, as cuing, 328n8
v. reason, 261
Western lexicon of, 257
emotional quotient
felt obligation to reciprocate, 259
in gift economy, 256–263
Mauss on, 261–262
empowerment (Tib. *dbang*). *See* Opening the Door to the Sky, xxi, 103, 272
emptiness (Skt. *śūnyatā*, Tib. *stong pa nyid*), 18, 44, 94, 176, 283, 307n57
Buddha teaching of, at Vulture Peak, xv
in Chöd ritual contexts, 44, *90*, 91
*ḍamaru* drum symbolizing, 253–254
defining, 302n14
during post-meditation period, 105
ethnomusicology and, 216–217
identifying, 199–200
imbued with understanding of, 70
meditation on, 57, 248, 281, 350n52
meditation on three spheres of giving, 248
in practice, 203
realization of, xxiii, 45, 208
three principle paths, one of, 73
Ven. Pencho Rabgey on, 200
enemies, 51, 172, 191, 203, 236
beings misperceived as, 71, 87, 133
as conceptual designation, 237, 348n30
inviting, 30
Enigma (music group), 108
enjoyments, 320n48
listening, 202
transforming, 84, 244
enjoyment body (Skt. *saṃbhogakāya*), 169
enlightenment (Buddhism)
attain in this lifetime, 44
*bodhicitta* as prerequisite to achieve, 6, 70
Chöd sādhana traverses the path to, 40
Machik Labdrön, on guiding hostile beings to, 70
rapidly attaining, 3
resolving to attain for others, 32
Ensa Ear-Whispered Lineage (dBen sa snyan brgyud), 42–43, 160–161
ensemble based monastic chant, 9, 57, 77–80, 188–189, 192
equalizing and exchanging self and others (Tib. *bdag gzhan mnyam brje*), 348n29
as method of cultivating *bodhicitta*, 44

equalizing and exchanging self and others *(continued)*
as taught in Stages of the Path (*lam rim*) discourses, 253
*See also* giving and taking practice (Tib. *gtong len*)
equanimity (Tib. *btang snyoms*), 253
basis for developing *bodhicitta*, 44
toward all sentient beings, 236
*Essai sur le don* (Mauss), 254, 350n1
ethical discipline (Tib. *tshul khrims*), *179*, 258
ethics, 25, 250, 269
in ethnographic research, 19, 299n50
Levinasian, 25, 269
Mahāyānist, 313n114
use of musical analysis, 95–96, 326n84
ethnoaesthetics, 20, 108. *See* ethnography
defined, 299n53
*See* Sugarman, Jane
ethnography
armchair, 146, 260, 267
changes in Buddhist studies, 300n61
ethical code, 19
practice of return, 19
reciprocity in, 19
recording, 43, 83, 96, 109
reflexivity, 15, 298n39
Spradley on "informant-expressed needs," 296n25
ethnology, 19, 108, 298n39
ethnomusicology, 279, 284, 297n29
and Buddhist ritual music, 53–56
on Chöd music performance, 17–19
on Chöd ritual practice, 9–22, 78–80
disciplinary blinders, period of, 19–22
emic perspective in, 15, 306n51
etic perspective in, 15
Knopoff on, 21, 110, 325n78, 326n84
methods of inquiry, 11
native and indigenous perspectives in, 10–11, 306n51
on oral tradition, 305n42
participant-observation, 11, 14, 106
ritual in, 106–110
role of, in lineage continuity, 324n77
study and training context, 11–12
on Tibetan ritual music, 9–10
transcription in, 95–96, 106–107
transmission in, 215
ethnomusicological methodology, 9–17
integrated approach to Chöd, 22
intimate context of apprenticing, 216
performance training in ritual as methodology
ritual mapping through musical analysis, 16–17
etic perspective. *See also* emic perspective
defining, 298n43
emic perspective combined with, 16–17, 298n43
in ethnomusicology, 15
Will on, 20
everyday life
Buddhist practice in, 7, 9, 26, 81–82, 104–106, 144, 262
Chöd ritual practice in, 236–248, 277
responses to, 217, 270, 274
*See also* daily practice
exchange. *See* gift and exchange
exorcism, 69

faith, 9, 36
belief form of, 341n3
bracketing, 127
cause of going for refuge, 74

cultivating, 74
developed, xxi
inspire through synchronous *ḍamaru* gestures, 155
in spiritual teacher (lama), 215
fear
cause for taking refuge, 73–74
elicited by sound of vultures' wings, xvi
of failure, 243–244
and faith, 74
imagery utilized for practice, 29
operationalization of, xxiii
originates in mind, 31
pacification of, 189
transmuting experience of, xxiii
when searching for the "self" seeking protection, 31–32, 300n2
fearful contexts, 29–30
habitual protective instinct arising in, 32, 55, 118
memorizing sādhana before going to *nyen sa*, 102, 286, 327n2
sites of Chöd practice, 32, 78, 238
feast (Tib. *tshogs*). *See also* distributions, banquets, *Gaṇacakra*, *gCod Tshogs*
feeling, 260. *See also* emotion
as aggregate of persons, 301n4
of obligation to repay a gift, 259
vulnerable, 5, 87, 116, 206, 209
Feld, Steven, 19
on groove, 297n34
on sound structure as social structure, 343n13
fieldwork, 14, 78, 96, 152, 216. *See* research methods, ethnography
fire puja, 23, 41
Fish, Stanley, 333n2. *See* interpretive community
five aggregates (Skt. *pañca skandha*, Tib. *phung po lnga*), 31, *178*, 300n4, 339n22
Five Ḍākinī Chöd Retreat, 23
flow, 54
Csikszentmihalyi Mihaly on, 14, 297n34
in kinetic aspects of ritual practice, 13–14
in meditative musical gestures, 61, 101–102, 200
melodic, mantric, and rhythmic, 54–55, 85, 100, 134, 243
physical and mental, in ritual process, 30, 223
quasi-trance-inducing *ostinato*, 148
rhythmic, maintained by *ḍamaru* drum and bell, 101, 129
forbearance, 179, 241–243, 258, 263. *See also* patience
*The Forest of Symbols* (Turner), 147
form aggregate (Tib. *gzugs kyi phung po*), 301n4. *See* five aggregates
form body (Skt. *rūpakāya*, Tib. *gzugs sku*), 92
fortunate human rebirth, 167–168
four classes of tantra (Tib. *rgyud sde bzhi*), 207
four distributions (Tib. *'gyed bzhi*)
giving Dharma (*chos kyi sbyin pa*)
manifold (*sna tshogs 'gyed*)
red (*dmar 'gyed*), 93, 118, 178, 320n41
white (*dkar 'gyed*), 87, 88–89, 92, musical score of, 115
four hundred meat offerings (Tib. *sha brgya zan brgya*), 23, (ransom ritual)
four kinds of enlightened activity (Tib. *phrin las rnam bzhi*), 26, 131–134, 185
as expressed in contrastive ways of playing drum, 188–191
transformation through, 191–192

four levels of Chöd, 44
inner (*nang*), 44
outer (*phyi*), 45
secret (*gsang*), 45
suchness/thatness (*de kho na nyid*), 45
four *māras* or demons (Tib. *bdud bzhi*), 244, 294n11, 335n25
four noble truths (Tib. *bden pa bzhi*), 187, 196, 200, 351n12
four ritual (Vajryāna) activities, 185–187
four seals/mūdras of Buddhism (Tib. *phyag rgya bzhi*), *86*, 93–94, 251
Khalkha Rinpoché on, how to contemplate during practice, 152
verse on (English translation), 94
verse on (Tibetan transliteration), 321n49
*Four Seasons* (Vivaldi), 328n4, 328n8
four schools of Tibetan Buddhism, 41, 304n34
Bonpo school's Chöd lineages, 303n29
having Chöd lineages, 41
shared core meaning of Chöd across, 151
four ways of going (Tib. *'gro tshul rnam bzhi*), 44
FPMT (Foundation for the Preservation of the Mahāyāna Tradition), 345n7
frame drum (*rnga*), 78, 81
(St.) Francis of Assisi, 252, 302n15
Frankfurt School, 325n81
freedom
from extremes, 199, 201
from cyclic existence (*saṃsāra*), 63, 122, 191, 205
Friedson, Steven, 67–68
friends, make with *ḍamaru,* 154, 223
frightening appearances
contemplating depending arising and emptiness of, 239
maintaining balanced mental disposition, 178
meditate on emptiness while blowing *kangling*, *178*
"see" and "hear" as if appearing in a dream, *105*
frightening sites. See *nyen sa* (Tib. *gnyan sa*), haunted sites
where spirits are said to live, 30–32, 327n2
full awakening, 191, 238, 316n12, 341n3. *See also* buddhahood, enlightenment
functions
and efficacy, 13, 29, 51
guiding question, 2
on individual and social level, 4
interrelated questions on, 29, 32, 101
of music in Chöd rituals, xxiv, 2, 23, 46, 53, 72, 113
of symbolism in music and meditation, 142–149
funerary rites, xvi, 327n3
Chödpa's role in, 9

*Gaṇacakra* (Skt., Tib. *tshogs 'khor*)
ritual feast gathering, xi, xxiv, 137, 332n34
Ganden Chöd Tradition, 52, 113, 160, 304n40
continuity and preservation of, 285
Gyalwa Ensapa, 42–43
institutional support for, 315n11
Khalkha Jetsun Dampa Rinpoché on, 326n1
*Lama Chöpa* Chöd sadhana, as white distribution, 318n31
lineage of, 41–45
oral tradition, stories, 246–247
rhythmic figures in, 42, 310n93
rituals in, 23

sādhanas in, 86–95
transmission of, 42, 216, 229–235, 347n23
Ven. Pencho Rabgey on, 42, 230, 243–244
Zong Rinpoché (Kyabje) on, 67, 134
Ganden Ear-Whispered Lineage, 42, 87, 161, 287
Ganden (dGa ldan) Monastery, 43, 304n33
Ganden Shartse Monastic College, xxviii, 345n14
*gCod*, xiii, 2. *See* Chöd
*gCod Tshogs* (Chöd sādhana), 43, 87, 135–136, 219, 341n46
Geertz, Clifford, 127
Gelongma Palmo, 186
Gelug (dGe lugs pa) School, 41, 43
on lineage, 304n40
Lama Tsongkhapa, founder, 187
masters on highest yoga tantra, 339n16
transmission of Chöd tradition in, 231–232
treatment of instruments, 157
Gelugpa Chöd Ḍākinī lineage, 131, 160, 232. *See* Troma Nagmo
Gelugpa Tradition, 41, 43, 157, 187, 231, 347n18
gender
no restrictions to practice Chöd, 78
of religious otherness (Orsi), 295n14
Gendün Chopel, 339n20
generosity (Tib. *sbyin pa*), 258. *See also* altruism, six perfections
of blood donors, 265
corporeal, Diprose on, 266–268
impossibility of, Derrida on, 266–267
perfection of, 248, 258, 272
practice of, 118
Geshé (Gen) Trinley, 113, 161, 188, 232, 306n50
Ven. Pencho Rabgey, sharing advice from, 275–276
Geshé (Tib. *dGe bshes*), levels of, 336n46
gestures (aesthetic)
*ḍamaru*, 223
mantras, 13, 56, 163
musical, 1, 101, 114, 149
mudras, 61
physical and sonic, 13
shared signals between practitioners, 218
*The Gift* (Mauss), 254, 259
central questions in, 262
gift economy, 270
emotional quotient in, 257–263
exchange in, 260–261
giving one's work and flesh, (in Mauss), 262
Mauss on, 256–263
reciprocity in, 257–263
self-interest v., 256–263
stages in, 354n54
gifting, 25
altruism in giving, 265–267
anonymous, 274
as antidote to suffering, 259–260, 273–275
cross-cultural comparative studies of, 256, 285
Derrida on, 266–267, 274
intentionality in giving, 255, 257, 265–271
Irigiray on, 269–270
Levinas on, 266–270, 272, 274
in Mahāyāna Buddhism, 69
Zemon Davis, 265–266, 273
*The Gift Relationship* (Titmuss), 265, 273

giving and taking (*tong len*), 88. *See also* equalizing and exchanging self with others
as *bodhicitta* practice, 251, 269, 320n43
subritual practice within a Chöd sādhana, *90*, 94
giving Dharma (Tib. *chos kyi sbyin pa*), 86, 93–95
Gluckman, Max, 146–147
Godelier, Maurice, 234
gods and ghosts (Tib. *lha 'dre*), 32, 156, 172–173, 206
"Going for Refuge," musical transcription of, *60*
gradual skills acquisition, 23–24. *See also* practice-level
in both, meditation practice and musical performance, 46–53, 143
in Chöd ritual music practice, 46–53, 143
on gradual path to enlightenment, 187, 269
Ven. Pencho Rabgey on, 280
grasping. *See* self-grasping
at extremes, 201
habitual, 157, 197
at an inherently existent "self," 31
great compassion, in Buddhism, 257–258
Great Mother, 33, *35*, *59*, 64, 92, 289. *See* Yum Chenmo
Grimes, Ronald, 293n3, 298n42
groove, 297n34
in Chöd ritual practices, 318n28
Feld on, 298
rhythmic, 277
group Chöd performance practices, 22, 308n67. *See also* solo Chöd performance practices
aesthetics of, 80–81
Chöd pedagogy, 217–218
importance of, in Chöd ritual practices, 317n23
musician/practitioner interactions in, 218
Ven. Pencho Rabgey on, 176
*gtong len*. *See* giving and taking, *tonglen*
Guenther, Herbert, 38
on *dohā* tradition, 303n23
on dualistic grasping, 198, 342n5
*Guide to the Bodhisattva's Way of Life* (Śāntideva), xvi
*gur* (Tib. *mgur*) tradition, 38–41, 173–174
See *mgur*, songs of meditative experience
*Guru Puja* (*bLa ma mChod pa*), 219
in Ganden Chöd Tradition, 318n31
guru-deity yoga, 45–47, 272
defining, 295n15
identity, 7–9, 65, 68, 45 205
The Dalai Lama on, 200
transmission, 215
guru-yoga, 66
how to see the lama, 45
invoking lineage lama's blessings, 88, *89*
singing melody as an act of, 54
*guru-śiṣya paramparā*. *See* master-disciple tradition
Gyalwa Ensapa Lobsang Döndrup, 42, 109
Gyatso, Janet, 66, 141, 299n46, 304n31
Gyürmé Losel, 139, 140–141, 161

habit memory, 312n109
habitual
attributing self-existence to phenomena, 31, 74, 87, 157, 202, 241, 263
egoic relationship to sensory experiences, 104, 276

mental states, 188, 247
patterns of thought, 205, 240
self-generatting identity of deity as antidote, 305n47
tendency to protect the body as "self," 32, 55, 118–119, 197
hagiography (Tib. *rnam thar*), 6, 302n19, 345n8
in Chöd studies, xxiv
liberation narrative, 208
literary genre of spiritual autobiography, 141
of Machik Labdrön, 313n114
hand gestures (Skt. *mudrā*, Tib. *phyag rgya*), 62, 163
happiness, 267
dedicating merit, 275
defining, 312n112
Dharma practice and, 93, 263
if encountering obstacles, 241
mind state of generosity leads to, 277
paying down karmic debt, 242
real as compared to worldly, 313n112
Harding, Sarah, 6, 66, 302n16, 313n114
harmdoers (Tib. *gdug pa can*), 5, 31, 55, 69–70, 88, 172, 189, 206
Harrington, Anne, 271–272
hatred anger (Tib. *zhe sdang*), 294n9. *See also* attachment, aversion
Hayagrīva, 186
haunted places, *nyen sa* (Tib. *gnyan sa*), 32, 54, 68, 70–71, 213
healing
Chöd rituals as, 4, 66–68
mandala construction as, 103
shamanic aspects in Chöd, 85, 86
suffering from self-interest, 255, 259, 270
heart-mind (Skt. *citta*, Tib. *sems*), 2, 286, 305n44
*Heart Sūtra*, xv, 301n12, 312n111
manner of recitation, 174–179
playing dharma instruments during recitation, way of, *175*
Helffer, Mireille, 164, 315n9, 337n52
Hertz, Robert, 71
Highest Yoga Tantra, 168
Chöd practice as, 3
controlling the dying process through, 166–169
Dalai Lama, teaching on, 339n16
deities of, 98
dying, dissolution of consciousness, 166–171
mantric recitation in, 165, 170–174
ritual practices of, 98, 190, 206–207
symbolic practices of, 144
transmission of, 97
Vajrayoginī, 319n40
Hinayāna, 204. *See* Theravāda
hindrances (Tib. *bar chad*). *See* interferers, obstructors, *phaṭ*
clears away, mantric utterance *phaṭ*, 55, 92, 191
internal and external, Machik Labdrön on, 285
Himalayas, 2, 238, 302n20, 303n29
Hinduism, karma in, 312n111
Hindustani music, 11, 38, 310n94, 325n80. *See* Indian Classical Music, Carnatic, *bol*
historiography, xxiv, 33, 75, 304n29, 351n12
Hobsbawm, Eric, 95–96
Holst, Gustav, 328n4
humanitarianism, 349n38
humanism, in ethnomusicology
Berger on, 11
Ellis, Catherine, on, 99
hyphenated identity, 15

iconography, 63. *See also* sonic iconography
  Beer on symbolism in, 143–144
  Nebesky-Wojkowitz, 76
  thangka of Machik Labdrön, 41, 120
  thangka image, 101
  visualizing music, 116
identity
  as ḍākinī, 48
  as a deity, 7
  in guru-deity yoga, 7, 9, 45
  hyphenated, as researcher, 15
  shifting notions of, Turner and Schechner on, 68
identitylessness, 150
ignorance (Tib. *ma rigs pa*, *gti mug*), 138, 150, 335n40
  antidote to, Chöd practice as, 203–204
  cutting off the root of, 16, 208
  not seeing the lack of inherent existence, 294n9
  as root delusions, 31, 157, 189
  as root of three poisons, 4
  "self-grasping," xxiii, 31
illness, 4. *See also* healing
  84,000 delusions in mindstream, as cause of, 189
  advanced rituals, to heal, 48
  Chödpas and, 238–239
  pacification of fear from, 189
  transforming, 4–5
  utilizing Chöd practice to heal, 4–5
  viewing as karmic ripening of causes, 4–5
illusory body (Tib. *sgyu lus*). See *Dedicating the Illusory Body* (sādhana), 56, 83, 84, 86
imagery. *See* visualization
  ferocious, 144
  meditative, 128
  musical, xvii, 113–123
  naturalistic, 114, 134–135
  ritual element of, 101
  selection by Machik Labdrön, 118–119
  terrifying, 29, 118, 121, 123, 239
  of vultures, xvi, 119–123
immersion, 11, 24, 47, 224–225, 233, 346n17. *See* fieldwork, ethnomusicology research methods
impermanence (Tib. *mi rtag pa*), 3, 121, 269, 309n78, 348n30
  of the body, 71, 199, 209
  *kangling* reminds one of, 54, 250
  recalling, 119, 123
  of sound, and all phenomena, 156
  theme in songs of spiritual experience (*mgur*), 40
  vultures symbolic of, xv–xvi
improvisation (music), 30, 79
imputed phenomena
  merely labeled, 203, 308n72, 322n52
  self as, 348
  symbolism, 163, 283
increasing (Tib. *rgyas pa*), *89–90*, 134–135, 185, 331n35. *See* four ritual Vajryāna activities
  internal and external aspects, 189–190, 192
India, 211–214
Indian Classical Music Traditions of musical transmission, 11, 38
indigenous. *See also* native
  exponents, 110, 295
  interpretations, 10, 23
  music aesthetics, theory of, 283
  music ritual traditions, Tibetan lineage holders of, 23, 325n78
  music transcription, issues in, 95–96
  perspective, 11, 46, 306n51
  ritual as cultural theatre, 68

understandings of skills acquisition, 53, 72–73
initiation ritual, 232. *See* Common Initiation of Opening the Door to the Sky, empowerment
inner Chöd practice, 44–46, 72–73, 99–100, 305n44
inner performance of visualizations, 3, 281
insider-outsider status, 4, 15–19. *See* emic, etic
insight. *See* wisdom
instrument classification system. *See* Sachs-Hornbostl
instruments. *See* musical instruments, implements
intentionality
altruistic, xxiii, 45, 66, 151, 183, 258, 268
in gift giving, 255, 257
as imupted symbolism, 283
in Mahāyāna Buddhism, 240, 313n114
in Mauss, reciprocity of the gift, 265–271
intentionally produced sound, 174–182
interdependence, xxiii, xvi, 157, 202, 294n9. *See* dependent origination
interdependent ritual elements, xviii
interdisciplinary, 26, 143, 271, 285
discourse, 249–251
ethnomusicology as, xvii, xxiv, 18, 29
integrated approach
to Chöd studies, 22–23
to practice of liturgy (sādhana), 125
to study of sound in context, 53
to symbolism in Dharmic instruments, 163
performative aspects, 279
interferers (Tib. *bgegs*) 88, 189, 191. *See also* obstructors
"intermediate" skill level. *See also* practice-levels, "beginner," "advanced"
in music and meditation, 46–47, 307n56, 309n73
intermediate state (*bar do*), 166, 168–9, 327n3, 338n4
internal intertextuality, 24, 56
interpretive anthropology, 127
interpretive community
among Chöd practitioners, 140–149
case study of *ḍamaru* symbolism, 160–163
context of, 141–142
defined, 25, 333n2
indigenous variation in, 147–148
oral tradition and, 151–152
sources of interpretation, 151–152
of symbolic attributions, 142–145
value of differing variations, 147–151, 163–164
interpretive paradigm, 20–21
intersubjectivity, 31, 268, 301n7
intertextual layering, 121, 281–283, 309n84
intradisciplinary imperialism, 20–21
intrinsic identity, rejection of, 13, 100, 239
inviting all beings, 30, 70, 249–251
itinerant nuns and monks, 7, 227, 297n30

Jackson, Roger R., 309n81
Jampel Shenyen, 43
*Jātaka Tales*, 274–275
Jesus Christ, 250–251, 341n3, 350n47
joy, elicited through Chöd practice, 54, 85, 232
joyous effort, 258. *See* six perfections
Judeo-Christian based traditions, 7, 40, 251

Kachen Lobsang Zopa (dKa' chen blo bzang bzod pa), 283
  written commentary on *phaṭ* 171–173
Kagyü (*bKa' brgyud*), 41, 170, 303n29, 304n32, 316n11
Kalu Rinpoché, 170
*kangling* (Tib. *rkang gling*). *See* thighbone trumpet
karma, 51, 167. *See* cause and effect
  Buddhist conception of, 247, 312n111
  help others avoid committing negative, 313n114, 339n18
  negative imprints, 3, 69, 217, 248, 349n43
  place of rebirth due to, 74, 167, 343n7
  positive imprints, 247
  purify, 4, *89*, 263
  ripening of, 242
  virtuous/non-virtuous, 133, 338
Karma Trinley (*Kar ma phrin las pa*), 38
karma. *See* cause and effect
karmic debt, paying down, xxiii, 5, 51, 69, 121, 237, 242, 269, 294n11
karmic imprints, 92, 187–188, 263, 312n11
  mantra and, 165
  negative, 5, 239, 242, 247, 251
  positive, 167
  potential, 226
Karnataka, 157, 211–212, 336n46
Kaufmann, Walter, 10, 333n7
Kelsang Gyatso (Seventh Dalai Lama), 94
Khalkha Jetsun Dampa Rinpoché (the Ninth), xvii, *153*, 158, 160–161, 219, 233, 296n27
  in Canada, teaching and giving initiations, 326n1
  Choepel la (son), 229
  on *ḍamaru* drum, 152–153
  on Ganden Chöd Tradition, 326n1
  on recording and disseminating Ganden Chöd ritual sadhana practices, 233
  on singing, 156
Khedrup Chojé, 43
Khedrup Gelek Pelzang, 172–173
kindness, of mother sentient beings, 5
King, Martin Luther, Jr. (Rev.), 274, 354n2
Kippen, James, 310n94, 325n80
Klein, Anne-Carolyn, 316n13
Kleinman, Arthur, 67
Knopoff, Stephen, 21, 110, 299n51
  on Ellis's intervention, 325n78
  on music analysis in ethnomusicology, 326n84
Kundeling (Kusho), 157, 160, 304n34
Kusali Chöd, 319n40
Kwan Yin, 186. *See* Buddha of Compassion
Kyirong (Happy Valley), 160
Kyotön Sönam Lama, 36

*la gyü* (Tib. *bla rgyud*). *See* lineage lamas
*Lam gyi gtso bo rnam gsum*. *See* three principle aspects of the path
*Lam rim* (*Stages of the Path to Enlightenment*), 4
  discourses, foundation of Buddhist path, 253
  parables expressed within, 245–246
  study and meditate on, as basis of Chöd practice, 45, 73
  three scopes of, 73, 314n120
  Tsongkhapa on, 338n8
*Lama Chöpa* (Tib. *bLa ma mChod pa*), "Offering to the Spiritual Guide" ritual, 84, 219

Chöd sādhana adapted from, in Ganden Chöd Tradition, 87, 318n31
lama (Skt. *guru*; Tib. *bla ma*), 8–9. *See also* lineage lamas
advice on graduated path, 50–52, 70
Chöd traditions of various, 232
in Ganden Chöd Tradition, 216
instruction from, 11, 16
on *Lamrim* studies, 73
*lung* from
melodies composed by, 21, 40, 119, 126
on musical practice variations, 149
permissions from, 43
qualified teacher, 30, 45, 62
role of, 64
root, 83, 164
seen as a buddha, 311n99
on singing melodies correctly, 113–114
transmission, to disciples, 243–244
viewed as inseparable from *yidam* / meditational deity, 92
Later propogation of Buddhism into Tibet (*phyi dar*), 187, 304n29, 347n22
Lauffer, Edward, 325n81
law of karma/causality, 237, 312n110. *See also* cause and effect
lay practitioner, 9, 33, 35, 78, *79*, 149, 209
Lessing, Ferdinand, 75–76
Levinas, Emmanuel, 25, 266–270, 353n33
absolute gratuity, 266
alterity, 269
on obligation to the other, 353n32
other-directed sensibility, 268–269
*lha 'dre* (Tib.), 320n48, 331n33. *See* gods and ghosts
Lidov, David, 328n4
lifespan, longevity, 190, 238
liminality. *See* Turner, communitas
Schechner on, 312n108
transformation of identity through ritual, 68
Turner's concept of, 68, 345n12
Limitless-Oneness, 51, 308n69
Lin, Yutang, 50–52, 308n69
lineage lamas (Tib. *bla rgyud*), 16, 18, 41–42, 61, 68, 88, *115,* 143, 149–151, 161
preservation of traditions by, 215–216
requests for blessings from, 92, 94, 133, 180–181, 287
singing and invoking names of, 43, 54, 135, 253, 304n40
List, George, 299n51
lineage holders, 4, 35, 125, 229, 309n86
lineage transmission, 3, 23, 149, 214, 304n31
Ling Rinpoché (Kyabje), 168
liturgies, 22, 40, 56–65, 77, 83, 95–100, 123–127
living traditions, xxxi
Beyer on, 75
differences, in symbolic attributions between, xxvi, 146
ethnographic engagement with, 139
"frozen," in exile initially during 1960s, 107
as interpretive communities, 140–142
living memory
of Chöd, through lama's instructions, 243
of Chöd, as practiced in pre-1959 Tibet, 4, 11
establishing land claims by remembering songs (Aboriginals), 98
Machik, recounting her previous lifetimes, 36

living memory *(continued)*
of pre-1959 Performing Arts traditions, in TIPA's repertoire, 324n71
shared among Tibetan exiles and refugees in Diaspora, 3
lived experience, 95, 180
ethnomusicology participatory method, 12
relying on one's practice to overcome fear, 180
local spirits, 103, 327n2. *See also* earth owners (*sa bdag*), *nāgas*
long-term meditators, 48–49. *See also* "advanced" practitioners
long lineage, *ring gyü* (Tib. *ring brgyud*), 43
Lopez, Donald, 6–7, 165, 296n20
loss. *See also* attachment
in dreamt milieu, 106
of identity, 212
of "self," 249, 308n72
taking a loss, 241, 349n43
willingness to accept, 71, 217, 252, 332n13
lotus, symbolizing renunciation, 63, 81
love, 23
and compassion, toward beings in *saṃsāra*
cultivating toward spirits, advice on, 314n115
equanimous, 237
Irigaray on, 269–270
Jesus's, in Christianity, 250–251
Machik Labdrön on cultivating, 70
loving-kindness, 250
*lu jin* (Tib. *lus byin*), 301n11. Chöd practice, as called in Mongolia
*lung*. *See* spiritual (scriptural) oral transmission

Machik Labdrön, xiii, xvi, 2–3, 33, 42, 144, 167
children and disicples of, 35, 316n12
compassion of, 302n15
early years, 33, 36
as emanation of the Great Mother (Yum Chenmo), 33
enlightenment of, 36, 316n12
on harmdoers, 69–70
on helping unembodied and embodied beings, 70
hostile spirits, her focus to pacify and liberate, 70
iconography of, *34*, *35*
lineages of, 41–44
melodies of, 114–116, 281
musical image composed by, 114–119
musical instruments held by, *34*, *35*, *145*
Padampa Sangyé and, xvi, *35*, 36, *37*, 71, 285
previous life, 36, 338n6
on self-grasping, 188
semi-wrathful expression, 185–186
three Indian swift-footed ācāryas, 36
visualization of, 64, 91
*Machik's Complete Explanation* (Harding), 313n114
Mādhyamaka-Prāsaṅgika, 294n9, 302n14, 314n118, 343n6
Mahābodhī Temple, 228. *See also* Bodh Gaya
Mahākāla, 133, 186
Mahākarunā, 313n114
mahāparanirvāṇa, of Machik Labdrön, 93–94
mahāsiddha (Skt., Tib. *grub chen*), 33, 35–40, *37*, 208
Mahāyāna Buddhism, 3, 5, 18, 36, 205
altruism, 151, 351n8
*bodhicitta* in, 262, 264, 272, 352n19
Chöd as practice of *bodhicitta*, 25

cultivation of compassion, 272
cultural background, 36
efficacy in, 300n1
generosity, 69
intentionality in, 240
obviates closed system of exchange, 69
other-directed sensibility in, 269
realization of paths common to sūtra and tantra, 190

mandala
body mandala offering, 84, 88, 91–92, 133, 328n5
colored sand, creating and dissolution, 103
as conceptual paradigm, in *Mandala of Sound* (Ellingson), 10, 23, 317n20
inner, 45
in preliminaries *ngön dro* (Tib. *sngon 'gro*), 45, 84, 88, 92, 226
in sadhana sequence, 92

mandala concept, 23
Ellingson on, 10

*Mandala of Sound* (Ellingson), 10, 296n21, 317n20

manifold distribution, *86*, 87–88, *90*, 93, 253, 319n39, 320n42

Mañjuśri (*'Jam dpal*). *See also* Yamāntaka, 98, 103, 133, 204
sādhana of, 204
Tsongkhapa consulted, Lama Umapa Pawo Dorjé as medium, 42–43
visionary lineage from, 43

mantra
*Āḥ*, 88, 92, 180–183
in *Dedicating the Illusory Body as a Heaped Offering*, 165
functions in Chöd ritual, 55, 58
*Gaté*, of *The Heart Sutra*, 177, *179*
layers of depth, *179*, 179–180
*Oṃ maṇi padme hūṃ*, visualization, *179*
of the Perfection of Wisdom, 26, 174–179, *175*
*phaṭ*, 166–170
transmitted between master and disciple, 165

mantric utterance, 165, 179–182. See also *Āḥ*, *phaṭ*
blessing imbued, 215
function of, in Chöd ritual, 58
vocal gestures, 13, 44, 54–55

mapping. *See* ritual mapping

*māra* (Skt., Tib. *bdud*), 244. *See* demons, four *māras*

Martin, Dan, 307n59, 320n46

master-disciple tradition. See *guru-śiṣya paramparā*, 4, 11, 22, 16, 72
inquiry and correction, process of, 25
mantra transmission within, 165
process of oral transmission, 17, 152
transmission (musical and Buddhist lineage), 12, 42
unbroken lineage, 72

Mauss, Marcel, 25, 69, 146, 254, 285, 350n1
on emotional quotient of a gift, 261–262
on the gift economy, 256–263
on reciprocity, 259–260
on self-interest, 256, 264–265
on socialism, 271
on suffering, 264–265

Mead, Margaret, 330n29
and Boas, Franz, 330n29

medical anthropology, 67–68, 265

meditation
on altruism, developing, 354n49
on *bodhicitta*, 281
on death and dying, 166–169
defining, to familiarize (Tib. *sgom*), 49
on emptiness, 248, 281, 350n52
giving Dharma (*chos kyi sbyin pa)*, 86, 93–95

meditation *(continued)*
on patience, 245–246
on renunciation, 281
Zong Rinpoché on, 313n115
meditational deity (Tib. *yi dam*), xiv, 7, 62, 144
Chenrezig, 186
co-extensive with practitioner, 7
meaning of, 305n47
receiving from lama, 7
Troma Nagmo as, 23
melismatic, 136, *137*, 344n2
Ganden Chöd melodies (Molk on), 304n34
melodies in Chöd as, 213
melody (Tib. *rta, dbyangs*), 54, 78, 101, 287–288. *See also specific topics*
*a capella*, 221
blessings and, 40, 42
in Chöd practice, 53–54, 82–83, 115–116, 122
*ḍamaru* drum, accompanying, 222–224
for dedicating merit, 226
in *Dedicating the Illusory Body as a Heaped Offering*, 126
incorporation of new, 125–127
of *kangling* (thighbone trumpet, practice implement), 104
lamas composing, 126
of Machik Labdrön, 114–116, 281
oral tradition of, 299n47
ornaments, 42–43, 46, 221
*phaṭ* mantra recitation and, 55, 85, 174
of Purchog Ngawang Champa Rinpoché, 126
relationship with text, xviii, 17, 24, 54, 59, 68, 97–98, *99–100*, 101–102
ritual mapping of, 123
slowing down of, 136–137
sonic iconography, xviii, 24, 116, 120–125
symbolism in, 282
teaching of, 221
tone-contour chant (Tib. *dbyangs*), 57, *79*, 98
transcription of, 109
transmission of, 299n47
*umdzé* selecting pitch for, 65
Ven. Pencho Rabgey on, 317n24
vocal range, *60*, 65, 78, *79*, 80
vultures depicted by, 121
Zasep Tulku Rinpoché on, 134
membranophone, 78, 317
memoir, *Mountains and Valleys of a Homeland: Memoir* (Ven. Pencho Rabgey), xvii
"mendicant's practice" 114, 227–228. *See also* "beggar's Chöd"
mental states, delusive, 187–188
mentally produced
aural music (Ellingson on), 148, 317n20
expansive visualized imagery, 56, 83, 86
ritual hooked implements, 206
merit (Tib. *bsod nams*), 190. *See also* wisdom (Tib. *ye shes)*
accumulation of, 187, 190, 212, 226, 248, 251, 253
dedication of, 88, *90*, 91
merit field (Tib. *tshogs zhing*), 61–62, 246
metallophone, 77, 317
*mgur* (*gur*) tradition, 9–10, 67, 124, 136. *See* songs of meditative experience
aspects of Chöd ritual practice, compared with, 40–41

song texts and commentaries, 303n27
Thupten Jinpa on, 302n20, 325n79, 332n44
vajra songs (Skt. *vajra gīti*, Tib. *rdo rje'i glu*), 128, 136
*mi rtag pa*. *See* impermanence
Middle Way, view of Nāgārjuna, 199
Mādhyamaka-Prāsaṅgika, 343n6
Milarepa, xiii. See also *mgur* tradition
didactic songs imbued with dharma advice, 107, 197
melodies of song-poems, 67, 164
Mind and Life Institute (MLI), 48–49, 73, 271
comparative studies of meditators, 344n28
contemplative sciences studies, 73
development of compassion, discourse on, 271
efficacy of meditation, correlated with experience level, 73, 344n28
nature of interdisciplinary dialogues, 307n63
mind of renunciation, 205
mind training, *lo jong* (Tib. *blo sbyong*), 88, 276–277, 320n43
mindfulness, 73, 204–205, 350n44, 354n50
mind. *See also* consciousness
and body, relationship between, 3, 68, 104
gross levels of, 167–169
habitually attributing independent existence to phenomena, 31
heart-mind, 2, 286, 305n44
nature of, 187
subtle levels of, 117, 166–170, 338n12, 339n18
mnemonic
in anapest rhythm, 55, 129, 130, 331n30
prosody, 2, 129–131
rhythm interwoven with text, 56, 58, 129–131, 133
seven-branch practice (meter, prose and rhythm), 129
vocables as, 176, 310n94
Molk, David, 304n34
monasteries, policy on, 294n6
monastic ensemble rituals, 77–78, 79
Chöd ritual practice, compared with, *79*
*mudrā*, 163
music, role of, in Chöd, 1–2
music training, in Chöd pedagogy, 218–220
musical analysis
as intervention, 98–99
revealing underlying mechanics of ritual design, 17
musical instruments/implements. *See also specific types*
in Chöd ritual practice, 77–78, *79*
construction of, 158
*ḍamaru* (drum), 139–164
*dril bu* (bell), 54, 78
functions of, 54–55, 72
*kangling* (thighbone trumpet), 80–81, 174–179, *178*, 249–251
Machik Labdrön holding, *34*, *35*, *145*
roles of nuns increasing, 316n13
as symbolic referents, 15, 149–151
in Tibetan ritual music, 316n14, 317n18
training in, 47, 152
treatment of, 157–158
musical notation. *See also* musical analysis
numbered musical notation, 213
tone-contour monastic (overtone) chant, 57, *79*, 98, 323n58
Western staff notation, 57–58, 109

musical transmission, 217–225, 229–234. *See also* apprenticeship
*a capella* versions in, 219, 221
Chöd pedagogy, 218–220
by digital media, 229
Ear-Whispered, 42–43
*guru-śisya paramparā*, 22, 72
near secret, 21
oral transmission in, 215–216
received from lamas, xvii
Shelemey on, 215–216
and spiritual transmission, 214, 233, 280, 284, 294n7
Zong Rinpoché on, 218–219
music-poetry correspondences, in Chöd sādhana, 56–71
mapping. *See* ritual mapping
Mustang region (Nepal), 120

*nāga* (Tib. *klu*), 199. *See also* harmdoers (Tib. *gdug pa can*), obstructors (Tib. *bgegs*)
illnesses caused by, 48
signs attributed to, 149
Nāgārjuna, 33, 314n118
commentaries on tantra, 168
disciple of Saraha, 301n10
Middle Way view, 199
received *Prajñāpāramitā Sūtras* from *nāgas*, 199, 342n5
utilizing natural stages of dying, 169
Nālandā University, 1, 350n52
*namtar* (Tib. *rnam thar*). *See* hagiography
narrative
constructed with literary devices, 24
dramatic, 90
dramaturgical, 102
dualistic, unknowingly, 38–39
reflexive, 214
native/indigenous perspective, 10–11, 23
non-native, 108
on performance practices, 151
through oral tradition, 217
nature
of buddhas, 8
of mind, symbolized, 86
of one's self, 13
of phenomena as mutually interdependent, 31, 113
of reality, xvi, 236
of suffering, 126
v. nurture, 128
Ndembu, 67
healing ritual practices (Friedson), 67
*mudyi* tree, symbolism, 147
reading social symbols as a musical score (Turner), 148
studying ritual as social organization among (Turner), 147
near lineage, *nye gyü* (Tib. *nye brgyud*), 43, 92
requesting and receiving blessings from, 136
singing lineage lamas' names, 135
Nebesky-Wojkowitz, René de, 9, 75–76, 295n17
negative karmic imprints, 3, 69, 167, 217, 248, 313n114. *See also* delusions
accumulated through this and previous lifetimes, 239
Chöd as counter-intuitive method for overcoming, 239
eliminating through specific ritual practices, 188
harmdoers' suffering due to, 5
shaving off like a razor, 251
negative actions, 4
of body, speech and mind, 94
ceasing, 187
Nepal
Ani Choying Drolma, 180

Chöd spread to, 2
Kopan Monastery, 240
monasteries rebuilt in, 3
Mustang region, 120
wood of *seng deng* tree to make *ḍamaru*, 222
Nettl, Bruno, 323n59
neural correlates, 49
new musicology, 20–21
*nges 'byung*. *See* renunciation
*ngön dro* (Tib. *sngon 'gro*). *See* preliminary practices
*ngo shi* (Tib. *dngos gzhi*). *See* actual practice
*ngo wa* (Tib. *bsngo ba*). *See* dedication of merit
nihilism, 199, 348n33
nirvana, 94, 200–201
nomenclature/naming practice, 41
non-virtues, 152
normative concepts within Chöd pedagogy, 10
loss of "self," 249
notation. *See also* music, transcription, ritual mapping
Tibetan chanting notation (Tib. *dbyangs yig*), 98
Western staff notation, 57–58, 109
numinosity, xxv, 21, 185, 196
nunneries
fundraising tours, Chöd performance repertoire, 235
rebuilding, policy on, 294n6
regularly scheduled Chöd practice at
nuns (Skt. *bhikṣuṇi*, Tib. *dge slong ma*)
Chöd practice demonstrations on fundraising tours, 347n19
musical roles, changing, 316n13
practicing Chöd, 78
visualizing oneself pre-odination, 209
way of practicing, 81
*nyams mgur*. *See* songs of meditative experience (*mgur*)
*nyams len gyi dngos gzhi*. *See* actual practice
*nye gyü* (*nye brgyud*), 43. *See* near lineage
*nyen sa* (Tib. *gnyan sa, gnyan khrod*), 68, 70–71, 327n2. *See* haunted places, frightening sites
*nyon mongs* (Tib., Skt. *kleśa*). *See* delusive mental states, afflictive emotions, 170, 187, 263, 341n5
Nyingma school, 41
Chöd liturgical repertoire, 316n11
Chöd melodies, 304n32

objects of refuge (Tib. *skyab yul*), 62, 64, 74, 88
objects
external and internal, 199
interrelated, 348n33
material 201, 343n15
mind needs one to work with, 51
not existent in the way they appear, 94, 263
ritual, 41
of self-grasping ignorance, 31
symbolic, 144
obligatory reciprocation, in gift economy, 257, 259–263
distinguished from generosity, 257, 267
obscurations (Tib. *sgrib pa*)
purified through visualization and utterance, 180
purifying, *91*, 92, 136, 212
obstacles (Tib. *bar chad*), 48, 88, 189
attitude when encountering, 241–242
avoiding, by correct treatment of Chöd *ḍamaru*, 157
clearing away, mantric utterance *phaṭ* as, 55, 165

obstacles *(continued)*
and enjoyments, recognizing nature of both, 244
how to remove, toward achieve realizations, 40
suffering, approach toward, 284
obstructors, harmdoers (Tib. *bgegs*), 189. *See also* interferers
occurs externally, ritual mapping internally, 24
*Offering the Body as Gaṇacakra* (*gCod Tshogs*), 137
*Offering to the Spiritual Guide* (*bLa ma mchod pa*) liturgy, 84, 87, 219
offerings (*mchod pa*)
to guests, in four distributions, 118. *See* four distributions
inner, outer, secret, 132
prayer flags, xii
seven branch practice, *89*, 129–133, 226
Old Testament, 266
old (former) body, 48, 69, 100, 115–118
compassionately regarding as food offering, 121
disassociated from, 92
*Oṃ Ma Ṇi Pad Me Hūm*, 179–180
omniscience, 7, 36, 302n18
path to, 8
Omzela, 164
108 Spring Wilderness Retreat (Tib. *chu mig rgya rtsa*), 23, 81
*Opening the Door to the Sky*, 45, 296n27, 305n46
*Oracles and Demons of Tibet* (Nebesky-Wojkowitz), 75, 295n17
ornamented melody, 60, 129
sung *a capella*, 221–222
oral instructions, 152
from Geshé Trinley, 275
on how to respond to visions, dreams, 239
from Khalkha Jetsun Dampa Rinpoché, on *ḍamaru*, 152
from Kyabje Zong Rinpoché, 113–114, 327n2
on the manner of utterance of mantra, 196
from one's Chöd Lama, 284, 288
and textual instructions, 2
from Ven. Pencho Rabgey, 196, 225, 218–229
oral tradition, 286
continuity of, 43–44, 279–289
ethnomusicology on, 305n42
in Ganden Chöd Tradition, 246
interpretive community and, 151–152
Kyabje Zong Rinpoché on, 113–114
of melody, 299n47
in musical transmission, 215–216
on vultures, 120–121
oral transmission, 17, 113
*guru-śiṣyā paramparā* method of, 4, 11, 38, 152
pedagogical discourse on skill, 29–30
of performance practices, 124
*umdzé* (chanting master) responsible for (Ellingson on), 57
Zasep Tulku Rinpoché, on Chöd, 67
ordinary attainments, 190
Orsi, Robert, 295n14
Öser Rinpoché (Lama), 327n27
*ostinato* patterns, 82–85, 101–102, 311n96, 318n28
flow and, 148
*ma dang lha yi khan dro*, 42, 62
rhythmic, 83
other-directed sensibility
of Levinas (Diprose on), 268–269
in Mahāyāna Buddhism, 269
other-interest, 271

othering, 250
outback, Australian
knowledge of songs as cultural survival, 323n61
outer Chöd, 44, 72–73, 99–100, *105*. *See also* inner, secret, suchness

Pacification Tradition, *Shijé* (Tib. *zhi byed*), xvi, 36–38
pacification (*zhi ba*). *See* four ritual activities, 185–187
of fear, 189
internal and external distinctions, 188–189
mapped, in sequence of subrituals, *89–90*
playing the drum, to effect, 341n5
of relations, through paying down karmic debt, 257
in ritual dramaturgy, 133
Ven. Pencho Rabgey on, 188–189
Padampa Sangyé (*Pha dam pa sang rgyas*), *35*, 36, *37*, 38, 41, 43, 285
founder of *zhi byed* (pacification) tradition, xvi
Machik Labdrön and, 71
teacher of Machik Labdrön, 36, 41, 43, 103
Padmasaṁbhava, 303n29
Pala. *See* Ven. Pencho Rabgey
Panchen Losang Chokyi Gyaltsen, 318n31
Panchen Lamas, 42, 318n31
Papua New Guinea, 19
*paramitās*. *See* six perfections
paranirvāṇa (Skt). *See* mahāparanirvāṇa
paradox
feeling of "I," even after body given away, 31
role of music in Chöd meditation practice, 2, 66, 113
participant-observation. *See also* ethnomusicology methodology
combining methodologies with, 11, 106
ethnographic-based methodology, 106
ethnomusicological performative approach to, 14
Shelemay on, 345n10
in varied pedagogical contexts, 12
path to enlightenment, 95, 131, 204–205
gradual, 269
*mgur* dharmic songs on, 302n20
in tantric context, 197
patience
advice on, from Ven. Pencho Rabgey, 244–245, 349n43
of Chödpas, 244–248
defining, 246
meditating on, parable of the monk, 245–246
perfection of, 179, 248
three spheres of (Tib. *bzod pa'i 'khor gsum*), 248
training in, 244–248
paying down karmic debt, 30, 121, 210, 242
with altruistic resolve, 285
by giving the body away, 51
Payne, Helen, 323n61
pedagogy. *See also* transmission
on *ḍamaru* accompanying singing, 221–222
experienced in apprenticeship, 11, 23, 106, 152
nuanced understanding of symbolism, 25
pedagogical discourse, 24
receiving oral commentary only after memorizing, 220

pedagogy *(continued)*
singing ornamented melody *a capella*, 221, with *ḍamaru*, 222
Ven. Pencho Rabgey's methods of training, 220–225
Zong Rinpoché (Kyabje), training in *ḍamaru* and singing, 221
perfection of generosity, 1, 118, 170, 248, 272
perfections (*pāramitā*) 118, 179–180, 190, 253–254. *See* six perfections, bodhisattva practices
Perfection of Wisdom (Skt. *Prajñāpāramitā*). *See also* Great Mother, emptiness
*Perfection of Wisdom Sūtras*, xvi, 33, 337n2
mantra, 175, 177
origin of, 301n12
personified as Yum Chenmo (Great Mother)
recitation of, as merit making, 33
"performance-*centered* practice," 24, 46–47, 72, 281. *See also* "practice-*centered* performance"
performance practices, 119–120
of *ḍamaru* drum, 152
defined (Béhague), 53, 80
group v. solo, 80–81
integration of, 124
learned through oral tradition, 220–222
of mantric utterance *phaṭ*, 171
of melody, mantra, and rhythm, 54–55
of ritual instruments, 54–55
primacy of, 124–125
performance studies xxiv, 14, 68. *See also* ritual studies
dramaturgical analysis in, 102, 297n29
ethnomusicological perspective enhanced by, 106
philosophy of Chöd and, 195
ritual as social drama (Turner on), 329n12
Schechner on, 68, 102
performance tradition, masked dances (Tib. *'cham*), 9
performance theory, 14
performative architecture, in Chöd sadhana, 41
permissions
from head of lineage, to contribute new melody, 125–126
to practice in a *nyen sa*, from earth owners (*sa bdag*), 103
permission ritual (Tib. *je nang*, *rjes gnang*). *See also* initiation, empowerment
personal transformation, 3
Pabongka Dechen Nyingpo, 126, 135. See *Lam Rim* discourses
approval of melody, 161
*phaṭ* (mantra), 165, 166–170, 283
clearing away obstacles, with utterance of, 165
comprised of two syllables, 171
Kachen Lobsang Zopa, written commentary on, 171–174
manner of utterance, 173–174
mapping, *99, 100*
at sectional transitions, 82, 85, 243
symbolizing sutra and tantra, 171
in transference of consciousness, 170–171
*tsam gcod phaṭ*, utterance before each subritual, 165, 173, 318n32
phenomenology
aspects of ritual practice, 208
Chöd as multifaceted, 30
Derrida, on gift and exchange, 267

phenomena, selflessness of, 70, *150*, 156, 300n2. *See also* selflessness
philosophical schools, 151, 187, 303n29
*phowa* (Tib. *'pho ba*). *See* transference of consciousness
*phrin las rnam bzhi*. *See* four ritual activities
*phyag rgya bzhi*. *See* four seals of dharma
physical body
  relationship to the "self," 18. *See also* body
*phyi dar*. *See* Later propogation of Buddhism into Tibet
physical illness, 4–5
physical effort, training in *ḍamaru*
*Pictures at an Exhibition* (Mussorsky), 328n4
places for Chöd practice, 30–32. *See* frightening sites; terrifying sites
*The Planets* (Holst), 328n4
poetry
  allusions, 2
  enlivened by music, 40
  meter, 38
  Tibetan poetics, 287–288
Pollock, Sheldon, 298n39
polyphony, 328n6. *See* drone polyphony
positivism, 261
positionality: in ethnomusicological discourse, 19
post-meditation period, *je thob* (Tib. *rjes thob*), 57, 104, *105*
potlatch (Mauss on), 264
power, 264
powerful (Tib. *dbang*) ritual activities, 185
  internal and external distinctions, 190
practice
  emotional state before v. after, 218
  experience in, 23
  medtiation, 49, 52, 64
  progressive advancement, 23
  of return, in ethnography, 19
  sessions, 104–106
  values of tradition, 18
"practice-*centered* performance," 24, 46–48. *See also* "performance-*centered* practice"
practice-level. *See* advanced, beginner, graduated path
  "advanced," 5, 41, 47–54, 169, 276
  "beginner," 46, 49–55, 68, 70, 72–73, 142, 149
  graduated training in Chöd, 46–54
  how gaining musical skill enhances meditative engagement in Chöd, 47
  "intermediate," 46–47
  in music and meditation, 46–47, 72–73, 307n56
*phowa*, 104, 167–169. *See* transference of consciousness
*Prajñāpāramitā Sūtra* (Tib. *shes rab kyi pha rol tu phyin pa*) 33, 165, 181, 199, 204
  *Āḥ* (mantric syllable) in, 88, 92, 301n12
  recitation while calling with *kangling*, *175*, 174–179
  six perfections in, 118
  *See also* Perfection of Wisdom, 33
*prāṇāyāma*, 288
Prāsaṅgika-Madhyamaka
*pratītya-samutpāda* (Tib. *rten cing 'brel bar 'byung ba*). *See* dependent arising, 39, 94, 283
prayer flag offerings, on Vultures' Peak, xii
preliminary practices (Tib. *sngon 'gro*), 87, 88, 94, 226
  body mandala offering, 84

preliminary practices *(continued)*
going for refuge and generating *bodhicitta*, 88
guru-deity yoga, 205, 215
requesting blessings from lineage lamas, 88, 135
seven branch offering practice, 129–135
preparing for nightly practice, 49–50
principal paths, three. *See* three principal paths
preservation, 229–230, 233–234
confluence with transmission and dissemination, 25, 214–216
continuity and change, in the context of, 284–289
of Ganden Chöd Tradition, 265
primary text, 25
primary sources, 128
prophecy, Machik on her previous life's body, 36
propogation of Buddhism in Tibet. *See* early period, later period
prosody, symbolism of, 29, 58
as mnemonic, 129
profane, 6–7
psychophysical aggregates (Skt. *skandha*, Tib. *phung po*), 30–31, 300n4
public performance v. spiritual practice, 225–229
Purchog Ngawang Champa Rinpoché, melodies of, 126
purification by mantra, 92, 181

*qawwali*, 107
Qureshi, Regula, 107

Rabgey, Pencho "Pala" (Ven), xvii, 4, 12, 42, 83, 131–13
on advanced practitioners, 196–197
on Chöd pedagogy, 217, 221
on *ḍamaru* drum, 153–155, *158*, 158–159, *162*, 223
*Dedicating the Illusory Body as a Heaped Offering* practiced by, 317n24
on dualistic grasping, 198–199
on emptiness, 200
on Ganden Chöd Tradition, 42
Gen Trinley and, 275–276
on giving the body, 274–275
on graduated skill, 280
on group performance, 176
lectures of, *227*
on melody, 317n24
name of, 297n28
on patience, 244–245, 349n43
on peaceful activity, 189
on resolving conflict, 349n43
on society, 224
studies of, 306n50
as teacher, 346n17
on tempo, 155
on visualizations, 153
Rabten, Geshé, 239–240, 348n36
Rājgṛha (Rājgīr), xii, xv. *See also* Vulture Peak
Ranger, Terrance, 95–96
*rasa*, 124–125, 131–134, 192
Ravel, Maurice, 311n96
realization (Tib. *rtogs pa*), 190
rebirth, 208–209
fear of next, as motivation for taking refuge, 73
in lower or upper realms, 8, 70, 73
Tsongkhapa on, 338n8
reciprocity
altruistic intentionality in Buddhism, 257–259
in ethnography, as research methodology (Spradley on), 19, 23
in gift economy, 257–263
Mauss, on social systems, 255–274

recordings field (audio, film, video), 96, 107, 110
albums for fundraising, by Ani Chöying Drolma and Steve Tibbetts, 226–227
audiotape cassette, 223
Canzio, Ricardo on, 143
by Chöd lamas, as teaching aids, 218–220
consumer recording technology, 25, 43, 83, 109
dampen harmonics of bell for, 219, 345n13
dissemination of, 25, 44
Kyabje Zong Rinpoché, 161
Lama Zopa Rinpoché, 345n7
as method of training, 220–224
pedagogically-oriented cassettes, 284
for preserving, 284
resistance to, 345–346n14
transmission conflated with dissemination and preservation, 229–231
videotape, 110, 219, 226
red distribution (Tib. *dmar 'gyed*), 86, *86*, 87, 88, 93, 320n47
reflexivity, 15, 141, 208, 214, 225
refuge (Tib. *skyab 'gro*). *See also* Three Jewels, three scopes of person
causes for 66, 73–74
going for refuge, musical analysis of subritual, 60–65
liberation from cyclic existence, as goal, 314n120
objects of (Tib. *skyab yul*), 62, 74
structural placement in sadhana liturgy, *178*
symbolic imagery in melody for, 13
in the Three Jewels, 74, 88, 93
Tsongkhapa's incantation for, 183
refugees, Buxa Duar camp, 83
Chöd practice in exile, 83
Tibetan exile community, 75, 213, 296, 324n71
reincarnation, 167
rejoicing, 129. *See* seven branch offering practice
in accumulated merits of buddhas and beings, 130, 132
relative stability, 159
relative truth. *See* conventional truth
relativity
cultural, 202
physical-cognitive, 202–203
of sound, 202–210
reincarnation, 167. *See also* rebirth
renunciation (Tib. *nges 'byung*), 190, 240–241, 247
attitude of, conjoined with bodhicitta, 18, 151, 182
cultivating, 104
fear, as cause for, 73–74, 123
lifestyle based on, 197
lotus flower symbolizing, 63
meditation on, 281
melody recalls, 123
three principal paths, 45, 73
weariness with cyclic existence, 18, 209
wish to be free of eight worldly concerns, 104
Roerich, George, 38
repetition, in Chöd music training, 65–66
requesting blessings from lineage lamas, 43, 88, *89*, 226, 308
research methods, 11–12. *See also* ethnography, fieldwork
apprenticeship as immersive ethnomusicological study, 11, 23
developing word-for-word translations of liturgies 12
five distinct stages of, 2
indigenous method, learning with master practitioners, 18

research methods *(continued)*
multisite ethnography, 12
reciprocity, 19, 23
sought advice from Tibetan scholars and lamas, 11
six different pedagogical contexts, 12
rhythm, 66, 101–102
in *Chöd Tshogs*, 135–137
*dram-dram* rhythm, 310n93xw
*lha-yi*, 310n95
as mnemonic prosody, in seven branch offering, 129–131
played on *ḍamaru*, 82–83, 94, 131
relationship with melody and text, 19, 59
rhythmic *ostinato* in Ganden Chöd, 310n93
six beat ostinato, *ma dang lha yi kang dro*, 42
synaesthetic, 131
tempo set by *umdzé*, 224
vocables, function in training, *100*, 310n94
rhythmic patterns
creativity within, 109
drumming, 47
exploring, 108
melodic, 56, 61
micro-beat rhythm, 42
physical movement to play *ḍamaru*
rhythmic cycle, "*ma dang, lha yi, kha(n) dro*," 62–64, 81–82, 84–85
rhythmic flow, 53–54
ritology, 298n42
ritual (Tib. *cho ga*), 7
Bell (Catharine) on, theory and practice, 13–15
efficacy, 12–14, 29, 50–53
ethnomusicological approaches to, 9–12, 17–22, 53, 106, 279
historiography of, in Tibetan studies, 75–76
instruments/implements of, 54, 72–74, 77–78, 243
layered intertexuality, 24, 55–56
as social drama, 68
Turner on, 146–149, 329n12
rite of passage, on group level, 345n12
*rkang gling* (Tib.). *See* thighbone trumpet
ritual studies (Tibetan Buddhism)
*Buddhist Himalaya* (Snellgrove), 75–76
*Cult of Tārā* (Beyer), 75–76
integrated approach to Chöd studies, xxv, 22
of monastic orchestral ensembles, 10–11, 75–76
*Oracles and Demons of Tibet* (Nebesky-Wojkowitz), 75–76
of vocal monk chant (*dbyangs*), 10, 77
ritual feast gathering (Tib. *tshogs*)
rituals
four hundred meat offerings (Tib. *sha brgya zan brgya*)
funerary, xvi, 9
going for refuge (Tib. *skyabs 'gro*), *35*, *60*, 61
sky burial (Tib. *bya gtor*), 327n3
success in, causes for, 13, 30, 48
ritual mapping, 24–25, 127–128, 283
approaches to, 125
of Chöd sadhana practice, 97–102
defining, 293n3
Grimes on, 293n3
of intertextual layers, 56, 101 121, 281–283
of melody, 123
of melodic layer, 101
motivations for, 128–129
of rhythmic layer, 101–102
in transcription, 97–98
of written liturgical layer, 123–124

ritual master, 86
advanced Chöd rituals, Tsongkhapa on, 48–49, 332n36
*Civilized Shamans* (Samuel), 319n35
ritual mastery, 70–71
ritual meditation practices, 143
ritual studies, 68
in anthropology, 195–196. *See* Turner
in ethnomusicology, 6, 297n29
kinesthetic v. synaesthetic experience, Bell on, 13–15
and performance studies, 68, 106. *See* Schechner
ritual music. *See* Buddhist ritual music, Tibetan ritual music, 6, 9–10, 22
Rizong Monastery, xvii
*rjes thob* (Tib.). *See* post-meditation period
*rnam thar* (Tib.). *See* spiritual biography (*namtar*)
root lama (Tib. *rtsa ba'i bla ma*), 83, 164, 336n51
of Pala, Geshé Trinley, 232, 272, 306n50
Rouget, Gilbert, *100*, 319n33
on trance rhythms, 323n64
Royal Ontario Museum, 22
*rta. See* melody
*rtogs. See* realization

*sadag* (Tib. *sa bdag*), 41, 103. *See* earth owners
*sa skya. See* Sakya school
Sachs-Hornbostel instrument classification system, 78, 317n18
sacred/profane, Durkheim on, 6–7
sacred sites (*gnas*), 44, 103, 238
sacrifice, 5, 294n11
body visualized as ransom (Tib. *glud*), 26, 69
bodhisattva actions of, in Buddhism, 248–249
imagery in Chöd, not harming any being, 294n11
*Jākata Tales*, verse on Buddha giving body to tigress, 274
Western misapprenhension of v. reality of Chöd practice, 85, 294n11
sādhana, xiv, 38, 50. *See also specific topics*
in the Chöd ritual tradition, 16, 22–23
as daily life practice, 104–106, 197
*Dedicating the Illusory Body* (Tib. *sGyu lus tshogs su sngo ba*), as case study, xxiv, 86–95
defining, 12, 300n3, 342n4
formal structure of, 21, 86–88, *89*, *90*, 91
in the Ganden Chöd Tradition, 86–87
generating *bodhicitta* before and within, 45
levels of; inner, outer, secret, suchness, 44–46
liturgical corpus of, 22, 87
liturgical poetry of, 17, 117–118
memorization of, 220–221, 306n53, 327n2
musical texture of, 54, 82, 116, 123
music-poetry corresopndences within, 56, 58, 118, 124
post-meditational periods, 103–105
practice of, 18, 40, 88–91
training step-by-step, 102
Ven. Pencho Rabgey on training, 220–224
word-for-word translations of, making, 12, 17, 220, 287–289
Sakya Paṇḍita Kunga Gyaltsen, 10, 137–138
Sakya school, 41, 303n29, 316n11

Śākyamuni (Buddha), 238, 301n10
applying of antidotes, teaching 188
enlightenment at Bodh Gaya, 228
Four Noble Truths, 187
second turning of the dharma wheel, xv
*saṃbhogakāya* (Skt.), 169
*saṃsāra* (Tib. *'khor ba*). *See* cyclic existence, conditioned existence
Samten Karmay, 85, 297n29
on shamanic rites, 319n36
Sanskrit, 63–64, 88, 175
*dohā* tradition of poetics, 38
Machik Labdrön's knowledge of, 36, 302n18
poetics in *mgur* tradition, Jinpa on impact of, 325n79
terminology, xiii–xiv
Śāntideva, 1, 258
*Bodhisattvacaryāvatāra* (*Guide to the Bodhisattva's Way of Life*), xvi
on guarding alertness, 247, 350n44
at Nālanadā Monastic University, 16, 1
on perfection of generosity, 1, 258–259
sentry at the doorway of the mind, 247
on vultures symbolizing impermanence, xvi
Saraha, 38, 301n10, 342n5
*Saraha's Adamantine Songs*, Braitstein, 303n27
Sarasvatī, xxvii
Sarnath, 187, 351n12
Savvas, Carol, 6, 43, 66, 304n40, 307n60, 332n36
*sbug chal. See* cymbals
*sbyin pa. See* generosity
*sbyin pa'i pha rol tu phyin pa. See* perfection of generosity
*sbyin pa'i 'khor gsum. See* three spheres of giving
scapegoat (Tib. *glud*), 69
Schechner, Richard, 68, 102, 329n12
dramaturgical narrative, 102, 297
on healing rituals, 68
performance studies, xxiv
ritual events as social drama, 329n12
Schools of Tibetan Buddhism, 41, 303n29
*See also* names of individual schools
scriptural knowledge, and ritual skills compared, 319n35
second turning of the wheel of Dharma, xv
secret level of Chöd practice, 3
self, 4–5, 204
appearance to the mind, grasping at 308n7
attachment to, 263
fearful of losing, 32, 49, 300n2
grasping at true existence of, 198
identification of body mistakenly as, 5, 201–202
Kyabje Zong Rinpoché on recognizing correctly, 197, 206
strong experience of, 201
self-cherishing (Tib. *bdag gces 'dzin*), 93, 269, 272
egotistical, 31, 153
Kyabje Zong Rinpoché on, antidote to, 314n115
*tong len* practice used to subdue, 348n33
self-existence, 151, *178*, 179, 199, 203
habitual attribution to phenomen as having, 31
phenomena lacking inherent, 247, 294n9
sound, as symbolizing lack of, 54
subtle perspective on, to reduce ego, 350n52
self-grasping ignorance (Tib. *bdag 'dzin ma rig pa*), 119, 125, 157, 197, 263, 294n11, 308n72
cutting root of, xvi, 31, 249
cutting through, 207–208

destruction of, 243
Machik Labdrön on, 188
as real enemy, 119
as root of cyclic existence, 263
self-interest
Buddhist approaches to reduction of, 257, 270–273
collective interest, 273
Dalai Lama on, 271
gift economy and Buddhism, distinction between, 256–263
gifting to heal, 273–274
healing the suffering from, 255, 264–265, 270, 273–275
Mauss on, 256, 264–265
as Western economic model, 256–257, 259
selflessness of persons, 300n2
selflessness of phenomena, 70, 94, 156. *See also* emptiness, dependent-arising
dependent arising reasoning, 113, 204
reasoning of the three spheres, 87, 281, 350n46
wisdom realizing, 150
semiotics, xxix, 328n4
semi-wrathful activity (Tib. *zhi ma khro*), 185–186
*sems pa*. *See* consciousness, mind
sentient beings (Tib. *sems can*), 88. *See also* transmigrators
altruism devoted to alleviation of suffering of, 6
equanimity toward, 44, 236, 253
inviting all, xxiii, 173, 249–251
kindness of, 5, 69
karma of, 69, 167
Sera Mey Monastic College, xxvii, 306n50, 346n17
Sera Monastic University, xxviii, 16, 295n17
Sermey Khensur Lobsang Tharchin, 168, 313n112
Sermey Khensur Lobsang Jamyang, xxviii, 16, 336n51
seven branch offering practice, *89*, 92, 129–134, *130*, *178*
in Chöd sadhana liturgy (translated), 331n32
verses of, 132
seven-step cause and effect instruction, 351n8
severance (*gCod*), 25, 31, 197. *See* Chöd
*sgom*, 49. *See* meditation
*gomchen* (*sgom chen*), 53
*Shadows in the Field* (Barz and Cooley), 15
shamanism, 5, 67, 69, 84–86, 319n35. *See also* trance
aspects of, 5, 84–85
Chöd ritual mistakenly viewed as, 69, 84–86
Geoffrey Samuel on, 319n35
healing and, 86
music studies of, 67
Samten Karmay on, 85–86, 319n36
Zasep Tulku Rinpoché on description of, 67, 319n37
Shelemay, Kay Kaufman
on participation in ethnomusicological research, 345n10
on transmission, 215–216
*Shi jé* (Tib. *Zhi byed*) School, 16, 36, 38, 285. *See also* Pacification Tradition
skull cup (Tib. *thod pa*), 39, 92–93, 316n14
skull drum (Tib. *thod rnga*). See *ḍamaru*
siddha, 309n86m, 312n102. *See also* adept, mahāsiddha
siddhi, of enlightened speech, 165
of knowledge, proof of Machik's realization, 302n18
singing (liturgical, vocal). *See also* chanting, tone-contour overtone chant

singing *(continued)*
a Chöd sadhana, 115–116
compelling melodies, 32
in darkness, having memorized liturgy, 50
dedication prayer, 133
determining pitch of vocal entries, 80, 245
dharmic advice, 40
enjoyment of, 85, 309n81
flow of, 100
graduated increase in pitch, 331n35
Khalkha Jetsun Dampa Rinpoché on, 156
learning performance utterances, 102
names of lineage lamas, 167
ornately, by training in vocal production, 56, 83
on pilgrimage, 126
umdzé leads, 80
Ven. Pencho Rabgey/Pala on, 83
vibrato, 56
vocal ranges, 78
six perfections (*pāramitās*), 17, 190, 254, 342n7
of ethical discipline, 179
of generosity, 1, 118, 170, 248, 258, 267
training in compassion, 272
of joyful effort, 301n11
of meditative concentration, 179
of patience, 248
in *Prajñāpāramitā Sūtra*, 301n11
of wisdom, 33
six realms of existence, 88, 93, 313n113
contemplation of suffering, 167, 180
mantric recitation while visualizing, *179*
sky burial, 91, 119, 307n59, 320n46. *See also* cemetery
Dan Martin on, ritual process of, 327n3
site for Chöd practice, 113
vultures invited to, xvi
*skyab yul. See* objects of refuge
Simmer-Brown, Judith, 301n6
*snga dar. See* Early dissemination of Buddhism into Tibet
Snellgrove, David, 75–76
social image, 238
social justice, 268
socialism, 264. *See also* utilitarianism
Durkheim on, 271
Mauss on, 271
social suffering, Bourdieu on, 267
solitary, 3, 80, 120, 246, 283
solo Chöd ritual practice, 22, 60, 78, 81–82
distinguished from group Chöd practice, 80
flexibility in performative aspects, 308n67
Sönam Lama (Kyotön), lama of Machik Labdrön, 36
songs of spiritual experience (Tib. *mgur*), 309n81
Chöd ritual practice compared with, 40–41
*mgur* tradition, 9–10, 67, 124, 136
popularization of song texts, 303n27
Thupten Jinpa on, 302n20, 325n79, 332n44
sonic iconography, xviii, 24, 58, 116–117, 125, 131, 282
tone painting as, 120
sound
emptiness of, 54
images, of vultures, xvi, 123, 156
impermanence of, 40, 121
phenomena interrelated with, 202
relativity of, 202–210
structure, 343n13
speech, as enhancing visualization, 13
purifying negative acts of, 88, 94, 166, 181

spiritual biography (Tib. *rnam thar*), 141, 208
spiritual teachers. *See* Chöd lama
spiritual practice, need effort in, 23, 197, 225–227, 233
spiritual realization (Tib. *yon tan gyi rtogs pa*) 190
spiritual transmission (Tib. *lung*), 231, 233
  training context, 4, 11
  woven together with musical transmission, 280
  *See also* musical transmission
spontaneous compositions, 108–109
  Milarepa *mgur* as, 107, 197
  Thupten Jinpa on, 79, 302n20
Spradley, James, 11
  on building reciprocity into methodology, 23
  listening to Tibetan consultant-expressed wishes, 296n25
*Stages of the Bodhisattva Deeds* (Asanga), 313n114
*Stages of the Path to Enlightenment.* See *Lamrim*
structural-functionalism, 2
Subaltern school, 298n43
subrituals, of a Chöd liturgy, 40, 44, 134
  performance practice, 226, 288
  *phaṭ* mantric utterance, at transitions between, 85, 243, 318n32
  seven branches offering practice, *130*
subtle mind/consciousness, 167, 339n18
suffering (Skt. *duḥkha*, Tib. *sdug bsngal*)
  Buddha taught antidotes to, xv
  cessation of, 187
  giving as antidote to, 259–260, 273–275
  relieving others from, in Mahāyāna path, 269, 281
  seen as "positive" result of practicing Chöd, 5, 238–241
  "self-grasping ignorance" as root cause of, 270, 273–275
  understanding causes of, 4, 240–241
  *See also* cyclic existence, conditioned existence
Sufism, 107
Sugarman, Jane, 20–22
  *See* ethnoaesthetics defined, 108, 299n53
Sujata, Victoria, 323n62
*śūnyatā* (Skt., Tib. *stong pa nyid*). *See* emptiness
*sutra,* defining, 301n9
symbolism
  in Chöd ritual practice, 140–149
  of *ḍamaru* drum, 140–141, 253, 282–283
  Ellingson on, 140–141, 144–145
  function of symbols at different levels, 142–143
  indigenous variation in interpretation of, 147–148
  intentionality in, 283
  learning, 12, 24
  melodic, 282
  musical, 113
  of sound and material, 156–157
  of thighbone trumpet, 249–250
  in Tibetan Buddhism, 143–149
  in Tibetan ritual music, 148–149
  Turner on, 147–148
  in Vajrayāna ritual practices (Jinpa on), 144
synchronic
  and diachronic, in anthropology, 334n19
synchronous
  instrumental rhythm, 82
  meter, 100
  playing of instruments as inspiring faith, 155

synchronous *(continued)*
structure, 14
study in British anthropology, 334n19
synchronizing
needs of people with goals of research, 296n25

*tābla*, 330. See also *bol*
Takten House, xxviii, 219, 306n50, 317n23
Talmudic thought, 266, 274, 353n33
tantra, defining, 293n4
Tantric Buddhism, 75, 313n114. *See also* Highest Yoga Tantra
Tantric Vehicle, 293n4. *See also* Vajrayāna
Tārā, *35,* 36
advice to Machik, 338n6
tape recordings. *See also* recordings (audio, field, film, video)
audiotape cassette, 219, 223
Lama Zopa Rinpoché (FPMT) Chöd CD/DVD, 345n7
videotape, 110, 219, 226
Tashi Lhunpo Monastery, 283
*tathāgatagarbha* (Skt., Tib. *de bzhin gshegs pa'i snying po*), 187, 295. *See* buddha-nature
teacher-student relationship, 4, 16, 18
technology, in Chöd pedagogy, 214, 223–224, 229
as musical transmission tool, 234, 284–286
tempo, 135, 221
accelerating slowly, 85, 94, *100,* 317n24
of *ḍamaru*, 140, 154–155
depth of meditation, affected by, 159–160
slow, while training, 335n34, 346n15
*umdzé* adjusts in practice, 80
Teng word-for-word transcription, 287–290
terminology, conceptual (in Buddhism), 198–202
testing
efficacy of Chöd method (through practice), 13
monk's mettle, in parable on patience, 245–246
as pedagogy, 223–224
text-setting, 58–66, 96, 108–109, 129–131, *132,* 134
*thangka*, *35*, *145*, 282
as holistic image, 101
Machik Labdron, *34*
Padampa Sangyé, *37*
Theravādan Buddhism, 190, 204–205
theory. *See also* music theory
Chöd, 122–123, 248–250
explanatory, 10
gift and exchange, 25–26, 69
indigenous, on Tibetan music asthetics, 283
Mauss' gift economy, 69, 267 270
of obligation, 255, 257
performance, 14
philosophical, 202
postmodern, 142
and practice, ethnomusicology, 16, 306
ritual, 6, 106
of substitution, Levinas on, 352
Talmudic, 353
turning into practice, 18
thighbone trumpet (Tib. *kangling*), 26, 30, 32, *37,* 81, 177, 213
calling forth beings with, *178*, 250
in *Dedicating the Illusory Body*, 174–179
inviting to the feast, 249
materials of, 316n17
role of, 54, 78

symbolism of, 249–250
visualization while calling, 250
Thönyön Samdrup, *35*, 345n8
three doors (body, speech, mind), 4, 242, 344n5
Three Jewels, 88, 93
three poisons (Tib. *dug gsum*), 4, 138. *See also* anger, attachment, ignorance
defined, 294n9
*Three Principal Aspects of the Path* (Tsongkhapa), 18, 136, 190, 247
on emptiness and dependent origination, relationship of, 201
Kyabje Zong Rinpoché on, 45
*Lam rim* (Stages of the Path) discourses, 136
root of Chöd practice, 18, 45, 73, 136, 319n37
Tsongkhapa (*Tsong ka pa*) on, 338n8
three rounds of subduing (Tib. *zil gnon skor gsum*), 44, 338n2
three scopes, persons practice according to, 73–74
three spheres of giving (Tib. *sbyin pa'i 'khor gsum*), 95, 253
contemplating mutual dependence of, 87, 254
Kyabje Zong Rinpoché on, 322n52, 350n46
in ritual sādhana context, 57, 281
way of meditating upon emptiness, *90*, 248
three spheres of patience (Tib. *bzod pa'i 'khor gsum*), 248
Thubten Yeshe (Lama)
on blame, 240
on dualistic grasping, 198
on mind, 163
Thupten Kelsang Champa (Acharya), 200–201, 340n31
Thupten Jinpa (Geshé), 67, 96
on Kyabje Zemey Rinpoché, 67
on *mgur* tradition, 302n20, 325n79, 332n44
on music transcription notation, 96
on symbolism in deity-yoga, 144
on Vajrayāna (Tantric Vehicle), 293n4, 339n16
Thurman, Robert, 170
Tibbetts, Steve, 226–227
Tibet, 3, 52, 140–141
Chöd ritual practice in, 1–4
lifeways, 8–9
Tibetan Buddhism, 286
Chöd lineages in, 143, 151
in daily life, 8–9
doctrine, 204–205
guru-deity yoga in, 215
iconography of, 143–144
interpretive communities, 141
Mahāyāna, 352n19
practice, 204–205
schools, 41
scholars of, 6, 141
symbolism in, 143–149
transmission of, 286, 290
Tibetan Diaspora, 3, 12, 186, 214, 238, 303n29
Tibetan Institute of Performing Arts (TIPA), 324n71
Tibetan music notation. *See* tone-contour chant
Tibetan ritual music studies, 7, 9–12, 17, 26
audible and imagined symbolism, Ellingson on, 148–149
contrasting genres, monastic orchestral ensembles v. Chöd, 77–78, *79*
gender roles, tradition and change, 77–78, 316n13

Tibetan ritual music studies *(continued)*
liturgical repertoire in monastic settings, 98
mandala concept, Ellingson on, 10, 23
*mgur*, 107
monastic liturgical ritual music, 77, *79*
and musical instruments, 78
nunneries, ensemble practices, 316n13
performance practices, group v. solo 80–82
*umdzé* (Tib. *dbu mdzad*), expertise of, 164
Tibetan ritual music, 9–10, 143. *See also* Buddhist ritual music
genres of, 77–78
instruments in, 78, 316n14, 317n18
Kaufmann on, 333n7
musical analysis of, 103
symbolism in, 148–149
Titmuss, Richard, 265–266, 273
Togden Jampel Gyatso (rTogs ldan 'jam dpal rgya mtsho), 43
tonal areas, 61
defining, 311n97
exemplified in analysis of "Going for Refuge" melody, 58–66
issues with musical analysis of non-Western musics, 61, 311n97
tone-contour overtone chant (Tib. *dbyangs*), 57, *79*
Ellingson on, 57, 323n58
Tibetan musical notation for (Tib. *dbyangs yig*), 98
tone painting, 24, 282. *See also* sonic iconography
aural analogy of natural phenomenon, 185
Machik Labdrön's use of, in Chöd melody, 114, 128
music composition technique, 24–25, 328n4
as sonic iconography, 120–121, 282
Vivaldi's use of, 328n8
of vultures' wings, 118
*tong len* (Tib. *gtong len*), 88, *90*, 251. *See* "giving and taking"
traditionalism, 95–96
trance, 84–86
*ostinato* (rhythmic and melodic) as potentially inducing, 84, 148
rhythm as physiological ground for, *100*
Rouget on, 319n33, 323n64
in shamanic contexts (Chöd outside of), 84–86
transcription
of Chöd melodies, 56–66, 127
in ethnomusicology, 95–96, 106–107
of "Going for Refuge" melody, *60*
insights from, 96–97
Nettl on, 323n59
observations through, 58
Western values and, 95–96
transcribing ritual music (benefits and drawbacks)
allows one to see complex web of events 134
concern with, applying West-writing-East paradigm, 21
as intervention for cultural survival, 98
as method of analysis and insight, 21–22
resistant to, 21–22
slows down visualizations and performance elements, 134
transcription as analysis
as descriptive tool, 97
as prescriptive tool, 98
ritual mapping, 97–98

transference of consciousness, *phowa* (Tib. *'pho ba*), 31, 47, 92, 104, 117, 166, 209
*phaṭ* in, 170–171
Rabgey on, 339n22
transformation
through Chöd practice, 236–241
within transmission, 253
transforming and offering body, 93
translation, Teng word-for-word method, 287
transmigrators (Tib. *'gro ba*), 112, 167. *See* sentient beings
transmission, 2, 284–285, 296n20. *See also specific topics*
in Buddhist studies, 215
conflated with dissemination and preservation, 25
continuity and lineage preservation, 285–290
for cultural survival, 229–235
digital recording technology, as medium for, 43
in ethnomusicology, 215
*guru-śiṣya paramparā* traditional method, 4, 11, 22, 38, 72
individualized one-to-one, 18
initiation, 12
learning by rote, tradition of, 20
listening to teachings, way of, 7
musical, 21–22, 214–217
of musical and meditation aspects, 22
oral, 3
passed on secretly, 42
pedagogical methods, xvii, 280–281
Shelemay on, 215–216
six pedagogical contexts of, 297n31
spiritual (*lung*), 11, 214–217, meaning in Buddhism
Troma Nagmo, 23, 131, 192, 205
truth body (Skt. *dharmakāya*, Tib. *chos sku*), 92
two truths (Tib. *bden pa gnyis*)
Acharya Thupten Champa on, 200–201
conventional, 54, 199–202, 204
ultimate, xv, 199–202, 204
*tshe ring po*. *See* lifespan, longevity
*tshogs zhing*. *See* merit field
Tsongkhapa, 38, 42–43, 48, 134, 182–183, 187
advanced methods in Chöd, 332n36
Chöd sadhana of, translated in Savvas, 307n60
on rebirth, 338n8
three principal paths
Tulku Urgyen Rinpoché, 227
Turner, Victor, 15, 67–68. *See also* ritual, Schechner, Richard
on communitas, 345n12
on liminality, 68, 312n108
on ritual, 329n12
on symbolism, 147–148
two wings of a bird (analogy), 95, 253
method and wisdom balanced as, 45
Tylor, E. B., 6

Umapa Pawo Dorjé, 42
unconventional
Akhu Jamyang, 252–253
Chödpa's life path, 9, 29
ultimate truth (Skt. *paramārtha-satya*, Tib. *don dam bden pa*), xv, 198–203, 204. *See* two truths
*umdzé* (Tib. *dbu mdzad*). 81, 140, 174, 224. *See also* music director, chant master, performance practices
*ḍamaru*, manner of performing, 160–164
dedication of research to (Bentor), 337n55
expertise, in ritual arts and aesthetics, 164

*umdzé* (continued)
- protocols for following, 218, 224
- ritual and musical guidance, providing, 218, 291
- role, setting and adjusting tempo and pitch, 224

Universal Salvation Vehicle (Mahāyāna), 191
utilitarianism, 256, 264

*vajra gīti*, 128, 136. See also *rdo rje'i glu, mgur*
Vajrabhairava (meditation deity). *See* Yamantaka
Vajravārāhī, *39*, 42, 91
Vajrayoginī, 45, 130
Vajrayāna, 3, 7, 9, 204, 247. *See also* tantra
- altruism as basis of path, 272–273
- defined, 293n4
- as diamond path, 254, 301n9
- guru-deity yoga in, 7, 177, 205–206
- symbolism in, 144

Vajrayoginī, *35, 39*, 305n48
- in aspect of Vajravārāhī
- *kusali*-like offering, Chöd as, 319n40
- Machik Labdrön, visualized as, 144
- seven branch practice offerings made to, 130
- visualization as, method of going, 206–207
- visualization for subduing beings at the *gnyan sa*, 206–207
- Yum Chenmo as aspect of, 45

Vandoor, Ivan, 10
variations
- in Chöd music performance practices, 149–160
- Chöd lamas on, 149
- environmental factors, 22
- permitted in practice, 22
- solo and group distinguishing between, 80
- socioeconomic factors, 22

variegated distribution. *See* manifold distribution (Tib. *sna tshogs 'gyed*)
varja songs (Skt. *vajra gīti*, Tib. *rdo rje'i glu*), 137
Vietnamese-American Buddhist communities, xxviii, 15–16
vigilance, 246–247
visualization, 101
- in Chöd ritual practice, 281–282
- while cutting, 209–210
- as ḍākinī, 329n14
- in *Dedicating the Illusory Body as a Heaped Offering*, 207
- deity yoga, 206
- of *Gaté* mantra, *179*
- of Machik Labdrön, 207
- of mantric syllable *Āḥ* purifying beings, 180–181, 318n32
- of music, 116–118
- Rabgey on, 153
- of Vajrayoginī, 207
- of vultures, 119
- while *kangling* is playing, 250

Vivaldi, Antonio, 116, 328n4, 328n8
vocable, 100, 310n94
vocal chants, 77–78
vultures, 117
- ḍākinī as, 119
- deceased person's body offered to, in sky burial, 327n3
- as emptiness symbol, xv–xvi
- meanings evoked by, 120–121
- melody depicting, 121
- musical depictions of, 114–115
- oral tradition on, 120–121
- poetic analogy of impermanence, in Śāntideva's *Bodhicharyāvatāra*, xvi
- sky burial, invited to, xvi–xvii, 119–120, 123

sound images of, 114
sound of wings, as reminder of impermanence, xvi–xvii
symbolic meaning of, xv–xvi, xviii
in tone painting, 118
visualization, conjuring fear of, 113–124, 119
Vulture Peak, xii
in photos, *xii*
sacred place where Buddha introduced doctrine of emptiness, xv–xvi
second turning of Dharma wheel, place, xv

Wallace, Alan, 301n7
Wang, Eugene, 329n13
warrior. *See* bodhisattva warrior
water burial, 327n3. *See* sky burial
*The Weight of the World* (Bourdieu), 267
Weiss, Sarah, 311n97
white distribution (*dkar 'gyed*), 57, *86*, 87–93, 320n47
"The White Distribution," *115* (music transcription of)
white offering, 118, 320n47
Will, Udo, 20–21
on emic and etic perspectives, 20–21
Willis, Janice, 309n86, 312n102
wisdom, 31, 45, 258
accumulations, merit and, 187, 226
Chöd melodies as, 114
dependent arising, 94, 254
emptiness, realization of, 104, *105*, 200
mantra embodying, 92
method and, 70–71, 95, 253–254
realizing selflessness, 150
symbolized, 54
women's roles in Buddhist society, changing, 316n13
word-for-word translation, Teng, 287–289
internal and external distinctions, 191
worldly happiness, 312n112
as suffering, 104
*See* eight worldly dharmas
worship, *See also* rituals of worship
faith-based, 9, 341n3
Judeo-Christian traditions, 7, 251
in Tibetan Vajrayana Buddhism, 7–8
Woser Rinpoché (Lama), 327n27
wrathful (Tib. *drag po*). *See* four ritual (Vajryāna) activities, 185–187
Kyabje Zong Rinpoché on, 332n40
written liturgy
ritual mapping of, 123–124
textual nature of, 280–281
Wylie transliteration, xiii, 320n48, 335n28

Yak Dance, 324n71
Yamāntaka (Vajrabhairava), 98, 103, 133, 204
*ye shes kyi tshogs*. *See* accumulation of wisdom
*yidam*. *See* meditational deity
*yon tan gyi rtogs pa*. *See* spiritual realization
Yum Chenmo, 33, *35*, 42, 45, 64–66, 144, 166. *See* Great Mother
verse of homage to, 200, 337n2
visualization of *Āh*, 180–181

Zasep Tulku Rinpoché, 58, 67, 220
on Chöd meloides as healing, 67
on melodies symbolizing nature, 134
pedagogy of, 231–232
on shamanic description, 319n37
Zemey Rinpoché (Kyabje), 67
*zhe sdang*. *See* hatred-anger
*zhi ba*. *See* peaceful mode
*zhi byed*. *See* pacification

*zhi ma khro. See* semi-wrathful mode
*zil gnon skor gsum. See* three cycle of subduing
Zong Rinpoché, (H.E. Kyabje), 5–6, 83, 120, 135–136, 163, 284, 306n50
  advice for beginner practitioners, 49–50, 280
  Chöd pedagogy of, 113, 166, 218–219, 221
  on Chödpas, 313n115
  on *ḍamaru* drum, 156–157, 161, 219
  on *dram-dram* rhythm, 332n40
  on *Lam Rim*, 73
  on meditation, 313n115
  on musical transmission, 218–219
  on oral transmission, 113–114
  on the self, 197, 206
  on three spheres of giving, 322n52, 350n46
  as *umdzé*, 219